The publisher and the University of California Press Foundation gratefully acknowledge the generous support of the Simpson Imprint in Humanities.

ITALY'S NATIVE WINE GRAPE TERROIRS

ITALY'S NATIVE
WINE GRAPE TERROIRS

Ian D'Agata

UNIVERSITY OF CALIFORNIA PRESS

University of California Press, one of the most distinguished university presses in the United States, enriches lives around the world by advancing scholarship in the humanities, social sciences, and natural sciences. Its activities are supported by the UC Press Foundation and by philanthropic contributions from individuals and institutions. For more information, visit www.ucpress.edu.

University of California Press
Oakland, California

Library of Congress Cataloging-in-Publication Data

Names: D'Agata, Ian, author.
Title: Italy's native wine grape terroirs / Ian D'Agata.
Description: Oakland, California : University of California Press, [2019] | Includes bibliographical references and index. | Description based on print version record and CIP data provided by publisher; resource not viewed.
Identifiers: LCCN 2018049276 (print) | LCCN 2018050702 (ebook) | ISBN 9780520964778 (ebook) | ISBN 9780520290754 (cloth : alk. paper)
Subjects: LCSH: Terroir—Italy.
Classification: LCC SB387.8.I8 (ebook) | LCC SB387.8.I8 D34 2019 (print) | DDC 634.80945—dc23
LC record available at https://lccn.loc.gov/2018049276

Manufactured in the United States of America

28 27 26 25 24 23 22 21 20 19
10 9 8 7 6 5 4 3 2 1

CONTENTS

PREFACE

Universities are the ultimate learning institutions, and our student days have left us all with memories (scars?) of long nights poring over our textbooks and of exams hazardous to our fingernails. Not all of the immense amount of knowledge I was exposed to in medical school has remained embedded in my neuronal network: but what did stick I have been using routinely in my wine writing since. One important lesson was learning to pick the right lunch spot. Really, it's a skill. One bright Sunday, I joined friends for lunch in the charming countryside of Frascati, near Rome, in a *fojetta* (the local—you might say native—word for *trattoria*). At precisely that moment in time somewhere on the other side of the world a butterfly must have fluttered its wings, and my life was steered in a completely different direction. The *fojetta*'s food was hearty, and the house wine much better than others served in similar dining establishments. In fact, so much better that I could not resist asking the *fojetta*'s owner, Alfonso, why this was so. He promptly pulled up a chair, joining us at the table (what can I say, Italy is a friendly place) to tell us all about his wine. My friends got into it, too (asking questions is just part of being a medical student, I guess . . .), and so it was that Alfonso doffed his apron, waved good-bye to his wife,

telling her he was off to the vineyards with us, and left her standing there (open-jawed) to (wo)man the busy lunch hour. I am not sure what the poor lady thought of the whole affair, but I do know that for the rest of us it turned out to be one great afternoon. Standing in front of a rickety maze of gnarly old vines of a local Malvasia grape that apparently nobody else in the area owned vines of anymore, Alfonso proudly told us that those rare, forgotten grapes were the "secret" to his wine's success. It didn't take a degree in ampelology to figure out what he was talking about: even to novices like us, those portly, speckled grapes glistening in the Roman afternoon sun were obviously different from all the other Malvasia grapes hanging around in vineyards surrounding Alfonso's small plot. "But for whatever reason," he added, "these grapes weave their magic only in this precise spot. I've tried replanting them near my house, but the wine just isn't the same." I remember that those words got me thinking. I was still thinking about them the next day, in class and later still that evening, while having dinner with my wine-loving girlfriend. You might say I haven't stopped thinking about them since. In fact, native grapes and the role of site specificity in wine have guided me, polestar-like, in a lifetime's journey devoted to wine.

As anyone who has read my earlier book *Native Wine Grapes of Italy* (D'Agata 2014a) knows, I have always been fascinated by native grapes, their histories and characteristics; simply put, if you don't know the grape varieties or cultivars (cultivars are cultivated grape varieties, as opposed to wild ones), you don't know the wines. One aspect that has always intrigued me most is the terroir-related expression of grapes in wines. F. Scott Fitzgerald said it best: "First you take a drink, then the drink takes a drink, then the drink takes you" (Fitzgerald 2011); if in a different sense than the one he was getting at, much the same thing happens with wine knowledge. When people try a wine they like, natural human curiosity drives many to learn more about it; that wine inevitably brings them to try other wines made with the same grape variety or from the same country. In time, these same people might wish to understand why Arneis wines from Oregon taste so different from those made in Italy. Others might find themselves scratching their heads as to why a Barbaresco producer's Asili wine offers obviously different nuances from that same producer's Barbaresco Rabajà (even though they might be told the wines are similarly made). For many of us, figuring out why such differences surface and what causes them is a huge part of wine's attraction. Of its magic, even.

With most writers, there is often a theme that is repeated throughout their work to varying degrees over time. And so it is with me. I have been fascinated by Italy's native grapes and their wine terroirs for close to thirty years, speaking about these topics in wine courses then writing about them, first in Italian wine periodicals and later for Stephen Tanzer's *International Wine Cellar* and as contributing editor of *Decanter* magazine; I now do the same as the senior editor of the website *Vinous* (www.vinous.com). Furthermore, native grapes and wines are my focus as the director of the Indigena festival held annually in Barolo, the Indigena World Tour, and 3iC (the Italian International Indigenous Center for Wine and Food Studies) wine and food school, also in Barolo.

All my life, I have never ceased to be amazed by how native grapes and their wines express a distinctive signature of place, what in Italy is aptly termed the *genius loci*, or "genius of place." Therefore, the book you hold in your hands is the logical, even inevitable, follow-up to *Native Wine Grapes of Italy* (*NWGI*); it is a summary of my adult-life-long search for the *genius loci*. A search for wines that are grounded in nature and that speak the voice of the land. Wines that explode in the glass with the colors and textures, the memories and souls, of specific places and people. Wines of intergenerational reach, so very different from many of today's liquid cultural relics with nothing to say. In *NWGI*, the quest was about learning in detail about Italy's myriad wine grapes—where they have come from, and what their wines are like. With *Italy's Native Wine Grape Terroirs*, we see them through a different looking glass, no longer on their own but through their interaction with specific places and human beings. And though *Italy's Native Wine Grape Terroirs* takes you down a totally different rabbit hole than *NWGI*, much like the latter book it is meant to be both an academic text and a quick reference guide to Italy's most interesting wines and significant (best?) terroirs. I am aware that the subject matter of this book is at times deeply rooted in scientific facts and data, but my hope is that you will enjoy spending time in its company anyway. That is, if our goldfish-like eight-second attention span allows it (McSpadden 2015).

Clearly, wines made from one specific site are not "better" than those made from a blend of grapes culled from many plots, just different; after all, we each have our own individual taste preferences, and there is no right or wrong way to enjoy wine. All wines send messages (of one kind or another), and my hope is that people will have fun not just in hearing these messages, but also in settling back and deciphering them. Such messages are the soundtrack of my life, and I hope this book will help you create yours. Native grapes, their specific terroirs and their wines, are all about learning from the past while looking to the future. This is because native wine grapes are the keepers of genes that contain the imprints of generations past: through the interaction with terroir, the immense wealth of genetic information contained within each cultivar's DNA is tweaked and modulated to give a different physical background to each wine. In the ultimate analysis, Italy's terroir-specific wines made from native grapes help us remember the past while living the present, but also shed light on what the future may hold. Theirs are the stories of Italy's wine yesterdays, todays, and tomorrows, and therein lie their charm and their importance. After all, it really would be a poor sort of memory that only works backward, as the White Queen tells Alice.

HOW TO USE THIS BOOK

This book covers wine terroirs that I believe to be relevant to the production not just of very fine wines, but of fine site-specific wines in Italy. Wines that speak clearly of a place, exhibiting what Matt Kramer in his magisterial 1990 *Making Sense of Burgundy* (which I believe to be one of the best wine books ever written) brilliantly defined as "somewhereness." I will analyze which Italian terroirs are most suited to giving outstanding world-class wines when planted to specific grape varieties, and why. Clearly, Italy has myriad native wine grapes and terroirs, and so my analysis of terroirs and grapes is forcibly shorter than it might (or should) be; I seize this opportunity to apologize to all my readers for having left out terroirs and wines that might be dear to their hearts. For example, given the many noteworthy wine terroirs in Piedmont and Tuscany alone, I could have easily limited the discussion to the terroirs of only those two regions. However, that would have short-changed many other Italian regions that are rarely written about but that have exceptionally interesting terroir-related wines to offer the non-accidental wine tourists among us.

There are two main parts to this book. Part 1 is an introduction to terroir, an attempt to make a highly complex and confusing subject more manageable and easier to understand.

There are four sections: "A Brief History of Terroir in Italy," "Italy's Wine Terroir: An Overview," "A Study in Terroir," and "The Italian Job." "A Brief History of Terroir in Italy" provides insight into the country's relatively thin historical background relative to the subject. "Italy's Wine Terroir: An Overview" delivers necessary background information on the country's topography, geology, and wines. "A Study in Terroir" addresses briefly how physical and nonphysical parameters of terroir interact with specific grapevines to give unique wines not replicable ad nauseam everywhere else. Clearly, this book's goal is not to provide an in-depth analysis of terroir in general, and so I refer you to one of the many fine tomes that offer more detailed information on this fascinating if complex subject. "The Italian Job" analyzes why it is that, though Italians love to talk terroir and crus, for the most part a real understanding (an acceptance, even) of these concepts proves elusive to the (unfortunately nonsilent) majority.

Part 2 is devoted to describing Italy's finest wine terroirs relative to a specific grape variety. Each entry bears the title of a different grape variety's name, but all entries carry the same subheadings so as to make reading and looking up information easier. The subheadings are: the grape variety; specific terroirs; and benchmark wines. The first subsection (grape variety) discusses the cultivar and why it may do well in specific terroirs and less so in others. The second (specific terroirs) addresses those terroirs where a specific Italian native grape variety does best; please note that in order to avoid repetition, in some chapters I refer you to another where the terroir has already been described (unless of course there are significant differences about it relative to that one cultivar). The third (benchmark wines) includes a list of those wines that are especially full of somewhereness; a three-star system is used to highlight those wines that are most "terroir-worthy" (where three stars are awarded to those wines that are most exemplary of that specific terroir, although all wines receiving stars in this book have merits or I would not have included them; a superscript capital *PS* (^PS) next to three stars indicates the most exceptional of all wines, where ^PS stands for *prima scelta,* akin to the French *hors classe*). The terroirs included in this book were chosen on the basis of the importance and uniqueness of the wines made in each and are the best sites in which to grow those specific wine grapes in Italy. For example, at roughly eighteen hundred hectares under vine, Zibibbo is a fairly common Italian wine grape; but I believe there to be only one true world-class terroir for the variety in Italy: the island of Pantelleria. Therefore, I will discuss just that one island terroir in this book. Clearly, the chapter titled "Nebbiolo" will obviously be longer than most, given the numerous famous terroirs linked to this variety—such as, for example, Barolo, Barbaresco, Carema, Donnas, and Valtellina. In Nebbiolo's case, I have had to stop short of addressing them all, because to have done so would have meant writing a book exclusively on Piedmontese wines. For now, space limitations have forcibly caused me to leave the discussion of, for example, Nebbiolo and Alto Piemonte, Primitivo and Manduria, Greco and Tufo, Cesanese and the Piglio/Olevano Romano areas until my next book.

IN CONCLUSION . . .

This book has been written with the goal of helping wine lovers discover Italy's wine terroirs in all their charm and intricacies. (Of course, this being Italy, where if something is complicated it's good and if it is more complicated it's even better, you just know it will be intricate going.) Over the years, thanks to the generosity and patience of producers and winemakers, I have assembled and tasted multiple samples of wines from specific sites (made with the same grape variety, with similar winemaking protocols, and from the same vintages in an effort to keep distracting variables to a minimum). Tasting them was invaluable in helping me understand what each specific site really could give relative to that one native grape. To the best of my knowledge, no other book on Italy's wines has ever described the wine microcosm that comprises Italy's terroir-specific wines to a similar degree. I am deeply indebted to the many wine producers who over the years were patient and kind enough to share their time and wines with me; but despite their help and best intentions, I realize I have only scratched the surface and have much more to learn and to understand. Or in the words of my favorite English-language poet, I have "miles to go before I sleep. And miles to go before I sleep."

Last but not least, I also wish to thank my editor on this project, Kate Marshall; the production editor, Francisco Reinking; and my copy editor, Carl Walesa; I am truly indebted to them all. Should you, my reader, like the book, it will also be their merit. And special thanks to my mother, who has been an inspiration all my life and will continue to be long after she is gone.

Introduction

DEFINING TERROIR

Walk into any wine bar today in Italy (or elsewhere, for that matter) and you will find the place so crammed with glass-swirling *terroiristes* it's almost immoral. It was not always so. Jean-Claude Berrouet, for over forty years technical director at J. P. Moueix (the producer of wines of near-mythical status such as Château Trotanoy, Château La Fleur–Pétrus, and, in California, Dominus, who is still today the consultant winemaker at Pétrus), is one of the wine people I respect and have learned the most from over the years. During one encounter with him in what others might have defined as my salad days of wine writing (I wrote about one such meeting in the "Ampelology" chapter of *Native Wine Grapes of Italy*, and not by chance, I do so again here), he was kind enough to discuss the subject of terroir at considerable length. As is often the case when I am around him, I had just finished saying something completely wrong; in such moments, Berrouet pauses, with the hint of a smile (probably trying hard to keep a straight face despite what he has just heard), looks straight toward you like a laser beam directed onto a stick of butter (and *you* are the butter), and says something so clear you never end up forgetting it. In this case, it was: "You know, Ian, back when I was your age, to say that a wine had a *goût de terroir* was seriously offensive."

The word "terroir" originally derives from the Latin word *territorium*, or "territory," but over time it lost that association and took on the meaning of the French word *terre*, or "earth"; therefore, back in the 1930s or 1940s, to tell someone his wine tasted of the earth was just about the best way to ensure you wouldn't be invited back to the house (which, depending on how you felt about the person and his or her wines, might have been a good thing). Dating back to the seventeenth century, the word "terroir" was used to refer to the soil and subsoil only, and anything tasting of the earth was frowned upon as being something rustic, or worse, unclean (Matthews 2015). In modern times, "terroir" has taken on a broader meaning, one that encompasses the highly complex interaction of grape variety, soil, climate, and human involvement in the production of distinctive wines from a specific site or area (Seguin 1986; Van Leeuwen and Seguin 2006). According to Michael Broadbent, who holds the title Master of Wine and is one of the world's foremost wine experts, wine is a product of man, but even more important are the earth—the soil and subsoil—and the climate, because there is little or no point in cultivating vines and making wine in a place not suited to *Vitis vinifera* (Broadbent 2003). It is only when grapevines have been planted in the right place that man's role becomes most important. Aubert de Villaine, the gentleman in charge at Domaine de la Romanée-Conti, in Burgundy, believes the same: there can be no great terroir without human beings allowing those very terroirs to express themselves to their fullest potential (de Villaine 2010).

The notion of terroir today includes all the features of a landscape and of the past and present societies that have, or have had, an effect on the wine you drink. Therefore, many different factors contribute to terroir in their own important way. Plant the same grape variety in two different areas, and they make remarkably different wines; plant them in the same area, and the wines can turn out noticeably different as well. All it takes is for one of the two plantings to be done in a shady area, and the other perhaps in an area exposed to the cold north. Clearly, a wine made from Nebbiolo tastes different from one made with Sangiovese, and more different still from one made with Cabernet Sauvignon. However, as many wine lovers know, plant Nebbiolo in Monforte d'Alba's Ginestra and Bussia crus (the real Bussia: an important matter I will broach later in this book; see the section titled "The Italian Job" in part 1 and the Nebbiolo entry in part 2), and the wines, though similar, will also differ. Clearly, terroir differences can change what a grape can give only to a degree. You cannot expect Sangiovese to give you the inky-black-hued wines of Merlot; no matter where you plant Sangiovese, that fact stays true. However, by planting it in appropriate soils and intervening with creative viticulture and winemaking techniques (judicious water deprivation, very low yields, cold soaks, and small oak barrels), you can certainly kick Sangiovese's wine color up a notch or two. Just remember that no amount of terroir will ever turn a 100 percent Sangiovese wine into a Merlot or Montepulciano doppelgänger (please note that I use that word not with poetic license but rather in its literal but oft-forgotten meaning). This is because the genetics of each grape variety determines what each can and cannot give: terroir (which includes the actions of human beings) can only modulate the end result.

Using different words: if the grape variety is the vehicle, then terroir is the driver. One cannot function well (at all, really) without the other. It follows that it doesn't matter if Riesling is the world's greatest white grape or not: Riesling being a cool-climate variety, if you should decide to plant it in one of the coastline vineyards of Sardinia, you have no hope of making a great wine, never mind hearing the voice of the land. The message will be hopelessly muddled, if not downright absent. Because wine is the end product of grapes grown in specific places, the metabolic composition of the grapes used to make that wine depends both on the genetic makeup of the grape and on its interaction with the many factors that characterize a specific terroir. Varying concentrations of sugars, organic acids, esters, flavonoids, anthocyanidins, and many other compounds in the grapes all affect the way a wine will taste. Some of these compounds are found within the grape to begin with and have their concentrations modified during the ripening process. Without any creative winemaking action, a wine tastes of peach because the grape used to make that wine has aromatic precursor molecules that through the winemaking process will liberate, among other molecules, γ-undecalactone, which smells of peach. It follows that the genetic element (the grape variety) is all-important in determining the aromas and taste of any wine and is the single most important factor in determining the terroir effect, while terroir's other factors help fashion wines distinctive of a finite area.

Taking Chianti Classico as an example, 100 percent Sangiovese wines made with grapes grown in Gaiole and Radda (two specific subzones of the denomination) are usually sleeker wines, and wines of greater total acidity, than those of Castelnuovo Berardenga (another Chianti Classico subzone). All three subzones are associated with magnificent but distinct wines: the differences are especially obvious when the wines from Gaiole and Radda are made with grapes grown in spots located at higher average elevations and with soils especially rich in calcium carbonate. In these areas, the interaction between strong ventilation rates and high calcareous soil content leads to slowed grape ripening and higher acidity levels in the grapes; in Castelnuovo Berardenga, where vineyards lie at lower elevations and calcium carbonate is not as abundant, such an effect is lacking. It is easy to understand why the wines from the latter subzone taste so different from those of the other two subzones.

But there's more to wine than just cultivar, geology, topography, and climate. Human beings, with their viticultural and winemaking decisions, also help fashion what a wine will be like. The winemaking process causes molecules to be newly formed, either by the transformation of preexisting precursor molecules in the grapes or by yeast activity in the must; for example, which yeasts one chooses to use will play a role in determining the expression of terroir in that wine. In fact, the degree to which the biochemical profile of a wine is changed depends not just on the yeasts performing normally, but also on the ambient conditions the yeasts find themselves in. (For example, in conditions of environmental stress, yeasts produce very different molecules than they would produce otherwise.) Viticultural practices are just as important: if a farmer chooses to let his vineyards produce twice as many grapes as those of another grower, it is likely his wine will taste more diluted. If in a hot climate one producer decides to remove all leaves from the vines

(thereby fully exposing the grapes to the sun's rays), that producer's wines will taste obviously different from one made with grapes kept under a cool, shady leaf canopy. Clearly, human decisions will also impact heavily on how a wine will taste. For example, in 2015, Anesi et al. found that viticultural practices (row direction and vine training system) and certain soil properties (pH and active lime) correlated with the composition of volatile metabolites in wines, which clearly leads to different-tasting wines. Terroir in a nutshell.

SCHRÖDINGER'S WINE

Looking for and finding terroir in wine is not the playground of a privileged few. At different levels, terroir in wine speaks to all wine lovers. I strongly believe terroir is more than a mere physical, viticultural, or winemaking concept leading to different biochemical outcomes. There are important cultural, intellectual, socioeconomic, ecological, and spiritual components to terroir. In this sense, my view is not different from the one voiced by Vaudour (2003), who wrote of terroir in terms of the socioeconomic, cultural, and ethnological meanings of a geographical place. For example, the intellectual aspect of terroir is huge: even after decades of drinking fine wines, many wine lovers remain mesmerized by the many nuances that great wines offer and the reasons such wines behave thus. Sardinia offers delicious Vermentino wines; but whereas a Vermentino di Sardegna is all about fruity charm, a Vermentino di Gallura (made with grapes grown on degraded granite soils highly characteristic of the Gallura region of Sardinia's northeastern corner) offers greater salinity and power. Why that is fascinates a subset of wine lovers on a wholly different level than just the hedonistic experience the individual wines provide. A well-made entry-level Alsace Riesling wine from just about any decent site is delightful, but one made with grapes from the Schlossberg grand cru is usually deeper and richer. However, because of differences in soil, exposure, and microclimate, Schlossberg Rieslings made from the summit, the middle, and the bottom parts of the Schloss-berg hill are very different wines. Part of the intellectual stimulation in wine resides in the discovery of (or rather, the attempt to discover) all the different facets that a specific terroir can showcase. For this subset of aficionados, wine is not just about making and drinking it, but also about *thinking* it: questioning and deconstruct-ing wine are highly enjoyable steps of the same game.

Though this approach to wine might come across as a little excessive to those just starting out in wine or not prone to intellectual games-manship, it isn't, really. Think of this in the same terms you would pasta. Some people go to a restaurant and just ask for a plate of pasta, limiting themselves to choosing a sauce they like, be it *carbonara, amatriciana,* or *cacio e pepe;* but an Italian, or anyone seriously into food, will also look at the specific pasta shape paired with the sauce. Pasta shapes are myriad, including *spaghetti, tagliatelle, fettuccine, bavette, penne (rigate* and *non rigate),* and oth-ers. The reason for so many different shapes is that each different sauce actually wants a differ-ent type of pasta, and vice versa: specific pasta shapes hold on to sauces in different ways, and in the end, the flavor and texture of what you are eating will be different than it would other-wise be. You didn't really think Italy has over one hundred codified and officially recognized pasta shapes just because someone had lots of imagination or free time on their hands, cor-rect? Just imagine that pasta shape is a matter of such importance that back in the 1980s, the famous pasta company Barilla hired no less than Giorgetto Giugiaro and his Italdesign Giu-giaro firm (Giugiaro is one of the world's fore-most designers: he has created the Volkswagen Rabbit; the DeLorean DMC-12, made famous by the *Back to the Future* movie franchise; numerous Maseratis and Ferraris; Apple com-puter prototypes; Nikon camera bodies; and other iconic elements of twentieth-century style) to create a new pasta shape. Which he did, wind-tunnel-like drawings and all, creat-ing "Marille"; that the curvy, inner-ridged cross

of *rigatoni* and *scialatelli* was less than success-ful than it should have been attests to the com-plexity involved in the apparently simple details, such as pasta shape, that create an ultimately satisfying taste experience. And so it is with wine grapes and terroir: details matter.

Terroir is also a cultural concept of signifi-cant socioeconomic impact, for, much as native grapes do, it speaks of specific places and people, their traditions and habits. In fact, both Aubert de Villaine and Jacky Rigaux (author, university professor, and one of the world's most knowl-edgeable people on all things Burgundy) go so far as to speak of a "civilization of terroir." After all, UNESCO created its World Heritage Sites with just this objective in mind: to preserve the cultural, historical, and natural landscapes. (Famous wine-production zones such as the Langhe and the Burgundy *climats* are World Heritage Sites.) The interplay between terroir and culture occurs everywhere. Basilicata's Agli-anico del Vulture, one of Italy's potentially great-est red wines, is completely different from Taur-asi, another red wine also made with Aglianico grapes grown on volcanic soil, but in Campania. Campania and Basilicata are two different places: the people are different, their histories are different, the land is different. The wines, too, are different, because each represents a spe-cific way of life, a specific memory. It's a cultural thing. This is true even within a region itself. Aglianico del Vulture made at five hundred meters above sea level near Maschito on reddish-clay soils should and does in fact taste different from Aglianico del Vulture made from grapes grown at six hundred meters above sea level on lava-rich soils near Barile, for example. (See the Aglianico entry in part 2.) Those who farm Mas-chito vineyards expect their Aglianico wine to speak of who they are and where they are from: they want, even need, their Aglianico to show-case the differences with respect to any Agli-anico wine made elsewhere. The common denominator is the grape variety—the first and most important step in any terroir-based wine; but much as Clint Eastwood's character in Ser-gio Leone's 1966 film *The Good, the Bad and the*

Ugly believes that every pistol has its own sound, Aglianico del Vulture from Maschito sings its own tune, too. And in so doing, it speaks of Maschito to the world. It follows that the socioeconomic impact of that terroir-specific wine will be felt in the community (in terms not only of wine sales, but also of increased tourism to the area and increases in sales of other local food products and handicrafts to visitors).

The concept of terroir also has ecological importance. Terroir-oriented viticulture is ecologically friendly: for example, the cultivation of vines high on the alpine slopes of Valle d'Aosta and Valtellina reduces the risk of erosion and helps to preserve them, reducing the risk of landslides. And the centuries-long cultivation of a specific grape variety adapted to a specific spot makes for a more eco-friendly agriculture than one where producers rip everything up just so they can plant the latest grape flavor of the month. Last but not least, terroir is a spiritual concept. Great site-specific wines speak of much more than just soil, climate, or viticultural practices. Potentially, they have an inspirational quality (from the Latin *inspirare*, "to breathe into"), breathing new life and new experiences into people and propelling them into, however briefly, a higher realm. It's a unique experience. Much as Schrödinger's cat confuted quantum superposition theory (a quantum system exists as a combination of dynamic states that can have different outcomes; hence a cat that may be simultaneously both dead and alive, which is unlikely), terroir-specific wines are, if you will, Schrödinger's wines. Their ability to live simultaneously in different states (the physical, the intellectual, the spiritual) is a random event that may or may not occur, and often doesn't. We are all the better for it when it does.

PART ONE

Understanding Terroir and Its Context in Italy

A BRIEF HISTORY OF TERROIR IN ITALY

A look at the history of terroir reveals a legacy that stretches back into antiquity. In France, where the concept of terroir is held in the highest and purest esteem, it reaches almost artistic form in Burgundy and Alsace. In fact, no serious wine lover would ever discuss Burgundian or Alsatian wines without referring, at some point in the discussion, to *climat* or terroir. It would be unthinkable, in fact. The wines of those regions live not just through the (very) specific grape variety they are made with, but through the (very) specific sites where that variety is grown, sites whose names most wine lovers know by heart. Burgundy's Musigny, Chambertin, Romanée-Conti, Montrachet, and Corton-Charlemagne are music to a wine lover's ears; and much the same can be said about Alsace's Rangen, Schoenenbourg, Hengst, and Brand, for example.

There are many reasons why France developed the "cru" ideal that so permeates its wine fabric. The most important is that the country was united early. (The birthdate of France, one of the world's oldest countries, is open to debate: some report it to be A.D. 486, when the Germanic Frank King Clovis I conquered all of Gaul, establishing the Kingdom of France; others place the country's birthdate in the ninth century, with the end of the Carolingian Empire; and still others set France's birth in the eleventh century.) Being a united front made it easier for France to rule upon viticultural and winemaking matters in a far-reaching way, as is demonstrated by the well-known edict of July 31, 1395, signed by Philip the Bold (Philippe le Hardi). Most wine lovers know this as the decree that wiped out Gamay from Burgundy's Cote d'Or, but in fact the edict covered numerous other aspects relative to fine wine production. Among these were admonishments not to abandon the better vineyard sites (which implies that people were aware, already then, that some viticultural sites were better than others, and aware of which sites those were) and to curtail manure use in the vineyards, in an effort to avoid excessive fertilization and high yields detrimental to wine quality. Later on, having an emperor didn't hurt the French wine cause, either: it was thanks to Emperor Napoleon III that the famous Bordeaux classification of 1855 came to be. Created in honor of the 1855 Exposition Universelle de Paris, it harked back to similar classifications of Bordeaux wines that had been available decades before, so the concept of classifying wines by price and/or quality was already well engrained in the French mentality (so much so that Napoleon I's 1804 *classification des vignes* in Germany was the basis for the Prussian State's vineyard classification of 1868). In Burgundy, the Roman Catholic Church, and especially the Benedictine and Cistercian orders, played a role of paramount importance not just in guaranteeing wine quality but also in establishing the identity of specific crus. Not all experts agree on the exact extent of the monk's influence in creating a "philosophy of terroir" (Matthews 2015), but monks and nuns certainly had the time and manpower to study their terroirs well (Brajkovich 2017). In tending to their vineyards uninterruptedly for over one thousand years, they created some of France's most famous vineyards and wines. Clos de Vougeot provides a very interesting take on the Burgundian cru concept. Perhaps inaccurately, it is generally believed that the monks had subdivided Clos de Vougeot into thirds (the top, the middle, and the bottom of the hill) based on the quality of the wine made in each part. (Certainly, Clos de Vougeot's lowest-lying vines suffer from drainage problems.) In fact, the monks had subdivided the *clos* into roughly fifteen different *climats* (for example, de la Combotte and Devant-la-Maison); and in wanting to make the best possible wines, they proceeded to assemble some of them in—perish the thought!—Bordeaux-like fashion (Kramer 1990). In fact, according to Bazin (2012), the use of specific place-names in French wine emerged late. For example, up to the eighteenth century, wines were bottled and sold as generic "Burgundy wine," regardless of origin; but it sufficed to know that a wine came from a specific site or plot of vines for it to have more value than another. As early as 1855, Jean Lavalle (the

author of *Histoire et statistique de la vigne et des grands vins de la Côte d'Or*, whose work helped create the first official ranking of Burgundy vineyards) distinguishes between specific place-names and classifies them according to wine quality; for example, he wrote that the wines of Mazis-Haut were better than those of Mazis-Bas. (Note that examples of such written historical site-specific evaluations relative to Italian wine vineyards are practically nonexistent.) With the establishment of the Appellation d'Origine Controlée system and the enactment of the Premier Cru law of 1942, such place-names became even more famous and embedded in everyday life. That Burgundy's *climats* and terroirs were officially recognized in 2015 by their inclusion on UNESCO's World Heritage List only crystallizes their relevance further.

The history of terroir in Alsace isn't much different from Burgundy's. That statement might surprise some readers, given that Alsace's wines are very strongly linked to the grape variety's name being proudly displayed on the label. And yet in Alsace, specific cultivars have always been associated with specific sites. The Romans were known to have planted vines around Andlau, in what today are known as the Kastelberg and Moenchberg grand crus (Stevenson 1993); and it seems only logical to infer that the Romans, who most likely did not build the largest empire mankind has ever known by being idiots, planted vines there, and not somewhere else, for a reason. Wines from the Steinklotz, Mambourg, and Hengst were mentioned as early as the sixth, the eighth, and the ninth centuries, respectively. More specifically, Alsace grand crus such as the Zoztenberg and the Goldert have long been famous for their high-quality Sylvaner and Muscat wines. Much like in Burgundy, regional unity did much to promote the Alsace wine brand and its reputation: the name Alsace, or *Alesia*, as the region was known back then, was reportedly in use as of A.D. 610. By the ninth century there were already 119 recognized wine-producing villages of note in Alsace; by the fourteenth century, that number had climbed to 172. And much like in Burgundy, monks tended to the vines. (There were over three hundred abbeys located throughout Alsace by the fourteenth century.) Some were linked to very famous wines. For example, in 1291 the Dominican convent of Basel bought vineyards in the Rangen, still today one of Alsace's most hallowed sites; and the abbot of Murbach thought enough of the Hengst (another of Alsace's most famous grand crus) to buy vineyards there in the ninth century.

By contrast, Italy did not become a nation until 1861, and that late start in the country sweepstakes explains partly why a true culture of wine terroir failed to develop. Things weren't always so: for example, the importance of terroir was not lost on the ancient Romans. (Of course, you might find yourself thinking that ancient Rome and modern Italy have very little in common, but we won't go there.) The Romans named their grape varieties and wines in many different manners (D'Agata 2014a), and place of origin was perhaps the most important of those; but even in ancient Rome it took a while for the idea of associating wine with specific places and sites to jell. As late as 121 B.C., no specific appellation was given to the produce of different localities, and jars or amphorae were marked with the name of the ruling consul; in 121 B.C. that person was Lucius Opimius, and hence a wine from that year was known as *vinum opimianum*, or Opimian wine. (Apparently, wines from 121 B.C. were highly thought of, thanks to the vintage's especially favorable weather.) Once areas associated with higher-quality wines began to be recognized, commercial considerations led to an increased use of appellation names, or *nomen loci* (names of places). *Falernum* (Falernian), *Pucinum*, *Mamertinum*, and *Vesbius* were just some of the most sought-after wines in ancient Rome; however, these names indicated the wine's region of origin, not the precise site where they were made. For example, *Pucinum* was the wine made in the vast area of Aquilea, a city in today's Friuli–Venezia Giulia region; *Vesbius*

was a wine made on the slopes of Vesuvius; *Mamertinum*, made near Messina in Sicily, was apparently one of Julius Caesar's favorite wines (Smith, Wayte, and Marindin 1890). The Romans also prized many wines made outside of the Italian borders; the production, import, and export of wine was so important in ancient Rome that the city boasted a wine market (*forum vinarium*) and a port (*portus vinarius*) entirely dedicated to wine-related activities (Dosi and Schnell 1992). Falernian, made in an area south of Rome on the border with modern-day Campania (the exact production area has been the subject of much academic debate), was not just one of the most famous wines of antiquity, but also one of the oldest examples of a wine with a clear-cut association with terroir. Falernian was divided into three quality levels: *Caucinum*, made from the grapes grown at the top of the hill (Caucinian Falernian, in English); *Faustianum*, from grapes grown on the middle slopes (Faustian Falernian; this was the most famous of the three, perhaps because these slopes belonged to Faustus, the son of the Roman consul, and later dictator, Sulla); and generic *Falernum*, from the vines growing at the base of the hill (the lowest quality of the three). Apparently, there were other ways by which to classify Falernian wines as well: Pliny the Elder distinguished three types: the rough (*austerum*), the sweet (*dulce*), and the thin (*tenue*); this being Italy, it will not surprise you to know that Galen recognized two types of Falernian only, the rough and the sweet; and that others wrote of yet another, called *severum*, a subtype of *austerum*.

With the fall of the Roman Empire, viticulture and winemaking were carried on in Italy as in the rest of Europe: mostly by monks and nuns who needed to make wine for the officiation of the Holy Mass. The monks allowed the local inhabitants to farm some of their landholdings, most often under a contractual agreement called the *pastenadum*; the farmer would plant and upkeep vines until they started bearing fruit, at which time the farmer had to turn over to the monastery a portion of the land or of his annual produce (generally ranging from one-seventh to one-tenth of the total amount). Another, much less popular, version of the *pastenadum* was known as the *pastenadum ad partionem*, in which the land planted to vines was divided in half between the two parties. However, because the parcels of land were invariably very small, and the poor farmers needed to stay on good terms with the church, the division rarely if ever took place as such (Leicht 1949). In general, it appears that the rental agreements were actually fairly favorable to the poor farmers; this is not surprising, for these agreements derived from the "level," a specific type of agrarian contract established in A.D. 368 by the Roman emperors Valentinian I and his brother Valens. (The former, who ruled from A.D. 364 to 375, is known as the last great Western Roman emperor; upon ascending to the throne, he made his brother Valens, or Flavius Julius Valens Augustus, the Eastern Roman emperor.) The two wished to improve the lot of the empire's poorer working classes by encouraging landowners to rent out their lands at a fair fee (but without a loss of ownership rights). Unfortunately, there was no requirement in the level contract that those renting had to improve the conditions of the land they were renting. For example, the medieval statutes of the towns of Alatri and Ferentino, in Lazio, show that the vineyard work a farmer was obligated to perform was minimal: pruning in March, sodding the ground in June, but little else (D'Alatri and Carosi 1976; Venditelli 1988). The amelioration of the rented plot's agriculture was an integral part of another agrarian contract—the *emphyteusis* (with which the level contract is often confused), which did require the renter to perform the work needed to improve the land (*ad meliora*) under contract. In fact, contracts stipulated with the church were usually of this latter type. For example, the monks insisted on low training systems, which would ensure better ripening of the grapes (climate change must not have been a problem then), and tight spacing of the vines, which helped both to improve

the quality of the wines made from those vines and to concentrate the farmer's work on a smaller piece of land, thereby making more land available for others to work. Apparently, the monks also furnished technical assistance, such as how to correctly build terraces on especially steep slopes. According to Vagni (1999), the monastery employed a *cellerarius*, who was in charge of the cellar, and *terraticarii*, emissaries of the monastery who would oversee the division of the year's crop when that time came. They were also in charge of communicating the date of the harvest, which could not begin before the monks gave the green light on the matter. For this reason, the *terraticarii* were also known as *nuntii*, from the Latin word *nuntius* (*nuntii* is the plural form), or "messenger." Thanks to these sorts of arrangements, viticulture seems to have thrived to a degree; for example, a medieval inventory of the episcopate (the territorial jurisdiction of a bishop) in Tivoli shows that there were fifty different vineyard contracts; most of these vineyards were of the *clausurae* type—that is, vineyard blocks that were closed off similarly to the walled and gated *clos* of France (Fabiani 1968). We also know that vineyards were protected, as much as possible, from vandals (Taglienti 1985). For example, chapter 29 of the 1544 statutes of the town of Grosotto in the Valtellina states that vineyards had to be "tense," or protected (Maule 2013). Interestingly, in some townships such as Castel del Planio, on Tuscany's Monte Amiata, the harvest date was set on separate days for different grape varieties; even back then it was apparent to all that cultivars have different ripening curves.

In medieval times, Italy's scenario was a far different one than that of France: Italy as such did not exist, but was made up of little city-states that were almost continuously at war with each other. One of the consequences of this was that the countryside was ravaged by rampaging armies, and so establishing the quality scale of (or even a list of) viticultural sites was not first and foremost on the minds of those for whom just surviving was a chore.

Furthermore, unlike Burgundy and Alsace, Italy has had very few Benedictine and Cistercian monasteries of note (Shepherd 1964) to help make and keep order among the vines—the result being that, unlike in Burgundy and Alsace, a "culture of terroir," so to speak, was never established in Italy (or at least not to the degree that it was in those two regions of France). In fact, in those few areas of Italy where monastery-related influences were present (for example, in Carema and Gattinara, in northeastern Piedmont), a history of greater attention to sites and of their documentation is obvious. The importance of terroir didn't escape everyone on the boot, however. This is obvious from the famous edict of 1716 by Cosimo III de' Medici, who officially identified the four viticultural areas of Tuscany that gave the best wines in his time. It is one of the world's earliest and most important documents specifically recognizing the privilege of place, and it clearly stated which these were: Carmignano, Chianti (the Chianti Classico of today), Rufina-Pomino, and Valdarno di Sopra.

In any case, for all the potential terroirs Italy possesses, such wines have become a reality in Italy only recently. The concept of "terroir" implies a spiritual and respectful tie to the land, and the use of mostly one grape variety to translate into the bottle the environmental and human factors it has been exposed to over time. There can be no terroir expressed when many different grapes are used in wildly varying proportions to make wines from very high yields, using often faulty winemaking practices and poor cellar hygiene. All of that has long been a problem in Italy. Another roadblock to recognizing the quality of site in Italian wines was that wine was mostly made by growing grapes by the method of *viti maritate* or *viti alberate* ("married vines" or "tree-bound vines") in which the vines ran free around a natural support such as a tree. Unfortunately, however "natural" a support a tree might be, it also provides copious shade to the grape trying to ripen below. Clearly, the resulting highly acidic, dilute potions were not the ideal vehicle by which to express a terroir's nuances. (Italy did away with the *viti alberate* only in the twentieth century, but they can still be seen in Campania's Asprinio d'Aversa production area.) Sharecropping, in which farmers got to keep only a small percentage of what they grew (a derivative of the old level contract, this arrangement was alive and well in Italy well into the 1960s), was also an impediment to recognizing or caring about site quality, for clearly sharecropping spurred poor farmers to grow as much as they could regardless of quality. Many vineyards were co-planted with other plant species, such as grains, vegetables, and other fruits—which clearly did not help matters any as far as wine quality goes. In Piedmont there did exist *vinee* (small parcels of land entirely devoted only to vineyards), but for the most part co-planting dominated, in the *sedimen* or *terrae aratoriae cum vistibus* ("arable land with a view") (Pasquali 1990). Furthermore, because Italian wines traveled poorly and weren't all that great, they lacked the important European markets that French and German wines could count on. The English and Dutch wine markets were knowledgeable and demanding, and wines from Bordeaux and Burgundy were of a stable quality standard, unlike Italy's.

Today, just as in other countries, Italy's wine terroirs are being increasingly studied via the use of the spatial modeling of terroir units, satellite-guided precision viticulture, and geographical information systems (GIS). Airborne and/or satellite images collected during the growing season can help predict variations in grapevine phenology. Thanks to this modern technology, "terroir zoning" of entire viticultural zones is now possible, with areas carved up into land units and territory units, allowing for the breakdown of broader areas into smaller ones that are easier to analyze and to tailor viticulture to. Such zoning methods are at the core of modern-day wine denominations (though, as we shall see, these usually leave a lot to be desired and often have little or no relationship to high-quality wines or sense of place; see the section titled "The Italian Job" below).

ITALY'S WINE TERROIR: AN OVERVIEW

Italy boasts a large array of different habitats, in which exposures, temperatures, altitudes, rainfall, and geological origins of the soils differ greatly. Vineyard locations range from the mountainous areas of the Alps, with high diurnal temperature variations, to hillsides with a continental climate and copious spring/fall precipitation, to Mediterranean climate zones (where the majority of Italy's vineyards grow) characterized by moderate temperature ranges, abundant rainfall in the winter and springtime, and, often, summer drought.

The myriad wine terroirs that characterize the country are a direct consequence of its topography and geological origin. Italy is mainly a country of mountains and hills; in fact, its surface area (324,000 square kilometers) is 38.7 percent mountainous, 39.7 percent hills leading up to those mountains, and only 21.6 percent flat plains. (This explains why only 30 percent of the country's cheese is made with cow's milk: there simply isn't that much space for cows to graze in.) Over time, viticulture in Italy has increasingly moved from the mountains to the easier-to-work hillside areas. It follows that Italy's wine terroirs may be categorized by altitude: there are wines of high mountain areas, wines of the hillsides, and wines of the coastal plains and inland flatlands. Examples of mountain wines would be the Blanc de Morgex et de la Salle (made with the Prié grape in Valle d'Aosta), the wines of Valtellina (made with Nebbiolo, locally called Chiavennasca, in Lombardy), and the Etna Rosso and Etna Bianco wines made on Sicily's famous volcano (made with the two Nerello varieties and Carricante, respectively). High hillside wines would be those of Piedmont's Langhe or Matelica, while wines of lower hillside areas would be those of the Collio in Friuli–Venezia Giulia and parts of Franciacorta. The wines of the flatlands or coastal plains include Emilia-Romagna's many different Lambrusco wines; the incredibly intense Nero d'Avola wines from Pachino, in Sicily's southeastern corner; the perfumed white wines of Venice's lagoon;

the wines of parts of the Franciacorta; and the magically great Vernaccia di Oristano from Sardinia.

Another possible breakdown of Italy's viticultural areas can be attempted by the geological origin of the area's main soil type. According to Cita, Chiesa, and Massiotta (2001), these include wines from marly arenaceous soils (such as those of the Langhe); wines from flysch formations (for example, Cinque Terre and Collio); wines from alluvial plains (most of the Lambrusco wines and Friuli Grave); wines of calcareous soils such as those of Soave Classico; wines from volcanic soils such as those of Etna or Vulture; and wines of the moraines (such as Gattinara and Franciacorta). In fact, Italy's geology is at times impossibly complex, and just about every major Italian wine derives from a unique geological formation. For example, Sardinia is characterized by an altogether different geology than the rest of Italy. The majority of its soils were created during the Primary era, roughly 650 million to 225 million years ago, or long before dinosaurs graced the earth with their presence. The Gallura region of Sardinia is characterized by extremely old, strongly granite soils, and such granite deposits are rare elsewhere in the country. By contrast, almost all the well-known viticultural areas of the Tuscan hills close to the Apennine mountain range were born during the Tertiary era, or between 65 million and 5 million years ago, and are mainly sandstone, sandy arenaceous, and calcareous. The hills of Irpinia, where world-famous wines such as Taurasi and Fiano di Avellino are made, are mostly clay rich. In the appendix, table 3 lists the geologic soil substrate of the major Italian DOCG (Denominazione di Origine Controllata e Garantita) wines described in this book, its age, and the geomorphology of the individual landscapes (adapted from Zangheri 2003). For those who are unfamiliar with DOC/DOCG terminology, these are two major Italian wine classifications: the DOC (Denominazione di Origine Controllata) and DOCG were modeled after France's AOC classification (Appellation d'Origine Controlée). In theory at least, the DOCG is the highest quality level in Italian wine.

A STUDY IN TERROIR

Grape variety and terroir are not the separate entities they are often said to be: wines are neither "of terroir" nor "varietal," because, quite simply, there is no terroir without grape variety, and vice versa. This is because the cultivar genetically determines what the wine will taste like but the environment in which the cultivar lives is characterized by many natural factors specific to the area that influence the grape's behavior, metabolism, growth, and development. Hence wines made from grapes that grow in a specific spot taste the way they do because these factors modify the juice in the berries in both absolute (quantity) and relative (quality) terms. It can be huge fun searching for terroir in the glass, but understanding its effect, its presence even, is a complex issue. In fact, Van Leeuwen and Seguin (2006) wrote that the difficulty in studying terroir on a scientific basis is mainly due to the large number of factors involved in determining it: these include not just the specific cultivar (or cultivars), the soil, and the climate of a given area, but also human-related factors, such as the history and socioeconomics of the *lieu* as well as the viticultural and oenological techniques employed. (Left all on its own, grape juice turns into vinegar, not wine.) It is not by accident that in *Matt Kramer on Wine* (2010), the author writes (extrapolating from a chapter he had written years before in his *Making Sense of Burgundy*), "Discovering the authentic voice of a particular terroir requires study."

Forty or fifty years ago, in Barbaresco and Barolo, the best sites for Nebbiolo vines were believed to be those areas where the snow melted first. A late-ripening variety, Nebbiolo needs a long growing season to weave all its magic; southern exposures and warm sites were, quite rightly, deemed best for it and were the most sought-after. However, a site's relative mesoclimates were just one of the many factors our ancestors took into consideration when deciding where to plant their vines. They were, in fact, far more knowledgeable in their grapevine planting than we usually give them credit for. Farmers were very aware of the flora that characterized each subzone, potential viticultural district, or vineyard, because that flora is an expression of the area's climate and soil. For example, local flora provides a wealth of information about the site's water capacity and temperature, as well as the physical and chemical characteristics present in the soil. Exaggerating somewhat, you wouldn't want to plant alpine flowers where palm trees grow, and observing what else grows in a specific spot helps you make informed decisions on what to plant, and what not to. The grape variety to be planted has to be ideally matched to the area you plan to plant it in—that is, it has to be what Rigaux (2018) has very insightfully termed *adapté* (adapted), in the sense of "ideally suited" to that specific habitat. After all, there's no sense planting Riesling where Nero d'Avola grows well, since those two grapes need completely different habitats. For example, cultivars thrive in very high mountain areas only if the exposure allows a rapid warming of the soils and surrounding air; likewise, in droughty areas pockets of clay in the subsoil (clay has water-retentive properties) are also very important vineyard aspects to consider. Clearly, not all wine grapes respond in the same manner to the same habitats. For example, there exists a huge difference in heat-unit requirements between the world's grape cultivars, and so what grows well on the hot plains of Sicily will not do as well in the cooler mountain reaches of the Valle d'Aosta (and vice versa). That human beings, all over the world, routinely try to force grape varieties to grow in environments in which they have never been present just because of market forces or their own egos is another story. (Again, see "The Italian Job.")

Grape Variety, DNA, and Terroir

Terroir's role in allowing grapes to achieve full polyphenolic ripeness and to develop their full aromatic potential (and hence that of the wines made with them) has long been recognized (Ribéreau-Gayon 2006). Terroir modulates the expression of the grape's genetic makeup, but wine will always taste (and should taste) of the grape used to make it. The terroir effect will be translated into different wine colors, aromas, and flavors as a result of where the grapes are grown and other terroir factors (for example, what human beings decide to do, or not to do); in other words, the colors, aromas, and tastes of wines made with the same variety in different places will vary (to a smaller or larger degree) depending on the environment and human decisions the grape is exposed and subjected to. Another way to express this is to say, in the words of Aubert de Villaine, of the Domaine de la Romanée-Conti, that the grape variety acts as an interpreter of the terroir it is planted in. After all, you wouldn't expect to get white juice from red beets or red juice from white grapes. You would also not expect your white Burgundy to smell or taste like a Gewürztraminer because whether you drink Montrachet, Corton-Charlemagne, Russian River, or Niagara, it's still always Chardonnay that those wines are made with and that you are drinking. Clearly, planting Chardonnay in four viticultural areas as diverse as those will unfailingly lead to wines that showcase (or should showcase) different nuances related to the diversities of those places. However, the differences we are talking about will be about, for example, the relative degree of fruity or of floral notes; getting one of those four Chardonnays to taste like Gewürztraminer, on the other hand, is impossible. In fact, many others besides myself have recognized the importance of the wine grape in determining the taste of wine (Robinson 2005). In Italy, wines made with Frappato are not supposed to taste like those made with Merlot; even better, a Frappato wine made with grapes grown near Vittoria will taste ever so slightly different from one made with grapes grown around Pachino, another town in Sicily (famous for its tomatoes, too), close to Vittoria. A sip of Nero d'Avola wine should not make you think

you picked up a bottle of Rhone Syrah by mistake. Rather, it should make you think that (a) you are drinking a hopefully lovely Nero d'Avola wine (which is probably the reason you bought the wine in the first place); and (b) you are drinking a lovely Nero d'Avola wine from Milazzo that is recognizably different from one made in Noto. A wine made with Malvasia di Lipari, from the drop-dead gorgeous Lipari (or Aeolian) Islands off the north coast of Sicily, should not make you think of a Malvasia wine from Emilia-Romagna—if for no other reason than that the two wines are made with different Malvasia cultivars: Emilia-Romagna's Malvasia di Candia Aromatica is a strongly aromatic grape (much like Moscato Bianco and Gewürztraminer), unlike the only lightly aromatic Malvasia di Lipari. In the best of all possible terroir-driven wine worlds, that Malvasia delle Lipari (confusingly, Malvasia di Lipari is the grape variety and Malvasia delle Lipari is the wine) ought to make you think not just of the Lipari variety and the Lipari Islands, but of the island of Vulcano rather than of Salina (or whichever one of the seven Lipari Islands the grapes were grown on).

Clearly, if you were to use the same grape variety to make wine in completely different areas of the world, the wines would be expected to share a family resemblance but to also speak of the different places they come from. If grape varieties were human beings, that might translate into different accents or different dress habits. In the case of wine, it will be about different colors, aromas, and flavors. Over the course of centuries, generation after generation, the genetic structure of wild and cultivated grapevine populations becomes unavoidably modified. Evolutionarily successful grape varieties adapt to specific environments and selection pressures (for example, human paradomestication efforts): the interaction between the physical, environmental, and human factors and the cultivar exerts an influence on the cultivar's DNA. Such interaction was intensified greatly once *Homo sapiens* started creating a new, stable agriculture (stable as in the sense of no longer nomadic). The domestication, cultivation, and breeding of plants and animals was an integral step in the formation of the *civitas,* or orderly society, in which the planting of vineyards no longer occurred in haphazard fashion, but knowingly, in sites apparently more suitable than others, to give tastier grapes and larger crops.

Clearly, random mutations can also contribute to the change in grape genotypes (Levadoux 1951). Indeed, Tarr et al. (2013) have shown that terroir influences the grape metabolome (that is, the total number of metabolites within an organism). Each grape variety is characterized by variety-specific deoxyribonucleic acid (DNA) that is transcribed and translated thanks to ribonucleic acid (RNA); Nebbiolo is different from Sangiovese because the two have totally different DNA. (If their DNA were identical, they'd be the same variety; therefore, we would not be calling one Nebbiolo and the other Sangiovese, but would use the same name for both.) The genetic patrimony of each grape variety codes for a variety-specific framework of colors, aromas, and flavors, and it is upon this genetically determined background that the other factors characterizing the specific terroir in which the grape variety is planted act to generate a terroir-specific expression of wine (in other words, a wine that clearly says it is made from that specific wine grape in that specific terroir). Using our example of Nebbiolo, the resulting wine will still be (or should be) recognizably Nebbiolo, but it will look, smell, and taste slightly different from a wine made with those grapes planted somewhere else. Think about it this way: the product of a wine's DNA is a canvas that is modified over the course of time by the climate, soil, exposure, altitude, humidity, soil pH, and all the other factors that are typical of that specific terroir.

The result is a wine that expresses the surroundings the cultivar has lived in, sometimes for many centuries. It is for this reason that those grape varieties that have lived in different environments for centuries are also those that have the largest number of biotypes. Biotypes

are examples of a grape variety that has adapted over time to its new environment and consequently looks and behaves slightly differently from the original mother plant; they have a slightly different DNA than the vine that was originally planted because of the increasing number of mutations in the DNA that have occurred over time (and, depending on the degree to which the DNA changes, will look more or less different; when the changes are really noteworthy, we speak not of biotypes but of different, new varieties). For example, the Nebbiolo that grows in Valle d'Aosta looks and behaves differently from the Nebbiolo that grows in Lombardy and also from the one growing in Piedmont, but all three are clearly Nebbiolos. Given that the Valle d'Aosta is an alpine and much colder area than Piedmont, it is only logical for the Nebbiolo growing there to adapt in time to that habitat. In fact, in Valle d'Aosta, Nebbiolo has a different name, Picotener, because people there believe it to be their very own. (Similarly, in Lombardy locals call Nebbiolo "Chiavennasca.") The length of time the variety has lived in new surroundings is also important: with grapevines planted in different places only a few years apart, terroir does not have the time to weave its magic in producing plants that look or behave differently. In slightly less poetic terms, what this means is that the specific terroir has not induced mutations in the grape variety's DNA (also known as genotype) that will in turn lead to differences in the cultivar's aspect (also known as phenotype) and viticultural behavior. It follows, and this is important, that understanding the effects of terroir in wines is difficult, if not downright impossible, unless one is fully aware of the most common aromas and flavors that characterize (or should characterize) wines made with a specific grape variety. Think about it: if you do not know what a Vermentino, Nerello Mascalese, or even a Merlot wine is supposed to look, smell, and taste like, how are you ever going to recognize if it is from Liguria, Etna, Napa Valley, or somewhere else? It would be much like trying to read and understand Sartre's *Huis clos* or Shakespeare's *Hamlet* without first having learned the alphabet.

Interestingly, most wine lovers *do* know that Sauvignon Blanc wines will smell of sage and green figs, and that Merlot wines will remind them of cocoa, chocolate, and dark berries. In fact, that is probably why they buy them: because those wines deliver aromas and flavors wine lovers like and look for in wines made with those grapes. This is one of the big advantages that wines made with French cultivars have over Italian wines; it is imperative that a similar knowledge base be built up for Italian wines made with many of the country's often little-known native grapes. Otherwise, the wines will inevitably remain the mysteries they are to most people (Italians included). Putting it another way, to fully understand any discussion (the discussion, in this case, being the one that is taking place between human beings and wine), you need to speak the language in which the discussion is taking place. The dialogue between two entities that don't speak the same language is the end of dialogue. This book wants to make sure that does not happen.

The Biochemistry of Grapes and of Wine

Only once the wine basics (color, aromas, flavors) that each cultivar can deliver have been filed away in one's tasting memory does it become possible (plausible, even) to try to figure out what terroir's effect might be on wine. In this we are helped by the fact that all of wine's colors, aromas, and flavors are due to specific molecules, and that the concentrations of these color-, aroma-, and flavor-associated molecules vary with terroir. Unfortunately, a specific aroma or flavor we might pick up in our glass of wine is not always traceable to one specific molecule (admittedly, that would make all this much easier): stating such clear-cut relationships is dancing perilously in the dark because a single molecule can be associated with multiple aromas and flavors (Chambers and Koppel 2013). For example, hexanal (an alkyl aldehyde) is usually reported to exude a grassy-green aroma: it has been found to do so in multiple fruits and vegetables, including tangerines (Miyazaki et al. 2012), blackberries (Du et al. 2010), and even olive oils (Tura et al. 2008). Of course, it is not unheard-of for scientists to agree to disagree, as in the case of Yilmaz (2001), who found that hexanal was associated with a green/grassy note in tomatoes, while Tandon (2008) did not. Hexanal can also be associated with oxidized and rancid aromas (Lee et al. 2001), so the spectrum of its associations is indeed large. It is also important to know that human perception will change when two or more molecules combine, and that hundreds of aroma and flavor molecules normally coexist in wine (Saenz-Navajas et al. 2012; Yoder et al. 2012). Furthermore, molecular interactions can lead to unpredictable results (Kurin, Mučaji, and Nagy 2012). For example, Bott and Chambers (2006) investigated which molecules were associated with a "bean" note. Very interestingly, neither hexanal nor *trans*-2-nonanal were found to evoke a memory of beans in a trained panel of experts; but when the two molecules were combined at even low doses, the "bean" quality became immediately obvious.

Unfortunately, studies on the aroma profile of native Italian varieties have not been especially numerous to date, and of the country's nonaromatic varieties even less so (Mannini et al. 2015); we therefore have to rely on the limited information that is available. Nevertheless, it behooves those who wish to understand the many different permutations of Italian wines to know at least a bit about the basic aroma and flavor molecules found typically in wines made from Italian native wine grapes. Many wine lovers all over the world are aware that the green bell pepper smell of unripe Cabernet Sauvignon is due to methoxypyrazine molecules; unfortunately, similar levels of knowledge about Italian native grapes and their wines are lacking. For example, wines made from nonaromatic grape varieties such as Trebbiano Abruzzese and Malvasia Bianca di Candia express mainly delicate herbal aromas. (Do not confuse Malvasia Bianca di Candia with Emilia-Romagna's similarly named Malvasia di Candia Aromatica.) These delicate herbal aromas are due to the presence of specific volatile aldehyde and alcohol molecules in the wines: examples of the former are 2-hexanal or 3-*cis*-hexenal, while 1-hexanol or 3-*trans*-hexenol are examples of the latter. (In biochemistry, the -*al* suffix indicates an aldehyde; the -*ol* suffix indicates an alcohol.)

Clearly, no grape variety smells of grass, and yet there are countless times we all pick up grassy notes in wines. This is because of the presence of aroma precursor molecules in the grapes that are turned via the winemaking process into new molecules that smell of grass or delicate fresh and dried herbs. Linoleic and linolenic acid are two such precursor molecules: when making wine with Trebbiano Abruzzese and Malvasia Bianca di Candia, those two polyunsaturated acids are modified by mechanical or enzymatic activities that free the aldehyde and alcohol molecules responsible for the herbal aromas typical of those two grape varieties and their wines (and in fact, typical of most nonaromatic wines). Neither of those two cultivars can deliver much in the way of tropical-fruit notes, even if the grapes are subjected to variously different viticultural and winemaking practices (see below). Therefore, the next time someone pours you a (rather laughably) highly scored or multi-award-winning Trebbiano d'Abruzzo (Trebbiano Abruzzese is the grape; Trebbiano d'Abruzzo is the wine) and the thing makes you think you stepped by accident into a papaya and mango jamboree, you will know that the wine, independently of how good it is, is not what it should be. This is because such a wine reflects the winemaker's signature, and the terroir, rather than amplified, is being distorted: no amount of terroir can or should turn something that is normally pale red into black, or lions into leopards, or make a Trebbiano d'Abruzzo smell like a tropical-fruit cocktail. In any case, a wildly interesting study by Spiers, Chen, and Lavidis (2015) has shown that the delicate aromas of freshly cut grass act on areas of the brain that have to do with memory and emotion, and in so doing apparently help reduce stress. More recently, Harada et al. (2018) have demonstrated the anxiolytic effects of linalool in lavender extracts in mice, and linalool is a terpen found in most wines (especially in those made with aromatic grapes). In fact, wine has long been known as a sedative (many Italian seniors have the habit of drinking a small glass of sweet wine at nighttime to help facilitate sleep), but it appears that our favorite liquid's capacity to relax may not be just an alcohol-derived effect. Terroir might play a role here, too. According to Hashizume and Samuta (1999), the altitude at which the grapes are grown plays a major role in the expression of methoxypyrazine molecules, and especially the amount of sunlight the grapes are irradiated with. (Sunlight is necessary to break down methoxypyrazines; if and when that happens, the overt green notes will be less obvious in wines.) It follows that, depending on the terroir the vines grow in, one can greatly reduce the presence of these molecules in the grapes, and ultimately in the wines as well. The relationship between stress relief and different linalool concentrations in wine might be a promising area of study as well.

The Date of Harvest and Other Terroir-Related Aspects in Wine

Back in my high school days at a private French school in Canada, one of the things that I found most fascinating in biology class (besides my beautiful teacher from Strasbourg) was the study of plant pigments. Everyone knows about chlorophyll, the substance responsible for the green color of plants, but I was much more attracted to xanthophyll and the carotenes. (What can I say? We all have our personal preferences.) My favorite color is lemon yellow, and xanthophyll (the name derives from Greek *xanthos* ["yellow"] and *phyllon* ["leaf"]) is the yellow pigment of plants. It is also one of the two major subgroups of the carotenoid class of molecules, characteristic of all plants. (The other subgroup is made up of the carotenes.) Carotenoids come in a variety of shades, but as their carrot-sounding name implies, their color hovers in the orange–red spectrum. (And after yellow, my favorite color is red, so the carotenoid group had a lot going for it in my teenage books.) Besides color, carotenoids are remarkably interesting for a variety of other reasons, such as being part of a plant's defense armamentarium, protecting it from photooxidation-related damages. Even more interesting for us wine lovers is the fact that carotenoids are the source of many enticing aromas present in the wines we drink. In order for such aromas to appear, carotenoids (highly conjugated polyene chromophores, most of which are made up of chains forty carbon atoms long) must be broken down into smaller chains of nine to thirteen carbon atoms, called norisoprenoids. It is norisoprenoids that give off the very intense, perfumed aromas of, for example, honey, resin, and tropical fruit (Ribéreau-Gayon et al. 2006; Mendes-Pinto 2009). To a greater or lesser extent, norisoprenoids are found in all wine grapes: but their concentrations are—you guessed it—genetically determined in each specific cultivar. And if you were to guess that different terroirs can modulate their expression, you would be right again. In fact, sunlight can break down the carotenoids in grape skins into norisoprenoids, and this is why wines made from late-harvested grapes will always remind you, to greater or lesser degrees, of dried apricots, superripe peach, figs macerated in alcohol, raisins, and honey (all norisoprenoid-related aromas).

In this light, it becomes much easier to understand the importance of the date of harvest when discussing wine, and why it is important to know, more or less, when the grapes were picked; otherwise, trying to draw conclusions about a specific terroir relative to the wines you are tasting is perilous. It is intuitively obvious to most wine lovers that two wines made with grapes picked one, two, or even more months apart will differ. One would normally expect the wine made from late-harvested grapes to be lower in acidity and taste riper, honeyed even; but why exactly is that so?

As shown by Razungles et al. in 1993, norisoprenoid formation is especially marked in overly ripe or air-dried grapes (norisoprenoid concentrations in grapes are normally low before veraison—the color change of berries as they begin to ripen—and increase after it has taken place), such as the grapes used to make late-harvest or passito (air-dried) wines. For this reason, when comparing dry white or red wines made from the same grape variety in more or less the same habitat and with the same cellar techniques, the exact time at which the grapes were picked becomes a fundamental datum for one trying to piece together the puzzle of terroir. When tasting two wines, if you don't know that one is made with grapes picked three weeks later than were those used to make the other, it becomes objectively very difficult to draw conclusions on what exact role the terroir might have played in the makeup of the two wines. And that is but one of the many terroir factors to consider. Crupi, Coletta, and Antonacci (2010) looked into carotenoid concentration in Puglian grape varieties such as Primitivo and Negro Amaro and found a positive correlation with the aromatic potential and varietal character of wines made with each. And they are just some of the researchers who have studied norisoprenoids in wine extensively over the years.

The story is much the same with many other aroma and flavor molecules. The note of camphor you might pick up from time to time is due to various molecules: one of the best known is vitispirane, which is usually found in only very low doses in young wines (Eggers, Bohna, and Dooley 2006). However, it can be found in high concentration even in young wines if the grapes used to make the wine were subjected to very different hang times, resulting in diverse degrees of grape ripeness. Vitispirane concentrations also increase as wines age in the bottle. Another example is the more or less intense floral smell of violet that characterizes many Italian red wines (and not just Italian, in fact): just think of a Brunello di Montalcino (made with 100 percent Sangiovese) or Barolo (100 percent Nebbiolo). This immediately recognizable smell of violet (and in part also of raspberry) is due to a molecule called ß-ionone, found in different concentrations in all wines (usually at a mean value of 30 micrograms per liter, well above its perception threshold of 4.5 micrograms per liter). However, ß-ionone's concentration varies greatly with the grape variety and even more so with the degree of ripeness of the grapes used to make the wine (Etiévant, Issanchou, and Bayonove 1983). Therefore, two Brunellos may be made exactly the same way in the same vintage, but if one starts from superripe grapes, the intensity of its violet aroma may be less than that of the wine made with grapes picked earlier in the season. In fact, a similar terroir effect on wine aroma can be reached in a different way: the superripe quality may be due not to one producer's decision to harvest late but to the fact that the grapes used to make the wine grow in the much warmer southeastern sector of Montalcino near Castelnuovo dell'Abate, as opposed to the cooler northeastern section around Torrenieri. In the ultimate analysis, the various factors that characterize a specific site can influence the wine you will end up tasting in myriad ways. Again, the degree to which this happens depends on the interplay between the specific variety and the other factors that help express terroir.

Aromatic Grapes, Wines, and Terroir

Although people speak and write about wines often having an "aromatic nose," the way the word "aromatic" is used in winespeak is often wrong. Clearly, all wines have aroma, but by definition, aromatic wines are only those made with aromatic grape varieties: in fact, grapes are divided into aromatic and nonaromatic varieties. Italy boasts numerous famous and less-famous aromatic grape varieties such as Aleatico, Lacrima, and Moscato Bianco. When we speak of aromatic wine grapes, we ought to mean only those cultivars that have significant concentrations of specific aromatic molecules.

These are mostly molecules of the terpene class: terpenes are hydrocarbon molecules made up of carbon and hydrogen atoms. (When the molecule contains other atoms as well, such as oxygen or nitrogen, these are no longer terpenes but terpenoids or terpenic alcohols.) Terpenes can be found in free or bound forms, and the two are very important in determining just how aromatic the finished wine will be. (The bound terpenes are not odoriferous per se but can be freed from their bond and therefore function as aromatic-molecule reservoirs.) Some of the best-known terpenes include α-pinene (it exudes a smell of rosemary) and limonene (as its name implies, it smells of lemon); some of the best-known terpenic alcohols include geraniol, which smells of roses and geranium; eucalyptol (or, more precisely, 1,8-cineole), which smells of eucalyptus; citronellol (a component of essential plant oils such as oil of citronella, obtained from lemongrass leaves like those of *Cymbopogon nardus* from Sri Lanka or *Cymbopogon winterianus* from Java), which has a delicate lemony smell; and linalool, which will remind one of musk, orange flowers, and roses.

Not all aromatic grapes have similarly intense personalities, and it is important to know why this is so, especially in the context of terroir wines. For example, Moscato Bianco, Malvasia di Candia Aromatica, and Gewürztraminer are strongly aromatic cultivars; Ruchè, Minutolo, Malvasia Istriana, and Aleatico are moderately to strongly aromatic; Malvasia del Lazio, Malvasia di Lipari, and Glera are mildly aromatic; and Malvasia Bianca di Candia, Chardonnay, Pinot Bianco, and Cortese are not aromatic at all. (The Chardonnay Musqué clone is aromatic, but otherwise Chardonnay is a nonaromatic variety.) It is possible to classify different grape varieties by their different absolute aromatic-molecule concentrations, such as their absolute terpene values (Mateo and Jimenez 2000). For example, anyone who has ever tasted a Muscat d'Alsace wine (almost always a blend of Muscat Ottonel and Muscat à Petit Grains, the latter better known in Italy as

Moscato Bianco) or a Zibibbo wine from Pantelleria knows them to be far more aromatic than wines made with Chardonnay or Syrah. However, free terpene concentrations account only partly for the aromatic expression of the finished wines. This is because bound terpenes can be freed from the molecules they are tied to (usually a sugar molecule) via either enzymatic activity or acid hydrolysis, meaning that some varieties can give wines that have greater aromatic potential than others. Since wine is an acid medium in which numerous enzymatic activities take place, terpenes are inevitably freed up over time (Williams, Sefton, and Wilson 1989). In the case of wines meant for early consumption, usually made with grape varieties that are not especially known for ageworthy wines (such as, for example, Piedmont's red-berried Malvasia di Casorzo), winemakers will actively try to free up terpenes such as citronellol via the winemaking process to make the wines more interesting (Di Stefano 2001). Therefore, unless one knows for sure that two Malvasia di Casorzo wines being compared were made by more or less the same winemaking procedure, it becomes impossible to conclude that one wine is more aromatic than the other as a result of the specific site it grows in. Similarly, winemakers working with one of Campania's two different Falanghina varieties will usually try to increase the aromatic aspect of the wines by picking the grapes slightly late to increase norisoprenoid concentrations, and will avoid filtration so as not to strip the finished wine of any of its aromatic potential. By contrast, the majority of winemakers will rarely proceed in the same manner with Greco or Fiano (two other white grapes of Campania), the wines of which carry more than enough aromatic clout as it is.

THE ITALIAN JOB

The Problem with Appellations

Wine should speak of a specific place, but often it doesn't even hint at where it's from. When that happens, wine is reduced to little more than a soft drink, something that is exactly the same no matter where you buy it; the soft drink industry's very success depends on an often secret formula for a drink that can be replicated everywhere. By contrast, wine emerges from a specific grape variety (or blends) and a specific area (and often a specific small section of land within that larger area). Barbaresco is a different wine from Carema or Gattinara, yet all three are made with Nebbiolo grapes. The differences stem from slightly dissimilar Nebbiolos growing in different environments, and that have adapted to their terroirs over the centuries (though each is still recognizably a Nebbiolo). The differences in the three wines are present, to a greater or lesser degree, even when the Nebbiolo grapes are similarly grown and vinified. The French were the first to devise officially recognized and defined viticultural zones separate from others. The system of the Appellation d'Origine Controlée (AOC), which saw the light of day in 1935, identifies a number of wine regions in the country based on the distinguishing features of the wines produced in each. By so doing, the AOC system essentially recognizes and fosters the existence of terroir. (In the context of this book's subject matter, it is not without interest that as early as 1932, within the Fédération des Associations Viticoles de France, a "Section des grands crus" was created, an initiative supported and broadcast by Senator Joseph Capus, France's agriculture minister from 1923 to 1924 [Le Roy de Boiseaumarié 1967]—a fact that denotes how France's political figures were behind the initiative from its inception.) The AOC guidelines were later used as a template for the creation of the appellation laws of other countries, ranging from Italy's DOC and DOCG system of *denominazioni* (the Italian word for appellations), founded in 1963, to the American Viticultural Areas (the AVAs, founded in 1980) of the United States, to the Vintner's Quality Alliance (VQA), a wine-support program of the province of Ontario (founded in 1989), and many others.

All appellation systems have the objective not just of broadcasting the precise origin of agricultural products (such as wine) traditional and typical to specific areas but also of protecting their integrity, traceability, and authenticity. All appellations have strict wine-production guidelines that wine producers have to follow in order for their wines to belong within the appellation; examples of the provisions typical of all these systems are the listing of the allowed grape varieties from which to make wine within the appellation, the maximum yields allowed, the aging requirements, and the date on which the wine can be first released for sale. Official tasting committees are set up that taste the wines annually to ensure that the wines are devoid of major flaws and typical of the area's traditional production. In this manner, denominations function (in an ideal world) as safety nets for the consumer and propel the development of previously sleepy rural communities by turning their wines into brands unique to each area. In theory, all the appellation-of-origin systems help establish not just an identity, but also value; whether they actually do so in practice is a completely different matter.

Unfortunately, for all their many merits, appellations are not problem-free. Far from it. In fact, Italy's denominations present wine lovers with numerous challenges. For one, much as in other countries, they were drawn up on the basis of administrative criteria, often with an eye to political convenience, and thus are often only loosely grounded in local geography or history (Fregoni 1998). This means that, despite what most politicians and producers would like you to believe, many DOCs and DOCGs make little sense and have only a tenuous link to the terroir they were meant to uphold and defend. Possibly even more damning to the credibility of many denominations is the simple fact that most are, in Italy and abroad, just too large. Clearly, because of the added value that a denomination supposedly brings with it, producers and politicians alike are prone to wanting to extend the size of denominations as much as possible—the end

result being, of course, that many denominations cover such large swaths of land that they become devoid of unifying features: wines made from thousands of hectares' worth of grapes have little in the way of common mesoclimate, geology, or history. For all intents and purposes, while the denomination usually maintains, even in such conditions, its legislative and consumer-safety functions, it loses any real connection it might have otherwise had with the land. The examples are almost too numerous to count. In Italy, Montalcino is a very well-known example of denomination largesse: whereas in the 1930s there were only four Brunello wines bottled and less than one hundred hectares of land devoted to Brunello production, today the Brunello di Montalcino DOCG is a truly laughable two thousand hectares large. To use one of Gertrude Stein's most famous quotes in a different context (actually one of my favorite quotes of all time), there is no longer any there, there. For this reason, in Sardinia, a cult producer such as Alessandro Dettori has chosen to not make DOC wines, preferring the Indicazione Geografica Tipica (IGT) category "Romangia." He reasons that the Romangia viticultural area has more of an identity, centered around the township area of Sorso and Sennori, where his vineyards are located. So it makes sense for him to label his wines with a less-important-sounding denomination. The recently created Menzioni Geografiche Aggiuntive (MGA) of Barolo and Barbaresco are a commendable attempt to put some order in the many single vineyards of those two famous wine areas. Unfortunately, many of those MGAs are also too large to have much meaning. For example, the prestigious Bussia cru has been so enlarged (at 297.7 hectares, it is now the second-biggest of all Barolo MGAs) that I often find myself thinking that if and when I were to plant Nebbiolo vines in front of my apartment in Rome, I'd call my wine Bussia, too, since almost everyone else seems able to do so.

Of course I jest, but I trust you see my point. Let me add that problems such as these are not specific to Italy: in California, an AVA such as Sonoma Coast is so large that few of the wines have much in common, while Alsace grand crus such as the Brand and Sporen have been conveniently increased in size over time by roughly fifteen and four times, respectively. All the world's the same, in this context. Clearly, the problem of denominations being too large could be addressed and fixed (somewhat, at least) by creating or identifying officially distinct subzones within the larger appellations, and to an extent this is being done (the Aglianico del Vulture denomination is an example); but not all producers choose to use the as yet lesser-known subzone names, so the problem remains. And, Italians being the creative and individualistic types that they are, many producers would rather make up a fantasy name for their wines without any mention of a specific site (especially if that site or subzone is viewed as being of lesser quality than others in the immediate area). Of course, another huge problem with MGAs is that only 85 percent of the grapes need to come from that specific vineyard area in order for the wine to benefit from the site's name on the label; in Burgundy, when a label states "Musigny" or "Échezeaux," 100 percent of the grapes have to come from that specific vineyard site. Not so with Barolo and Barbaresco, two of Italy's most famous wines. And they wonder in Italy why French wines have the reputation theirs lack.

In fact, it's not just the size of denominations that is often too large; the ampelological guidelines (the number of different grape varieties allowed) of each denomination are often problematic as well. It seems like some DOCs in Italy allow just about every grape variety known to man within their borders. For example, estates producing the wine called San Gimignano Rosso (made in the surroundings of that beautiful medieval town) can choose to use Sangiovese, Cabernet Sauvignon, Merlot, Syrah, and Pinot Nero in varying proportions (50 percent Sangiovese minimum), and can add another 15 percent of just about any red nonaromatic cultivar they can think of provided

it's allowed in Tuscany. Of course, the same producers might prefer to bottle instead a San Gimignano Sangiovese, a San Gimignano Cabernet Sauvignon, a San Gimignano Merlot, a San Gimignano Syrah, and/or a San Gimignano Pinot Nero; and so the place has at least six completely different red wines made there. Of course, this being a free world, anyone can do as they see fit, but it strikes me that creating a brand value for the red wine of San Gimignano, never mind trying to describe a local specific wine terroir, would be next to impossible. Of course, there are other viticultural zones in Italy where something similar is allowed. Another problem with denominations is that the government committees created to enforce and ensure that the winemaking standards, traditions, and the organoleptic profiles of the wines are maintained have virtually abdicated their role. Today, for a wine in Italy to be refused DOC or DOCG status is a rare thing indeed: the wine has to present truly major flaws for that to happen. For example, nowadays a slew of very lightly colored Cerasuolo d'Abruzzo wines (historically always a very dark pink or almost pale red in color) are given DOC status anyway. This is happening because the paler-than-pale Rosé wines of Provence are now selling like hotcakes, and Rosati wines such as Abruzzo's Cerasuolo are at a competitive disadvantage with their (perceived) too-dark pink hue. Unfortunately, this is not the way to have anyone view your wines as the product of a serious belief in the local terroir or history.

Grasping at (Terroir) Straws

Understanding, implementing, and defending terroir is not easy. It certainly cannot be done if politicians cave in to every producer's whim just because a particular wine or wine style sells well at a particular moment. For example, did you know that the likes of Pinot Nero, Petit Verdot, and Chardonnay are allowed on Etna? The point is not that up to 15 percent nonaromatic white grapes are allowed into the Etna Bianco blend (again, it's a free world); the point is, What is that 15 percent doing there to begin with? To be crystal clear, Etna is one of the most special wine terroirs in the world, associated mainly with only four grape varieties that give unique wines there. For the most part, these are two white grapes, Carricante and Minnella Bianca; and two red grapes, Nerello Mascalese and Nerello Cappuccio. But Minnella Bianca is very rare nowadays, and there is not that much Nerello Cappuccio, either. The piercing lemony flintiness of a good Carricante wine is not easily forgotten (admittedly, Carricante can be too much of a good thing at times), and neither are the perfumed fragrances that emerge from a well-made Etna Rosso. No wines in Italy (or anywhere else in the world, for that matter) are even remotely similar to these two Etna beauties. So what do the Sicilians do? Rather than protect and uphold the uniqueness of the area, perhaps by initiating an official classification of specific subzones to showcase the different nuances characterizing these great wines, they plant Pinot Nero and Petit Verdot on Etna's slopes. It's not that these are lousy grape varieties (they are not, of course); it is just that there was no need to plant them on Etna. Does it never occur to anybody in Italy that red Burgundies are made only with Pinot Noir (and Beaujolais only with Gamay)? That white Burgundies are inextricably tied to Chardonnay? Why is it that nobody in Burgundy clamors to plant Durif or Malbec? Why does nobody in Chablis ask to plant Petit Manseng or Zibibbo? In Italy, nobody seems to realize that this drive to try their creative hand at what others do so much better is ultimately nothing more than a hapless diminution of the country's own grape varieties and terroirs. Honestly, if even on Etna, a truly special place, you cannot do without planting Pinot Nero, you might as well hang a sign around your neck that clearly states, "Yes, I know my grapes and I are inferior, but I desperately want to show you that I can play with the big boys." *Puh-leeze.* In general, Italy needs to do a better job of broadcasting and protecting its wealth of different grape varieties, many of which are specifically associated, as are their wines, with specific terroirs. For example, there are seventeen different Malvasia varieties in Italy, mostly unrelated. (Only four share relatively close familial ties.) Almost all are very intimately linked to a specific region: Malvasia di Lipari grows only on the Lipari Islands of Sicily; Malvasia di Candia Aromatica is mainly associated with the Emilia part of Emilia-Romagna; Malvasia di Schierano is located in and around the town of Castelnuovo Don Bosco, in Piedmont (where it gives the almost magically perfumed Malvasia di Castelnuovo Don Bosco wine), and basically nowhere else; Malvasia Istriana is linked to Friuli–Venezia Giulia . . . and yet, in many cases Italian law states that the wine label read "Malvasia" only. For example, the dry white wine of the Lipari Islands is officially labeled as Salina Malvasia only. So, just for the sake of argument and precision, let us recapitulate: there is a unique grape variety that nobody else has, not just in Italy but anywhere else in the world (Malvasia di Lipari); it can give an absolutely delightful dry wine and an outstanding sweet wine on the Lipari Islands—a wine that speaks intimately of one specific neck of the woods (in general, of the Lipari Archipelago; specifically, of Salina, Vulcano, or one of the other Lipari Islands where the grapes are grown). And what is the decision? People can call the dry wine "Malvasia" only (in this case, Malvasia Salina or Salina Malvasia). In Lazio, where at least two different Malvasia varieties grow, many generically label their wine as "Lazio Malvasia." Please excuse me while I throw my hands up into the air and bang my head against the wall a few times.

The inability (the unwillingness, really) to grasp the true meaning of the word "terroir" in Italy is shown by other damning observations and facts. Did you know that Italy's supposedly best and most important wine category (the DOCG) does away with preexisiting subzones? Believe it or not, if and when a wine gets elevated to DOCG status, the subzones are eliminated officially. Clearly, with "promotions" of that ilk one is better off not getting promoted at all, and this is precisely what many in Italy are starting to realize. This is why the Rapuzzi family was willing to leave no stone unturned to defend their Cialla subzone when the Picolit DOCG was created, and managed to resist successfully. In the end, they are and will always be better off. By contrast, producers in Rosazzo gave their Picolit subzone up—something that even Orfeo Salvador, who was retired at the time but had been a longtime key political figure in Friuli–Venezia Giulia wine, characterized by telling me, in his typically nuanced, refined House of Lords–type English, " [T]hose producers are morons" (especially given the fact that Rosazzo had a long history of excellence in Picolit production). Do you also know there are roadblocks to using the term "old vines" or *vecchie vigne* on wine labels in Italy? The official excuse is that too many were getting carried away with what they determined to be an old vine, and wines from less-than-Methuselahan-type plots were being embellished with the "old vines" moniker. The answer to that problem, though, is not to eliminate the possibility of declaring that a wine is made from old vines. Rather, you determine officially what "old vines" are: thirty, forty, fifty years old? Hardly a Herculean task, correct? Wait, it gets better. In recent years, all sorts of roadblocks have been placed on using the term *"vigna"* (vineyard) on wine labels in Italy. Undoubtedly, there were less-than-forthcoming individuals who used to label their wine as a *"vigna* something-or-other" when this was not so (in other words, giving the impression the wine was the product of a single vineyard when it was not), and that is, at the very least, admittedly deceitful. The answer, however, is not to make it impossible for people who do have single vineyards of note to indicate that fact on their wine labels, but to create rules (and enforce them) by which such use is regulated and monitored. Clearly, those who make huge volumes of wine from large expanses of land are quite happy with the way things stand now, but it is hard to accept that terroir really matters in a country where even using the word "vineyard" on your label is made difficult.

In fact, at times Italian producers themselves are their own worst enemies. At a recent conference, those in charge at one Aglianico del Vulture estate in Basilicata objected to my trying to break down the Vulture subzone by townships because, according to them, soils varied too much across the denomination—"every fifty feet or so." Clearly, only in Italy must this be a problem, given that in Alsace, Burgundy, the Mosel, and Bordeaux, people have had no problems speaking of wines of Gevrey-Chambertin or of Pauillac or of Thann or of Forst for centuries. Furthermore, in most countries, one usually first learns the differences between, say, Pommard and Volnay, and only then moves on to learn the differences in the wines of Rugiens and Épenots (both Pommard vineyards). Of course, Italians always know better, and so similarly logical and easy frameworks in which to work are unappreciated. In Italy, producers and politicians would like you to accept the fact that a vineyard is a cru just because they say it is. In fact, the majority of Italian producers refer to almost any single vineyard they own as a "cru." You can understand why they would like to think that, but it is just not so. Don't take my word for it: according to Oxford dictionaries, a cru is "[a] vineyard or group of vineyards, especially one of recognized superior quality"; such recognized quality derives from centuries of observation and wine sales. In Italy, vineyards devoid of history are talked up by their owners as being vineyards of note, when what they really mean is that in their experience (and practically nobody else's), the specific vineyard gives different and supposedly better wines than those made from other vineyards. Speaking of a "cru" becomes objectively difficult when nobody else makes wines from the site and winemaking there goes back only a few years (while famous French monopole vineyards often boast centuries of history). Corton-Charlemagne is one of the world's best-known white wine crus, and documentation exists of wines made there for hundreds of years. This is also true of the Bernkasteler Doktor, the Scharzhofberger, the

Forster Jesuitengarten, the Rangen, the Brand, the Clos de Vougeot, and many other world-famous crus; not so in the case of most Italian vineyards. In Italy, the only person to have ever spoken or written about specific wine sites with any regularity was Luigi Veronelli, Italy's most famous wine writer, who did much to advance knowledge about Italy's best wines (Veronelli 1964, 1995). But while he named and evaluated many of Italy's crus, even his books dealing with the subject confusingly mix together the names of specific sites with those of estate brands (which is all right if the latter wines are made only with grapes from single crus, but that is not necessarily the case). Still, I started paying attention to names such as Rocche, Villero, and Monprivato thanks to him, for that sort of attention to detail was to be found practically nowhere else in Italian wine-writing circles at the time. The fact that I had to figure out which were true crus and what the wines made from each were like is another matter and doesn't lessen Veronelli's role as a precursor in the least.

Yet another issue is that any classification of sites by quality level strikes fear in the hearts of many in Italy. The fear that one's piece of land may be evaluated poorly in an eventual quality classification (with all its attendant consequences) is a very serious matter. Take, for example, Piedmont producers of Nascetta; or Friuli–Venezia Giulia producers of Pignolo. These are two examples of very rare Italian wines for which clear-cut terroirs of special note have been officially identified: those producers who own Nascetta vines within the boundaries of the municipality of Novello, and those whose Pignolo vines fall within the jurisdiction of the Rosazzo zone, can label their wines, respectively, as "del Comune di Novello" and as "Pignolo di Rosazzo." This has led to almost comical levels of resentment: one producer in Piedmont recently told me he had decided against planting Nascetta in his vineyards because his vineyards were not within the Novello township, and then his wine would not have had the right to the "del Comune di

Novello" label. Because he did not want to be stuck with a second-class-citizen image (in his view) by having to use a more generic denomination such as Langhe, he opted to plant another white variety in the same place instead. Do not make the mistake of shrugging off the above anecdote as an example of one person's sorry lack of synaptic connections, because this is a behavior and a way of thinking you will come across time and again in Italian countrysides. And you want to talk terroir with these people?

After all that, some good news. For the most part, the younger generations taking over the helm of their family wineries are increasingly aware of site-specific wines and are fine with others making wines from the same named sites. For example, producers of Teroldego Rotaliano are looking for a new name by which to identify their wines—one that emphasizes a link to the specific terroir of the Rotaliana plain. In Piedmont, producers of Barbera d'Asti have commendably created an outstanding set of production guidelines for their Nizza wines (previously called Barbera d'Asti Superiore Nizza); the name Nizza is far easier to pronounce than the old one, and it is well linked to a specific, finite area within the much larger Barbera d'Asti production zone. (See the Barbera entry in part 2.) Of course, producers should leave the name of the grape variety on the back label at least, but the importance of this seems to escape many in Italy. The fact is that Barbera and Teroldego are names instantly recognized abroad (whereas Rotaliana and Nizza are not), and help propel sales. Most famous sommeliers, importers, and wine experts I have talked to over the years believe that the grape variety should be visible on back labels (at the very least), while people become familiar with the specific terroirs.

Another big but only recently identified problem relating to terroir-specific wines (and in fairness, this is a concern not just in Italy) is the matter of site-specific biotypes (more precisely referred to as ecotypes). There is an increasing awareness that site-specific biotypes produce unique wines that speak of finite places, and that they need to be protected. Planting newly developed grapevine nursery clones in areas where ecotypes have lived for centuries leads to local gene-pool dilution and contamination. In other words, the purest possible expression of that specific local terroir as translated by vines that have lived and adapted to that specific area over centuries is being corrupted by the new arrivals. For example, Cannonau wine quality has been greatly damaged by haphazard plantings on Sardinia of Tocai Rosso (now known as Tai); Tai was planted in good faith because scientists believed that the Veneto's Tai and Sardinia's Cannonau were genetically identical. Maybe so, but the former has adapted over the centuries to a cold and wet habitat, while the latter has always thrived in a marine, hot, droughty one. At the very least, to expect a grapevine from the Veneto to give good results or even just behave like the grapevine does in Sardinia is foolhardy. Furthermore, the area of Jerzu in Sardinia is characterized by many ungrafted, century-old vines and is a true grand cru for Cannonau. These very site-specific Cannonau grapevines give wines that are highly specific to Jerzu. Local producers such as Fratelli Loi are understandably besides themselves that Cannonau nursery clones from outside Sardinia are allowed in Jerzu; in fact, they do not want vines even from other parts of Sardinia to be planted there, and really, you can't blame them. The damage done, and being done, to ecotypes and specific wines has only recently been grasped by scientists and wine producers alike. The good news is that genetic research has advanced such that ecotypes can now be identified by combining different genetic tests (Meneghetti et al. 2012); these have been used, for example, to distinguish between Italian and Croatian biotypes of Malvasia Istriana and between the Malvasia Nera di Brindisi and Malvasia di Lecce grapevines of Puglia. More recently, this panel of tests has been used to distinguish between the Serprina ecotype of Glera typical of the Colli Euganei in Veneto near Padova from the Glera of the Prosecco production area farther east (Meneghetti et al. 2014). Producers are no longer forced to plant generic grapevines that are not those historically grown in their area. Other countries besides Italy are also aware of the need to protect ecotypes. For example, the recently born Burgundian Association pour la Sauvegarde des Biotypes des Cépages has identified over 550 Pinot Noir and over 350 Chardonnay biotypes and strives to make better grapevines available to growers everywhere. So far, these biotypes have been distinguished as Très Fin, Fin, and Supérieur (Aubert de Villaine, private communication). This undertaking aims to help growers avoid using clonal selections developed over the years mainly with an eye to large production volumes, increased disease resistance, and early-ripening qualities. But planting Pinot Noir clones such as the 777 or 677 everywhere has led to a standardization of Pinot Noir wines all over the world; similarly, an overreliance on early-ripening Chardonnay grapevines is a handicap in these times of climate change because finished wine complexity is invariably limited. Paying greater attention to biotype specificity will ultimately lead to more site-specific and hopefully better wines. After all, terroir in your glass conveys a broad, beautiful landscape that suggests endless possibilities, a chance for everyone to realize their dreams. Provided you don't standardize the landscape to begin with, that is.

PART TWO

The Grape Varieties and Their Specific Terroirs

Aglianico

THE GRAPE VARIETY

Given its Greek-sounding name, Aglianico (which closely resembles the Italian word *ellanico*, "Hellenic") was long believed to be a very ancient wine grape that arrived in Italy with the Greeks; however, most linguists agree that the Italian word *aglianico* cannot derive from the word *ellanico*. The earliest the name Aglianico appears in print is most likely in a 1520 archival document attesting ownership of vineyards planted to *Aglianiche* (as in *uve aglianiche*, "aglianico grapes") to the Count of Conversano and in a mid-sixteenth-century reference to the Aglianico wines of the Monte Somma. After that, Aglianico is written about more often (Acerbi 1825; Viala and Vermorel 1909). Aglianico is one of Italy's three greatest red grapes, along with Nebbiolo and Sangiovese, but unfortunately, dubious winemaking has made it hard for Aglianico to show off its true wine colors. It can be used to make a plethora of different wine types: light, easygoing entry-level wines; ageworthy collectibles; and even sparkling, sweet, blush, and white wines.

In the nineteenth and twentieth centuries white wine was commonly made with Aglianico by quickly removing the juice from the skins (a few producers still make such wines), and the grape's high natural acidity is also ideally suited to the production of sweet and sparkling wines. Aglianico's quality is attested to by the large number of nursery clones available to growers. (Clearly, no nursery would have engaged in selecting so many different Aglianicos if they were not likely to sell.) So, depending on which clone or biotype of Aglianico is being considered, the variety generally has medium-small, pyramidal, usually winged, compact bunches and small, round, dark blue-black berries equipped with thick skins.

The three phenotypes of Aglianico that one should remember are those of the three main Aglianico biotypes grown today: Campania's Aglianico di Taurasi (grown near Avellino, in the mountainous Irpinia section of the region) and Aglianico del Taburno (grown near Benevento, to the north of Avellino), and Basilicata's Aglianico del Vulture. These three are supposedly genetically identical, but one quick look tells you they are different biotypes, and their genomes undoubtedly present differences that more in-depth genetic studies would show. There are other, rarer biotypes of Aglianico that might be worth getting to know as well (Monaco and Branca 2016). These are Aglianico Lasco or Aglianico a Sbrinzuli, genetically identical to the very rare variety called Gralluopolo (Aglianico Lasco is characterized by smaller grapes, a loosely packed bunch, and an earlier ripening curve than other Aglianico biotypes); Aglianichello, now almost extinct because of its very small bunch and grapes (obviously, farmers were not impressed); and Aglianico Trignarulo (another extremely rare Aglianico, its presence limited to the countryside around Calitri), characterized by small blue grapes that recall the *spina trigna,* a rare local variety of plum. A late-ripening variety (November harvests are not rare, especially for Aglianico del Vulture), Aglianico benefits from long, warm autumns, which are also helpful in lowering this variety's naturally high acidity and ensuring optimal tannin polymerization. (Aglianico is certainly not short of tannins.)

The three most famous wines made from Aglianico carry the names of the three main biotypes and are called Taurasi, Taburno Aglianico, and Aglianico del Vulture, but there are very good to excellent Aglianico wines made in other DOCs, such as Campania's Cilento and Sannio. No matter where it grows, Aglianico will always deliver a big, strapping red wine, but with considerable finesse (unless grapes are picked too late) thanks to its underlying acidity. Unfortunately, some Campanian producers apparently still believe that *riserva* wines must be made from practically overripe grapes, which is a shame. Normally, Aglianico wines are also firm, minerally, savory, and ageworthy. Pre-fermentation macerations help intensify color and the variety's typical red- but also black-fruit aromas. (The use of hyperreductive winemaking techniques helps avoid burning off aromas.) When young, Aglianico wines also have strong balsamic notes that can be muted by oak and age. (Small and large oak barrels are both fine with Aglianico, but best not to exaggerate with new oak.) Interestingly, all Aglianico wines (but in my experience, especially so the Taurasi and Aglianico del Vulture) have aromas and flavors that are reminiscent of Nebbiolo-based wines. (For this reason, Aglianico wine has reportedly long been used to help strengthen weak vintages of famous wines made in northern Italian and non-Italian climates.) In fact, young Aglianico wines offer red cherry, violet, rose, red berries, and licorice, much like Nebbiolo wines. So it cannot surprise anyone that according to Genovese et al. (2005a), these aromas are the result of the presence of ß-ionone, linalool, ß-damascenone, and ethyl cinnamate. The presence of the latter among molecules in Aglianico wines is important, because we know it is present in Nebbiolo wines as well (see the Nebbiolo entry), providing supportive evidence that wines with at least partly similar aroma profiles can be produced with the two cultivars. Just as interestingly and along the same lines, it is important to know not only that Aglianico is rich in furaneol (a molecule that smells of strawberry and that is also found in Nebbiolo wines), but also that much of it is bound, and is released only slowly into its free form with time. This is important: it helps understand why Aglianico wines maintain a strongly red fruity personality even with age (Gambuti et al. 2005); the slow release means the strawberry flavor develops over a long period of time. Esters are also important in the formation of the typical perfume of Aglianico wines (Piombino et al. 2004). Last but not least, since Aglianico can express methoxypyrazines when not especially ripe, green aromas and flavors reminiscent of the unripe Cabernet cultivars are possible in Aglianico wines, though I have rarely come across them. Should we find them in an Aglianico wine, we will know that, at the very least, the wine is from a bad vintage, a not particularly talented winemaker, or a not especially memorable terroir.

SPECIFIC TERROIRS

Unlike Nebbiolo and Sangiovese, Aglianico can give delightful ageworthy wines in almost any terroir, be it high up in the mountains or down by the seashore. Aglianico performs especially well in volcanic sand and conglomerate-rich, generally loosely packed soils that contain vigor and ensure medium or low grapevine productivity. Not surprisingly, Taurasi, Taburno, and Vulture are all eponymously linked to nearby extinct volcanos: how this mineral environment may translate exactly into finished wines remains unclear, but it is obvious to even minimally experienced tasters that this specific geologic origin has a huge impact on the way Aglianico wines taste. There is no doubt that producers who work more or less the same way, with the same clones and biotypes and with similarly old vines but planted on different soils (such as alluvial sands or volcanic ashes), make completely different wines. Furthermore, wines born on different volcanic sites also differ: Taurasi expresses flinty, red rose, and sour red cherry notes; Taburno, leather and tobacco; and Vulture, rich plum, red and black cherry, and crushed rock. The three different volcanic matrices would appear to have a direct impact on the way the wines from those three areas taste. Clearly, since the best Aglianico wines are made from grapes growing in high mountain vineyards, a potential problem for farmers might be achieving optimal grape ripeness in difficult vintages.

On this subject, an interesting study by Scaglione, Pasquarella, and Boselli (1998a) analyzed the sugar concentration, pH, titratable total acidity, and weight of Aglianico grapes and found that all parameters were positively correlated with heat units, leading the authors to estimate that Aglianico needs roughly 1990 growth degree days (GDD) to ensure musts of 23° Brix, with pH values of 3.1 and at least 7.5 grams per liter titratable acidity. (GDD, or the Winkler index, is an estimate of the energy available for plant development, and is a heat index used to predict when a crop will reach full ripeness.) However, reading the study carefully tells you that these findings pertain to Aglianico grapes in the study's area of Lapio only, in itself one of the coolest and highest Taurasi production subzones. I daresay what is true of Lapio is not exactly true of Venticano or Paternopoli (other, warmer Taurasi production areas; see "Taurasi" below). I wonder if the results would have been the same had the grape source in the study been different. Interestingly, study data showed that grape-sugar accumulation in Aglianico was most sensitive to total heat units, while both acidity and especially pH were less influenced by this measure. This confirms what most wine lovers already know from empiric observation: Aglianico wines showcase remarkable acidity even when made from grapes grown in areas far warmer than Lapio.

Taburno

Campania's Taburno area is less famous than its regional stablemate Taurasi, since up until the 1980s wine was mostly a quantitative affair in this neck of the Aglianico woods (with not only Aglianico vines but also canopies of other cultivars common). How times change: today, there are many outstanding wines made in the denomination, such as those made with the Coda di Volpe Bianca grape. The Taburno denomination has a high-quality terroir; the Taburno Aglianico DOC was awarded in 1986 and the DOCG in 2011. There are thirteen municipalities associated with Taburno Aglianico production (the entire territory of the municipalities of Apollosa, Bonea, Campoli del Monte Taburno, Castelpoto, Foglianise, Montesarchio, Paupisi, Torrecuso, and Ponte, and parts of the territories of Benevento, Cautano, Tocco Caudio, and Vitulano), located mainly on the eastern side of Mount Taburno, where soils are mostly clay-calcareous and where there can be diurnal temperature variations even greater than in Taurasi. In fact, an in-depth analysis by the regional government (Regione Campania

2009) has demonstrated five different soil types in the Taburno denomination, of which only four are especially involved with viticulture. They are: (1) the marly-calcareous and marly-sandstone soils of the Sannio; (2) the clay soils of the high Sannio and high Irpinia areas; (3) the alluvial terraces of the high and middle Volturno River basin; and (4) the lower slopes on internal-area calcareous reliefs. Of these, the most important is the first, with 7,180 hectares, of which 29 percent are under vine. For the most part, the Taburno area also has considerable summer rainfall (on average one thousand millimeters per year, with peaks of sixteen hundred millimeters per year), and a generally cooler microclimate than Taurasi (according to Terribile's 2016 data, the coldest month of the year is February, with the warmest months being July and August, in which daily temperatures average 15–17°C [Winkler index, 1969–2225]), so Taburno's Aglianico wines are marked by particularly high total acidity levels, an austere mouth feel, great freshness, and delightful fragrance. In fact, the other name for Taburno Aglianico (used more often than not by locals) is Aglianico Amaro, where the *amaro* in this case has nothing to do with bitterness but refers to acidity. (Of course, the acidity makes the tannins stand out more.) There are also terroir-related differences between wines made in different sections of the denomination that are not difficult to recognize when one is tasting blind. The northeastern section of the Taburno Aglianico denomination is the one that has been most planted over the years: Torrecuso is the township with the largest number of hectares under vine of the whole denomination (roughly twelve hundred hectares). The other communes in this section of the denomination boasting large expanses of vineyards are Foglianise, Paupisi, and Vitulano. Most vines there lie at four hundred meters above sea level, and are east facing. The microclimate is a little warmer than elsewhere in the denomination, and the soils are typically calcareous-clay. By contrast, vines in the southern section of the Taburno

denomination between Bonea and Montesarchio grow at much higher altitudes, roughly five hundred meters above sea level; many are planted higher, at six hundred meters above sea level. It follows that this subzone has a much cooler mesoclimate and the Aglianico wines are characterized by higher acidities and more-austere mouth feels (partly also due to the soil's higher calcareous content). Throughout the Taburno DOCG, Aglianico grapes are picked in the second half of October and the first ten days of November. An absolutely typical descriptor of Taburno Aglianico is a note of tobacco, one that is not especially typical of Taurasi or of Aglianico del Vulture. Another descriptor that is typical of Taburno Aglianico is a delicate herbal or aromatic underbrush note, again not that typical of the other two main Aglianico wines. Clearly, such nuances are lost when overripe grapes are used. Overall, I find many of the Taburno wines to be more monodimensional than the other two, better-known Aglianico wines, but there are many outstanding wines to be had.

BENCHMARK WINES

La Rivolta Taburno Aglianico***, Cantina del Taburno Aglianico Bue Apis***.

Cantina del Taburno Aglianico Delius**.

Fontanavecchia Taburno Aglianico*.

Taurasi

In 1993, Taurasi was named southern Italy's first DOCG wine. In fact, there is very little "southern Italian" about Taurasi at all (save for wines made by those producers who use overripe grapes and sweet oak in an effort to "internationalize" their wines by making soft, high pH, chocolaty wines). Since Taurasi is not all that warm a place, wines that are overripe and excessively high in alcohol should not be the norm. Taurasi is a DOCG whose wines actually have a clear link to their respective terroirs, and these can be broken down by commune (there are seventeen communes or townships in the

Taurasi denomination) just like in Burgundy or Bordeaux. This makes understanding Taurasi's terroir and its wines much easier. (See below.) Though not small (one thousand hectares in total, but only half or so are under vine), Taurasi is not an especially large DOCG, either. It is cut in half by the Calore River and has a very hilly topography, with mostly small vineyard pockets located at a dizzying array of altitudes, exposures, gradients, and vineyard extensions. It's a situation that makes for many potentially different meso- and microclimates. (The Antonio Caggiano estate has a huge map of the Taurasi DOCG on its winery wall on which the various subzones are very clearly seen.) In Taurasi, Aglianico is the main red grape variety, though Piedirosso is also grown. (Taurasi can be made with 85 percent minimum Aglianico, but almost all the best wines are 100 percent Aglianico.) Altitudes range from three hundred to almost eight hundred meters above sea level, though most vineyards lie between three hundred and six hundred meters above sea level. It follows that diurnal temperature variations are very marked; and though summer days can get warm (13.5–15.5°C), snow is not uncommon in the winter and can at times be very heavy. The coldest month of the year is February and the warmest is August. Taurasi's Winkler index ranges from 1750 to 2150 and its Huglin index from 2200 to 2600. In fact, according to Terribile's outstanding and scholarly 2016 overview, a more precise calculation of the Winkler index (in this book, Huglin and Winkler indices are reported in degrees Celsius) as a yearly average from 2006 to 2015 shows this value to be 1931, 1950, and 1881, respectively, for the three most important Taurasi macroareas—differences not at all insignificant. Rainfall is less copious here than along Campania's coastline (estimated by Terribile to hover between six hundred and one thousand millimeters per year), with most rain falling in November and December, followed by the March–April period. The June–August period sees the least rainfall. The cool late-season environment contributes to protracted, late harvests that in Taurasi commonly take place in

late October or early November. However, because of the denomination's highly varied topography and the huge differences in the altitudes at which the grapes grow, there can be two to three weeks between the harvest in warmer and cooler parts of the denomination. Training methods include cordon spur and Guyot, with an average interrow distance of 2.4 meters, and 1 meter between vines. Most interesting are the old cultivation methods that can still be observed in the area such as the *alberata taurasina* or *alberata tennecchia*. Taurasi's soils are highly complex: while sharing the same calcareous-clay base, there is a highly variable presence of volcanic elements such as lapilli, tuff (do not confuse the similarly sounding tuff with tufa: tuff is of volcanic origin; tufa is a porous limestone), pumice, and ash. Depending on the subzone being considered, varying degrees of alluvial sediments are also present. Regional government data (Regione Campania 2009) break the Taurasi soil types down into a complex system of seven macroareas, of which four are devoted to viticulture: (1) marly-calcareous and marly-sandstone soils of the Sannio and Irpinia; (2) clay soil of Irpinia; (3) marly-calcareous and marly-sandstone soils of the high Sannio and the Sele River valley; and (4) clay soils of the high Sannio, the high Irpinia, and the high Sele River valley. Of these, it is the first two areas that have the greatest amount of land under vine: 12.4 percent and 5.6 percent of their 9,917 and 4,964 hectares, respectively. (By contrast, the other two areas amount to, respectively, only 1,943 and 1,246 hectares, of which only 3.6 percent and less than 1 percent, respectively, are under vine.) According to Luca Palumbo's more recent and highly interesting Viticultural and Enological Sciences faculty thesis of 2012, there are mainly four major soil substrates in Taurasi: marly sandstone; clay and clay-calcareous; sands and conglomerates; and fluviolacustrine/alluvial. It appears that the two factors that exert the greatest influence on the quality of grapes from Taurasi are the altitude and the physical/chemical characteristics of the soil, while exposure appears to play a slightly less important role. Vines in Taurasi grow mostly at three different altitude levels: 300 meters, 400 meters, and 500 meters above sea level. (In fact, the previously mentioned data from Regione Campania described vineyards mostly at heights between 437 and 521 meters above sea level, and judged areas higher up to be devoid of Aglianico vineyard interest.) The consequences are significant: apparently, Aglianico grapes grown at the highest of those three levels ripen slowly, have difficulty accumulating sugars, and have the highest total acidity levels. Grapes growing along the lowest band ripen earliest, and not surprisingly, these wines usually have the highest alcohol levels and the most intense color, while the vines planted between those two extremes tend to give wines with characteristics that are, appropriately enough, intermediate.

By contrast, technological maturity seems to be mostly related to the diverse soil substrates. Clay and calcareous soils containing various amounts of silt give more ageworthy, deeper-colored wines. (But really inky monovariety Aglianico wines à la Merlot or Montepulciano are a red flag.) Wines from grapes grown on such soils and substrates have good but not exceptional intensity of red and blue fruit descriptors (red cherry, blueberry, blackberry). Aglianico grown on Taurasi's alluvial fluviolacustrine soils (in the denomination, these are found mostly below 400 meters above sea level), provided yields are kept judiciously low, tends to give wines that have good balance if not memorable intensity and power, slightly lower total acidity, and higher alcohol concentration than when grown on the other two soil types. The wines are marked by strongly recognizable notes of red and blue fruits, just as are those born on conglomerate and sandy soils. Last, soils characterized by marls and sandstone push Aglianico to give potentially higher yields; these wines are not especially complex (and have generally lower alcohol concentration and higher total acidity). Unless the producer chooses to intervene in the vineyard to curb such vigor, the resulting wines will be ideal for early consumption, offering plenty of early appeal and less staying power. In a really interesting 2010 study by Mazzei et al., Aglianico wines made from grapes grown in three different Aglianico vineyards were compared to analyze the influences of the different terroirs. Microclimate and topography differed slightly at the three sites, but the wines were made following the same winemaking protocol so as to eliminate this confounding variable. The researchers analyzed six metabolite concentrations in the wines: α-hydroxyisobutyrate, lactic acid, succinic acid, glycerol, α-fructose, and β-d-glucuronic acid. Multivariate analyses demonstrated that the differences present among the three wines were related to microclimate and the soil type (specifically, the soil's carbonate, clay, and organic-matter content). The three Taurasi vineyards were located in Case D'Alto (vineyard C), Coste Morante (vineyard S), and Macchia dei Goti (vineyard M). All three vineyards (reportedly harboring only the Aglianico di Taurasi biotype, which is important) were planted in the same year (1982), on the same rootstock (1103 Paulsen), with a spurred cordon training system at a (somewhat low) density of two thousand vines per hectare. Vineyard C is four hundred meters above sea level and has coarsely textured, mostly sandy soil (over 80 percent volcanic ashes and pumices on cinereous platforms), rich in nitrogen and organic carbon, with good drainage. Vineyard S is 325 meters above sea level, and has clay-calcareous, slightly alkaline soil with average exchangeable potassium and a good carbon/nitrogen ratio. Vineyard M is located at 340 meters above sea level, and is mainly characterized by calcareous-clayey soil rich in exchangeable calcium and potassium. (Soils from vineyards M and S are fairly similar, with 27.6 percent and 30.3 percent clay and 21 percent and 22.8 percent silt, respectively.) At cationic exchange capacity (CEC) values of 26.3 (vineyard C), 29.3 (vineyard S), and 24.4 (vineyard M) milliequivalents per one hundred grams of soil, fertility of the three vineyards was comparable. (CEC is a measure of soil fertility that reflects a soil's ability to hold on to and supply important plant nutrients like the positively charged cations calcium, magnesium, and potassium.) The vinifications were carried out at the very high quality Contrade di Taurasi/Lonardo estate: the principal component analysis (PCA) elaboration of the 1H nuclear magnetic resonance (NMR) spectra of the three wines showed significant molecular pattern differences in each (the largest differences being relative to lactic acid, α-fructose, and glycerol). Since the three wines in the study were mostly the product of different soils, this study's results suggest that soil difference was the main factor determining the differences in the three wines. Clearly, soil cannot be taken to have been the only cause for the measured differences, for slight topographical variations and yeast activity could also have contributed in part to the study's results. (At least some of the metabolites investigated, such as lactic acid, succinic acid, and glycerol, may have derived from must and wine-yeast interaction.) An especially interesting aspect of this study is that one of the three wines was markedly different in its metabolite profile from the other two (all three wines were made in the 2005 vintage), implying that mesoclimate also plays a large role in the expression of site specificity. In fact, the wine presenting the biggest analytical diversity was located at the highest altitude with slightly different recorded average temperature and humidity values. Last but certainly not least, NMR spectroscopy combined with chemometric methods showed that an Aglianico wine made in the Taburno area (and therefore deriving from different soils than the three Taurasi sites included in the study) showed statistical differences from the wines in the study, further providing terroir backers with evidence that diversity in similarly made wines exists not just within production zones (the three Taurasi sites) but across them, too (Taurasi and Taburno). I'll drink to that.

The Taurasi Subzones

Taurasi is especially fascinating because the wines made within its various subzones smell and taste obviously different: the legislative powers that be could and should have proceeded to a zonation and classification system of the denomination years ago. In my opinion, the Taurasi production zone can be divided into four main subzones, and a number of today's Taurasi wines can be readily assigned to each subzone (clearly not those made with blends of grapes grown in different parts of the denomination). However, what should be a fairly straightforward task (that of assigning wines and estates to different subzones), given the altitude, commune, and soil data at our disposal, turns out not to be as easy as it first appears, most likely because viticultural and especially winemaking techniques used in the denomination are quite varied (much more so than in the Vulture, for example). The easiest Taurasis to spot blind are those of the fourth (or southern) subzone, because the high altitudes are reflected in very sleek, flinty wines; the greatest difficulty lies with the third subzone, in which unifying traits between wines are harder to come by.

THE NORTHWESTERN SUBZONE

The northwestern Taurasi subzone is situated to the left of the Calore River at the denomination's lowest altitudes (roughly 300 to 350 meters above sea level), and includes only three communes: Pietradefusi, Torre Le Nocelle, and Venticano. It is important to remember these names because wines from this subzone are relatively easy to recognize (if made from grapes grown only there). This subzone's microclimate is relatively warm: Aglianico is harvested earlier than elsewhere in Taurasi (usually by mid-October). Slopes are not especially steep, and soils are fairly homogenous (mainly marl with a little loose loam and sand, especially toward Venticano, where water stress can pose problems, and less so at Pietradefusi). The alkaline and subalkaline soils have plenty of organic matter, high levels of potassium, and low levels of phosphorus. In my experience, these Taurasis are broader, fleshier, and especially earthier than all the others (as expected, given the specific minerals in the soil and the area's mesoclimate); but they have also sneaky age-worthiness, managing to age well despite also offering relatively early appeal. One of the best estates is Struzziero, located in Venticano; the Aglianico grapes used by the talented Clelia Romano, owner of the famous Colli di Lapio estate, also come from Venticano, as are those of Traerte's Aglianico. (Traerte is a new winery run by a group of friends, with ultratalented Raffaele Troise, of the now defunct Vadiaperti estate, making the wines.) Struzziero, Traerte, and Colli di Lapio are among the very best producers of Taurasi. (Struzziero is the more traditional of the two, with at times slightly funky wines, but of great depth and texture; Colli di Lapio's wines, if not quite endowed with the same fleshy, chewy texture, are more modern, suaver, and cleaner; Traerte's style falls in the middle.) Another solid up-and-coming estate using grapes from this subzone is I Favati.

THE WESTERN SUBZONE

Lapio, San Mango sul Calore, Montemiletto, and Montefalcione (whose vineyards lie at four hundred to five hundred meters above sea level) are the municipalities to the west. This subzone is famously devoted to Fiano production: in fact, the communes of Lapio and Montefalcione are the only two Taurasi townships also included in the Fiano di Avellino DOCG. However, locals always say that Lapio was once much more famous for its red-wine production (though I point out that this might simply be because Fiano had virtually disappeared and red wine grapes were the only ones growing in the area; see the Fiano entry). Slopes are steep, and harvest occurs at the end of October or beginning of November. Soils are mainly clay but contain the DOCG's most copious volcanic elements (pumice, for example). These very refined, flinty wines have very good flesh and power, but less so than those of other subzones. Terredora's Taurasi Fatica Contadina is a good example of Taurasi from this subzone (grapes grown in the famous Campore cru).

THE NORTH-CENTRAL SUBZONE AND THE SPECIFIC TAURASI DISTRICT

This subzone is situated to the right of the Calore River: the communes are Bonito (the farthest north of all the Taurasi townships), Fontanarosa, Luogosano, Mirabella Eclano, Santangelo all'Esca, and Taurasi. Soils have a higher proportion of gravel mixed with clay. There is also a strong component of volcanic ash in this subzone, especially around the hamlet of Taurasi; the latter's terroir differs considerably from that of the rest of the subzone, and so, much as I classify Lamole and Panzano as separate wine districts within Greve in Chianti (and you should, too), I also view Taurasi proper as a separate district within the larger Taurasi denomination. Slopes of this subzone are not especially steep (but steeper than those of the left bank of the Calore in the northwestern subzone), the microclimate is a little cooler, and the topography is more rugged, with narrower valleys and smaller vineyard plots, less sunshine, and larger expanses of forest. Though cooler, the mesoclimate is not especially rigid; the Aglianico harvest occurs later than in the northwestern subzone, but the grapes are picked still relatively early (from the end of October through the beginning of November), and olive trees confirm a certain temperate bent to the weather. A high-quality estate near Fontanarosa is Di Prisco, while star winemaking consultant and university enology professor Luigi Moio's Quintodecimo estate is the most famous in Mirabella Eclano. (Mastroberardino owns a vineyard in the vicinity where they cull grapes for their Taurasi Naturalis Historia.) Like the rest of this subzone, the area around Mirabella Eclano has high potassium and low phosphorus levels in the soil, and is especially low in organic matter. Even separating the territory of the hamlet of Taurasi into its own district (see below), the north-central subzone is still the most heterogenous of Taurasi, and both the wines and habitat can differ remarkably. Often the reason is the vastly different viticultural and enological techniques used; and as if that weren't enough, the subzone is probably too large. For example, the hamlet of Pietradefusi is situated at roughly 500 meters above sea level, whereas Mirabella Eclano is found at 350 meters above sea level, and such a difference in altitude has large consequences for the finished wines of each municipality. This is further compounded by differences in soils within the subzone: for example, Pietradefusi's are stonier, and Mirabella Eclano's are sandier. So in the ultimate analysis, current differences between the wines of this subzone reflect individual producer choices as much as the diversities in climate and soils. For example, Antonio Caggiano's famous Taurasi Macchia dei Goti and Feudi di San Gregorio's Taurasi Piano di Montevergine could not be any more different; the former is sweeter, suaver, and more luscious; the latter more austere and flinty. Each is a lovely Taurasi in its own right, but the two really do not seem like they come from the same subzone at all.

THE DISTRICT OF TAURASI

At roughly 350 to 400 meters above sea level, the average elevation at which Aglianico grows in the Taurasi hamlet's territory is lower than that of the rest of the north-central subzone. The topography is also less rugged, with flatter slopes and different soils, deep and rich in organic matter and mostly calcareous with a strong volcanic ash component. In my experience, these wines often have greater depth and better balance than those made with grapes from the rest of the subzone. The Taurasi district can be further subdivided into four microareas that correspond to four plateaus, some of which are historically linked to famous wines: Piano di Montevergine (at about 350 meters above sea level), Contrada Paludisi (at roughly 340 to 370 meters above sea level), Contrada Case d'Alto (at 390 to 400 meters above sea level), and last but certainly not least, the very famous Piano d'Angelo (at 430 to 440 meters above sea level). All four plateaus are characterized by strong volcanic and loamy elements, good drainage, and plenty of sunlight. They are true grand crus for Aglianico production, especially Piano di Montevergine, Case d'Alto, and

Piano d'Angelo. The 1968 Mastroberardino Taurasi Piano d'Angelo is one of Italy's greatest wines of all time; today the outstanding Guastaferro estate sources grapes there. According to Raffaele Guastaferro, Piano d'Angelo's soil is especially characterized by a noteworthy sand content. Cantine Lonardo / Contrade di Taurasi Vigne d'Alto is also a modern masterpiece.

THE SOUTHERN SUBZONE

Taurasi's southern subzone snakes out in the high valley of the Calore River, and includes the townships of Castelvetere sul Calore, Paternopoli, Castelfranci, and Montemarano; soils are more loamy and clay-rich (at Castelfranci, a typical soil breakdown might be loam 55 percent, clay 25 percent, and sand 20 percent), and vines generally grow at about five hundred to six hundred meters above sea level, with some vineyards planted as high as seven hundred meters above sea level. Clearly, this area has a much cooler climate than Venticano's (or that of the rest of the Taurasi denomination, for that matter). Aglianico is picked the latest here: mid-November dates are not unheard of even in these days of climate change. Salvatore Molettieri's famous Cinque Querce vineyard is located in this subzone; other fine estates with vineyards in this area include Boccella, Mastroberardino, Michele Perillo, and Luigi Tecce. The wines are some of the slowest to mature of the whole denomination (never touch a bottle until five to six years after the harvest), and are also some of the most powerful Taurasis (for example, Tecce's mouth-coating Polifemo bottling from vines near Paternopoli).

Taurasi's Best Crus

Based on my tastings of the last thirty years or so, and the studies of old documents and the comments made by producers and winemakers over the years, I offer the following list of exceptional vineyard sites for Taurasi, listed by commune:

Castelfranci: Contrada Baiano (outstanding Aglianico terroir, with clay, lapilli, and gravel); Contrada Valle (differently from Baiano, more sand and tuff). Those who know Italian wine well are aware that in the early to mid-twentieth century, when a lot of Aglianico wine found its way into Piedmont and France, it was actually the wine from the communes of Castelfranci and nearby Montemarano (and not that of Taurasi proper, better known thanks to its train station, since that is where the wine was shipped from) that was most sought after by those trying to improve their anemic reds.

Lapio: Campore. (Some producers and experts value this cru for Fiano, too, but I disagree, finding Fiano wines from Campore to be too broad, ripe, and tropical. This is an example of Italy's lack of credible and accurate official vineyard classifications not helping anybody out; by contrast, Campore's heavy clay soil and full south/southeast, sunny exposures make it an outstanding Aglianico vineyard.)

Montemarano: Jampenne (the area in which Salvatore Molettieri's famous Vigna Cinque Querce Aglianico vineyard is found, but Perillo also owns a vineyard in this cru); Torre. Veronelli (1995) reported that the areas of Baiardo, Chianzano, and Conte Corbo were also very good, but I need to investigate this further.

Montemiletto: Vigna Quattro Conìfini. (Gabriella Ferrara of the Benito Ferrara estate makes an outstanding Taurasi from this site.)

Taurasi: Coste; Piano di Montevergine; Contrada Paludisi; Contrada Case d'Alto; Piano d'Angelo.

BENCHMARK WINES

Contrade di Taurasi Vigne d'Alto***, Contrade di Taurasi Coste***, Guastaferro Primum***, Mastroberardino Radici***, Quintodecimo Vigna Gran Cerzito***, Salvatore Molettieri Riserva Vigna Cinque Querce***.

Benito Ferrara Vigna Quattro Confini**, Colli di Lapio**, Contrada Vini**, Di Prisco**, Perillo**, Pietracupa**, Rocca del Prin-

cipe**, Tecce Polyfemo**, Terredora Fatica Contadina**, Fratelli Urciuolo**.

Boccella Taurasi*, Colli di Castelfranci*, Di Marzo*, Di Meo* (Fontanarosa), Feudi di San Gregorio Piano di Montevergine*, I Capitani*, I Favati* (Cesinali), Il Cancelliere* (Montemarano).

Vulture

Mount Vulture is an extinct volcano that dominates northern Basilicata in the province of Potenza and is geologically older than Mount Taurasi and Mount Taburno. It is so named because its characteristic and instantly recognizable summit of seven peaks is said to transmit the impression of a large bird of prey with its wings spread out, but as I have said and written before, this likeness is no doubt much easier to appreciate after one has imbibed very large amounts of the local Aglianico wine. Which, given how good some of it is, might not be such a bad thing. Aglianico del Vulture is potentially one of Italy's (the world's, even) greatest red wines, but shoddy winemaking and a difficult past twenty years have kept the wine off the radar of collectors and wine lovers. Unfortunately, local producers did not capitalize on a series of positive events at the turn of the new century. For a variety of reasons, that promise was not sustained (among the problems: the Aglianico del Vulture DOC itself, which is just too large; too many and too similar Aglianico wines made at each estate; no white wines of note; bad oak, or too much of it when of good quality; and, with few exceptions, little or no team spirit between producers), and so the area fell on tough times. The one Michelin-starred restaurant in Barile came and went, the beautiful hotel in which it was housed (the Locanda del Palazzo) was sold to Campania's Feudi di San Gregorio and shut down, and producers Angeletti, Basilisco, Basilium, Giannattasio, Il Nibbio Grigio, Macarico, Paternoster, Tenuta del Portale, and Tenuta Le Querce were sold, ceased activity, or took a break before reemerging recently. The good news is that the last five years have seen an energetic new generation taking over their family wineries: Carbone, Grifalco, Madonna delle Grazie, Musto Carmelitano, and Vigna Mastrodomenico are some of the most exciting estates to have appeared on the Italian wine scene in some time. The Vulture has a long and distinguished history as a source of very fine wines, and just as with Taurasi, local old-timers still regale all those within earshot with stories of their Aglianico wine sold off in bulk and transported by train to more-northern lands.

In fact, the surface of Vulture's potential has only been scratched. I have visited the Vulture something like forty-five to fifty times in the last eighteen years (I kid you not), and I know its terroir like the insides of my pockets. From a general standpoint, the Vulture's production area is open toward the Adriatic Sea, ensuring a cooler mesoclimate than Taurasi's, which looks out toward the Tyrrhenian Sea. Mount Vulture also creates a barrier to the extremely hot winds blowing in out of Africa, which is important given that the summer months can be particularly droughty in this part of Basilicata. However, the high content of clay-rich volcanic tuff in the Vulture's soils that are located at higher altitudes allows for water to be released slowly when environmental conditions become too dry. Clearly, an expanse as vast as that of the Vulture boasts many diverse terroirs, and it is genuinely thrilling to discern these different terroirs in the glass. The first step is to learn the names of the townships within the denomination: Acerenza, Atella, Banzi, Barile, Forenza, Genzano di Lucania, Ginestra, Lavello, Maschito, Melfi, Palazzo San Gervasio, Rapolla, Rionero in Vulture, Ripacandida, and Venosa. That is easier to do than it looks because only a few of these communes are associated with wine. The communes of Acerenza, Atella, Banzi, Genzano di Lucania, Lavello, and Palazzo San Gervasio have no Aglianico producers of note; some have even few Aglianico vines. You can certainly go to Palazzo San Gervasio, as I have, and see the pretty late-nineteenth-century Fontana Cavallina (once

voted one of Italy's thirty-three most beautiful fountains); what you will not see is many Aglianico vines. Another important thing to know is that the Vulture, much like the Etna or Taurasi, has a number of *contrade* historically linked to exceptional wines; in fact, locals referred to the best grape-growing sites of the Vulture as *"prime zone"* (meaning "first zones" or "first choice" areas), indicating an awareness, at least among locals, of the area's best terroirs. Over the last fifteen-year period, producers have talked with me about these at length, and newcomers to the Vulture wine scene are now getting into the act. For example, the Aglianico del Vulture wines of the talented Piccin brothers (Grifalco estate) carry a clear indication of the township where the grapes come from. In 2005 their first wines from the communes of Ginestra and Maschito were named Aglianico del Vulture Daginestra and Aglianico del Vulture Damaschito (where the "Da" means "from"). A list of *contrada* names of the Aglianico del Vulture denomination is officially recognized, and producers are free to use these names on their labels, provided of course that the grapes were really grown in those *contrade*. Though this is certainly a positive step, fairness dictates that I mention that a number of important Vulture estates, such as Fucci and Grifalco, would have much preferred the indication of township on the label (and the Piccin brothers have cleverly proceeded to do so anyway) because they believe the *contrada* names are currently completely unknown to most wine lovers (hard to argue that) whereas the townships are easier for people to identify, remember, and understand. Of course, this being Italy, there are those in the Vulture who disagree with the use of both townships and of *contrade*, preferring to try to pull the wool over the eyes of wine lovers by going on about how special their single vineyards are (when nobody throughout history seems to have thought so; for that matter, nobody does today, either). Admittedly, it will take time and producer and regional-government effort to have people learn the *contrada* names; currently it's one thing to say, "This wine is from Barile or Venosa," and quite another to say it is from Piano di Carro or Gelosia. (But they have the same problem in Barolo: more than one foreign wine expert has complained to me over the years that having to remember almost two hundred MGA [*menzioni geografiche aggiuntive*, or "additional geographic characterizations"] names makes little or no sense when it is far easier to remember that La Morra and Barolo make lighter-bodied wines than do Monforte or Serralunga d'Alba.) Still, I do not believe one should be overcome with negative thoughts on the matter. (Some of the Vulture's smaller producers view this unwillingness to identify townships as another attempt by the Vulture's bigger estates and co-ops to stifle zonation attempts that, in their view, might actually be of use to people.) Being the "glass is always half full" type, I think just the fact that the *contrade* have been officially recognized and are included in the denomination production guidelines is a major step. Producers now need to work together to categorize the characteristics of the wines of each *contrada*. In the end, it will not be any different from having to learn about Barolo's Cannubi, Vigna Rionda, and Rocche.

Aglianico del Vulture Subzones

I think the easiest way to break down the Vulture's terroir is into subzones (divided into Upper, Middle, and Lower Vulture) and then by township, since the aroma and flavor profiles of the Aglianico del Vulture wines made from grapes grown in each township differ. Once the differences between the townships are committed to memory, the next step is to learn the characteristics of the wines of the *contrade*. Much like in Bordeaux and Burgundy, where one would never say that Margaux is better than Pauillac or that Musigny is better than Gevrey-Chambertin, it is the same in the Vulture, where it is not a matter of one terroir being better than another, but rather that each provides a different take on the Vulture's wines. The three most important communes of the Vulture are Barile (at the top of the volcano),

Venosa, and Maschito (the latter two slightly lower down the slope). Keep in mind that "higher" and "lower" are very relative terms on the Vulture, where distances are short. (It is the never-ending winding roads that you drive along up and down the mountain that make you think otherwise.) So, for example, Barile lies at 620 meters above sea level and Venosa at 420 meters above sea level, but the latter's vineyards climb both downward and upward from the city. It also helps to know where the townships are located relative to Mount Vulture's summit: the municipalities of Barile, Rionero in Vulture, and Rapolla are located close to the volcano's summit; Venosa and Maschito are located farther away from the summit (which is not exactly the same as saying "lower down": the Vulture is a broad-based, slowly sloping volcano); the vineyards of Forenza, Ginestra, and Ripacandida are situated between these two extremes. (The towns of Forenza and Ripacandida are located on outcroppings at higher altitudes than Barile and Rionero in Vulture, but these two are situated right below the seven peaks, whereas Forenza and Ripacandida are farther removed from the summits.) For the most part, the most reputed Aglianico vineyard sites on the Vulture are those located between four hundred and five hundred meters above sea level, closest to the volcano's summit, but Aglianico vineyards are not rare on Vulture even at altitudes of six hundred meters; some ventilation is essential, given the characteristics of the Aglianico grape (as discussed above); and given that diurnal temperature variations in the Vulture can be as much as 20°C, the leaf canopy works for longer hours during Aglianico's long, protracted growth cycle. Therefore, geology and soil types on their own are not enough to correctly identify subzones in the Vulture, since altitude and exposure play significant roles, too. However, knowing the geologic origin of the soils is an important first step, because the origin of soils closer to the volcano's peaks (such as in the communes of Barile, Rionero in Vulture, Ginestra, and Ripacandida) differs from that of the soils of Maschito and Venosa. The soils of the communes close to the volcano's summit originate from volcanic eruptions that happened at least 133,000 years ago and that ejected volcanic ash at great distances; the ash then compacted and consolidated, forming tuff. (Remember, do not confuse tuff with tufa.) By contrast, the areas of Maschito and Venosa were formed from deposits of a large lake that covered that part of the Vulture during the Quaternary period. Therefore, these soils are the result of the compaction of gravel, fine and coarse sands, and conglomerates, resulting in a mostly tufa-rich soil. I caution readers that classifying the Vulture into two major wine-producing areas in this manner does not sit too well with those producers who fear that their estates will be saddled with a "lesser" subzone. "Better" and "lesser" in the Vulture almost always refer to just how close a vineyard is to the summit of the volcano and the presence or lack of volcanic soil there: soils with strongly volcanic elements are thought to be most suited to Aglianico. Consequently, the farther removed you are from the Vulture's summit, the less likely your vineyard's soils are to be strongly volcanic in nature, making them second-class citizens in the minds of many wine lovers, experts, and even producers. Volcanic elements present in Maschito and Venosa soils originated from the far-reaching ejection of pumice, lapilli, and ash during eruptions and from lava streams flowing down the volcano's slopes to reach the eastern territory of Venosa; but clearly, volcanic elements are more abundant closer to the top of the volcano. However, the view that the best sites for Aglianico del Vulture are the mountain top's volcanic dark soils is fallacious at best. I can make a very good case that the best Aglianico del Vulture wines of all are those of Barile and Maschito, but the latter has anything but black soil (I am partially daltonic, but even I can tell it is reddish.) So the issue of where the lava actually did get to (or did not) is moot. Therefore, differentiating between Aglianico del Vulture wines made in the subzone of Venosa and Maschito and those of Ginestra, Ripacandida, and

Rapolla, Forenza, Barile, and Rionero is possible and accurate thanks to the geological differences present in the two large subzones. The lithological properties of the soil are not by themselves enough to distinguish between wines from the Vulture's subzones: exposure, altitude, slope gradient, and other terroir-related parameters play an essential role in what the Vulture's grapes and wines will be like. Gerardo Giuratrabocchetti of the Cantine del Notaio estate proved as much in the 1990s when he set up experimental vineyards in five different communes. The vineyards he studied are at about 450 meters above sea level, and exposures, slopes, and all other parameters (save for soil) were comparable. Results of tests showed that the major differentiating factor between wines was when the grapes were picked: delaying the harvest by two, four, and six weeks had the most impact on the wines (and in fact this is the guiding principle behind Cantine del Notaio's wines: the various Aglianico wines they make are distinguished by harvest date). While the study showed that soil alone does not make for highly different wines on the Vulture, the combination of different altitudes, exposures, soil, and Aglianico biotypes allows for very different wines in the denomination's subzones. The following is my breakdown of the Aglianico del Vulture subzones based on where the communes are located and the characteristics of the wines made in each.

UPPER OR HIGH VULTURE

Barile: At 620 meters above sea level, this town is at the epicenter of Aglianico del Vulture production. Historically, Barile has always been intimately linked with Aglianico vineyards, while Rionero in Vulture was always the home to *négociants* (more than to vineyards). In fact, Barile's coat of arms shows a barrel (*barile* is Italian for "barrel," and the town was once a barrel-making center) inserted between two fir trees and a grape bunch. Barile is characterized by the *scescio*, the long row of century-old cellars built above ground to store wine (unlike

Rionero in Vulture, where cellars are below ground; Rapolla's cellars are also located above ground). The countryside of Rionero in Vulture, though it closely resembles Barile's, presents noteworthy differences in topography, microclimate, and soils; but the wines still resemble those of Barile, sharing a strongly flinty-mineral connotation to the floral red and blue fruit aromas and flavors. In this trio of communes (Barile, Rionero in Vulture, and Rapolla), Rapolla's wines are always the broadest and softest (a relative term with Aglianico wines), with a fleshier mouthfeel, though they still offer the flinty-savory blue and red fruit nuances typical of the other two communes. The softer, richer personality of Rapolla's wines is most likely due to its generally lower-lying vineyards (Rapolla lies only at 447 meters above sea level); its more open and breezier topography; a sunnier, warmer mesoclimate; and higher clay-loam soil content. The slightly more herbal, aromatic note of Rapolla's wines may also be due to the wealth of perfumed field herbs growing in the commune's vineyards; for example, I can vouch that there is plenty of wild rocket growing in the Rapolla vineyards.

CENTRAL OR MIDDLE VULTURE

Atella: At five hundred meters above sea level, this village is slightly removed from the other Vulture subzones. It is situated close to the two lakes of Monticchio—one of Basilicata's most beautiful natural sites and well worth a visit. Soils are clay-loamy, and the microclimate is relatively cool. The wines are less flinty and broader than those of Barile, but less fleshy and savory than those of Rapolla. There is considerable potential here.

Forenza: I believe this territory to be one of the two or three greatest in all the Vulture. Many true grand crus for Aglianico del Vulture are located here, but few are known. Having found, over my years of tasting in the cellars of estate after estate, that the best vats of wine are always those made with one specific grape variety (or blends) from the same specific area year after year, I realized that this is no accident.

Simply put, the barrels of Aglianico wine from Forenza are always the best or close to the best at every estate I have tasted at over the years, and that cannot be the result of chance. Furthermore, over the years tasting in the Vulture, locals have always sung the praises of Forenza's terroir. Forenza highlights how treacherous it is to assume that you know where towns and vineyards lie relative to the volcano's peaks. Even though it is only a few kilometers from Maschito, Forenza lies at a whopping 836 meters above sea level, so it's actually higher up than Barile and Rionero in Vulture (the road to the town seemingly does nothing but go straight up; as an aside, you will find there is a very good pastry shop on your left as you drive upward), whereas in general, vineyards lie at lower altitudes (roughly 450 to 580 meters above sea level). The reason Forenza is essentially unknown to wine people (even in Italy) is because there have never been major wineries in the area, and those who do own vineyards there, such as Armando Martino, did not emphasize site specificity much. Forenza's mesoclimate is cooler than that of most other parts of the Vulture, and snow is not rare there come winter. Summers are fresh and dry, but the rainy autumns can be Forenza's Achilles' heel. The wines are some of the deepest and balanced of the Vulture, with a flinty-mineral undertone (but less than Barile's wines).

Ginestra: By contrast with Forenza, Ginestra has always been associated with fine Aglianico grapes and wines; the town is located at 564 meters above sea level, but the vineyards lie between 500 and 600 meters above sea level. Soils are mainly clay-calcareous tuff, and there is plenty of open space and sunlight.

Ripacandida: Located at a much higher altitude (620 meters above sea level) than Ginestra; perched high on a rocky outcropping, the town is easy to spot. (Besides visiting the vineyards, which lie below town at lower altitudes, I recommend stopping at the San Donato church, the nucleus of which dates back to the twelfth century and whose lovely sixteenth-century frescoes are the work of a Giotto student.) Ripacandida's wines are more austere in their floral exuberance than those of Ginestra (which are fleshier and more savory), but neither have the depth or complexity of those of Forenza.

LOWER VULTURE
Northern Sector
Melfi: Historically the most important town of the Vulture area, Melfi was at one time the capital of the Duchy of Apulia (in 1059), and papal councils were held there. Emperor Frederick II proclaimed the Constitutions of Melfi (or *Constitutiones Augustales*) in 1231, and its officials were allowed to levy taxes, and in so doing greatly increased Melfi's size and wealth. By contrast, quality Aglianico viticulture is only recent there. Melfi lies at 532 meters above sea level, and soils are mostly calcareous-loamy clay. The Aglianico wines can be a little straightforward but with good tannic backbone; I would rate them of premier cru quality at best.

Northeastern Sector
Lavello: Lavello is located at 313 meters above sea level in the flatlands at the foot of the Vulture. The area is open and breezy and well exposed to sunlight, with lightly reddish soils rich in clay and potassium. The Aglianico wines from Lavello are very linear and simple, and offer early accessibility; but reaching physiologic ripeness is difficult here in some vintages.

Eastern Sector
Maschito: The extremely red-tinged clay and gravelly soils of Maschito are instantly recognizable. Large jagged rocks (very different from the round and smooth rocks of fluvial origin) are abundant, making Maschito's steep slopes hard to work; the vineyards lie mostly at five hundred meters above sea level. Maschito's are unique among all Aglianico del Vulture wines, spicy and fleshy, with ripe red fruit and sweet pipe-tobacco aromas and flavors of extreme intensity immediately distinguishable from all other Aglianico del Vulture wines. As a learning tool, if you compare Grifalco's Aglianico del Vulture Damaschito to Fucci's Aglianico del Vulture Titolo, the difference between the wines of Maschito and Barile will jump out at you immediately. Importantly, the wines from the Maschito subzone made by different producers all share the same traits, which speaks of a definite terroir. According to Christian Scrinzi, winemaker of Terre degli Svevi (owned by Gruppo Italiano Vini), every time he tastes different samples of Aglianico del Vulture blind, he always rates the Maschito wines best, and you hear similar statements everywhere in the Vulture. The greatness of Maschito and its Aglianico del Vulture is showcased by Paternoster's famous Don Anselmo bottling: though still exceptional, it no longer reaches the heights it attained in the late 1990s (when it was the best Aglianico del Vulture of all: witness the 1997, a simply grandiose wine); the reason is a change in the source of grapes. In the new century, Paternoster had to stop using the Maschito grapes they had always rented and switched to those of another vineyard. The differences in aromas and flavors between the "before" and "after" wines are obvious.

Venosa: By far the prettiest of all the Vulture's towns, Venosa is a place where you will enjoy taking a walk. The birthplace of the Roman poet Horace (65–8 B.C.) and home to a beautiful Aragonese castle built by Pirro del Balzo in 1470, it is also the township with the largest extension of vines in the Vulture. Vineyards lie below and above 400 meters above sea level; the town itself lies at 415 meters above sea level. The brownish-tan-colored soils are mostly pebbly loamy clay with pockets of volcanic elements, and so there are obvious dark-colored spots. Be careful: the towns of Venosa and Maschito are close to each other, and so the tendency is to lump together their wines, but that should be avoided because the wines of each are quite different. Aglianico ripens earlier in Venosa than anywhere else in the Vulture: therefore, Venosa's grapes usually boast the highest sugar concentrations and its wines sport the highest alcohol levels of all Vulture wines. A good Venosa Aglianico has more of a red color compared with the purple-red of

Vulture Aglianicos from Barile or Ginestra; the aromas and flavors are mostly of ripe red fruit (red cherry, strawberry) but with only a hint of the sweet spiciness of Maschito or the flintiness of Ripacandida or Barile wines. Venosa's wines are generally more linear, but there can be noteworthy differences between wines made in the large Venosa territory relative to their polyphenol concentrations. It is also important to know the vintage characteristics of Venosa's wines. Its vineyards lie mostly on flatlands rather than hillsides; therefore, water drainage here can be a problem compared with that in Barile or Rionero.

The Contrade and Best Crus

BARILE

Gelosia: This large *contrada* is probably best split up in a northern sector (close to Rapolla) and a southern sector. The wines from the former are more floral and fruity, the latter more savory and earthy. Historically, the most famous wines from this *contrada* were made by Michele Cutolo at his Basilisco estate (and sold in 2010–11 to Campania's large Feudi di San Gregorio winery). Today, thanks to Viviana Malafarina, who now runs Basilisco with passion and competence, the estate is trying to highlight differences in its Aglianico del Vulture wines via single vineyards. But I respectfully submit that it would be far more useful for everyone, Basilisco included, if people first got to learn—just as they do in Burgundy, Bordeaux, and the rest of the world—what the wines of Barile are mostly about, then those of Gelosia, and only then single-vineyard wines, provided they really are that noteworthy.

Gorizza: Well known to locals for the quality of its grapes and wines already in the 1800s (the Giannattasio winery conserves an 1872 agricultural surveyor's document detailing the extent of vineyards and olive groves in the "Tenuta La Gorizza"), I have always found Gorizza's wines to be fleshy and sweet yet refined. In my books, this is a very high quality premier cru site, possibly a grand cru.

Macarico: Located at about five hundred meters above sea level, this vineyard site always gives large-scaled, deep, flinty Aglianico del Vulture wines marked mostly by notes of blue fruit and balsamic oils. The most famous Macarico wine was made by Rino Botte at his Macarico estate (he named it after the *contrada*), now owned by Gerardo Giuratrabocchetti of the famous Cantine del Notaio, but Giannattasio has made some outstanding Aglianico del Vulture wines with grapes from this site, too.

Rotondo: This cru takes its name from the Villa Rotondo, a once beautiful but now run-down building. The vineyard area has long been associated with Paternoster (sold in 2016, Paternoster is now owned by Veneto's Tommasi estate) and lies at roughly 550 meters above sea level, characterized by dark-colored clay-calcareous soil with small stones. The wine is always refined yet powerful, brimming with red fruit aromas and flavors complemented by hints of balsamic oils and aromatic herbs. It's a unique site that combines the Vulture's two souls—flinty minerality and ripe red fruit—as few others do.

Titolo: The Titolo is the one grand cru *hors classe* of the Vulture denomination. It is mostly owned by the Elena Fucci estate. (A local farmer owns a few plots of vines, but he does not produce wine for commercial sale.) The Titolo is situated next to one of the Vulture's summits (only one kilometer away), which means that it is cooled by cold winds blowing down from the volcano and that the dark clay-loam soils are exceptionally lava-rich. (One of the Vulture's main lava flows passed immediately south of the Fucci estate.) The vines lie at roughly six hundred meters above sea level, in a much fresher and better-ventilated area than others (as anyone standing in the vineyard and not wearing a light sweater, even in the summertime, will realize immediately).

FORENZA

San Martino: A true grand cru for Aglianico del Vulture, San Martino is situated at roughly 560 to 590 meters above sea level on mostly volcanic sandy soils with high manganese and iron content (friable sulfur-rich stones are also common); below the top layers, gravel and compacted volcanic ash dominate. Given the high sand content of the soil, these are not the most structured of Vulture wines, but they are extremely elegant, showcasing wonderful perfume and floral lift. Grifalco owns two hectares of sixty-to-seventy-year-old vines. (Their Damaschito wine is made with fruit from this vineyard situated on the border with the Maschito area, but in my humble view, the wine should really be called Daforenza.)

GINESTRA

Piano dell'Altare: This site is located at an average of 440 meters above sea level with a 12 percent slope gradient, though vineyards can climb much higher (590 meters). The soils are mostly clay with a volcanic tuff substrate. In my experience wines made from this site are well balanced and elegant, intensely floral and never too high in alcohol.

MASCHITO

Caggiano, Casano, and Cerentino: Both Caggiano and Casano are situated just below 500 meters above sea level, while Cerentino is located lower down, at 380 to 400 meters, though a section of its vines climbs to slightly more than 500 meters above sea level. These Maschito crus give very different wines. Casano (430 to 520 meters in elevation) has a mostly western exposure, with more loamy clay above and increased gravel and limestone tufa at lower elevations: its wines are characterized by good structure and color, are less floral, and are never too high in alcohol. Caggiano's vineyards climb up to 540 meters above sea level; the soil has less loam and looks white thanks to a higher calcium carbonate content. Its wines are slightly neutral when young but have good acidity and citrus lift. I may be

wrong, but grapes from this cru might represent very good blending agents. Unlike Casano and Caggiano, Cerentino (not to be confused with the very similarly named Celentino, which is another *contrada* of the Vulture) has a flat topography. The soils are mostly clay. From 1998 to 2003, Cantine del Notaio's famous Aglianico del Vulture La Firma was made with grapes picked only in Cerentino; beginning in 2004 the wine became a blend from different sites and so the cru's name was dropped from the label.

RAPOLLA

Caselle: A very famous Aglianico vineyard that I would rate an exceptional premier cru, in the same vein as Gevrey-Chambertin's Clos St.-Jacques and Chambolle-Musigny's Les Amoureuses. Vineyards lie at roughly four hundred meters above sea level on gray-colored volcanic clay soils that are loosely packed. There is a lot of wild rocket that grows in the vineyard: perhaps this is why, besides exceptional balance and a suave mouthfeel, I also usually find aromatic herbs complicating the sour red cherry aromas and flavors (very Nebbiolo-like, in fact) of Caselle wines. Donato D'Angelo has made many beauties from this vineyard over the years.

RIONERO IN VULTURE

Cugno di Atella: One of the higher vineyards in the denomination, lying at an altitude of 490 to 550 meters above sea level, with a 25 percent slope gradient. Many of the vines here were planted with a north–south orientation. The soils are a mix of sand and siliceous volcanic ash, with a volcanic tuff substrate. The wines are some of the most tactile and savory of the whole denomination, but also quite refined.

RIPACANDIDA

Piano del Duca: The vineyards here have a mostly east/southeast exposure and lie at altitudes of four hundred to five hundred meters above sea level. The slope gradient is roughly 20 percent. Soils are mainly siliceous volcanic ash with a volcanic tuff substrate. The wines can be flinty but angular at times.

VENOSA

Fronte Cantina, La Sbarra, Notarchirico: In my opinion, Notarchirico is another top-notch premier cru like Caselle, characterized by looser soils with some gravel and much ventilation; the wines recall those of Maschito. By contrast, Fronte Cantina and La Sbarra, characterized by deeper, more fertile soils, give less structured and fleshy wines that offer more in the way of elegance and higher total acidities. The Aglianico del Vulture grapes from these two sites are highly typical of the Venosa area. (Terre degli Svevi owns vineyards on all three sites but blends them together, so unless you taste the single wines prior to the making of the final blend like I do, it becomes objectively harder to understand what each terroir can give on its own.)

BENCHMARK WINES

Elena Fucci Titolo***[PS].

Cantine del Notaio La Firma***, Donato D'Angelo Canneto***, Grifalco Damaschito***, Paternoster Don Anselmo***.

Basilisco Cruà**, Basilisco Fontanelle**, Cantina di Venosa Carato Venusio**, Cantine del Notaio Il Sigillo**, Grifalco Daginestra**, Musto Carmelitano Pian del Moro**, Musto Carmelitano Serra del Prete**, Paternoster Rotondo**, Terre degli Svevi Serpara**, Terra dei Re Nocte **.

Armando Martino Pretoriano*, Laluce Zimberno*, Terre degli Svevi Re Manfredi*.

Barbera

THE GRAPE VARIETY

Roberto Conterno (of Giacomo Conterno) states, in his usual self-assured style: "Barbera is one of Italy's greatest wine grapes." Just by looking at the numbers, I would have to say a lot of people agree with Roberto: Barbera is Italy's third-most-planted red cultivar and one of the top five, all colors considered. According to Tempesta and Fiorillo (2011), in 1970 the number of hectares under vine to Barbera was almost the same as that of Sangiovese and Cataratto (which we now know actually comprises a family of three slightly different grapes); at the time, these were Italy's three most-planted wine grapes. (It is only in the 1980s that Sangiovese became by far the most-planted grape variety in Italy.) Barbera is common not just in Italy (20,759 hectares) but all over the world (another 12,500 hectares), confirming it as a highly reputed wine grape: as recently as 1990 it was the world's fifteenth-most-planted wine grape (Anderson 2014), and it still ranks in the world's top thirty-five. (Previously surveyed grapes of Charbono in Argentina had been mistakenly identified as Barbera, partly explaining the latter's decreased hectarage over a short period of time.) Barbera's popularity is shown by more than just arid data: for example, few Italian wine grapes boast more clones than does Barbera. Remember that no nursery would have bothered with the expense of creating clones if it didn't think there would be people interested in buying them. (The problem with most of the Barbera clones available today is that they are too productive.) Another indirect piece of evidence telling us Barbera is a pretty hot-to-trot grape is the copious amount of laboratory work undertaken to have it parent new wine grapes. Once again, it is safe to assume that no scientist worthy of his or her graduated cylinders would ever choose a cultivar with serious flaws as the potential parent of new grape crossings. And so it is that the list of Barbera crossings is a long one, too. Barbera is one of the proud parents of Albarossa, Cornarea, Ervi, Incrocio Terzi 1, Nebbiera, Nigra, Prodest, San Michele, and Soperga. Of these, Incrocio Terzi 1 has met with some success, but it is Albarossa (Barbera × Chatus) that is one of the all-time most successful crossings. In this light, Prunotto's Bricco Colma and Chiarlo's Albarossa are just two examples of delightful Albarossa wines, fleshy and redolent of ripe red cherry and spicy tobacco nuances. Last but not least, that Barbera is a highly thought-of variety is demonstrated by the large number of Barbera-something varieties that exist in Italy: Barbera del Sannio, Barbera Sarda, and Barbera Bianca are all distinct and unrelated. Clearly the name Barbera helps sell, and so people everywhere wish to give their own local grapes a boost by associating them with Barbera.

Barbera's name derives either from *barbaro* ("barbarian") due to its deep red color or from *vinum berberis*—an astringent, acidic, and deeply colored medieval drink. The grape originates in the Monferrato area of Piedmont (in the province of Alessandria), where its presence is documented as early as the seventeenth century. In fact, DNA profiling studies presented in 2003 by Schneider, Boccacci, and Botta have shown that Barbera does not share close genetic ties with any other Piedmontese wine grape. Very vigorous and drought resistant, Barbera is susceptible to spring frosts and very sensitive to fanleaf virus. A very deep purple color, a virtual absence of tannins, and high acidity are the hallmarks of Barbera wines. The variety's pigments were first studied in depth by Sakellariades and Luh (1974), then by Cravero and Di Stefano (1992): the pigments have a high total anthocyan content, malvidin (a dark pigment, unlike peonidin and cyanidin) being the most common anthocyanidin; even more important, 47 percent of Barbera's anthocyanidins are of the conjugated form (p-cumarates [22 percent] and acetates [25 percent]), which explains why the color of Barbera wines is very stable over time. Barbera's pips are characterized by lower tannin concentrations than those of most other Piedmontese wine grapes, and its higher concentrations of pip epicatechin compared with pip catechin means that Barbera is less likely to give aggressive wines (Novello 2005). Barbera's pips tend to ripen at different rates, and so, come harvest, grapes usually reveal some green pips next to fully ripe brown ones: according to Mario Olivieri, winemaker at Marchesi Alfieri, this depends mostly on the soil Barbera is planted in. Barbera is resistant to saline environments: a study performed in California indicated that Barbera behaves similarly when planted on highly saline and nonsaline soils (Mielke and Dutt 1977). Even more interestingly, a study from Arizona compared soil salinity tolerance of ungrafted Barbera vines on the one hand, and Barbera vines on different rootstocks and reared in a greenhouse setting on the other. The soils were irrigated with solutions sporting different salt concentrations (0.45, 2.5, and 5 millimhos per centimeter, respectively): ungrafted grapevines were less resistant to the soil's salt load than grapevines grafted onto Kober 5BB and Ramsey rootstocks (Arbabza-deh-Jolfaee 1982). Kober 5BB-grafted Barbera vines also appear more resistant to cold weather than do ungrafted vines (Bandinelli et al. 1986). Barbera is a late-ripening variety, but this can vary based on the viticultural decisions taken at each estate. For example, a study on ten different Barbera vineyards in the Monferrato that were green-harvested at veraison (with elimination of 16 to 39 percent of the distal bunches) reported decreases in both malic acid and total acidity in the musts. With bunches reduced by 30 percent or more, optimal grape ripeness was achieved eight days earlier (Corino et al. 1991). Though when left to its own devices Barbera tends to ripen late, it is a variety that likes warm temperatures; even better, it likes constant warm temperatures (unlike Nebbiolo, which thrives instead on strong diurnal temperature variations). Heat is important with Barbera for very specific reasons: when I write anywhere in this book (or when I mention in public) that a variety "likes heat," I am not just throwing that phrase out lightheartedly; rather, I am addressing a link between a physical parameter of terroir and specific grapevine physiology that is worth knowing about. For example, Barbera grown in hot, droughty environments is characterized by a very high percentage of fertile buds (80 percent), which is not the case when it is grown in humid, wet ones; in the former type of habitat, the fertility index is close to 2 and the index of real fertility is 1.3 (Forlani, Gioffré, and Coppola 1981). In cool habitats, bud fertility increases from the base up to the seventh–thirteenth nodes, after which it begins to fall in linear fashion (Khalil 1961). You understand why it is so critical for farmers to have that piece of information and how this genetically determined Barbera grapevine trait will eventually play out in the Barbera grape's expression of terroir in the glass.

Heat is important with Barbera for another reason, too. Unlike many other cultivars, Barbera has a very good ability to recover from hail episodes (clearly, depending on just how disastrous the hail episode), ensuring decent productivity within the year in which the hail episode took place, and almost normal production levels the following year (Eynard et al. 1975; Gay, Eynard, and Almondo 1985). That is the sort of information that greatly affects planting, training, and pruning decisions. Most important, Barbera has the Riesling-like quality of producing decent-quality wines even at high yields, though getting it to put out waterfalls of wine isn't the way to go about either making good wines or identifying terroir-related nuances in them. Stefano Chiarlo of the Chiarlo winery explains that Barbera wines *have* to have high alcohol levels (at least 14 percent); otherwise, the wine risks being boring and nondescript (though from a scientific point of view, we still do not understand why that is). Not surprisingly, results presented by Ummarino and Di Stefano (1996) showed Barbera's biochemical profile to be strongly influenced by the number of pips in its grapes. The authors reported that in Barbera grapes an increase in the number of pips from one to three is accompanied by a 50 percent increase in berry mass and a 25 percent increase in total polyphenol content, while (and perhaps even more relevantly in Barbera's specific case, given its high acid personality) tartaric and malic acid concentrations remain unchanged. Boselli, Volpe, and Di Vaio

(1996) reported similar results and also found that the skin anthocyans decrease (by 16 percent, in this study) as do the pip polyphenols (by 37 percent). The same paper reports that the increase in pips is associated with increased calcium and magnesium concentrations in the grapes. In lighter soils, Barbera becomes extremely sensitive to boron and potassium deficiencies, leading to discolored leaves and smaller berries (Scienza et al. 1981), while the acidity tends to remain high. In fact, the mellow mouthfeel of Barbera wines is the result of the combination of the variety's genetically determined lower absolute tannin concentration, high alcohol and acidity, and soil types. In the ultimate analysis, it is important to know and remember that Barbera wines are distinguished by three main features: deep color (purple-red), high acidity, and seemingly, an absence of tannins. These characteristics bring consequences. As a result of its weak tannic strength, many producers oak their Barbera wines more or less gently, though some oak fetishists can get carried away. Those who know what they are doing use oak to increase the wine's complexity and spiciness: Barbera's intensely showy fruitiness can be a little one-dimensional in its exuberance, and so oak may make Barbera wines more interesting. Actually, Barbera does express linalool (reminiscent of sweet lavender, rose, and bergamot) and α-terpineol (reminiscent of lilac, pine, lime, wood, and flowers), and so it has actually long been known that the grape can give wines with aroma profiles that are more than about fruit (Usseglio-Tomasset 1969). The high acidity explains why Barbera has always been made as a sparkling wine, too (Barbera *mossa* or *vivace*; these qualifiers are usually found on the bottle's back label). You will find that fewer wines in Italy match better with *panini al salame* or *al prosciutto*. In general, Barbera wines are lovely right after or up to four years from the vintage and there is little to gain by holding on to them, since the variety does not give especially ageworthy wines. Only those oaked wines made with the idea of standing the test of time should be cellared for more than six to eight years, and even then you risk pushing your luck with all but a select few.

SPECIFIC TERROIRS

Barbera d'Alba

Generally speaking, Barbera d'Alba is bigger, richer, and fleshier than Barbera d'Asti and Barbera del Monferrato, which are lighter, fruitier, and have sharper tannins and higher acidity. Barbera d'Alba benefits from high-quality wine-making across the board, but since the best spots around Alba are reserved for Nebbiolo, Barbera does not always get the chance to show its best there. (This is worth knowing, given that in the minds of many people an association with "Alba" in any wine's name automatically makes that wine better than others.) In fact, Alba is probably not where the best Barbera wines are to be found, although its Barberas can be luscious, rich, and very likable. Many producers will say that Barbera d'Alba tries to play, or is made to play, the "Barolo card" a bit too much, in that it is so big and fleshy that it can stand in for the more famous wine. And yet, that very quality can be Barbera d'Alba's downfall, for many want their Barberas to be lively, juicy, and fun to drink, not luscious and rich. Also, be aware that crus famous for Nebbiolo are not necessarily as good for Barbera. Sergio Germano, of the Ettore Germano estate in Serralunga d'Alba, has a good point: "Paiagallo, which has a dark, rich, heavily organic clay soil, is a much better site for Barbera than Sarmassa, which has more white calcareous-clay soil." The lesson is that a famous Barolo cru (Sarmassa) is not always the solution to making better Barbera wines. That fact recognized, there are sites that have long been associated with especially fine Barbera wines in Alba.

The Best Barbera d'Alba Crus

This list could easily get very long, but these are sure bets:

Cerretta (Serralunga): Very deep, perfumed wines with darker aromas and flavors than the Barbera wines of Barolo or Castiglione Falletto. A richer and denser structure as well (but not hard, as it is with Serralunga's Nebbiolo wines). The Giacomo Conterno estate makes a must-have wine.

Fossati (Barolo): The white soils generate fresh wild red berry and sour red cherry aromas that are delicate and floral; Dolcetto is also extremely perfumed here.

Gallina (Neive): Famous for Barbaresco, but the fleshy, luscious, and concentrated Barbera wines are also very noteworthy.

Ginestra (Monforte): A true grand cru not just for Nebbiolo but for Barbera, too, Ginestra gives powerful, intensely perfumed wines redolent of violet and blue and black fruit. These are benchmark Barbera wines.

Paiagallo (Barolo): A site that maintains the variety's piercing nature but softens it, giving balanced, deep wines.

Piedicucche (Novello): Dark soils rich in clay and iron give Novello-typical structure to the wines.

Rocche di San Nicola (Novello): An extremely steep vineyard just above the tall cliffs that plunge down to the streambed that flows toward Monchiero. Plenty of sun, heat, and ventilation: perfect Barbera habitat. Sandrone grows Barbera here.

Scarrone (Castiglione Falletto): Simply outstanding site for Barbera, a true grand cru: actually an outstanding site, period, given that locals have always considered it to be part of the Rocche di Castiglione (one of the ten best crus in Barolo). Scarrone surrounds the town of Castiglione Falletto by almost 360 degrees, with the south-facing sites planted to Nebbiolo and the rest to other varieties. (Barbera is the most planted.)

Pozzo (La Morra): Renato Corino and Roberto Voerzio make very impressive wines in small volumes from this site. Voerzio's is a cult wine, and is one of the best Barbera d'Alba wines made each vintage: it stands to reason that the site is an especially worthy one for the variety.

Vietti Scarrone***PS.

Brovia Sorì del Drago***, Del Tetto Superiore Rocca delle Marasche***, Giacomo Conterno Cerretta***, Giacomo Conterno Francia***, Roberto Voerzio Riserva Vigna Pozzo dell'Annunziata***.

Paolo Conterno La Ginestra**, Renato Corino Vigna Pozzo**.

Barbera d'Asti

The Barbera d'Asti denomination is about two hundred thousand hectares large, extending over the hillside terrain in the province of Asti and the hillsides in the western sector of the province of Alessandria. That translates into a whopping 118 communes in the Asti province and another 51 communes in the Alessandria province within the denomination. And even though the wine can be made in only 116 communes of the former area, that's a lot of land, and a lot of wine. True, Barbera d'Asti offers something for everyone, but with so much wine pumped out, it cannot all be of the same high quality. In terms of production volume, only Asti produces more bottles of wine a year in Piedmont. But when it's good, Barbera d'Asti is simply a great wine (it must be made with 90 percent minimum Barbera), and is exactly what I reach for when I want to drink an effusively fruity, cheerful, juicy red. Barbera's chameleon-like personality (it can give wines of early and juicy appeal and more full-bodied oaked wines) allows estates to make at least two if not three or four different wines. The simple, entry-level Barbera wine can be still or bubbly, and usually does not see any oak. Barbera d'Asti Superiore must be aged at least twelve months before release, of which six must be spent in oak. Some estates make special selections of Barbera d'Asti Superiore, usually sold with a fantasy name; though they are supposed to be the estate's best Barbera wine, this is not always the case: some can be too oaky. A famous winery such as Braida chooses to label its world-famous Barbera Bricco dell'Uccellone and Bricco della Bigotta simply as Barbera d'Asti, followed by the fantasy name.

Clearly, a large denomination such as Barbera d'Asti has highly varied terroirs. After ten years of discussions, field studies, and micro-vinifications, three Barbera d'Asti subzones have been identified, all located south of the Tanaro River: Colli Astiani, Nizza, and Tinella. The most important of these subzones, from both a qualitative and a historical perspective, is Nizza (see the Nizza entry), located southeast of the city of Asti; it covers the entire territory of eighteen townships including Calamandrana, Agliano, Nizza Monferrato, and Vinchio. Currently, roughly forty estates produce a Nizza: the wine is 100 percent Barbera as of the most recent production guideline modifications (in 2014). Previously the wine had to be a minimum of only 90 percent Barbera (though estates belonging to the Associazione Produttori del Nizza always made 100 percent Barbera wines only); eighteen months' minimum aging is required before release for sale (of which six have to be spent in oak). Riserva wines need to spend thirty months in oak, which is frankly a little too much for many of the wines, which taste overly oaky. The Tinella subzone, located southwest of Asti, is centered around the towns of Calosso and Costigliole d'Asti. Production guidelines are the same as those of Nizza, save for a longer minimum aging requirement (twenty-four months instead of eighteen). The Colli Astiani subzone is situated immediately south and southwest of Asti; in terms of aging requirement, production guidelines are almost the same as Tinella's, but this subzone demands a minimum of 90 percent Barbera. To date, so few estates are making Tinella or Colli Astiani wines that it is difficult to draw any reasonable conclusions about their wines and specific terroirs.

Barbera d'Asti: Townships and Specific Wines

The shape of the Barbera d'Asti denomination recalls a stylized interpretation of the North and South American continents. Given that it is such a vast area, drawing hard and fast conclusions about finite portions of the denomination's terroir is simply not possible, though numerous studies have analyzed the characteristics of significant sections of the denomination. Cellino and Soster (1998) identified five major areas within the Barbera d'Asti production zone around the townships of Vignale Monferrato, Costigliole d'Asti, Vinchio, Costigliole Monferrato, and Castel Boglione. (Vinchio and Castel Boglione fall within the Nizza subzone today, but at the time of this study the Nizza DOCG had not yet been officially delimited.) Forty different vineyards in the five areas were studied, with twenty different vinifications made. Analysis of the vineyards under study revealed that the Barbera vines growing in the different communes had reliably identifiable "within-commune" morphological features and behavior patterns (in other words, features and behaviors that were individual to each commune).

Castel Boglione: The Barbera vines have medium vigor, medium-high productivity, and very large leaves and bunches.

Costigliole d'Asti: These Barbera vines were characterized by strong vigor, medium productivity, and medium-small leaves and bunches.

Costigliole Monferrato: Strong vigor, medium-high productivity, large leaves, and very large bunches were common to these Barbera vines.

Vignale Monferrato: Very strong vigor, high productivity, and large leaves and bunches were also typical of the Barbera that grew here.

Vinchio: These Barbera vines showed medium-low vigor, high productivity, medium-sized leaves, and medium-small bunches.

Interestingly, in this study, almost 90 percent of the grapevines were found to be hit by Grape Leafroll-Associated Virus 3 (GLRaV-3), much less so by Grape Leafroll-Associated Virus 1 (GLRaV-1), and not at all by Grape Fanleaf Virus (GFLV). The researchers were careful to choose plants that did not exhibit signs of viral infection for this study, and productivity was strong throughout all vineyards. At the Barbera d'Asti Symposium held during the sixth edition of the Collisioni Vino & Food Project Festival held in Barolo each July, a presentation by Longo (2017), based on work by Di Stefano et al. (2001), classified Barbera d'Asti's soil into four major types: S1 (silty-clay, silty-marly, silty-arenaceous), S2 (sandy-marly, sandy-arenaceous), S3 (Villafranchian soils), S4 (sandy, ancient terraces). The data were relative to wines made with grapes from forty different vineyards growing on the four soil types and showed significant correlation between soil granulometry, total acidity, and alcohol (results evaluated by analysis of variance, or ANOVA). For example, sandy soils are associated with Barbera wines characterized by lower alcohol and higher acidity levels, while the converse is true of wines made from grapes grown on the sandy-clay and loamy-clay soils (higher alcohol and lower acidity levels); wines made from sandy-compacted sands and sandy soils had instead the highest total acidity levels. In my experience, it is currently possible to distinguish between the Barbera d'Asti made with grapes grown on fine textural soils (silty-clay and silty-marly) and those grown on coarse textural soils (sandy-marly, sandy, and sandy-arenaceous). In this light, limestone content of the soils is also associated with a specific type of Barbera d'Asti, characterized by a color, aroma, and flavor profile different from all the others. Therefore, the Barbera d'Asti denomination can be subdivided into two macroareas distinguished by soil texture and limestone content. Within these two macroareas, there are at least six different subzones characterized mostly by different soils. And while attributing specific soil-related characteristics to many Barbera d'Astis is not easy because producers (especially the larger ones such as Bersano, Chiarlo, and Coppo) blend grapes from different areas to make the most balanced wine possible, in the case of others it is possible to do so (especially with smaller estates that own fewer vineyards).

1. Rocchetta Tanaro, Vigliano d'Asti, Montaldo Scarampi, San Damiano d'Asti, Castagnole Monferrato, Roatto: Barbera d'Asti made from mainly sandy soils (or type S2): differently from Barbera d'Asti made with grapes grown on the *terre bianche* (S1 type), these wines are initially more purple in color, evolve more rapidly, and usually have lower tannin, total acidity, and alcohol levels.

2. Costigliole d'Asti, Castagnole Lanze, Cocconato, Moncalvo, Alfiano Natta, Grazzano Badoglio, Calliano, Ricaldone, Maranzana, Cassine: These are Barbera d'Asti made from mainly calcareous soils (or type S1), the so-called *terre bianche*. They are richer in tannin, have bigger structures and higher alcohol levels, and evolve more slowly. In general, they show more ruby-red colors and have aromas that are not just ripely fruity, but also earthy and herbal.

3. Barbere del Basso Monferrato (Vignale, Sala Monferrato, Cella Monte, Cerrina Monferrato, Odalengo Piccolo, Odalengo Grande, Murisengo, Mombello Monferrato, Serralunga di Crea, Ponzano Monferrato): Soils in this part of the Barbera d'Asti subzone are geologically much older. They were formed during the Miocene and emerged during different stages, including the Aquitanian (roughly 23 million years ago), the Langhian (roughly 16 million years ago), and the Tortonian (roughly 11.6 million years ago). The soils are very calcareous in nature, made up mainly of marls and/or marls and compacted sands. There are also more clays, loam, and rocks (the so-called *pietre da cantoni*—rocks that originated from marine sands). Since fertility is higher, vines grow faster and the wines have an usually deeper color, more structure, and higher total acidity. They are not especially easy to drink when young and need to be cellared, but evolve beautifully. They are not unlike Nizza wines made from marly soils.

According to Fabio Teoldo, general coordinator of the Consorzio Barbera d'Asti e Vini del Monferrato, and Soster himself, a possible association between soil type and wine can be made for the estates shown in table 1 in the appendix, but these are generalizations, not set in stone. (In some years estates might choose to blend grapes from other sites so as to make the best possible wine.)

BENCHMARK WINES

Accornero Bricco della Cima***, Bersano Superiore***, Braida Bricco dell'Uccellone***, Braida Bricco della Bigotta***, Franco Ivaldi La Guerinotta***, Olim Bauda La Villa***.

Bava Libera**, Braida Ai Suma**, Cascina Castlet Superiore Passum**, Il Falchetto Barbera d'Asti Superiore Bricco Paradiso**, Olim Bauda Superiore Le Rocchette**, Vinchio Vaglio Serra Vigne Vecchie**.

Franco M. Martinetti Bric dei Banditi*, Giacomo Scagliola Bric dei Mandorli*, Guasti Clemente Superiore Boschetto Vecchio*, Scarpa La Bogliona*, Tre Secoli San Pietro*.

NIZZA

Nizza is the highest-quality Barbera d'Asti there is. Born in 2008, the Barbera d'Asti Superiore Nizza DOCG became simply and more manageably called Nizza *tout court* in 2014. Riserva and single vineyard (*vigna*-something) wines are also allowed. Nizza wines are made from 100 percent Barbera grapes (as of 2014, when the production guidelines were changed from the previous 90 percent minimum Barbera requirement) grown in a small subzone of the Monferrato, under stricter production and viticultural guidelines. It is a Barbera d'Asti made with grapes grown in the territory of eighteen townships in the province of Alessandria south of the Tanaro River, an area that has historically been linked to high-quality Barbera. The eighteen communes are Agliano Terme, Belveglio, Bruno, Calamandrana, Castel Boglione, Castelnuovo Belbo,

Castelnuovo Calcea, Castel Rocchero, Corti-glione, Incisa Scapaccino, Moasca, Mombaru-zzo, Mombercelli, Nizza Monferrato, Rocchetta Palafea, San Marzano Oliveto, Vaglio Serra, and Vinchio. From the beginning, the official Nizza production guidelines were well laid out and strict (some producers believe too strict). Impor-tantly, the majority of Barbera vines in the DOCG are rather old (fifty years or more). All of which means Nizza is potentially the best and most serious of all Barbera d'Asti wines. Of course, there are problems, too: for one, many Nizza wines tend to be over-oaked, though there are welcome signs this situation is improving. Another problem is that although Nizza is meant to be the top of the Barbera d'Asti production pyramid, not all producers have chosen to make a Nizza or to use the name on their wine label (despite the fact that the Barbera wine they make could be so labeled). Vineyards in the Nizza DOCG are mostly planted at 150 to 350 meters above sea level. Even though the Nizza area is not large, the soil geology is varied. The northern part of the Nizza subzone is characterized by mainly sandy, sandy-marl, and fine sand and silty soils, while marl- and sandstone-rich soils are prevalent in the southern half of the DOCG. The resulting wines showcase these differences well. Along general lines, and to make it easier to interpret any Nizza wine you may drink, the communes in the DOCG and their dominant soil types are shown below.

The Nizza Subzones and the Townships

Northern sector (sandy, sandy-marl, and fine sand and silty soils): Belveglio, Bruno, Castel-nuovo Belbo, Castelnuovo Calcea, Cortiglione, Incisa Scapaccino, Mombaruzzo, Mombercelli, Vaglio Serra, and Vinchio.

Southern sector (mainly marl and sandstone soils): Agliano Terme, Calamandrana, Castel Boglione, Castel Rocchero, Moasca, Nizza Monferrato, Rocchetta Palafea, and San Marzano Oliveto.

This subdivision is remarkably accurate and one of the easiest to remember among Italian terroirs, and it really does help in placing the wines within one group or another. However, I find two subzones too limiting for the establish-ment of a link between specific Nizza terroirs and all the wines made nowadays, since there is some overlap between different soil types. And so I further subdivide Nizza's two sectors into four band-like segments based on the prevalent soil types. In my experience, these four bands correlate with the wine made from grapes grown in each, and, with a little practice, you should be able to find somewhereness in the Nizzas you drink (provided, of course, that you know exactly where the grapes were grown).

From north to south, the four band-like seg-ments are as follows:

1. Northern Upper Band (sandy soil): Very sandy, or strongly sandy-loam and/or loamy-sandy soils characterize this sector of the Nizza DOCG. Such soils are absolutely typical of the communes of Cortiglione, Incisa Scapaccino, and Vinchio, plus parts of the communes of Mombaruzzo and Mombercelli. Drought can be a problem in this part of the Nizza DOCG due to the excellent drainage. These Nizza wines are the highest in acidity, usually less complex than others, but offer early appeal. That said, they age surprisingly well. Outliers in this portion of the Nizza DOCG are the towns of Cortiglione, Belveglio, and Bruno, which, besides sand, also have reddish iron-rich clays; vineyards are scarce, and I know of no commercially available wine made entirely from these clay soils. Microvinifications I have tried over the years showed the wines to be neither as refined nor as ageworthy as the majority of Nizza wines of the northern sector.

2. Northern Lower Band (sandy-marl and sand): Soils with strong percentages of loamy-silt or loamy-sand and marl. They are typical of the communes of Castelnuovo Belbo and Castelnuovo Calcea, and parts of the communes of Agliano Terme, Mombaru-zzo, Mombercelli, and Nizza Monferrato.

The wines from this band will be "medium" in most respects: medium-bodied, with medium-deep color and medium total acidity levels. (For example, the color may be only medium-deep purple-red.) Much depends on exactly where the estate owns its vineyards: those that farm grapes on soils with a much higher marl content than sand will clearly make deeper, richer wines. In fact, I find these Nizzas to have the most varied aroma and taste profiles.

3. Southern Upper Band (mostly marl): Soils characterized by silt and marl with small amounts of permeable clay. They are typical of the communes of Agliano Terme, Castel Rocchero, Moasca, and San Marzano Oliveto and parts of the commune of Castel Boglione and Nizza Monferrato. These wines tend to have strong mineral and earthy nuances, are long-lived, and are quite deep in color. They are some of the most refined Nizzas of all.

4. Southern Lower Band (mainly sandstone): Soils characterized mainly by permeable marl and sandstone and located in the southernmost portion of the Nizza DOCG. A very hard and superficial compacted substratum means roots here cannot dig as far down as in the other three parts of the Nizza denomination. These soils are typical of the communes of Calamandrana and Rocchetta Palafea and parts of Castel Boglione. The wines are similar to those born off sandy soils but are in my experience much deeper, more complex, and slow to open. These are potentially great Nizza wines that require patience.

Nizza's Best Crus by Townships

The following are specific sites or vineyards within each township that I have found over the years to be associated with noteworthy site-specific wines:

Agliano: Rocche, Salere (characterized by mostly marly soils; however, please note that the summits of these hills have chalk-sulfur deposits that give the wines a flinty-mineral edge that is not altogether typical of the grape variety).

Nizza: Bricco Cremosina (mostly sandy soils; this site is near Castelnuovo Calcea); San Nicolao (very marly); Villalta (very marly).

Vaglio Serra: L'Annunziata (very sandy).

BENCHMARK WINES

Bersano La Generala***, Dacapo***, Erede di Chiappone Armando Ru***, La Barbatella La Vigna dell'Angelo***, Michele Chiarlo Cipressi***, Olim Bauda***, Vietti La Crena***.

Bava Piano Alto**, Berta Paolo La Berta**, Cascina Garitina 900** (mostly sandy-marly), La Gironda Le Nicchie**, Villa Giada Bricco Dani Agliano** (calcareous-clay with sulfur and chalk).

Cantina Sociale Di Nizza Ceppi Vecchi* (mostly clay sandy soils), Cantina Sociale Vinchio Vaglio Laudana* (mostly sandy soil), Cantine Tre Secoli *, Cooperativa Mombaruzzo* (mostly sandy-loamy), Guasti Clemente*, Ivaldi Dario 1613* (mostly clay-limestone-sandy), Vinchio Vaglio Serra*.

Biancolella and Forastera

THE GRAPE VARIETIES

Biancolella

Biancolella is a typical native variety of Ischia, called San Nicola and Teneddu on the nearby islands of Capri and Procida, respectively. Some experts believe Biancolella was brought to Ischia by Eubean Greeks in 770 B.C.; more-modern evidence of Biancolella's presence on the island is from 1867, when Giuseppe D'Ascia wrote about it in his *Storia dell'isola d'Ischia*. Cipriani et al. (2010) have shown that Biancolella is probably a parent of Sanlunardo (another Ischia native white grape), while an earlier study by Costantini et al. (2005) suggests it is closely related to Falanghina Beneventana. In the vineyard, Biancolella is characterized by early budding and flowering and is the Ischia native grape that grows at the highest altitudes (up to six hundred meters above sea level). Most commonly used is the 1103 Paulsen rootstock (ideally suited to mountain environments), plus the old 5BB and SO4. According to Andrea D'Ambra (owner of Ischia's most

storied and largest wine estate), it was Giovanni Dalmasso, one of Italy's all-time most famous ampelographers, who was the first to distinguish between two biotypes of Biancolella, the *verace* and the *selvatica*, but perhaps owing to its secluded island habitat, Biancolella has not been the object of much academic study. Nevertheless, the *verace* is apparently characterized by a more loosely packed bunch than the *selvatica*, which is stockier and more compact. However, when D'Ambra tried growing Biancolella Verace in more fertile soils, it became full-bodied just like *selvatica*, so it appears that the different phenotypes are the result of an environmental selection process (terroir, in a nutshell). Biancolella wines are always lightly golden tinged, with strong white flower and thyme aromas, offering flavors of fresh herbs, spearmint, grapefruit, and oregano, plus a noticeable saline quality. In warmer years, nuances of pineapple and grilled plantain are not uncommon (but I stress: nuances, not orgies; and any Biancolella wine redolent of tropical fruit should get you wondering). If poorly made or the product of high yields, wines can be lean. With age (roughly five to eight years from the vintage date), a subtle petrol note similar to Riesling's develops. Graceful and precise, the wines are normally enlivened by a juicy acidity that provides good lift and freshness. In fact, when Biancolella wines are especially rich, broad, and almost fat (all atypical traits of these wines), locals believe a larger percentage of Biancolellone was used in the blend. Of course, just what Biancolellone might be exactly is anyone's guess: maybe Biancolella Verace grown in more fertile soils or a distinct variety of Biancolella. (And you thought that drinking Biancolella wine was all there was to it?) Biancolella wines are not blessed with palate-burning levels of acidity, but they can age remarkably well; having tried numerous bottles of Biancolella wines from the 1970s and 1980s over the years, I know they can hold up spectacularly well. Remember that wines labeled as DOC Ischia Biancolella are 100 percent Biancolella, whereas Ischia Bianco wines are blends.

Forastera

Forastera's name (called Uva dell'Isola on the nearby island of Procida) is derived from the Italian *forestiera,* or "foreigner," because Forastera was brought to Ischia in the mid-1800s (D'Ambra 1962); in fact, while D'Ascia (1867) does not mention Forastera's presence on the island, Frojo (1878) does. According to Andrea D'Ambra, Forastera grapes are characterized by sugar accumulation and total acidity levels that are modest at best, and this even when grown in highly different terroirs. Forastera is planted on SO4, Paulsen, or Kober 5BB rootstock, whereas 420A has been mostly abandoned due to its low productivity. Compared with Biancolella, Forastera grapes and wine have always been thought of as a little rustic, but I think that assessment is harsh; and now that producers have started to get their heads around Forastera's charms, an ever-increasing number of monovariety Forastera wines are produced. (The grape had been previously looked at as mostly a blending agent.) In fact, that Forastera

deserved better should have been obvious to all thanks to the noteworthy "Cimentorosso" Forastera wine made by D'Ambra from 1988 to 1995. (The name was changed to Euposia in 1996, but today the wine is simply labeled "Forastera.") In fact, while "Euposia" was a fantasy name, "Cimentorosso" was not: it is a specific place-name (and as I shall discuss below, one of the best Forastera crus in all of Ischia). A good Forastera wine is delicately herbal (wild fennel, oregano, mint) and always saline, with hints of ripe Golden Delicious apple and dried apricot. It has a richer mouthfeel and a more savory quality than the lighter-bodied, more citrusy and penetrating Biancolella wines.

SPECIFIC TERROIRS

Although a little Biancolella and Forastera grow on the Campanian coast, Ischia is the best terroir for Biancolella and Forastera.

Ischia

You have got to love a place where one of the best wines is made from a vineyard (Vigna del Lume) lying by the sea at the bottom of a hill so steep that it is impossible to carry the grapes back up the same hill (and so the grapes are loaded onto a boat and taken back to the winery by sea). Or a place where the most famous vineyard (Frassitelli) is so steep in its top portion that just standing, never mind picking grapes, is impossible (and so a monorail train is necessary to bring the grapes down to more manageable slopes and gentler heights). All that, and a whole lot more, is the magic that is Ischia and its wines.

Ischia is located roughly twenty-nine kilometers southwest of Campania's coast and Naples. It is where Italy's oldest Greek colony, Pithecusa, was established, and that was the island's first known name. Later it was called Aenaria (courtesy of the ancient Romans); the name Ischia (Iscia, actually: it derives from the Latin word *insula,* or "island") first appears in A.D. 813 in a letter sent from Pope Leo III to

Charlemagne. Roughly trapezoidal in shape and volcanic in nature, Ischia has been associated with quality viticulture since ancient Roman times. (Rome's second emperor, Tiberius, was fond of its wines, for example.) In fact, despite its island reality, it is agriculture and not fishing that has historically been the mainstay of Ischia livelihood (though it is tourism today). Agriculture so permeates life on Ischia that its delightful cuisine is not dominated by fish or shellfish; rather, meat and vegetables are the name of the game here. The island's iconic dish is *coniglio all'ischitana,* a heavenly preparation of pan-roasted rabbit, lemon, capers, and rosemary. (In my experience, everybody but die-hard Bugs Bunny fans swoons when they try it.) In fact, Ischia is a very green island, beginning with its beautiful gardens. The generally very fertile soils have plenty of humus; that feature, combined with the mineral-loaded water the island is famous for (Ischia is a hot-springs paradise, and thermal baths are a big part of its tourism industry) have made the reputation of the island's vegetables: a typical Ischia saying is that those lucky to own island orchards or vegetable gardens are rich, because the vegetables and fruits (fava beans and tomatoes especially) are famously tasty and have always fetched high prices.

Closer to our hearts, viticulture—not just agriculture—has always enjoyed pride of place on Ischia, the wines of which are actually made where they say they are (perhaps differing, dare I say it, from those of some other famous tourist-magnet islands). Ischia boasted as many as one thousand hectares of vineyards already in the 1960s, and even though this number has been whittled away to the current four hundred hectares, the fact is that you actually *do* see vineyards on the island. (You also see the old terraces of abandoned vineyards that serve as testimony of the island's viticultural glory days.) More important, despite Ischia's gorgeous landscape, eye-piercingly beautiful azure sea, and vacation-home destination, viticulture is unlikely to disappear on the island, since the remaining vineyards are located on impervious cliff-like

outcroppings where nobody will ever go building a home or hotel. (Besides, there is a building freeze, as there should be.) The island's geography is dominated by Mount Epomeo (which covers 34.5 percent of the island's surface), a huge mass of mostly green volcanic rock jutting out 785 meters into the sky, surrounded by other, lower-lying hilly ridges. It is a blessed terroir for wine, and in fact Ischia's wines are increasingly successful (not just in Italy) every year. (All the better island estates are already sold out of wine by summer's end.) Even better, newcomers and old hats alike are taking steps to making terroir-related differences clear in the wines they sell. In this respect, climate is all-important in shaping Ischia's viticultural habitat. Mount Epomeo is high enough to protect agricultural areas on its south-facing side from the wet and windy weather that batters its northern face. Furthermore, thanks to the rain-shadow effect, when the cold mountain air blows around the top of the mountain and starts moving downward toward the sea, it warms up and becomes drier. These wind currents are an example of "rain-shadow winds"—warmer drainage winds that blow downward along an incline, such as from a mountaintop, a glacier, or a plateau. (Other rain-shadow winds include the chinook and the foehn.) Therefore, these are not technically katabatic winds (from the Greek word *katabatikos,* "moving downward"), a term previously used to include all downward winds but today limited only to cold air currents, such as the bora, typical of Italy's northeast and the Adriatic, or the Santa Ana in Southern California. So it is not surprising that Ischia's vineyards are mainly planted on Mount Epomeo's southern flank. The latter has a very recognizable green color due to the volcanic tuff (absolutely typical of Ischia) formed during an eruption that took place roughly fifty-five to thirty-three thousand years ago. (The green color is a characteristic of volcanic elements that have been in contact with seawater for a prolonged time period: Mount Epomeo's green tuff is believed to have remained underwater until twenty-eight thousand years ago.) This tuff is rich in sulfur, manganese, and iron. (Though it may come as a surprise given iron's more usual association with red soils, it is this metal that is mostly responsible for the green hue.) Since Ischia is of volcanic geothermal origin, hot springs are everywhere: in fact, on a clear day you will see wisps of smoke arising from different hillsides. Locally called *fumarole,* these are gusts of hot, humid air blowing up from deep below the surface through vents in the ground (showcasing just how thermally active Ischia's underground is). The combination of Ischia's high mountain vineyards and the extremely rich mineral content of its soils and water are features that doubtless contribute to the considerable potential for complexity of flavor and perfume of the island's wines.

The Ischia Subzones

The best way to remember Ischia's wine subzones is by township, of which there are six: Barano d'Ischia, Casamicciola, Forio, Ischia (made up of Ischia and Ischia Porto), Lacco Ameno, and Serrara Fontana. Sant'Angelo is a hamlet in this last commune and is situated in the most beautiful part of an already very beautiful island; another important hamlet of Serrara Fontana is Panza, where most of the few remaining vineyards of San Lunardo, another local native white grape variety, still grow. Lacco Ameno and Casamicciola are situated on the island's north coastline; Ischia is to the east; Forio to the west; Panza is to the southwest; Barano d'Ischia, Serrara Fontana, and Sant'Angelo are in the southern part of the island.

Based on work done by Zamboni, Iaconi, and Bozzalla (1997) and others, in addition to the wealth of knowledge of Andrea D'Ambra and that of a few other island grape growers and winemakers, plus my own experience tasting all the island's wines during my annual visits over the last fifteen years, I believe the island's geology allows the subdivision of Ischia's wine production area into five distinct subzones: (1) Casamicciola, Lacco Ameno, Forio, and Panza; (2) Ischia; (3) Barano d'Ischia; (4) Serrara Fontana and the central-south sector of the island; and (5) Serrara Fontana and the southwestern

sector of the island. (These two Ischia territories are both located in the commune of Serrara Fontana, but I distinguish between them because of slightly different soils and because the wines made in each are recognizably different from each other.)

CASAMICCIOLA, LACCO AMENO, FORIO, AND PANZA

The territories of these four communes correspond to the northwestern flank of Mount Epomeo. Small towns in this area boasting noteworthy vineyards include Fango, Monte Nuovo-Pannoccia, Monte Corvo, and Pietra Martone. At the highest altitudes Ischia's green tuff dominates (and is used to make building blocks for walls and buildings; its green color seems to follow you around the island), while lower down it is two different tuff formations that become prevalent: the tuff of the Frassitelli area (Frassitelli being a famous Ischia forest of acacia trees growing near the town of Serrara Fontana) and the Pizzone tuff (the Pizzone being an area of fumarole activity not far from the Monte Cito, just off to the side of a holm oak forest). The lowest part of the Mount Epomeo flank that segues into the coastline soils is characterized by thick deposits of degraded tuff, boulders, and loam. The best vineyard sites are those located at mid and high elevations, where the flank's soils are rich in pumice, clay, silicate, zeolite, and high concentrations of alkali elements (most notably, potassium and sodium). The presence of zeolite (which belongs to the same structural class as feldspar) is especially interesting since this mineral forms when volcanic ash falls into an alkaline water source during an eruption. It is highly porous and therefore characterized by very good water retention (holding up to 60 percent of its weight in water) and soil aeration; furthermore, it hangs on to heavy metals and toxins such as arsenic, thereby making them unavailable to plants (Velde and Barré 2009). There are many *fumarole* here (especially in the areas of Monte Cito, Monte Buono, and Bocca). An especially well known *fumarola* is the Bocca di Tifeo near Montecorvo, which you can get to by taking the Via Pietra Brox, a country road flanked by vineyards of Tenuta Arimei, which up until 2018 was owned by the Fratelli Muratori (who bought the vineyards from the noble Milone family in 2001), of Franciacorta fame. Another well-known *fumarola* is the one of Monte Cito, easily reached by taking the Via Crateca (formerly called "Via De'Carri," because it was always packed with chariots and carts loaded with, among other things, wine). The soil here is especially interesting: one look shows it to have different colors, ranging from orangy to yellowish to reddish and even white, hinting at a noteworthy mineral presence. Clearly, the combination of hot springs beneath the surface and hot vapor and gases emitted into the air from the ground makes for a very warm mesoclimate; since Panza's mostly south-facing vineyards bask in a hot environment, red grapes do well there, too.

ISCHIA

The vineyards of this subzone are planted on the eastern flanks of Mount Epomeo on the ridge of hills near Campagnano and Monte Vezzi, characterized by a very different geology than that of the western flanks. Here the typical green tuff is absent: the soil is a mix of lava and pumice rich in trachite (an igneous volcanic rock formed by the crystallization of iron, magnesium, and calcium minerals) and the Formazione di Pigniatello, a geologically different tuff from Mount Epomeo's famous green one. Vineyards are planted on very steep slopes (easily 40 percent or more of which require the building of terraces with stone walls—what locals call *parracine,* from the Greek words *para,* meaning near, and *oikos,* meaning "house"). Over the years, I have found this to be an area not especially meaningful as far as great wines go—good ones, yes; great ones, maybe not. Let's just say it is an area of premier crus rather than grand crus. Or that I am wrong.

BARANO D'ISCHIA

This subzone covers the lower-lying ridges sloping from the center of the island toward the eastern coast near the areas of Piedimonte (Piejo) and Fiaiano. Soils are not especially homogeneous in this sector, consisting of a varied mix of volcanic elements including pumice and cinerite (compacted volcanic ash). The area of Fiaiano is one of the island's greatest grand crus of all for Biancolella.

SERRARA FONTANA AND THE CENTRAL-SOUTH SECTOR

Soils in this subzone (which, for accuracy's sake, actually extends slightly into Barano d'Ischia's territory, too) are a mix of colluviums, volcanic debris, silt, and loam. The soil granulometry is rather large, and drainage is good. Slopes are steep, and so it is necessary to set up terraced vineyards (some of the most beautiful on the island, actually).

SERRARA FONTANA AND THE SOUTHWESTERN SECTOR

This subzone extends from Ciglio, Succhivo, and Cava Petrella in the territory of Serrara Fontana. It is where you will find the *belvedere di Serrara,* which offers one of the most beautiful and truly unforgettable views from anywhere in Ischia (and there's a cute little bar with tables set up right up against the fence separating you from the cliff-like plunge below). The soils here are mainly yellow tuff rich in pumice, clay, and trachytes, with a high potassium content.

The Best Crus of Each Township

I have been visiting Ischia regularly (at least once a year, more often than not two to three times a year) for the past fifteen years and have walked and climbed up more of its vineyards than my joints care to remember. I absolutely love the island and its people, and consider it one of my homes away from home. I have personally become involved in resurrecting a number of the island's native grape varieties (free of charge) with the help of Giancarlo Carriero, owner of the five-star luxe Albergo Regina Isabella (the island's best hotel and a world-class spa), who along with his wonderful staff has embraced my ideals of helping foster and save the island's biodiversity. This while also creating new job opportunities for Campania's youth through the creation of new and exciting wines from old grapes. (The project has moved forward, with Professor Luigi Moio now acting as consultant enologist in collaboration with Nicola Mazzella, whose winery is the site of the specific vinifications.) What all this means is that over the course of more than a decade of scouring the vineyards in the hunt for the practically unknown San Lunardo, Coglionara, Arilla, Cannamela, and Guarnaccia Ischitana cultivars, I was also able to learn where the best sites for the much more common Biancolella and Forastera are located. In general, the eastern areas of the island have always been most famous for Biancolella, while the western areas around Forio are reputed as a source of excellent Forastera. An Ischia grand cru is undoubtedly Fiaiano di Barano; I say this not just based on tasting evidence, but on historic truths as well; for example, this is the area of Ischia where *negozianti* looked to buy grapes from and make wines. Boats and ships loaded with Ischia's wine have long set sail from Ischia Ponte—in the direction of Naples (in the case of the island's white wines) or toward La Spezia (with Ischia's red wines, made with Sangiovese and/or Piedirosso).

Biancolella's Best Crus

Barano d'Ischia: Bosco dei Conti, Testa (that part of the Testa area that is in the hamlet of Fiaiano), Toccaneto, Pietra Sparaina (a hamlet in Buonopane).

Casamicciola: Castiglione, Maio.

Forio: Spadara, Mortola, Piellero, Montecorvo, Bocca, Cimmentorosso, Cuotto, Chignole. I may be wrong, but slightly less qualitative but still noteworthy sites include Fumarie and Pannocchia.

Ischia: Piano Liquori, Pignatiello, Grotta di Terra, Costa del Lenzuolo. According to

Andrea D'Ambra, this is where some of the most refined of all Biancolella wines are made. (I can totally vouch for the Costa del Lenzuolo—in my estimation, another one of Ischia's grand crus.)

Lacco Ameno: Fango di Sopra, Mezzavia, Pannella.

Serrara Fontana: East-southeastern slope: Aito, Casale, Eschia, Martofa, Rio, Rufano; south-southwestern slope: Calimera, Ciglio, Frassitelli, Succhivo.

Forastera's Best Crus

Barano: Bosco dei Conti, Candiano, Chiumanno, Ciglio, Felice, Fiaiano Frassitelli, Monterotto, Montevetto, Sparano, Testaccio.

Forio: Bocca, Calitto, Cimmentorosso, Cuotto. An especially good area for Forastera is just below Calitto, where the soil is rich in phosphorus and potassium and low in nitrogen.

Ischia: Bosco dei Conti, Pignatiello.

Serrara Fontana: Eschia, Martofia, Rufano.

Slightly less qualitative but still noteworthy sites for Forastera are Casamicciola's Campomanno, Chianatella, and Fasaniello; Ischia's Piano Liquori and Torri; and Lacco Ameno's Cetragnola and Pannella. Again, I could be wrong, but don't think so.

BENCHMARK WINES

Antonio Mazzella Biancolella Ischia Vigna del Lume***, Cenatiempo Biancolella Kalimera Ischia***, D'Ambra Biancolella Ischia Frassitelli***, D'Ambra Ischia Forastera***.

Antonio Mazzella Ischia Forastera**, Cenatiempo Ischia Forastera**, Giardini Arimei (Arcipelago Muratori) Passito Secco dell'Isola d' Ischia Pietra Brox**.

Carricante

THE GRAPE VARIETY

Carricante is one of Italy's three or four greatest native white cultivars in that wines made with it offer amazing complexity and noteworthy longevity (the latter a trait shared by very few other Italian white natives, including Fiano, Trebbiano Abruzzese, Timorasso, and Verdicchio). Talk of high quality is surprising given the variety's name: "Carricante" derives from *caricare,* as in "to load up" (most likely a cart or donkey) with grapes—a nod to the cultivar's capacity for very high productivity if left to its own devices. Carricante grows in Sicily, mostly near the city of Catania; specifically, it is intimately linked to Mount Etna, and thrives at its highest altitudes, where Nerello Mascalese does not reach optimal ripeness. (This is why star consultant winemaker Salvo Foti, the single biggest expert on Etna grapes and wines, refers to Carricante as a "default" grape, with farmers planting it only in areas where the Nerello varieties won't grow. Foti then quickly adds, "But Carricante is the only Sicilian white cultivar that was born to make dry white table wines, unlike Grillo, the Catarrattos, and Insolia, which were selected to make Marsala; and Moscato Bianco, Zibibbo, and Malvasia di Lipari, which were selected to make *passito* wines.") Carricante's bunch is usually medium-large, cylindrical-conical, and long, with elliptical berries covered with little bloom. The berries have thick skins but are easily sunburned. There are two clones (CR-7 and Regione Siciliana 2) and at least two known biotypes (simply called A and B); neither one appears to be especially resistant to common vine diseases—Carricante's Achilles' heel. For the most part, it thrives in extreme climate conditions, where rain and low levels of sunlight are common. This is why Mattia Catania, of the outstanding Gulfi estate, says Carricante exhibits behaviors that remind him of Chenin Blanc and Riesling (two other varieties that don't mind humidity and shade). Carricante wines have an extremely intense lemony and mineral character that can be positively shocking to those who try a glass without knowing what to expect; you might say Carricante takes its high-acid habit to a risky extreme. The wine is characterized by low potassium concentrations, very high total acidity, and very low PH (values of 2.9 to 3 are common) due to high malic acid concentrations. (This is why most producers choose to harvest it as late as possible and put the wine through malolactic transformation.) Carricante's unique acid-saline-lemony equilibrium is a character trait local Etna people refer to as *muntagnuolo*. The simplest way to describe a good Carricante wine is as a dry Riesling look-alike, expressing flinty and diesel-fuel aromas along with notes of lemon, lime, broom, botanical herbs, green apple, and unripe apricot. The variety can express (independently of site) significant concentrations of 1,1,6-trimethyl-1,2-dihydronaphthalene (TDN), which is associated with the diesel-fuel note typical of Riesling wines, and 4-vinyl guaiacol (herbal, spicy, clove-like aromas and flavors). Their aromatic expression increases with time due to acid and enzymatic hydrolysis leading to the release of previously bound forms of these molecules over time. In my experience, Carricante always converts those that were initially skeptical into believers. It is truly one of the world's best white wine grapes, and its wines have all the hallmarks of greatness: complexity, ageworthiness, minerality, and lightness of being, yet noteworthy concentration.

SPECIFIC TERROIRS

Etna

The memories of those who visit Etna are not made just of unique wines, but also of a kaleidoscope of colors unique to the area. White is the blanket of snow that permanently caps Etna's highest reaches; black is the volcano's positively lunar landscape; greens ranging from pale to emerald to very dark are everywhere; and yellow is the color of the broom flower, one of the most typical sights on the volcano (the other being the beautiful red, black, gray, and white chukar partridge, unfortunately rare today—a sign of the sorry times we live in). But what strikes me most about the Etna is how the volcano dominates life in an all-pervasive manner; to people here the volcano is much more than "just" a mountain, but rather a living entity, a companion with which one lives through both good and bad times. For example, the inhabitants of Catania, Sicily's second-largest city, over which the volcano has towered for centuries, refer to it simply as *"la montagna"* (or "the mountain," in English). In fact, I have practically never heard any local refer to Etna as a volcano. Still today, I distinctly remember an evening in 2001 or 2002 (all right, not so distinctly then) when Salvo Foti's son Simone, then eight years old, during a private tasting organized at a friend's home to discuss the state of Etna viticulture, looked up to his dad and whispered, "So, Dad, how does everyone else in Italy manage to get by without *la montagna?*" And so it is with Etna.

The Etna denomination is crescent shaped (a "C" written backward), arching around the volcano that sits in its center. Viticulture is limited to the volcano's upper reaches (essentially between four hundred and one thousand meters above sea level) because urban sprawl has taken over at lower altitudes. The decrease in vines has been significant: for example, at the end of the 1800s Etna produced over one hundred million hectoliters of wine and boasted about fifty thousand hectares of vines. Today, there are only two thousand hectares in the denomination with only seven hundred hectares in production, and about two million bottles are produced annually (2010 data, Istituto Regionale Vino e Olio). Furthermore, Carricante accounts for only a small portion of the hectares under vine; whereas there were more than four thousand Carricante hectares in 1915, there are only fifty today (though hectarage is increasing, given the quality and success of the wines).

Mount Etna is Carricante's home and the only terroir in which it gives wines of world-class quality. Though the cultivar does grow in other parts of Sicily (where its presence was already documented in centuries past), it was never a favorite with Sicilian farmers. (Its tendencies to give wines that were both low in alcohol and high in total acidity were unacceptable flaws in poorer times, when wine was a source of calories.) The fact is, Carricante likes, perhaps even needs, extremely high altitudes to thrive. It grows on both the eastern and southern slopes of the volcano (at altitudes of 700 to 900 meters above sea level on the former, and as high up as 1,050 meters on the latter). However, it really is most typical of the eastern slope of Etna, from Viagrande to Sant'Alfio, where rain and cold weather are most abundant and where it gives the best wines: not by chance, Etna Bianco Superiore wine can be made only from grapes grown on the eastern slope. Carricante's appearance elsewhere on Etna is really only a recent development; according to Foti, when locals speak of their old Carricante vines on Etna's northern slope, it is because they don't recognize that most of the time they are likely growing something else (Grecanico, probably— which is a charitable way of explaining why so many Etna Bianco wines taste nothing like Carricante). For example, Benanti's outstanding Etna Bianco Superiore Pietra Marina, despite bearing the name of a specific *contrada* on Etna's northern slope in the territory of the Castiglione di Sicilia township, has never been made with grapes grown there (if you can believe that's even allowed: what can I tell you? This is Italy) but rather from the outstanding *contrada* of Caselle on the volcano's eastern flank. And as good as some Carricante-based wines from the Arcuria *contrada* on Etna's northern slope can be (Arcuria is in the township of Castiglione di Sicilia), it is important to realize that Carricante was never grown much there; simply put, the northern slope is not Carricante's historical area of production. That today estates best known for their Etna Rossos increasingly produce Carricante wines from northern-slope townships such as Randazzo and Castiglione di Sicilia has more to do with convenience rather than true quality terroirs for Carricante. (Clearly, an estate making Etna Rosso wines from vineyards it owns in *contrade* like Rampante or Muganazzi on Etna's northern

slope finds it much easier to just plant Carricante where it already owns vineyards. But those are not the best terroirs for Carricante; and just as one thinks of a Burgundy from Musigny as potentially better than one from Marsannay, the same logic should apply to Italian wines—but rarely does, because so little is known about Italy's wines terroirs.)

Clearly, the presence of the volcano shapes the local climate in multiple ways. Towering above (at 3,329 meters above sea level, it is the highest active volcano in Europe), Etna interferes with air circulation, creating characteristic lenticular cloud formations (stationary lens-shaped clouds) such as altocumulus standing lenticular clouds (ACSL) and the *contessa dei venti* (which translates in English to "countess of the winds"), a series of layered lenticular cloud cumuli that have the shape of flattened almonds. The area's wind currents can't help but be modified by the presence of the large mountainous cone; such modifications are specifically related to exposure. For example, the eastern side of Etna is the one closest to the sea, and temperature differences between the mountain's surface and the surrounding air create anabatic and katabatic wind currents that blow up and down the mountain slopes, respectively. (For example, katabatic [cold downslope] winds are generated by the temperature difference between the cold mountain surface and the warmer surrounding air.) These air currents merge with sea–land breezes, making for a highly windy environment: Etna's average wind speed is two to four meters per second, which is twice that of Barolo, for example. The eastern side of Etna is not just the coldest but also the wettest: this is because the volcanic mass intercepts the cold and humid currents blowing in from the Ionian Sea that feed the precipitation systems. Sicily is battered by many different winds: in this case it is the easterly *grecale* wind and the southeasterly *scirocco* wind that contribute to bringing rain to the eastern and southeastern flanks of Etna. Etna's eastern slope is the wettest (two thousand millimeters of rain per year compared with the eight hundred millimeters of the northern slope). By contrast, the driest sections of Etna are its western, southwestern, and northwestern flanks (in decreasing order of dryness). The area's average temperature also changes depending on which side of the volcano is under consideration: at the same moment of the day, average temperatures in vineyards on the northern slope are one degree Celsius lower than those on the rest of the volcano, while average temperatures on the southern slope are at least one degree Celsius higher than those in flatland vineyards. Average temperatures on the eastern slope (Etna's coldest) are much lower than they are in the rest of Sicily (temperatures of 0°C being common even at budbreak). Diurnal temperature variations are noteworthy, and can exceed 30°C in the summer months. However, the wealth of dark, almost black-colored volcanic soil helps capture and store heat during daytime; its release during colder moments of the day and especially at night helps make the vineyard microclimate warmer than it would be otherwise. The old bush vines (grown according to the *alberello* training system) typical of Etna also help grapes ripen in a hostile climate, since they offer the grapes a 360-degree exposure to the sun. Furthermore, keeping grapes low to the ground also ensures they capture more heat radiating up from the ground. Around Zafferana Etna, situated in the southeastern sector of the Etna denomination, the coldest month of the year is February and the warmest is August. Most of the rain there falls from September to April. Nevertheless—and for what this may be worth, given the fact that the different sides of the volcano play such a major role in the area's climate—the average daily temperature on Etna over a twelve-month period ranges from 12°C to 17.5°C (Winkler index, 1250–2300; Huglin index, 1650–2850). All this means that there can be at least twenty days of difference in reaching full polyphenolic maturity on the different sides of the volcano (and up to a 2° Brix difference in sugar concentration in grapes picked).

Centuries of eruptive activity on Etna have led to the layering of lava coats of different age and mineral composition, and this profound geologic diversity contributes greatly to the different aroma and flavor profiles of Etna's wines. However, not all of Etna's volcanic soils are conducive to successful viticulture, depending in large part on the volume of the pyroclastic flows and where they occurred, as well as the age of the lava flow. The locals use the term *sciara* to refer to a lava flow. The youngest *sciare* (the plural of *sciara*) are barren expanses of molten rock with little biochemical or microbiological activity; it takes centuries for the surface to erode into topsoil and for microbes to create humus and organic matter necessary to support plant life. Clearly, at higher altitudes, where microbial activity is less strong, or in those area where human agricultural activity has also been less present, soil formation occurs at a slower rate. This is why few vines grow on the barren western and northwestern expanses of Etna (characterized by very little topsoil). One of the few and most recognizable forms of Etna plant life that do thrive in the barrens is the broom, a very pretty yellow flower. And although broom in Italy is immediately associated with Sicily and Etna, various species of the tribe live elsewhere in the country (for example, in Sardinia and Tuscany) and the Mediterranean basin. In fact, the common broom (*Cytisius scoparius;* one of several genera in the tribe *Genisteae*) was the emblem of the Plantagenet kings (Plantagenet deriving from *planta genest,* from *Genisteae*). Studying where broom grows provides a very good idea as to where the youngest lava flows are situated; those swaths of land are not ideal for viticulture. The fact that there are at least three different species of broom living on Etna and thriving at different altitudes in different parts of the volcano further states the case for terroir as an integral component of all plant life. Carricante thrives on mostly sandy and well-aerated soils, allowing for easy root penetration. Etna's soil granulometry is varied, ranging from very fine sands such as those of the Caselle and

Verzella *contrade* to the small and medium-sized pieces of pumice typical of Monte Serra and Monte Gorna in the volcano's southeastern sector. The best Etna soils are rich in allophane (water-storing) clays derived from volcanic cinders, and this means the vines have some respite during the often droughty summer months. Furthermore, soils rich in allophane clays have better cation-exchange properties; and because such soils also contain loam, they are much more fertile than volcanic soils would normally be. Clearly, not all of Etna has the same soil composition: for example, a typical soil composition of vineyards located near Castiglione di Sicilia, in the northern sector, shows 78 percent sand, 10 percent loam, and 12 percent clay, whereas vineyard soils of the southern sector's Viagrande area are 88 percent sand, 4 percent loam, and 8 percent clay. Soil color varies from gray-brown to black, resulting from different mixes of degraded lavas of different age and deposited pyroclastic eruptive materials such as lapilli, ashes, and sands. The locals use the term *ripiddu* instead of "lapilli," and never fail to point out that soils rich in these very small pieces of pumice are characterized by very good drainage (though drainage varies depending on the flank of the volcano). Ashes are especially fine and loosely packed and ensure that soils become fertile faster than if they consisted of just lava or pumice. Clearly, periodically working nitrogen-containing organic material into the ground to offset the moderate to high potassium concentrations typical of many volcanic soils is a good idea. Etna's soils are mostly low in nitrogen and calcium, have moderate concentrations of potassium, phosphorus, and magnesium, and have high concentrations of iron and copper (Foti 2011).

The Etna Subzones and the Contrade

The Etna is best divided into three subzones, which are nothing more than three of the volcano's flanks: the northern, the eastern, and the southern. In each of these there are *contrade* or vineyard districts, and within each of these, specific crus of note. But the best crus for Carricante differ from those that are most suited to the Nerellos, if for no other reason than that they are mostly located on the volcano's eastern sector or slope. The epicenter of Carricante production on Etna was always the commune of Milo, where a number of high-quality *contrade* are located: Caselle, Finaita, Nespola, Praino Crisafulli, Rinazzo, Villagrande, and Volpare. Of these, the real Carricante grand cru is Caselle, loaded with old vines and situated between 900 and 920 meters above sea level. (At this altitude, Nerello Mascalese does not ripen well.) The wines have a naturally high acidity and a very lemony personality, such that malolactic transformation is necessary to avoid making unbalanced, shrill-tasting wines. They also need to be aged at least three or four years (depending on the vintage) in order to show their best, and can last ten or more in a good cellar. Look for Carricante under the guise of Etna Bianco wines: Etna Bianco and Etna Bianco Superiore. Unfortunately, the former can be made with only 60 percent minimum Carricante and the latter 80 percent, but clearly the best wines are the Etna Bianco Superiore made with 100 percent (or close to it) Carricante. Etna Bianco is a good wine (in some cases, very good), but it is just that: nothing more than a *bianco*. Like it or not, the inclusion of up to 40 percent other varieties modifies completely the aroma and flavor profile of Carricante to the point that the variety becomes almost unrecognizable, so that seems like a missed opportunity to me.

The Best Carricante *Contrade*

Eccezionale Sceltissima (Grand Cru *Hors Classe*)
Township of Milo: Caselle.

Eccezionale Scelta (Grand Cru)
Township of Milo: Fornazzo, Pianogrande, Rinazzo, Villagrande, Volpare. (The Benanti estate will be releasing a Contrada Rinazzo Carricante wine in 2020.)
Township of Santa Maria di Licodia: Cavaliere.
Township of Viagrande: Blandano.

Benanti Etna Bianco Superiore Pietra Marina***PS, I Vigneri Etna Bianco Superiore Vignadimilo***PS.

Pietradolce Etna Bianco Archineri***, Tenuta delle Terre Nere Cuvée delle Vigne Niche Calderara Sottana***, Tenuta delle Terre Nere Cuvée delle Vigne Niche Santo Spirito***.

Benanti Etna Biancodicaselle**, Cottanera Etna Bianco**, Graci Etna Bianco Arcuria**, Gulfi Sicilia Caricantj** (a rare Carricante wine not from Etna but from southeastern Sicily; richer and riper but less typical than Etna wines), Tenuta di Fessina Etna Bianco A'Puddara**.

Calcagno (Calcaneus in the United States) Etna Bianco Ginestra*, Girolamo Russo Etna Bianco Nerina*, Planeta Sicilia Bianco Eruzione 1614* (with 10 percent Riesling), Planeta Etna Bianco* (barrique-aged for the international set), Tenuta di Fessina Etna Bianco Erse*, Tornatore Etna Bianco Pietrarizzo*.

Cornalin

How much do I love the Valle d'Aosta and its wines? So much that when I was told that Renato Anselmet had made a wine from the rare Broblanc biotype of the Cornalin variety (back in 2001 or 2002, I don't remember which), I dropped everything, hopped into my car, and drove eight hours straight to taste the wine from barrel. I remember Anselmet's amusement at my driving all the way from Rome just to taste a wine made from a grape nobody had ever heard of (he kept asking me if I did not wish perhaps to also taste his other, more famous wines), and yet I was very happy to have done so. Still today I am proud to say I am the first non-Valdostano wine writer to have ever tasted the Broblanc wine. (Anselmet labels it "Broblan," without the "c.") And whereas Petit Rouge is the most-planted red grape and Fumin viewed as potentially the best of the region's red-grape lot, Cornalin is possibly the region's hottest grape currently. Such popularity is the result of wines that, while pleasantly smooth yet full-bodied, are never marred by the green streaks or the funky smells that can affect Fumin and Petit Rouge wines (either when made from physiologically unripe grapes or if subjected to excessively reductive winemaking). Cornalin's name derives from *corniola*, a mountain gemstone. (Other, less poetically inclined minds think it originated from the town of Colignola, one of the of initial Cornalin centers of cultivation.) Cornalin's presence has been documented in the Valle D'Aosta for centuries; it was apparently very common in the eighteenth century but fell out of favor in the nineteenth, and by the twentieth it risked extinction. Cornalin was saved from that sorry fate because of its morphological similarity to Petit Rouge, with which it was interplanted in the vineyards. So when nursery personnel came knocking on estate doors looking for Petit Rouge grapevines to reproduce and propagate, they often unknowingly took Cornalin vines as well. This is a rare example where making an ampelographic mistake was actually beneficial, helping maintain the region's biodiversity. Local old-timers have always told me that Cornalin grew most commonly in the countryside around Charvensod and Chatillon; its Broblanc biotype was more common around Aymavilles, Jovençan, and Gressan (*broblanc* is the local patois dialect word for "white stalk," a distinguishing feature of this biotype, though Cornalin's lightly tan-colored stalk isn't especially dark, either). Why Cornalin fell out of favor is unclear: after all, the variety accumulates high levels of sugar and assures copious crops every year; unlike Petit Rouge, it also withstands excessive sunlight very well (sunburn not being an issue with Cornalin). Readers ought to be aware that the Cornalin of Italy is not the same variety as the Cornalin of the Swiss Valais, which is Rouge du Pays, a distinct grape. (Italian Cornalin is called Humagne Rouge in the Valais.) Morphological studies and genetic tests have confirmed not just that Cornalin and Humagne Rouge are identical, but also that Petit Rouge and Mayolet are the grandparents of Cornalin. Cornalin's return to prominence was thanks to Valle d'Aosta's Institut Agricole Régional: after locating old Cornalin vines back in 1997, massal selections were propagated in experimental vineyards. (Believe it or not, the researchers identified fifty-nine different biotypes of Cornalin; there are four that are more or less common today.) Cornalin wines offer a fleshy but refined and smooth mouthfeel, with red cherry and red berry aromas and flavors typically complicated by hints of tobacco and spices.

SPECIFIC TERROIRS

Monovariety Cornalin wine is named Valle d'Aosta DOC Cornalin: for an in-depth description of the Valle d'Aosta terroir, see the Mayolet entry.

BENCHMARK WINES

Anselmet Broblan***, Grosjean Cornalin Vigne Rovettaz***, Feudo di San Maurizio Cornalin***, La Vrille Cornalin***.

Cave des Onzes Communes Cornalin**, Chateau Feuillet Cornalin**, Les Granges Cornalin**, IAR Cornalin**, Rosset Cornalin**.

La Source Cornalin*.

Corvina, Corvinone, Rondinella, and Molinara

THE GRAPE VARIETIES

Corvina

With the exception of Molinara, most cultivars used to make Valpolicella, Amarone della Valpolicella, and Recioto della Valpolicella have names related to birds. Corvina, Corvinone, Rondinella, and Oseleta are named after the dark color of a bird's plumage or their behavior (a fondness for sweet grapes). Corvina means "little raven" (from *corvo*, "raven"), but paradoxically, the wine made from Corvina is never superdark or black, just as those made with the also dark-sounding Pinot Noir are not black, either. Corvina is a vigorous and dependable producer, capable of delivering very large yields, but it is a difficult variety from a viticultural perspective. Delicate and very disease prone, it is sensitive both to excessive humidity and to water stress; furthermore, its grapes are prone to sunburn. Corvina does not fruit on the first few buds of the cane, and so it needs plenty of space; this fact, coupled with its disease sensitivity, means that exposing it to air currents and distancing it from the ground's humidity are not just a good idea, but necessary. For this reason Corvina is still trained mostly with the *pergola veronese* system. (Typical of the Veneto, this training system has grapes grow high above ground with a horizontal arm, differently from Trentino's *pergola trentina*, which has an upwardly angled arm and grapes lying lower to the ground.)

Corvina's main claim to fame, and the reason why it is much loved and planted in the Veneto, is that it takes extremely well to air-drying, something that is not true of other varieties, and especially not of Cabernet Sauvignon and Merlot, which tend to produce bitter molecules when air-dried (Zenoni, Guzzo, and Tornielli 2012). Corvina often has trouble reaching adequate sugar concentrations and alcohol potential, and so producers will either late-harvest (weather permitting) or perform strong green harvests (even 50 percent of the bunches being removed at the time of the berry color change) to help Corvina concentrate sugar. Its wines are characterized by an extremely intense red cherry aroma and flavor (more intense than in most Italian red wines) that wins over many fans. According to Garner (2018), "Low fermentation temperatures bring out all sorts of fruit aromas such as cherry and raspberry in particular and background notes of hedgerow fruits, and between the lovely freshness of a Valpolicella *annata* through to the inimitable style of Amarone, there's nothing quite like it." Corvina is also characterized by very fine tannins, but not much of them, so a 100 percent pure Corvina wine cannot, and should not, remind you of a tannic behemoth. Corvina is the most important grape in the Valpolicella, Amarone della Valpolicella, and Recioto della Valpolicella wine blends. (For example, Corvina must total anywhere from 40 to 80 percent of the blend.) Therefore, it is hard for wine lovers and even experts to taste a 100 percent Corvina wine because there are not many made; Giovanna Tantini's is lovely, but others have only very rarely reminded me of what I think a 100 percent Corvina wine should taste like—something also noted by another fine wine expert (Belfrage 2001). Sweet spices, herbs, and balsamic notes are also typically found in 100 percent Corvina wines: a recent report by Ferrarini (2014) confirmed that spices (nutmeg, cinnamon, and cloves) are an important component of the best Corvina wines.

The red fruit notes for which Corvina is famous are due to furaneol and β-damascenone (Tosi et al. 2012). You will not be surprised to learn that furaneol is also called strawberry furanone and is commonly found in, you guessed it, strawberries. (It is also partly responsible for the aromas of tomatoes and fresh pineapple, but at high doses it actually takes on an unpleasant smell.) The role of β-damascenone is interesting: originally classified as a rose ketone (Simpson and Miller 1984) exuding a strong aroma of rose, it also contributes aromas of dry plum, honey, and dark berries. It is found in all wines, and though its perception threshold varies, in a wine matrix it was determined to have a perception threshold of four to seven micrograms per liter (Pineau et

al. 2014). However, β-damascenone is found at levels that are below this threshold in red wines (one to two micrograms per liter) and above it in white wines (five to ten micrograms per liter); because of this, it is believed to have an indirect impact on red fruit aroma in wine either by lowering the perception threshold of volatile molecules that have a red fruit aroma or by increasing that of methoxypyrazines, which mask other aromas with their intense grassy, bell-pepper aroma. The 2014 study by Pineau et al. also found that in hydroalcoholic solutions (in which β-damascenone's concentration is one thousand times lower than it is in wine), it enhanced ethyl-cinnamate- and ethyl-caproate-related fruit notes and masked the herbaceous aroma of 3-isobutyl-2-methoxypyrazine (IBMP). In doing their research, the study's authors also confirmed a previous finding by Ferreira et al. (2002) that β-damascenone can act as a red fruit aroma facilitator. Ethyl cinnamate and ethyl caproate both contribute red cherry and candied strawberry aromas in many red wines. (See the Nebbiolo entry.) Furthermore, the fact that it helps mask the aroma of methoxypyrazines provides further food for thought about supposed 100 percent Corvina wines marked by green bell pepper or other herbal notes. Last but not least, β-damascenone concentrations increase with shading: this tells me that using the pergola system is not without merit, given that shade is everywhere under a pergola. (Pergola-trained vineyards are nice places to hang out under on a hot summer day.) A winemaking technique that can also increase β-damascenone levels is cold maceration with pump-overs (passing the must over the skins with a pump) (Cai et al. 2014).

Perhaps Corvina's biggest claim to fame is an almost unique suitability to air-drying. (As stated previously, this is not true of all grape varieties.) And so the aroma portfolio of Corvina wines can differ depending on whether air-dried grapes were used in part, wholly, or not at all. The dehydration process concentrates aromatic molecules: among these, lactones such as γ-nonalactone and 4-carboxyethoxyγ-buttyrolactone play an important part in characterizing the wine's aromatic profile, conferring a note of coconut. Even more important, *Botrytis cinerea* (noble rot) has a noteworthy effect on the aroma profile of Amarone, and there is a positive correlation between level of fungal infection and the concentration of molecules such as N-(3-methylbutyl) acetamide and sherry lactone (Fedrizzi et al. 2011). Findings such as this shine the spotlight on just how important the presence or lack of noble-rot-affected grapes is when evaluating (and scoring) Amarone and Recioto wines. Personally, I have found over the years that less-experienced wine tasters who are not aware of the fact that Amarone can in fact be made with partially botrytized grapes tend to dislike or be taken aback by wines in which noble rot's presence is marked. Clearly, all this is important relative to the discussion of terroir in Amarone and Recioto wines, because not all sites give grapes that are as suitable for air-drying (Tornielli et al. 2010), and even fewer are prone to the development of noble rot. Many producers, fearing the oxidative effects of *Botrytis cinerea* in wine, have moved to reduce the presence of noble rot in Amarone, if not eliminate its presence altogether. In so doing, their wines gain in color but lose in overall glycerin content, making the wines less velvety and voluptuous; quite often, these same estates will also reduce maceration times and the length of the dehydration process in an effort to obtain grapes with lower sugar concentrations and lower potential alcohol levels. In my view, such tactics are rarely helpful when not downright counterproductive. Such wines almost invariably taste unpleasantly austere and tough, even bitter, and they still boast noteworthy octane strength; it is one thing if the Amarone is naturally austere and tannic, another to force it to become something that both the genetic background of the grapes used to make it and the specific terroir do not mean it to be. Such behavior is an example of estates reacting to perceived market desires (dry wines sell better than sweet ones nowadays), but it betrays both the spirit of the wine

and its specific terroir (for example, where noble rot occurs naturally and contributes a different expression of site that is typical of it; noble rot is not exactly rampant in all vineyards). Older Amarone bottling can show off a hint of camphor, too (due mostly to 4-terpineol) and of black pepper (due to rotundone), according to Ferrarini et al. (2015). Actually, a fresh note of black pepper is typical of young Corvina wines, too (and the rotundone data help all us wine tasters feel good about ourselves), but I stress that it is nothing like the peppercorn note of, for example, wines made with Schioppettino, Vespolina, or Grüner Veltliner, in which rotundone concentrations are some of the highest of all wine grapes.

Last but not least, possible notes of smoke and licorice in the wines are due to phenols such as 4-ethylguaiacol and 4-ethylphenol. Also be aware that Corvina has many different biotypes (unless further genetic testing determines them to be distinct from Corvina), such as Corvina Rizza (probably a Corvina affected by fanleaf virus) and Corvina Gentile (high quality but rare nowadays, its presence limited to very old vineyards at higher altitudes). So how "Corvina" performs in different terroirs (and hence what its wines are like) may be at least partly related to the Corvina biotype or biotypes or nursery clones planted. On this subject, an extremely interesting recent study by Anesi et al. (2015) investigated the effects of terroir on a single clone of Corvina (clone 48) in seven different vineyards in three different macrozones over three years. The authors reported that, even accounting for the different vintages, and slightly different viticultural practices, the three macrozones showed distinct terroir-specific signatures in the fruit composition of the grapes studied. Furthermore, grapes from each individual vineyard within an individual macrozone were characterized by specific chemical markers. For example, stilbene molecules characterized vineyards located in the Lake Garda macrozone (where soils are low in clay but have average amounts of soil-exchangeable potassium), while a specific subset of flavonoids characterized vineyards in Soave and Valpolicella (where soils have low concentrations of clay, total lime, and exchangeable potassium), and all the different vineyards and macrozones were characterized by different anthocyanin profiles. Therefore, it appears that greater soil fertility leads Corvina to partly modify the expression of its metabolites: the cultivar will express specific metabolites in some terroirs and not in others. The end result is different Corvina wines that are reflective of the different terroirs in which each population of grapes grew. Furthermore, in the study, the individual vineyards within each macrozone were easily distinguishable by the specific metabolite signatures of the wines made in each, which is proof of the logic for (some, not all) single-vineyard wines. Interestingly, flavonoids such as myricetin glycosides and various flavanones (dihydrokaempferol and naringenin glycosides) did not especially characterize any of the vineyards under investigation, suggesting that specific terroir-related factors act upon only parts of the grape's metabolic machinery. This study's results also suggest that, rather than bringing about huge changes in only one or two metabolites, terroir's effect is enacted via small modifications in concentration of many different secondary metabolites. This is consistent with tasting experience whereby fairly similar terroirs are most often associated with only nuanced changes in the wines made there: a Corvina wine made with grapes from Fumane will be only slightly different from one made with grapes grown in nearby Sant'Ambrogio di Valpolicella, much like a Charmes-Chambertin is only mildly and not radically different from a Griotte-Chambertin.

Corvinone

Corvinone (meaning "big raven"; the *-one* suffix in Italian refers to a larger size) is not related to Corvina: it is neither a Corvina clone nor a Corvina biotype but a distinct variety—a fact proven some time ago (Cancellier and Angelini 1993; Vantini et al. 2003). So beware of those

(and there are many) who keep saying that the two varieties are related, because that is simply wrong. (The fact that numerous wine people keep saying so—in public, no less—is revealing on many other different levels, but let us not go there.) Corvinone's area of distribution was always mostly the flatland and hillside vineyards of the Valpolicella Est: in these sites it has lower yields and more loosely packed bunches. It's a cultivar typically characterized by asynchronous maturation of berries within the same bunch as well as by bunches of different sizes growing on the same grapevine, forcing the estate to resort to costly and time-consuming hand sorting of the grapes. Monovariety Corvinone wines are practically nonexistent, since the variety is always blended with small to large percentages of Corvina to bolster the latter variety's tannic framework: the two varieties are planted together directly in vineyards, and the legal production guidelines allow up to 50 percent Corvinone in making Valpolicella, Recioto, and Amarone della Valpolicella. I have tasted numerous experimental batches of 100 percent Corvinone over the years thanks to university and private projects, and these tend to show variable profiles—most commonly, a very intense red cherry flavor (at times even stronger than of Corvina wines), but also a tannic spine often just this side of unpleasant, with a green streak. It is a variety whose fortunes are declining: whereas it was quite popular twenty years ago, I find increasingly that producers are reducing its presence in both the vineyards and the wines.

Rondinella

Easy to recognize in vineyards because of its characteristic leaf but especially because of its small, slightly curved, compact bunch and round berries (Corvina has oval berries), Rondinella, for all practical purposes, grows only in the Veneto. The variety takes its name from the swallow (*rondine* in Italian means "swallow") or, more precisely, a small swallow (because the *-ella* suffix in Italian is a diminutive, just like *-ino*). In fact, Rondinella has dark-colored grapes (deep bluish-black), just like the plumage of the swallow. Documentation of Rondinella's presence in the Veneto is relatively thin and does not go that far back (to the best of my knowledge, none prior to 1882), which is surprising given how popular the variety is among grape growers today. Rondinella's surge to prominence was no doubt helped by the fact it took very well to American rootstocks after the onslaught of phylloxera (and not every cultivar does: for example, Malbec had a very difficult time adapting—one of the major factors behind the grape's demise in France, where it was once much more common than it is today). Rondinella has endeared itself to farmers over the decades because of its cold and drought resistance and its very reliable productivity; clearly this helps farmers hedge their bets, given that the temperamental and delicate Corvina grape is nowhere near as *simpatica* to work with. On the other hand, the debate is open relative to Rondinella's exact contribution to Valpolicella and Amarone blends. (The official production guidelines allow 5 to 30 percent Rondinella in Valpolicella, Recioto, and Amarone.) Some producers insist that the cultivar adds a complicating herbal nuance to finished wine blends that would otherwise be lacking in Corvina- and Corvinone-only wines (though not everyone is convinced). Nevertheless, we do have indirect evidence that Rondinella is highly thought of because there are a large number of nursery clones available, including R 1, ISV-CV 73, ISV-CV 76, ISV-CV 23, VCR 32, and VCR 38. This is a sure-fire sign that Rondinella has fans, for no nursery that wants to stay in business bothers to select multiple clones of a variety that is not going to sell. Another sign of the renewed interest in Rondinella is that there are now monovariety wines produced with it, and this was not the case just a few years ago (D'Agata 2014a). Last but not least, Rondinella is very important in the production of the sweet Recioto della Valpolicella, because it accumulates sugars with greater ease than do the other Valpolicella varieties; that also contributes to its hanging around vineyards (literally).

Molinara

I love Molinara, and I think it is a shame that producers in the Veneto have done away with it as much as they have. In the very misguided quest to produce always bigger and blacker wines that nobody wants to drink anymore (by themselves or with their dinner), Molinara risks going the way of the thylacine (or Tasmanian wolf, now extinct). In fact, as recently as 1950, in what were less wine-scores-driven times, Montanari and Ceccarelli wrote of Molinara's importance to the local economy and recommended that more of it be planted. Unfortunately, Molinara has fat pink berries with plenty of juice that do not allow the making of dark, fleshy wines. Those muscular wines were all the rage in the 1990s and early 2000s, and so Molinara vines were uprooted everywhere. A real shame: Molinara has long been a part of the Veneto countryside (it was already described by Pollini in 1824 and Di Rovasenda in 1877) and is a red grape that produces light-bodied, natural rosé wines that are delightfully juicy, floral, spicy, and saline (the latter quality explaining why Molinara is locally called *ua salà,* or "salty grape"). It does not have the polyphenols to give big, burly, dark-colored wines. In fact, Strucchi (1908) believed it to be a Veneto biotype of Grignolino. I think it is a very pretty grape: its name derives from *mulinara or mulino* ("mill," in English), where they used to mill flour and make bread. In fact, Molinara grapes are covered in a powdery white bloom so that they look as if dusted in flour. Different clones of Molinara exist (R 2, ISV-CV 87, ISV-CV 100, ISV-CV 3, VCR 12); in general, all have medium-size bunches and berries, the former slightly pyramidal and the latter round-oval in shape. One big drawback is that Molinara's skin becomes much thinner and easily degrades over time, making the grapes unusable. "Therefore, it requires very accurate, work-intensive viticulture," says Fratelli Speri's Paolo Speri (who likes to add it is the best tasting of all Veronese grapes). Molinara is very sensitive to soil potassium deficiency, while it's resistant to most diseases except gray rot. It needs lots of space to grow (another factor limiting its interest for farmers) and requires very well ventilated sites since excessive humidity is a real no-no. (Look at where the Molinara is planted the next time you visit a winery: you will notice that the old Molinara vines are planted on the outskirts of the vineyards, where it could benefit from a stronger wind effect.) I believe that abandoning Molinara (for example, it is no longer obligatory to include it in Valpolicella, Recioto della Valpolicella, or Amarone, but can make up as much as 10 percent of the blend if the producer so wishes) will likely prove to be a grave mistake on the part of more than one Veneto denomination. Drinking 17 percent alcohol Amarones regularly at mealtime is nobody's idea (at least no one I know) of a good time, and continuing on this slippery slope opens Amarone to the risk of becoming a wine with a great future already behind it. Other areas in the Veneto that were once rich in Molinara, like Bardolino, have also done away with it, again in an effort to produce bigger red wines in the belief that that is what the market wants. And Bardolino's fortunes aren't exactly flying high, either. There is a lesson in wine terroir here: Bardolino's many sandy areas do not allow for wines of great power to be made, so clearly, a little (or a lot) of Molinara allows for graceful wines to be made, in tune with the area's specific terroir. Of course, such logic is often lost on many producers who push their terroirs to try to give all sorts of unrealistic wines. The most famous Molinara wine of all is made by the Quintarelli estate, whose wines are cult items. The Serego Alighieri estate, owned by Count Pieralvise Serego Alighieri, a direct descendant of Dante Alighieri (the author of the *Divine Comedy*, arguably Italy's most famous work of literature), owns a special biotype of Molinara (named biotype Serego Alighieri) characterized by a smaller and more compact bunch. It's a slightly richer, spicier, high-quality Molinara, but paradoxically even lighter in color than usual (hence its name, Molinara Ciara—where, in dialect, *ciara* signifies "light-colored").

Santa Maria Valverde is one estate whose wines have plenty of Molinara.

Oseleta

Yet another of the many *uve uccelline* ("bird grapes") of Italy, Oseleta has cylindrical-pyramidal-shaped, very compact bunches. It is a rustic variety and so fairly disease resistant. Oseleta has only recently climbed back to fame after having been abandoned by growers in Valpolicella for the better part of the last century. (In fact, the variety's presence was not documented much before 1900.) Farmers lost interest because of its small berries that do not yield much juice. (There is even less juice than one would expect because Oseleta has more pips per single grape than most cultivars; the additional pips take up space.) And as air-drying further reduces available juice from Oseleta grapes, large amounts of it are not used in Amarone production (and for the same reason, monovariety Oseleta wines are also likely to continue being scarce). However, Oseleta does have a number of distinguishing features separating it from all other grapes of the Veneto that make it a very interesting cultivar for the region. For one, its tannic clout is such that it has taken over the role of providing backbone from Cabernet Sauvignon and Merlot in Valpolicella and Amarone. In my experience, I have found that Oseleta provides Valpolicella and Amarone with different flavor profiles and textures than does Merlot or Cabernet Sauvignon. With a little patience and dedication, it becomes very easy to recognize whether either a Cabernet variety or Oseleta has been added to Amarone. Raffaele Boscaini of Masi believes that adding even just 5 percent of Oseleta will change a wine completely; by comparison, it takes at least a 15 percent addition of Rondinella to do the same. Oseleta was first replanted in 1985. (Credit must go to Sandro Boscaini of Masi for having been the one to rediscover it.) It was first included in the Masi blend of a wine called Toar and then made an appearance in an impressive 100 percent Oseleta wine called

Osar; Celestino Gasperi of the Zymé estate also makes two world-class wines with it (called Oseleta and Oz). Because the variety has only recently come to attention, the best terroirs for it are a matter of conjecture, but we do know it prefers gravelly and sandy soils with good drainage (but with a modicum of water-retentive capacity). In my experience, wines that are all or mainly Oseleta have almost inky-ruby hues and exude grapey and violet aromas and delicate herbal and blackberry flavors, complicated by nuances of tar, fresh herbs, and cinnamon. There is always an aromatic green streak in the wines that can become unpleasant if physiological ripeness was not achieved, but otherwise it adds noteworthy complexity and elegance to the wines made with it, which are always quite tannic.

SPECIFIC TERROIRS

In 1968, in a move analogous to the one that led to the creation of a Chianti and a Chianti Classico many years before, the original Valpolicella production area was greatly increased in size, so as to create more than one "Valpolicella." So there are now three Valpolicella zones: Valpolicella Classica (to the northwest of Verona, it includes the communes of Fumane, Marano di Valpolicella, Negrar, San Pietro in Cariano, and Sant'Ambrogio di Valpolicella—the five towns at the historic center of the Valpolicella area); Valpantena (north of Verona, it is a narrow, roughly twelve-kilometer-long valley that runs parallel to the Valpolicella Classica denomination and includes the townships of Grezzana and part of the Verona territory itself); and Valpolicella Est or Allargata (allargata means "widened") (made up of the Squaranto, Mezzane, d'Illasi, Tramigna, and d'Alpone valleys; communes located in this denomination include Colognola ai Colli, Illasi, Mazzane di Sotto, San Martino Buon Albergo, Tregnago, and the remaining portion of the Verona territory). I will analyze the two Valpolicella denominations (Valpolicella Classica and Valpolicella Est) that I know best, and whose wines I have always

liked most. I am in good company, too: Michael Garner, author of the splendid *Amarone and the Fine Wines of Verona* (2018), states that "the eastern part of Valpolicella is highly underrated, the higher reaches of Mezzane di Sotto and Illasi in particular." That recognized, there are some truly outstanding wines made in the Valpantena as well, such as Brigaldara's Amarone della Valpolicella Case Vecie, from grapes grown around Grezzana and Cavolo.

Valpolicella Classica

The Valpolicella Classica is where the largest critical mass of outstanding Valpolicella wines are made. There are many fine wines made in both the Valpolicella Valpantena and the Valpolicella Est, but the Valpolicella Classica's terroir holds a number of advantages over the other two denominations. One is that it is the denomination closest to Lake Garda: the lake captures heat during the day and releases it at night, which translates into warmer breezes blowing off the lake. This leads to potentially dry sunny and breezy Septembers and Octobers (good if you have to air-dry grapes). Another advantage is that the Valpolicella Classica is characterized at least in part by volcanic soils (the presence of which is usually associated with more-complex wines). The Valpolicella Classica production zone looks something like the outstretched fingers of a hand, with three main parallel valleys running in a north–south direction. Small *progni* (the local word for "streams" or "small rivers") flow through the three valleys, which are easily identified by the name of the main commune within each: Marano, Negrar, and Fumane. Each of the three valleys has its own microclimate, and the interaction between each valley's microclimate and specific soils leads to potentially very different wines being made. Climate is especially relevant to the styles of Valpolicella and Amarone made here: for example, the proximity of Lake Garda to the western part of the Valpolicella Classica (around Sant'Ambrogio di Valpolicella) makes for highly different wines than those typical of its eastern reaches (around Negrar, for example). Garner (2018) states that "[v]ariations in average temperatures between the western parts of Classico, close to Lake Garda, and those to the eastern reaches of Valpolicella can be as much as four degrees Celsius": that temperature differential makes its presence felt in the wines. The valleys begin up high in the Lessini Mountains, at about 700 meters above sea level, but vineyards grow mainly between 150 and 500 meters above sea level. Historically, slopes with southeast exposures were believed best for Recioto production, whereas southwest-facing slopes were thought best for Amarone production. Unfortunately, over the last twenty years or so, few estates make this distinction anymore, and an important element of terroir has gone lost (simply because everyone wants to make the strongly selling Amarone nowadays; unfortunately, making wines grounded in terroir is another matter).

The geology of the Valpolicella Classica is complex. Its soils were formed mainly during the Jurassic (199.6 million to 145 million years ago) and in the Cretaceous (145 million to 66 million years ago), as well as partly in the Paleogene period (66 million to 23 million years ago) and the Eocene epoch. (See table 2 in the appendix.) Generally speaking, favored vineyard sites for Valpolicella, Amarone, and Recioto della Valpolicella production are those of the hillsides and foothills, where soils are mostly reddish and brownish in color, compact and calcareous in nature. (Most often the reddish soils arose in the Jurassic, whereas the brownish ones are Cretaceous in origin; the latter's darker color derives from a small presence of basalt.) Lower-lying vineyards grow on essentially alluvial deposits of the Adige River and of the streams that hurtle down from the Lessini Mountains. The soil structure changes with the river's course: for example, soils in the upper reaches of the streams are characterized by a gravelly component and a larger soil granulometry. Hillside vineyards are planted on soils that have different calcareous elements (marly clay, calcarenites) but that at times can have poor drainage. The foothills are characterized by good drainage but also better water-retention capacity than the hillside vineyards (Scienza et al. 2008). It is these areas where the *marogne*—the typical stone walls of the Valpolicella that are used to delimit vineyards—appear in full force. The lower reaches of the Valpolicella Classica have a warm microclimate thanks to the natural barrier to cold winds blowing in from the north provided by the Lessini Mountains. However, despite the presence of the olive trees, the Valpolicella area does not have a true Mediterranean climate, which as defined by Wladimir Köppen (a famous Russian climatologist who devised one of the world's most used climate-classification systems, in which climates are labeled with two- or three-letter combinations, such as Cs or Dfc, which stand for the Mediterranean and Subarctic climates, respectively) is one in which less than 30 percent of the annual rainfall occurs during the winter (Sommers 2008). In fact, in Valpolicella that number is much higher: about 55 to 60 percent of the annual precipitation falls in winter. Rainfall varies with the altitude, ranging from 850 millimeters per year in the flatlands to 1,200 millimeters per year at five hundred to seven hundred meters above sea level, while precipitation is slightly less in the high mountain zones (900 to 1,000 millimeters per year). The rainiest months of the year are October and May, whereas the driest is February, followed by July. Rainstorms and hail episodes are not rare in the summer, but this is mostly true of the non-Classica Valpolicella areas. Not surprisingly, temperatures are highest in August and lowest in January; the mean daily temperature is 13–15°C. The Winkler index is 1900–2300, and the Huglin index is 2300–2750 (data from Portale Valpolicella.it).

The Subzones of the Valpolicella Classica

I believe that, in the manner of the Haut-Médoc, the Valpolicella Classica and its wines can be divided into five subzones named after their most important commune. Subdividing the denomination in this manner is much easier to do than in other parts of Italy—such as Chianti Classico—because the geology of the Valpolicella Classica, though still complex, is a great deal more uniform. Over the years, I have also found that there are very clear relationships between the wines made in the various subzones, and well-defined and easy-to-trace terroir-specific factors. Two such factors are the altitude at which the grapevines grow and their proximity to Lake Garda. In the nineteenth and twentieth centuries, and to some extent still today, the Valpolicella Classica was alive with individuals making wine for home consumption; they knew their area's vineyards quite well, and used to trade grapes among themselves in order to make the best possible wine, or one that was to their personal taste. Gianpaolo Speri of Fratelli Speri recalls his grandfather Benedetto paying the various farmers who lived in his area a visit from time to time and always making a point of trying their homemade wines. In this manner he had a good idea of where to buy the best grapes in each vintage: one year it would be the Molinara grapes grown, say, by Francesco, and in another year those grown by Mario—and the same with all the other cultivars used in the Veronese wine blends. Most of the time, though, he found that it was always the same farmer who grew the best Molinara, while another was always the one who had the best Corvina, and so forth.

SANT'AMBROGIO DI VALPOLICELLA
Sant'Ambrogio di Valpolicella is the westernmost subzone of Valpolicella Classica and is characterized by mainly calcareous soils of sedimentary origin. Despite the fact that vineyards are planted anywhere between 120 and 450 meters above sea level, grapes grow at low average altitudes in this subzone—roughly 180 meters above sea level. (Sant'Ambrogio di Valpolicella is at 174 meters above sea level.) In fact, about half the vineyard area in Sant'Ambrogio di Valpolicella is on the flatlands. Vineyards are mostly south-facing (50 percent), but eastern (30 percent) and western

exposures (20 percent) are common, too. Hamlets worth knowing in this subzone (because they are linked to very good wineries and wines) are Gargagnago, Monte, and San Giorgio. I find the wines from the Sant'Ambrogio di Valpolicella subzone to be less dark in color (bright red to deep ruby) and lower in overall acidity than those of the other subzones; they also often tend to have a savory quality, perhaps due to veins of marble (a calcareous metamorphic rock) present in the soil, but that's just my theory. The wines made from grapes grown at the higher altitudes are not unlike those of the western slopes of Fumane: much more expressive aromatically, even pungent, and more austere than wines made from Sant'Abrogio di Valpolicella grapes grown at lower altitudes. In fact, wines from these higher-placed vineyards of the subzone offer noteworthy refinement, and prove highly enjoyable even at a young age. Some estates worth knowing: Masi and Serego Alighieri.

SAN PIETRO IN CARIANO
San Pietro in Cariano is the southernmost commune in the Valpolicella Classica, and therefore it is very close to Verona. (The city of Romeo and Juliet is only twelve kilometers away.) Most of this subzone's vineyards are located on flatland alluvial soils, although there are hillside vineyards such as at Castelrotto, at 170 meters above sea level; the town of San Pietro in Cariano is at 151 meters above sea level. From a viticultural and winemaking perspective, these are the most interesting and potentially high-quality vineyard sites, with as much as 20 percent clay and a strong limestone presence. Most vineyards have southeastern exposures, but some face north. There are hamlets worth knowing, such as Castelrotto, Pedemonte, and San Floriano; the latter especially makes wines that are distinctive enough to have made me consider the option of separating it from the subzones and assigning a "district" category to it, much as I have done with Lamole and Panzano in Chianti Classico. The wines offer plenty of early appeal, a supple texture, and noteworthy balsamic and spicy

nuances, but there are fairly large differences present in wines made from this subzone. For example, the wines made at Castelrotto are different from those made with grapes grown in other parts of San Pietro in Cariano. Some estates worth knowing: Lorenzo Begali, Brigaldara (San Floriano), Buglioni, Nicolis, Speri, Tedeschi, Tommasi, Luigi Vantini (San Floriano), Venturini, and Zymé.

FUMANE

Like Sant'Ambrogio di Valpolicella, about 60 percent of Fumane's vines grow on hillsides (40 percent on flatlands), at an average altitude of two hundred meters above sea level. (The town of Fumane is found at that altitude, too.) Sandwiched between the subzones of Sant'Ambrogio di Valpolicella to the west and the Marano subzone to the east, Fumane is located in the northern part of the Valpolicella Classica immediately above the San Pietro in Cariano subzone. At 110 people per square kilometer, or 300 people per square mile, it is one of the least densely populated subzones of the denomination. (By comparison, San Pietro in Cariano has a density of 640 people per square kilometer, or 1,600 people per square mile, and Sant'Ambrogio di Valpolicella has one of 500 people per square kilometer, or 1,300 people per square mile.) The subzone presents other distinguishing features. The soils are mostly calcareous, and the valley is the least narrow of the three in Valpolicella Classica, and so the wines, though they don't lack for power (they are denser and more powerful than those of Sant'Ambrogio), also boast truly delightful and very typical spicy and floral notes (especially when made with grapes from the eastern side of the subzone; wines made with grapes grown in the western part generally are gentler and bigger, perhaps with better overall balance). The aromatic nature cannot come as much of a surprise given that the town's name derives from *fumo*, or "smoke" (though I never find much of a smoky presence in the wines). Some estates worth knowing: Allegrini and Stefano Accordini.

MARANO

The Marano subzone is located in the northern part of the Valpolicella Classica denomination right above San Pietro in Cariano, with Fumane to the west and Negrar to the east. The city of Verona is only about fourteen kilometers removed from Marano della Valpolicella (the town's official full name). The soils differ quite a bit from those in the other subzones, especially in the central portion of the subzone, where volcanic basalt elements locally known as *toari* are common. Vineyards face mostly southeast and southwest and are planted between 300 and 400 meters above sea level. (In fact, Marano is one of the highest of all the Valpolicella Classica communes, situated at 318 meters above sea level.) There are noteworthy diurnal temperature ranges in this subzone, and the wines are perfumed—almost aromatic, in fact—with very good acid lift. These are the wines in which Corvina's red cherry aromas and flavors jump out at you the most, but I have also always found nuances of dried plum, underbrush, and flint, giving the wines an aromatic and extremely refined quality. Some estates worth knowing: Ca' La Bionda, Giuseppe Campagnola, Michele Castellani, and Novaia.

NEGRAR

Negrar is the largest of the Valpolicella Classica subzones and therefore boasts greater topographical complexity than the others. For the same reason, there are numerous hamlets that are worth knowing because of their high-quality wines: Arbizzano, Cerè, Jago, Mazzano, Montecchio, Santa Maria, and Torbe are all worth remembering. The Negrar subzone can be divided into three parts: a flatland area to the south, where vines grow at about 80 to 100 meters above sea level; and a northern, hillier area that can be subdivided into eastern and western sections. (The town of Negrar itself is located at 180 meters above sea level.) This hillier area gives the more interesting wines that are perfumed, downright fragrant. (Generally speaking, there's a bit more sand in Negrar than in other subzones of the Valpolicella Classica.) The wines are always elegant, but to make clear-cut inferences as to the wine's link to the local terroir, you need to know where the grapes that are used to make the wine grow within the subzone, since there are large variations in style due not just to individual estate viticultural and winemaking decisions, but also to how large and diversified the subzone is. Some estates worth knowing: Cantine Bertani (Arbizzano), L'Arco, Le Ragose, Quintarelli (Cerè), Roberto Mazzi, and Viviani.

Noteworthy Crus of Valpolicella Classica

Campolongo (Marano), Creari (Fumane), Gargagnago Alto (Sant'Ambrogio di Valpolicella), *Marega* (Fumane), Mazzano (Negrar), Monte Olmi (San Pietro in Cariano), Calcarole (Negrar), *Le Ragose* (Negrar), Monte Ca' Paletta (Cerè in Negrar), Monte Fontana (San Pietro in Cariano), *Ravazzol* (Marano), Novare (Negrar), Palazzo della Torre (Fumane), Poiega (Negrar), San Floriano (San Pietro in Cariano), *San Giorgio* (Sant'Ambrogio di Valpolicella). (Italicized names refer to sites that are also especially good for Recioto della Valpolicella production, and not just for Valpolicella and Amarone).

BENCHMARK WINES

Amarone: Quintarelli***PS.

Bussola TB***, Bussola TB Vigneto Alto***, Masi Campolongo di Torbe***, Masi Mazzano***, Santa Maria Valverde***, Serego Alighieri Vajo Armaron***, Speri***, Stefano Accordini Acinatico***, Tedeschi Capitel Monte Olmi***, Tommasi***, Zymè***.

Allegrini**, Ca' La Bionda**, Musella**, Venturini**; Giuseppe Campagnola*, Marion*, Villa Novaia*.

Recioto: Quintarelli Recioto della Valpolicella Classico***PS, Bussola***PS.

Valpolicella Est

Val d'Illasi

I doubt I will offend anyone by writing that the Val d'Illasi was essentially brought to notoriety by Romano Dal Forno and his absolutely amazing wines. The Val d'Illasi produces both Soave and Valpolicella DOC wines, and its two main townships are Illasi and Tregnago; viticulture is practiced on both the hillsides (25 percent) and plains (75 percent). Most of the grapes are sent to the local cooperative (the Cooperativa di Illasi). Pesavento Mattioli (1996) writes that viticulture in the Val d'Illasi was historically always florid. The Val d'Illasi is just one of the many long and narrow valleys that run in a north–south direction in the extended (or *allargata*) Valpolicella zone (though I think the name of this DOC area ought to be Valpolicella Est, since *allargata* is too easily misinterpreted to mean something pejorative) stretching from the Lessini Mountains toward the plains around Verona. The Val d'Illasi starts off at roughly 1,650 meters above sea level in the Mount Carega group of peaks and spreads out southward for roughly thirty-five kilometers and joins the Mezzane Valley in the fluvioglacial plain of the Adige River. (Just as the Arno flows through Florence and the Tiber through Rome, the Adige flows through the city of Verona.) As the river moves south, the valley broadens progressively, while its topography is characterized by numerous natural uprisings that, moving south, become gentler and lower in altitude. The higher reaches of the Illasi valley around the town of Tregnago have mostly gravel-sandy soils with large diameter alluvial elements, while south of the town of Illasi the soil is mostly loamy-clay. Though carbonate salts are present throughout the entire Valle d'Illasi, they are especially abundant in the loamy-clay areas south of Illasi, while the hillsides are richer in lime. The water table lies at different depths throughout the Valle d'Illasi and is closest to the surface in the southern reaches of the denomination. Interestingly, while the water table rises while moving south, annual rainfall increases in a northward direction (for example, it is 819 millimeters per year in the Zevio area, 1,039 millimeters per year at Tregnango, and 1,506 millimeters per year at Giazza). Meneghel (1979) mentions that the most northern parts of the valley receive as much as 2,000 millimeters per year of rain, but this portion of the valley is of little interest to wine lovers. Numerous excellent studies have documented the geomorphology of the valley (Fabiani 1913; Pasa 1954; Meneghel 1979; Sauro and Meneghel 1980); Failla et al. (1998) presented interesting data in a Valle d'Illasi zonation study. These researchers studied possible links between viticulture, climate, and soil by using sensory analysis of wines made there. Reference vineyards (six used to make Soave and another nineteen red grape Valpolicella vineyards) were followed over three years (1993–95), and parameters such as yields, rate of vegetative growth, and ripening curves were analyzed. Microvinifications were performed and the wines evaluated. For the most part, vineyards were very comparable, though I point out that the vineyards examined were of slightly different ages: the Soave vines ranged between ten and twenty-five years old; the Valpolicella vines, between ten and fifteen years old. There was also some rootstock deformity between vineyards: in both the Soave and Valpolicella vineyards under study, numerous rootstocks other than 420 A were also present (1103P, 41B, and 140 Ru for Soave; 41B and 140 Ru in the Valpolicella vineyards). The authors believed that such differences were not significant, but the interpretation of the results is clearly made slightly more difficult. Soil type and altitude were found to be the most important parameters determining wine quality, with the lower-lying vineyards (less than 280 meters above sea level) planted on soils that were richer in sand than clay deemed to give the best wines. For the most part, wines showed aromas and flavors of strawberry, spices, and dry herbs of varying intensity and complexity.

BENCHMARK WINES

Amarone: Dal Forno***[PS].

Roccolo Grassi***, Tenuta Sant'Antonio Campo dei Gigli***.

Trabucchi**.

Recioto: Dal Forno***[PS].

Roccolo Grassi***.

Dorona

THE GRAPE VARIETY

Dorona is also known as Garganega Grossa, but it is best not to use the latter name because Dorona and Garganega are distinct (though closely related). Furthermore, there are many biotypes of Garganega, some of which are in fact quite large, characterized by very big bunches (especially when grown in flatland vineyards on very fertile soils) and berries. As a result, confusion among Garganega-something biotypes, Garganega, and Dorona is likely. In fact, as its name implies, Dorona does have large bunches and grapes: in a not-too-distant past it was most appreciated as a table grape. Dorona had other synonyms, too—Garganega dall'Oro (in the Colli Euganei), Garganega Piramidale, Garganegona—but Dorona is the name typically used for it on the islands of the Venetian lagoon, where, thanks to the Bisol family, the variety has been brought back home. According to Di Vecchi Staraz et al. (2007), Dorona may be the result of a natural cross between Garganega and Bermestia Bianca, a table grape from Emilia-Romagna. Dorona grows in the Veneto, but it is rare: researchers from the University of Verona have located it on the Sordato estate in Selva di Montebello, and a similar but different variety on the estate of Ca' Piovene in Toara. Thanks to the Bisol family, it appears to have also returned to one of its original homes: Venice and its lagoon. Since Dorona is a vigorous variety that produces abundant yields regularly, a long cane-pruning system is best. Dorona has demonstrated low sensibility to fungal diseases—in particular, botrytis—with a long conservation capacity either on the vine or once harvested, which explains its past use as a table grape.

SPECIFIC TERROIRS

Venice and Its Islands

Like everywhere else in medieval times, religious communities that settled in Venice and its territories grew grapevines, since wine was necessary to celebrate the Holy Mass. There were as many as twenty-four monasteries in Venice's lagoons: therefore, vineyards and grape varieties were not exactly scarce. Furthermore, the presence of monasteries also ensured the study and the upkeep of the local varieties. (See part 1 of this book.) In 2010, research teams from the Universities of Milan and Padua, as well as of the Centro di Ricerche per la Viticoltura di Conegliano (CRAVIT) and the University of Berlin along with the Consorzio Vini Venezia, set up experimental vineyards on the island of Torcello as well as in the convent of the friars of the order of the Carmelitani Scalzi, adjacent to the church of Santa Maria di Nazareth, better known as "degli Scalzi," one of the most noteworthy examples of Baroque Venetian architecture in the city. The grapevines that were planted in these two vineyards were painstakingly selected from eleven different sites located all over Venice's territory, including the north lagoon (the islands of Torcello, of delle Vignole, and of Sant'Erasmo; on the latter island, Michel Thoulouze makes an outstanding Malvasia Istriana and a Fiano white wine blend called Orto di Venezia), the city of Venice itself (most people are not aware that Venice's buildings harbor some of Italy's most beautiful gardens within their walled confines: unfortunately, the majority are not open to the public), and the south lagoon (Lido Alberoni, San Lazzaro degli Armeni, and Pellestrina). In wildly interesting results, sixty-eight different grapevines were tested and twenty-five different DNA profiles were identified. Of these, twenty-two were of known varieties (only twenty of which were *Vitis vinifera:* fourteen wine grapes and six table grapes). To further give you an idea of the incredible biodiversity that was commonplace on these islands, a white cultivar called Rushaki was found on San Lazzaro degli Armeni: it is a white table grape that doubles as a wine grape, and was most likely imported to Venice from Armenia. (It was created in an Armenian laboratory in 1932 by crossing the Mskhali and Sultanina varieties.) In 2002, Bisol came across what he thought was a funny-looking grapevine in a garden on Torcello while sightseeing there with friends. Bisol was fairly sure he had never seen the grape before, and so he decided to look into the matter further by having the mystery vine's DNA analyzed. Upon discovering that it was Dorona, he began searching for it on other islands of the Venice lagoon as well, tracing its presence mostly on Sant'Erasmo. He selected vines from the latter island and planted them at the ancient Scarpa Volo estate (where Bisol has created a delightful country hotel called Venissa) on Mazzorbo, a pretty island joined by a wooden footbridge (the *ponte longo,* "long bridge") to Burano, a bigger island bursting at the seams with charm, famous for its colorful homes (the *buranelli*) and exquisitely delicate lace. Though Burano is the better-known island today, Mazzorbo itself was no slouch in the importance department in medieval times: its name derives from *maiurbium,* or *magna urbe* (great or big city).

The Venice lagoon is one of the world's truly magical places: walk around in Venice and its islands in the off-season late at night, when there is virtually nobody around, and you'll feel catapulted into a seventeenth-century graphite-and-ink drawing. Having spent my adolescent summers in Friuli thanks to the maternal side of the family, Venice was a regular weekend getaway, and to this day there is simply no place on earth that I like or know better. In fact, the Venice lagoon is an amazing ecosystem and a remarkable lesson in wine terroir. Wine production was common in the Venice lagoon in medieval times, though clearly large vineyards were out of the question given that space was limited. For this reason, the area was characterized by the presence of the *brolo veneziano,* the term for a small plot of land that was vineyard, orchard, and vegetable garden all in one. A series of clever dikes and canals allowed for the control of water flow in and out of the *brolo,* and over the centuries the plants of the lagoon adapted to a highly saline environment. (In this respect, it is interesting that Venice's vegetables and fruit have always been much sought after for their savoriness and intensity of flavor, something still true today.)

BENCHMARK WINE

Venissa Dorona**.

Durella

THE GRAPE VARIETY

Durella is native to the Veneto's Monti Lessini, where it was known as Uva Durasena in the thirteenth century. But according to some producers and grape historians I have talked to over the years, the variety might have been known even in ancient Rome. In any case, it is an old variety and the parent of other local varieties such as Bianchetta Trevigiana (Cipriani et al. 2010). Durella's name derives either from its tough skin or its just-as-tough high acidity (*duro* in Italian means "hard"), since it boasts high malic acid concentrations. Another possibility is that the *duro* refers to anger or rage (and given how high in acid some Durella wines are, I can see how some short-fused tasters might be left less than happy). Durella is a rustic variety characterized by very stable, copious production volumes and extremely high total acidities—the main reasons why farmers have always loved it. By comparison, Garganega (the other grape variety that grows in the same part of the Veneto as Durella) is a wimp, and farmers could not count on it for a living. Very importantly, Durella does not drop its acidity levels as does Garganega (or Glera). However, its wines do have a tendency to oxidize easily, in which case they become an unsightly orange color. Therefore, limiting oxygen contact during the winemaking process is of utmost importance; the very interesting thesis work by Girardi (2008–9) showed that the activity of the polyphenol oxidase enzyme (involved in the premature browning of musts) in Durella is comparable to that of Garganega and lower than that of Cortese, for example. In my experience, Durella gives high-acid wine blessed with delicate aromas and flavors of minerals, white flowers, and fresh fruit (especially green apple and lemon) and low alcohol (rarely exceeding 12 percent, and mostly hovering between 10.5 and 11 percent). The wines go well with many vegetable and fish dishes; those made with extended contact with lees pair well with white-meat dishes as well.

SPECIFIC TERROIRS

Lessini Durello

Durella is used to make both sparkling wines (the majority) and nonsparkling wines, and the Lessini Durello area of the Veneto is where it grows best. Nonsparkling wines made with Durella are labeled Veneto or Monti Lessini Durella (the still dry wines) or Monti Lessini Passito or Monti Lessini Durella Passito (the sweet wines). The sparkling wines can have small percentages of other grapes such as Chardonnay, Garganega, or even Pinot Noir blended in, but most producers are making 100 percent Durella wines. Lessini Durello is made in nineteen communes in Vicenza and six in Verona near the Lessini Mountains, on mainly volcanic soils. The wines offer much bigger structure and much higher acidity than Prosecco, along with notes of honey, orchard fruit, and resin, complemented by strong lemony mineral nuances, plus noteworthy aging capacity. Broadly speaking, Lessini Durellos offer a very different taste sensation than any other Italian sparkler. Unlike Prosecco, Lessini Durello wines are devoid of the charming aromatic touch that makes Glera wines so irresistible. They are also much less creamy than Proseccos (the good Proseccos, at least) and other Italian sparkling wines such as Franciacortas, but have much better acidity and lift. Unlike Franciacorta, though, Lessini Durello wines can be made both via the Martinotti-Charmat method (like most Proseccos) and, most often, by secondary fermentation in the bottle in the manner of Champagne. Unfortunately, labels and back labels do not always make this distinction clear, though the term *riserva* usually refers to a wine made by secondary fermentation. The DOC is young (1986); the consortium of the Lessini Durello was born only ten years later and, happily, has done a good job of promoting the variety's merits and encouraged its planting. The members of the Soave consortium's board over the years (Lessini Durello wines fall within the promotional duties of the Soave consortium) deserve credit for having stuck with and promoted what is a smaller denomination and its wines, even when they could have conveniently forgotten about this part of their job. That is to their credit.

The Lessini Durello terroir can give wines exhibiting noteworthy differences in aroma, flavor, and texture depending on where in the denomination the grapes are grown. Vineyard land is scarce for a number of reasons: hills are often too steep to work in a cost-effective manner, large protected forests cannot be cut down to make room for vineyards (the nature lover in me applauds), and cold microclimates mean a lack of sufficient sunlight hours. Over the years, the flatlands have been turned over to housing, with vineyards limited to higher hillside slopes. (Grapes are grown as high up as 550 to 600 meters above sea level.) Slope gradients can be steep, as high as 70 percent, but are mostly between 10 and 30 percent; terraces are often necessary. The wines are very different depending on the type of soil on which Durella is planted: there are two main soil types in the denomination: volcanic, and a calcarenite-sandstone mix. (Volcanic soils are located mostly in the heart of the DOC.) The volcanic soils are fine-grained and are devoid of rocks, gravel, and limestone; they are not very permeable and are marked by poor drainage, but the available water capacity in this area of the Lessini is good. The climate is not especially warm, thanks to cold air currents and air masses that stagnate on the hillsides rather than reach the flatlands below: the average daily temperature per year is 12.5°C. Temperatures rise to 18°C on average during May to October, but that is not high compared with the temperatures of most Italian viticultural areas during the same time period. A positive is that diurnal temperature variations are noteworthy: there can be a difference of as much as 14°C in day–night temperatures during the ripening period. Winters tend to be cold, summers hot and humid but short (Huglin index, 2150). At 1,225 millimeters, annual rainfall is high; 65 percent of all the rain falls during the grapevine's vegetative period. The typical training system in this part of the Lessini is the pergola, which allows for optimal grape ripening (18° Brix is attained easily) while maintaining high acidity even with widely spaced vines (2,000 to 2,500 vines per hectare). And so these grapes almost always clock in an astounding nine grams per liter total acidity or more (you realize why the grape is suited to sparkling-wine production), of which three grams per liter are of malic acid, accounting for the strong note of green apple that so characterizes Lessini Durello and Veneto Durello wines (at least those that do not undergo malolactic transformation). Another common descriptor of a well-made Durella wine is white flowers. Not surprisingly, then, research has shown that Durella grapes are especially rich in linalool, nerol, and β-ionone. By contrast, the western and eastern portions of the Lessini Durello DOC (those corresponding to the Val d'Alpone and the Val Leogra and Mount Malo areas, respectively) are characterized by calcarenite and sandstone soils. (These are also typical of the lower Chiampo Valley.) Very differently from the Lessinia's volcanic soils, root penetration is limited by the relatively high bedrock. (Whereas in Lessinia's volcanic soils, roots dig down for a meter or more, in these soils they descend to fifty centimeters at most.) Because there are plenty of rocks and gravel within the soil, available water capacity is low to average and drainage is good; differently from the volcanic areas of the DOC, limestone content is also quite high, with as much as 10 percent active lime. For these reasons, vineyards are planted mostly at lower altitudes in this part of the Lessini. Slopes are also less steep, often not more than 10 percent. Different training systems are used and planting densities are generally higher than in the volcanic areas (four thousand vines per hectare). The microclimate is much warmer, too, with annual average daily temperature of 13.5°C and an average of 19°C from April to October (Huglin index, 2340). Annual rainfall is 1,152 millimeters, with 70 percent of that amount falling between April and October (coinciding with the grapevine's vegetative period). The Durella grapes have even higher acidity levels (they reach 12.5 grams per liter total acidity easily, with about 4 grams per liter of malic acid). Though linalool, nerol, and β-ionol are still the most common aromatic molecules found in Durella grapes grown on these soils, the wines exhibit even stronger green-apple notes than those born of volcanic soils, while being much less flinty and floral. They also offer a stronger citrus note.

BENCHMARK WINES

Lessini Durello (sparkling wines): Fongaro Brut***, Fongaro Pas Dose Guerrino***, Marcato Brut 36 Mesi***, Marcato Riserva Extra A.R.***.

Ca' Rugate Riserva Amedeo**, Casa Cecchin Nostrum**, Tonello 60 Mesi**.

Monti Lessini or Veneto Durello (still wines): Casa Cecchin "Il" Durello***, Casa Cecchin Pietralava*** (Durello late harvest).

Corte Moschina Sui Lieviti Purocaso*.

Erbaluce

THE GRAPE VARIETY

Erbaluce has one of Italy's prettiest grape names, deriving from the words *alba* (dawn) and *luce* (light): "the dawn's light," in reference to the cultivar's very pale, almost translucent green grapes (that are "pale as the dawn's light"). Another possible origin of the cultivar's name is *albaluce*: a local legend would have it that Albaluce was a fairy who blessed the townspeople of Caluso with this specific wine grape as her gift. First described by Croce in the seventeenth century as *erbalus* or *albalux*, it has also been called Bianchera, Albaluce, and Ambra (or "amber," in English: the pale grapes turn amber-gold when fully ripe or air-dried). In fact, a local name in dialect is *bianc-rousti* or *uva roustia* ("roasted grape") in reference to the golden-amber color of the grapes. (Erbaluce is famous as the ingredient of the local outstanding *passito* wine.) Erbaluce's most common synonym is Greco or Greco di Caluso, but it would be better to abandon this use because Greco and Erbaluce are distinct varieties. Erbaluce's budbreak is early in the season, and so spring frosts are a threat. Despite high vigor, Erbaluce is not an especially fertile variety (the first buds don't fruit), and it is very susceptible to most vineyard diseases (as well as to soil magnesium deficiency), so yields are both low and irregular. Depending on the clone or massal selection, Erbaluce's grape bunch is medium size, elongated, and cylindrical, with medium-large, round, thick-skinned berries; a higher-quality Erbaluce biotype described by Tedeschini in the 1930s was characterized by a pink stalk but was sickly and poorly productive, and so it disappeared by the mid-twentieth century. Since Erbaluce needs plenty of room to expand, airy canopies (called *topie* in the Canavese region where Erbaluce grows) are the most suitable training system. Despite its being a high-acid variety, a thick wall of leaves is necessary to protect Erbaluce's grape bunches from too much sunlight, and hail is always a possibility in this part of northern Italy. That said, deleafing is practically mandatory for grapes to reach optimal ripeness.

Apparently, it was Francesco Orsolani who first tried to make sparkling wines with

Erbaluce in 1968, in an effort to duplicate the success and easy-drinking charm of sparkling wines that were very successful in Italy at that time. It is likely that others in the area also thought that the grape's high natural acidity made it an ideal candidate for sparkling-wine production; in fact, Remo Falconieri of the outstanding Cieck estate once showed me a thick-staved barrel that his grandfather used to make sparkling wine in. The key about Erbaluce's acidity is that it does not drop precipitously even as the grapes overripen or air-dry, which distinguishes it neatly from varieties such as Passerina in which the acidity in the grapes drops very quickly.

The most famous Erbaluce wine is the DOC Erbaluce di Caluso (Piedmont's first white DOC wine, awarded in 1967), but good, too, are Colline Novaresi Erbaluce (or Bianco) and Coste della Sesia Erbaluce, also DOC wines (note that these latter Erbaluce wines, produced outside of the official Caluso DOC zone, cannot be labeled "di Caluso"). However, Erbaluce has always been most famous for its outstanding sweet wines. Erbaluce's berries have thick skins, ideal for air-drying: in fact, Mas and Pulliat (1874–79) documented that this part of Italy once used to make *vins de paille*, just like in France. True late-harvest wines that offer pleasant if delicate aromas and flavors of apricots, peach, and acacia honey are rare, given the region's climate. Most common are the luscious *passito* wines, offering bittersweet chestnut honey, almond, dried fig, and saffron flavors that linger on the long tropical-fruit aftertaste. (A noteworthy tannic bite is undoubtedly Greco-like, one of the reasons that likely led to the use of the erroneous synonym.) A very interesting study by Giordano et al. (2009) studied the aroma and flavor molecules of Erbaluce di Caluso *passito* wines. In this study at least, the Caluso *passito* wines presented higher contents of organic acids (especially malic acid), metabolites from noble *Botrytis cinerea* (laccase, glycerol, gluconic acid, and benzaldehyde), and low contents of total polyphenols compared with other well-known Ital-

ian sweet wines like Liguria's Sciacchetrà and Sicily's Passito di Pantelleria. Among the volatile components, normal fatty acid ethyl esters (ethyl hexanoate and ethyl octanoate), branched-chain esters (ethyl 2-methylpropanoate, ethyl 2-methylbutyrate, and ethyl 3-methylbutyrate), and benzaldehyde characterized Caluso *passito*, which accounts at least in part for the aromas and flavors of apple (ethyl hexanoate and ethyl octanoate) and pungent pineapple skin and apple peel (ethyl 2-methylbutyrate) and almond (benzaldehyde), which in my experience can be extremely intense in Caluso *passito* wines. Not surprisingly, since Erbaluce is not an aromatic variety, concentrations of terpenes were low compared with concentrations of ethyl esters, ethyl acetates, and alcohols.

SPECIFIC TERROIRS

Caluso

Caluso is where the best Erbaluce wines in Italy are made. In fact, the Erbaluce di Caluso wines (DOC already in 1967 and DOCG in 2010) were so highly thought of that specific communes were identified as the source of the best grapes as early as the nineteenth century. In his outstanding treatise on the wines of the province of Ivrea (1838), Lorenzo Francesco Gatta documents that the white grapes and wines of the towns of Settimo Rottaro, Caluso, Orio, and Lessolo were especially prestigious and sought after, fetching ten times the price of the local red wines. The most expensive of all were the sweet wines made from grapes air-dried well into February or even March. The Caluso production zone is located in the Canavese area of Piedmont (where the famous Nebbiolo-based red wine Carema is also made), less than an hour's drive north of Turin on the way to the Valle d'Aosta. It is landlocked between the Valle d'Aosta and the Alps to the north, again the Alps to the west, the Po River valley to the south, and the Serra Ivrea chain of hills to the east, which separates the Canavese from the province of Biella (the Biellese). Another important natural landmark, the Dora Baltea River, flows through the Erbaluce di Caluso production zone. In general, the production area is characterized by three concentric moraine hill ranges. The outermost and oldest is the San Michele–Borgo group, dating back to the lower Pleistocene (1,650,000 to 730,000 years ago); it is located in the Biellese area north of the Serra di Ivrea. It is characterized by sandy-gravel soils that derived from fluvio-glacial sediments. The second landform system, called the Serra group (formed roughly 730,000 to 130,000 years ago), the largest of the three, is associated with the long Serra of Ivrea hill chain, ranging in altitude from the 900 meters of Croce Serra to 250 meters above sea level at the beautiful Lake Viverone. From here the group of hills moves in a circular fashion, first in a southwest and then in a northbound direction; in fact, moraines make up the hills of Moncrivello, Viverone, Mazzè, Caluso, and Cuceglio, and part of the hills near Parella at the entry of the Valchiusella. The Serra group is where most of the Canavese vineyards lie, planted on brownish-yellow, thin glacial deposits. The third landform, the Bolnego-Strambino (formed 130,000 to 95,000 years ago), is the innermost and youngest, with very sandy, thin soils featuring irregular sandy and silty deposits typical of towns such as Brolo, Albano, and Strambino. All three of these hillside formations resulted from tectonic movements during subsequent glaciations that took place during the Pleistocene period and were once classified (from youngest to oldest) as the Wurm, Riss, and Mindel glaciations. (Readers should take note that this classification is now considered antiquated and is no longer used to describe the basin formation south of the Alps.) The denomination is characterized by cold winters and hot summers, with noteworthy diurnal temperature ranges in September (Winkler index, 1510–1570). Rainfall is not especially abundant throughout the year (roughly nine hundred to twelve hundred millimeters per year). Vineyards lie at an altitude of 250 to 350 meters above sea level, mostly trained with the classic

pergola canavese system, but an increasing number of producers are trying to switch over to cordon spur or Guyot systems in an effort to diminish labor costs. The soils have either acid or subacid pH levels, are nutrient poor, but are rich in potassium and phosphates. They are strongly sandy-gravelly, and therefore have very good drainage. As in other viticultural areas with strong potassium soil content, such as in the vineyards of Forst in the Palatinate (or Pfalz, as the area is known in wine circles), I find a certain savoriness and tactile mouthfeel to Caluso's best Erbaluce wines. Today's official production zone is larger than it was classically and includes thirty-six communes (thirty-two in the province of Turin, and four in the provinces of Biella and Vercelli). It has the shape of a semicircle, with the city of Ivrea in the middle and the main production areas of Caluso to the south and Lake Viverone to the east. Grapes grown around Lake Viverone may have trouble ripening and wines are usually fresh and lighter-bodied than others made in the area; Caluso's are thicker and riper but also showcase the best balance of all. The wines from the Borgomasino area fall somewhere between these two extremes, though I admit that only the most experienced tasters out there will be able to pick out these differences. Interestingly, Caluso's sweet *passito* wines have significant concentrations of 4-terpineol and 1,4-cineol (Giordano et al. 2009); the latter molecule offers spicy-balsamic and resinous-floral scents, both typical findings in Caluso *passito* wines. The concentrations of such molecules vary not just because of different grape-growing sites, but also with length of the air-drying process and age (their concentrations decreasing over time). Also, Caluso *passito* wines show high concentrations of laccase and gluconic acid, typical of noble rot metabolism, and these findings are usually absent in other Italian *passito* wines such as Sciacchetrà and Passito di Pantelleria. The presence of noble rot in Caluso *passito* wines speaks of the differences in the various terroirs. (The township of Caluso is the warmest in the denomination.)

Erbaluce di Caluso's Best Crus by Township

The list below includes the names of what I have long thought were some of the best sites (and the townships in which they are found) for Erbaluce production of the last thirty years. I have always been a huge fan of this grape and wine, and so I used to visit the area regularly during my university years and try as many Erbaluce di Caluso wines as possible.

Caluso: Baiarda, Barbetta, Casetto, Castellazzo, Crose, Feralda, Montasso, Pero (at a slightly lower altitude), Sant'Andrea, Sant'Antonio, Santa Croce.

Candia Canavese: Colombaio.

Piverone: Cariola.

San Giorgio Canavese: Misobolo.

Other noteworthy sites: Madonna, Quaro, Viassola.

Readers beware that there are wines made currently bearing the name of a specific cru (for example, Baiarda) but the wine is not made with grapes coming just from that cru.

BENCHMARK WINES

Bruno Giacometto Erbaluce di Caluso***, Bruno Giacometto Erbaluce di Caluso Passito***, Cellagrande di San Michele Erbaluce di Caluso Tardif***, Cieck Erbaluce di Caluso Misobolo***, Ferrando Vendemmia Tardiva Solativo***.

Cellagrande di San Michele Erbaluce di Caluso San Michele**, Cieck Erbaluce di Caluso San Giorgio**, Ferrando Erbaluce di Caluso Cariola**, Ferrando Erbaluce di Caluso Passito**, La Masera Erbaluce**, Orsolani Erbaluce di Caluso Vigneto Sant'Antonio**, Podere Macellio Erbaluce di Caluso Passito**, Tenuta Roletto Erbaluce di Caluso Passito**.

Benito Favaro Erbaluce di Caluso*, Cantina Cooperativa Erbaluce di Caluso*.

Erbamat

THE GRAPE VARIETY

Erbamat is a little-known grape variety that was just getting ready to step into the limelight when I was wrapping up my *Native Wine Grapes of Italy* book. At the time I and everyone else (producers included) had had very little if any experience with this cultivar in Franciacorta. What a difference four years makes. Erbamat is still nowhere near becoming a household name, but now I have enough scientific, experimental, and anecdotal data to make discussing Erbamat not just interesting and useful, but necessary. I write "necessary" because the variety looks to become important in Franciacorta relative to the region's fine sparkling wines. Franciacorta has been remarkably successful in establishing a regional identity for very high quality sparkling wines made by secondary fermentation in the bottle *à la* Champagne (16.5 million bottles per year and 116 estates—numbers that vouch for the success I speak of). In fact, people now walk into a wine store or a restaurant and ask directly for a "bottle of Franciacorta," just as they would "a bottle of Champagne," rather than asking for a generic sparkling wine. However, Franciacorta has one potential Achilles' heel: it is a rather warm place in which to be making sparkling wine. Given these times of encroaching climate change, total acidity levels in the area's wines have been a concern for some time. Enter Erbamat, a little-known local native grape that has one big advantage over the region's Pinot Nero, Pinot Bianco, and Chardonnay: laser-like acidity that gives lemons a run for their money. Clearly, Erbamat is not only about acidity; it also has enough texture (just) and nuance to make a fine potential addition to the Franciacorta blend. First mentioned in 1565 by Agostino Gallo as a typical variety of the Brescia countryside, the cultivar's original name was Alba Matte and later changed to Erbamat (*matt*, a reduction of *matta*, or "crazy": the grape may be thought to be so because of its high acidity). In fact, Erbamat grapes have anywhere from three to six grams per liter of malic acid. Actually, I have been told by researchers that Erbamat and Alba Matta are not quite the same grape: the former is more likely a biotype of the latter, which grows in Trentino and around Lake Garda, but not in Lombardy; so perhaps Alba Matta was transported suitcase-style to Lombardy and then mutated over the centuries to give Erbamat. By any stretch, Erbamat is a still-rare Italian native grape: there were zero hectares reported in Italy prior to 2000 (which can't be correct, because the cultivar has always hung around northern Italian vineyards, if in small quantities) and a whopping twenty-five hectares as of 2000. Erbamat still wines are made in the Veneto around Lake Garda: for instance, the Comincioli estate has had considerable success with a wine called Perlì, a still Erbamat–Trebbiano Valtènesi blend (the latter being a local biotype of Verdicchio). Erbamat is characterized by a delicate, nonaromatic nose, by being a late ripener, and by its high total acidity levels. Soils must not be too rich and fertile or Erbamat wines become heavy; even worse, the variety tends to become too vigorous and then the grapes rot easily. (It is very sensitive to common vine diseases.) Performing malolactic transformation appears to increase the complexity of Erbamat wines, since too much malic acid simplifies the wine greatly. Erbamat flowers over a long period (fifteen days or more: by comparison, Chardonnay and Pinot Nero tend to flower at the end of May or the beginning of June in Franciacorta vineyards, and Erbamat does so from the middle to the end of June). In fact, Erbamat is usually picked in October, and thus far, to the best of my knowledge, over the last ten years or so nobody in Franciacorta has harvested it before September 20, even in very warm vintages. This is good news for Franciacorta, where climate change has caused harvests to take place sooner and sooner. (Silvano Brescianini of the Barone Pizzini estate tells me that in the last twenty years they have lost one month in hang time.) "In the 1980s it would have been unthinkable to plant Erbamat in Franciacorta, since it would have been physiologically ripe only by mid-November; today it is perfectly suitable to our terroir," he reasons. It has been written that Erbamat is identical to the Verdealbara cultivar

(Robinson, Harding, and Vouillamoz 2012), but, no doubt through a failing of mine, I have found no mention of this in any peer-reviewed scientific paper—the minimal acceptable standard in any serious scientific community. In fact, at the time of writing, Italy's National Registry of Grape Varieties lists the two wine grapes separately and does not state that they are synonymous (and I point out that the registry *does* list synonyms): Erbamat is number 418 in the registry and was officially inserted there on March 27, 2009; by contrast, Verdealbara is number 401 and was officially inserted on January 9, 2007. The former is allowed only in the DOCG Franciacorta, whereas the latter is allowed in three IGT denominations: Trevenezie, Vallagarina, and Vigneti delle Dolomiti. Furthermore, the ampelographic descriptions in the registry do not match at all, disagreeing on less-than-trivial matters such as the shape and size of the leaf, shape and degree of compactness of the grape bunch, size of the bud, cross section and color of the shoots, amount of bloom on the grapes, and a good deal more. Last but not least, the 2013 edition of the "International List of Vine Varieties and Their Synonyms," published by the Organisation de la Vigne et du Vin (http://www.oiv.int/public /medias/2273/oiv-liste-publication-2013-complete.pdf), also does not list the two varieties as synonymous and has them listed in different slots—Erbamat at number 1084 (last updated on October 18, 2011) and Verdealbara at number 3808 (also last updated on October 18, 2011). So although we may one day find out otherwise (as we often do), at least for the time being, there is no reason to consider the two varieties as identical. In any case, Franciacorta producers and their outstanding consortium have been studying Erbamat for about ten years (in collaboration with the University of Milan); the bulk of the viticultural and winemaking experiments began in 2009, with five Franciacorta estates involved initially (Barone Pizzini, Ronco Calino, Ferghettina, Castello Bonomi, and Guido Berlucchi). The number has since grown to six estates (one going so far as to make an experimental 100 percent Erbamat sparkling wine meant for study: it cannot be sold as a Franciacorta as Franciacortas can have no more than 10 percent Erbamat in the blend). Three different training methods and five deleafing regimens were investigated (such as deleafing on one side of the row only at veraison or before flowering) under the guidance of Professor Leonardo Valenti. Grape berry sugar and total acidity and other biochemical parameters were monitored at regular intervals. The study provided numerous interesting findings: for example, in the Franciacorta terroirs under study, Erbamat's veraison proceeds very slowly, taking up to a month. (In fact, the variety does not reach full color change until mid-September.) The variety is characterized by high vigor (but interestingly, as its vigor rises its fertility decreases, so reining in Erbamat's natural vigor is a must); it has a very compact bunch, meaning that in weather-challenged years it can be a rot magnet.

SPECIFIC TERROIRS

Franciacorta

Franciacorta is a DOCG sparkling wine made in the Franciacorta production zone located about an hour's drive east of Milan. Specifically, Franciacorta's geographical boundaries are sealed by morainic hills, the Mella River and the Valtrompia to the east, the Oglio River to the west, the shores of the Lake Iseo to the north, and Mount Orfano and the start of the Padana Plain to the south. There are 18,000 hectares and nineteen communes (of which Erbusco is the most famous and important, at least given the number of Franciacorta estates that are located there); currently 2,800 hectares are under vine (plantings are 82 percent Chardonnay, 14 percent Pinot Nero, and 4 percent Pinot Bianco, with Pinot Bianco slowly on the rise), plus another 350 hectares of Curtefranca, the area's DOC still wine. Up until recently, the only wine grapes allowed to make Franciacorta were Chardonnay, Pinot Nero,

and—differently from Champagne and most other sparkling-wine regions of the world— Pinot Bianco (there is very little if any Pinot Meunier grown in Italy), but now Erbamat is part of the Franciacorta equation, too. The name Franciacorta derives from the medieval *curte francae*, a reference to the area being a tax-free haven in medieval times. Though modern-day production in Franciacorta began only in the 1960s, it is an area where wine has always been important. In fact, a most important document attesting to sparkling-wine production in Franciacorta is the *Libellus de vino mordaci*, written in 1570 by Girolamo Conforti, a medical doctor from Brescia, that is one of the first texts ever written (some experts insist it is the first) on the production of sparkling wine by secondary refermentation in the bottle and its effects on the human body. (Did you know that doctors have a long and distinguished history as gifted writers? Anton Chekhov was a practicing physician most of his life, and a list of some other pen-happy MDs includes François Rabelais, Sir Arthur Conan Doyle, John Keats, John Locke, and Michael Crichton.) In any case, in 1967, when the DOC was instituted, there were only 11 estates signed up to make Franciacorta. (Compare that number with the current 116!) In 1995, the new DOCG decreed that Franciacorta is the name allowed only for wines made by secondary fermentation in the bottle; all still wines of the area are now called Curtefranca Bianco or Curtefranca Rosso. (These had been previously called Terre di Franciacorta Bianco and Rosso, but not surprisingly, producers thought it best to change those names, which could easily engender confusion relative to the area's main player, Franciacorta sparkler.) Since the beginning, Franciacorta and its wines have met with unbridled success. Corn and wheat used to grow in the flatlands, but those fields of gold (I spent part of my childhood in Bergamo, not far from Brescia) have been mostly replaced with vineyards. Most importantly (and in very big contrast to other wine-production areas of Italy, which, not surprisingly, haven't achieved anywhere near the success of Franciacorta), producers mostly get along and work together toward their common goals. Results of such commendable teamwork include the establishment of the toughest sparkling-wine production guidelines in the world, as well as two of the best zonation studies (Bogoni et al. 1997; Panont and Comolli 1998) ever implemented by any Italian denomination (if of a headache-inducing complexity; take my word for it). Ideally, it would be important to remember Franciacorta's nineteen communes or at least the most important ones; this helps in understanding Franciacorta wines, just as trying to understand the wines of Bordeaux or the Mosel is made easier by knowing a little about Pauillac and Margaux, or of Piesport and Urzig.

Franciacorta is characterized by a gentle topography resulting from three concentric rings of hills that run essentially east to west, south of Lake Iseo, creating numerous mesoclimates leading to very diverse base wines. Franciacorta's altitude varies from 127 meters above sea level at Brescia to 850 at the Sella dell'Oca, but for the most part the gently sloping hills hover around 250 meters. From a viticultural perspective, Franciacorta was mapped early on: in 1912, subzones were identified by the Consorzio Antifillosserico Bresciano. In modern times, the consortium began performing its own zonation study in 1992, and so we know that Franciacorta's landscape is made up of three main topographical formations: hillsides, foothills, and high plains. In (very) general terms, Franciacorta's hillsides are softly rounded and were formed during the Mesozoic (262 million to 66 million years ago) and Cenozoic (66 million years ago to the present) eras and are characterized by mainly marly and marly-calcareous soils with varying amounts of loam, compacted sands, and conglomerates and very little clay present. The foothills are constituted mostly by morainic deposits (till) organized and modeled by the tectonic movements (advances and retreats) of the glaciers. They are characterized by a complex mix of sandy loam, red clays, and gravel elements (with a presence of larger

stones, even boulders, that varies from subzone to subzone), running in a band-like fashion around the lake, with the younger, more recently deposited layers found closest to the lake and the older ones farther removed from it (so much so that the foothills can be subdivided into three specific morainic areas: antique, middle, and recent). Last, the high plains are mostly fluvioglacial deposits that segue from the hills and foothills into the flatlands to the south. The majority of Franciacorta's potentially best vineyards are located on the hillsides and the foothills; interestingly, the original production guidelines established that vines could not be planted above 496 meters above sea level (something producers are likely going to modify, since climate change clearly wasn't much of a problem back in the late 1960s or 1970s). And climate *is* important in Franciacorta: relatively mild in the winter but not especially hot in the summer, the area experiences diurnal temperature variations that are not especially marked. Budbreak in Franciacorta occurs earlier than one would normally expect for such a northern land. (The presence of olive trees showcases the temperate nature of the area's climate.) Franciacorta's metereologic data were analyzed by Panont and Comolli (1998) by factoring in the contributing effect of the many geographical and territorial variables present (soil cover, exposure, gradient, distance from the lake) according to the methodology illustrated by Lazzaroni and Mariani (1997). Normally, the warmest months of the year are July and August, whereas the coldest month is January. The mean daily temperature ranges from 12°C to 13.5°C during the year, although there is some discrepancy in the various Winkler indices I have found in different publications, ranging from 1500 to 2300 in Panont and Comolli (1998) to 1600 to 1950 in Scienza et al. (2015). The latter research group reports that Franciacorta's Huglin index is 2050 to 2400. Annual rainfall is about 1,000 millimeters, with roughly two-thirds (or about 650 to 700 millimeters) falling from March to the end of October (data: Consorzio Tutela Franciacorta), but it tends to be more abundant in some parts of Franciacorta than in others; for example, the central southern part of the denomination gets much less rain than the rest of the denomination. Summer drought is not common, because even in dry years, Franciacorta rarely has less than 300 millimeters of rain per year. It is this very abundance of rain that explains why oidium and peronospora are a problem in Franciacorta.

Franciacorta Subzones

The easiest manner in which to think of Franciacorta is to divide the production area into two large sectors: the eastern and the western. The heart of the Franciacorta production zone centers around the town of Erbusco, where many of the most famous wineries are located; other towns that are found in this sweet spot are Cortefranca, Cazzago, and Adro. Two specific districts whose wines are slightly different from all the rest can also be identified within the denomination. One is the area of Paderno, Passirano, and Provaglio d'Iseo, a thin strip of land sandwiched between the eastern sector and the heart of the Franciacorta production zone next to the Monte Orfano in the south (an area characterized by a unique microclimate, where rainfall is on average two hundred millimeters less a year than in the rest of Franciacorta); the other is the small area of Paratico and Capriolo, in the northwestern corner of the denomination.

THE EASTERN SECTOR

In general, Franciacorta's most elegant, freshest wines are made with grapes grown in the eastern sector, characterized by a cooler microclimate and higher altitudes than the rest of the Franciacorta production zone. It is an especially beautiful part of Franciacorta and easily the most rugged, with steep slopes and relatively high altitudes, with vineyards planted as high as 450 meters above sea level. (Only a swath of the eastern sector's countryside, around Rodengo Saiano, is made up of flatland vineyards.) The communes of the eastern sector are Cellatica, Gussago San Martino, and Rodengo Saiano to the south (close to Brescia), and Monticelli Brusati and Ome to the north (the coolest area in Franciacorta, where the freshest wines are made). In general, all Franciacortas made with grapes grown in these communes will be marked by higher acidities, more refined textures, and pomaceous orchard fruit as opposed to tropical nuances. Knowing that, it seems rather strange that this part of the Franciacorta was actually most famous for its red wines up until recently. (Cellatica, Gussago San Martino, and Rodengo Saiano are the only Franciacorta communes included in the Cellatica red-wine DOC.) Some wineries worth knowing: Casa Caterina (organically grown grapes and bio wines), Ca' del Vent, Castelveder, Andrea Arici/ Colline della Stella, Majolini, and Villa. (But like all estates in Franciacorta, most own vineyards all over the denomination, so finding an "eastern-sector somewhereness" in the wines is not automatic: you have to know exactly where the grapes used to make the wine grow— information estates are happy to release.) Soils are mostly compact calcareous or marly clay. The Paderno, Passirano, and Provaglio d'Iseo district runs from the town of Iseo in the north down past the splendid Torbiere del Sebino to Provaglio d'Iseo and Passirano (with its hamlets Fantecolo, Camiglione, and Monterotondo) and Paderno Franciacorta. This area is best thought of as producing Francicortas that fall somewhere in between the fresher, more vertical wines of the eastern sector and the broader, richer wines of the western sector. The best estates in this area are Il Mosnel, Bersi Serlini, and Mirabella.

THE WESTERN SECTOR

The northern part of the western sector is generally hillier than the southern one, which spreads down toward the Montorfano. The major townships here are Erbusco, Colombaro di Cortefranca, Cazzago, and Adro. It is in this northern part of the western sector that Franciacorta's best or at least most famous Chardonnay sparklers are made. Cortefranca's countryside is very interesting because it includes four small townships: Colombario to the north, Timoline to the east, Borgonato to the south, and Nigoline to the east. Of these, Colombario appears to be hillier and to have the cooler microclimate. Adro and Erbusco also have permeable soils characterized by the presence of round river stones. Some estates worth knowing: Battista Cola, Villa Crespia-Fratelli Muratori, Cascina San Pietro, Castel Faglia, Corte Aura, Montenisa-Marchesi Antinori, Ronco Calino, Barone Pizzini (at Timoline), Guido Berlucchi and Fratelli Berlucchi, Bellavista, Ca' del Bosco, Cavalleri, San Cristoforo, and Uberti. Estates such as Lantieri de Paratico and Ricci Curbastro are located near Paratico and Capriolo and tend to make tactile, round Franciacortas.

Franciacorta Crus

As noted earlier in this section, Franciacorta and terroir have always gone hand in hand. As early as the first decade of the twelfth century, the abbey of San Nicola di Rodengo and its Cluny monks were replanting vines and cutting down forests, but at the time the vines were being co-planted amid other crops. In the first decades of the twelfth century, vineyards were often surrounded by stone walls (much like the *clos* of Burgundy and Champagne). In the thirteenth century new vineyards were planted near the monastery of Leno and Collebato, where the bishop of Brescia was already known to own vineyards. (The Mass was apparently officiated with wines made from grapes such as the Groppellos and local grapes generically called Vernaccias.) The choice to plant vineyards at Collebato is an interesting one, for that is a fairly hilly, hard-to-work area: both the bishop of Brescia and the abbot of Leno and Collebato owned many other, easier-to-work lands in the plains, such as those of Bagnolo. Therefore, it appears that people were cognizant of the fact that specific hillsides and slopes gave better wines, even though they might require more work (Archetti 1997; Villa, Milesi, and Scienza 1997).

Today, as mentioned above, identifying a terroir effect in Franciacorta's wine can be difficult in most cases because the majority of estates blend together grapes from many different communes; it is possible only in those rare instances where the estate is using grapes from a single commune, district, or sector only. And to try to identify terroir in Franciacorta relative to Erbamat is downright impossible, for too little is known about the variety and how it performs and will perform in the area. Clearly, more time is needed to accumulate data and learn where the variety will perform best. It does not take a degree in science to figure out that it is those farming Franciacorta's western sector that need Erbamat the most; people in Monticelli Brusati, less so. To shed some light on this subject and in an effort to determine the characteristics and quality of different Franciacorta terroirs and their wines relative to Erbamat, I set up a series of tasting tests over the years to analyze what Chardonnay, Pinot Nero, and especially Erbamat wines taste like when made with grapes grown on different soils in different parts of the denomination. I am greatly indebted to Silvano Brescianini, then vice president of the Franciacorta Consorzio (and named president in 2018) and also part owner of the Barone Pizzini estate, who was patient and interested enough to help me on this project. In fact, such was his enthusiasm that he called in Professor Valenti for the tastings, as well as Pierluigi Donna, a longtime collaborator of Valenti's and one of Italy's foremost viticulture experts. It is one of those opportunities anyone with an interest in wine and in science cherishes forever.

Franciacorta is made up of six vocational soil units that the Consorzio Tutela Franciacorta summarizes as follows: shallow moraines, deep moraines, fine deposits, fluvioglacial deposits, and two different types of colluviums. I realize occasional wine lovers might balk at this almost granular degree of detail, but these soil types exert an influence on the finished wines in easily recognizable ways: with a little experience, guessing correctly where the grapes used to make the Franciacorta you are tasting or drinking come from is not as hard as it might seem.

Shallow moraines: Thin soils found on top of crests that are the earliest ripening and lowest yielding of all; the acidity in the grapes drops gradually but regularly, and the pH of these grapes at harvest time is often the highest when compared with that of grapes picked in vineyards planted on the other soil types. Sugar accumulation tends to be uneven, so identifying the right time at which to pick the grapes is essential. Chardonnay base wines (wines that will later undergo secondary fermentation in the bottle) made on moraine soils tend to be the most complex of all and are usually redolent of ripe tropical fruit notes (mango, banana) but also flowers and dried fruits.

Deep moraines: Medium to medium-deep soils located mostly in the foothills. Grapes are characterized by medium pH levels and generally high sugar buildup. Wines are similar to those made with grapes on the shallow moraines, which means they offer vegetal-spicy nuance and not much in the way of floral notes.

Fine deposits: Mainly deep loamy or loamy-clay soils with generally poor drainage; productivity is high, as shown by an increase in the number of bunches and in bunch weight. The sugar buildup and acid breakdown tend to slow down in the grapes toward the end of the growing season, and so come harvest time these grapes show some of the lowest pH levels and sugar concentrations. (That may not sound great, but remember that neither is necessarily a bad thing when it comes to sparkling wine.) Mostly, the wines are floral (chamomile flowers), while spices and dry herbs are uncommon.

Fluvioglacial deposits: Mainly sandy-gravelly soils with pockets of clay push strong productivity (as shown by an increase in the number of bunches per plant and in bunch weight), but harvest times are not especially early. Sugar buildup and acid degradation follow nonlinear progressions, and at harvest time sugar concentrations are usually low compared with those of grapes grown on other sites, while the pH values fall in the intermediate range. These Chardonnay base wines are very similar to those made with grapes grown on fine deposit soils in that they are quite floral but not especially complex.

Colluviums: Very deep clay-rich soils found mainly in the foothills and on the high plains; vineyards planted on the latter tend to yield much larger crops and grapes with higher total acidity than those planted on the former. Grapes grown on such soils in the foothills behave like those grown on deep moraines, while those from the more distal colluvium soils show high sugar concentrations and low pH values. Wines offer early appeal and sneaky complexity, offering notes of candied yellow fruit (pineapple, peach, banana) and honey.

The above information is useful in helping to analyze wines of the Franciacorta, but unfortunately, practically all the information we have today is relative to Pinot Noir and Chardonnay microvinifications. However, this helps us understand Erbamat's eventual behavior in Franciacorta's terroir, too.

ERBAMAT IN FRANCIACORTA WINES

The following is a summary of a tasting of monovariety Erbamat samples (still base wines) from Franciacorta wineries over the course of 2016, 2017, and 2018. I selected those wines made from grapes harvested more or less at the same time (to reduce confounding variables; in general, all the wines in the analysis were made with grapes picked in the first two weeks of October). Given the limited amount of data available, and to average out for vintage effect, I performed statistical analysis on the wine scores I attributed to the wine samples in the three years, and distilled a summary of the tasting notes relative to each specific vineyard source and vintage that you will find below. To the best of my knowledge these are the first published data in a nonacademic publication on a large sample of Erbamat wines from Franciacorta in three successive vintages. (Samples appear in order of vineyard sites, from north to south, in the Franciacorta denomination.)

1. From a vineyard in Timoline (Barone Pizzini estate): Extremely pale straw yellow. Very lovely freshness on the nose, then less obviously acid on the palate but still rather shrill. A lime, white flower, and green-apple bonanza. The vines are planted on deep moraine soils with veins of chalk (but at Barone Pizzini they plan to change their planting strategy, having come to the conclusion that Erbamat performs better on thin moraine soils, where it tends to yield less heavy-set, chunky wines).

2. From a vineyard in Calino close to Ca' del Bosco (Ronco Calino estate): richer, sweeter, and longer than sample number 1. Very clean; also has a bit more body than the first sample. Finishes long and saline, with very good balance.

3. Monte Orfano (Castello Bonomi): White peach, saline, very long. Lovely freshness; rather juicy. Also larger and fleshier than samples number 1 and 2. Features a late hit of spice.

A GLIMPSE OF WHAT THE FUTURE MAY HOLD
The following are summaries of experimental "Franciacortas" with varying percentages of Erbamat in the blend. In order to reduce confounding variables, all tasting notes refer to wines still on lees, and all the wines described here were made with grapes grown in one commune (Timoline) and on one estate only:

2014 (40 percent Erbamat, 30 percent Chardonnay, 30 percent Pinot Nero; 24 months on the lees): Very tart, fresh, and precise; very citric but perfumed and "mineral." Actually, a lovely sparkler with sneaky complexity and concentration.

2012 (60 percent Erbamat, 20 percent Chardonnay, 20 percent Pinot Nero; 48 months on the lees): A whopper! Big, fat, and spicy; very rich mouthfeel, with a ferrous, savory quality. A hint of bruised apple on the nose hints at a slight incipient oxidation. This complex, rich sample shows that Erbamat can offer more than just acidity.

2011 (80 percent Chardonnay, 20 percent Erbamat; 60 months on lees): Complex, rich, round; impressively long and saline. Strongly dominated by ripe yellow fruit. (The good 2011 vintage helps.)

BENCHMARK WINES
Clearly, for all the reasons that have been discussed above, there can be as yet no "benchmark" Franciacorta Erbamat wines.

Fiano

THE GRAPE VARIETY

Practically extinct as recently as the 1940s, or at the very least forgotten, Fiano delivers a range of wines, from light to full bodied, dry to sweet, easygoing to very ageworthy, that few other Italian white grapes can match. The age-worthiness of Fiano wines is not to be underestimated, since these wines easily improve for eight to ten years in bottle. One of Italy's oldest cultivars, Fiano, some experts believe, was one of the *"viti apiane"* cited by Pliny and Columella. (However, the majority believe these were Moscato Bianco.) Twelfth-century documents show that King Frederick II, during his stay in Foggia (Puglia), bought Greco, Grecisco, and Fiano wines for private consumption. Records kept by Guglielmo De Fisoni in 1861 indicate that King Carlo d'Angiò II bought sixteen thousand Fiano vines and had them planted in the royal vineyard at Manfredonia (Scienza and Boselli 2003). So it appears that Fiano has been hanging around Italian vineyards for some time. Credit must go to Antonio Mastroberardino for having brought Fiano back from oblivion and getting farmers to

believe in it. Fiano has mostly medium-small, compact, pyramidal-shaped bunches, and usually one wing; the grapes are also of medium size and oval, with thick, yellow-green skins that can be covered in brown spots when ripe. Fiano is characterized by low productivity (its basal buds are infertile), and so it needs specific pruning techniques. Very vigorous and with a tough skin, it is usually harvested from the end of September to mid-October. (When grown by the seaside or in much warmer climates, it can be picked at the end of August.) Its late-ripening nature can pose problems in the cool Apennine microclimate, but its thick skins enable it to resist better than other varieties. The best-known wine is DOCG Fiano di Avellino, made in close to thirty townships around Avellino, though there are many other Fiano wines made in Campania and in the rest of Italy (Basilicata, Puglia, Sicily). However, it is in parts of the Fiano di Avellino DOCG that truly world-class expressions of Fiano wine are reached. In my view, volcanic soils are best for Fiano, allowing the formation of piercing mineral and delicate green-apple and white-peach nuances (this despite what you might be told or will read elsewhere about hazelnut aromas appearing only over time or when Fiano is grown on very sandy soils). In fact, Fiano is very site sensitive, and its wines differ greatly depending on where the grapes grow. It is rich in geraniol and linalool (these terpenes explain the wine's floral note), but the presence of free alkyl-2-metoxypyrazines and volatile phenols also explains the toasty note that Fiano wines develop with age (Moio 2012). Moio's research team at the University of Naples has also found significant concentrations of many other aromatic molecule precursors, such as terpin-4-ol, β-damascenone, 1,1,6-trimethyl-1,2-dihydronaphthalene (TDN, the molecule associated with Riesling's diesel-fuel aromas), and 1-(2,3,6-trimentilfenil) buta-1,3-diene (TPB); TDN and TPB are responsible for aromas of wild fennel, broom, and acacia—all typical descriptors of Fiano wines. In fact, when Fiano wines are still young, they exude mostly fermentative aromas (banana, grass), but three to four years after the vintage, diesel, iodine, and smoky notes emerge. Fiano's aroma profile shows good balance between the floral and fruit components—differently from Falanghina Beneventana and Greco, which are dominated by fruit notes of various types (Moio 2012). In fact, notes of musk, mint, and fern are also typical of Fiano wines. (I stress mint and not menthol, the latter being a characteristic descriptor not of Fiano wines but rather of Falanghina Flegrea wines or those Falanghina wines made in especially cool microclimates.) Interestingly, despite the fact that Fiano can express methoxypyrazines just as Sauvignon Blanc does (especially 3-isobutyl-2-methoxypyrazine and 3-isopropil-2-methoxypyrazine), it is extremely rare to find a Fiano wine that smells and tastes of green bell pepper, cut grass, sage, or rosemary. In my experience, when grown at high altitudes and in cold microclimates, Fiano wines offer penetrating, absolutely memorable aromas of lemon verbena and jasmine; in these cases, it is more than likely that ethyl cinnamate plays an important role in contributing to the generation of these aromatic nuances. Especially musky versions of Fiano are

more common when the grape is grown in especially warm areas; the musky note results from above-perception-threshold values of terpin-4-ol (Lamorte et al. 2007), which might actually remind many people of nutmeg, too. Some Fiano wines are downright smoky (akin to burned vulcanized rubber); some experts believe this smoky odor to be due to a reductive tendency and to be caused by increased thiol concentrations (benzenemethanethiol, for example) and perhaps 4-vinyl-guaiacole. Other producers long in the tooth have told me that they think that when said smoky note is too intense, another grape variety is being (unwittingly) used. Genovese et al. (2007) studied the aroma molecules of sweet Fiano wines (both late harvest and air-dried) and found these to be nerol, geraniol, and linalool (which express hints of orange flowers and rose, for example); lactones such as γ-nonalactone (coconut), δ-decalactone, and γ-decalactone (apricot); and 1-octen-3-ol (mushroom). These authors concluded that differences in the molecules present or their concentrations are due to the air-drying process, which concentrates the aromatic compounds already present in the Fiano grape but at the same time enables an easier transfer of these from skins to must during the winemaking process. In fact, part of Fiano's appeal is that, depending on growing conditions, it can give dry or sweet wines. (But the dry wines are much better: Fiano is not an aromatic variety, and so its sweet wines are not that interesting.) In the ultimate analysis, the most typical Fiano wines are those offering refined aromas of green apple, pear, and honey (and hazelnut, in due course), and little smoke. Wines made with grapes picked in cooler microclimates and in the manner of Mastroberardino (a two-week maceration/fermentation at 18°C maximum) are usually just so.

SPECIFIC TERROIRS

Fiano di Avellino

The Fiano grape variety reaches its qualitative zenith in the Avellino zone and in the Fiano di Avellino DOCG. (The DOC dates back to 1978, when there were only five hectares of Fiano planted in total; the DOCG was awarded in 1993.) The Avellino province is a landlocked mass of land enclosed by Campania's Sannio Beneventano region to the north and east, Puglia and Basilicata to the east, Campania's Salerno province to the south, and the province of Naples to the west. Most likely, Fiano is a native of the area of Lapio (the variety's name may in fact derive from Appia, then transformed to Apiano, and finally Lapio), a small town located east of Avellino at roughly 590 meters above sea level and one of the real grand cru areas for the variety. The Fiano di Avellino DOCG extends over twenty-six municipalities; the largest of Campania's denominations at 430 hectares (of a possible 550 total hectares), it is not so packed with grapevines. The DOCG territory covers the valleys of the Sabato and the Calore Rivers, the foothill slopes of the Mount Partenio, and the hills that look toward the Vallo di Lauro. Even though it's a drive of only a few hours or so from the beautiful Campanian coast, this is a highly mountainous area with more than a couple of peaks pushing 2,000 meters above sea level. It's also a very cold part of Italy, at least in the late fall and winter: snowstorms are not uncommon in the winter months, and the average daily temperature is only 13°C. Diurnal temperature variations are high, and so are annual precipitation levels (one thousand to twelve hundred millimeters per year; most of the rain falls in four months of the year: in the fall at harvest time and winter). Vineyards lie between 300 and 650 meters above sea level; the soils all have a strong clay-calcareous base with volcanic elements, but range from loosely packed to quite compact depending on the section of the denomination.

Based on my years of tasting experience, I would say that Fiano wines can have three basic profiles: the Fianos of the clay-dominated soils of the towns of Lapio and Montefalcione, which give pristine, mineral, lacy wines; the fruity, lighter-bodied wines offering early appeal typical of wines born of the very loosely packed sand-rich soils of the areas around the towns of

Cesinali and Santo Stefano del Sole; and the downright ripe, intensely fruity wines marked by smoky or *fumé* notes of Montevergine, Sant'Angelo a Scala, Summonte, and Capriglia (where vineyards are situated at about four hundred meters above sea level). I stress smoky, and not especially mineral. Locals tell me that the soils of these four communes are richer in calcareous conglomerates than the others and also have a thin layer of volcanic ash on the surface that is believed to account for, or at the very least contribute to, the smoky notes found in some of the wines.

The Fiano di Avellino Subzones

THE SOUTHERN SECTOR

Most of this part of the DOCG was planted to vines recently (say, in the 1990s), when Fiano di Avellino became a hot commodity. Municipalities in this sector include Aiello del Sabato, Atripalda, Cesinali, Contrada, Forino, Mercogliano, Monteforte Irpino, and part of Avellino (where the cash crop had historically been hazelnuts). For the most part, vineyards grow at low altitudes, roughly 300 to 350 meters above sea level, on gently rolling hills with soils that have a strong sand component. Not unexpectedly then, these are the Fiano grapes that ripen the earliest; the wines usually have lower average total acidity values and are generally less complex and the fastest maturing.

BENCHMARK WINES

Cantina del Barone Fiano di Avellino Particella 928**, I Favati Piatramara Etichetta Bianca**.

THE EASTERN SECTOR

From north to south, this sector includes the municipalities of Lapio, Montefalcione, Candida, San Potito Ultra, Parolise, Salza Irpina, Sorbo Serpico, Santo Stefano del Sole, Santa Lucia di Serino, San Michele di Serino, and Manocalzati. Most of the vineyards here were planted in the 1970s and 1980s, save for Lapio, which is the original home of Fiano and from where the original vines were selected and propagated all over Campania. It has a much cooler microclimate than the southern sector, with vineyards planted at altitudes of 400 to 550 meters above sea level (and even higher at Santo Stefano del Sole). It is a beautiful, still very wild part of Campania, with very steep slopes, oak forests, and lots of animals running around. (Watch out for the boars if you drive at night.) Grapes are rarely picked before October. The soils are mostly heavy clay-calcareous, with limestone and volcanic elements. This subzone is a vast one and in my view must be further broken down into the districts of Lapio and Candida, two viticultural areas that have completely different soils, exposures, and gradients from the rest of the subzone.

BENCHMARK WINES

Mastroberadino Fiano di Avellino Stilèma***PS.

Mastroberadino Fiano di Avellino Radici***.

Feudo di San Gregorio Fiano di Avellino Pietracalda**.

FIANO DISTRICTS: LAPIO AND CANDIDA
Lapio
As Clelia Romano has told me numerous times, the grandest cru of all Fiano grand crus (Lapio, that would be) was once more famous for its red or sweet wines. The high quality of the grapes from this area is confirmed by the fact that nowadays everyone wants to buy grapes from Lapio (and this despite the fact that the grapes cost much more than those from other communes). But not all of Lapio was created equal. Lapio has two slopes, and they differ greatly in terms of time of harvest, soil type, and exposure. The slopes of the *contrade* Campore, Verzara, and Valloni look to the south toward Chiusano San Domenico and are very steep and clay-rich. Despite what others will tell you, I strongly believe it is actually a much better place to grow Aglianico than Fiano. (Not by chance, Lapio and Montefalcione are the only communes of the Fiano di Avellino DOCG where you can also make Taurasi.) The vine-

yards in the *contrade* Pezze, Scarpone, Tognano, and Arianello (the last two are the most important and, for my money, give the best Fiano wines of all) look north toward Montefalcione. The clay-calcareous soil is much more loosely packed, gravelly, and volcanic. The central portion of the Lapio subzone has a different soil still—richer in loam and alluvial deposits (especially at the lower altitudes) that end up merging with those of the eastern sector. This is a cool-climate subzone with diurnal temperature variations of 20°C or more and plenty of wind blowing through at all times. The Fianos of Campore, rich, heavy, and with tropical-fruit notes, are not to my liking, whereas I adore those of Arianello, with their cool, Nordic flair. Granted, they don't have the flesh and body of some other Fiano wines, but you cannot have everything in life. Rocca del Principe's Tognano bottling is a recent attempt at bottling a Fiano from a Lapio cru, but the wine is so marked by its prolonged contact with lees that it speaks of the winemaking method as much as it does of the place where the grapes grow.

BENCHMARK WINES

Colli di Lapio Fiano di Avellino***PS.

Joaquin JQN 2013 Piante a Lapio***, Quintodecimo Fiano di Avellino Exultet*** (since 2012; 2011 and before: **), Rocca del Principe Fiano di Avellino***, Rocca del Principe Fiano di Avellino Tognano***.

Candida
A sheltered amphitheater with a very characteristic marly-calcareous soil loaded with small white rocks that give the place its name (*candida* from candid, as in white), but despite the whitish look, soil limestone concentrations are not especially high. Nevertheless, Candida is a real grand cru for Fiano. Maura Sarno is an extremely passionate, talented lady, and in just a few vintages her wine has quickly risen to the top of the hierarchy of Italy's best white wines. Michele Contrada's Fiano is instead much more wild and savory.

Tenuta Sarno Fiano di Avellino***PS.

Contrada Fiano di Avellino**.

THE NORTHERN SECTOR

From east to west, the communes are Pratola Serra, Montefrèdane, Grottolella, Capriglia Irpinia, and the northern halves of the territories of Avellino and Manocalzati. Vineyards are planted at 350 to 400 meters above sea level. The soils are rich in tuff and clay; the Sabato River contributes to a climate that makes for bigger, more savory Fiano di Avellinos. I like these wines, and the producers I suggest below are some of Italy's (never mind Campania's) most talented.

BENCHMARK WINES

Pietracupa Fiano di Avellino***, Traerte Fiano di Avellino Aipierti*** (Traerte was previously known as Vadiaperti).

Traerte Fiano di Avellino**.

THE NORTHWESTERN SECTOR

Sant'Angelo a Scala and Summonte are most associated with famous Fiano wines. The vineyards hug the foothills of Monte Partenio and lie as high up as 450 to 650 meters above sea level (especially at Summonte). Summonte's rigid weather, high diurnal temperature differences, and very poor, rocky soils are probably the factors most contributing to the unique profile of its wines. (The grapes really pack in the sugar, and so these big, bold Fiano wines are nothing like you might expect from their cool climate and mountain habitat.) These are also some of the smokiest Fianos of all and some of the most ageworthy, too.

BENCHMARK WINES

Marsella Fiano di Avellino***PS.

Ciro Picariello Fiano di Avellino**.

Fumin

THE GRAPE VARIETY

Fumin has always been highly thought of in the Valle d'Aosta. Lorenzo Francesco Gatta was the first to describe the cultivar fully in 1838, but its existence in the region had already been documented prior to this date as Fumin was one of the most abundant grape cultivars of the Alta Valle and the Media Valle (the high and central valleys) of the region. Gatta famously described two different Fumins, which led to a great deal of confusion over the centuries; he mistakenly believed one of the two Fumins he identified to be Freisa. Other grape luminaries of centuries past also believed Fumin and Freisa to be related, but today we know the two are not. In reality, there are two biotypes of Fumin, which Bich (1896) named the *maclo* (male) and *femella* (female); the latter was the more regular producer and was believed to give the better wines. In fact, Fumin is related to Vuillermin, another high-quality native grape of the Valle d'Aosta. (Fumin is most likely the parent because its existence in the Valle d'Aosta was documented before that of Vuillermin:

Fumin in 1785, Vuillermin only in 1890.) Viticulturally, there are many reasons why farmers loved Fumin. It is a very cold-resistant variety, and so was typically planted in vineyards facing north, where no other variety could be planted due to the cold. It is also a disease-resistant variety, and since it is neither early budding nor early flowering, it is not easily victimized by spring frosts and flowering-related problems such as millerandage and berry shot, which reduce fruit set and yields. Depending on which biotype is planted, Fumin is both vigorous and a generous yielder. Unfortunately, for unclear reasons, Fumin fell into disfavor with some experts in the twentieth century, who recommended against planting it, and it seriously risked extinction. Thanks to work done by the Institut Agricole Régional (IAR), which replanted old vine massal selections in the 1970s, Fumin is now a household name again. (The Les Crêtes winery was the first to bottle a 100 percent Fumin wine in 1993.) Today most farmers plant it facing fully south and usually not above six hundred meters above sea level in order to ensure maximum grape ripeness. Both the bunches and the grapes are small to medium in size; the latter are covered in bloom (in fact, Fumin's name derives from its thick whitish bloom, which gives it a smoky look: Fumin is a reference to *fumo*, or "smoke"). Along with Petit Rouge, Fumin is the most-cultivated red variety of the Valle d'Aosta, and its plantings are increasing annually. A well-made Fumin has a very deep color, and aromas and flavors of red and blue fruit, black pepper, quinine, and flint. Unlike Petit Rouge, it delivers tannins in spades. Its wines can exude some strangely foxy and wet fur aromas and also harbor a rather mean green streak if the grapes are not fully ripe, and for this reason some producers choose to air-dry the grapes (though in my view this limits this wine's unique traits and standardizes the production somewhat). The best approach is, weather permitting, to let the grapes hang out before harvest as long as possible. I believe Fumin is one of Italy's most exciting native grape varieties and the wines to be unique and really quite special (but I believe that even more of Vuillermin and Mayolet).

SPECIFIC TERROIRS

Valle d'Aosta

Aymavilles

This charming mountain town has the largest extension of vineyards of any other such place in the region. Part of its territory is located within the Parco Nazionale del Gran Paradiso (one of Italy's most beautiful national parks) and so is one of the more pristinely kept viticultural areas of Italy. Aymavilles is located on the left bank of the Dora Baltea at 640 meters above sea level, with mostly west/northwest/east exposures. (The area of Les Crêtes has a 360-degree exposure and is an especially sunny site.) The mesoclimate here is very dry and windy, and disease pressure is minimal; soils are typically those of the central valley, with a high percentage of sand and loam, a little limestone, and very little if any clay. (For a full description of the Valle d'Aosta terroir, see the Mayolet entry.) Fumin is usually grown at lower altitudes than other red varieties of the Valle d'Aosta, typically between 400 and 600 meters above sea level; in fact, the wines differ mostly because of the altitude and the exposure, rather than because of soil differences. Of the various sites where Fumin grows in the Aymavilles area, the Coteau La Tour is known to be one of the best crus for the grape. It is not without importance to realize that Aymavilles is an especially favored viticultural site and that many of the Valle d'Aosta's once-forgotten native grapes that have made a comeback used to live here in forgotten isolation prior to being rediscovered (mostly thanks to the groundbreaking work, energy, and passion of Costantino Charrère, owner of the well-known Les Crêtes winery). The first-ever Prëmetta wine also saw the light of day thanks to Charrère and his Aymavilles winery. (At the time, Les Crêtes didn't even exist; the wines were simply labeled "Costantino Charrère.")

BENCHMARK WINES

Les Crêtes La Tour***, Grosjean Fumin Vigne Rovettaz***, Grosjean Fumin Vigne Merletta*** (sold entirely in the USA), La Crotte de Vegneron Esprit Follet***.

Elio Ottin**, Feudo di San Maurizio**, Lo Triolet**.

Anselmet Fumin*, Chateau Feuillet*, IAR*, La Vrille*, Les Granges*.

Garganega

THE GRAPE VARIETY

Garganega is the twelfth most commonly grown wine grape in Italy (2010 data); it grows especially in the western part of the Veneto (around the towns of Soave and Gambellara), but also in Lombardy, Emilia-Romagna, Lazio, Umbria, and Sicily (where they call it Grecanico Dorato). When planted in fertile flatland soils, Garganega develops easily recognizable huge, long bunches that can produce embarrassing volumes of insipid, neutral wine. However, limiting yields and planting Garganega in the right soils have revealed the variety's true potential. Garganega's main claim to wine fame is its association with Veneto's famous Soave Classico wine, but wines made in the Soave area are among the oldest documented in Italy. Garganega is mentioned as early as the thirteenth century by Pier de' Crescenzi, who described it growing in the regions of Bologna and Padua. Later, it was described at length by numerous experts over the centuries, from Pollini (1824) to Cosmo (1939). We actually know that Garganega is one of Italy's oldest cultivars because

it holds a first-degree relationship with many Italian wine grapes, including Trebbiano Toscano, Albana, Malvasia Bianca di Candia, Marzemina Bianca, and Catarratto Comune (Crespan et al. 2008). Crespan's study also confirmed previous study results by Di Vecchi Staraz et al. (2007) that Garganega and Grecanico Dorato are identical. Garganega is also a parent of Puglia's Susumaniello, which is a natural Garganega × Uva Sogra crossing. Garganega has strong intravarietal variability; therefore, there are many biotypes. Most commonly, Garganega has a large, very long grape bunch (reaching up to twenty-five centimeters in length and 500 grams in weight, with an average of 185 grams), usually pyramidal-conical in shape. Garganega is very vigorous (yields need to be reined in), but it is sensitive to winter cold and common grapevine diseases, and it suffers desiccation of the stalk. It is trained mainly with the *pergoletta veronese* system. In rainy years Garganega wines are on the thin side and so some wineries resort to concentrators, but hot weather is no better, because it kills the expression of the grape's aromas. The most famous Garganega wines are DOCG Soave and Gambellara, but DOC Bianco di Custoza wines can be very enjoyable as well. Clearly, Soave is the most famous wine and is made east of Verona, its territory spanning an area from San Martino Buon Albergo to San Bonifacio; the Soave Classico zone, centered around the towns of Soave and Monteforte d'Alpone, is located to the north of San Bonifacio. Garganega is sometimes blended with 10 to 30 percent other varieties such as Trebbiano di Soave (which is a local biotype of Verdicchio). Unfortunately, Chardonnay and Sauvignon Blanc can also be added, but those two grapes easily overpower Garganega's delicate aromas and flavors. In the immortal words of Leonildo Pieropan, "[H]eaviness is not a characteristic of the Garganega grape and its wines should not be so either." Great wine made with 100 percent Garganega will remind you of white flowers, almond, and green and yellow apple. Since the cultivar has plenty of tartaric acid, its wines have a sweeter mouthfeel than wines that have higher malic acid concentrations. Honeyed notes are instead typical of late-harvested or air-dried Garganega grapes (as they are of most superripe grapes due to the breakdown of carotenoids and the buildup of norisoprenoids). (See "A Study in Terroir" in part 1.) In over thirty years of tasting wines from reputable producers such as Pieropan, I have never found banana to be a strong descriptor of the wines, even when made from especially ripe or late-harvested grapes. Even then, I point out that even Pra's Monte Grande Soave Classico, made from grapes the stalks of which are severed a month ahead of their being picked (and so they air-dry directly on the vine), rarely boasts anything more than a faint hint of banana. So that should tell all of us something (and norisoprenoids be damned). But what do the scientific data say, you ask? Apparently a floral character is always present in Soave wines (Ubigli 2010), especially rose and acacia flowers, due mainly to linalool, geraniol, nerol, and α-terpineol; violet nuances are the result of the presence of β-ionone. Notes of almond, spices, and balsamic oils are most likely due to the presence of methyl salicylate (Versini et al. 1991). Recently, highly interesting data have been published by Tomasi et al. (2015) relative to the differences found in Garganega wines made by different training methods. What this research team found is that Garganega wines made from grapes grown with the traditional pergola Veronese (a type of canopy) have higher concentrations of norisoprenoids (aromas of yellow peach and exotic fruit), phenylethanol, and benzylic acid (alcohol molecules that remind one of rose petals). By contrast, espalier-trained Garganega vines appear to express more terpen derivatives (of linalool, to be precise). The researchers conclude that the former wines have a less-pronounced nose and offer sweeter notes of almond, honey, and broom. Results from research presented by Pezzotti, Tornielli, and Zenoni (2015) on grapes grown in the area of Colognola, Sarmazza, Roncà, and Pressoni showed that where the Garganega grows makes a great deal of difference to both grapes and wines; for example, the high-quality Pressoni area is characterized not only by the largest sugar accumulation in grapes, but also by accumulation that continues unabated during all the phases of the maturation cycle. In fact, transcriptomic analysis revealed that grapes in Pressoni were characterized by the largest amount of activated genes during ripening. In other words, the terroir of Pressoni causes more genes to be turned on, and their expression is greater, than in other locations where Garganega grows. Apparently, the genes most affected by the activation process were those involved in lipid and polyphenol metabolisms, which are all-important for the aromatic and nutritional development of the grapes. Even more interesting was the observation that a number of genes involved in plant defense, especially those directed against oxidative and heat stress, were activated preferentially in Pressoni compared with other sites. Because the latter is a volcanic area characterized by darker soils and a generally warmer microclimate, it is tempting to speculate that in such potentially stressful habitats Garganega relies on the activation of genes useful in self-defense. Last but not least, this highly interesting study also showed that within the population of genes that were activated in the Pressoni site (and activated not at all or not to the same degree elsewhere), there were genes involved in ion transport. Given the highly mineral nature of volcanic soils, it is absolutely fascinating to postulate that such gene activation might have some as-yet-not-understood role in the development of aromas and flavors specific to volcanic soils when Garganega is grown on such soils.

SPECIFIC TERROIRS

Soave Classico

Starting at the Soave–San Bonifacio highway exit, Soave Classico encompasses fifteen hundred hectares and forty official crus among the chains of hills that run from Soave (and its hamlets of Castelcerino, Castelletto, Costeggiola, and Fittà) to Monteforte d'Alpone (with its hamlets of Brognoligo, Sarmazza, and Costalunga), at altitudes as high as 320 meters above sea level. Soils are a mix of mainly volcanic or marly elements, and it's a very different reality from that of the plain (associated with dilute wines from excessively generous yields). In few other Italian wine denominations is the importance of soil as obvious as it is in Soave Classico. As early as 1939, Dalmasso, Cosmo, and Dell'Olio presented a detailed study of the Soave area's soils and climate, thereby updating work that had been done in the previous century by the Accademia di Agricoltura, Scienze, e Lettere di Verona. Today, most experts and some wine lovers are well aware that the whitish, calcareous, limestone-rich soils of the Soave township give refined, even delicate wines of sneaky concentration while Monteforte d'Alpone's very dark, almost black volcanic soils give wines that are more powerful and spicy. Training methods also exert an influence: grapes grown with the area's traditional *pergola veronese* (canopy) system usually deliver wines of greater aromatic complexity, whereas those trained with the more modern Guyot system tend to give more-powerful, broader wines. According to Ponchia et al. (2010), the two main factors that contribute easily recognizable traits in the finished wines are altitude and soil type—so much so that Soave Classico's vineyards can be divided roughly into four territorial units: noncalcareous alluvial plains, calcareous plains, volcanic hills, and calcareous hills.

Noncalcareous Alluvial Plains

The noncalcareous alluvial plains have deep soils rich in loam and clay, where roots dig deep—a meter or more below the surface. These soils are typical of the plain of Monteforte d'Alpone, with vineyards usually located at between thirty and one hundred meters above sea level and on essentially flat terrain (2–4 percent gradients). On this type of soil, keeping the yields low is everything, since the fertility and good water-storage capacity can make Garganega grow like a weed. Roots are able to dig deep, which allows the vines to stand up to water stress much better than do the calcareous plains in front of Soave (characterized by coarser granulometry and less clay). The average daily temperature (18.8°C) is lower here than on the hillsides but is higher than that recorded in the Soave plain, which is even colder (Winkler index, 1820; Huglin index, 2240). Annual precipitation is about 748 millimeters; roughly 53 percent of the annual rainfall is unleashed during the vine's vegetative cycle. Well-made wines (that is, those not from ridiculously high yields) offer delicate and at times simple aromas and flavors of yellow apple and plum, complicated by subtle white-flower and spicy notes.

Calcareous Plains

The calcareous plains are those of the town of Soave. The area borders on the east with the Soave Classico vineyards and on the west with Colognola ai Colli; the soils are mainly loamy on the surface, with limestone deeper down. (Chalk content increases with soil depth.)

Vineyards grow at 30 to 120 meters above sea level, but those toward Illasi and Colognola ai Colli are at slightly higher elevations. Annual precipitation is 704 millimeters (52 percent of which falls during the growing period). The Winkler index is 1768, and the Huglin index is 2036. Wines made from grapes grown on these soils are more often than not redolent of ripe yellow fruit and even honey, but also have the signature limestone citrusy acid kick that extends the flavors on the back end, adding noteworthy refinement in the process. Often the wines can hint of violet, whereas strawberry and red-fruit notes are rarer.

Volcanic Hills

As good as some of the wines made on the first two soil types can be, there is no doubt that the two best sites on which to grow Garganega grapes are the hillsides. Volcanic (basalt-rich) hills are most common in the eastern part of the denomination, east of an imaginary line that connects the town of Soave to Monte Bastia. Vineyards lie at elevations of 50 to 550 meters above sea level and can have extreme 70 percent gradients, and they are some of the oldest of the denomination. (About 50 percent of the vineyards are over thirty years of age.) The annual temperatures are higher than in other parts of this denomination (Winkler index, 1920; Huglin index, 2400). The annual rainfall is nine hundred millimeters (half of that amount falling during the vegetative season). In general, topsoils here are not especially deep, and the grapevine root penetration is blocked by the mother rock. These soils are especially sensitive to water deprivation and low heat units in the month of July—two conditions that greatly reduce sugar accumulation in the grapes. Soave Classico wines from these soils can be rich, spicy, and ripe, but with a definite floral nuance, plus a strong saline note at the finish. The wines also often hint at a balsamic nuance due to methyl salicylate, a molecule that gives off notes of underbrush and resin and that, as we have seen, is found in the Garganega grapes. Sweet spices such as cinnamon are also

discernible, thanks to the benzenoid content of the grapes. Most importantly, these are some of the thickest, richest Garganega wines of all.

Calcareous Hills

The limestone soils are roughly eighty centimeters deep (roots have a hard time digging farther because of the presence of an impermeable mother rock layer) and have only average water retention—a problem in droughty summer months. Limestone content can be high, with 10 percent active lime not rare. Annual rainfall is 903 millimeters, 54 percent of which falls during the vine's vegetative period. The average annual temperature is 14.5°C (Winkler index, 1954; Huglin index, 2402). When all the stars are aligned and the growing conditions are just what the doctor ordered, the wines showcase extremely complex noses, with an intense note of white flowers (jasmine, buttercup, peony) and citrus notes thanks to the presence of terpineols; the best wines usually have high acidity and a good saline spine, not to mention uncommon precision, clarity, and cut. However, fully south-facing vineyards produce grapes with a high content of norisoprenoids, and so ripe tropical-fruit notes can also be found in the wines.

Soave Classico's Best Crus

There are many outstanding Soave Classico sites, some of which have become famous all over the world because their names are associated with what are some of Italy's best white wines. Unfortunately, some other sites are just a little too big to easily grasp the terroir behind them: for example, though I like most of the wines from the Castelcerino site that I try, I would be lying if I told you that I know what a wine from Castelcerino is supposed to taste like. Getting one's head around this extremely large site and its wines—it comprises 180 hectares in the Soave Classico and another 135 in the Soave Colli Scaligeri—is admittedly difficult (even for someone like me, who visits Soave three or four times a year).

Soave

Calvarino: Thirty-three hectares under vine (of forty-one in total) for what is the single most famous site in all of Soave Classico (and for what it's worth, my favorite Soave wines of all). The vines are planted anywhere from 49 to 215 meters above sea level on loamy clay, with calcareous inclusions and basalt within the substrate. The west-southwest-facing slope has a gradient of roughly 25 percent. Colombare is another important site, as is the Monte Becco, both just above the famous Calvarino. Pieropan's Soave Classico Calvarino is the single best Soave of all (it is a 70/30 Garganega and Trebbiano di Soave blend).

Fittà: At 155 hectares (of which roughly 75 hectares are under vine), this is a large site that straddles both the hill's summit and its slope. Fittà lies between 64 and 312 meters above sea level, and its vines, facing south, east, and west, are planted on mainly clay-loamy soils with a basalt substrate. The slope becomes very steep near the summit; otherwise the general gradient is 10 to 30 percent. Suavia makes an excellent Le Rive cru bottling from this site: insiders know that it is a wine that ages very well and can be at times intensely mineral in its aroma and flavor profile.

Monte Tenda: Twenty-three hectares in total, of which ten are under vine, with an elevation of thirty to one hundred meters above sea level and mostly south/southeast exposures. Soils are not especially deep and mostly clay-calcareous in nature. Marcato makes a lovely Soave from this site.

Monte Tondo: Located south of Soave, this is an area where limestone dominates the subsoil, already present one hundred centimeters below the surface. This cru is fifty-six hectares large (of which roughly forty-eight hectares are under vine) and has an elevation of thirty to one hundred meters above sea level. The vines have mostly south-southeast exposures and grow on clay-rich soils. Bertani's lovely Sereole bottling is made from grapes grown on this site, and the wine expresses well this southernmost outpost of the *classico* zone and its gently rolling landscape. The terms "gentle" and "soft" apply to the wine's peachy fruit profile, but I point out that, based on the Sereole wines I have tried, Monte Tondo can give wines of noteworthy longevity.

Rocca: Roughly fifty-four hectares, of which forty are under vine, at an altitude of 70 to 170 meters above sea level; the vines have southern and western exposures mostly. This especially beautiful vineyard is located very near the Castello di Soave, where the soil is mostly calcareous; but the substrate changes as one moves eastward in the cru, with basalt inclusions appearing and also steeper slopes. Pieropan's La Rocca is the best oaked Soave Classico.

Monteforte d'Alpone

Foscarino: One of the truly great sites in Soave Classico, it includes the smaller crus of Palestrello, Pigna, and Ponsara. It is 130 hectares large (with 105 hectares under vine) and straddles both the hill's summit and the slope at an altitude of 80 to 289 meters above sea level; the vines face mostly south, east, and west, and slopes get steeper up toward the top of the hill. Basalt is a typical presence within the soil. Inama has made some grandiose Soave Classico wines from this site over the years; the Montetondo estate also farms grapes here.

Froscà: Located on the first set of hills west of Monteforte d'Alpone, this small site (only thirty hectares, of which twenty-five are under vine) has fairly homogenous deep volcanic basalt soil and very little or no calcareous elements. The cru's elevation is 40 to 160 meters above sea level, and the vines mostly face south-southeast. Gini is the estate most associated with this cru.

Salvarenza: Situated just below Froscà, Salvarenza differs from the latter because of a greater limestone content in its soil, especially at midslope. It is a steep and small cru (twelve hectares in total, of which ten are under vine), and again, the estate most associated with it is Gini, whose Salvarenza Vecchie Vigne Soave is one of the denomination's (Italy's, really) best wines.

BENCHMARK WINES

Pieropan Calvarino***^{PS}, Pieropan La Rocca***^{PS}.

Gini Salvarenza Vecchie Vigne***, Inama Vigneto du Lot***, Inama Foscarino***, Prà Monte Grande***, Prà Staforte***.

Agostini Vicentini il Casale**, Coffele Alzari**, Coffele Ca' Visco**, Filippi**, Nardello Monte Zoppega**, Nardello Meridies**, Nardello Vigna Turbian**, Suavia Monte Carbonare**.

Recioto di Soave: Pieropan Le Colombare***, Nardello Suavissimus***; Gini Renobilis**, Tamellini**.

Glera

THE GRAPE VARIETY

Glera is the grape behind Prosecco, Italy's most popular wine currently. And demand is such that new vineyards are being planted all the time, even where they shouldn't be. Until recently, the variety was known as Prosecco as well, but the latter name is now used only to describe the wine. Glera is most likely a native grape that originated in the Carso Triestino area in Friuli–Venezia Giulia (where the town of Prosecco is located) and from there moved into the Veneto's Treviso area (the heart and home of modern–day Prosecco production) and then farther east into the region's volcanic Colli Euganei, where the grape is called Serprina. However, local producers refuse to accept that their Serprina is a biotype of Glera, insisting that the two are distinct; and data recently presented by Meneghetti et al. (2014) bear this out. (By using a combination of genetic tests one can differentiate between Serprina and Glera.) There are two main varieties—Glera Tondo, which is the more common, and Glera Lungo; but the latter's plantings are declining because it gives a less aromatic wine. There exist two biotypes of Glera Tondo: the Balbi (characterized by a loosely packed bunch) and Cosmo (with a more compact bunch). The Balbi biotype (also known as Glera Bianco) takes its name from Count Marco Giulio Balbi Valier, who selected it on his estate at Pieve di Soligo. Apparently, not just the Veneto had many Glera subvarieties (Sannino 1913): Friuli–Venezia Giulia also had its own populations of Glera biotypes. Importantly, it is possible to distinguish between the various populations of Glera specific to local environments, making for potentially very site-specific wines (Calò et al. 2000; Meneghetti et al. 2014). Glera has medium to strong vigor but a medium-low resistance to dry conditions. Its leaves are subject to sunburn in very hot sunny environments. It is sensitive to soil potassium deficiency and even more so to magnesium deficiency. It is an early-budding variety but ripens late: the grapes are picked between mid-September in flatland vineyards and in early October in vineyards at higher altitudes. Training systems depend on the area of cultivation (flatlands or hillsides), and those most often used are Sylvoz, Guyot, and *cappuccina* (double-arched cane). By contrast, training systems that require short pruning, such as free cordon or spur cordon, are not ideal, because yields become alternatingly high and low year after year. Pruning Glera takes skill because it tends to create, rather than scar tissue, necrotic masses that block vascular-lymphatic flow and can kill the plant. Glera is a lightly to moderately aromatic grape variety, and among the charms of Prosecco are the lovely aromas due to terpineols and benzenoids that are found in both free and bound forms. The benzenoids are especially important. (Benzyl alcohol and β-phenylethanol explain the notes of geranium, rose, and spices that can be picked up in the better Proseccos.) Interestingly, it is the second most abundant group of aromatic molecules in Glera—the terpenes—that mark Glera wines most: geraniol, 8-hydroxygeraniol, and 8-hydroxylinalool are present at significant concentrations and help explain the strongly floral and fresh fruit (citrus) aromas that Glera wines are famous for. All those vineyards located in cooler microclimates give Proseccos that are redolent of these aromas, whereas vineyards with full southern exposures in warmer microclimates tend to produce grapes that are richer in norisoprenoids, meaning that the wines will be marked more by ripe and even tropical-fruit aromas and flavors. Last but not least, remember that the traditional recipe for Prosecco wine was one-third each of Glera, Bianchetta Trevigiana, and Verdiso, because each was believed to contribute something special to the final wine. Perera was also much used in Prosecco blends of the eighteenth and early nineteenth centuries. Modern-day Prosecco allows only a maximum 15 percent of the other grapes, in the belief that Glera is the best variety of the lot. Glera is undoubtedly a high-quality cultivar and can make a fine Prosecco by going solo, but sometimes the sum is more than the individual parts. For example, Perera gives a very perfumed wine; Verdiso contributes acidity; Bianchetta Trevigiana adds structure and roundness. (Marchiori makes an outstanding series of such monovariety wines.) The official production guidelines allow small percentages of Chardonnay and Pinot Bianco in the blend, but this is a mistake, in my opinion: Chardonnay tends to overpower Glera's delicate charms, while Pinot Bianco adds a refined minerally elegance that, though delightful, is not typical of Prosecco. Of the two, Pinot Bianco is undoubtedly the better addition to a Glera-based wine, but I still think that native grapes are the best choice: the resulting Proseccos are much more true to type and ecotypical. Of course, the native grapes are not free of problems, either: for example, Perera is especially sensitive to *flavescence dorée*, a vineyard disease of the twenty-first century that requires the uprooting of all affected vines. (It is caused by a bacterium called *Candidatus Phytoplasma vitis*, the vector of which is the leafhopper *Scaphoideus titanus*, and there is currently no cure. Infection can kill young vines and reduces the yields of old vines.)

Prosecco is made by the Charmat-Martinotti method, and so there is a technological aspect that can also affect wine expression. This is because when making Prosecco, the must is fermented with selected or natural yeasts at controlled temperatures in stainless-steel vats. There, it matures for usually up to ninety days (and even more) on the lees, after which it undergoes secondary fermentation in steel pressure fermenters or autoclaves and bottled (unlike Champagne, where secondary fermentation occurs directly in the bottle). Therefore, the time the wine spends on the lees will greatly affect the aroma and flavor profile of the wines: there is a huge difference, for example, between a wine that sits on the lees three months and one that spends six months on the lees (the latter is referred to as a Charmat Lungo method), and that change is not due to any environmental or site-specific factors. Further muddling the expression of terroir in Prosecco is the fact that over the last ten years the traditional method of secondary fermentation in the bottle has become popular again (called either Prosecco *sul lievito* or *sui lieviti,* or Prosecco *sul fondo*). Glera wines made by fermentation in the bottle taste richer, but also more austere, yeasty, and earthy than those made by the Charmat-Martinotti method, without the delicately aromatic and floral note that so typifies Glera wines. I am among those who think that Glera's bright, fruity charm is somewhat lost in the process. Like Champagne and all other sparkling wines, Prosecco comes in different levels of dryness, labeled Extra Brut (the driest), Brut, Extra Dry (off-dry), and Dry (the sweetest, though thanks to the carbon dioxide and the acidity, the wine never seems frankly sweet). In tune with the changing times that want drier wines, Prosecco has become less sweet in style, and increasingly Brut and Extra Brut Prosecco wines are made. However, I believe the best Prosecco by which to showcase Glera's attributes and the terroir it grows in are the Extra Dry Proseccos. I find they are always better balanced than the Extra Brut and Brut Proseccos. In fact, at the time of writing, the Valdobbiadene DOCG doesn't even recognize the Extra Brut category (and that tells you something right there), so producers making such wines have to use other names such as Dosaggio Zero (Zero Dosage) or resort to identifying their wines as Vino Spumante di Qualità.

SPECIFIC TERROIRS

Prosecco as we know it today was officially born with Antonio Carpanè in 1868, who was the first to apply the Charmat-Martinotti method to Glera and turn Prosecco into a sparkling wine. I am sure Prosecco's founder never imagined that his creation would one day enjoy sales on which the sun never seems to set. As a result of Prosecco's huge popularity, more and more bottles are produced every year; but a good thing can be taken too far, and so it has been with Prosecco, much of which today is correctly made but ultimately uninteresting and bland. A great Prosecco is truly a thing of beauty (and totally deserves its worldwide success); but not all Prosecco wines are worth writing home

about. First, Prosecco is made in two Italian regions (Veneto and Friuli–Venezia Giulia), on the territory of (count 'em) nine provinces and 556 (that's right: 556!) communes. I trust you will agree that is an enormous tract of land, and to expect products of similar quality level is insane.

There are four denominations of Prosecco forming a pyramid of quality. The base of the pyramid is made up of the Prosecco DOC, which encompasses the aforementioned 556 communes and roughly twenty-five thousand hectares of land. Soils there can vary from the leaner ones around the Piave River to the more fertile lands of the *pianura padana* and the sandy expanses near Venice. Commendably, the Prosecco DOC consortium is working toward the creation of official subzones that will distinguish between the Prosecco wines made there. Though there are some decent Prosecco DOC wines made, for the most part they are simpler everyday quaffs with only average depth, complexity, or interest factor. The next step in the pyramid is Prosecco Treviso, a DOC wine that can be made in ninety-five townships. Again, quality is wide-ranging in this category (how can it not be, with 95 communes involved?), but it can offer a step up in depth compared with entry-level DOC Prosecco. The two most important categories of Prosecco are the two DOCGs, named, respectively, Prosecco Asolo (or dei Colli Asolani) and Conegliano Valdobbiadene Prosecco Superiore. The former denomination extends over roughly one thousand hectares, while the latter is about eight thousand hectares large (sprawling over thirty-five communes) but is unquestionably where the greatest, and I do mean *greatest*, Proseccos are made. The positive in this scenario is that for once, the Italian DOC/DOCG system actually works: the DOCG wines are the best, as it should be.

Valdobbiadene Conegliano

The Valdobbiadene Conegliano DOCG Prosecco area occupies the northernmost corner of the province of Treviso, on the border with the province of Belluno and within a valley that has an east-northeast to west-southwest direction. The Dolomite Mountains to the north protect the vineyards from cold winds while reducing the risk of spring frosts, and the Venice lagoon to the south further tempers the microclimate thanks to warm northerly breezes. It is a very pretty part of Italy, especially in the Valdobbiadene subzone, with charming villages perched on wooded, very green hillsides of incomparable beauty.

The Conegliano Valdobbiadene production area is characterized by a series of hills that run east–west, closed off by the Piave River to the west and the Crevada stream to the east. The Soligo River splits this area in two, creating a western and eastern subzone: Valdobbiadene to the west and Conegliano to the east. Valdobbiadene can be further divided into two districts: the northern district of Valdobbiadene and Miane, and the southern district of Vidor and Farra di Soligo (which is close to the Conegliano subzone). The Conegliano subzone also has two different sectors: the western one, where the vineyards of Pieve di Soligo, San Pietro di Feletto, and Refrontolo are located in the north and where those of Conegliano and Susegana are more to the south; and the eastern one, where Vittorio Veneto and Colle Umberto are located. Of course, there is a fifth district, the most famous of all: Cartizze, undoubtedly the one grand cru *hors classe* of the Prosecco world, but it deserves to be treated separately from the rest of the DOCG.

In fact, Prosecco DOCG wine is made from vineyards that grow in only fifteen townships. They are, moving from west to east, Valdobbiadene, Vidor, Miane, Farra di Soligo, Follina, Cison di Valmarino, Pieve di Soligo, Refrontolo, San Pietro di Feletto, Susegana, Tarzo, Conegliano, Vittorio Veneto, Colle Umberto, and San Vendemiano. Perhaps even more useful and important is to remember the names of some of the hamlet and smaller localities that are associated with the best vineyards and wines of the Valdobbiadene subzone: the hamlets of San Pietro di Barbozza, Santo Stefano, Villa, Teva,

Follo, and Guia; and the smaller localities of Saccol, Guietta, and Col (around Valdobbiadene) and of Combai and Premaor (around Miane). Cartizze is located around Santo Stefano, San Pietro di Barbozza, and Saccol.

Historically, Valdobbiadene and Conegliano have always been linked together because many (not all) producers blended grapes from Conegliano (that provide more body) with those from Valdobbiadene (which gave more finesse and perfume). Experimental studies comparing Glera grapes grown in the Valdobbiadene and the Conegliano sectors specify differences on the basis of the concentration of aromatic precursor molecules. Of the three main classes of these molecules (benzenoids, terpenes, and norisoprenoids), it is the benzenoids that reach the highest concentrations in Glera grapes from both sectors of the DOCG. Grapes from Conegliano have higher benzenoid levels than do those of Valdobbiadene, which in turn are instead richer in terpenes (Tomasi and Gaiotti 2011). Benzenoids give aromas of rose, geranium, and spices, and these are in fact descriptors that I commonly associate with Proseccos from the Conegliano area, which are always much spicier than those from Valdobbiadene. That Conegliano and Valdobbiadene should give radically different wines is easy to imagine, given the clear-cut topographic, microclimatic, and geological differences that characterize the two subzones. Whether the blended wines are better than wines made from only Conegliano or Valdobbiadene grapes is most likely a matter left to individual taste preferences, and not unlike the diatribe concerning classic Barolos compared with those made from specific *menzioni geografiche aggiuntive* (MGAs). Personally, I absolutely love the penetrating fragrance of the best wines from Valdobbiadene, but I can see why others might prefer wines from Conegliano.

The hills of Conegliano area run north–south, are not especially steep, and have soils that are mainly morainic or clay-loamy in nature; grapevines are trained either with the old Sylvoz system (used especially on fertile low-lying hills and in the plains) at densities of 2,200 to 2,750 vines per hectare; or, in more modern vineyards, with the Guyot system, with a single fruiting cane (ten to thirteen buds) at a much higher density of plantation. By contrast, Valdobbiadene is characterized by vineyards that run mainly east–west on at times extremely steep hills (with gradients of even 80 percent: one look at this essentially mountain viticulture and you realize immediately why high-quality DOCG Prosecco cannot be an inexpensive wine); soils are mostly marly and conglomerate in nature. Training systems are the classic *cappuccina* system (double-arched cane), planting densities are 3,000 to 3,500 vines per hectare, and yields are naturally quite low. The most commonly used rootstocks are those that push vigor such as the Kober 5BB, 110 Richter, and 1103 Paulsen, all perfectly suited to tough, dry hillside slopes and to the fact that in this viticultural area most growers practice in-vineyard vine replacement when they have to replace vines—and so the 420A rootstock is less popular than it might be otherwise. However, recent data show that its use has been increasing lately, especially in deeper, more fertile soils (Tomasi, Gaiotti, and Jones 2013). An important characteristic of Glera is that, like Riesling, it supports high crop yields without its wine becoming insipid, which means that it does offer growers some degree of site tolerance. However, it drops its malic acid concentrations very quickly during the ripening phase, and its expression of aromatic compounds is very weather and site sensitive. The climate of the two communes differs slightly. In general, Conegliano is characterized by higher summer daytime temperatures, but diurnal temperature shifts are generally high, and minimum temperatures can be especially marked, since Conegliano's flatter topography allows for the collection of masses of cold air. The Winkler index is 1200–1900, and the Huglin index is 1650–2400; Valdobbiadene's districts have slightly different values, reflecting differences in the local climates. And so, in the northern part of Valdobbiadene, in both its districts, the Winkler index is generally 1880 and the Huglin index, 2260 (not unlike those of Conegliano); but in the southern part of the Valdobbiadene subzone and the Susegana area of the Conegliano district, the Winkler index is 1780 and the Huglin index, 2300. Furthermore, over the last sixty years, climate change has made its presence felt with an increase of 184 degrees in the Winkler index, plus all phenologic stages of the vine's growth cycle are now happening two to five days earlier on average (Fila et al. 2010). Rainfall is generous between April and November, whereas it hits its lowest trough during January. Valdobbiadene is generally rainier than Conegliano (roughly by 20 to 30 millimeters each month); over the course of a year, Conegliano has 600 millimeters of rain, while there are 750 millimeters at Col San Martino and Farra di Soligo and 800 millimeters in Valdobbiadene, especially in areas closer to the Piave. Interestingly, in the Valdobbiadene district, roughly 67 percent of the rain falls between mid-March and mid-October; in the Susegana district it is 75 percent; in the Vittorio Veneto district it is only 60 percent. Annual mean temperatures range from 9.5°C to 13°C.

Compared with other Italian denominations, the geology of the Valdobbiadene Conegliano area is easy to grasp. Soils are essentially of four types; marls, conglomerates, clays, and moraines. Marly soils give outstanding Proseccos, redolent of white flower and white stone fruit notes, and a strong aromatic quality due to high concentrations of monoterpenes such as linalool and geraniol. These are some of the most floral Prosecco DOCG wines of all (they offer broom, mimosa, chamomile, and jasmine) and also exhibit very good structure and depth. In fact, from a biochemical standpoint, these wines are characterized more by monoterpene molecules than norisoprenoids, explaining their freshness. These are typically the soils found around Valdobbiadene, especially in the northern district; this will not surprise anyone with experience drinking the Proseccos of the Valdobbiadene area, which are the most piercingly, fragrantly floral of all

Proseccos. In fact, these soils are also found in large parts of the Conegliano subzone, which is logical enough since all Prosecco wines exude floral and white stone fruit aromas and flavors to a degree; what changes mostly from zone to zone is the intensity and complexity of the same. Conglomerate soils are characterized by various depths of topsoil, slopes are often steep, and vines usually face south. These soils push the grapes to ripen early: Glera grapes here are usually picked ten to fifteen days before those planted on other soils. These Proseccos are usually fragrant and fresh (typical fruit descriptors like apple and white peach are common in these wines, as opposed to floral findings such as mimosa), but are not especially deep or complex. In droughty years, these Proseccos can develop strong notes of very ripe, even exotic, fruit. Typically, these soils characterize the southern half of Valdobbiadene and the Susegana district. Moraine soils are mostly typical of the Vittorio Veneto district, but can be found in an area just north of Conegliano and to the south of Vittorio Veneto, especially between Ogliano and Carpesica di Vittorio Veneto. They are characterized by compacted sands, and therefore water reserves are usually low: supportive drip irrigation may be necessary. The harvest usually takes place in mid-September. Areas with these soils are characterized by some of the highest diurnal temperature variations of the whole DOCG, and though grapes accumulate sugars easily, total acidity levels tend to be on the low side in droughty years. The day–night temperature variations favor the production of monoterpenes, which yield wines with citrus and floral notes, and the high daytime temperatures lead to the formation of benzenoids and norisoprenoids (aromas and flavors of ripe fruit). Generally, these wines tend to be more delicate than those of other areas. Last but not least, clay soils are mostly typical of the Conegliano township, especially around San Pietro di Feletto and Refrontolo. These clays often have a reddish coloration and are weakly acid or neutral. Thanks to the excellent water reserves, crops are potentially large, with grapes characterized by good sugar and acid buildup. September rains can be problematic in this specific subzone, in which case the aromatic potential of the wines is lessened. These are some of the broadest Proseccos of all, with an interesting mix of floral notes (iris, buttercup, daisy) and riper fruit notes of yellow melon and pear, often with menthol hints.

Le Rive: The Specific Crus of Valdobbiadene Conegliano

Producers and local government institutions have always been aware of the uniqueness of the Conegliano and Valdobbiadene Prosecco, and invested in years of research and zonation studies that have led to the identification and establishment of forty-three official single-vineyard sites called *rive*. The *rive* are beautiful vineyards, and probably give the best wines of all, but are extremely difficult and costly to work. By comparison, whereas flatland vineyards require roughly 120 hours or less of work per hectare, Valdobbiadene's *rive* single vineyards can require as much as 700 or more hours. (Hours of work per hectare is a unit of measure indicating the number of hours worked on a hectare over the course of twelve months.) Clearly, the steeper the slope, the more hours are required, while flatland, machine-harvested vineyards are obviously easier and faster to work, and require fewer work hours. A few of my favorite *rive*:

Col San Martino (Farra di Soligo township; located in a central-south position in the denomination, it is medium-large, located at 280 meters above sea level; the soil is mainly calcareous conglomerates)

Colbertaldo di Vidor (Vidor township; southwest in the territory; small, located at 200 meters above sea level; calcareous conglomerates)

Farra di Soligo (Farra di Soligo township; central-south position; large *riva* located at 280 meters above sea level; soil of calcareous conglomerates mixed with marl)

Ogliano (Conegliano township; central-south position; small, at 150 meters above sea level; glacial deposits rich of stones)

Pieve di Soligo (Conegliano township; central position; large, at 150 meters above sea level; colluvial calcareous deposits)

Soligo (Farra di Soligo township; central-south position; small, at 180 meters above sea level; marls and conglomerates)

BENCHMARK WINES

Silvano Follador Brut Nature***[PS].

Adami Superiore Asciutto Rive di Colbertaldo Vigneto Giardino***, Bisol Crede Brut***, Bisol Vigneti Del Fol Extra Dry***, Bortolomiol Superiore Ius Naturae***, Marchiori Superiore Extra Dry***, Masottina Extra Dry Rive di Ogliano***, Nino Franco Superiore Vigna della Riva di San Floriano***, Ruggeri Superiore Vecchie Vigne***.

Andreola Superiore Rive di Soligo Mas de Fer**, Adami Superiore Bosco di Giga**, Fratelli Bortolin**, Bortolomiol**, Bosco del Merlo Extra Dry Millesimato**, Col Vetoraz** Frozza Col d'Orso**, Le Colture Superiore Extra Dry**, Ruggeri Giustino B**, Sorelle Bronca Extra Dry Particella 68**.

Cartizze

The most famous Prosecco of all is Cartizze, made from grapes grown on 106 hectares in the heart of the Prosecco zone. It is from this hallowed piece of land that truly *hors classe*–quality Prosecco can be made. The name of Cartizze is of uncertain origin, with most experts believing that it derives from *gardiz* (a dialect word for the canes on which grapes were air-dried to make sweet wines) or perhaps *cardus* ("cardoon" in English), a plant that grows commonly in the local vineyards. Another possible source is the ancient name of a locality called *caurige*, which first appears in a 1362 notary document (Graziotin 2016). Cartizze's reputation is such that it was until recently Italy's most expensive piece of vineyard land (Barolo crept ahead as of 2017), costing an estimated €800,000 to €950,000 per hectare. It's only a theoretical value, because nobody who owns land in Cartizze sells any; by comparison, in Valdobbiadene land cost is roughly €650,000 per hectare. All this means that some individuals are prone to want to make Cartizze no matter what. So better to stick with known producers when choosing your Cartizze. Cartizze is not just the most elegant and deepest of all Proseccos, but also fuller bodied and always carries a little residual sugar due to the sunlit slopes, on which grapes really pack in the sugar. Therefore, Cartizze usually tastes off-dry, with penetrating, extremely pure nuances of white peach, jasmine, and powdered rocks; some wine lovers complain that the wine is just too sweet, but frankly, getting dry or *nature* Cartizze just right is a balancing act achieved by only a few very talented producers (Bisol or Silvano Follador, for example). The Cartizze denomination can be subdivided into fifteen rather homogenous subzones, of which the main communes are Santo Stefano, San Pietro di Barbozza, San Giovanni, and the hamlet of Saccol. The soils were formed roughly twenty million to seven million years ago and are mainly calcarenite based and not especially deep; water drainage is quite good.

BENCHMARK WINES

Col Vetoraz***[PS], Silvano Follador Nature***[PS].

Adami***, Bisol***, Bortolomiol***, Ruggeri***.

Andreola**, Le Colture**.

Grechetto di Todi and Grechetto di Orvieto

THE GRAPE VARIETIES

Also known as Pulcinculo, Strozzavolpe, Occhietto, and Montanarino Bianco, Grechetto has two distinct varieties: Grechetto di Todi and Grechetto di Orvieto, the former better known as Pignoletto (Filippetti, Silvestroni, and Intrieri 1999). Therefore, speaking or writing of a generic "Grechetto" variety, as many do, is of no use to anyone, so readers, beware. The fact is that producers, wine writers, and even scientists fall into this trap because the two varieties have long been erroneously thought of as clones (and identified as such: you will find when you visit wineries that producers still refer to Grechetto di Todi as Grechetto clone G5 and to Grechetto di Orvieto as Grechetto clone G108). This is also partly because the two are usually co-planted in the field. (People thought they were clones of the same variety.) In any case, the name "Grechetto" should mean Grechetto di Orvieto only (D'Onofrio and Scalabrelli 2015). The two are distinct varieties that were given the "Greco-something" moniker, most likely with the intent of cashing in on sales

(Greco wines being some of the most sought after in antiquity). Grechetto di Orvieto's loosely packed bunch makes it ideal for sweet-wine production (and most Orvieto Passito wines are top-heavy with it), something that the stocky, compact Grechetto di Todi bunch is less than ideal for. Of course, this being Italy, you will always find one or two producers dissenting from what everyone else says, and they will tell you that, no, Grechetto di Todi's thick skins allow the grapes to be harvested late, and therefore it's just a perfect variety with which to make sweet wines. (In the study of wine grapes, it helps to be the patient type, and all the more so in Italy—either that or enjoy counting to ten, often.) Of the two Grechettos, Grechetto di Todi (or Pignoletto) is grown mostly in the Emilia portion of Emilia-Romagna, but is abundant in the Umbrian countryside, too, where it is also known as Perugino or Pulcinculo. It is a much less vigorous variety than Grechetto di Orvieto. Because its basal buds are not very fertile, to train it by cordon spur means ending up with a lot of greenery and very few grape bunches. What Grechetto di Todi needs is a

Guyot pruning system; in this case, it will be characterized by much more regular productivity and better-quality grapes with higher extract and acidity values. No matter how one chooses to train or grow Grechetto di Todi, its grape bunch is always smaller and stockier, and weighs much less, than Grechetto di Orvieto's. It also gives wines that are very easy to distinguish from those made with Grechetto di Orvieto: thanks to its wealth of polyphenols, Grechetto di Todi wines are always tannic (in this they are very Greco-like), dense, and more complex than those made with the Orvieto variety. There are numerous nursery clones of this variety available: the ICA-PG clone is a much-planted one because it is very resistant to powdery mildew and botrytis, though in hot, humid years it can drop its acidity very quickly if allowed to get overripe (Borgo et al. 2004). Given their tannic backbone, these wines can be judiciously oaked, though as Niccolò and Bernardo Barberani have found over the years at their Barberani estate (perhaps Umbria's best), larger, used barrels are a better fit for Grechetto di Todi wines than barriques, where the oak can camouflage Grechetto's delicate aromas and flavors and exacerbate its tendency to display a phenolic edge.

By contrast, Grechetto di Orvieto has a much larger, long bunch that is immediately recognizable from that of Grechetto di Todi in vineyards. It is also very loosely packed, and its grapes have thin skins (so it really is completely different from Grechetto di Todi). Wines made with it offer early appeal, with hints of white flowers, yellow apple, and lime, with generally high acidity; lesser examples (such as when the wines are the product of high yields) can be tart and neutral. Grechetto di Orvieto wines are always simpler and lighter bodied than those made with Grechetto di Todi, and can be at times marked by a strong note of chamomile, even camphor, that not everyone likes. Most importantly, it is this variety that strikes me as being the one able to offer thiol-related notes of grapefruit and passionfruit; not so Pignoletto (Grechetto di Todi), the wines of which are not

especially marked by thiol notes even when hyperreductive winemaking techniques are used (in my experience, at least). Unfortunately, all research papers (save one) that I have tracked down over the years fail to state exactly which Grechetto variety is being written about. Clearly, since the two Grechettos are often co-planted in vineyards, it is logical to assume that most often study results apply to a population of the two Grechettos (which is not an ideal manner by which to reach significant conclusions relevant to the single cultivars). In fact, a very interesting study by Esti et al. (2010) analyzed sixteen different wines from two consecutive vintages (2005 and 2006) made by seven different Lazio and Umbrian producers on the basis of 133 aroma and flavor descriptors. The most common descriptors in the Grechetto wines were apple, acacia flower, banana, pineapple, herbaceous, apricot, and peach. (Gooseberry, guava, grapefruit, and other thiol-related aromas and flavors were mentioned less than 50 percent of the time in individual tasting reports.) In this study, the single most important terroir-related factor in determining Grechetto wine aroma and flavor profiles was found to be the "clone" of Grechetto used (the study used the term "clone," as was common at the time), whereas in fact they were studying different varieties altogether. Two wines in the study were 100 percent Grechetto di Todi (unfortunately, there were no monovariety Grechetto di Orvieto wines included); another was 80 percent Grechetto Poggio della Costa, a local biotype of Lazio (which in my experience offers very different aromas and flavors from those of the Umbrian Grechettos). The study's results bear these impressions out: Grechetto wine made with the Poggio della Costa biotype was the only one to showcase mineral nuances (not typical of Umbrian Grechetto wines, but very characteristic of wines made with the Lazio biotype, which grows in an area where soils are very volcanic), whereas the monovariety Grechetto di Todi wines expressed notes of banana and other tropical fruits that were absent in the wines made with the other two Grechettos under study. These findings are also consistent with my own experience: all the experimental monovariety Grechetto di Orvieto wines I have tried over the last fifteen years were generally marked by herbal, pomaceous orchard-fruit, and lemony notes, with little in the way of tropical attributes to speak of. However, because some Grechetto wines produced over the years have smelled of guava, passionfruit, and gooseberry, recent studies have analyzed the presence and concentration of thiol precursor molecules in Grechetto must and wines. Cerreti et al. (2015) investigated the presence of glutathione and cysteine conjugates in Grechetto and Malvasia del Lazio grapes, and compared these results with those obtained in Sauvignon Blanc grapes. (Sauvignon Blanc was included in the study as it is the variety that has the highest concentrations of these thiols.) A second objective of the study was to determine thiol kinetics during ripening in order to predict the ideal harvest time for each variety such that grapes can be picked with the maximum thiol concentration. Quantitative automated liquid chromatography–electrospray ionization–tandem mass spectrometry (LC-ESI-MS/MS) analysis revealed that in Sauvignon Blanc, glutathione conjugate precursors are found in lower concentrations than are the cysteine conjugates (in accordance with previous results published in 2010 by Roland et al.) and that such a difference is not present in the Grechettos and in Malvasia del Lazio—two varieties in which concentrations of these precursor groups are much lower than in Sauvignon Blanc. (Whereas the cysteine/glutathione conjugates ratio is three to one in Sauvignon Blanc juice, it is one to one in the two Italian native grapes.) More interestingly, the concentration of a specific cysteinylated thiol, cysteine-3-sulfanhyl-hexan-1-ol (cys-3SH), is eleven and twenty-eight times higher in Sauvignon Blanc grapes compared with the Grechettos and Malvasia del Lazio, respectively. I don't know about you, but these are the sort of scientific findings that provide me with more than just a *quantum* of solace, as I have never, and I mean never, found that a truly monovari-

ety Malvasia del Lazio wine ever exudes meaningful passionfruit, guava, box-tree, or grapefruit aromas and flavors. By contrast, the study does confirm that Grechettos can produce wines that offer a similar aromatic profile, though not of the intensity commonly associated with Sauvignon Blanc wines. Furthermore, the highest concentration of thiol precursor molecules in Grechetto grapes is found when these reach 22° Brix. Relative to human factors associated with terroir expression in wines, Cerreti et al. (2017) analyzed thiol expression in both Grechetto grape must and in wines made from Grechetto grapes that had been grown with different training systems (royat cordon and Guyot). Results showed that thiol precursor concentrations are higher when Grechetto grapes are trained with the former system; however, these higher concentrations do not translate into higher concentrations of volatile thiols in the finished wines. And so, at least based on these study results, it does not appear that the choice of training system in itself will cause the production of Grechetto wines with greater aromatic oomph.

SPECIFIC TERROIRS

Colli Martani

The Colli Martani are located to the east of Todi, and the Colli Martani denomination falls within the entire territory of the townships of Gualdo Cattaneo and Giano dell'Umbria as well as parts of Todi, Massa Martana, Monte Castello Vibio, Montefalco, Castel Ritaldi, Spoleto, Bevagna, Cannara, Bettona, Deruta, and Collazzone—all in the province of Perugia. The DOC was instituted in 1988, and later modified and updated in 2003 and 2009. Unfortunately, the "updates" local politicians like to talk about are often detrimental; for example, the introductions of Chardonnay and Sauvignon Blanc were hardly enlightened moves. Though Colli Martani wines can be made in all colors—including *rosso, bianco,* Trebbiano, Grechetto di Todi, Sangiovese, Cabernet Sauvignon, Merlot, Sauvignon

Blanc, Chardonnay, Riesling, sparkling wine, Vernaccia Nera, and Vernaccia—the only two that are of any real interest are the Grechetto and the Vernaccia Nera wines.

Though the two Grechetto varieties grow all over Umbria, they are actually indigenous to Orvieto and Todi, and not to the other Umbrian production areas, such as for example Lago di Corbara or Montefalco. (The historic local white grape of the latter was Trebbiano Spoletino, not the Grechettos.) As its name implies, in Umbria Grechetto di Todi is especially linked to Todi, a very pretty and well-kept medieval town (definitely worth a vacation or visit, by the way) located twenty kilometers (roughly twelve miles) to the southeast of Perugia in southwestern Umbria. The soils are essentially a mix of calcareous rocks (marly limestone, marl, and siliceous limestones) of marine origin. These Grechetto wines (mostly blends of the two varieties, as has always been common in Umbria) boast nuances of white flowers, herbs, and fresh citrus fruits, with very delicate frames and saline finishes. Poor examples are lean and nondescript.

BENCHMARK WINES

Peppucci Grechetto Colli Martani**.

Antonelli San Marco*, Arnaldo Caprai Grecante*, Romanelli*.

Orvieto

It is really unfortunate that an ocean of lean and insipid Orvietos has been produced for decades, reducing the wine in the minds of most people to the level of an afterthought. And though Orvieto is unlikely to be mentioned by anyone when the subject of Italy's best white wines or ageworthy collectibles is broached, it is a denomination that can produce much better wines than generally believed. No, I do not mean Montrachet-type complexity or nostril-piercing intensity of aromas. But top estates such as Barberani, Sergio Mottura (his single-vineyard Grechetto wines especially), and Palazzone all demonstrate that a good Grechetto wine can be just that, and age—in some cases, even four to six years after the vintage. Orvieto wines (classico or not) are a blend of the Grechettos, Procanico (a local Trebbiano Toscano biotype generally believed to be a higher-quality wine grape than the original), Verdello, Drupeggio, and other varieties still. For those readers who would like to know if the Orvieto they are enjoying is more top-heavy with Grechetto di Todi or with Grechetto di Orvieto, a general rule of thumb is as follows: any especially tannic Orvieto not aged in oak (a few are) speaks of a strong presence of Grechetto di Todi, which as we have seen tends to give a chewy, fleshy mouthfeel to any wine it plays more than a minor role in; by contrast, a more citrusy, lighter–bodied wine might be hinting at a greater Grechetto di Orvieto presence. (Keep in mind that the latter variety does not give wines as lean or as herbal as those where Procanico dominates.) Last but not least, remember that no other viticultural zone in Italy is as blessed when it comes to noble rot as Orvieto. Plenty of Botrytis cinerea forms there, thanks to the nearby Rivers Tiber and Paglia, the manmade Lake Corbara, and wide temperature swings between early and late morning. In fact, the words muffa nobile (Italian for "noble rot") are an integral part of the official DOC designation for Orvieto late-harvest wines (and in fact are indicated on the labels of these wines: Orvieto Classico Superiore Passito Muffa Nobile).

Not many people are aware that the Orvieto production zone actually straddles two Italian regions, Umbria and Lazio, and therefore can be made in the territories of two communes: the province of Viterbo in Lazio, including the countryside of the towns of Castiglione in Teverina, Civitella D'Agliano, Graffignano, Lubriano, and Bagnoregio; and the province of Terni in Umbria, which includes the territories of the towns of Orvieto, Allerona, Alviano, Baschi, Castel Giorgio, Castel Viscardo, Ficulle, Guardea, Montecchio, Fabro, Montegabbione, Monteleone d'Orvieto, and Porano. Clearly, it is in Umbria that most Orvieto is made (only about 10 percent of Orvieto is made in Lazio), but it should be noted that Lazio's production is very high in quality. The Orvieto denomination is characterized by four soil types (sandy clay, volcanic, alluvial sands, and a mix of yellow compacted sands and conglomerates) of either sedimentary or volcanic origin. The sedimentary soils are mainly clay-sandy in nature and are most typically found in the eastern reaches of the denomination and to the northwest of the city of Orvieto itself. (These soils are richer in clay, and compacted clays at that, and the wines reflect this, being characterized by big structures.) For the most part, these soils have a good CEC (cationic exchange capacity) and a healthy limestone content. The volcanic soils are typical of the southwestern portion of the denomination: west of the Paglia River and just south of where the Tiber joins the Paglia. They are especially typical of the Lazio portion of the Orvieto denomination (not surprisingly at all, given that the denomination edges toward Lake Bolsena, which originates from a volcanic crater). These soils are very poor in organic matter and have virtually no limestone but are rich in ignimbrites (see the glossary), lava, and tuff, with a high potassium content and a pH that hovers around seven. These are soils more suited to later-ripening varieties, and though the early-ripening Grechettos can have a tough time accumulating sugars when planted there, the wines can be quite perfumed. This is also the part of the denomination most associated with noble-rot formation. By contrast, the lowest-lying vineyards of the Tiber River valley, of the shores of Lake Corbara, and of the Paglia River basin have soils that are alluvial in origin; differently from the other two, though, the soils of the Paglia River basin are also characterized by the presence of large rocks. In general, the soils of the banks of the Paglia and Tiber were formed in the Pliocene period (roughly five million to 1.7 million years ago), whereas the terraces located at slightly higher altitudes are more recent, dating to the Pleistocene. There is an average limestone and organic-matter content, a good CEC, and a presence of both loam and clay. The yellow compacted sands, sandstone, and conglomerate soils of the townships of Murotondo, Cerreto Civitella, and Salviano are characterized by low organic matter, a slightly alkaline pH, low CEC, and low available-water capacity (so water stress can be a problem in droughty years). Vineyards lie between 150 and 350 meters above sea level; even in these times of climate change, planting the local native grapes anywhere higher would be courageous, since the likelihood of grapes not reaching optimal physiologic ripeness is high. Rainfall is roughly 850 to 1,000 millimeters a year, and diurnal temperature variations are not that marked, especially in the ripening phase. The Winkler index is 1850–2350, and the Huglin index is 2300–2650. Training systems used are the double-arched cane and the Guyot. Planting densities are generally low (commonly twenty-five hundred to three thousand vines per hectare). Procanico is generally harvested in the first half of October, the Grechettos after the third week of September. (By comparison, Chardonnay in this area is picked as early as mid-August—hardly the stuff by which wines of mind-bogglingly complexity are made.) The main problem with the Orvieto denomination has always been the quality of the majority of its wines—a fact mostly due to there being far too many big nonregional and regional bottlers churning out an ocean of mediocre, boring stuff. Note that Orvieto wines do not necessarily have to be dry, and in fact the off-dry versions (Orvieto Abboccato, Orvieto Amabile) were by far the most popular right up until the 1980s.

BENCHMARK WINES

The list below does not mention, or rates poorly, those Orvieto wines that smell and taste too strongly of Chardonnay and Sauvignon Blanc. If producers wish to use those grapes, they are of course welcome to, but they should spare us the use of the word "Orvieto" on the label. If someone buys a wine labeled Orvieto, they are not looking to drink a Chardonnay or a Sauvignon Blanc wannabe, because otherwise they would just go out and buy a wine labeled Sauvignon or Chardonnay.

Orvieto and Grechetto wines (dry): Barberani Luigi e Giovanna***, Palazzone Campo del Guardiano***, Sergio Mottura Grechetto Poggio della Costa***.

Castello della Sala San Giovanni della Sala**, Decugnano dei Barbi Il Bianco**, Palazzone Terre Vineate**, Sergio Mottura Grechetto La Tour a Civitella**, Sergio Mottura Vigna Tragugnano**.

Argillae Panata*, Cantina Altarocca Arcosesto*, Custodi Belloro*, Foresi*, Palazzone Grechetto Grek*.

Orvieto and Grechetto wines (sweet): Barberani Calcaia Muffa Nobile***PS.

Decugnano dei Barbi Muffa Nobile Pourriture Noble***, Palazzone Orvieto Muffa Nobile***.

Custodi Orvieto Pertusa Vendemmia Tardiva**.

Grignolino

THE GRAPE VARIETY

Grignolino takes its name from the Piedmontese dialect word *grignolè,* which refers either to grimaces or the grating of the teeth (made when one bites into the high-acid and tannic Grignolino grape), or to pips (because Grignolino has more pips per berry than other cultivars: three when most others have two). In fact, Grignolino is a recent name: the variety used to be also known as Balestra, Verbesino, Arlandino, Rossetto, or especially Barbesino (though there exists evidence that Barbesino was also the name of a wine made from a blend of Grignolino, Barbera, and Freisa). Now found only in Piedmont, Grignolino used to be common in both Piedmont and Lombardy, but it is very rare in the latter region today. Centuries ago, the cultivar was not just abundant but also well regarded: even in the thirteenth century there were strict laws in place punishing severely all those harming Barbesino vines. Grignolino wines were especially popular because of their pale hue and refined mouthfeel that distinguished them from all the other wines of the time, which were either much darker (those made with Barbera) or bigger and richer (Nebbiolo wines). Back then, Grignolino was popular in a sparkling-wine version as well, a wine category the variety seems well suited to given its intrinsically high acidity. The variety craves well-exposed sites with plenty of sunlight, and such top real-estate spots are usually reserved for varieties that bring better financial returns, such as Nebbiolo. Grignolino also needs well-ventilated areas, because its compact bunch poses rot-related problems. Whereas today Grignolino has virtually disappeared from the Langhe, in the nineteenth century the majority of Grignolino wines were produced there by estates that bought the grapes grown in the Astigiano and Monferrato. However, there were always very good to great Grignolino wines made in the Langhe with grapes that grew there. (Bartolo Mascarello made a great Grignolino wine, for example.) Grignolino bunches are roughly medium to large in size, very long, and pyramidally shaped, with up to three wings. The grapes are medium-small with thin pale blue-red skins. Unfortunately, there is a huge amount of intravarietal variability, and many Grignolino phenotypes exist. This is due partly to mutations that have built up over time, leading to different morphologies but also numerous clones (a sure-fire sign that Grignolino was highly thought of; otherwise, no nursery would have bothered to reproduce it). Not especially resistant to diseases, it also yields very little juice (a logical consequence of having small berries and plenty of pips) and suffers from asynchronous maturation: consequently, bunches sporting a kaleidoscope of different-colored berries are common, with greenish grapes hanging side by side blue and pinkish-red ones. This is why it is necessary to curb Grignolino's natural high vigor, for high yields are an almost virtual guarantee of not achieving optimal ripeness. Unfortunately, Grignolino is very sensitive to the grapevine *flavescence dorée* phytoplasma, and many splendid old vineyards have been killed in recent years. (If you hear someone sobbing in the distance, that's me.) The wines are characterized by graceful frames, high acidity and tannins, and mainly floral aromas and flavors, with subtle red-berry and cherry nuances lingering nicely. Such traits made Grignolino an unfashionable grape in the last thirty years, when its pale red-pink color, lack of obvious sweet, ripe, and soft fruit flavors, and very high acidity and tannins were a ticket to nowhere. In fact, wine novices often mistake Grignolino wines for Rosatos; even worse, the wine's typical garnet edge does not communicate just how well Grignolino wines can age. In fact, it is deep red Grignolino wines that should worry everybody, for that's not normal, despite what you might be told: Grignolino's pigments are not easy to mobilize, and long macerations are not the answer because of the risk of making a very bitter wine. The aroma and flavor profile of Grignolino wines brings to mind fresh flowers (small wild roses and violet), small red berries (strawberry, raspberry, sour red cherries), and spices such as white pepper (not the black pepper more typical of Syrah wines, for example). The wines are always very fresh and crisp, with noteworthy but not unpleasant tannic bite. Low alcohol levels (most usually 12 or 12.5 percent) and an absence of oak aging are typical of entry-level Grignolinos, though the low alcohol levels are mostly the result of the wrong choice of Grignolino biotypes or clones; Grignolino wines can pack 14 percent alcohol like all other red wines. Recently, producers in the Monferrato Casalese have "resurrected" the traditional Grignolino wine of a few centuries ago (made by oak aging for up to two years in large barrels). The wine is called "Grignolino Storico"; it is made in the manner of roughly two hundred years ago by applying very long macerations (up to two months) and aging in large oak barrels for as much as two years. These Grignolino wines are rich and dense, and interestingly, using oak judiciously does not overpower Grignolino's delicate fruit aromas and flavors. Accornero is a producer who manages to oak Grignolino splendidly (his Grignolino del Monferrato Casalese Bricco del Bosco Vecchie Vigne is a work of art), but not everyone in the denomination is as gifted. Grignolino makes a splendid food match with the likes of white-meat dishes (rabbit, chicken, veal), fatty foods of all kinds, and soy-sauce-enhanced dishes. Grignolino wines are also the best match in the world for *vitello tonnato, lingua in salsa verde,* and *agnolotti,* either *alla piemontese* or *al sugo di carne*—archetypal dishes of Piedmont's delightful, refined cuisine.

SPECIFIC TERROIRS

Like Riesling, Pinot Noir, and Nebbiolo, Grignolino is an excellent translator of soil types—a fact that was well known to famous Italian grape luminaries of the past: for example, Di Rovasenda thought the wine was "extremely fine" and specified that the variety needed specific soils to show its best (1877). In fact, Grignolino wines express a huge diversity of aromas and flavors, depending on the biotype and where the grapes are grown. It is therefore not surprising that Grignolino has always been strongly associated with specific terroirs and crus. Grignolino wine denominations include Piemonte Grignolino, Grignolino d'Asti, and Grignolino del Monferrato Casalese, but the last two are most famous.

The Grignolino Wines of the Langhe

You want to talk terroir? It cannot be a fluke that the Grignolino wines from the Langhe, while rare today, were all so good: the Langhe is really a grand cru spot for this grape variety, but unfortunately the area is totally devoted to Nebbiolo nowadays (understandably). Castiglione Falletto (Bricco Boschis, where a very good Grignolino wine is still being made today), Monforte d'Alba (the Pianpolvere Soprano and Bussia crus were famous for their Grignolino), Serralunga d'Alba (the wine called Grignolino di Rivette was especially famous: Rivette is a famous Barolo cru in the Serralunga subzone), and Neive (from the Cortini area) were all linked to memorable Grignolino wines. But the grape used to do well everywhere in the Langhe, as mentioned previously about Bartolo Mascarello. Today, Grignolino is grown mostly in the provinces of Alessandria and Asti.

Grignolino d'Asti

Marco Crivelli, one of the most talented producers in Italy, has a funny terroir story to tell. Years ago, he asked a local farmer if he could buy a part of his vineyards. The farmer answered, "Sure, no problem": but he would sell him only that section of vines growing on red soils (iron-rich clays), and not any of his vines growing on white soils (mainly loam, clay, sand, and limestone). Taken aback by such a firm stand, Crivelli naturally inquired as to why the farmer felt so strongly about the issue. The farmer's reply? "Sorry, but I am keeping all my plots on white soils because I like to drink Grignolino." There's no better summary of terroir than that.

The Grignolino d'Asti denomination is located immediately south of the Grignolino del Monferrato Casalese denomination, spreading eastward (where it borders Nizza Monferrato) and southwest (where it touches the province of Cuneo). Wine lovers and insiders know to specifically look for the Grignolino d'Asti wines of Portacomaro, Moncalvo, Castello di Annone, and Costigliole d'Asti (all these towns fall within the Asti province), all true grand cru areas for the variety. Grignolino wines tend to be tannic and high in acidity, but since the best areas for Grignolino in Asti can be very sandy, the wines from there are especially fragrant and perfumed, and surprisingly ageworthy, too. The best sections in which to make Grignolino d'Asti are the ridge of hills that run from Costigliole d'Asti to Rocchetta Tanaro and then to Castello di Annone, and the hills of Portacomaro and Migliandolo. Historically, a number of outstanding Grignolino wines were made in the Asti province: the most famous of all was the Grignolino di Migliandolo, a grand cru of the larger Portacomaro subzone, of which it is a hamlet. Migliandolo was a commune itself up until 1837; its name derives from *milledolium*, meaning "one thousand," or *mille*, "mugs"—a reference to the town's strong viticultural tradition. Another origin might be *mian deux*, or "two miles," since that was the distance separating Migliandolo from the town of Asti, the most important city of the area. Unfortunately, with the fall from grace of all Grignolino wines in the 1980s and 1990s, the hill of Migliandolo was turned into a building site, and so homes stand today where I remember vineyards once growing—a real shame. (But as one very keen producer observed, it tells you a lot about Migliandolo's favorable exposure/mesoclimate that homes were built there and not in Asti.) In fact, Grignolino di Portacomaro was also much sought after, since it had the reputation of being the most magically perfumed Grignolino wine of all. In 2014, the town of Portacomaro dedicated a Grignolino vineyard to Pope Francis because he had publicly mentioned liking Grignolino; the vineyard is just two kilometers away from Bricco Marmorito, the home of the grandparents of Pope Francis. (Need I say that local Grignolino wine sales have increased with the pope having voiced his opinion on the matter?) Besides the Grignolino di Migliandolo and that of Portacomaro, there were at least two other well-known Grignolino wines of the Asti zone, all of which spoke of a specific, local terroir: Grignolino della Rocchetta (made with grapes grown around Rocchetta Tanaro) and Grignolino di Saraprone (made with grapes grown around Castagnole Monferrato, on the hill of Saraprone). Of these two, the Rocchetta wines were, and are, famous for an intense note of red cherry that is deeper than that of most Grignolino d'Asti wines and for an absolutely unique note of white pepper. By contrast, the Grignolino di Saraprone wines always struck me as being much spicier than other Asti Grignolino wines. The list below (and the one detailing Grignolino del Monferrato crus) is based on work by Veronelli (1995) and my own experience, accumulated over thirty years of tasting Grignolino wines and listening to producers (and their staff) like Paolo and Franco Angelini, Giulia Alleva, Raffaele Bologna, Marco Canato, Carlo Cassinis, Paolo and Ernesto Casalone, Beatrice and Marco Gaudio, Fabio Marinoni, Domenico Ravizza, and Diego Visconti.

Specific Crus

Asti: Rotondino, Valdeperno.

Casorzo d'Asti: Casaletto, Moncucchetto.

Castagnole Monferrato: Montiò, San Pietro Realto, Saraprone, Valvinera.

Castello di Annone: Tagliata.

Grazzano Badoglio and Penango: Bisoglio, Podere dei Mossetti.

Portacomaro: Bodina, Borlotto, Migliandolo, Miravalle, Sassia, Serra, Vadonia.

Rocchetta Tanaro: Garbera, Limonte, Rollone, San Bernardo.

BENCHMARK WINES

Braida Grignolino d'Asti Limonte***PS, Crivelli Grignolino d'Asti***PS, Incisa della Rocchetta Grignolino d'Asti***PS.

Evasio Garrone***, Santa Caterina Monferace***.

Agostino Pavia**, Franco Roero**, La Fiammenga**, Montalbera Grigné**, Santa Caterina Arlandino**, Tommaso Bosco Grignolino d'Asti**.

Castello di Neive*, Francesco Rinaldi*, Fratelli Giacosa*.

Grignolino del Monferrato Casalese

The Monferrato (from the Latin words *mons ferratus,* meaning "hill of iron") can be divided into the Monferrato Casalese or Basso Monferrato (Lower Monferrato), the Monferrato Astigiano (divided into Upper and Lower Monferrato Astigiano), and the Alto Monferrato (Upper Monferrato of Acqui, Ovada, and Gavi). Despite its *alto* designation, the latter is actually located farthest south (because it was once common practice in Italy to attribute geographical names in an order based on proximity to the sea) and extends from the Val Bormida down to the Ligurian Apennines. The Monferrato Casalese is therefore the one situated farthest north; the denomination's boundaries are the Po River to the north, the Tanaro River to the east, and the Grignolino d'Asti denomination immediately to the south. Important townships in the denomination (worth remembering in order to understand this wine's terroir) are Rosignano, Sala, and Cella Monte to the north and Camagna, Vignale Monferrato, and Grazzano to the south; Casale Monferrato and Ozzano also boast significant terroirs. Though it is not technically within the denomination (because of a bureaucratic error at the time the official production zone was drawn, but likely soon to be fixed), the town of Lu Monferrato, to the south just beyond the denomination's borders, is also very relevant in any discussion of the terroir of the Grignolino del Monferrato Casalese denomination. However, because the commune's territory falls outside of the official denomination, these Grignolino wines are labeled Piemonte Grignolino (instead of Grignolino del Monferrato Casalese), but they are, to all effect, Monferrato Casalese wines. Both Grignolino denominations, d'Asti and Monferrato Casalese, have soils that offer different mixes of sand, loam, and calcareous clay. Generalizing somewhat, it is useful to think of the Grignolino d'Asti denomination as being dominated by sand and the Monferrato Casalese production zone as more calcareous marly-clay (very differently from the Asti area, there is little sand in the soils around Alessandria). In fact, most of the soils in the Monferrato Casalese where Grignolino grows look whitish in color (the *terre bianche*), and the wines are relatively bigger (if Grignolino wines can ever be truly qualified as "big"). The Monferrato boasts a great diversity of calcareous marls, the most important two belonging to different geologic formations: the older Formazione di Casale Monferrato (formed 57 to 36 million years ago in the Lower-Middle Eocene), and the more recent Gruppo di Pietra de Cantoni (including the Formazione di Cardona and the Formazione di Antognola formed 17.5 to 14 million years ago). The former formation, more common in the northern part of the denomination, is much harder (cement-like), while the latter has lower calcium carbonate concentrations and more clay, breaking down when exposed to air and water, and is more common in the southern reaches of the denomination. The different terroirs of the Grignolino del Monferrato Casalese are easy to recognize in the wines, with a little practice. This wealth in different terroirs is showcased by the numerous and various outstanding Grignolino wines that were once made in the Alessandria province, all identified by a specific place-name: Grignolino del Castelletto (made with grapes grown around Castelletto Merli); Grignolino di Corteranzo (made with grapes grown around Murisengo); Grignolino di Olivola (made with grapes grown around Olivola); Grignolino di San Giorgio (made with grapes grown around San Giorgio Monferrato); Grignolino di San Pancrazio (made with grapes grown around parts of the communes of Terruggia Monferrato and of Rosignano Monferrato). All these wines were made

within the boundaries of today's Grignolino del Monferrato Casalese. I love Grignolino, one of my favorite grape varieties, and have been drinking wines made with it incessantly for the past thirty years. I therefore have a very good idea of how the terroir of the Grignolino del Monferrato Casalese production zone is best subdivided. There are five macroareas: Colline del Po, Lu Monferrato, Valle Cerrina, Valle Ghenza, and Vignale Monferrato. Each one of these is very clearly linked to recognizable, area-specific wine types. The Winkler index is similar in the five macroareas (around 1800); the central portion of the denomination is warmer and drier, whereas the areas bordering the Po River (where the towns of Rosignano Monferrato and Ozzano are found) are more humid and rainy. Most of the vineyards lie between 250 and 400 meters above sea level. Though some knowledgeable experts, like Franco Angelini of the Paolo Angelini estate (one of the best producers of Grignolino wine anywhere), believe that Vignale and Lu are one macroarea based on topographical similarities and geographical proximity, I believe differently, for the simple reason that I find the wines made in each area too different. Lu Monferrato's Grignolinos are by far the lightest of all Grignolino del Monferrato Casalese wines. They have quite a bit in common with the finer wines made in the Grignolino d'Asti denomination: tellingly, the wines of Tenuta Santa Caterina, made in the area of Grazzano Badoglio, in the Asti denomination, are very similar to those of Lu, and in fact the vineyards of these two townships are not that far removed from each other. The five macroareas have the following characteristics:

Colline del Po: a band-like area that runs parallel to the Po River, with mostly clay soils that give bigger, darker-colored Grignolino wines that have structure but less finesse. This is the Saint-Estèphe of the Grignolino del Monferrato Casalese production zone. An especially large area, the territory of the town of Ozzano pushes southward almost like a nail driven into the heart of the Monferrato

Casalese production zone. Therefore, even though the estates of Cantine Valpane (in the town of Ozzano) and Marco Botto (in the town of Sala Monferrato, basically a stone's throw away from Ozzano) ought to fall within the Colline del Po' macroarea, their vineyards are planted on soil types that are much more typical of the Valle Ghenza (and so these two estates make wines more typical of the latter macroarea). The Paolo Angelini estate owns vines in both the Colline del Po and Valle Ghenza macroareas and blends them; importantly, he owns vines on the Bricco Robiano (in Valle Ghenza), one of the best crus of the whole denomination, which explains why the estate's Grignolinos are often characterized by a bit more refinement than those made with only Colline del Po wines. Producers worth knowing: Paolo Angelini (town of Ozzano), Castello di Gabiano (town of Gabiano).

Lu Monferrato: Has a warmer and less rainy microclimate than other sections of the denomination; its vineyards lie at slightly lower altitudes, on average (about two hundred meters above sea level or less). Soils are mixed calcareous clays that give especially pale-colored, light-bodied, and saline wines. Even by Grignolino wine standards, the wines of Lu are remarkably light in texture and color (medium-light pink to dark pink being their normal hue). Very refined, if not especially deep, and with just a little practice, *anyone* can recognize them as coming from Lu. This is the Margaux of the Grignolino del Monferrato Casalese production zone. Producers worth knowing: Casalone and Tenuta San Sebastiano/De Alessi.

Valle Cerrina: Probably the single most difficult area to characterize in just one wine style, with vineyards planted at various altitudes (humidity becomes a factor) and with many different soil mixes (generally there is plenty of marl). These are usually the latest grapes to be harvested in the Grignolino del Monferrato Casalese denomination (even though the difference might be just a few days). Though it is difficult to draw firm conclusions about the

area's style of wines, I think these are some of the spiciest of all Grignolino wines. Think of this as the Pessac-Léognan of the Grignolino del Monferrato Casalese production zone (more Pessac than Léognan, actually). Producers worth knowing: Pierino Vellano (town of Camino) and Tenuta Tenaglia (town of Serralunga di Crea).

Valle Ghenza: Located in the heart of the Grignolino del Monferrato Casalese denomination. Documents dating back to 1248 mention the "Valle Ghensa." Soils here are mostly calcareous, though some sections have a good amount of clay. Therefore, these Grignolino wines are some of the most floral and well-balanced wines of the whole denomination, with a bright savory (rather than saline, which is more Asti-like) quality, with a juicy red-cherry component. Some of the wines from this area can be very similar to those of the Colline del Po; in fact, the Grignolino wines by Cantine Valpane and those of Marco Botto (as I explained above, these should be viewed as typical of the Valle Ghensa rather than the Colline del Po) are very similar in aroma and flavor profile to the wines of Vicara and Castello d'Uviglie. This is the Saint-Julien of the Grignolino del Monferrato Casalese production zone. Producers worth knowing: Castello d'Uviglie (town of Rosignano Monferrato) and Vicara (town of Rosignano Monferrato).

Vignale Monferrato: This is, in my view, the grand cru area of the denomination, with wines that have it all: depth, concentration, balance, and above-average complexity. They are also some of the darkest colored of all Grignolino wines (but remember that "dark Grignolino" is an oxymoron, because the wines are anything but). Throughout history, only Portacomaro of Grignolino d'Asti has enjoyed as lofty a reputation as Vignale's wines. In fact, about twenty years ago, there was a movement to have the town's territory officially recognized as a specific, separate Grignolino ("Grignolino di Vignale"), but fortunately, cooler heads prevailed and a larger, less splintered denomination was created that is easier to market and understand. The soils are mostly a mix of calcareous clays. This is the Pauillac of the Grignolino del Monferrato Casalese production zone. (To be clear, I mean the southern sector of Pauillac, the one where the two Pichons and Latour are located, not the Moussas sector of Pauillac.) Producers worth knowing: Accornero, Gaudio, Il Mongetto, and Marco Canato.

Franco Angelini believes that the wines from the five macroareas are distinguishable by the different intensity of aroma and flavor descriptors, and therefore I include below, with his permission, the breakdown as he sees it (save for the aforementioned difference in view we have relative to Lu and Vignale). And besides maintaining a distinction between Lu and Vignale, I have also taken the liberty of adding the "florality" descriptor to his list, since I think it is a sine qua non of all Grignolino wines.

Wine characteristics (from fleshiest and darkest to lightest) in relation to townships:

Color: Valle Cerrina, Colline del Po, Valle Ghenza, Vignale, Lu.

Spiciness: Valle Cerrina, Colline del Po, Valle Ghenza, Vignale, Lu.

Structure: Colline del Po, Vignale, Valle Cerrina, Valle Ghenza, Lu.

Elegance: Valle Ghenza, Vignale, Lu, Colline del Po, Valle Cerrina.

Florality: Lu, Valle Ghenza, Vignale, Colline del Po, Valle Cerrina.

The Best Crus

Casale Monferrato: Magnano, Pozzo Sant'Evasio.

Castelletto Merli: Cabiola.

Lu Monferrato: Capletta (Cappelletta), Samnent (San Benedetto).

Olivola: La Presidenta (this is where Bruno Giacosa used to buy grapes and his version of Grignolino wine was simply outstanding), Màndola, Ròccolo.

Ozzano Monferrato: Bricco Robiano.

Rosignano Monferrato: San Bastiano, Bricco dell'Uccelletta.

Sala Monferrato: Canestrina.

San Giorgio Monferrato: Besso.

Vignale Monferrato: Bricco del Bosco, Bricco Mondalino, De Bernardi, Rudifrà, Vignotto.

BENCHMARK WINES

Accornero Bricco del Bosco Vecchie Vigne***PS.

Accornero Bricco del Bosco***, Gaudio / Bricco Mondalino Bricco Mondalino***, Paolo Angelini Casalese Arbian***, Vicara***.

Cantina Valpane**, Casalone La Capletta**, Castello di Uviglie**, Davide Beccaria Marco Botto**, Marco Canato Celio**, Pierino Vellano**, Tenuta San Sebastiano Piemonte Grignolino**.

Pio Cesare* (made with grapes from the Rosignano area).

Malvasia Bianca di Basilicata

THE GRAPE VARIETY

My love for native grapes and what they stand for is exemplified by this grape variety even more than others. That is because I am personally responsible for having initiated its return from oblivion, with the help, passion, and foresight of the fine people at the Cantina di Venosa. In 2000, there was no monovariety Malvasia Bianca di Basilicata being bottled (although there was one wine apparently made mostly with Malvasia Bianca di Basilicata that was being sold commercially: the Topazio, by Consorzio Viticultori Associati Vulture, labeled as a Basilicata Bianco). The grape had been all but forgotten and was used to make local wine blends that nobody ever spoke of (much less wrote about). And yet I knew Veronelli loved its wines and called both grape and wine "Malvasia del Vulture," going so far to suggest pairing it with provolone cheese and even with octopus in chili-pepper-spiced tomato sauce (Veronelli 1981). Historically, white Malvasia wines in Basilicata were made with grapes from vineyards located above five hundred meters above

sea level, especially those on the mountain slopes past the Potenza–Foggia railway tracks. Over the years, during my walks on the rugged terrain of the Vulture volcano, it was obvious that the white Malvasia growing there was unlike any other I had seen anywhere else (I write "white Malvasia" because there is also a dark-berried Malvasia Nera di Basilicata). Not only did it look different (a very long, scrawny bunch with smaller-than-average berries, it is a little like Malvasia di Lipari), but the wine made by local farmers was different from that of the Lipari Islands or any other Malvasia variety I had tried before. Locals told me that in the past Malvasia Bianca di Basilicata was often blended into Aglianico wines to add freshness, whereas today it is most often blended with Moscato Bianco to make either dry or sweet wines. Apparently, it is hardy and resistant, though sensitive to potassium and magnesium deficiencies as well as oidium.

In 2001, just as I had done previously with Lazio producers relative to Malvasia del Lazio, I began urging all those in the Vulture willing to listen to consider looking into bringing their local variety back to everyone's attention. The problem was that Malvasia Bianca di Basilicata had been reduced to only a few scattered vines mixed in with others in often abandoned sites; consequently, individual family estates would never be able to bottle the wine in any meaningful quantity. Thankfully, the Cantina Sociale di Venosa, a forward-thinking social cooperative led by winemaker Luigi Cantatore, understood the merits of the idea and the project, initiating a Malvasia Bianca di Basilicata selection and propagation process. With over five hundred members scouring through their vineyards, it was more than likely they would succeed in producing a Malvasia Bianca di Basilicata wine again. So it was: D'Avalos was born, and since followed up by the even better Verso Bianco, a truly lovely wine. Thanks to Cantina di Venosa's example, Eleano, with their Fedra wine, and many others have followed suit, and I am both happy and proud to report that Malvasia Bianca di Basilicata is back, with more estates looking to make a wine from it. We now know that there are at least two biotypes of Malvasia Bianca di Basilicata growing in the vineyards. That of the Rapolla area is different from that of the Venosa area, and guess what: their wines are different, too. Just imagine: only fifteen years ago we knew nothing about this grape and wine, but thanks to the passion of wine people working together, a new grape and wine have been born again.

SPECIFIC TERROIRS

Basilicata

Venosa and Rapolla

The Malvasia Bianca di Basilicata of the Venosa area grows on mostly white clay-calcareous soils (actually, an even mix of 30 percent clay, 35 percent sand, and 35 percent loam) in which the limestone helps provide freshness and a savory lift to the wines. This particular biotype is especially vigorous, and the 157 rootstock is used to help contain its natural proclivity. Differently from other Malvasia Bianca di Basilicata biotypes, the Venosa has a stocky bunch and very thin-skinned grapes (you can practically see the pips from outside the grape); most importantly, it is a more neutral grape variety than the biotype of Rapolla and other areas, something I had noted in the past (D'Agata 2014). Venosa's wine is fresh and juicy, with a strong note of sweet citrus fruits (lime, tangerine) and minty herbs, but shows neither the notes of cinnamon, white pepper, and nutmeg nor the fresh citrus (orange, lemon, and grapefruit) more typical of the wines made with other Malvasia Bianca di Basilicata biotypes.

BENCHMARK WINES

Cantina di Venosa Verso Bianco***; Cantina di Venosa D'Avalos**, Eleano**, Terra dei Re**.

Malvasia di Lipari

THE GRAPE VARIETY

Italy's seven Lipari islands (also known as Aeolian islands) of Lipari, Salina, Panarea, Vulcano, Stromboli, Alicudi, and Filicudi form a volcanic archipelago that has been the home of the Malvasia di Lipari grape variety for many centuries. There is ample documentation attesting to this wine grape's cultivation on the islands, and how important it was in the production of raisins and wines. Cupani (1696) documents that wine called *malvagia* had been produced on the islands since the first century B.C. at least, though we cannot be sure it was made with the Malvasia di Lipari documented on the islands since the seventeenth century. In fact, the islands were originally more famous for their different types of raisins: *passolina* and *uva passa*. The former is made with Uvetta di Corinto (a raisin of very small size, a little like the grains of black pepper), used mostly in food preparations (not just desserts), whereas the latter was made with white grapes, much larger in size and without seeds (unlike Uvetta di Corinto). With the onslaught of phylloxera,

which appeared on the islands in 1891 (Baroncini 2016), most of the island vineyards were wiped out (so much for the infernal louse not surviving in volcanic soils), leading to a mass exodus of people who went to look for work elsewhere. The loss of island population was worse on the smallest of the Lipari islands, with as many as 80 to 90 percent of the locals abandoning Alicudi, Filicudi, and Panarea. (Vulcano, also very small in size, did not share the same fate—only because it was never much inhabited to begin with, given its nondormant volcanic state and ongoing eruptive activity.) In the 1970s and especially the 1980s, viticulture was brought back to the island archipelago: only this time, it was wine's turn to be the main player. Raisins are still made in the Lipari archipelago, but they are the less prestigious and visible agricultural product of the islands. (The islands have since become famous for their excellent capers, too.)

Malvasia di Lipari is immediately recognizable due to its very scrawny, elongated, cylindrical (rarely cylindrical-conical) grape bunch and round berries with thin skins. The variety has always been described just so—for example, in the *L'Illustrazione Italiana* reportage on the Aeolian Islands (Ristuccia 1957), where it was reported as having "grappoli lunghi, radi e dorati [grape bunches that are long, sparse, and golden]." This is a very important point to know about Malvasia di Lipari—that that's what the variety looks like and has always looked like. So when you walk about vineyards on the Lipari Islands, that's also what you should expect to see in any "Malvasia" vineyard you might walk about in. A landmark and oft-cited 2006 study by Crespan et al. indicated that Malvasia delle Lipari (the variety's correct name is Malvasia di Lipari; the name Malvasia delle Lipari that is used in the study title is just plain wrong: it refers to the wine made from the variety) is identical to Sardinia's Malvasia di Sardegna, Calabria's Greco Bianco (called in the study by its synonym of Greco di Gerace), Croatia's Malvasia Dubrovačka, Madeira's Malvasia Cândida, and Spain's Malvasía de Sitges. (Madeira's Malvasia Cândida Roxa and the Malvasía Rosada of the Canary Islands are two red-berried mutations of the latter variety.) The trouble is, I've never talked to anybody in Calabria who has told me they think their Greco Bianco variety is identical to Sicily's Malvasia di Lipari; and regional diatribes and parochialisms aside, it's hard not to agree with them. Though there are clear-cut morphologic similarities between Greco Bianco and Malvasia di Lipari, there are also enough differences to make one raise at least an eyebrow (or two) at their supposedly being identical varieties. Most importantly, the wines made from each have nothing in common, and it does not take any great deal of experience to realize that the thick, resiny, and tannic palate presence of a Greco Bianco wine is not even distantly related to the lithe, fresh, juicy, and delicate mouthfeel of a Malvasia delle Lipari. It may just be a case of ecotypes, or those biotypes that have evolved over the centuries in specific, highly different habitats (which is most likely what happened in the genesis of Malvasia di Sardegna, which, differently from Greco Bianco, at least does look a little something like Malvasia di Lipari), changing their phenotypic aspect over time in response to different environmental pressures. However, I point out that when supposedly identical varieties give wines that taste completely different from each other despite similar winemaking methods employed, a number of scientists have stated that the grape varieties in question ought to be considered distinct, even though genetic testing at the current state of our scientific knowledge might determine the varieties under examination to be the same (Pelsy et al. 2010; Emanuelli et al. 2013). Another study that looked at monoterpene glycoside profiles of different Malvasia samples (Malvasia Bianca Lunga, Malvasia del Lazio, and Malvasia di Lipari) showed that there was no similarity between the first and the other two Malvasia varieties. Instead, both Malvasia del Lazio and Malvasia di Lipari shared similarly high furan/pyran linalool concentrations; and the two diverged greatly on the basis of the concentrations of 7-hydroxygeraniol (high in Malvasia di Lipari, virtually nonexistent in Malvasia del Lazio—differently from geraniol levels, which were relatively high in both). The study confirmed that Malvasia di Lipari is the most aromatic of the three varieties. The grapes in this study were picked in the same vineyard in the same vintage, and therefore such environmental and viticultural factors were not confounding variables; therefore, it seems likely that observed differences in the monoterpene levels were due to the genetics of the individual varieties (Flamini 2013). From a viticultural standpoint, Malvasia di Lipari is an early-budding variety susceptible to spring frosts and to powdery mildew. It's a very irregular producer, and worse (for farmers), low-yielding; it thrives on volcanic soils but is not very vigorous.

SPECIFIC TERROIRS

The Lipari Islands

Over the years, my voyages to the Lipari Islands have taught me a number of things. For one,

I do not use the word "voyages" lightly: I have been stranded on these beautiful islands more than once in the last thirty years when the hydrofoils were unable to leave port and venture out into the blue wrath of Neptune, aided by Eolus, the Roman god of winds. (It is not by chance that the islands carry the name they do.) All clouds have a silver lining, though, and frankly, spending an extra day or two on these beautiful isles was something I have never complained about. How beautiful? Beautiful enough to be listed as a UNESCO World Heritage Site in 2000. In Sicily there are fourteen estates producing Malvasia delle Lipari wines and at least sixty grape growers. At last report, the hectares under vine to Malvasia di Lipari are sixty-five (ISTAT data, 2010), located mainly on the island of Salina; but the grapevine has recently reached Vulcano, Panarea, and Stromboli as well. Over two hundred thousand bottles a year of Malvasia delle Lipari are produced, most of which is in the sweet Passito or air-dried version (about 80 percent of the total annual production volume; the remaining 20 percent is fortified, or *liquoroso naturale*). Honeyed and sweet but offering very delicate fresh peach, dried apricot, orange peel, and sweet spicy and herbal nuances that are lifted by remarkable freshness for such a hot-weather wine, Malvasia di Lipari wines are unique in the panorama of southern Italian wines. The dry wine made with this variety, simply labeled Salina Malvasia, is an outstanding dry white wine in which the resiny, aromatic note of the variety adds noteworthy complexity to the saline, floral aromas and flavors.

Over the centuries, the Lipari Islands became famous for their production of raisins and Malvasia wines. Commerce transaction volumes of *passolina* and *uva passa* were not small: in 1800, sixteen thousand barrels of both were sent from the Lipari ports off to northern lands. In 1832, there were reportedly fifteen hundred people earning their living from viticulture or vineyard-related work on Stromboli alone. (To put that number into perspective for you, Stromboli is a marvelously beautiful, rugged island, but as far as islands go, it is not exactly the size of Australia, and there are only five hundred people living there today.) At the same time (1832), there were about 350,000 kilograms of *passolina* produced a year in the entire Aeolian archipelago. That business was booming in the Lipari raisin sector is further demonstrated by the fact that only a few years later, in 1850, a whopping 903,229 kilograms of *passolina* were sent off from the port of Messina. Admittedly, that's a lot of raisins; by contrast, wine production appears to have been less copious than that of raisins, at least until the mid-nineteenth century: in 1847, there were a reported three hundred barrels sold of what we would call today Malvasia delle Lipari wine. Though there were undoubtedly many vineyards on the islands, the islanders' incomes were mostly derived from the raisining of grapes, not from turning them into wine. Unlike today, when the bulk of Lipari wine grapes grows on the island of Salina (historically always the greenest of the Aeolian isles), with very small pockets on a few others (Vulcano, Stromboli, Panarea, and Lipari), other islands had a florid viticulture at the end of the seventeenth century (Campis 1980). At that time, Lipari, Salina, Panarea, and surprisingly, Filicudi (known as Fidicudi at that time) were apparently covered with vineyards.

It appears that English seafaring merchants were big buyers of raisins (but wine, too) from the islands, as documented, for example, in the 1637 and 1638 books of a Samuel Bootheuse stating at least one merchant company in Leghorn was well "furnished with zibibbi." Arthur Penington was another merchant based mainly in the port of Messina who also traded in "zibibbi" in the seventeenth century (La Greca 2016). In fact, in the 1600s, raisins were divided into different quality classes, and the English merchants paid for them accordingly: those of the Aeolian isles were highly thought of. The most sought after were the raisins of Corinth (then known as "currants"), produced in the Ionian islands mainly; next in order of quality were the "raisins of the sun" or *"raisins solis*," made with grapes grown in Spain; in third place, the "raisins of Lipari," followed by the raisins of Smyrne (also known as sultanas); and last, the "raisins of Malaga," also from Spain, and the cheapest of the lot. Prices paid for these raisins ranged from the 44 pence per hundredweight for the "currants" to the 33 pence per hundredweight fetched by *raisins solis* and the 28 pence per hundredweight of Lipari raisins (a hundredweight being 112 pounds [or 50.8 kilograms]). Malaga raisins were only paid 20 pence per hundredweight.

Although raisins were all-important for the commercial well-being of the Aeolian archipelago back then, it is very clear that it was not just Lipari's raisins that were exciting the palates of those times. In 1776, Michel-Jean de Borch (despite the sound of his name, he was of Polish nationality) writes of the "many grapes used to make wine on the islands of Folicudi, Alicuri, Vasselucco, Panarea and le Saline." (Clearly, Folicudi and Alicuri are today's Filicudi and Alicudi; Vasselucco is a small rocky outpost known as Basiluzzo today but not big enough to be listed as one of the Lipari Islands; "le Saline" was the term employed back then to describe the islands of Salina, Lipari, and Stromboli together.) Just a few years later, in 1788, another world traveler, Jean de Lévesque Burigny, writes that the local Malvasia made a wonderful, much-sought-after wine. Another believer in the quality of Lipari Malvasia wine was one of Italy's greatest scientists of all time, Lazzaro Spallanzani, who spent thirty-five days on the Lipari Islands in 1788. He documented (Spallanzani 1793) that the variety's yields were low and that only about two thousand barrels of "outstanding" wine were made a year, almost all of which was exported; in fact, Spallanzani lamented that he had trouble finding the wine on the island for his own libations. Ever the scientist, he also described in some detail how the Malvasia grapes were grown and how the wine was produced at the time. The most common training method was the *pergola* (canopy), which provided the hanging grapes with protective shade from the hot Mediterranean sun;

interestingly, Spallanzani mentions that Abbot Gaetano Trovatini was one of the few growers to have chosen an espalier system, which made it easier for him to plant wheat in between the rows of vines. (Everyone else planted vegetables on the ground beneath the canopies.) The grapes were picked at full maturity and air-dried on cane mats for eight to ten days, then pressed in *palmenti* (the typical winemaking cellar structures of southern Italy and its islands, many of which are still visible today), and the must fermented in wood barrels. In 1853, professors Antonio Prestandrea and Pietro Calcara (La Greca 2009) described the agriculture of the Lipari Islands and stated clearly that "Malvasia wine" was the archipelago's most important product at the time. This observation was confirmed by Michele Lojacono Pojero, of the Royal Botanical Gardens of Palermo, when he visited the islands in 1877–78: he pointed out how what looked to be "sterile and ungrateful volcanic lands" guaranteed instead "delicious wines of maximum alcohol level" (Lojacono Pojero 1878). Like others before him, Lojacono Pojero reported that Salina was more fertile and produced more grapes and wine than did Lipari, as well as that Stromboli was "entirely covered with vineyards."

With the advent of phylloxera, Malvasia delle Lipari wine production fell noticeably, with only small, almost anecdotal amounts made on Salina and Stromboli. According to one detailed report, only fifty hectoliters of Malvasia di Lipari wine were being produced a year by the end of the 1920s and the beginning of the 1930s (Speranza 1953). In 1929, in an effort to ward off the danger of this wine disappearing forever, it was recommended that the few winemakers left on the islands associate together to form a consortium in order to help reduce costs and better market the wine, since the few small producers left were not able, on their own, to increase and improve production or promote the wine (Paulsen 1929). It was especially thanks to the efforts, energy, and passion of Nino Lo Schiavo that the Malvasia di Lipari variety and the wine did not disappear altogether. In 1930 a first meeting was held, and in 1942 the name "Malvasia di Lipari" became official (though that has been since changed: today, the specific grape variety is called Malvasia di Lipari, whereas the wine is called Malvasia delle Lipari). Proceedings at the time were slow because already then producers were aware that not all the islands made Malvasia wine, and that the best terroirs for the variety were the islands of Salina and Stromboli. Some feared, not unreasonably, that use of the name Lipari would bring to mind the name of one of the Lipari Islands (Lipari) that had never been much linked to Malvasia wine production. But the name "Malvasia di Lipari" was already in use at the time: for example, the 1931 *Guida gastronomica italiana,* by the Touring Club Italiano (an enogastronomy guide), advised, "Malvasia di Lipari: Outstanding wine made with the Malvasia variety grown on the Eolian islands, especially on the islands of Salina and Stromboli." Finally, it was decided to use the Lipari Islands' names not only to identify the wine (given that the archipelago was better known than any one single island; therefore, its use was more likely to help awareness and sales of the wine) but also to allow the indication of the island where the wine was made, such as Salina or Stromboli.

To their credit, the island producers did not sit around twiddling their fingers while the meetings went on (and on) in order to come to a decision, and in 1931, Nino Lo Schiavo, Giuseppe Re, and Giuseppe Giuffrè founded the "Società della Malvasia," which would bottle, label, and sell Malvasia wine from the islands. The initiative met with success: records show that by 1939 roughly 50 percent of all Malvasia wine made on the islands (amounting to ninety-six hundred liters) was being sold by this company. By 1940, yearly production of Malvasia wine had climbed back up to four hundred hectoliters. In 1952, of sixty-eight new vineyards planted on the islands on fourteen hectares, ten were planted to Malvasia di Lipari. Business was so good that others tried to get in on the act—for example, Domenico Bella-

chioma and Giovanni Randazzo, who created their own company with a bottling facility in Messina. (In other words, they were bottling the wine outside of the islands, something that with a little more foresight would not have been allowed.)

Soils on the islands are rich in phosphorus and potassium and low in nitrogen. Average annual rainfall is 600 millimeters (of which 440 millimeters are concentrated in the autumn and winter months). Winds are mainly from the northwest (the *maestrale*), west (the *ponente* wind), and southeast (*scirocco*). The Huglin index is 2900. There are 160 hectares of grapevines on the islands, of which 95 are planted to Malvasia (67 on Salina, 18 on Lipari, the rest divided up between Vulcano, Stromboli, and Panarea). The Malvasia grapes grow from the flatlands up to 350 meters above sea level.

THE LIPARI SUBZONES (OR THE INDIVIDUAL ISLAND TERROIRS)

In the 1700s, vineyards and orchards were planted as high as one hundred meters above sea level on Stromboli and Panarea, while they were planted up to three hundred meters on Salina, Lipari, Alicudi, and Filicudi. Very interestingly, even in the eighteenth century, the inhabitants of the islands grew specific grapes in specific parts of the islands only, and various authors described where on the islands each grape variety grew best (Rodriquez 1841; Lojacono Pojero 1878). Interestingly, other grapes were also used to make a sweet "Malvasia" wine on the various Lipari islands, but the superiority of the wine made with authentic Malvasia di Lipari grapes was such that the latter's wine cost almost twice as much as any other made. (Whereas the Malvasia delle Lipari would cost fifty lire per hectoliter, a wine made with other, less expensive white grapes would cost twenty-nine lire, and one made with common red grapes would cost only twenty-two lire.) By the first half of the nineteenth century, specific island terroirs were also starting to get recognized: relative to "le Saline," these were the *cuntrade* (or *cuntrate*, both Sicilian dialect for *contrade* ["crus"], the plural form of *contrada*)—a word that is commonly used in southern Italy to signify subzones. In his delightful (and remarkably precise) article "Breve cenno storico sull'isola di Lipari," Carlo Rodriguez (1841) lists the best *contrade* of the islands based on the quality of their grapes: Capo (the place now known as Capo Faro, on the island of Salina), Gramignazzi, Lene, Lingua, Malfa, Pollara, and Stromboli.

Filicudi and Alicudi

Though some vines were planted on these two islands (more so on Filicudi), Spallazani reports that there was no Malvasia planted there in the eighteenth century, which seems strange, given what others had written. Today neither island is known for its vineyards, and as of the writing of this book, no Malvasia wine is being made for commercial sale from either island. Racheli (1983) has written that it is a shame viticulture has not been brought back to these two little islands, given the large number of terraces "that have been built by our ancestors and that now lie abandoned."

Lipari

Well known in the seventeenth and eighteenth centuries for its large extension of vines, Lipari boasted two areas—Piano di Conti and I Piani Grandi—that the abbot Francesco Ferrara deemed especially good for Malvasia production (Ferrara 1810). Lojacono Pojero (1878) wrote that the island's *contrade* associated with quality wine production were Castellaro, Maduro, Piano Conte, and Varisana (on Lipari). I would humbly submit that Castellaro is still a quality area today (though even better in my opinion for the Corinto Nero variety than for Malvasia di Lipari); look for the very good wines of Tenuta di Castellaro, for example. Did you know that Lipari's wine was the source of inspiration for one of California's oldest wine brands, Liparita? According to La Greca (2016), William Keyes, a geologist who settled in the Napa Valley, found the terrain there to remind him of Lipari's, and so he decided upon the "Liparita"

name for his estate. His wine was the first California wine to win a gold medal at the 1900 Paris Exhibition.

Panarea

At 3.4 square kilometers, Panarea is the smallest of the Lipari islands. (Some consider Basiluzzo the eighth Lipari island, and in that case it would be the smallest of the lot; but most everyone classifies the Lipari as a seven-island archipelago.) It is also the most fashionable of these islands, attracting a remarkably well-heeled and a young, hip clientele, and becoming a tourist hot spot in the summertime, with hotels packed to the rafters and a navy of boats and yachts moored in its bays. The highest peak on Panarea is the Punta del Corvo (421 meters above sea level). Andrea Pedrani is the only one making a Malvasia di Lipari wine on the island, in Contrada Ditella: he first made a dry version (called L'Insolita) in 2011 with the help of a winemaking colleague (Nino Caravaglio of the eponymous Salina estate), then followed up with the more typical, sweet version. Pedrani's estate is called La Vigna di Casa Pedrani, and its Malvasia vineyard lies at only 70 meters above sea level. Though it is much too early to tell what viticulture and the wines of Panarea are like in comparison with those of the other Lipari islands, from what I have been able to observe in these first few years of wine production, the harvest occurs generally a little earlier there than it does on Salina, and always before the end of September. Panarea also boasts numerous olive trees, which tells us that the climate is rather mild. The wine seems more graceful and perfumed, with higher acidity, than those made on the other Lipari islands.

Salina

Viticulture on Salina dates back to very ancient times indeed. Fossilized pips have been found in archaeological digs at Portella di Salina; these pips were of both *Vitis vinifera silvestris* (the wild grapevine) and *Vitis vinifera sativa* (the cultivated grapevine) and date back to 1450 B.C. At the very least, it appears that wild grapevines were being domesticated in this part of the archipelago. Writing in 1816, William Henry Smyth noted that "Salina's Malvasia has no peers." Lothringen (1893–96) wrote that Malvasia di Lipari was produced especially on Salina and Stromboli, and that on Salina, the areas of note for Malvasia di Lipari were Malfa and Santa Marina. By contrast, the areas of Puorri, Quadara di Lingua, Ramignazzi, Satana, Sierru I Viscotti, Vaddi I Chiesa (known as Valdichiesa today), Vadduni a Castagna (all near the town of Malfa), and Pollara, he wrote, were best for the "uva mostale nera"—black grapes of various varieties. Interestingly, though Malvasia was harvested from the end of September to the beginning of October on the other Lipari islands, on Salina the harvest could last until the end of the month, since apparently it was where the grapes ripened best. At roughly twenty-nine square kilometers, Salina is not exactly small. (Unless you like *really* long walks, you most definitely need a car or scooter to drive around if you wish to see all of the island.) It is the greenest and richest in water of the Lipari islands, taking its name from a lake near Santa Marina; the small body of water was once famous for the quality of its salt (and hence the island's name of *salina,* or "from where salt is extracted"). Salina also boasts two of the highest peaks of the archipelago: the Monte Fossa delle Felci (962 meters in height) and the Monte dei Porri (860 meters). It is these two mountains that explain Salina's ancient Greek name of Didyme (which is also the name of Tasca d'Almerita's dry Salina Malvasia), which means "twins": looking at them from the northeast, the two mountains do look almost identical. Not just Salina's topography, but also its geology is especially different from that of the other Lipari isles, and there are different soils in different sections of the island. For example, though there is mostly volcanic sand between Lingua and Santa Marina (both towns are right by the seaside), above Santa Marina (toward the town of Leni) there is more clay, and grapevines planted there suffer less in droughty years. In my experience, it is because of this clay that Malvasia wines made with grapes grown in the higher vineyards of the northern half of the island tend to have slightly more alcoholic power. This is partly due to the fact that the grapes ripen better (more evenly) thanks to the clay, which helps diminish water stress. Clearly, Malvasia di Lipari grapes grown in the area of Lingua and Santa Marina also ripen earlier, so producers will usually harvest these grapes early so as to avoid too rapid a drop in total acidity. In most vintages, by harvesting in the third week of August (say, around August 22 or 24), and by following this with the more or less customary one month of air-drying, the Malvasia delle Lipari wines made will still clock in at about seven grams per liter total acidity (depending, clearly, on the vintage conditions and individual producer's wine style: but the former do not vary much on a yearly basis on Salina or the other islands, and the latter cannot push the grape harvest much beyond the end of September). Nevertheless, at Valdichiesa and Leni (situated at roughly four hundred meters above sea level), where it is shady and cool, the harvest always takes place one month later than it does at Lingua. The *contrade* of Capo Faro and Ramignazzi are also fairly late ripening. Last but not least, Salina is strongly characterized (more so than the other Lipari islands) by very strong diurnal temperature variations. In general, there is a large difference in Salina's minimum and maximum temperature range of January and August (11–15°C and 24–30°C, respectively). Rainfall is most copious in the winter (eleven days of rain on average each month in December and January), less so during springtime, and hardly at all during summer (on average, July has 0.6 days of rain); in fact, most of the rain falls within a fifty-to-ninety-day stretch in the winter.

Stromboli

Stromboli is a cute little rock of an island; it is my favorite member of the Lipari clan, instantly recognizable by the permanent wisp of smoke that emanates from is crater top—a reminder that this is one of Italy's five still-active volcanos, and a potentially very dangerous one. (Its peak is at 926 meters above sea level, the second highest in the Lipari archipelago.) Based on all the information I have gathered, Stromboli's was one of the Lipari's highest-quality Malvasia di Lipari wines. As early as the eighteenth century, Malvasia grapes were preferentially planted near the marina, with exposures ranging from north to east. Wine grapes destined for "common wine" (*vino comunale*) were planted on the flanks of the volcano, where there was a colder microclimate. William Henry Smyth first visited the Lipari Islands in 1815, and immediately began writing about them and their wine; according to him, Stromboli had very fertile soil and grapevines planted "quite high up the mountain" (Smyth 1824). More importantly, he defines the Malvasia wines as "of the Mediterranean's best." In 1865, Francesco Lawley distinguished between a Malvasia di Salina, a Malvasia di Lipari, and a Malvasia di Stromboli wine; to the best of my knowledge, the wine of no other Lipari islands ever received the honor of being called by the island's name. According to Lothringen (1893–96), Malvasia production on Stromboli was most noteworthy in the Cuntrata San Vicienzu. Unfortunately, the horrific eruption of 1930 destroyed all of the island's vineyards, and only recently has viticulture started to make a comeback on this little island. To date, there are 1.5 hectares of Malvasia di Lipari planted, all belonging to the Caravaglio estate. However, a quick visit to the island confirms that land ideally suited for grape growing is not scarce; there are many old terraces still visible. Nino Caravaglio, who is a huge believer in Stromboli's winemaking potential and would like to see it brought back to its glory days, maintains these terraces, and walls could easily be rebuilt. To date, there are still no Stromboli subzone Malvasia di Lipari wines being made.

Vulcano

Vulcano takes its name not from *Star Trek* but from Ephestus, god of fire, who Thucydides tells us lived in Hyerà (or Vulcano, in Latin). Long a sleepy little isle mainly known as a place where other island inhabitants took their sheep and goats to graze, Vulcano is most famous nowadays for beautiful see-and-be-seen beaches like Baia Negra in the Porto di Ponente, and Asino Beach in the Bay of Gelso. It is, of course, dominated by its volcanic peak (499 meters above sea level). Wheat, capers, legumes, and grapes have always been the main agricultural products, but viticulture is making a noteworthy comeback on the island. Paola Lantieri, a Palermo doctor and later a manager of a family supermarket chain, bought the "house of the pink geraniums" at Punta dell'Ufala, on the southern side of the island, in 1994 (and finished restoring it in 2001). Along with viticulturalist Alessandro Accardi and winemaker Vincenzo Angileri, she soon started making Malvasia delle Lipari and a dry Salina Bianco. The wines are excellent, and are recognizably different than those made on the other islands. Soils on Vulcano are rich in sulfur, and this distinguishes them neatly from those of Salina, which are not. Like Salina, though, Vulcano also has pockets of clay that helps grapevines weather periods of drought—not exactly rare in the archipelago. In my years of puttering around the island, I can say that some areas strike me as being fresher than others. For example, the area around the Porto Levante crater is certainly one of the cooler spots on the island. Grape-growing areas of note include Piano (at 300 meters above sea level); Lentia, where grapevines grow at about 150 meters above sea level; and Ufala, where the best wine of the island is made by Paola Lantieri, and where grapevines grow at roughly the same altitude as Lentia, an area of extinct volcanos.

BENCHMARK WINES

Malvasia delle Lipari (sweet wine): Caravaglio Passito***, Casa Pedrana Passito***, Gaetano Marchetta Passito***, Lantieri Vulcano Punta dell'Ufala***.

Salina Malvasia (dry wine): Caravaglio Infatata***, Caravaglio***, Casa Pedrani Il Vino del Comandante***, Gaetano Marchetta L'Insolita***, Lantieri***.

Malvasia di Sardegna

As mentioned previously, Malvasia di Sardegna is believed to be identical to Malvasia di Lipari, but it is probably more accurate to say that Malvasia di Sardegna is a biotype of Malvasia di Lipari (if they are not distinct varieties). The two grapes do share noteworthy morphological similarities, but the wines are different. Though Malvasia di Sardegna grows in different parts of the island (220 hectares as of 2009), in the countryside of Alghero, Bosa, Cagliari, and Sorso, the one grand cru is Bosa, in the Planargia zone of Sardinia. Malvasia di Bosa is a DOC (the wine can be *amabile* or *dolce, spumante, riserva*, and *passito*), but the IGT Malvasia Planargia is also very good. The communes of Malvasia di Bosa DOC are Bosa (utterly pretty), Flussio, Magomadas, Modolo, Suni, Tinnura, and Tresnuraghes—all in the province of Oristano. The towns with the largest number of hectares under vine are Magomadas and Modolo; the whole denomination is characterized by terraced hillsides overlooking the blue sea below. The vineyards are situated at various altitudes (mostly between 70 and 170 meters above sea level), made up of very old bush vines of rickety old plants that are thrilling to see. Soils are mostly potassium-rich calcareous tufa, tuffs, and fluviolacustrine deposits, but there are also arenaceous limestones, molasses, marbles, sandstones, and conglomerates. The climate is arid warm and coastal, with mild winters, summer temperatures above 30°C in the months of July and August, and an average annual temperature between 17°C and 18°C. The golden-yellow wines are redolent of almonds, hazelnuts, ripe apricot, peach nectar, and aromatic herbs, only adding to the magic of a visit to the area, one of Italy's prettiest viticultural areas. Some of the wines are made in an oxidative style resembling Vernaccia di Oristano, such as the Malvasia di Bosa Riserva of Columbu and of Oggianu, but the wines are very different if for no other reason

than that Malvasia di Sardegna and Vernaccia di Oristano are grapes that give very different wines. Also, and differently from Oristano, in Bosa they never use large barrels as aging vessels (seven hundred liters at most; either oak or chestnut), and cellar temperatures tend to be more constant and the cellar air more humid. The oxidative wines are also less marked by flor (a thin film of yeast that forms on the wine's surface that helps control the wine's oxidation rate over time) than is Vernaccia di Oristano. That said, the best Malvasia di Bosa is Columbu's Alvaréga, and it is not made in an oxidative style. This wine ages extremely well, twenty years-plus not being a stretch at all (D'Agata 2018).

The Best Malvasia di Bosa Crus

The following list of crus was arrived at thanks to discussions with the Columbu family and other local *vignaioli*. Unfortunately, I cannot say I have tasted microvinifications from most of these sites as I have in most other parts of Italy, but I am currently in the process of trying to set these up over a number of consecutive vintages.

Bosa: Campèda (a grand cru), Pischinas, Silàttari (historically a grand cru also for Girò, a now very rare Sardinian sweet red wine that deserves to be much better known).

Modolo: Coloras.

Magomadas: Frau, Nigolosu, Pianu, Sa Pittuda, Su Filigalzu.

BENCHMARK WINES

Giovanni Battista Columbu Malvasia di Bosa Riserva***PS.

Angelo Angioi Malvasia di Bosa Salto Di Coloras***, Emidio Oggianu Malvasia di Bosa***, Fratelli Porcu Malvasia di Bosa Secco***, Fratelli Porcu Malvasia di Bosa Dolce***, Giovanni Battista Columbu Malvasia Alvarega***.

Malvasia Istriana

THE GRAPE VARIETY

Malvasia Istriana is one of seventeen different Malvasia varieties that call Italy their home. It is a remarkably interesting cultivar that gives some of Italy's best dry white wines, at once intensely mineral and aromatic. (Unlike Malvasia di Lipari and Malvasia del Lazio, Malvasia Istriana is not used to make sweet wines.) For the longest time, it was believed that this cultivar was a Greek import, one of the many Malvasia-something grapes brought over supposedly from the area around the city of Monemvasia in Greece by the seafaring Venetians. In fact, this long-held belief was proven wrong thanks to a fascinating 2005 study by Pejić, Maletić, and Naslov, who demonstrated that the Italian Malvasia Istriana grapevine does not share any genetic ties with at least twenty-eight Greek varieties. We also know that Malvasia Istriana is distinct from Malvasia di Sardegna (Crespan et al. 2006) and therefore from Malvasia di Lipari, too, given that Malvasia di Lipari and Malvasia di Sardegna are supposedly identical (although they are not: see the Malvasia di Lipari entry), and that it is related to Malvasia di Lipari, Malvasia Bianca Lunga, and Malvasia Nera di Brindisi (Lacombe et al. 2007). Morphologically and enologically, Malvasia Istriana is unlike any other Malvasias grown in Italy. Depending on the nursery clone or biotype observed, the grape bunch is medium-sized, cylindrical, with one very small wing, and loosely packed, with round berries characterized by thin but resistant, yellow-green skin. Intravarietal variability is frequent and so it is not surprising that the grapes look and behave differently. Malvasia Istriana is hardy and very resistant, though oidium is problematic. It is a fairly adaptable grape, for it performs equally well in the hilly vineyards of the Collio and the Colli Orientali, in the very poor, rocky soil of the Carso, and in the flat, gravelly riverbed plains of Friuli–Venezia Giulia's Isonzo River basin. The variety wants well-draining soils, and so those containing high percentages of clay are not suitable for Malvasia Istriana. For this reason, Malvasia Istriana is usually planted in the highest portions of hillside vineyards, where water drains easily. This grape's naturally high vigor needs to be kept in check, because at high yields

Malvasia Istriana and its wines lose most of their appeal. (For example, the grape fails to broadcast its aromatic nature.) Nowadays it is hard to find a Malvasia wine from Friuli–Venezia Giulia that is not aromatic: many are so spicy, fruity, and floral they actually seem to want to "out-Gewürz" Gewürztraminer. The real nature of the grape has been revealed thanks to lower yields, which are roughly half today what they used to be twenty or thirty years ago. It is a reductive variety, and avoiding the formation of off odors is important; furthermore, unless the grapes are picked at optimal ripeness, Malvasia Istriana's wealth of polyphenols leads to unpleasant aromas of cauliflower or chrysanthemum. At the same time, the high levels of norisoprenoids in the skins mean that lightly air-drying the grapes or late-harvesting them will greatly increase notes of apricot, peach, and wisteria in the wines. After three years from the vintage, the norisoprenoid component becomes even more noticeable, as does the presence of 1,1,6-trimethyl-1,2-dihydronaphthalene (TDN), which has the aroma of kerosene or hydrocarbons and also characterizes Riesling wines. I repeat, however, that grapes need to be fully ripe for the wine to exude such aromas and flavors.

SPECIFIC TERROIRS

Malvasia Istriana is a grape variety on the way up, and plantings of it are increasing everywhere in Italy. And I do mean Italy—not just Friuli–Venezia Giulia. Time and again I have had producers tell me that they had just finished planting a hectare or two of Malvasia Istriana. Which is just dandy in Friuli–Venezia Giulia, but all too often they tell me they are doing so in Puglia or Basilicata—which is not fine, given that those two regions of Italy have their own long-forgotten Malvasia cultivars to boast of (Malvasia Bianca and Malvasia Bianca di Basilicata). Clearly, Malvasia Istriana's value as a high-quality cultivar is finally being recognized, its wines sell well, and everybody's happy to jump on the bandwagon, but it pains me to see that other cultivars are now being passed by in its favor with no thought to

what is being done not just to the local biodiversity but also to pride of place. The take-home message, of course, is that Malvasia Istriana really is one great wine grape. Most Friuli–Venezia Giulia Malvasia wines are very good to outstanding, with very few duds to be had: one reason is that the majority of Malvasia Istriana vines planted in the region are old, though that is bound to change now that the cultivar is hot once again. Just remember that, much like Tocai Friulano (that's the cultivar) and Friulano (the wine), the variety is called Malvasia Istriana, but the wine is unfortunately called Malvasia only, with the denomination attached. So it is Collio Malvasia, Friuli Colli Orientali Malvasia, Carso Malvasia, and so forth. Carso, Friuli Colli Orientali, Collio, and Friuli Isonzo are where the most famous FVG Malvasia wines are made. Carso Malvasia is a mineral smorgasbord, a wine of wonderful levity and of welcome austerity (indeed, it is probably the most minerally-tasting wine of Italy). Collio Malvasia is potentially at once dense and refined, rich and fragrant. Isonzo Malvasia, due to the denomination's much warmer microclimate, is atypically full-bodied and can reach highish alcohol levels (14.5 to 15 percent is not uncommon). Friuli Colli Orientali Malvasia wines are usually riper and softer than those of the Collio, and some have a hint of residual sugar behind. Malvasia Istriana seems to have found a welcome home in the little-known Friuli Annia and Friuli Aquilea denominations, which up until recently, with little viticultural history to speak of, functioned mainly as a laboratory for every cat and dog of a variety one could plant. Only of late have producers begun to focus on a few varieties that seem better suited to their respective terroirs: of these, Malvasia Istriana seems like the real item. Last but not least, another important thing to know about Malvasia Istriana wines from Friuli–Venezia Giulia is that there many such wines are generically labeled "Venezia Giulia," rather than carrying a specific denomination. So, for example, the outstanding Malvasia wines from Kante (normally associated with the Carso) or I Clivi (made from vines that are eighty years old) are both labeled "Venezia

Giulia." Why producers choose to do so has to do with personal choices that vary with each one of them, but most often it means the grapes are not entirely from just the Carso or just the Collio, for example.

Collio

For a description of the Collio's terroir, see the Ribolla Gialla entry.

The Best Crus of Malvasia Istriana in the Collio

The Malvasia wines of the area of Spessa, Russiz, and Russiz Superiore are especially famous: the first two areas have a warmer mesoclimate, while Russiz Superiore is usually colder by at least 1°C. Harvest times will vary between these areas (roughly two weeks). Famous winemaker and consultant Gianni Menotti does not believe there is one specific high-quality area in the Collio "just for" Malvasia Istriana; according to him, unlike Oslavia for Ribolla Gialla, where the two (site and variety) seem to have been made for each other, a similarly Malvasia Istriana–specific area in the Collio has never been prominent historically. Undoubtedly, there are areas of the Collio where Malvasia Istriana seems to grow better and the wines are fuller and more complex. Over the years, by combining information gleaned from producers and work previously done by Veronelli (1995), I have compiled a list of the better Collio Malvasia Istriana sites; the names of these sites do not usually appear on labels since the grapes may be blended with those from other sites, in order to make more wine, for example. The names of Collio's great sites for Malvasia Istriana are as follows:

Brazzano: Vigneto Selezione Italo & Bruno.

Capriva: Russiz.

Cormons: Monte Quarin, Roncada, Pradis.

Farra d'Isonzo: Campagnis.

Gorizia: Ucizze e Draga.

Lucinico: Ripis.

San Floriano: Lasko, Runk, Uklanci.

BENCHMARK WINES

Borgo del Tiglio Malvasia Selezione Italo & Bruno***[PS], Doro Princic (etichetta blu)***[PS].

Alessandro Pascolo***, Borgo del Tiglio Malvasia***, Ca' Ronesca***, Clivi Vigna 80 Anni***, Ronco dei Tassi***, Schiopetto***.

Dario Raccaro**, Vosca**.

Blazic*, Fiegl*, Gradis'ciutta*, Muzic*, Venica & Venica Petirs*, Picech*, Pighin*, Subida di Monte*, Tenuta Stella*, Villa Russiz*.

Friuli Aquileia

The DOC Friuli Aquileia involves a long, thin strip of land that stretches from Aquileia to Trivignano Udinese, by way of Cervignano del Friuli and Palmanova. Sixteen communes are included within its boundaries. There are two main characteristics of the Aquileia territory that have a great impact on its wines: it is a coastal area, and so its southern boundary is essentially formed by the Adriatic Sea, and it comprises a huge variability of soils that often change multiple times within a short distance. The soil range runs the gamut from pure gravel to yellow marls to brownish clays; for simplicity's sake they can be summarized into three major types. In general, the closer one moves toward the Torre stream (calling it "river" is far too generous), the more likely it is to run across gravel- and sand-rich terrains; by contrast, the soils from just south of Cervignano and extending to Aquileia and Fiumicello are mostly made up of yellowish-looking marl, a mix of varying proportions of clay and sand. Aquileia's third-most-common soil type is sand, found along a thin band of sandy soil that is typical of the area running from Aquileia to Grado and its beautiful lagoon. Thanks to Aquileia's proximity to the sea, the climate is essentially temperate, and temperatures rarely dip below 0°C in this part of Friuli–Venezia Giulia; snow is practically unheard-of. The warm bora wind that blows in an east-northeast direction also helps remove any stagnating humidity, and fog is common only in autumn and in winter (when it is actually not a rare event). Annual precipitation is concentrated mostly in the spring and fall seasons and is not copious, so water stress can be a problem come summer (usually quite hot for brief periods) in those areas characterized by a low presence of clay. Diurnal temperature variations are not that marked in the Aquileia DOC. All these features combine to explain the area's wines: generally medium-bodied (but those producers who do not crop low make some of the thinner, more dilute wines of Friuli–Venezia Giulia), without the penetrating perfume of the best from the Collio or the Friuli Colli Orientali, with a pleasant savoriness (at times even salinity). The wines of Aquileia are only recently starting to come into the mainstream, but awareness of them (and their specific characteristics) is still low among wine cognoscenti—despite Aquileia's ancient history of real wine excellence (in fact, less than the awareness of any other Friuli–Venezia Giulia denomination). Strabonius wrote that during the Roman republic and empire, Aquileia was not just a production area of very fine wines (home to the famous *Pucinum*), but also an important commercial wine hub, with significant trade directed especially to the empire's eastern provinces along the Danube. The exact grape makeup of *Pucinum* is unknown, but the majority of experts believe that it may have been produced with an ancestor of Refosco del Peduncolo Rosso that grew by a small freshwater spring called Polzino, located near Scodovacca (a hamlet of Cervignano del Friuli) and Villa Vicentina. The area has always been famous for the quality of its Refosco del Peduncolo Rosso wines, thanks to a favorable mesoclimate and clay-rich soils. There are plenty of old documents that attest to a flourishing culture of wine in and around Aquileia through the fifth and sixth centuries right up to the age of the Patriarchy of Aquileia and the Republic of Venice. Today there are many interesting, up-and-coming estates, and their wines (especially those made with Refosco del Peduncolo Rosso and Malvasia Istriana) are worth getting to know.

Ballaminut*, Donda*, Tarlao Ninive*, Tenconi*.

Friuli Carso

Not many wine lovers realize that there is more than one Carso in Friuli–Venezia Giulia: the Carso Goriziano and the Carso Triestino. It is the latter that is best known, no doubt thanks to very particular wines and charismatic producers (Kante, Zidarich, and Skerk, among others) that have helped put it on the map. In fact, the two Carsos have similar geologic origins, their main difference being in their respective proximity to the sea: the Carso Goriziano is more inland, and this, combined with minor differences in soil, may account for differences between the wines (which for the most part resemble each other quite a bit). The two main soils of the Carso were formed from the degradation of different geological substrates and therefore have different chemical and physical properties: they are the red clays and the classic Friuli–Venezia Giulia whitish marl sandstone known everywhere in the region as *ponca*. These two soils are also found across the border in the Istria Slovena (Slovenska Istra) and Istria Croata, but I caution readers that though there is also a Slovenian Carso or Kras, the Italian Carso and Slovenian Carso are not the same. One reason is that though the latter also has *ponca* soils (for example, around the villages of Vrabce and Stjak), these are of a different geologic origin, having derived from the Vipacco Basin and not the Istrian Basin like Friuli–Venezia Giulia's *ponca*. In fact, things are a bit more complicated, because in Friuli–Venezia Giulia there are many different *ponche* (just as there are many different flysch formations; see the Ribolla Gialla entry). In Friuli–Venezia Giulia, the *ponca* of the Istrian Basin is found only in the southern part of the Carso denomination, on the hills above Trieste and Muggia right up to the border with Slovenia. The red clays derive from the degradation and subsequent sedimentation of the calcite in the classic Carsic whitish rocks.

The infiltration of water leads to the leaching out of calcareous elements, and the silicate impurities accumulate in channel-like depressions called *doline* or *polje*. The soils that form in this manner have no carbonates; are rich in iron, calcium, magnesium, and aluminum; and are low in potassium and organic matter. The soil pH is either neutral or lightly acid. Clay tends to accumulate in the deeper layers (up to 70 percent of the total), while sand is not abundant (5 percent); the highly porous calcareous bedrock means water retention capacity is not exceptional. The Italian Carso's soils are also quite shallow, with very little topsoil to speak of. (By contrast, these soils in Istria are as much as two meters deep.) The white soils are a type of *ponca* that is locally called *tasel*. This is not a mere difference in semantics, but reflects the fact that the Carso's *ponca* has a different geologic base, having originated in the Istria Basin instead of the Julian Basin or the Vipacco Basin like the rest of Friuli–Venezia Giulia. I do not wish to appear to be too granular about such matters, but these different geologic origins translate into some very practical diversities. The *tasel* has a larger percentage of marl than of sandstone, compared with other Friuli–Venezia Giulia *ponche*. The lower amount of sandstone means that these hills are at a greater risk of erosion, which clearly has repercussions on the local landscape (where terraces are often necessary). The calcareous elements are also leached out with greater ease, which means that, depending on the limestone content, these soils will have either neutral or alkaline pH values, and this clearly brings consequences for the wines. These soils also have a stronger loamy presence and are rich in potassium; they have better water-retention capacity than the red soils, and so vines are less likely to go into water stress. Another important difference between the red and white soils is that the former tend to give wines with more-polished tannins and a lower concentration of catechins (which, when too copious, can impart a bitter aftertaste). Given the tendency of Carso producers to make wines by prolonged macerations, it follows that it is grapes grown on red soils that are most suitable for maceration, while those of the white soils risk becoming excessively chewy, astringent, and bitter. In fact, the wines from these two soils could not be any more different. Those made with grapes grown on the red soils are very vertical wines (extremely perfumed, with shrill acidity and noteworthy tannins but considerable refinement, too); those born off the marly-sandstone soils are more horizontal (rounder and fleshier, almost opulent by Carso standards, but with very good acidity and refinement). The latter wines are ready to drink sooner, while those made with grapes grown on the red soils need at least three to four years of cellaring after the vintage date. Unfortunately, no estate has yet taken up the challenge of producing individual wines from the two different soils. (There is currently some debate in the Istria Croata on which soil type is best for Malvasia Istriana, but not much in Italy.) Clearly, there are reasons why this is so: for one, most estates of the Carso are small, family-run enterprises that do not have large numbers of hectares from which to make too many different wines. Another reason is that producers, understandably enough, have preferred so far to broadcast the characteristics of one Carso, given that it is fairly distinctive as it is. The following step will be to dig deeper into Carso's diversity and produce specific wines from specific subsoils, thereby making the Carso and its wines even more interesting to wine lovers.

BENCHMARK WINES

Castelvecchio Venezia Giulia***, Kante Venezia Giulia***, Skerk Venezia Giulia***, Zidarich Venezia Giulia***.

Friuli Colli Orientali (FCO)

For a discussion of the Friuli Colli Orientali terroir, see the Picolit and Schioppettino entries.

BENCHMARK WINES

Miani***PS, Meroi Zitelle***PS.

Paolo Rodaro***.

D'Attimis Maniago**, I Clivi Malvasia Venezia Giulia**, Petrucco**, Scarbolo**, Scubla Speziale**.

Guerra Albano*.

Friuli Isonzo

It is the beautiful Isonzo River, where I spent a good chunk of my adolescent summers fishing for trout, that gives its name to the Isonzo denomination. Not surprisingly, the soils of the area are a classic gravelly-alluvial mix. There are only roughly forty-five centimeters of top-soil, and then immediately below, the gravel appears. Some sections of the Friuli Isonzo are richer in limestone and others in iron. (Clearly the latter, reddish-colored soils are very easy to recognize, especially in the summer when it's dry.) Differences such as these have led the Friuli Isonzo denomination to be subdivided into two subzones: the Rive Alte and the Rive di Giare. The Rive Alte are those of the cooler, right side of the Isonzo River and are a mix of mainly iron-rich clays and gravel with a little limestone. The Rive di Giare soils are located on the left bank of the Isonzo, closer to the sea, are characterized by mainly white gravel and sand, and are richer in limestone. A number of producers I have interviewed over the years have always told me more or less the same things when it comes to Malvasia Istriana and the Isonzo. Giorgio Badin, owner of the high-quality Ronco del Gelso estate, maintains that having rocky, nutrient-poor soils low in clay content and choosing the correct rootstock are of paramount importance in determining whether one will have success with this cultivar in Friuli Isonzo. For example, the best root-stocks are the mid-vigorous ones, since they handle water stress better, and in Friuli Ison-zo's gravelly terrains that is a point of funda-mental importance. Gianfranco Gallo, of the well-respected Vie di Romans estate, also thinks that soils must not be excessively deep for Malvasia Istriana to show its best; he draws the cutoff at 150 centimeters deep; otherwise, he says, the variety's naturally high vigor takes over and it will then produce dilute grapes.

Isonzo's mesoclimate is one of the most reg-ular in all Friuli–Venezia Giulia. Located at roughly the forty-sixth parallel (like Burgundy, for example), Isonzo is characterized by a rather warm climate: for example, daily temperatures are on average 10°C higher than Burgundy. The Alps shield the Isonzo's vineyards from the cold northern winds, and the warm marine breezes blowing up from the nearby Adriatic also help create a warm microclimate (actually downright hot, in the summer). Clearly, diurnal tempera-ture variations aren't as strong as in the Alps, for example, but are large enough to ensure wines with crisp aromatics. Luminosity is also exceptional in Isonzo. The combination of warm temperatures and extreme light account for many of the characteristics of the Isonzo wines, most of which are fleshy, tactile, and rich, tend-ing toward robust alcohol levels (alcohol levels of 14 and 15 percent being common in Isonzo's white wines). It also rarely rains in Isonzo, a fact of key importance with Malvasia Istriana. Unlike other areas in Friuli such as Grave, parts of which can receive up to two thousand milli-meters of rainfall a year, Isonzo is doused with only about seven hundred to eight hundred mil-limeters of rain per year, and this liquid refresh-ment is concentrated mainly in spring and fall. Taking into consideration the last decade or so, only 2010 and 2014 can be viewed as especially rainy vintages in Isonzo.

BENCHMARK WINES

Ronco del Gelso Vigna della Permuta***, Vie di Romans Malvasia Istriana Friuli Isonzo Dis Cumieris***.

Drius Malvasia Friuli Isonzo**.

Brandolini Malvasia Friuli Isonzo*, Renzo Sgubin Malvasia Friuli Isonzo*.

Mayolet

THE GRAPE VARIETY

Costantino Charrère is one of Italy's most important figures in wine, a really great man who has single-handedly done more for the Valle d'Aosta's wines than anyone else. In fact, if we are able to talk about monovariety Mayolet wines today, it is only thanks to him (and the Institut Agricole Regional), who basically resurrected it. Unfortunately, Mayolet has an extremely compact bunch, and it is very hard to work with because rot is always a risk, and Charrère, as much as he loves and believes in native grapes, considers Mayolet to be a pain. It is one of the few varieties he has given up on for the moment, waiting for the development of more loosely packed Mayolet biotypes (and he correctly points out that Italy's government should fund and encourage such research). However, Mayolet's qualities are not lost on many in the region, and I now see that more producers than ever before are thinking of making a Mayolet wine, so I have hope that the wine's many charms will keep winning over consumers and experts alike. Mayolet's name

likely derives either from *mayola*, meaning "young vine," or from the Mayolet family (still a common family name in the Valle d'Aosta today). Mayolet is one of the region's oldest varieties, and for this reason it is related to other Valle d'Aosta cultivars: it is most likely the parent of Vien de Nus and of Vuillermin, and the progeny of Prié. Mayolet was first mentioned in the *Cahiers de la cave* of the Passerin d'Entrèves in 1787 (and not, as reported elsewhere, by Arguettaz, the curate of Valpelline, in 1822). Gatta (1838) wrote that the variety was common around Aymavilles, Sarre, and especially Saint-Pierre; Bich (1896) concurred, writing that Mayolet was one of the region's oldest known cultivars. There were once over one hundred hectares planted to Mayolet between Charvensod and Saint-Pierre (Berget 1904). Mayolet is the most precocious red of the Valle d'Aosta's cultivars, and so it is usually the first to be picked; it also likes growing at high altitudes, where it has no trouble ripening. Monovarietal Mayolet wine is exceptional, and completely different from any other Valle d'Aosta red, more aromatic and lighter styled (only Vuillermin shares a similar aromatic note): a good Mayolet wine is light to medium bodied, with spicy, floral, and very aromatic nuances of violet, blueberry, blackcurrant, and mountain flowers, with notes of cinnamon and white pepper.

SPECIFIC TERROIRS

Valle d'Aosta

Because the Valle d'Aosta is a mountainous region, one would expect very cold weather to be a given. However, things are not quite so dire. The region is an oasis of sorts, blessed with a continental subtemperate climate locked within a larger area characterized by an alpine climate. The coldest month of the year is January; the warmest months, July and August. And although the temperature difference between summer and winter is considerable, it is less than in areas of eastern Europe or central Asia at the same latitude due to the mitigating effect of the warm Mediterranean Sea. Importantly, this effect is stronger in the western Alps (where the Valle d'Aosta is situated) than it is in the central Alps (where we find the Valtellina, another important Italian mountain viticultural and winemaking district). The annual average daily temperature range in the Valle d'Aosta is 10–13°C, but clearly, the region's viticultural areas located at the highest altitudes, such as those where the Prié variety grows around the pretty town of Morgex (at twelve hundred meters above sea level), have lower mean temperatures (roughly 9.5°C). In fact, a characteristic of all mountain climates is the strong temperature variability that exists between different spots, even when these are just a short distance apart: a situation that arises from a combination of multiple factors such as the altitude, the exposure to the sun, the direction of the prevailing winds, and the low relative humidity rate of the air. The region's Winkler index is 1050–1950, and the Huglin index is 1450–2450.

The Valle d'Aosta is one of the rare places on the southern (or Italian) side of the Alps that has an east–west orientation. (Most of the Alpine valleys run north–south; other exceptions to this rule are the Valtellina in Lombardy and the Val Venosta in Alto Adige—all famous for their wines.) The practical consequence of this orientation is that water availability for crops is relatively low, a condition resulting from a number of factors. First, the mesoclimate of areas running parallel to a mountain chain is typically one of irregular rainfall patterns (and not exactly copious rainfall at that); in this scenario, humid air masses tend to dump rain mostly on the mountainous slopes external to the internal valley area (a situation known as the Stau phenomenon). When these masses finally reach the internally situated valley, they do so with very little humidity or liquid refreshment to offer. (This is known as the foehn effect: when air passes over mountains, the valleys on the downwind side are usually hit by strong downslope winds that are both warm and dry.) Most of the rain in the Valle d'Aosta falls in the autumn (in October and November) and in the spring (April and May); the period from July to September is the driest (with July seeing the least amount of rain). So a lack of water is a real concern for the Valle d'Aosta's farmers.

The topography of the region's vineyards also gets in on the act, making an already difficult situation worse. This is because most of the Valle d'Aosta's vineyards are located on south-exposed slopes where solar radiation is at its strongest (hence evaporation rates are noteworthy), and the absence of depressions or amphitheaters means that cold air does not accumulate. Katabatic air currents compound this by clearing the vineyard environment of any residual stagnating cold air. Last but not least, a potential for serious water stress is made more likely by the loosely packed moraine soils characterized by a large granulometry and poor water-retention capacity. And yet, it is rare to see grapevines in the Valle d'Aosta showing signs of water stress. Leaves are practically always green and crisp thanks to a continuous subterranean water supply derived from snowmelt and the area's rainfall (more frequent and abundant than on the valley floor). The water table runs deep (easily seven to eight meters below ground), sliding along the surface of the Valle d'Aosta's bedrocks (granite, gneiss). The ground's humidity levels are further contributed to by occasional pockets of loamy-clay molasses that act as sponges, storing rainwater and releasing it in dry conditions, when the grapevines need it most. The latter situation will remind knowledgeable readers of Bordeaux, and of Pétrus, especially; and they make pretty good wines there, too. Mayolet, like all the other red varieties of the Valle d'Aosta save for Nebbiolo (which grows mostly in the lower valley or Bassa Valle), grows mostly in the central valley (Media Valle) and on both sides of the Dora Baltea River. Mayolet vineyards are found from Saint-Vincent to Avise (but especially from Nus to Arvier) up to eight hundred meters above sea level. There are numerous excellent DOC Valle d'Aosta Mayolet wines made; plus, the variety is a bit player in the Torrette blend (which is at least 70 percent Petit Rouge, but it can use a little of Mayolet's aromatic kick).

BENCHMARK WINES

Feudo di San Maurizio***PS (utterly irresistible; this is the benchmark Mayolet wine).

Di Barrò Vigne de la Toule*** (from the Toule and Condemine vineyards at 850 meters above sea level in Saint-Pierre).

Cave des Onzes Communes** (delightful, inexpensive, well-made wines in general), Co-Enfer Vin des Seigneurs**.

Co-Enfer Triskell* (a rare Mayolet sparkling wine), IAR*.

Montepulciano

THE GRAPE VARIETY

Don't get confused: Montepulciano is a grape variety, whereas Vino Nobile di Montepulciano is a Tuscan wine made mainly with Sangiovese, not Montepulciano. Montepulciano grows everywhere in central Italy today, but it is most associated with the Marche and Abruzzo. And although in the Marche's limestone-rich Conero area it can give massively structured wines of some interest, the best Montepulciano wines are from Abruzzo. Abruzzo Montepulciano was first mentioned in 1792 in the travel diary of Michele Torcia, archivist of King Ferdinand IV, though exactly where Montepulciano originates from has been the matter of some conjecture. Whereas it used to be accepted that it might have been brought to Abruzzo from Tuscany, most researchers and scientists I have spoken to over the years believe that Montepulciano was born in Abruzzo's cold, mountainous Val Peligna (Peligna Valley, in English). This makes sense, too, if you stop to consider the characteristics of the grape. Montepulciano has no problem building up sugar, but its pip tannins ripen only very slowly, and so it needs to be planted in cold microclimates that will allow slow, even ripening to give truly interesting wines. Unfortunately, the variety has been planted everywhere in Abruzzo, even where it is far too hot, and that makes producing truly world-class wine from Montepulciano impossible. Asynchronous maturation is another difficulty presented by Montepulciano, with grapes of different color (hence different ripeness levels) in the same bunch. Of course, Montepulciano has many positives, and this explains why it is one of Italy's five most-planted grape varieties. For example, it boasts huge quantities of anthocyanins, so its wines are never short on color; this is why Abruzzo is famous for its own special brand of *rosato* wine (called Cerasuolo) that is more like a pale-medium red than pink, and its deep hue is arrived at with little or no maceration of the skins. Montepulciano's red wines can be cheap and cheerful or brooding and concentrated, offering something for everyone. It adds up to its being a very popular grape, as attested by the almost endless number of nursery clones available, but unripe pip tannins remain the

Achilles' heel of many Montepulciano wines, a problem compounded by lavishing on new oak from small barrels in the hope of camouflaging the unripe-pip-derived green streak. Many oaky charmless Montepulciano wines requiring extended bottle age never actually round out their tannins. A talented new generation of producers taking over their family estates is moving away from oak-aging their entry-level Montepulcianos (the best of which can now be outstanding and almost Pinot Noir–like) and using oak sparingly for their *riserva* wines, while paying greater attention to their estate's viticulture (in order to attain greater pip tannin maturity). Great Montepulciano wines offer very strong red-cherry aromas and flavors, so much so that flowers are hard to come by on an initial olfaction. According to Sagrantini et al. (2012), the red-cherry notes are due especially to ethyl hexanoate, octanoate, and decanoate (all of which are amplified by the presence of ß-damascenone).

SPECIFIC TERROIRS

Colline Teraman

Though this is a DOCG, I find the area too large, too clay-rich, and too hot to make truly great wines (though exceptions exist).

L'Aquila

Viticulturally, the L'Aquila province (or the Aquilano, in Italian) is made up of two important subzones: Ofena to the north, and the Val Peligna to the south. Of the two, it is the Val Peligna that is more important for Montepulciano (unlike Pecorino, for which the opposite is true). The grape has therefore had centuries to adapt to the specific Val Peligna terroir, and this goes a long way in explaining its highly refined Montepulciano wines. Ofena gives fleshier, richer Montepulciano wines that showcase very good balance and are some of the best made anywhere in Abruzzo. In fact, L'Aquila makes Abruzzo's best Cerasuolos.

Montepulciano d'Abruzzo: Cataldi Madonna Tonì*** (from Ofena), Praesidum***(from the Val Peligna).

Cerasuolo d'Abruzzo: Praesidum***.

Cataldi Madonna Piè delle Vigne**.

Casauria and Vestina

The province of Pescara has produced a number of excellent Montepulciano wines over the years. Its two subzones, Vestina (or Terre dei Vestini) and Casauria (or Terre di Casauria), were introduced in 2006. There are twenty-one communes or municipalities within the first and seventeen in the second. Of the two, Casauria has the stricter qualitative production guidelines: its Montepulciano d'Abruzzo wine has to be 100 percent Montepulciano (that of Vestina can be made with 15 percent other red nonaromatic grapes blended in), the yields are lower (a not exactly low ninety-five quintals per hectare compared to one hundred), and the minimum alcohol by volume is 12.5 percent (as compared to 12 percent in Vestina). The wine has to age for eighteen months prior to release for sale, nine months of which it spends in oak; *riserva* wines need to be aged for thirty months before sale. Vestina does boast a high-quality Montepulciano wine district: Loreto Aprutino. Casauria, located to the south of the Vestina area and west of Pescara, is more mountainous, extending westward into the Apennine Mountains. (Alanno, Bolognano, Cugnoli, Popoli, and San Valentino are important wine towns in the area.) Casauria's vineyards look both eastward toward the sea and westward, the latter sites located in a far cooler microclimate. Wider day–night temperature variations are the norm in Casauria and so its white wines are fresh, minerally, and potentially ageworthy, while its Montepulciano wines can be some of Abruzzo's most refined. Many of Abruzzo's very best—as well as up-and-coming—wineries, such as Filomusi Guelfi, Tiberio, and Valle Reale, are based here. The Casauria district extends on two slopes of a range of hills running northeast to southwest that have their epicenter in the town of Torre de' Passeri. On the southern slope we find the towns of Tocco de Casauria, Bolognano (where the Zaccagnini estate is located), and, much farther west and inland, Popoli (where the Valle Reale estate is found). On the northern slope there are the vineyards of, from east to west, Alanno, then Cugnoli, and finally Pescosansonesco. Alanno's and Cugnoli's terroir represents a transition zone between Vestina and the rest of Casauria; the eastern exposure looks to the sea, much like Vestina's, but the area is more mountainous and extreme in its viticulture (the landscape being not unlike that of Alta Langa, for those who live and die by Piedmont), like the rest of Casauria. Soils are mainly clay marls with an increasing percentage of rocks and gravel as the altitude climbs. Vineyards at Alanno and Cugnoli lie at about 300 to 360 meters above sea level and are divided up between Contrada La Vota (where the Tiberio winery is located) and at Colle Grande/Oratorio (where the Castorani estate is found). On the other hand, the vineyards of Pescosansonesco climb up as high as 500 meters above sea level and dig their roots in far rockier soils. The Montepulciano wines of Casauria are especially interesting, and can be some of the most refined and lithe of the region, almost Pinot Noir–esque in their perfume and silkiness (the latter a descriptor rarely associated with Montepulciano wines).

BENCHMARK WINES

Tiberio Colle Vota***[PS].

Tiberio***, Valle Reale***.

Filomusi Guelfi** (the winery is physically located in Tocco de Casauria).

Loreto Aprutino (a district of Vestina)

You do not need to be a huge Italian wine expert to come to the conclusion that Loreto Aprutino is an exceptional terroir for Montepulciano. Just realizing for a second that it is there that Valentini makes its Montepulciano d'Abruzzo, one of Italy's truly iconic wines, or that the two impressive Montepulciano d'Abruzzo crus by Torre dei Beati also hail from grapes grown there, has to mean something. In general, vineyards lie between 250 and 350 meters on mostly clay soils with a very good presence of limestone. The area's topography is not marked by especially steep slopes, since erosive phenomena have been limited in time. It lies roughly twenty kilometers from the sea, and a channel effect is created that causes winds to blow in from the sea, tempering the area's mesoclimate. The best vineyard area in the Loreto Aprutino zone is close to where the Tavo River's flow abruptly changes from a southwesterly (when the river flows through its more-rugged mountainous habitat) to a northeasterly direction (after which it flows in a practically linear direction toward the sea) while joining the Fino River to form the Saline River. The vineyard area looks somewhat like an enlarged "V," and most of Torre dei Beati's and Valentini's vineyards are located on the slopes looking out toward the vertex of the "V." The soils are fairly homogenous throughout the area (there are certainly some differences, but a standard composition might be clay (34 percent), loam (38 percent), and sand (28 percent), and so the biggest differences in the wines result from changes in vineyard exposure, slope gradient, and altitude. The area's Winkler index (calculated based on data from 1951 to 2009) is 2077; the annual rainfall (also calculated on the basis of data from 1951 to 2009) is 430 millimeters during the vine's vegetative period (April to October). These Montepulciano wines have greater density, spice, and flesh than those of Casauria (more Bordeaux to Casauria's Burgundy, if you will) but also very good balance.

BENCHMARK WINES

Valentini***[PS].

Torre dei Beati Cocciapazza***, Torre dei Beati Mazzamurello***.

De Fermo Prologo**(since 2015) *(before).

Moscato Bianco

THE GRAPE VARIETY

Moscato Bianco owns the distinction of being the only grape variety to be grown in every region of Italy. This cannot surprise anyone given that it makes some of the country's most-loved wines, like Asti and Moscato d'Asti. But there are other noteworthy Italian wines made with this cultivar: Chambave Muscat and Chambave Muscat Flétri in the Valle d'Aosta, Moscadello di Montalcino in Tuscany, Moscato di Noto and Moscato di Siracusa in Sicily, and Moscato di Trani in Puglia are just a few examples, all made with local biotypes of the variety. Moscato Bianco is very popular outside Italy, too, with myriad wines made practically in every winemaking area. The list of synonyms it is known by shows, how popular this cultivar is: for example, in France, Muscat Blanc à Petit Grains (Muscat de Frontignan, Muscat de Lunel, and Muscat d'Alsace are variants), and in Greece, Moschato Samou. It is such an ancient variety that it has spawned a huge number of other Moscato grapevines: in short, every other Moscato variety you may know is a descendant of Moscato Bianco, and that includes the red-berried Moscatos as well, such as Moscato Rosa and Moscato di Scanzo (see the Moscato di Scanzo entry). There are many historical references to its presence in Piedmont: for example, the 1511 statutes of La Morra protected their Moscato Bianco vineyards, and a 1539 document tells of "vines of Moscatello" bound for the Duke of Mantua. Just imagine that the Consortium of Moscato d'Asti and Asti was formed in 1932, two years before Barolo's. Though everyone loves the wines, the grape is not the life of the party. For example, Moscato Bianco prefers cool climates: although it can thrive in warm climates (provided there is some respite from the heat) such as in Sicily's (Moscato di Noto, Moscato di Siracusa) and Sardinia's (Moscato di Sardegna wine and/or Muscateddu), its best wines come from northern, cooler climates. But it is a late ripener, and in northern regions such as Piedmont this means less-than-fun times come autumn. Moscato Bianco has a very thin skin, and so rot is always a scary possibility, though its characteristic loosely packed bunch helps in this regard. It has smaller-size grapes than most other Moscato varieties and so provides farmers with less juice from which to make wine. Last but not least, it is also a delicate variety, succumbing easily to most vineyard diseases and pests, such as oidium and peronospora. Despite all those drawbacks, its popularity is attested by the numerous nursery clones available: the small-bunched CN 4, the very aromatic CVT CN 16, the medium-size-bunched and thick-skinned VCR 3, and the medium-small-bunched and moderately compact CVT 57 and 190 are just some of the many in a long list.

SPECIFIC TERROIRS

Moscato d'Asti

The Moscato d'Asti denomination extends over ten thousand hectares, fifty-two communes, three provinces (Cuneo, Asti, and Alessandria), and three well-known territories: the Roero (one commune), the Langhe, and the Monferrato (the latter two comprising the other fifty-one communes). This makes for myriad different terroirs sandwiched between the Tanaro and the Bormida Rivers, ranging from the softer, gentler topography of the Langhe to the steeper slopes of the Valle Belbo and the Valle Bormida. A look at a map of the denomination shows it to look like an irregular rectangle with two appendages in its westernmost portion (in correspondence to Serralunga d'Alba and Santa Vittoria d'Alba). These two appendages, added later to the original production zone, might lead cynics to cry foul given that the two very large and politically important wineries of Fontanafredda and of Cinzano are located in the former and the latter towns, respectively (and to add further fuel to the fire, Santa Vittoria d'Alba, where Cinzano is based, is the only town of the fifty-two included in the denomination that is located on the left side of the Tanaro River, all others being located to its right). Nevertheless, Santa Vittoria d'Alba has been named one of the three official subzones for Moscato d'Asti, along with Canelli and Strevi. The Moscato d'Asti denomi-

nation's soils were formed during the Cenozoic era, which began roughly sixty-six million years ago (see tables 2 and 3 in the appendix); all the area to the right of the Tanaro formed during the Miocene epoch (roughly 25 million to 5.3 million years ago), while Santa Vittoria d'Alba and the Roero (of which the town is formally a part) formed 5.3 million to 2.5 million years ago, during the Pliocene epoch. Relative to the age of geologic formation, the soils of the Moscato d'Asti DOC on the right of the Tanaro differ, too: those in the province of Cuneo (where the Langhe is) were formed in the Langhian stage (15.9 million to 13.8 million years ago), while those of the Asti and Alessandria provinces were formed during the Serravallian stage (13.8 million to 11.6 million years ago). This means that the soils of Santa Vittoria d'Alba are mostly calcareous-sandy, those of the Cuneo province mostly marly-white calcareous with clay inclusions, and those in the Asti and Alessandria portions of the DOC more characterized by compacted calcareous sands that are especially suited to Moscato Bianco. According to star producers Aldo Vajra, Paolo Saracco, and Pietro Ratti (whose father, Renato, wrote about Moscato Bianco), to whom I have talked about this specific subject over the years, the variety does best on marly clay soils—specifically, those formed in the Middle Miocene period. Strucchi and Zecchini (1895) wrote that farmers have been aware of this fact for some time. Not by chance, the areas of Canelli, Santo Stefano, and Loazzolo are considered to be true grand crus for Moscato Bianco, and all boast soils formed during the Middle Miocene, very lightly chalky and limestone rich. Similar soils are also found in the provinces of Alessandria and Cuneo but not to the same extent, due to a higher presence of clay (though Moscato Bianco, always fairly adaptable, thrives there, too). The variety has historically been cultivated between 220 and 300 meters above sea level, but nowadays vineyards are mostly planted between 150 and 400 meters and higher (ranging from the 160 meters at Cassine to the 600 meters of San Donato di Mango). Given the importance of

Moscato Bianco for the local economy throughout history (in the 1600s, Moscato Bianco wines cost twice as much as other local wines), this is one of the few viticultural areas of Italy for which we have documents identifying which Moscato Bianco vineyard areas had the best reputations. At the end of the 1800s, the communes of Strevi and Canelli were considered especially worthy. In the 1970s, four basic subzones had been identified, and they are still valid today:

1. Santo Stefano Belbo, Castiglione Tinella, Camo, and parts of the territories of Mango and Cossano Belbo: this subzone gives the medium-bodied wines that are the most perfumed (floral) and refined Moscato d'Astis of all. Mango's vineyards, at five hundred meters above sea level or above, are some of the denomination's highest.

2. Canelli, Calosso, and San Marzano: slightly more full-bodied Moscato d'Astis that, differently from those of the first subzone, are fruitier (citrus) than floral.

3. Calamandrana and eleven nearby communes: full-bodied, structured Moscato wines characterized by notes of very ripe fruit.

4. Cassine, Strevi, and Acqui: from the Alto Monferrato, balanced wines characterized by delicate fruity nuances.

In general, the Langhe has a warmer microclimate, so its Moscato d'Asti wines are richer and broader than those of Canelli, Santo Stefano Belbo, and certainly Mango. In fact, Canelli's association with Moscato Bianco is so strong that the variety is actually known all over the world as Muscat Canelli. A good Moscato d'Asti always reminds me of orange blossoms, grapefruit, pear, sage, rosemary, and vanilla. It can be still or lightly sparkling (*frizzante*) and quite sweet (up to 120 to 130 grams per liter residual sugar), and good examples are always long on flavor and short on alcohol (never more than 5.5 to 6 percent alcohol). Don't confuse it with Asti, a fully sparkling wine made in the same area that has a slightly higher alcohol content (but never more than 9.5 percent alcohol) and is more off-dry. A separate category of late-harvest (*vendemmia tardiva*) Moscato d'Asti wines exists, too.

The Best Moscato d'Asti Crus

I have tasted enough Moscato d'Asti in my lifetime and consequently enough bubbles to make me worry I might fly away some day. Despite having studied the matter at hand long and hard and with much gusto, it remains difficult to pinpoint the best vineyards for Moscato Bianco in Piedmont because many producers do not do single-vineyard wines, preferring to blend their grapes together. A good example is Paolo Saracco, by far the most talented and best Moscato d'Asti producer there is today (he blends the wines from different sites); in his and similar cases, I have had to resort to tasting from vats and tanks over the years. The list below includes a mix of my own discoveries over the years as well as many sites that others also thought (according to historical documentation) were just swell Moscato Bianco vineyard areas. Unfortunately, trying to gain information on this subject from most of the denomination's producers is very difficult because most do not have experience with wines made in other sections of the denomination. Consequently, their views are pertinent only to the immediate areas where they grow their grapes.

Calosso: Crevacuore, Moiso, San Siro.

Canelli: Moncalvina, Monforte, Sant'Antonio (ever since the 1700s, the most famous Moscato Bianco "cru" of all; the name does not refer to just one site but rather to the whole set of hills that extend to the north of Canelli. The site is characterized by extremely calcareous soil, not much wind, and a southwest exposure).

Castagnole Lanze: Biancospino, Bricco Quaglia (two names made famous by the La Spinetta winery).

Castiglione Tinella: Caudrina (at 280 to 300 meters above sea level, the vines face south-southwest on whitish-bluish tufa soils called locally *toèt,* with a little calcareous sand; very perfumed, persistent Moscato Bianco wines); di San Bovo (grown on a hill 390 meters above sea level, Moscato Bianco was probably already growing here in medieval times); La Vignassa (410 meters above sea level, southeast exposure; probably planted to Moscato Bianco since hundreds of years ago).

Cossano Belbo: Rovere, San Pietro, Scorrone (the latter an especially good site in rainy years due to the low clay content of the soil; Rovere and San Pietro give very complex, aromatic and full-bodied Moscato Bianco grapes and wines).

Mango: Bricco Riella, Terrabianca (as the name implies, these highly calcareous, whitish soils give high-acid, perfumed wines of real breed).

Santo Stefano Belbo: Alisan, Bauda, Moncucco (Bauda is easy to see on the left as you drive toward Canelli; it gives powerful but perfumed Moscato Bianco wines. Moncucco is one of the most famous crus of all, beautifully terraced and now linked to the Fontanafredda estate that bottles a wine with its name), Reisau, Sant'Elena.

Strevi: Valle Bagnario (one of the most famous Moscato crus of all along with Canelli's Sant'Antonio; it has tufa-sandy soils and relatively high temperatures, contributing to uniquely rich Moscato wines famous as early as the eleventh century).

BENCHMARK WINES

Paolo Saracco***PS, Paolo Saracco Moscato d'Autunno***PS.

Bera Su Reimond***, Elio Perrone Sourgal***, L'Armangia Canelli***, La Spinetta Bricco Quaglia***, La Spinetta Biancospino***, Rizzi Vendemmia Tardiva Frimaio***, Romano Dogliotti La Galeisa***, Romano Dogliotti La Caudrina***, GD Vajra***.

Borgo Maragliano**, Braida Vigna Senza Nome**, Ca' d'Gal Canelli Sant'Ilario**, Ca' d'Gal Vitevecchia**, Ca' del Baio**, Cascina Castlet**, Cascina Fonda Bel Piano**, Chiarlo Nivole**, Cogno**, Gianni Doglia Casa di Bianca**, I Vignaioli di Santo Stefano**, Il Falchetto Ciombo**, Il Falchetto Tenuta del Fant**, Marenco Scrapona**, Marrone Solaris**, Rivetto Vittoria**, Rizzi**, Scagliola Volo di Farfalle**, Vietti Cascinetta**.

Bava Bassa Tuba*, Giacomo Scagliola Canelli Sifasol*, Il Botolo*, Matteo Soria*, Mongioia*, Santero*, Terrabianca*.

Chambave

Historically, Moscato Bianco has performed remarkably well in the Valle d'Aosta (going back thirty years, I have tasted an almost endless number of great Moscato Bianco wines from this region), the forerunner of which was the fantastic Chambave Muscat by Ezio Voyat. The area's wines have always been characterized by a very refined, penetrating quality and a degree of purity not found in other Moscato Bianco wine of Italy. The wine can be made in the communes of Châtillon, Pontey, Chambave, on the right bank of the Dora Baltea River; and in Montjovet, Saint Vincent, Châtillon, Saint-Denis, Chambave, and Verrayes on its left bank. (The vineyards of Chambave and Châtillon straddle both sides of the river.) The production area is not an easy one to work in, with water stress a major risk in most vintages. The soils are mostly moraine sands (sand 70 percent, loam 25 percent, clay 5 percent), with high levels of iron and molybdenum and medium-low levels of calcium and magnesium. Interestingly, the Chambave viticultural area (especially the countrysides of Montjovet, Saint-Vincent, and Chatillon) is characterized by bush vines and cordon spur training systems as opposed to the canopy that dominates the low valley. (For a more detailed description of the Valle d'Aosta terroir, see the Mayolet entry.) Rootstocks used include the 110 Richter, which seems to perform well there. Muscat Chambave is less juicy and less intensely fruity than Moscato d'Asti but is spicier, with a richer texture. When the product of air-dried grapes, it is labeled *flétri* (or *passito*). There is essentially one major producer in the area, La Crotte de Vegneron (La Vrille is one of a handful of individual family-run estates also making excellent Chambave Muscat); Andra Costa, La Crotte's technical director, has proceeded to divide the territory where La Crotte's members own vineyards into three subzones homogenous for altitude, exposure, and slope gradient. The fist subzone starts at the Dora Baltea River and rises to 580 meters above sea level; the vines have mostly southeastern exposures and are planted on the left bank of the river. Zone 2 is characterized by vineyards at 580 to 650 meters above sea level and is the one that is currently giving the best results; two specific cru areas have been identified here: Grenel and Quichet. Zone 3 includes the highest-situated vineyards (800 meters above sea level or more—an altitude that guarantees crisp acidity and plenty of freshness to the finished wines).

The Best Chambave Muscat Crus

Champlain, Chamdianaz, Parleaz, Poyaz, Tercy.

Brunet (fraction Cretaz) and La Vigne des Junod (fraction Grangeon) are vineyards in the commune of Verrayes.

BENCHMARK WINES

La Crotta di Vegneron***, La Crotta di Vegneron Chambave Muscat Flétri Prieuré***, La Vrille Chambave Muscat Flétri***, La Vrille Chambave Muscat***.

La Crotta di Tanteun e Marietta Chambave Muscat*, Rosset Terroir Chambave Muscat*.

Noto

Moscato di Noto became a DOC wine in 1974, but it was absorbed into the Noto DOC when it was born. The legislation calls for the wine to be made with 100 percent Moscato Bianco (though charmingly and in typical Italian fashion, after that they go on using only a vague, and incorrect, "Moscato" term). Now, if it were me writing these regulations and guidelines, I would lose no opportunity to make clear that Moscato di Noto is made with a Moscato Bianco uniquely adapted through the centuries to a finite, specific part of the island—since this would only help crystallize in everybody's minds that it is a rarer, site-specific biotype and, ultimately, a more valuable product not available from anywhere else in the world. Moscato di Noto can be made in dry, sparkling, and sweet versions. The sweetest are those made as Passito wines from air-dried grapes, and, depending on the process of air-drying chosen, there can be different styles of these sweet wines. Air-dry it in the sun (no picnic, given the variety's thin skins), and the wine will have a darker color, riper aromas and flavors, and hints of caramel (plus traces of volatile acidity due to incipient oxidation); air-dry it inside in humidity and a temperature-controlled environment and the wine is a mightier gold in hue, with fresher profiles (white flowers, fresh grapefruit, only a touch of orange marmalade). Both can be exceptional wines: indeed, I think it is by far the best wine made by Planeta, an estate that has made its fortune and name with the likes of Chardonnay and Merlot. (For a more detailed description of the Noto terroir, see the Nero D'Avola entry.)

BENCHMARK WINES

Marabino Muscatedda***, Planeta***, Riofavara Notissimo***.

Marabino Moscato della Torre*.

Moscato di Scanzo

Moscato di Scanzo is one of my five favorite Italian wine grapes and wines. Undoubtedly the memories of the halcyon days of childhood play a role, given that my life essentially started out in Bergamo, one of Italy's most beautiful cities, and the countryside of which is the epicenter of Moscato di Scanzo production. In fact, Bergamo's countryside (not all that famous wine-wise today) was highly thought of for the high quality of its wines in centuries past: for example, land planted to vines cost twice as much as that planted to other crops (Sansovino 1575; Jarnut 1980). Moscato di Scanzo, the grape, gives Moscato di Scanzo, the wine, and it really is one of Italy's greatest (and unfortunately, rarest) wines. It is Italy's smallest DOCG, only thirty-one hectares in all, with only thirty-nine producers making about sixty thousand bottles a year. The grape and wine's name derives from the town of Scanzorosciate, itself a combination of Scanzo, a centurion in Julius Caesar's army, and *ros*, Greek for "cluster of grapes." Local historians maintain that the grape and wine were already typical of this corner of northern Lombardy in ancient Roman times: we have no way of knowing if the two really are that old, though Don Celso Lotteri, the parson of the town of Villa, wrote that in the first century B.C. the Roman founders of the towns of Villa, Scanzo, and Rosciate believed their local red grapes special and began production of a Moscato wine that quickly became one of the most expensive of those times (Lotteri 1852). A 1340 document attests to the grape growing locally, so it has been hanging around Bergamo for a very long time indeed. In the sixteenth and seventeenth centuries, Moscato di Scanzo was one of Italy's most famous wines, and it graced the tables of the royal courts of kings, queens, czars, and emperors. A letter dating December 15, 1784, tells us an architect native to Bergamo, Giacomo Quarenghi (responsible for many of Saint Petersburg's most beautiful buildings, including the Winter Palace), donated the wine to Catherine the Great. (Quarenghi is such a well-regarded and important figure that Russia released a commemorative stamp in 1994 honoring the 250th anniversary of his death.) Still in the eighteenth century, prices for Moscato di Scanzo were quoted on the London exchange (one gold guinea a barrel then; but the wine was so popular that its price had increased to fifty guineas a barrel by 1850). Moscato di Scanzo is one of the many descendants of Moscato Bianco. (It appears the other parent might have been Aleatico, but this is not yet certain.) Moscato di Scanzo is an aromatic red grape with a medium-size, long, loosely packed pyramidal-shaped bunch, with medium-size dark blue-black berries with very thin skins. It has good disease resistance, but is susceptible to gray rot; part of its popularity is due to the fact that it doubles as an excellent table grape, but the wine is so successful and expensive that its grapes cannot be used that way anymore. It ripens later than other red-berried Moscato varieties or Aleatico, usually in late September to early October.

SPECIFIC TERROIRS

Moscato di Scanzo

Moscato di Scanzo is made with 100 percent Moscato di Scanzo grown only in the territory of the similarly named denomination, corresponding to the territory of the small town of Scanzorosciate, near Bergamo. The official guidelines further specify that the wine cannot be made from flatland vineyards and that the grapes have to air-dry for at least twenty-one days to achieve a minimum 240 grams per liter sugar. (The wine has to have at least 50 to 100 grams per liter residual sugar.) The Scanzorosciate area has always been believed to be especially favorable to this grape variety, and so was officially recognized as a subzone in 1993; the DOC dates to 2002 and the DOCG to 2009. (In particular, the hill of the Tribulina hamlet has always been highly regarded by locals for the quality of its wine.) The geology of northern Lombardy is especially complex, but the Scanzoriosciate area stands out because of the presence of the *sass de la luna*, a calcareous marl

formed during the Cretaceous period (145 million to 66 million years ago) of the Mesozoic era. Found in Lombardy mostly between the city of Varese and Lake Garda, it is especially abundant in the countryside of Scanzorosciate; it can run from a few meters to three hundred meters deep, on a base of maiolica (a microcrystalline or micrite limestone) and Lombard silica containing calciferous substrate. The best Moscato di Scanzo wines are made from grapes grown on this very friable, nutrient-poor soil in which vines grow slowly and with difficulty because there is very little topsoil. The combination of specific soil, hilly topography, and the unique microclimate of the area gives an especially perfumed and refined wine. Moscato di Scanzo is planted at relatively high altitudes (usually around 350 meters above sea level), most often with the pergola or canopy trellising system: besides warding off the risk of excessive sunlight and heat (remember, Moscato di Scanzo has thin skins) and of rot (it helps to train these grapes away from the ground, where humidity stagnates), the canopy also protects against the risk of hail. Rootstocks of choice in the area are Rupestris du Lot (ideal in rocky habitats), Kober 5BB (typically used in the 1960s), and 420A (resistant to soil lime and ideal for hillside viticulture). The Scanzorosciate area is remarkably beautiful and dotted by very small vineyards hugging the slopes; large vineyards are rare (most are subdivided in many plots), and most are extremely old. For example, De Toma (a family that descends from the Mandelli family, which had bought land from Giulio Quarenghi, son of the famous architect Giacomo) owns 2.5 hectares of Moscato di Scanzo divided among eleven different plots; one plot of vines dates back to 1922, another to 1969, and the average age of the vines is roughly forty-two years. Estates here are small, producing at most between one thousand and four thousand bottles per year. A well-made Moscato di Scanzo wine is a paragon of balance, combining penetrating rose and violet aromas with nuances of cinnamon, nutmeg, white pepper, bay leaf, red berries, and red-cherry syrup. It is light and lively and never excessively sweet. I want to be crystal-clear about this: Moscato di Scanzo wines by De Toma and Pagnoncelli-Folcieri are little known, but are two of Italy's forty or fifty best wines.

The Moscato di Scanzo Subzones and Best Crus

Not surprisingly, since the production area is very small, there is not enough Moscato di Scanzo planted in large enough holdings for anyone to have ever made single-vineyard Moscato di Scanzo wines. There are at least three different subzones within the DOCG territory as we know it: the area surrounding Mount Bastia, an eastern section, and a central-western section. Spicy red-berry aromas and rich flavors are typical of wines made around the Monte Bastia; wines from the eastern section are fruitier and more mineral, while central-western wines are richer and thicker, expressing cocoa and black-fruit (blackberry, prunes) notes rather than the variety's usual red-fruit nuances. If grapes grown here were used to make your Moscato di Scanzo, get ready to have some terroir-related fun.

BENCHMARK WINES

De Toma***PS, Pagnoncelli-Folcieri***PS.

La Brugherata Doge***, La Rodola***.

Il Cipresso**, La Corona**; Biava*.

Valcalepio

A very similar wine to Moscato di Scanzo is Valcalepio Moscato Passito, mainly because it is also made with the Moscato di Scanzo variety on the hills of the Valcalepio area in the province of Bergamo (between the Seriana and Cavallina Valleys, on the left side of the Serio River), not far from Scanzorosciate. Geographically, the Valcalepio name applies to all the hills of the eastern part of Bergamo province; enologically, it corresponds to a much bigger area—the territory between Lake d'Iseo and Lake Como. Simplifying greatly, the northwest-

ern part of the denomination is characterized by soils that have a higher content of schistose clay and silica, while the northeastern section has mostly calcareous clay soils. Actually, the local geology is a great deal more complex, and I have spent long hours poring over geologic maps trying to figure out how best to break the area down in order to group its wines in a way that is easy for people to remember. There are two types of *sass de la luna* present (classic and calcareous), as well as Sarnico sandstone, flysch of Bergamo, flysch of Pontida, and radiolarite (a hard, fine-grained homogenous sedimentary rock), among still many more different formations, and so the task is, to say the least, not exactly an easy one. The eastern section has a generally warmer microclimate than the western; annual precipitation is eleven hundred to twelve hundred millimeters, but the volume has significantly reduced since 2003. Most commonly, the sweet red wine made in the Valcalepio from Moscato di Scanzo is simply called Valcalepio Moscato Passito (differentiating it from the lovely air-dried Moscato Giallo wines also made in this area that are not part of the Valcalepio DOC; see the Moscato Giallo entry). The Valcalepio Moscato Passitos can be labeled with a specific town's name if the grapes used to make them grow within that jurisdiction: for example, Moscato Passito di Gandosso, Moscato Passito di Castello di Grumello, and others. (The towns are Albano Sant'Alessandro, Carobbio degli Angeli, Cenate Sotto, Gandosso, Grumello del Monte, and Torre de' Roveri, all a stone's throw from Scanzorosciate.) In general, I find the Valcalepio Passito wines to be less floral but to have richer mouthfeels than Moscato di Scanzo; they can be remarkably good wines.

BENCHMARK WINES

Castello di Grumello***, La Rovere di Torre de' Roveri***, La Tordela***, Pecis Argo***.

Caminella Passito Rosso Dolce Goccio di Sole**.

Moscato Giallo

THE GRAPE VARIETY

Moscato Giallo is the least common of the "big three" Moscato wine grapes of the Moscato family (the others being Moscato Bianco and Moscato d'Alessandria or Zibibbo), to which practically all other Moscato varieties are related. While Moscato Bianco adapts to just about any terroir (it prefers cooler climates but manages to do well in reasonably hot ones, too) and Zibibbo thrives in hot, droughty environments, Moscato Giallo wants truly cold surroundings. Therefore, in Italy it lives only in the Veneto, Trentino–Alto Adige, and Friuli–Venezia Giulia. In Alto Adige it is usually referred to by its German name, Goldenmuskateller (not to be confused with the Gelber Muskateller of Germany and Austria, which is Moscato Bianco). Beware that in Sicily, old-timers will occasionally speak of their Moscato Giallo, but the variety they are actually talking about is Moscato Bianco (the latter's berries become golden when really ripe, hence the mistaken "giallo" reference). Moscato Giallo is either a grandchild or half-sibling of five other Moscatos (Moscato di Scanzo, Moscato Rosa del Trentino, Moscato di Alessandria, and Muscat Rouge de Madèire) or Moscato-like varieties (Aleatico)—all of which originated in Italy; and since it is an offspring of Moscato Bianco, Moscato Giallo is a true Italian native wine grape. It has large, long, pyramidal-shaped, loosely packed bunches with one to two wings, and round, thick-skinned bright-yellow berries. It ripens early in the season (from late August to mid-September), a good thing given its northern habitat. It is a fairly resistant variety (much more so than Moscato Bianco), though springtime cold and rainy weather are a real problem because the variety is prone to *millerandage*. It gives the best results in calcareous or volcanic soils, and therein is one clue as to where the best terroirs for it might be located in Italy. According to Usseglio-Tomasset (1966), Moscato Giallo is characterized by higher concentrations of pulp linalool than Moscato Bianco (and Gewürztraminer, Riesling, and Zibibbo, too), and other researchers have confirmed this finding.

SPECIFIC TERROIRS

Italy's best-known Moscato Giallo wines are those of the DOC Trentino Moscato Giallo and the Alto Adige Moscato Giallo (though labels may read "Goldenmuskateller"). These absolutely lovely wines are most often sweet, and only rarely does one find great dry wines, such as the outstanding ones from Alto Adige's Manincor and Lageder wineries (the latter is more off-dry than classically dry). However, in Trentino and Alto Adige, there is no history of specific crus for the variety, which was usually planted along with other varieties by passionate wine producers. Instead, the Veneto has long been associated with an outstanding Moscato Giallo wine specifically associated with one main and easily defined terroir, the Colli Euganei.

Colli Euganei

The Colli Euganei (or Euganean Hills, in English) are one of the many volcanic denominations of the Veneto. (The Colli Berici and parts of Soave would be others.) They are located immediately southwest of the city of Padua, about twenty-five and one hundred kilometers away from Venice and Verona, respectively. The Colli Euganei were named Veneto's first regional park in 1989 and are characterized by a hilly landscape dotted with almost perfectly conical-shaped hills (eighty-one in number) roughly three hundred to six hundred meters high. The Colli Euganei take their name from the Euganei tribe that had settled the area before the Romans arrived and took over (today, a *"euganeo"* in Italy also refers to someone from Padua); I will add, given that most wine lovers are also food lovers, that Padua is blessed with one of Italy's best, most famous, and oldest cafés, the legendary nineteenth-century Caffé Pedrocchi (which is most certainly worthy of a pit stop when you're wine hunting in the area). Another settler in the area was one of Italy's most famous literary figures, Petrarch, who lived in Arquà from 1369 until his death. (Believe it or not, the town actually incorporated his name into its own, and so it is now called Arquà Petrarca.) The Colli Euganei also inspired another famous literary figure, poet Percy Bysshe Shelley, the author of "Lines Written among the Euganean Hills."

The Colli Euganei were initially formed roughly forty-three million years ago when submarine eruptions during the Upper Eocene epoch led to basalt flows mixing with marly deposits. A second round of magmatic activity then took place thirty-five million years ago and shaped the area as we know it today. These eruptions took place in the Lower Oligocene epoch and were characterized by highly viscous lava (due to high silica and low magnesium and iron concentrations) that led to the accumulation of deposits rich in trachyte (volcanic rock rich in feldspar and, to a lesser extent, quartz) and rhyolite (not to be confused with the Nevada ghost town of the same name; in this context rhyolite refers to a pink-gray volcanic rock rich in silica and, to a lesser extent, quartz and sanidine). Trachyte deposits are easily found in many hills and small mountains of the area such as the Monte Grande, Monte Gemola, and Monte Altore, while rhyolite characterizes the area of Monte Venda (which, at six hundred meters above sea level, is the highest peak in the Colli Euganei) and Monte Cinto. However, the Colli Euganei are not characterized just by the presence of volcanic rocks, but also by sedimentary rocks of marine origin that gave rise over time to limestones and calcareous marls. The oldest such sedimentary rock of the Colli Euganei is red ammonite (actually more purple-red than red in hue), which was formed during the Jurassic period (201 million to 145 million years ago); it was followed by the deposition of *biancone* (a fine-grained limestone deposited in the Lower Cretaceous period, or roughly from 145 million to 100 million years ago), *scaglia rossa* (deposited from the Upper Cretaceous, or 100 million to 66 million years ago, to the Lower Eocene, or roughly 55 million to 48 million years ago), and Euganean marls (which have a high clay content and were deposited in the Lower Eocene and Oligocene, or 33.9 million to 28.4 million years ago). In terms most relevant to grape growing and winemaking, it is important to remember that the Colli Euganei denomination is characterized by essentially two major soil types: volcanic and calcareous marl (with a small section where alluvial soils dominate). Moscato Giallo has long called the Colli Euganei home (Zamorani et al. 1987). The Moscato Giallo is planted there especially on the calcareous marls of sedimentary origin. The Colli Euganei have a relatively warm microclimate, and for this reason various red wine grapes have long been planted here, such as Cabernet Franc. The hillside slopes with a southern exposure actually have a warmer microclimate than do the flatlands (what is known as the thermal belt effect), and diurnal temperature variations are not especially marked. The average daily temperature is 13°C; the Winkler index is 1800–2100, and the Huglin index is 2300–2550. The average rainfall is 858 millimeters per year, with a range of 650 to 1,000 millimeters per year. About 62 percent of the area's rain falls between mid-March and mid-October, though the wettest periods are spring (April and May) and fall (October and November).

In the Veneto, there has always been a wine called Moscato Fior d'Arancio, actually made with Moscato Giallo and not with the rare Moscato variety actually called Moscato Fior d'Arancio (according to a 2001 study by Crespan and Milani, Moscato Fior d'Arancio is related to little-known Moscato varieties such as Moscato Jesus and Moscato Bianco Grosso), which is not grown in the Veneto. By contrast, Moscato Bianco is found in the Colli Euganei, and so Moscato Giallo and Moscato Bianco are the main Moscato players in the DOC wines Colli Euganei Moscato Fior d'Arancio and Colli Euganei Moscato, respectively. Over

the years, I have conducted taste tests on Moscato Giallo wines made from grapes grown on the different soils of the Colli Euganei. In my experience, wines from alluvial soils (which have an alkaline pH and varying amounts of limestone, gravel, and clay) are often darker in color than the other area soils, and have a strongly ripe fruit presence on the nose and palate. In many ways, these strike me as the least "muscaty" wines of the area. Wines from calcareous marly soils are usually the area's most complex wines, with a plethora of aromas and flavors ranging from the variety's typical grapefruit notes to more delicate notes of apple, pear, and sweet spices. Wines from volcanic soils are, as might be expected, savory, clean, crisp, with an almost flinty quality the other two wine types lack. They also strike me as floral and minty.

BENCHMARK WINES

Borin Moscato Colli Euganei***, La Montecchia Colli Euganei Passito Donna Daria***, Maeli Spumante Colli Euganei***, Maeli Vino Spumante Metodo Classico Moscato Giallo Dilà***.

Vignalta Spumante Fior d'Arancio**.

La Montecchia Veneto Bianco Passito Acinidoro**, Locatelli Caffi Moscato Giallo Fior d'Arancio Passito Elix**.

Cantina Tramonte*.

Valcalepio

Though it is not officially included in the Valcalepio DOC near Bergamo (though, rather curiously, it is in the Colleoni or Terre del Colleoni DOC and the "della Bergamasca" IGT, both near Bergamo), Moscato Giallo does remarkably well in the Valcalepio production area. I would say this is one of Italy's best-kept wine secrets. Clearly, the terroir around Bergamo is obviously suited to Moscato Giallo, given the quality of the wine I have tasted from there over the years. Both dry and sweet Moscato Giallo wines are made and are excellent; certainly, while the sweet wines deliver expected levels of luscious sweetness, it is the perfumed, pungently spicy but refined dry wines that are especially noteworthy. (For a discussion of the Valcalepio terroir see the Moscato di Scanzo entry.)

BENCHMARK WINES

Pecis Laurenzio***.

Caminella Bianco da Uve Stramature Goccio d'Ambra**, Eligio Magri Lucentio**, Eligio Magri Vino da Tavola Bianco da Uve Stramature**, La Rovere Elisir**.

Sant'Egidio Marinele*.

Nebbiolo

THE GRAPE VARIETY

Is Nebbiolo Italy's greatest native grape? Most wine lovers and wine experts would answer a resounding yes. Nebbiolo (mostly written with only one "b"—Nebiolo—right up until the 1960s, when its spelling was changed officially) is used to make Italy's most famous wines—namely, Barolo and Barbaresco—but also the often great wines of Boca, Carema, Donnas, Gattinara, Ghemme, and Lessona, among others. However, while Barolo and Barbaresco must be strictly 100 percent Nebbiolo, the other wines can also be blends of Nebbiolo and small percentages of local cultivars (Croatina, Uva Rara, Vespolina, Rossola, and/or Brugnola). One of Italy's oldest cultivars, Nebbiolo takes its name most likely from *nebula*, the Latin word for fog (*nebbia*, in Italian), modified over time to *nubiola* and *nibiol*; fog is common in the vineyards of Piedmont late in the season when Nebbiolo finally ripens. Otherwise, Nebbiolo's name might derive from the abundant bloom of its grapes (given that the grapes look like they're covered by fog). The name "Nebbiolo" actually appears in the literature much before "Barolo" or "Barbaresco" do. "Nibiol" dates back in the literature to 1268: a document shows that the Castellano di Rivoli (the lord of the castle of Rivoli) placed an order for such wines. By contrast, mention of a wine referred to as "Barol" appears for the first time only in 1751 in an order placed by Piedmontese diplomats in London who were looking to import the wine (D'Agata, He, and Longo, in press, 2019).

The best Nebbiolo wines are known for their almost magical perfume of sour to ripe red cherries, delicate sweet spices, and red rose petals that is penetrating and can be downright unforgettable. With age, characteristic notes of tar develop that add complexity. An interesting study has recently shown that only when the Nebbiolo grapes have reached optimal ripeness or superripeness does the red cherry aroma take on a truly decadent note; otherwise, an aroma and flavor of sour red cherry and fresh red berries dominate (Gerbi et al. 2016). This is not surprising, for in my experience Nebbiolo speaks mostly of sour red cherry rather than superripe red cherry; ripe or superripe red cherry aromas and flavors are generally the product either of hot to very hot years (which are unfortunately becoming the norm) or of the *vignaiolo* deciding to push the ripeness envelope by harvesting later than usual (and, most often, unnecessarily). In fact, you never find the ultraripe red cherry note in wines from Gattinara, Carema, or Donnas—cool-climate environments of many northern Italian lands where poor Nebbiolo just tries its best to ripen fully (at least this was true before the advent of climate change). It is very interesting to know that the sour red cherry, raspberry, and strawberry notes and the sweet spice aromas (most notably, cinnamon) found in great Nebbiolo wines are due to the presence in the wines of, among other molecules, ethyl cinnamate (more accurately known as ethyl-3-phenylprop-2-enoate), ethyl dihydroxy cinnamate, and other chained ethyl esters. Ethyl cinnamate is the ester of cinnamic acid and ethanol, and is typically found in the essential oil of cinnamon. (It is noteworthy that pure ethyl cinnamate has an aroma of cinnamon, complicated by balsamic and red fruit nuances, all of which can be characteristic of a fine Nebbiolo wine's aromatics.) In fact, Ducruet (1984) reports an association between ethyl cinnamate and an aroma reminiscent of cherry-kirsch (a nuance also very typical of wines made by carbonic maceration), while Versini and Tomasi (1983) associate ethyl cinnamate with strawberry and raspberry notes especially. Also, it is often said that the nose of great red Burgundy is similar to that of Barolos and Barbarescos: fascinatingly, ethyl cinnamate and ethyl dihydroxy cinnamate are important players in the aroma of Pinot Noir wines as well. In an extremely interesting study investigating the effect of grape maturity on aroma-active compounds in Pinot Noir wines made from grapes at three different levels of ripeness in two different vintages, it was found that both berry ripeness and vintage significantly affected the aroma composition of the final wine, with concentrations of the two secondary metabolites decreasing with increased ripeness

(Fang and Qian 2006). Important information on the aromatic molecules present in Nebbiolo wines was recently also supplied by Petrozziello et al. (2011), who reported the presence of terpenes such as citronellol, linalool, α-terpineol, and geranic acid in Nebbiolo wines, accounting for this cultivar's capacity to give at times truly inebriating floral aromas. By contrast, while tar is often mentioned as a key descriptor of Nebbiolo wines, in my experience this aroma is found almost only in Nebbiolo wines with some age on them. It is rarely if ever present in young wines. And in fact we now know, thanks to work by Bordiga et al. (2014), that Nebbiolo wines boast noteworthy concentrations of ß-myrcene, eucalyptol, p-cymene, and limonene—all of which can remind one of piney, balsamic aromas. This is a very relevant finding, for pine and balsamic nuances can mimic a tar-like note; in my experience, these two notes are often mistaken for a generic "tar" descriptor by less-than-experienced wine tasters. Another interesting consideration in this setting is that although Barolo and Barbaresco age magnificently well, in time they tend to become less overtly fruity but spicier and tarry (unlike wines made with Aglianico, for example; see the Aglianico entry). One of the reasons this happens is that the concentration of β-damascenone (a molecule that helps to augment the intensity of red-fruit notes) decreases markedly over time in Nebbiolo wines (Petrozziello et al. 2011). Call me a medical science geek all you want, but knowing this sort of stuff helps convey a greater understanding of the Nebbiolo wines we drink.

A fascinating aspect of Nebbiolo and its different terroir-related expressions is its great genotypic and consequent phenotypic variability, as shown by the existence of numerous Nebbiolo subvarieties or biotypes; of these, Bolla, Lampia, Michet, and Rosé have always been the most common. In fact, we know now that Nebbiolo Rosé is not a subvariety of Nebbiolo at all but a distinct cultivar (Botta et al. 2000). Clearly, it is extremely closely related to Nebbiolo (Schneider et al. 2004). Nebbiolo Michet (the name Michet derives from the dialect word *micca,* or "loaf of bread," which is what the small, cylindrical, and tightly packed bunch of Michet will remind you of) is not a distinct Nebbiolo subvariety either, but rather Nebbiolo Lampia hit by grape fanleaf virus (GFLV). Unlike other virus-affected grapes, Michet has survived well in most Barolo and Barbaresco vineyards because producers almost unanimously agree it gives an even better wine than Nebbiolo Lampia (which is a very reliable producer and capable of giving a high-quality wine on its own; but many producers vouch that Michet is even better, quality-wise). It is a situation similar to that of Sangiovese T19, which is also virus affected, but most Tuscan producers you talk to will tell you it is the Sangiovese "clone" that gives perhaps the best of all possible Sangiovese wines. The interesting thing about Michet is that it does not necessarily have lower yields than Lampia: usually, lower productivity is the hallmark of a virus-affected grapevine, which, by definition, is diseased and therefore less healthy and strong. Not so with Nebbiolo Michet, apparently: according to Gay et al. (1981), Nebbiolo Michet actually can at times be more productive than Nebbiolo Lampia—a strange twist on normal viticultural behavior, and documented in Barbera grapevines as well. (Average yield increases of 26 percent and 19 percent, respectively, were observed in GFLV-infected vines of Barbera and Nebbiolo.) The data also showed that the viral condition does not alter Michet's biochemical parameters much: in this study at least, the decrease in the sugar content of the grapes was of only 3 percent and 1 percent in the virus-affected Barbera and Nebbiolo, respectively. (Anyway, Michet has been put through thermotherapy to rid it of the viral presence, and so there are now virus-free Michets.) According to Mannini, Credi, and Argamante (1994), Michet grapevines, once cleared not just of GFLV but of grapevine fleck virus (GFkV) as well, offer higher vigor, earlier breaking of dormancy, and increases in yield by as much as 50 percent.

Differently from Nebbiolo Michet, the plantings of Nebbiolo Bolla have sharply declined in recent decades, and so this Nebbiolo biotype has largely been forgotten and most of today's wine lovers do not know of it at all. Its story is an interesting one, however. The Bolla's main problem was excessive productivity (Nebbiolo is a vigorous cultivar, and this vigor needs to be reined in), and therefore its wines were never paragons of high quality. And so, while very common in Langhe vineyards of the 1940s and 1950s, Bolla's use has since been disallowed by the official production guidelines, and so the grape is rarely seen or heard about anymore. The subvariety takes its name from the man who first discovered it: Sebastiano Bolla, a grower in the Santa Maria fraction of La Morra. Of course, you might not be surprised to learn that another version of this story exists (doesn't it always, in Italy): according to some in the Langhe, there never existed a Nebbiolo Bolla; rather, it was a fabrication of Bolla himself. According to what many local old-timers have told me over the years, it might be that Bolla, who was much sought after for his recognized talent in successfully grafting new plants onto old ones, found it extremely convenient to let people believe that he owned a special, genetically different Nebbiolo that would guarantee especially large yields. (As we know, the latter was always a highly desired trait in any grape variety by poor farmers relying on their annual crop to eke out a living.) By so doing, Bolla ensured himself a steady stream of business during his day as everyone sought his services and his generously productive Nebbiolo variant.

Unfortunately, there is not much Nebbiolo Rosé left in the vineyards nowadays (in the Langhe, at least), which is a huge shame. As its name implies, Nebbiolo Rosé has pale red, dark pink berries (its wine is not much darker); it is an irregular producer, and its wines are less fruity and fleshy but more perfumed and higher in alcohol than those made with Nebbiolo Lampia. For this reason, in the 1980s and 1990s, when wines characterized by darker-than-dark colors, high pH, and rich, thick textures were most in demand, almost every Barolo and Barbaresco estate proceeded to rip out all the Nebbiolo Rosé in his or her vineyards. In those sorry times when graceful, nuanced wines were routinely penalized in favor of vulgar behemoths, Nebbiolo Rosé vines did not stand a chance; but Nebbiolo Rosé gives wines of mesmerizing perfume and haunting balance, and those producers in whose vineyards it still grows are intelligently nurturing it. Plantings in the Langhe are apparently increasing slightly, and there are at least two 100 percent Nebbiolo Rosé wines made today that I know of, all outstanding wines in their own way. (See the Nebbiolo Rosé entry.)

In a fascinating 2015 study by Mannini et al., highly interesting findings relative to the diverse expression of three different Nebbiolo clones in three different Piedmontese denominations were shown. Over the course of three vintages, the researchers compared Nebbiolo 63, Nebbiolo CVT 308, and Nebbiolo CVT 415 planted in Lessona (in Alto Piemonte), La Morra (in Barolo), and Neive (in Barbaresco). The Nebbiolo 63 was planted just in La Morra and Lessona, while the CVT 308 and CVT 415 clones were planted in all three denominations. Grapevine morphological and biochemical parameters (bunch weight, number of bunches per plant, pH, total sugar, total acidity, total flavonoids, and anthocyanins concentrations) of all three Nebbiolos in each of the three terroirs were assessed, as well as the biochemical composition of the wines (including pH, total acidity, and total polyphenol concentrations) made with each Nebbiolo clone in the distinct terroirs under study. A comparison of the clones revealed that Nebbiolo CVT 308 and CVT 415 behaved *very* similarly, with comparable grape and wine parameters within the same denomination. (For example, the pH/total acidity values of wines made with CVT 308 and CVT 415 planted in Neive were 3.56/3.56 and 5.6 grams per liter/5.4 grams per liter, respectively.) Clone-related differences remain (of course, or there wouldn't be any point in having different clones to plant), but the clones behaved very differently when planted in different terroirs. For example, the Nebbiolo CVT 308 and CVT 415,

when planted in Lessona, gave wines with pH/total acidity values of 3.30/3.42 and 6.6 grams per liter/6.9 grams per liter, respectively. Clearly, the *same* Nebbiolo CVT 415 clones planted in a totally different terroir (Lessona instead of Neive) gave wines that were fairly different, at least in terms of higher acidity and lower pH values of the Lessona Nebbiolo wines. This finding indicates that terroir seems to have a bigger effect on the finished Nebbiolo wines than does the choice of clone (*or* at least, it does in the case of specific Nebbiolo clones, such as CVT 415). By contrast, some Nebbiolo clones appear to be more "terroir-resistant" than others, such as clone CVT 308, the wines of which showed similar biochemical parameters when grown in places as different as Neive and Lessona. Differently from Nebbiolo CVT 308 and CVT 415, Nebbiolo clone 63 behaved in very homogenous fashion in all three terroirs (similar biochemical results were recorded in wines made in the different terroirs), confirming its greater environmental stability—something already empirically well known to farmers. I can vouch for the fact that CVT 415 especially is very unstable in its behavior relative to the terroir it is planted in; as I noted in *Native Wine Grapes of Italy*, about ten to twelve years ago I became aware of a systematic lack of perfume and atypically intense color in Barolo wines made with members of the 400 series of Nebbiolo clones (clones selected from Picoteners grapevines growing in the Valle d'Aosta). It is important to realize that, when specific clones and biotypes are planted in new environments, they may produce wines that are different than expected, and this does not always take centuries to occur. And so the Picoteners that behave like Dr. Jekyll in the Valle d'Aosta and Alto Piemonte's Carema (where they give lovely light-red-hued, perfumed wines) turn into Mr. Hyde in the Langhe (where they give very dark Nebbiolos that lack perfume). In fact, the only Barolo I can think of that is truly a grand wine despite being made with Picotener clones is Malvirà's Barolo from the Boiolo vineyard. And as for the Jekyll and Hyde thing, I am not sure anyone knows why, yet. Short of doing a séance and asking Robert Louis Stevenson, I guess.

SPECIFIC TERROIRS

Nebbiolo does not adapt especially well to just any terroir, though it does better outside of the Langhe than is commonly believed. Witness for example the at times outstanding wines of Gattinara, Lessona, Donnas, and Carema (and even some wines from South Africa, Chile, and California). For the most part, however, Nebbiolo is a homebody. In Italy, it grows in three other regions besides Piedmont: Valle d'Aosta, Lombardy, and Sardinia (and in fact, only in specific parts of those four regions.) Not all the wines made in those areas are something to write home about; and most Nebbiolo wines made outside of Italy are not even reminiscent of the variety. To showcase the aroma and flavor palette that Nebbiolo is capable of painting in different places, I will in this section discuss the following Nebbiolo terroirs: Barolo, Barbaresco, Carema, Donnas, Roero, Valtellina, and the little-known Albugnano. Unfortunately, owing to geological and climatic diversity, the Alto Piemonte's denominations, such as Boca, Bramaterra, Fara, Gattinara, Ghemme, Lessona, and Sizzano, are too complex a subject to tackle with the necessary depth in this book. To do so would mean writing an extremely long opus that would essentially be a Piedmontese wine treatise, which was not the intent with which I set out to write the book. (The Alto Piemonte, as well as other wine terroirs of Italy not discussed here, will be the subject of a future book.)

Albugnano

How many of you have heard of Albugnano and its Nebbiolo wines? Not many, I bet: it is a rare Nebbiolo wine made in the province of Asti. (We tend to automatically equate Nebbiolo with Alba, but centuries ago Nebbiolo was commonly grown in the Asti area too.) In fact, Albugnano's relative obscurity is one of the reasons why I wished to broach a discussion about its terroir;

and in so doing I hope to bring this very beautiful, still ruggedly wild part of Piedmont and its delicious wines to life for wine lovers everywhere. The small Albugnano DOC (only twenty-two hectares) includes the communes of Albugnano, Pino d'Asti, Castelnuovo Don Bosco, and Passerano Marmorito: it is a small enclave of Nebbiolo vines in Monferrato's northwestern reaches, right on the border with the province of Torino. Topography in this neck of the Piedmontese woods is of the utmost importance, for the Albugnano hills are much higher (over four hundred meters above sea level) and steeper than in any other part of the northern Monferrato area. The mainly marly soils were formed roughly twenty million to fourteen million years ago during the Langhian and Burdigalian stages of the Miocene epoch. This means the soils of Albugnano were formed immediately before those of the Tortonian stage (11.6 million to 7.25 million years ago) and the Serravallian stage (13.8 million to 11.6 million years ago) that characterize Barolo and Barbaresco (see table 4 in the appendix). Nevertheless, the soils of Albugnano share noteworthy similarities with the Saint Agathe marls of the Tortonian stage (when the soils of the Barolo townships of La Morra and Barolo and most of the Barbaresco denomination were formed). However, Albugnano's light-colored, medium-packed soils differ from those of the Tortonian stage in that their uppermost layers have higher levels of tufa and sand than do the classic Saint Agathe marls. Besides the soil, another important aspect by which to define Albugnano's terroir is the different slopes on which the Nebbiolo vines grow. A hilly ridge runs through the denomination, and Nebbiolo vines are planted on both slopes: the slope that looks toward Castelnuovo Don Bosco is characterized by a gentler topography, with greater exposure to light, while the slope that looks in the direction of Berzano San Pietro has a narrower conformation, with forests dominating the almost mountainous landscape. Furthermore, in the Albugnano denomination Nebbiolo is grown from 200 to 540 meters above sea level;

therefore, the combination of different soil types, exposures, altitudes, and gradients leads to diverse Albugnano Nebbiolo wines. The climate is a relatively cool one and fairly rainy. (In fact, Albugnano is the rainiest denomination of Asti province, with an average 834.9 millimeters of rain per year from 1962 to 1998.) The wines can be very pleasant, though clearly the area's producer talent level is not comparable to that of the Langhe: reminiscent of the Nebbiolo wines of Donnas and the Valtellina (also mountain habitats), the best Albugnano wines are charming and medium-bodied, with a savory quality and tactile, earthy presence that distinguishes them neatly from Barolo and Barbaresco. The wines have a certain wilder, sleeker, chewier quality that does make them very Asti-like, as opposed to the smoother, riper offerings of Alba province. Typical aromas and flavors include red cherry, blackberry, mountain herbs, and minerals. (Albugnano Superiore wines are aged twelve months or more in oak and offer more palate presence.) In 2017, the Associazione Vignaioli Albugnano 549 was created (the president is a producer, Andrea Maria Pirolo, and there are currently thirteen members in the association) with the goal of promoting the Albugnano territory and its wines in Italy and abroad. (The "549" in the association's name refers to the number of meters above sea level at which the town of Albugnano is located.) The member estates are also busy working on a new set of official production guidelines for Albugnano wines that are meant to improve upon those established twenty years ago: the goal is to have the association members produce wines that are 100 percent Nebbiolo only and aged in oak for a minimum of eighteen months, plus another six in bottle. The denomination has plenty of good intentions and I daresay potential, too, though the capacity to produce wine is currently limited (two hundred thousand bottles a year).

BENCHMARK WINES

Albugnano and Albugnano Superiore (the commune where the estate is located is in

parentheses): Ca' Mariuccia*** (Albugnano), Tenuta Tamburnin*** (Castelnuovo Don Bosco), Roggero Bruno e Marco** (Albugnano).

Maurizio Calcagni** (Albugnano), Mosso Mario** (Moncucco Torinese), Perotto Orietta** (Albugnano), Nebbia Tommaso** (Albugnano), Pianfiorito** (Albugnano), Vai Mario** (Albugnano).

Alle Tre Colline* (Albugnano), Cascina Quarino–Cantina Fasoglio* (Aramengo), Terre dei Santi* (Castelnuovo Don Bosco), Mosparone* (Pino d'Asti).

Barolo

While the Barolo production zone is said to be in the Langhe area, it is actually situated in the Bassa Langa (the Low Langa), hemmed in by the Tanaro River to the north and west, and by the Alta Langa (High Langa) to the south. The origin of the name Langhe is unclear. One hypothesis holds that the word derives from the word *lingua*, which means "tongue"—a reference to the elongated, tongue-like projections of the hills slowly sloping down to the Tanaro River basin. Another hypothesis is that the Langhe derives from the Celtic word *londe* or *landu* (which means "noncultivated land") or from *langates*, the name of an ancient Ligurian tribe that apparently first colonized the area millennia ago (Magnoli 2004). Barolo as we know it is a relatively young wine, its history starting around the 1830s. In fact, the Langhe had long been more famous for the quality of its wheat (Casalis 1834). Before then, because of archaic winemaking and less than pristine cellar habits and equipment, Barolo was often sweet and fizzy: not surprisingly, stuck fermentations were a routine occurrence. There was a dry Barolo wine, too, the "Barolo Vecchio," the *vecchio* being a reference to its dry taste (probably not by design but because, having been left longer in barrel, any residual sugars were completely fermented by still-active yeast cells). At that time Barolo was not made to be aged, no doubt because it would spoil soon after bottling. It was in the 1830s, with the arrival on the scene of Francesco Staglieno, an army general whose hobby was winemaking, and of Louis Oudart, a French *négociant,* that Barolo entered its modern age: temperature control, cleaner barrels, attention to avoiding oxidation, and the routine use of glass bottles were just some of the innovations brought by these two enlightened gentlemen. Staglieno went so far as to write an important winemaking manual, the *Istruzione intorno al miglior metodo di fare e conservare i vini in Piemonte* (1835). Clearly, the production of clean wines with some aging potential was the first and most necessary step in allowing Nebbiolo's penchant for giving wines redolent of somewhereness to become apparent at last.

That some vineyards and areas were associated with better Nebbiolo wines was already clear to our ancestors. In fact, the first attempt at a delimitation of the Barolo production zone dates back to 1883, in Lorenzo Fantini's seminal *Monografia sulla viticoltura ed enologia nella Provincia di Cuneo.* (You can admire a copy, under glass, at the Michele Chiarlo estate in the middle of the Cerequio cru.) Fantini believed that the Barolo production zone should include Barolo, Castiglione Falletto, Perno, and Castelletto Monforte and only parts of Verduno, Novello, La Morra, Grinzane, Serralunga, and Monforte. Interestingly, that delimitation was very close to the modern-day one; in fact, it was essentially confirmed in its entirety in 1909 by the Comizio Agrario and again in 1926 in the then-government's *Decreto sui vini tipici.* But already back then, some believed in the usefulness of smaller-size denominations: for example, the citizens of Barolo and Castiglione Falletto were unhappy with the largesse of the approved production area, for at that time the original if not best Barolo was believed to be the one made in those two townships. For a while, the idea of creating a Barolo Classico zone was toyed around with (not unlike what happened in Tuscany, with the creation of a very large Chianti zone, separate from Chianti

Classico), but it was eventually rejected. And so it was for Ferdinando Vignolo-Lutati to come to the rescue, with his all-important *Sulla delimitazione delle zone a vini tipici.* Vignolo-Lutati was an aristocrat and a cultured man (he was a botanist and a chemist) whose family owned much land in and around Castiglione Falletto. Over the course of twenty years, he mapped out the soils and Nebbiolo vineyards of the Barolo production area: he believed that it was not possible to classify wines on the basis of subjective tasting evaluations, but he did not place much stock in meteorological data either (given the Langhe's irregular weather patterns). He championed the characteristics of the soil as being the factor that most determined wine quality, and his was the first geologic survey of the Barolo production zone ever performed. It is a remarkably accurate work.

The Barolo Townships and Their Geology

Most wine lovers are familiar with the townships of the left and right banks of Bordeaux, such as Saint-Estèphe and Pomerol, as well as the names of the most important towns of the Côte d'Or, like Musigny and Vosne-Romanée. They are also more or less acquainted with the basic wine style associated with each commune of Bordeaux and Burgundy. The same level of knowledge goes a long way in appreciating Barolo to its fullest. The villages of the Barolo production area are eleven: Barolo, Castiglione Falletto, Cherasco, Diano d'Alba, Grinzane Cavour, La Morra, Monforte d'Alba (Monforte for short), Novello, Roddi, Serralunga d'Alba (Serralunga for short), and Verduno. Barolo's different communes are usually associated with one of two main wine styles linked to two main soil types generally referred to as Tortonian and Helvetian. In fact, this is not correct on a number of levels. First, Helvetian is an old name and should be substituted by Serravallian. Second, Tortonian and Serravallian soils do not exist: rather, those two terms refer to stages of the Miocene epoch of the Neogene period (see table 4 in the appendix); hence the accurate statement is that Barolo's geology is made up of soils that were partly formed during the Tortonian and Serravallian geologic stages. Third, Barolo's soils were also formed during the Messinian stage. Drawing an imaginary line diagonally from the northeast to the southwest in such a way that it passes immediately to the right of the town of Barolo neatly separates Barolo's production zone into two halves. (The Alba–Barolo road can be used in place of the imaginary diagonal line.) Very loosely, land to the right or to the east of this diagonal line/road was formed during the Serravallian stage: the townships of Castiglione Falletto, Monforte, Serralunga, Diano d'Alba, Roddi, and Grinzane Cavour are located there. Serravallian soils are sandstone-based, whitish-chalky-beige in color, loosely packed arenaceous and sandy layers alternating with calcareous marl and limestone. In general, the mineral elements that are prevalent in Serravallian soils are iron and phosphorous; the iron presence can give these soils a deeper reddish-gray hue. This is part of the DOCG where the majority of ageworthy, austere, and tannic Barolos are made. The territory to the left or west of the imaginary line/road is where the communes of La Morra, Barolo, Verduno, Cherasco, and Novello lie and is home to soils partly formed during the Tortonian stage. Such soils have an obvious bluish-gray tint to the naked eye and are made of calcareous marl mixed with sand. They are more fertile than Serravallian soils, and are especially rich in magnesium and manganese. (These minerals account for the soil's blue-gray shade.) Readier to drink, more graceful, and rounder Barolos are made there. Finally, parts of the townships of Verduno and La Morra lie on soils of Messinian origin that are found in the northwestern part of the Barolo denomination; the soils are sandy, smectite-rich, and gypsiferous (chalky marls derived from gypsum-sulfur formations). This is where you find the most approachable and softest of all Barolos (which does not mean simpler or lesser, just more overtly floral and with early appeal). As a general rule (very general), while the Barolos of Verduno, Barolo, and La Morra can be drunk as early as six to eight years after the harvest (reasonable drinking windows might be eight to twenty-five years in most vintages), Barolos from Monforte d'Alba and Serralunga d'Alba are best approached ten years from the vintage (apt drinking windows might be twelve to thirty-five years). Based on this breakdown, you would naturally assume that the wines of Serralunga, Monforte, and Grinzane ought to be bigger and more structured than those of Barolo and La Morra; and you would be correct, more or less. However, Novello sits on the left side of our imaginary line, too, just like Barolo and La Morra, and therefore its wines should express characteristics linked to soils of the Tortonian stage. In fact, its wines taste nothing like those of La Morra: for the most part, Novello Barolos are characterized by much tougher tannins and mouthfeels, and are among the biggest Barolo brutes when young. (See the "Unità di Novello" subsection of the "The Geologic Units of the Barolo Denomination" section below.)

However, the actual classification of Barolo soils and their composition is much more complicated than the simplistic Messinian-Tortonian-Serravallian breakdown. The regional government of Piedmont sponsored a remarkably interesting if complex study on this subject, clarifying the various geologic levels and sublevels that Barolo can be divided into (Soster and Cellino 1998). Based on the lithology of the soils, not their geologic origin, the Barolo production zone can be divided into four macro soil areas and nine different geological units. The wines you drink correlate more precisely with this breakdown than they do to the simplistic breakdown by geologic origin. Proceeding east to west, or from the oldest to the youngest, there is first the Formazione di Lequio (Lequio formation), made up of alternating layers of reddish-gray compacted sands and gray silty marls, and typical of Serralunga d'Alba (especially) and a few parts of Monforte d'Alba. This mix of yellowish sands and grayish compacted sands is cemented together by carbonate salts, and is generally characterized by excellent water capacity due to the sand-loam presence. This formation is associated with extremely refined but powerful Barolos in which the red-fruit notes dominate. Moving west, we find the Arenarie di Diano (Diano sandstone), formed in the heart of the Serravallian stage; these are blends of gray-brown to yellowish compacted sands and gray sandstone, typical of the townships of Castiglione Falletto and parts of Monforte d'Alba. This is very noteworthy in terms of the Barolos we drink: for even though both formations (the Lequio and the Diano sandstone) were born during the Serravallian stage, they are quite different in their mineral and textural aspects and consequently so will be the wines made with grapes grown there. Farther west still, in an area that covers mostly the townships of Barolo, La Morra, and Verduno (but not all of Verduno and La Morra), we find the *marne di Sant'Agata* (Saint Agathe's marls), formed in the Tortonian stage; these blue-gray marls are rich in magnesium and manganese carbonates. (For precision's sake, I point out that their color is blue-gray below the surface and bluish-gray-white on the surface.) Locally known as *tov,* their composition is roughly 55 percent clay, 30 percent very fine sand, and 15 percent limestone. Drainage can be a problem here due to a degree of water impermeability, but slope gradients are such that adequate water runoff is ensured; choosing the right rootstock is of key importance, since these soils can have surprising concentrations of active lime. Marly soils such as the Saint Agathe's marls give rise to very typical Barolos rich in red-fruit aromas and flavors (pomegranate, sour red cherry, raspberry, strawberry) that often exhibit a balsamic nuance. Last, the *formazioni gessoso-solfifere* (gypsum-sulfur formations) are mostly sandy deposits with chalk and soft sulphate (gypsum). The term *gessoso-solfifero* was first used by Selli in 1960. (It has now been changed to *complesso caotico della Valle Versa,* but most everyone continues to use the old, more manageable, term out of habit.) These formations are soils found in parts of La Morra, Verduno, and Cherasco and were formed during the Messinian stage.

The strong presence of sands in the gypsum-sulfur formations means these are the softest, fastest-maturing Barolos of earliest appeal. When well made, these wines show lovely balance and, though not exactly "blockbusters," can be very enjoyable.

The Geologic Units of the Barolo Denomination

The most accurate way by which to link Barolo's wines to geology is by knowing the geologic units on which the vineyards grow. Unfortunately, these nine different geologic units, if very precisely characterized, are extremely complex and difficult to remember and do not conform to single townships or easy-to-pinpoint natural or manmade landmarks. Therefore, committing to memory where they are found exactly (and hence which crus are located on which unit) is an almost Herculean task. I also believe that the choice of geologic unit names was not especially enlightened, since the potential for confusion is too great: a number of superfamous Barolo crus are situated on geological units the names of which do not correspond to the township with which they are historically associated or to which they belong administratively. For example, one of the geologic soil units is called the Unità di la Morra (La Morra Unit): as we shall see, not every La Morra cru is situated on La Morra Unit–type soils, for example. But, confident in your thirst for knowledge and your willingness to better grasp the nuances of the Barolos you enjoy drinking, I herewith present a breakdown of the nine geologic soil units (*unità*) of the Barolo production zone.

1. UNITÀ DI SERRALUNGA (SERRALUNGA UNIT)

Soil: Lequio formation. Location: corresponds mostly to, but not to all of, the township area of Serralunga d'Alba; its northern limit is just above the Gabutti cru. In an example of the potential for confusion I mentioned just now, the famous Serralunga crus of Prapò, Ceretta, and San Rocco are not situated on a soil belonging to this geologic unit. (Clearly, it would be only natural to assume that a cru of Serralunga such as Prapò would be situated on the Serralunga geologic soil unit, but not so.) However, if you know anything about the wines of Serralunga, you realize immediately why this revelation is meaningful: wines from these crus taste different from those of other parts of Serralunga, and this is because they have (all other factors being equal) a different soil. To make matters even more difficult than they already are, the Serralunga geologic unit spills over into Monforte d'Alba on the left bank of the Talloria stream (and so the Monforte crus of Pressenda, Castelletto, and La Villa are located on Serralunga Unit soils, despite being associated with Monforte in the minds of knowledgeable wine lovers and belonging administratively to the Monforte township).

2. UNITÀ DI CASTIGLIONE (CASTIGLIONE UNIT)

Soil: Arenarie di Diano d'Alba. Location: This is the geologic unit of eight different areas within the Barolo denomination. The biggest of these eight covers a large swath of land in Monforte moving toward Castiglione Falletto. Other areas of the denomination that are characterized by this geologic unit are a section just east of La Morra (Gattera is a famous La Morra cru located on this unit; so you have the confusing situation of a famous La Morra cru the geologic unit of which is called "Castiglione"); a section southeast of Barolo; and an area just south of Fontanafredda in Serralunga (and so the vineyards of the Serralunga crus of Prapò, Cerretta, and San Rocco grow on the Castiglione Unit rather than the Serralunga Unit, as mentioned previously). In fact, while all of Castiglione Falletto's most famous crus (such as Bricco Boschis, Fiasco, Monprivato, Rocche, and Villero) are logically enough (and mercifully, I would add) sitting on the geologic unit (Castiglione Unit) that bears their commune's name, important crus of Monforte such as Ginestra and Mosconi are not, belonging instead to the Barolo Unit (which is of course characterized by a totally different soil than that of the Castiglione Unit).

3. UNITÀ DI LA MORRA (LA MORRA UNIT)

Soil: mainly Saint Agathe's marls, but pockets just south of La Morra are characterized by gypsum-sulfurous deposits of Messinian origin. Location: one of the easiest units to locate geographically, since it corresponds roughly to a long vertical band that runs immediately east of Verduno in the north, Barolo in the center, and Novello to the south. Famous crus situated on this geologic unit include Monvigliero (a cru of the commune of Verduno); Arborina, Brunate, and La Serra (crus mostly of La Morra, though a small piece of Brunate spills over into the Barolo commune); Rué and Liste (Barolo commune); and Le Coste and Merli (Novello commune).

4. UNITÀ DI BAROLO (BAROLO UNIT)

Soil: Saint Agathe's marls. Location: this is the largest of all the geologic units, divided up into four areas that are situated as follows: Barolo to Castiglione Falletto; southeast of Verduno (no corresponding major crus); northeast of Castiglione Falletto in the direction of Grinzane Cavour (the Riva cru, subdivided between Serralunga and Diano, has mostly this geologic unit; same with La Rosa, which extends partly over this geologic unit and partly over the Castiglione Unit); and east of Monforte d'Alba (where Mosconi and Ginestra are located).

5. UNITÀ DI NOVELLO (NOVELLO UNIT)

Soil: there are two main soil types in this geologic unit: in the north, Saint Agathe's marls dominate, while in the south it is mostly the Lequio formation. Location: the area between Novello and Monforte. The most famous cru found on this land unit is Novello's Ravera. It is very important to know this fact, for you immediately grasp its consequences. Even though Novello is located on the left or west side of the imaginary line dividing the soils of Tortonian from those of Serravallian origin, one understands now why Novello's wines can be much harder, tougher, and more rigid than those associated with La Morra or Barolo. Not surprisingly then, wines born from grapes grown on the portion of Novello's soils of Lequio formation (exactly the same as that of Serralunga, a subzone also known for tougher-than-tough Barolos when young) will also be structured and tough at first, and have more in common with wines of Serralunga than those of La Morra, for example.

6. UNITÀ DI VERGNE (VERGNE UNIT)

Soil: Saint Agathe's marls. Location: an area roughly situated north of Novello and west of Barolo. Happily, here there is some correspondence with the location of specific sites and the geologic unit; famous crus that belong to the Vergne Unit are those of Bricco Viole and La Volta (both of which are clearly linked to the town of Vergne, a hamlet of Barolo).

7. UNITÀ DI VERDUNO (VERDUNO UNIT)

Soil: Messinian gypsum-sulfur soils. Location: an area extending southwest of Verduno. The topography is of gently sloping hills that are not especially steep. Interestingly, the best crus of the commune are not situated on this geologic unit, but on La Morra Unit soils.

8. UNITÀ DI BERRI (BERRI UNIT)

Soil: deposits of Messinian origin. Location: an area immediately west of La Morra. Calling things as they really are means writing clearly that there are no Barolo crus of any note here, and knowing the geologic reality of the production zone helps understand this. The less-than-stellar Brandini cru has recently surged to some fame, but I am not sure that this fame is warranted. The site is situated on this geologic unit, where Piedmont's outstanding hazelnuts, not Nebbiolo, ought to be planted.

9. UNITÀ DI GALLO D'ALBA
(GALLO D'ALBA UNIT)

Soil: alluvial deposits of recent origin. Location: the flatlands along the banks of the Talloria stream. These are mostly alluvial soils typically found outside of Serralunga d'Alba and below Grinzane Cavour, characterized by strong water retention; though most often planted to

crops other than grapevines (such as Piedmont's famous and very high quality Tonda Gentile hazelnut), Nebbiolo vineyards can also thrive provided soil fertility is kept at a minimum and good water drainage is ensured.

The Barolo Landscape and Mesoclimate

Barolo is only a few kilometers south of Barbaresco, separated from it by Diano d'Alba's very high quality Dolcetto vines, but the topography and climate of the two most famous Nebbiolo areas of all could not be any more different. Barolo is essentially a horseshoe-shaped basin that is cut in half by a ridge that leads off from Castiglione Falletto in the direction of Monforte. As a result, the Barolo production area is split into two valleys. The western valley runs from Gallo d'Alba to Barolo and includes La Morra. The valley's eastern border is delimited by two streams; the Talloria dell'Annunziata, which separates La Morra from Castiglione Falletto; and the Bussia, which separates Barolo from Monforte. The eastern or Serralunga valley is where the towns of Castiglione Falletto, Monforte, and Serralunga are all found, and it is walled off between two ridges: one the aforementioned ridge that runs from Castiglione Falletto to Monforte, and the other making up the eastern border of the valley. (Wine lovers visiting the area have driven at one time or another on both these ridges, since there are roads on top of both.) The vineyards lie mostly between 150 and 400 meters above sea level, though some crus climb higher up: for example, La Morra's Serradenari is situated at 450 to 540 meters above sea level. In fact, the highest peaks in Barolo do not go much farther up than that. (The Bricco del Dente, just behind La Morra, is 553 meters high, while Bricco Tappa, just north of Monforte, is 1,801 meters high).

Barolo has a Continental climate tempered by its protected inland status as well as by the small streams that flow through it, such as the Talloria. Throughout the year, the average daily temperature runs from 12.5°C to 14.5°C and diurnal temperature variations can be as high as 18.5°C (Winkler index, 1750–2150; Huglin index, 2000–2450). Water reserves are at their lowest between August 5 and August 25, but, at about eight hundred to nine hundred millimeters per year (the southern reaches of Barolo are rainiest), most of the rainfall is concentrated in October and November and again in April and May. The least amount of rain falls from July to September, but drought is rare in Barolo. The area is not especially windy, though due to its extremely hilly nature, the presence of anabatic and katabatic breezes is important in determining how early the vegetative cycle will start up again in the spring. This is one of the reasons why the gradient is an important factor when evaluating Barolo vineyards.

Barolo: The Art of the Blend

Crus have never been a way of life in Barolo, though there has always existed a keener sense of somewhereness here than anywhere else in Italy. Of the 170 Barolo vineyard sites officially recognized today, only the Cannubi vineyard was so famous that its name was placed on a wine's label as early as 1752—and just "Cannubi"; no "Barolo." The first modern bottlings from Barolo sporting a cru name appeared only in the 1960s thanks to Beppe Colla and Alfredo Currado, but for the most part placing the vineyard's name on the label was an infrequent happening. In fact, Barolo's very history is one that could be summarized as "the art of the blend." From the beginning of the 1900s right up to the 1950s–60s, the Barolo market and its sales were the playground of mediators and large firms, all of whom were understandably much more interested in establishing their family name or brand than in making Barolos that spoke of a specific place. There are many positives to making Barolo with a blend of grapes from the different communes, for choosing grapes from different townships allowed firms to make wines along the lines of their own house style (as Champagne houses do with their cuvée blends, for example). Those who wanted structure in their wines went to Serralunga, for example, while those looking to make a more genteel Barolo might have chosen

grapes from La Morra. Another advantage of blending grapes from different communes was that firms could tweak the relative percentages of grapes from each commune based on how the vintage had been in every single subzone. Therefore, in a year when weather might have been especially challenging in La Morra, producers would opt to buy more grapes from Monforte, for example. It was only in the 1980s that cru names began appearing on Barolo bottles, and soon thereafter at a truly alarming rate (some names having only a tenuous link to reality).

In 2010, the Barolo Consorzio introduced the *menzioni geografiche aggiuntive* (MGA)—an Italian term that translates to "additional geographic characterizations." (The Barbaresco Consorzio introduced them sooner, in 2007, giving Barolo's neighbors bragging rights at least on the matter of zonation.) While the MGA names refer to specific Barolos crus (some of which are historically quite famous), they are really best thought of as districts, since the majority are much too large to be viewed as just one vineyard or a cru site of limited size. For example, at 297.97 hectares, the Bussia MGA of Monforte is clearly a huge expanse of land with too many differing exposures, microclimates, gradients, altitudes, and soils for it to be considered just one site or a cru. Furthermore, since the Barolos made within Bussia are altogether different wines, speaking of a Bussia somewhereness is admittedly problematic. (Of course, that does not stop people from trying to do just that, especially those who have to sell the wines.) When all the discussions and deliberations in the town halls regarding how to carve up the specific vineyard sites of the Barolo production zone had finished, the wounded had been counted, and the smoke had cleared, it had been decided that there were going to be 181 MGAs, of which 170 are vineyard areas (the MGAs) and 11 are village designations. As a result of the new MGA guidelines for Barolo (and Barbaresco), the word *vigna* ("vineyard" in Italian) can be used on labels only if the vineyard is located within one of the official MGAs;

also, its name has to appear on the label in association with its corresponding MGA. For the most complete and in-depth analysis of all the MGAs of Barolo, I refer you to Masnaghetti's map book of Barolo, which details the individual MGAs to a degree never attempted before (Masnaghetti 2015). The introduction of MGAs was a necessary and, for the most part, welcome step. By the 1990s the "cru" movement had gained such momentum that some truly strange, even unacceptable, things were starting to happen in Barolo. For one, the popularity of cru-labeled wines was such that some producers were not above, or below, giving a vineyard name to a wine that was not in fact made from grapes picked in a single vineyard. Another problem was that many producers were charging a premium for just about any wine sporting a cru name, regardless of whether the particular vineyard quality merited the high price. For the most part, the MGA confines have been drawn up well, save for a few well-known examples that are not especially valid (the aforementioned Bussia, for example). Though I believe it is a shame that many small high-quality sites have lost the right to be named as such on wine labels, it is true that delimiting MGAs of slightly larger size means that Barolo doesn't have several hundreds of different vineyard names for wine lovers to remember. In this light, the 585 premier crus of Burgundy's Côte d'Or and Côte Chalonnaise must have acted as a silent admonishment to many a Barolo legislator; and even though Barolo tried to tighten things up somewhat, there are still 181 MGAs to contend with (admittedly, still a pretty large number). That said, while the wine geek in me decries the disappearance of some once-famous vineyard names, I can totally understand how the silent majority probably prefers things as they are now.

Of course, the absence of a wine-quality hierarchy in Barolo based on site-specific or vineyard designations is a shame, but in today's world such an undertaking would be a monumental task for anyone to attempt. For the most part it is also really a false problem, because the twelve or fifteen top crus of Barolo have long been documented and are well known to most everyone, producers included. Clearly, this also means that any Barolo cru can be talked up (especially so when a well-thought-of producer buys land there) despite its never having been known for the quality of its wines. Examples include Arborina, Ceretta, and Ravera di Novello, all of which do boast outstanding sites within their boundaries (and each has been associated with some very fine wines over the years). But the fact remains that, even taking climate change into account, they are not vineyard districts that have ever enjoyed the reputation of, say, Brunate or Villero. With Burgundy wines, for example, it almost never happens that generic *villages* wines or those from lowly premier crus are scored higher than those of Montrachet or Richebourg; but with Barolo (and all other Italian wines) it happens routinely.

The Barolo Subzones

LA MORRA

At 828.59 hectares under vine (2017 data, Regione Piemonte), La Morra does not own the largest extension of vineyards in the Barolo production area. (Those bragging rights belong to Monforte and its 1,031.12 hectares.) But it is the township that has the largest extension of Nebbiolo vines that are used to make Barolo (532.22 hectares). There are thirty-nine MGAs in La Morra, and it is the commune that produces the most Barolo annually. Blessed with the highest altitude of all the Barolo communes, La Morra doesn't just produce outstanding Barolos of relatively early appeal and grace, but also shields the whole production zone from cold winds blowing in from the Tanaro. So although La Morra has always been looked upon favorably for the high quality of its wines, all of us wine lovers also owe it a major thank-you for its unheralded but important topographical role. The two roads that head east out of La Morra help situate its Nebbiolo vineyards and aid in understanding the different wine styles made in the commune. The road that heads out in a northeasterly direction toward the Santa Maria hamlet of La Morra is where you will find the tiny conglomerate of houses that make up Roggeri; here are vineyards such as Rocchettevino and Bricco San Biagio. The latter, situated between 220 and 290 meters above sea level, has a full range of exposures, from southeastern to full southern (the best) and southwestern; it is characterized by soils that have one of the highest sand contents of all Barolo, and the wines are accordingly rigid, perfumed, and light-bodied—a graceful style of Barolo quite unlike any other made anywhere else in the denomination. The Ciabot Berton estate has been bottling a Barolo Bricco San Biagio for a number of years now for study purposes; they don't release it for sale as such (it ends up forming the backbone of their estate Barolo), but I have tasted individual bottlings of it kept aside for study purposes on numerous occasions, and I think it's a lovely wine. It is a wine of huge didactic value. (It is an eye-opening experience for beginners to taste a Barolo Rocchettevino side by side with a Bricco San Biagio.) That said, those looking for power and flesh in their wines are better off sticking with Barolos from elsewhere. Rocchettevino, the slope of which is divided in two parts, has vineyards growing anywhere from 280 to 440 meters above sea level, with mainly eastern exposures (with the lower-lying slope looking northeast). Although it has been the source of some outstanding Barolos in recent times (namely, from Gianfranco Bovio and Ciabot Berton), it is one of those Barolo crus that have jumped to fame only in the last fifteen years or so. (Historically, Rocchettevino had always been better known for outstanding Dolcetto wines.) So this is one example where climate change has been beneficial to Barolo. The road that heads out toward the Annunziata fraction of La Morra takes you right by a number of very fine, even outstanding, Barolo vineyards: Rocchette, Rocche dell'Annunziata, Conca, and what used to be called Gancia. Rocche dell'Annunziata (240 to 385 meters above sea level) is the first of show, arguably not just the best site in all of La Morra (Brunate and Cerequio lovers will argue that

statement), but one of the five or six best in the whole Barolo production zone. This is a real grand cru in just about every aspect: as far as I am concerned, it is worth its weight in gold. The site has a southeastern exposure in its higher reaches, while it faces south and southwest lower down. Rocchette and Gancia are examples of what were once relatively well-known Barolo crus that have disappeared with the official launch of the (rather large) MGAs. (Not surprisingly, Rocchette was made a part of Rocche, while Gancia is now a part of Bricco Luciani.) And yet there were some lovely wines made from both those crus. Gancia especially gave highly spicy but refined Barolos thanks to the calcareous-sandy soil; in truth these are also characteristics of wines from the Bricco Luciani, as anyone who has tried Silvio Grasso's wine from this site (when Filippo and the family do not get too carried away with the oak) knows only too well. A study in terroir is offered by the differences present in the outstanding Barolos from the Mauro Molino estate: their Bricco Luciani (again, the vines that used to make their excellent Barolo Gancia are now part of this MGA) could not taste more different from what used to be their Barolo Gallinotto (now a part of the Berri MGA)—a much more structured, linear wine, darker in color than the Bricco Luciani and also characterized by a strong menthol note more typical of Gallinotto's wines, especially in their youth. By the way, do not confuse the Borgata Gallinotto, a clustering of houses in the Berri MGA (very closely located to those of the Borgata Berri) with the Cascina Gallinotto, located in the midst of the Giachini MGA in another part of the La Morra subzone and that, though it bears the same name, has nothing to do with what we are discussing here. North of the Annunziata hamlet is where the well-known vineyards of Arborina, Monfalletto, and Gattera are found. Arborina (250 to 320 meters above sea level, with a good southern to southeastern exposure in its most central portion) is a site made famous by Elio Altare, one of Barolo's more talented producers. That said, it is a lesser cru that, had it not been for Altare's skill and Italian "wine experts" who praised it shamelessly, would never have had its Warholian fifteen minutes of fame. The name of the cru itself derives from *arbor* or *arboretum*, Latin for "tree" or "forest"—a clear-cut indication that growing vines there had never crossed anybody's mind. In this respect, it is enlightening to try, side by side, the same vintage of Altare's Barolos from the Arborina, Brunate (with grapes sold to him by Marco Marengo of the Matteo Marengo estate), and Cannubi crus. As good as the Arborina is (it is a fine wine), there is absolutely no comparison between it and the other two wines, for the Brunate is obviously much deeper and more complex, and the Cannubi a marvel of nuance and balance. That's a lesson in terroir if there ever was one, folks. The Cordero di Montezemolo estate makes lovely wines from both the Monfalletto and Gattera crus. The Monfalletto site is immediately recognizable because of the centenary Lebanon cedar tree that is one of Barolo's most visible and best-known identifying landmarks. The area south of the road going to Annunziata and to the southeast of La Morra is a south-facing slope that looks to Barolo and is where two of the most famous of all Barolo crus are located: Brunate and Cerequio. Brunate (230 to 405 meters above sea level, with southern to southeastern exposure) is, in the minds of many experts, one of the five best vineyards of all Barolo. Unlike most La Morra Barolos, Brunate wines also deliver a good wallop of power along with the grace and charm typical of La Morra. (No doubt, the fact that Brunate is a fairly warm site and its soil has a much higher clay content—almost 40 percent in parts of the vineyard—and a lower sand content than other vineyards in the area helps account for the power.) However, climate change is wreaking havoc, and Brunate is becoming almost too warm (though it was never especially cool to begin with); I find that I am increasingly less impressed by the wines made there in hot years. This applies even more to Cerequio (290 to 400 meters above sea level), recognizable by the fleshy nature of its wines and a strong bal-

samic note (and this is true of all seven producers who make wine there). But Cerequio is even hotter than Brunate; and so despite this vineyard having perhaps the highest historical reputation of all (Lorenzo Fantini rated it as *sceltissimo* rather than just *scelto*), I am not sure modern-day wines always merit a similarly lofty appraisal.

BAROLO

Barolo is the only commune of the Barolo production zone that was not built atop a hill (in fact, the town sits down low in an amphitheater), but it boasts an especially beautiful castle (which once used to be the feudal property of the Marchesi di Falletto) that is now the home of Collisioni (www.collisioni.it)—Italy's biggest annual music, literature, and wine and food festival—as well as of the beautiful Enoteca Regionale del Barolo. Barolo boasts 343.20 hectares under vine (261.49 of which are devoted to Nebbiolo for Barolo production) and thirty MGAs, some of which, like Cerequio and Brunate, are shared with La Morra. The town is indelibly associated with what is the most famous cru of all Barolo: Cannubi. Considered by many to be the very best of all the Barolo vineyards (but just as many would completely and successfully argue that statement), Cannubi experienced such fame that producers have always been inspired to use the Cannubi name in any way possible. And, much as with Montrachet and Puligny-Montrachet in Burgundy, we have Cannubi Boschis, Cannubi San Lorenzo, Cannubi Valletta, and Cannubi Muscatel along with Cannubi, which I have qualified in the past as Cannubi proper or Cannubi *centrale* (D'Agata 2014b). The historical Cannubi extends from the Cascina Viganò to the Cascina Ferrero. Despite this piece of common knowledge, many producers today will tell you that it was common for their parents and grandparents to refer to their vines as being in, or to call their wine simply as, "Cannubi," even though their vines were actually a part of Cannubi Valletta or Cannubi San Lorenzo; apparently, there was not the habit back then of being so precise with these names. (Cynics might say that it was convenient to be just so.) The irony is that, much like Montrachet, Cannubi itself is not a guarantee of greatness in the glass: in fact, many Barolo Cannubis are downright disappointing. For example, great wines are made in Cannubi Boschis (Luciano Sandrone made the site famous, but Francesco Rinaldi's Cannubi is almost all Boschis, too), Cannubi San Lorenzo (for example, Ceretto's outstanding version), Cannubi Valletta (Giacomo Fenocchio's is more than just outstanding), and Cannubi Muscatel (where Cascina Bruciata makes a lovely wine). The perceived greatness of Cannubi proper is in the vineyard's location, seeing as it was long believed to lie at the crossroads of where Barolo's main two geologically different soils, the Tortonian and Serravallian, meet. Therefore, it was believed that the wines stemming from Cannubi combine the perfumed velvetiness of the grapes grown on soils from the Tortonian stage with the power and backbone of those born from grapes grown on soils of the Serravallian stage. It's not so, of course: modern geologic studies have shown that the Cannubi vineyard sits on mainly Saint Agathe's marls of the Tortonian stage. The one single factor that most characterizes Cannubi is its relatively high sand content (35 percent) compared to the rest of the area. (The average for the whole Barolo zone is 31 percent, but it is generally lower in soils of the Tortonian stage.) This sandier nature assures excellent drainage, which explains why Cannubi wines are particularly great in rainy years, and less so in droughty years. Water stress is not a problem where the water table does not run too deep: in the central portion of Cannubi it is only six to eight meters down, and so vines do not suffer stress even in very warm years. The sand component is also responsible for Cannubi being a relatively early-ripening site. Another important factor making the central portion of Cannubi so much better than the others is how windy it is, with nonstop daytime breezes helping ward off disease pressure. For example, Chiara Boschis of Chiara Boschis/E.

Pira states that she has never seen downy mildew in her Cannubi vineyard, and Emanuela Bolla of Serio e Battista Borgogno also confirms that parasite or disease pressure is very rare in the Cannubi proper. All this being said, many Cannubi wines can often disappoint. Droughty years are problematic, and Cannubi can push vigor: keeping yields low is of paramount importance in making wines that showcase the magic that Cannubi can work. At best, Barolos from Cannubi proper are a sublime fusion of striking perfume and ripe silky fruit; at worst, thin, light, and rapidly evolving. The vines range in altitude from 220 to 330 meters above sea level. Exposures and altitudes at which the vines grow vary greatly, too. The other vineyard of note in the Barolo commune is Sarmassa—in my books, a grand cru to all effects. The soil of Sarmassa gives big-structured wines that age remarkably well, though the soil composition of Sarmassa varies greatly from spot to spot (some parts being much richer in clay than others). Sarmassa also has a unique topography: it is a cru with two peaks, so the part of the vineyard known as Bricco Sarmassa, which in other vineyards would be the highest part of the cru, in the case of Sarmassa is but one of the two summits. To the west, in the hamlet of Vergne, is the Bricco delle Viole cru (390 to 480 meters above sea level, boasting two diverse exposures: vines just below the road face east to southwest, and those just above the same road look south-southeast). It is a high-quality cru, where the likes of G. D. Vajra and Mario Marengo are making standout wines. At 45.74 hectares, Bricco delle Viole is not an exactly small MGA; 73 percent is under vine, and 81 percent of it is planted to Nebbiolo, which indicates it is a very good site for the grape. (By contrast, and for comparison's sake, about 50 percent of Serralunga's Boscareto is planted to Nebbiolo, which clearly indicates that parts of it are not exceptional for this cultivar.) Some of the most perfumed Barolos of all are born from Bricco delle Viole; Vajra's 1999 and 2001 are simply spectacular wines, for example. Costa di Rose is another vineyard in the Barolo township worth knowing—not because its wines are especially famous or memorable, but because they are very different from those made everywhere else in this township. In effect, the highly sandy soils of the Coste di Rose vineyard (250 to 310 meters above sea level) are similar to those of the Lequio formation, and this explains the rigid structure of the wines made there, all of which need bottle aging to round out and fleshen up in order to show their best.

CASTIGLIONE FALLETTO

Castiglione Falletto is the Barolo subzone more or less at the heart of the production zone, and for such a strategically important commune, it is surprising that it has so little land under vine: 220.62 hectares, of which 144.99 are devoted to Nebbiolo for Barolo production and 75.63 are planted with other wine grapes. The latter number is more than a third less than that of La Morra, almost a third less than Monforte, and about half the vines of Barolo. Vignolo-Lutati believed the Castiglione Falletto terroir to be a very homogenous one, and in fact the wines of this commune are some of the most balanced of all Barolos. In other words, Castiglione Falletto Barolos exhibit characteristics that are typical of the Barolos from La Morra as well as those of Serralunga. It's also a subzone characterized by very solid winemaking, with a bevy of very talented if not especially flashy producers. Furthermore, two of Barolo's greatest crus of all, Rocche and Villero, are located here, and a third, Fiasco, doesn't lag far behind the best. Another feather in Castiglione Falleto's cap is that the official zonation of the commune was done especially well, with only twenty-two MGAs.

Castiglione Falletto is one of the easiest Barolo townships to get around in. Its crus can be easily broken down in those of two sectors, located on the eastern and western slopes of one main ridge that runs north to south (roughly moving from Alba down toward Monforte). On the eastern slope, which is the one with fewer vineyards, the crus of Piantà, Pernanno, Scarrone, Pira, and Rocche run from north to south. With the creation of the MGAs, crus such as Cerroni and Lipulot were fused with others (Cerroni in Pernanno, Lipulot into Rocche), which is just as well, since they weren't especially famous and no memorable Barolos were made bearing their names. By contrast, the western slope of Castiglione Falletto boasts one famous cru after another, starting north with the Parussi cru, and then, in succession, Montanello, Bricco Boschis, Monprivato, Codana, Vignolo, Solanotto, Villero, Brunella, Fiasco, Altenasso, Serra, Mariondino, and Pugnane.

Some of these sites deliver truly memorable Barolos. Rocche di Castiglione was simply known as Rocche before 2010, but the cru's name has been officially changed in order to avoid confusion with La Morra's just as famous Rocche dell'Annunziata. The Rocche di Castiglione vineyard (320 to 350 meters above sea level) faces mostly southeast and is very steep: one small parcel is exposed fully south. This exposure sets it neatly apart from Villero, Castiglione Falletto's most famous other cru, which has a mostly southwest exposure. Rocche is a remarkably thin strip of sandy land, producing some of the most perfumed and balanced Barolos of all, but Barolos that also have real power (which, for example, the graceful wines of Cannubi proper or of Santa Maria in La Morra lack). In the new, modern classification of the Barolo MGAs, Rocche di Castiglione has been extended to the western slope of the Castiglione Falletto ridge, but that is historically inaccurate, because the cru on the western side was always known as Serra. In truth Serra, though less famous than Rocche di Castiglione, was always a top-quality site, and very similar in soil composition to Rocche for the most part (though the soil of Rocche can vary in color and mineral content depending on where you sample it). For example, gray, almost bluish marls dominate the northern section of the Rocche MGAs right up to the border between Serra and Mariondino; then the hue lightens in the direction of the Monforte border, where the soil's sand content increases further, thereby contributing to the paler color. Numerous great wines have been made over the years from Rocche di Castiglione, such as Vietti's Rocche bottling and Brovia's "Rocche dei Brovia" Barolo. Giovanni Sordo now makes an interesting Rocche as well. Castiglione Falletto's western slope is where a number of noteworthy crus are found. The first of the well-known Barolo crus here is Bricco Boschis, of which the Cavallotto family is practically the sole owner (their beautiful home and winery is perched right atop the cru), but in fact both Vietti and Roccheviberti also own very small parcels of vines in the Bricco Boschis. The Bricco Boschis is a medium to large Barolo cru where vines grow between 230 and 340 meters above sea level; and since it is essentially a round hill, it offers multiple different exposures (south-southwestern for its most central portion; the side that looks out to Serralunga faces east, while the other faces west-northwest). Over the years, terroir lovers have had a field day thanks to the hard work and passion of the Cavallotto family, who over the years have vinified many different Barolos from three different portions of this cru. Right across the Bricco Boschis is one of the most famous Barolo crus of all, Monprivato, which slopes down eastward. Monprivato's vines range in altitude from 240 to 310 meters above sea level and have a mainly south-southwestern exposure. It is a cru made famous by the Giuseppe Mascarello and the Sobrero estates. When Violante Sobrero sold his vineyards to Mascarello (including some in Villero, another prestigious cru), Mascarello remained the sole producer of Monprivato Barolo for many years, and many were in the mistaken belief that nobody else owned land there. Not so: today, two other producers can boast vineyards in Monprivato: Giovanni Sordo owns a small rectangular plot of vines up high close to the road and is making an acclaimed wine from this site, while Terre del Barolo farms a small triangular plot known as Banadona that was first planted to vines at the turn of the new century (first with Dolcetto, and since 2003, Nebbiolo). Villero is one of Castiglione Falletto's largest crus, with vines

ranging in altitude from 240 to 350 meters above sea level, with a mainly southwestern exposure in the central part of the cru (while the northern and southern reaches look west-southwest). One of Barolo's top ten or fifteen crus, it has had numerous owners, and hence there have been many fine Villero wines to try over the years. Differently from Rocche, Villero's wines are much more tannic and ageworthy, with almost Monforte-like elements; over the years, the best wines have almost always been made with grapes grown in the cru's upper reaches. Noteworthy wines include those of Giuseppe Mascarello, Giacomo Fenocchio, Cordero di Montezemolo (his marvelous Enrico VI Barolo is all Villero), and Vietti. Tellingly, both Vietti and Mascarello choose to bottle Riserva wines from this site; also, some memorable Bruno Giacosa Barolos were Riservas from this site. (The Giacosa 1978 Riserva is magical wine, but the 1988 and 1989 white-label, non-*riserva* wines are excellent, too.) Brunella (280 to 320 meters above sea level, with a mainly southwestern exposure) is owned solely by the Boroli family, and since its wines are at least partly similar to those of Villero (La Brunella itself is a natural prolongation of Villero cru), they had always used the Brunella grapes for their Villero bottling. (Boroli now bottles an excellent Barolo Brunella.) Right below Codana, Fiasco extends from Brunella higher up and Altenasso down below, and its flask-shaped contour is well known to Barolo lovers. Characterized by a hot microclimate, the cru derives its name not from the flask-like shape of the site but from the habit of the local vineyard workers of bringing flasks of water with them to work there. The vines grow at between 225 and 275 meters above sea level; Fiasco's higher slopes, with a southwestern exposure, are of especially high quality (owned by either the Paolo Scavino or the Azelia estate).

MONFORTE

Monforte is a very large subzone with 1,031.12 hectares under vine, of which 441.55 hectares are planted to Nebbiolo vines for Barolo. (Only

La Morra, among the Barolo communes, has more hectares under vine devoted to Nebbiolo.) Unlike other Barolo townships, the Monforte politicians decided to limit the number of crus, and as early as the mid-1990s had identified a maximum of ten MGAs. This decision, while undoubtedly making it easier to understand and remember the crus of Monforte, has the disadvantage of creating extremely large crus, such as is the case with Bussia and Bricco San Pietro, the second-largest and largest MGAs of all, respectively. Monforte is shaped roughly like a two-pronged triangle, with Castiglione Falletto to the north, Barolo and Novello to the west, and Serralunga to the east; it essentially covers the south-central part of the Barolo production zone. It can be divided into two by the road running from Monforte to Alba, which divides the area into an eastern and a western sector (where the hamlets of Castelletto and Perno, respectively, are found). The southeastern section of Monforte is where two of the commune's top-quality Barolo sites—Ginestra and Mosconi—are located, with the very good Le Coste di Monforte close by. All three sites are characterized by soils with the highest sand content of all Monforte as well as one of the lowest concentrations of clay. Ginestra is an extremely famous cru for wines of uncompromising fleshiness, warmth, and power (the antithesis of Bussia wines), made famous by outstanding Barolos such as Clerico's Ciabot Mentin Ginestra, Paolo Conterno's Ginestra and Ginestra Riserva, and the Conterno Fantini Sorì Ginestra. The key to Ginestra is, in my opinion, knowing that it is the cru's vines growing at its highest elevations that give the greatest wines, because Barolos made farther down the slopes tend to show progressively less-refined tannins (which in fact have never been Ginestra's selling point). After all, it is not by chance that Domenico Clerico's Barolo Ginestra and Conterno Fantino's Sorì Ginestra wines are made from grapes picked on the cru's highest slopes. The Barolo Casa Matè by Elio Grasso, Conterno Fantino's Vigna del Gris (a great wine but which is always noticeably the lesser Barolo in the Conterno Fantino stable), and Paolo Conterno's Ginestra bottlings are made from grapes grown at similar altitudes but also slightly lower down the slope. Outstanding wines all, so altitude may not play such an important role in Ginestra after all. No Monforte cru no longer with us is more famous than Pajana, but actually it had historically always been considered to be a part of Ginestra (290 to 540 meters above sea level, with the best sections of the slope having a south-southeastern exposure). Pajana's microclimate is fresher than Ginestra's—which, coupled with the lower-lying vines (the Pajana portion of Ginestra sits at 300 to 370 meters above sea level, with a mainly southern exposure), means more-austere, bigger wines than the fleshier ones typical of Ginestra. Clearly, the most famous Barolo Pajana of all was Domenico Clerico's, but Renzo Seghesio also made a good one. Mosconi (350 to 460 meters above sea level) is a rather large site with the best-placed vines having southern to southeastern exposures. It has recently come to prominence because many producers have bought land here and are now making a Barolo Mosconi of their own. Witness, for example, Chiara Boschis, who never used to bottle one (her famous Barolos were the Barolo Cannubi and Via Nuova, the latter a blend of different vineyards), or Conterno Fantino, who had never made anything but a Vigna del Gris and a Sorì Ginestra but started bottling a Barolo Mosconi as of 2004. Perhaps the most famous Barolo Mosconi of all was never identified as such: Domenico Clerico's Percristina bottling was named after Domenico's young daughter, who passed away at a very young age. Barolo lovers know that Rocche dei Manzoni's funnily named Barolo Big 'd Big was also made all from Mosconi grapes. Mosconi was once a very small site, and there undoubtedly used to be a sense of somewhereness in wines made from grapes grown there, but today, at 75.95 hectares, it is not really so small anymore (only a little more than 50 percent of Mosconi is planted to Nebbiolo). Chiara Boschis's Mosconi is made with grapes grown in what used to be the Conterno cru, a very clay-rich site that performs particularly well in hot, droughty years thanks to its water-retentive capacity. In fact, it's not too hard to pick out a Barolo Mosconi in a blind tasting, since they all have a fleshy mouthfeel and a strong balsamic note that is unmistakable. Below Mosconi is the cru once simply known as Ravera, but now called Ravera di Monforte to help avoid confusion with the Ravera MGA of Novello. It is a medium-small site with vines growing at 230 to 450 meters above sea level. Flavio Roddolo and Cascina Chicco (their wine was called Barolo Bricco Rocca) also made some good wines from here.

The western sector of Monforte is both big and complicated; it could be subdivided into four microareas. The historical heart of the Bussia MGA is the Bussia Soprana, with the three near-mythical Aldo Conterno crus of Colonello, Cicala, and Romirasco. This part of Monforte is characterized by soils with relatively high sand, medium clay, and low limestone content and high iron concentration. Located between 290 and 390 meters above sea level, Conterno's three famous sites are very different one from the other, as a quick walk in the vineyards will show immediately: Colonnello has a southwestern exposure and an unbelievably fine, sandy soil (not unlike what you see when walking on a beach); Cicala has a southeastern exposure and much-richer compact clay soil (Cicala's name derives from the cicadas—*cicale* in Italian—that live in the nearby forest and that seemingly never stop singing); Romirasco faces southwest and is the highest of these three world-famous crus and the one that gives the most complete, deep wine. Aldo Conterno Barolos from the 1970s and 1980s rank among Italy' s best wines ever; after a period of adjustment due to a new generation taking over and finding its way, these wines are in top form again. Gabutti also has a southwestern exposure, which is no surprise given that it is the natural prolongation of the Romirasco cru. More south still and to the west is the area where the Dardi and Pianpolvere Soprano

crus were located; lower down, Arnulfo and Visette were two other good crus, the latter providing a very mineral Barolo of real power and sneaky refinement. Attilio Ghisolfi's was the best-known wine made from the site. (Now that Visette is part of the Bussia megacru, the wine is labeled Bussia Bricco Visette.) Pianpolvere Soprano is a site that has a very sandy soil (*polvere* meaning "dust" or "powder" in Italian) similar to that of the Colonnello; Bruno Giacosa, perhaps the most famous Barolo and Barbaresco producer of all, told me many years ago that it is, in his opinion, the best cru of all Barolo. (Giacosa made a Barolo Riserva labeled Bussia, but that was reportedly made with grapes picked in this cru, in 1974, 1975, 1978, and 1979.)

SERRALUNGA D'ALBA

In 2008, Serralunga boasted 465 hectares under vine (311 hectares of Nebbiolo); the rest were planted with Dolcetto (46.5 hectares), Barbera (33 hectares), and Moscato Bianco (30 hectares), plus various other grapes used in Langhe wine blends (43 hectares). By comparison, Serralunga has 500.10 hectares under vine today (346.19 of Nebbiolo), so the town maintains a copious number of other grape varieties in its fold. It is a large township with thirty-nine MGAs; but while Serralunga is currently very trendy, only a handful of producers make truly benchmark wines. Serralunga's vineyards can be divided between those of the eastern slope and of the western slope: of the two, the eastern slope has the fewer and less-famous vineyards. The western slope rises steadily upward, and can be divided roughly into three sectors. The first has the lowest-lying vineyards (for example, Baudana is located between 250 and 350 meters above sea level; the second is higher up (crus such as Marenca and Rivette are located at 280 to 355 meters and 320 to 385 meters above sea level, respectively); and the third sector rises steeply upward (for example, the outstanding cru Falletto, solely owned by Giacosa, is found at 330 to 425 meters above sea level, and farther south, the Nebbiolo vines of the likewise excellent Francia cru grow at 360 to 445 meters above sea level). Falletto's central core looks south, while the extremities have southwestern or western exposures. It is made up of roughly thirteen parcels of vines, of which three to four always give the deepest wine. Francia, at the southernmost tip of the Serralunga production zone (only Arione is farther south) is the source of memorable Barolos (for example, the ultrafamous and superexpensive Barolo Riserva Monfortino). The Barolo Francia is the "other" Barolo made from this cru by Giacomo Conterno (this estate is the sole owner of Francia); in my view, much as in the Moueix stable Chateau Trotanoy was dwarfed by Pétrus, Francia suffers at the hands of its more famous sibling. It should not really do so, given that it is a magical wine in nearly all vintages (and the 1989 and the 1994 are about as good as any Barolo can get). Francia's vines grow at 360 to 445 meters above sea level and face west-southwest, save for a small section that looks east-southeast. The altitude and the luminous, well-ventilated amphitheater make for a cooler microclimate and outstanding wines in warmer years, too (though it shouldn't escape attentive Barolo lovers that Monfortino is rarely made in truly hot years: for example, no 2003, 2007, 2011, or 2012 vintages were made). Francia is also a very good site for Barbera: talented Roberto Conterno grows it in the lower-lying slopes as well as on the eastern part of the slope close to the Cascina Francia. Lazzarito's vines grow between 300 and 390 meters above sea level, with mostly southern and west-north-western exposures. It is a site that gives very powerful, austere Barolos of noteworthy complexity and depth. For example, the 1982 Fontanafredda Lazzarito is one of the best wines ever made by Fontanafredda; Vietti's Lazzarito is almost always his most austere wine, even more than the Villero—a *riserva*, which has more flesh. Not all of Lazzarito gives the same wine, however: in my view, this cru can be subdivided into La Delizia, which a few experts consider a part of the Parafada cru (but historically, it was never thought to be so), Lazzarito

proper, Lazzaraisco (farther down the slope), and Santa Caterina. (Guido Porro, a talented if little-known producer of very solid, dependable Barolos, used to make Barolos from each of these last two sites, though with the MGA names now official, these two sites no longer exist as such, having all been turned into Lazzarito.) The heart of the Lazzarito cru is what I refer to as Lazzarito proper, around the Cascina Lazzarito (also known as Santa Giulia). You won't be surprised to know that it is the section that locals have always told me is the best for Nebbiolo, one that gives the greatest of all Lazzarito Barolos. Pure Serralunga in style, they represent Lazzarito at its fullest and best: big, steely, slow to mature, and world-class. Prapò is the cru on the eastern flank of Serralunga that I believe to be a grand cru for Nebbiolo. The vines grow between 280 and 370 meters above sea level and have either southern or southeastern exposures. Prapò is actually a direct continuation of the Cerretta cru, but has for the most part a much better exposure than most of the (too) large Ceretta MGA. Cerretta's name probably derives from *cerro,* or "oak." (There are many oak trees in the periphery of the MGA—not at all a bad thing given their link to the white truffle that the Alba area is famous for.) It is an extremely popular cru of late; many well-known Barolo producers have bought land here and started making wine recently (for example, G. D. Vajra and Giacomo Conterno). However, it has become a much larger cru than it used to be because a series of smaller crus such as Cerretta Piani were fused with Cerretta proper. Which means that not all the vineyard positions in Cerretta are of the same quality level, and hence, neither are the wines (though they all carry the name Cerretta). The most famous cru of all Serralunga is Vigna Rionda—the name probably a corruption of *"vigna rotonda,"* which is how the vineyard's name appears on labels of wines from the late 1960s and 1970s. Is Vigna Rionda (as of 2011, and the official naming of the Barolo MGAs, its name ought to be written as one word: Vignarionda) the best Barolo cru of all? For many Barolo lovers such as myself there is no doubt that this cru stands out, much as Romanée-Conti does in Burgundy. Hallowed vines grow between 250 to 360 meters above sea level and have a mostly south-southwestern exposure, save for the small parcel that looks toward Monforte d'Alba (and therefore faces west). Interestingly, while everybody considers Vignarionda to be the best of all Serralunga crus, a *grand hors classe* if you will, its wines are not so typical of Serralunga, at least in the sense of being austere, steely, tough-as-nails brutes when young. Rather, the wines of Vignarionda, no matter who makes them (be it Luigi Pira, Massolino, or Bruno Giacosa), have always been characterized by a fleshy, sexy, and tactile mouthfeel that is quite unlike that of any other Serralunga Barolo. Clearly the depth and complexity achieved by Bruno Giacosa from this site's Canale-owned vines make a case for this being the best Barolo site of them all. Giacosa made a Barolo Vigna Rionda, most often as a red-label Riserva, in the following vintages: 1967, 1968, 1970, 1975, 1978, 1982, 1985, 1989, 1990, and 1993. It is only fair and historically accurate to write that many in that list rank among the greatest Italian red wines ever made. Of course, there are still other sites in Serralunga worth knowing, since they, too, give excellent wines. Margheria Barolos are sweet and floral: Luigi Pira's version is outstanding. Unfortunately, Ornato, solely owned by Pio Cesare, kicks the "sweetness thing" up a notch or two, with fleshy wines strongly marked by balsamic and cocoa-like notes (too balsamic and too cocoa-like, for me); it's a big, impressive mouthful of wine that wins over a lot of admirers upon first tastes, but it is a Barolo that has really never reminded me much of Nebbiolo, and I much prefer the grace and refinement of Pio Cesare's Barbaresco Il Bricco, from the Bricco di Treiso cru.

VERDUNO

Up at 380 meters above sea level, with beautiful views over portions of the Tanaro River valley and the Roero, Verduno not surprisingly has as its nickname the "Sentinel of the Langhe." The name "Verduno" itself is of Celtic origin, and means "flowery hill." You could joke that it ought to be changed to "vineyardy hill," since Verduno now boasts 198.16 hectares under vine, of which slightly more than half (109.80 hectares) are planted to Nebbiolo. (Verduno accounts for 5 percent of the total annual Barolo production.) Verduno's soil was formed during the Tortonian stage and is composed of the type of Saint Agathe's marls that extend southward through the Monvigliero cru down to Brunate and Cerequio in La Morra. Verduno is characterized by a slightly warmer microclimate and less rainfall than other areas of the Barolo production zone. There are eleven MGAs in Verduno, many of them the source of excellent Barolos: the best MGAs are those located immediately to the east of the town of Verduno and are arranged snugly together like the three prongs of an upside-down fork. Monvigliero is by far Verduno's most famous cru and one of the fifteen or twenty best in all of Barolo; it is a medium-large site characterized by soils that are roughly 40 percent loam, 30 percent clay, and 30 percent sand, and lies at 280 to 350 meters above sea level, with a full range of exposures (the best sites in this MGA being those fully south facing). San Lorenzo di Verduno (located at 210 to 280 meters above sea level) is a medium-size site with a mostly south-southwestern exposure), and its wines are different from those of Monvigliero. Interestingly, it is not the soil differences that contribute most to the diversity of wines from the two crus (they have fairly similar soils, different from those of other Verduno MGAs such as Rocche dell'Olmo or Neirane, which are sandier and loamier sites, respectively), but rather the microclimate, exposure, and gradients of each. (San Lorenzo di Verduno is less steep than Monvigliero.) Both Monvigliero and San Lorenzo di Verduno give extremely refined Barolos—a trait due in no small measure to their geographical location, since they are among the first sites to be hit by the winds blowing in from the Tanaro (which help characterize the specific microclimate of this sector of Verduno). It is a situation very similar to that of Barbaresco, also known for elegant wines of generally lighter structure than most Barolos. In fact, this very elegance that is innate to the Verduno MGA (and the Monvigliero–San Lorenzo di Verduno section in particular) is one of the reasons why there was never much Nebbiolo Rosé grown in this commune; the Barolos from here did not need the perfumed, elegant touch of Nebbiolo Rosé. There are two main reasons why I think that Monvigliero is a truly unique site (I am not sure its greatness has yet become apparent to all): first, it produces extremely refined Barolos of uncanny floral perfume (at times almost decadently so). Some producers (who do not make a Barolo Monvigliero, mind you) have told me over the years that they believe Monvigliero's often unforgettable, pungently fragrant nose of aromatic herbs and flowers is due to the fact that estates in the area do not destem the Nebbiolo grapes prior to pressing them. However suggestive this hypothesis may be, I know for a fact that many producers of Monvigliero Barolos do destem, so the presence of stems cannot account wholly for the magical perfume that characterizes the best Monvigliero Barolos. The second reason why I am so impressed by Monvigliero is that it is just about always the best or second-best Barolo made at every estate fortunate enough to own or rent vines in the MGA. It cannot be an accident that things are so. For example, Paolo Scavino had long made outstanding Cannubi, Rocche dell'Annunziata, and Fiasco (Bric del Fiasc) Barolos, but his Monvigliero was as good as if not better than the other Barolos in his portfolio right from the first vintage. Sordo, who has an incredible lineup of Barolos sporting single MGA names, also makes a good Monvigliero—always one of the two or three best wines in his lineup.

NOVELLO

Novello owes its Barolo fame to Elvio Cogno. Had it not been for him, nobody would have thought of planting much Nebbiolo in this commune, always known for Barbera and Dolcetto. Of course, now that producers have bought land in Novello and are making Barolo (of Novello's 221.68 hectares under vine, 182.101 are planted to Nebbiolo), everyone is writing these wines up in glowing terms, but the fact remains that unless you are a big believer in the effects of global warming, there is little reason to think of Novello as a potential source of top-end Barolos (at least at the present time). Novello, situated below Barolo, is an open amphitheater where the hail hits first, prior to the air currents losing energy and drying up; for example, in those years when Novello gets hail, the vineyards of Barolo hardly see any. As always, there are exceptions to such general statements, and there are standout crus in Novello. Of the seven MGAs of Novello, the three best known are Bergera-Pezzole, Sottocastello di Novello, and Ravera; the latter produces Barolos that rank with the best especially when made with grapes from a specific section of this very large MGA, essentially corresponding to the Bricco Pernice plot (owned by the Cogno estate). Ravera ranges in altitude from 300 to 405 meters above sea level, and the best sections have either a south-southeastern or south-southwestern exposure (the latter of which is Bricco Pernice's). An excellent Barolo from Bergera-Pezzole to look for is made by Le Strette. Novello's Barolos are all characterized by very structured mouthfeels thanks to chewy, massive tannins that remind one of those of Serralunga but without their nobility; very differently from most Serralunga Barolos, however, the better Novello wines have a fleshy (at times slightly chunky) mouthfeel even when young.

CHERASCO, DIANO D'ALBA, GRINZANE CAVOUR, AND RODDI

At 2.2, 19.79, 58.88, and 24.21 hectares of Nebbiolo vines, respectively, Cherasco (one Barolo MGA, Mantoetto, and 22.48 hectares planted to wine grapes other than Nebbiolo), Diano d'Alba (three Barolo MGAs and 490.56 hectares planted to varieties other than Nebbiolo), Grinzane Cavour (eight Barolo MGAs and only another 32.53 hectares planted to cultivars other than Nebbiolo), and Roddi (one Barolo MGA and another 94.51 hectares planted to non-Nebbiolo wine grapes) are clearly the least famous Barolo communes. Diano d'Alba is a grand cru area for Dolcetto, and has only a couple of noteworthy Barolo crus: Sorano (shared with Serralunga) and Gallaretto. Grinzane Cavour gives very tough, highly structured wines that can age well but that never develop, in my experience, the complexity or layered depth of the greatest Barolos; La Spinetta's Campé (from the Garretti MGA) is probably the most famous Grinzane Cavour Barolo of all, but as much as I love La Spinetta's Moscato d'Asti wines (truly some of the best of all), I am not a fan of their Barolos (or Barbarescos), finding them always marred by too much oak (and very balsamic oak at that). Roddi has only one MGA, Bricco Ambrogio, and it gives solid, well-rounded wines even in off years such as 2002, but the wines are not especially exciting. The Paolo Scavino estate has done much to bring Bricco Ambrogio wines to everyone's attention.

BENCHMARK WINES

The following is a very short list for which I have selected only one wine per estate and limited myself to three-star wines; otherwise, the list would have been too long.

Bruno Giacosa / Azienda Agricola Falletto Vigna Le Rocche Riserva***PS, Giacomo Conterno Monfortino***PS.

Aldo Conterno Romirasco***, Boroli Villero***, Cavallotto Riserva San Giuseppe***, Ceretto Rocche Bricco Rocche***, Chiara Boschis Barolo Mosconi***, Ciabot Berton Rocchettevino***, Conterno Fantino Ginestra***, G. B. Burlotto Monvigliero***, Giacomo Fenocchio Villero***, Mario Marengo Brunate Vecchie Vigne***, Marrone Bussia***, Giuseppe Mascarello Monprivato***, Massolino Vignarionda***, Francesco Rinaldi Brunate***, Giuseppe Rinaldi Brunate***, Rivetto Briccolina***, Luciano Sandrone Aleste***, Paolo Scavino

Rocche dell'Annunziata Riserva***, Sylla Sebaste Bussia***, G. D. Vajra Bricco delle Viole***, Vietti Rocche***.

Barbaresco

The first mention we have of a Barbaresco wine dates back to 1799 (Cavazza 1907), when the Austrian army defeated a French army on the plains of Genola; two days later General De Melas ordered, from Barbaresco, "*una carrà* of excellent Nebbiolo wine" (one *carrà* being the equivalent of about 492 liters). Barbaresco as such began to blossom in 1894 thanks to Domizio Cavazza, the dean of the Scuola Enologica di Alba (the Alba Winemaking School), who bought the castle of Barbaresco and adjacent vineyards. In the same year he founded, with a few of the local winemakers, the Cantina Sociale di Barbaresco (the ancestor of today's Produttori di Barbaresco co-op) and began to tirelessly promote the wines of the area, elevating them to the same fame as that of Barolo. According to Cavazza (1907), many others contributed to facilitating knowledge about Barbaresco and its wines: Carlo Rocca; Carlo Pagliuzzi, from Alba, who was the first to bring Barbaresco wines into Switzerland; the Luigi Calissano estate, whose Barbarescos won numerous awards at wine fairs of those times; and others. Unfortunately, Cavazza passed away prematurely in 1912 and Barbaresco fell on hard times, leading to the Cantina Sociale di Barbaresco going out of business and mediators buying Barbaresco's Nebbiolo grapes to use in making even better Barolos. In those days, there was still no law governing the origin of grapes used to make a specific wine. (Of course, there are many whispers that, even today, Barbaresco supplies Barolo with grapes when the latter has bad vintages, and vice versa, but of course we know something like that would never happen in Italy.) Interestingly, in 1988 there were 482 estates making 28,000 hectoliters of wine from 500 hectares of vines (Garner and Merritt 1990), while today there are 746.46 hectares and annual production is roughly

2.5 million bottles (or over 180,000 hectoliters). In 2007, Barbaresco's different crus were officially recognized (the so-called Menzioni Geografiche Aggiuntive, or MGA), and these sixty-six hallowed sites are now recognized on labels. For the most in-depth analysis of the Barbaresco MGAs, I refer you to Masnaghetti's map book (Masnaghetti 2016). In any case, the MGAs did not come a moment too soon: locals have long known that some sites in Barbaresco always deliver better grapes than others—much like in Burgundy, where a patchwork of premier crus and grand crus also exists. I am a huge fan of Barbaresco, and I think it is an underrated relative of Barolo: in fact, my top ten Nebbiolo wines from Langhe would favor Barolo over Barbaresco by only a slight margin. If I have only one caveat about Barbaresco relative to Barolo, it is that the former production area does not have the wealth of talented, bigger, and very organized producers of the latter.

Terroir in Barbaresco plays a major role in fashioning Nebbiolo wines that are different from those made anywhere else. Actually, terroir is the very reason Barbaresco exists. In fact, it was always obvious to the locals that the Nebbiolo grapes from Barbaresco gave different wines from those of nearby Barolo, and so it was inevitable that sooner or later there would be a push to bottle separate wines from this specific area. The area was defined in 1926 and then enlarged in 1933 to include Neive. In fact, much as with the Marchese Fracassi in Barolo, who lobbied hard, and ultimately successfully, to have Cherasco included within the official Barolo production zone, so it was with Barbaresco, where Count Riccardo Candiani, the owner of Castello di Neive, also lobbied long and hard, to have Neive included in the Barbaresco production zone. At last, his efforts were met with success.

Barbaresco and Barolo are similar in that they are both 100 percent Nebbiolo wines. After that, I would say, the similarities end. First and foremost, Barbaresco is not a feminine wine, and descriptions along those lines reveal a real lack of both imagination and knowledge. Simply put, Barbaresco is one of the world's more structured wines, and in blind tastings many Barbarescos are routinely mistaken for Barolos: so much for "feminine." The lighter-styled personality that Barbaresco has come to be associated with is the result of this wine being aged one year less in wood than Barolo and having a slightly less massive mouthfeel. Undoubtedly, Barbaresco is mellower, and readier to drink sooner, than Barolo. This is very much the consequence of its terroir, a very different terroir than that of Barolo. Barbaresco is located roughly three kilometers northeast of Barolo but is a world apart. It is much smaller than Barolo, with only four communes or townships (compared with Barolo's eleven): Barbaresco, Neive, Treiso, and San Rocco Seno d'Elvio (an administrative hamlet of Alba, and therefore sometimes referred to just as Alba, mistaken though this is). The Barbaresco production zone's hills are generally much softer and lower-lying (mostly 150 to 300 meters above sea level, though there are vineyards in the Treiso commune that climb up close to 500 meters), and the gradients less steep. The production area is much closer to the Tanaro River—a fact that has important consequences because it contributes to making Barbaresco's a much warmer macroclimate than Barolo's. Therefore, Nebbiolo ripens sooner in Barbaresco than in Barolo (usually by about two weeks). The wines are also ready to drink sooner (though they can age magnificently well: properly cellared Barbarescos from the 1940s and 1960s are still a thing of beauty). The soil and not just the macroclimate play major roles in this early-drinking, or "approachable when young," quality of Barbaresco, since the area's soils are almost all compact gray-white marl and limestone formed during the Tortonian stage—a soil mix that is known to give sooner-ready-to-drink wines. The soil of a small area in the southern sector of Treiso is instead characterized by the presence of the Lequio formation typical of Serralunga, and this contributes to the austere, almost rigid (when young) character of some Treiso Barbarescos. Speaking generally, Barbaresco's soils contain more clay than Barolo's and have a somewhat more even distribution of minerals.

The Barbaresco Subzones

BARBARESCO

In general, the wines of the Barbaresco commune are the most balanced of all Barbarescos, and have always been recognized for being quite distinct from those made in the other three communes. In fact, there was a time when Barbaresco tried to resist the enlargement of its wine's production zone to include townships such as Neive (Manzo and Trucchi 1927). Even then, differences in geology were cited, perhaps misguidedly, as an important reason that Neive should not be allowed to make a wine called "Barbaresco." Barbaresco's production zone was once vast. Cavazza (1907) writes that the territory of Barbaresco denomination was 1,700 hectares large, but stresses how the majority of this land belonged to four hamlets under control of the parish of Treiso, where the soils, according to Cavazza, were too rich in clay and too cold for Nebbiolo to perform well. (Cavazza reports that the territory of the commune of Barbaresco was then 700 hectares large, much of it under vine.) Barbaresco's fortunes changed for the worse with the death of Cavazza, and vineyard extension dropped over the decades following his demise. More recently, there were 217 hectares and 132 growers in the commune of Barbaresco in 1988, and today there are 246.58 hectares planted to Nebbiolo (and 103.08 hectares planted to other wine grapes). The town is recognizable from a distance because of its tower, built on foundations that might date back to ancient Roman times. The latest incarnation of the tower was built as a lookout post where fires could be lit to warn the populace of invaders; of course the fires could be lit for other reasons, too, such as the one that was lit in honor of the king of Italy's arrival. (Which would have been just fine if the fellows who decided upon this action didn't also think it a good idea to burn the tower's original furniture to light that fire. A real shame, but I guess those were other times and we shouldn't judge them by today's standards.)

The greatest expanse of this commune's best crus is located south of the town, toward the hamlets of Tre Stelle and Treiso. A ridge immediately south of Barbaresco is where the crus of Secondine, Pajé, and Muncagota (formerly known as Moccagatta) are found, but for the most part these are second-tier crus. Secondine, a good-quality south-facing site but no more than that, is where Gaja's San Lorenzo wine is made. (In the words of the man's inimitable, charming, bombastic style, Angelo Gaja once joked to me: "Of course I had to call my wine something else, I certainly didn't want to be associated with anything called second.") The best cru in this part of Barbaresco is probably the very small Pajé, once called Paglieri (as in a pile of straw—*paglio* in Italian—most likely), where both the Cantina dei Produttori di Barbaresco and Roagna have long made delicious ageworthy wines that are some of the most refined of all Barbaresco. Slightly higher up and with a more westerly orientation is Muncagota, where the Produttori cooperative produces a very good Barbaresco cru and where of course the Minuto family owns the Moccagatta estate (and in fact, the cru had to be given the dialect name Muncagota because the Minuto clan, somewhat understandably, were not inclined to give up a name that they had worked long and hard to establish). Farther south and more or less parallel to this row of crus is another, loaded with some of Italy's greatest names in terroir. Moving west to east, these are Pora, Faset, Asili, Martinenga, and Rabajà. These last three are the true grand crus of the Barbaresco commune. Faset and especially Pora give lovely Barbarescos, but the depth and complexity of the best wines of Asili, Martinenga, and Rabajà are often hard to match even for the best from Barolo. Asili is steep and mainly southeast-facing, Martinenga is a swath of land that moves gradually from southwest to southeast, while Rabajà has a southwestern exposure and is characterized by a softer, broader topography, which also helps explain the cru's much warmer mesoclimate (compared to Asili). The soil is about 40 percent clay, 35 percent limestone, and 25 percent sand, and yet the wines from Asili and Rabajà could not be any more different—the former refined and even austere, the latter fleshy and rich, with a truly signature note of cocoa that for once is not due to the oak regimen used by producers. Both are exceptionally great expressions of Nebbiolo and of Barbaresco. It is interesting to note how the Martinenga's two subplots echo the characteristics of these two famous vineyards. Besides his classic Martinenga Barbaresco (characterized by at least 20 percent Nebbiolo Rosé in the blend, which explains the wine's light color and perfumed nose), the Marchesi di Gresy also bottles a Gaiun and a Camp Gros Barbaresco. The former is located right next to Asili, while the latter's vines lie on the border with Rabajà. Wouldn't you know it, but Gaiun is the firmer of the two, and also the more refined, while Camp Gros is the fleshier and more chocolaty. Southward of Martinenga is the Rio Sordo cru (once also called Rivosordo, but practically never nowadays), a low-lying, mainly southwest-facing cru that gives Barbarescos of exceptional smoothness and drinkability in the best vintages. A very good premier cru rather than a grand cru, it produces wines that always boast rich notes of tobacco and underbrush but never quite have the complexity or depth of Asili and Rabajà's best; but when they are good, they are probably the single most enjoyable and balanced of all Barbaresco wines even at a young age. Overlooking the Tanaro and close to the border with Treiso lie the Roncagliette and Roncaglia crus. The former is best known for being the site where Gaja makes his Sorì Tildin and Costa Russi Langhe wines—soon to become once again, like the Sorì San Lorenzo, Barbarescos. (Apparently the new generation taking over at Gaja has decided that it's time to get back into the Barbaresco fold.) A series of hills that start at the border with Neive to the north and east of the town of Barbaresco make up the area where Barbaresco's three other best-known crus are found. Ovello is the northernmost, and is notorious for giving broad, fleshy, but slightly chunky wines that rarely if ever

develop the complexity of the best sites; next comes Montefico; and then, more south, Montestefano. Of these, Montestefano is an exceptional site: climate change has been good to it, in that its slightly cooler microclimate guarantees wines of both body and finesse that are never marred by cooked aromas and flavors even in the warmest years (something of a problem with even some famous Barbaresco sites that are situated at lowish altitudes). This northern part of the Barbaresco commune is characterized by more-compact, clay-rich soils, and all the wines made here are tougher and more austere when young, but Montestefano wines can develop a degree of finesse and complexity that is quite memorable, and is really perhaps as close to a grand cru among premiers as there is in all of Barbaresco.

NEIVE

The commune known for the most powerful, full-bodied Barbarescos of all, Neive produces wines whose mouthfeel and tannic structure are still resolutely Barbaresco. It is also the largest township of Barbaresco, even though it produces less Nebbiolo wine: in fact, Neive was long famous also for its Barbera, Dolcetto, and especially Moscato Bianco wines (though it is a little too warm to me to make truly stellar Moscato Biancos). For this reason, Neive has never had as much Nebbiolo under vine as Barbaresco: in 1988, there were only about 150 hectares planted to Nebbiolo (as compared with the 220 hectares of Barbaresco, for example). In fact, even today, while 271.74 hectares in Neive are planted to Nebbiolo, a whopping 447.41 hectares are planted to other grape varieties. Neive's geology is complex: moving southward from the town, where sites like Cotta and Basarin are found, soils have more sand (with less limestone and clay) than Barbaresco's, but Neive's more northerly sites, such as where the Santo Stefano and Gallina crus lie, are richer in clay. In general, it is true that Neive's soil is characterized by a generally higher sand content than that of the other Barbaresco townships, accounting for a certain firmness of the wines in their youth. (This is especially true of those wines made with grapes from the farthest eastern reaches of the Neive township, characterized by Lequio formation soils.) Neive is the most beautiful of all the Barbaresco towns, especially the narrow streets and charming storefronts of its old medieval town perched high up above the new town that spreads out below. Of Neive's numerous crus, only a few are truly famous and linked to memorable wines. Those that are well known are some of the greatest Nebbiolo wines of all, and I do not mean just Barbaresco. The crus that I most like from Neive are Cottà, Currà (once also called Chirra), Gallina, Santo Stefano (and Albesani), and Serraboella. All of these save for Serraboella are located in the western sector of Neive. Santo Stefano is the greatest of all Neive crus; it is solely owned by the Castello di Neive (Bruno Giacosa long bought grapes here to make his very famous Santo Stefano wines) that had gone uncultivated for roughly 150 years, only to be replanted roughly 60 years ago. It is situated in the central part of the much larger Albesani cru, at about 200 to 250 meters above sea level. Santo Stefano is one of the five greatest crus of all Nebbiolo-dom, Barolo included; it can deliver remarkably deep, complex, luscious, and balanced wines that are very similar to what an ideal blend of the best wines from Rabajà and Asili might taste like. Albesani (160 to 270 meters above sea level) is a very good cru in itself. The most northernly site of all the Neive crus, it has a southern to southwestern exposure in its central part (where Santo Stefano is located), and looks west at its corners; those sections that look north to northwest are less suited to growing Nebbiolo. Albesani Barbarescos are well balanced and suave, but have been somewhat unfairly overlooked due to Santo Stefano's fame. (Bruno Giacosa's 2009 Albesani is an excellent wine full of early appeal, for example, and Castello di Neive wines from this site are quite fine, too.) The high quality of Albesani is further demonstrated by another subzone within its confines: that of Borgese, at about 320 meters above sea

level, where Piero Busso has long made an interesting, if perhaps slightly too balsamic, Barbaresco of note. Immediately south, the Gallina cru (170 to 250 meters above sea level and about fifty-two hectares large) is a depression lying between two peaks; the vines with the best exposures look southeast to southwest. Barbarescos from the Gallina site are known for being very rich, thick, even chunky, but boast early appeal; Ugo Lequio and La Spinetta make the most full-throttle wines from Gallina, while Parroco di Neive and Bruno Giacosa used to make somewhat more refined, less in-your-face versions. To the southwest of Neive lies Cottà, a large, sunny MGA (190 to 345 meters above sea level), closest to the Barbaresco commune, and not surprisingly, its wines are those that are most Barbaresco-like; the best exposures are those that look west to southwest, but tannins can be slightly rustic at times, even in the best wines. Currà is about twenty-three hectares large and one of my favorite Neive MGAs of all: I especially love the wines of Sottimano from here, but Cantina del Glicine made many memorable Currà wines as well; and of course supremely talented Bruno Rocca is now making wines from this site, too. Small and very homogenous, Currà lies at 220 to 300 meters above sea level, situated just below what was once known as the Pastura cru (not to be confused with the Angelo Pastura estate); it has a protected topography and a warmer microclimate that contribute a riper red-fruit syrup note mixed in with a penetrating red-flower note. And yet, the Barbarescos from this site are also very fresh, thanks to a strong, rather uncommon degree of minerality that is quite apparent in some vintages. In short, Barbarescos from Currà are wines of real refinement. Basarin is another well-known, large vineyard in this section of Neive, but frankly, the site has always been much more suited to Dolcetto, and I have always believed its lofty reputation for Barbaresco to be a tad of a stretch. However, it is true that the Moccagatta estate has always managed to make very good wines from Basarin and that many estates have now bought vineyards there. Southeast of Neive are the tiny hamlets of Serra Boella Inferiore and Serra Boella Superiore, on a series of spurs that reach into the valley of the Tinella River. The Serraboella cru (250 to 450 meters above sea level), made famous by the outstanding wines of Cigliuti and Pasquero (Vietti's well-known Barbaresco Masseria is made from Serraboella grapes, and some vintages, like the 1989, are memorable), is another of my favorite Barbaresco sites of all. Its whitish-colored slopes that overlook Neive have western to southwestern exposures (and are where the grapes that make the MGA's best Barbarescos grow); otherwise exposures run east to northeast. These are some of the fleshiest yet refined Barbarescos of all, with an intensity of pure red fruit and sweet spices that is really unforgettable.

TREISO

I think Treiso is one of the prettiest spots of the Langhe, and it is my favorite one in which to take a stroll. Treiso as a wine-production zone is complex and not easy to generalize about. For example, the characterization of the area as having a much cooler mesoclimate that explains the steely, high-acid nature of many of its wines is one of the most common misconceptions regarding Italian wines. For although many of Treiso's vineyards lie at high altitudes, not all do (Rombone, for example). Up until the 1950s, Treiso was part of the Barbaresco commune, but it deserved to be separated from its more famous neighbor if for no other reason than that its wines are, for the most part, completely different from those of Barbaresco. In 1988, Treiso counted about one hundred growers and ninety-five hectares of Nebbiolo vines; the paucity of Nebbiolo vineyards can be explained by the fact that the commune has a much cooler microclimate and Nebbiolo didn't always achieve full polyphenolic ripeness in Treiso. In fact, Treiso has always been very famous for outstanding Dolcetto wines. (In my view, of all the Barolo and Barbaresco, Treiso is the best source of Dolcetto wines.) Today there are 182.74 hectares in Treiso planted to Nebbi-

olo, and another 350.91 hectares planted to other cultivars. However, it's the Barbaresco that gives Treiso its fame, and the zone can be divided in two. The northern, lower-lying sector of Treiso close to the border with the Barbaresco township has a much warmer mesoclimate and, not surprisingly, gives richer, broader Barbarescos that are close to the town of Barbaresco's in style, while the western-southern sector is characterized by a much cooler mesoclimate, with the Nebbiolo grown at higher altitudes giving wines of remarkable perfume and grace. Simply put, there is nothing quite like the Nebbiolo wines of this part of Treiso. One of the reasons why Treiso's Barbarescos are so austere in their youth is that, unlike the rest of the production zone, the soils here are in great part of the Lequio formation, and not the Saint Agathe's marls that typify Barbaresco and give rounder, softer, earlier-maturing wines. Furthermore, the high altitudes and cooler, windier microclimates mean that the best sites of Treiso are actually located at midslope, and not in the *bricchi*, or summits, that are so coveted elsewhere in Barbaresco (and Barolo). The most famous vineyards of Treiso are undoubtedly Pajoré and Rombone in the northern sector, and Bernadotti, Rizzi, and Nervo in the southwestern sector. Pajoré (210 to 340 meters above sea level, with a mainly west-southwestern exposure in its central part) is the most northerly of the Treiso crus and also its best. It is quite steep and large (forty-two hectares), with a poor, marly soil that gives wines of great power, depth, and complexity; however, only a small portion of the grapes find their way into bottles carrying the Pajoré namesake. Pajoré was made famous by Giovannino Moresco and his Podere del Pajoré; the last vintage of this wine was the 1979, and the vines have been since farmed by Gaja, who bought the property but who unfortunately does not bottle a wine carrying the Pajoré name. (Sottimano makes an outstanding Barbaresco Pajoré.) Moresco's holdings were also famous because they made up what was supposedly a 100 percent Nebbiolo Rosé vineyard—a supposition that Gaja has always disputed, telling me repeatedly that there was no more than 50 percent Nebbiolo Rosè there. At least a good portion of the Pajoré grapes go into Gaja's regular Barbaresco (to my taste and way of thinking, by far his best wine). To the west of Treiso are Bernadot (also once called Bernardot, Bernardotti, and San Bernadotti) and Bricco di Treiso, two of the steepest crus in all Barbaresco, almost precipice-like. (Rizzi, farther west still, is another very steep site.) Bernadot (320 to 400 meters above sea level, with a southern exposure in its best part) is the natural prolongation of the Nervo cru, which has the same orientation. A small and in my mind very underrated site, it is a natural amphitheater blessed with a mesoclimate that is warmer than what the cru's high altitude implies; Bernadot Barbaresco wines neatly combine refinement, concentration, and power. The best-known wine from this site is the one by Ceretto, but Mauro Mascarello made at least one beauty from here that I remember well (the 1978 being a work of art). The Bricco di Treiso (thirty hectares large, 340 to 405 meters above sea level, with a south-southwestern exposure in its best section) is the source of Pio Cesare's best wine (though its overly fleshy and balsamic Ornato Barolo is more famous). Bricco di Treiso is a very high, cool site, but thanks to mostly southern exposures and the open amphitheater-like shape ensuring great luminosity, there is usually very good ripening of the Nebbiolo grapes in most vintages. The wines made here are some of the most elegant and steely wines of all. Rombone, a cru made famous by Bruno Nada of Fiorenzo Nada, lies west of Pajoré and immediately north of the Bricco di Treiso, of which it is practically a lower-lying prolongation (190 to 315 meters above sea level, with a mainly southwestern exposure in its best sections). A large MGA (forty-seven hectares), not all of Rombone is well exposed and ideal for quality Nebbiolo wine production, but when the grapes are grown in the right spots, such as in the lower-lying, wind-protected areas, Rombone gives completely different and highly memorable

wines from Treiso's other sites: earthy, tannic, and compact wines that have more in common with the wines of the Barbaresco commune than they do with those of Treiso.

SAN ROCCO SENO D'ELVIO

This pretty little hamlet has plenty to brag about. For one, its Barbarescos offer outstanding price-to-quality value, since they are usually much less expensive than other Barbarescos. Also, the town is famous because it is the reported birthplace of a Roman emperor, Publio Elvio Pertinace (A.D. 126–193). The "Seno d'Elvio" part of the hamlet's name is also a stream that runs through the Treiso production zone, and like the Talloria and the Cherasca Rivers, it is a tributary of the Tanaro. Today, San Rocco Seno d'Elvio is administratively considered to be a fraction of Alba; hence San Rocco Seno d'Elvio and its wines are often referred to as being "of Alba"—a big mistake in my view. If the town ever wants to create an element of distinction for itself, and especially for its very fine and different Barbarescos, it should live separately from Alba itself. For one, this means that being known as the birthplace of the Emperor Pertinace is something local producers should broadcast more, since it is to their advantage. Also, the first-ever bottle carrying the Barbaresco name on the label dates back to 1870; it can be seen at Cascina Drago, located in San Rocco Seno d'Elvio. Today, there are apparently 45.54 hectares planted to Nebbiolo and 880.27 planted to other grape varieties. (But these statistics include vineyards in Alba, too; by comparison, in 1988 San Rocco Seno d'Elvio had only 80 hectares under vine, of which 38 were of Nebbiolo.) In my experience, the Barbarescos of San Rocco Seno d'Elvio are wines of mostly early appeal, perhaps less complex than those of the other three communes but for the most part offering a charmingly soft mouthfeel, and quite accessible in their youth. In this respect they are very different from Treiso's high-acid, austere wines or Neive's fleshy behemoths. Which all goes to show just how complex understanding terroir in wines can be: the soft, approachable nature of this hamlet's wines clashes with the fact that the soils are of the Lequio formation, which gives austere wines, especially in their youth.

San Rocco Seno d'Elvio does not boast any famous crus of its own, and shares most with Treiso. However, this does not mean that the township is devoid of great sites for Nebbiolo. In fact, the best section of the Rizzi MGA (commonly associated with Treiso) actually lies within the San Rocco Seno d'Elvio boundaries. The best slopes for growing Nebbiolo in Rizzi (200 to 300 meters above sea level and quite steep) are those looking southwest to south, and the latter especially belong to San Rocco Seno d'Elvio. The wines are very classic and austere in their youth but develop splendidly, and the best examples are by the Rizzi estate, owned by the Dellapiana family. Two other noteworthy sites that San Rocco Seno d'Elvio shares with Treiso are Montersino and Meruzzano. Both are very large MGAs (Meruzzano is the second largest in all Barbaresco), and so inferring specific terroir characteristics is difficult unless you know exactly which portion of the MGA the grapes used to make the wines come from. Montersino rises from 220 to 420 meters above sea level and features myriad different exposures; vineyards on the slope that looks toward Rocche Massalupo are softer but have a cooler microclimate, while some segments of the cru that look in the opposite direction, toward Meruzzano, are sunnier and steeper. My favorite Montersino wines made from grapes grown on the calcareous-clay, sand, and sandstone soils within the boundaries of San Rocco Seno d'Elvio are those made by Albino Rocca, which showcase neatly the elegance of this commune's wines. Meruzzano is an even larger cru, with vines growing anywhere between 250 and 490 meters above sea level, and with myriad exposures (though the best sites within this large MGA are those found between the hamlets of Meruzzano and Camairano). As with Montersino, most of the Barbarescos produced are with grapes from the larger portion of the cru, which falls within the boundaries of Treiso.

(Look for the outstanding Meruzzano and Montersino Barbarescos from Orlando Abrigo, though for accuracy's sake I should mention that the estate's vines fall within the boundaries of Treiso, not San Rocco Seno d'Elvio.) San Rocco Seno d'Elvio does boast one MGA of its own, Rocche Massalupo—a name that had not been used before the 2011 MGA designation. It is a medium-large MGA, located between 200 and 300 meters above sea level, with various exposures. The best portions are probably those that look toward the Montersino cru. Very good wines from Rocche Massalupo grapes are being made by the Lano and Manuel Marinacci estates (the latter wine is called Pajà); Luigi Oddero and Armando Piazzo also own vines in this MGA, and Orlando Abrigo has also bought vines there recently, so this is one cru we will be hearing a lot more of.

BENCHMARK WINES

With one exception, I include only one wine per estate and one per commune, limiting myself to three-star wines; otherwise, the list would risk being too long for this book.

Bruno Giacosa / Azienda Agricola Falletto Asili Riserva***PS, Bruno Giacosa / Azienda Agricola Falletto Rabajà Riserva***PS.

Albino Rocca Montersino***, Marco e Vittorio Adriano Sanadaive***, Bruno Rocca Rabajà***, Ca' del Baio Asili***, Ceretto Asili***, Cigliuti Serraboella***, Cisa Asinari Marchesi di Gresy Camp Gros***, Gaja*** (the Barbaresco, not the fantasy-named wines), Giuseppe Cortese Rabajà Riserva***, Nada Fiorenzo Rombone***, Orlando Abrigo Meruzzano Vigna Rongalio***, Poderi Colla Roncaglie***, Produttori di Barbaresco Montestefano Riserva***, Sottimano Pajoré***.

Carema

Carema, northern Piedmont's last viticultural outpost before the Valle d'Aosta, is one of the most bucolic and prettiest places in Italy, not to mention home to outstanding Nebbiolo wines famous as early as the sixteenth century. The area is characterized by the Picotener Nebbiolo biotype, which gives remarkably lithe, graceful wines that are, however, characterized by sneaky concentration and a steely backbone. There also used to be Pugnet growing in the area (another Nebbiolo biotype), but it produced very little, and so farmers phased it out. The interesting thing about Carema is that practically all the vineyard owners there (with the exception of the Ferrando family of the eponymous estate) are part-time only; they all hold a second job that allows them to survive. Currently there are only about 16 hectares of Carema DOC, and 13.5 of those hectares are under direct control of the Cantina Produttori and its seventy-one members. (Ferrando is currently the only private producer of Carema, but others are about to launch theirs.) That means that the average holdings in Carema are 0.2 hectares (or 2,000 square meters), which are actually subdivided even further within the same ownership. This is because families try to hedge their bets by owning parcels in different areas of Carema in order to reduce the risk of losing their entire crop to hail. (Mercifully, hail is not common in this part of northern Piedmont; but when you own so few vines, reducing even that amount of risk is important.) Locals need another job to get by: with only fifty thousand to sixty thousand bottles produced a year depending on the vintage, it is hard to make ends meet. Of course, things were not always so: in the early twentieth century there were 120 hectares of vines, and even as recently as 1967 there were 38 hectares under vine, and the Cantina Produttori (founded in 1960) only oversaw 6 of those. Carema is 100 percent Nebbiolo, though up to 15 percent other grape varieties are admitted in the blend, although both the Ferrando family members and a number of growers of the co-op have told me, "We will never do it, for we want to maintain typicity and our history, even though that may mean drinking something garnet-red, at a time when such

color is still a drawback in red wine." For students of the subject, and many wine lovers in general, Carema's terroir is highly interesting. The area is mostly characterized by terraced vineyards hugging steep slopes, but it is not all like that. For example, the area situated between the highway and the *strada statale* is characterized by a loamy soil that is not of morainic origin, and Nebbiolo does not ripen especially well. In Carema's best sites for Nebbiolo, the soil is mostly calcareous clay. The highest vines in the denomination are planted at 550 meters above sea level; sadly, when you gaze at the Carema landscape, abandoned terraces much higher up are everywhere in sight (vineyards used to grow at an ambitious 700 meters above sea level), but, being too hard to work and too far from town, they were the first to be abandoned. Since the Carema production zone is essentially an amphitheater, vines face southeast, south, and southwest, and in some vintages the difference in ripeness between grapes grown with southeastern and southwestern exposures is obvious in the wines. This is true even if those vines are only one hundred meters apart. Clearly, it is the southwestern exposure, more protected from the cold winds blowing through the Carema Valley and having the benefit of sunlight from morning to late afternoon, that is best here for Nebbiolo. The Nebbiolo harvest usually takes place in the second half of October; interestingly, Carema has a lot less snow than southern Piedmont; the locals tell me that this is very different from forty years ago, when there was much more snow. (Average temperatures were much lower then, and so snow hung around much longer.) Carema has less snow than one might expect from such a northern land, mainly because of the circulating air currents that do not allow its formation. Rainfall in Carema is also less than it is in other northern Piedmont denominations such as Gattinara. Along with Ferrando, it is the Cantina Produttori di Carema that is the main defender of this great Nebbiolo terroir and wine. As of 2010, the co-op has started making an entry-level wine (black label) aged two years (one of them in bottle), along with their Carema Riserva (white label), first made in the 1990s—a selection of the best lots, aged eighteen months in large oak casks. (Chestnut wood is no longer used but was once common in the area; in a sad sign of the changing times, one reason why chestnut is not used anymore is that there is nobody left in the area that knows how to make the barrels.) To maintain typicity, the co-op in 2010 stopped using barriques (which they had started using in 1995). Strangely enough—and rather unfortunately, I may add—at Ferrando they use a black label for the *riserva* wine and a white one for the entry-level wine (the exact opposite of what the co-op does). In fairness, and for the sake of precision, Ferrando's black-label wine is not a *riserva* but a *"selezione"*; still, situations like these only lead to consumer confusion—something that a small production area like Carema can ill afford. That said, Ferrando is one of Italy's best wine estates, with a portfolio of truly outstanding wines to choose from (and the Erbaluce wines are fantastic, too; see the Erbaluce entry). The estate's first vintage (then known as Luigi Ferrando) was the 1957; the black label was introduced in 1962. Ferrando rents plots from four families who take care of the roughly forty-year-old vines following the Ferrando guidelines; the grapes grow in some of Carema's best sites (Siey, Silanc, Runc, and Piole). To the family's credit, they are recuperating old parcels of vines that have been abandoned and where the forest has taken over.

Carema's Best Crus

I love Carema and have visited the area numerous times. The list of the area's best sites is one I have compiled after years of visits and interviews and of tasting microvinifications of area wines. To the best of my knowledge, there is no such list available anywhere else, and even Luigi Veronelli, Italy's leading wine expert, in failing to list any crus for this denomination, did not offer such data (Veronelli 1995). The cru names listed here are toponyms that are historically known and accepted. Cru wines might not be a good idea for Carema: the area under vine is just too small, and for the moment at least, blends of grapes from different sites probably make the best wines. Ferrando, for example, does not believe that bottling wines from individual sites is the way to go, and they say so on the basis of experimentations carried out in the past. Still, it is fascinating to know what each one of the better sites can give. And who knows? Perhaps one day there will be more hectares under vine so that a single-vineyard Carema will be made once again.

Airale: An amphitheater of potentially very high-quality Nebbiolo wines but very small (and with only 250 inhabitants), boasting excellent exposure. (Airale has a northwestern exposure and is very protected from the winds.) The southern segment of Airale is more precisely referred to as Piano.

Laurey: Also has a northwestern exposure, which gives more protection against the winds and gives balanced, suave Nebbiolo wines. This is hardly surprising since, at 500 to 550 meters above sea level, the vineyards lie at one of the highest altitudes in the denomination.

Piole: Relatively smooth, medium-bodied Nebbiolo wines with a characteristic earthy note.

Pozzalle: In the central part of the denomination at four hundred meters above sea level, this site has a warmer mesoclimate, with vines facing fully south. The wines have the potential for being some of the richest and deepest of all Carema.

Siey: These vines face more to the east, where the sun is born. The Caremas are some of the sleekest and most refined (a denomination not short on this quality trait). Chianej Piano is a specific part of Siey that is probably a grand cru within the cru. Ferrando made a cru Carema wine from this site in the 1974 vintage, but because it was characterized by a very pale color, it lacked appeal.

Silanc: Characterized by very steep slopes, sandy soils (the sand content is roughly 60 percent), and a relatively warm microclimate for the area, Silanc is one of Carema's potential grand crus. It is also blessed with an especially warm mesoclimate. For example, Silanc is on average 3–4°C warmer than Piole. (Mid-February, when it's 17°C in Silanc, it's only 13°C in Piole.) This site was another one that Ferrando attempted to make single-vineyard Carema wines from (Giuseppe, the grandfather of the current Ferrando generation, thought so highly of this site that he bought vines in Silanc as soon as he could), but for some reason the wine was never as good as it should have been, and so after a trial or two as a solo bottling, they have gone back to making blends of Nebbiolo picked from different sites.

Vairola and Nerere: These two are located in the central part of the Carema denomination and have a southern exposure. Wines tend to be fuller-bodied and slightly savory.

Villanova: An area immediately outside the historic center of Carema and located at midslope where the old town of Carema was once situated (but then evacuated and abandoned due to a landslide).

BENCHMARK WINES

Cantina Produttori di Carema Etichetta Bianca***, Ferrando Carema Etichetta Nera***.

Cantina Produttori di Carema Etichetta Nera**, Ferrando Carema Etichetta Bianca**.

Orsolani Carema Le Tabbie*.

Donnas

Much like Carema and mountain viticultural areas in general, where fragmented land ownership makes cooperation a viable necessity, Donnas wine from Valle d'Aosta is mostly the product of a high-quality local co-op. It was founded in 1971 by forty original members (today there are seventy-four), all of whom own vineyards around Donnas, Pont-Saint-Martin, Perlo, and Bard. The Nebbiolo vines grow mostly in Donnas and Pont-Saint-Martin. (The vineyards of Perlo are a northern prolongation of those of Pont Saint-Martin.) The average altitude of the vineyards is 350 to 500 meters above sea level at Pont-Saint-Martin, 320 meters in Donnas, and 500 meters in Perlo. Just as in Carema, vineyards in Donnas once grew at 600 to 700 meters above sea level, but have been slowly abandoned (which explains why Perlo has fewer vineyards than the other two towns); to their credit, the members of the Cave Cooperative de Donnas are busy reclaiming at least those abandoned vineyards at lower altitudes. Donnas boasts a total surface area of 25 hectares; the average size of individual plots is 0.3 hectares (or three thousand square meters), but many own less than 0.1 hectares and only a few more than 0.4 hectares. Another problem is that these surface areas are very fragmented, so that even those who own three thousand square meters may have their vines divided up into four distant parcels, which makes working this area especially tough. The co-op is working with the local institutions to favor the trading of distant parcels between owners so as to create larger estate vineyards, but clearly, this is a very hard thing to accomplish. In an exciting development, a brand-new producer has appeared on the scene, Luciano Zoppo Ronzero, owner of the Pianta Grossa estate, now making Nebbiolo wines from 2 hectares of vines in Donnas and Pont-Saint-Martin (at the time of writing, he had not yet released a Donnas, but was planning to). The Valle d'Aosta Nebbiolo is the Picotener biotype perfectly adapted to this environment where it gives delightful wines. The Picotener group includes the one typical of Carema (Nebbiolo Picotener 308, which is characteristically small-bunched and winged) and the 400 series. The 423 (also winged, but less frequently than the 308) is the most common in the area, though to the best of my knowledge there is not enough planted in one finite area to push people to want to try making a pure monobiotype Donnas. (This actually might be easier to accomplish in another Valle d'Aosta denomination known for

Nebbiolo, Arnad-Montjovet, since there, the espalier and Guyot training systems are in place (rather than canopies) and so they have entire rows of Picotener 423 planted there. The Pugnet biotype of Carema, as well as a "male" and "female" Nebbiolo, were also once common in Donnas, all characterized by the loosely packed bunches typical of Picotendro (the 423 may be a direct descendant of one of the two). That Picotener does not have a compact bunch is important, for it makes possible the air-drying of grapes (in the manner of the Valtellina's Sfursat) if one wishes to do so (partly air-dried wines is an old Donnas tradition), since Picotener's loose bunch lessens the risk of rot attack in the cool and potentially wet late autumns of the Valle d'Aosta. People have tried to replant the male and female biotypes of Picotendro, but the resulting wines (from vines that are fifty years old) have failed to impress, at least thus far. Nevertheless, the 308 and 400 series do very well in Donnas; by contrast, the latter have been a complete disaster when planted in the Langhe (atypically dark in color, with no perfume: see Barolo subchapter). Magic of terroir, you might say. For one, Alba's territory has alkaline soils that are much richer in clay, while Donnas's soils are lightly acid and are mostly sandy-gravelly, with little clay. These Picoteners are simply not adapted to the Langhe's habitat and should not be planted there; we have seen his happen time and again in Italy. (See the introduction to this book.) The rootstock is also important: in Donnas they use the 420A, which drives the roots down (though for reasons that are as yet unclear to me on a scientific basis, Nebbiolo longevity is lower with this rootstock in Donnas). Donnas's climate is especially favorable to viticulture. A strong air current blows down from the valley of Gressoney and does not allow air to stagnate, and so the fog of Piedmont never forms here, and average temperatures are often mild. The growth cycle is longer in Donnas than in Piedmont. (Bud break may occur at the end of January, while the harvest is at the end of October.) The characteristics of a good Donnas Nebbiolo wine are a pretty, light-red color, less-showy

Nebbiolo aromas than those found in Barolo or Barbaresco, but lovely, pristine mouthfeels and very good persistence. Clearly, at these northern latitudes the most important factor in determining the characteristics of the wine is the vintage.

The Best Donnas Crus

Anyone who knows me even a little is aware that the Valle d'Aosta is my favorite Italian region and I go there every chance I have; even better, I love Donnas and its wines and have tasted them extensively over the last thirty years. The Cave has tried to harvest grapes from single spots and sites in order to make cru wines, but for a variety of reasons, this is never easy with co-op realities. Gatta (1838) mentioned specific areas of Donnas such as Reisen (a corruption of *raisin*) as being especially good. (And with a name like that, how could it not be?) Jocularities aside, Reisen is a completely sheltered site that is not too steep; however, it is not especially well-ventilated and so tends to be humid. Other potential Donnas crus are Rovarej and Ronc-de-Vacca (Rondevacca), as well as Ronc, the low part of the hill to the east of Donnas but still situated at 450 meters above sea level and therefore the most-ventilated site; its slopes are so steep that a monorail train is needed to bring grapes down to the valley floor. One last site that has real cru potential is the area of Bard, which is less sunny than Donnas in general. Bard ought to be divided into two sections, located in front of and behind the medieval fort that Bard is famous for. The area in front of the fort is very much like Donnas, while the slopes behind the fort are more similar to those of Ronc, but the latter have been largely abandoned both because they are very steep and because most of the area's youngsters have left.

BENCHMARK WINES

Cave Cooperative Donnas Vieilles Vignes***, Donnas Barmet***, Donnas Napoleon***.

Pianta Grossa Nebbiolo Dessus**.

Roero

Differently from the Langhe, which is on the right bank of the Tanaro River, the Roero is located on its left-hand side. Roero is a denomination that includes twenty-three communes in the heart of the Piedmont region, halfway between Asti and Cuneo. Traditionally under Savoia family rule, Roero derives its name from the noble family of the same name from Asti. Thanks to its sandy terroir rich in sea-fossil residue, Roero gives Nebbiolo wines that have lighter frames and that are potentially more fragrant than the Langhe's. The sandstone and sedimentary rocks of marine origin composed of limestone, clay, and sand make for a soft and permeable setting. Roero is much wilder and less manicured than Barolo: forests and wild game are everywhere. The climate is generally warmer in Roero (by as much as 3–9°C), and the harvest usually takes place one or two weeks earlier than it does in Barolo. Be aware that the Nebbiolo d'Alba denomination also covers Roero, and therefore Roero producers can choose to label their wines with either the Roero or the Nebbiolo d'Alba name.

The Roero Subzones

In March 2017, the Roero Consorzio presented the official Menzioni Geografiche Aggiuntive (MGA), the list of Roero crus. In my view, the denomination can be broken down into different subzones. There is one main band running from west to east that includes the townships of Santo Stefano Roero, Monteu Roero, and Vezza d'Alba to the south; this sector then stretches eastward through the area of Canale and toward Castellinaldo and Castagnito. Soils change from west to east, ranging from the mostly sandy soils of the first three communes to the heavy clay soils of the last two: Canale's soils fall between these two extremes, and the townships' wines certainly reflect their different respective origins. Here is a list of those you need to know.

Canale: The biggest and most important township of the denomination, it is also the one with the most vineyards (370 hectares, 240 of which are registered to the DOCG). Of these, the lion's share are planted to Arneis (175.62 hectares), with Nebbiolo some distance behind (63.10 hectares). The soil tends to be on the sandy side, with blue-gray loamy inclusions and as much as 20 percent clay in parts of the township. The soils and wines of Canale can be thought of as "in between" those of the western zone (Santo Stefano Roero, Monteu Roero) and those of the eastern zone (Castagnito, Castellinaldo). Wines made from grapes grown within the Canale township but toward Priocca and the eastern side are bigger and savory, while those made in the eastern boundaries of the township are more refined and mineral.

Castagnito: This township has an especially marly soil that is very cold and clay-rich, with veins of chalk running through it that is ideal for the production of large-bodied Arneis wines that, though big and savory, are not exactly the last word in refinement. Still, it is historically viewed as a very good site for the variety, and in fact 58.34 hectares are planted to Arneis and only 6.4 to Nebbiolo.

Castellinaldo: At 260 hectares under vine (of which roughly 120 hectares are registered for DOCG wine production), this is the Roero township with the second-largest extension of vines. Much like nearby Castagnito, there is much more Arneis planted than Nebbiolo: 107.88 hectares in Castellinaldo are planted to Arneis, and only 12.3 to Nebbiolo. However, unlike Castagnito, which has more-homogenous soils, the Castellinaldo territory can be divided on the basis of two main soil types. The southeastern sector, covering an area located roughly between Bric Cenciurio and Bric Zoanni and Priocca, is characterized by a gentler topography and marl-rich soils containing very high percentages of sand and especially limestone; and the northwestern sector (toward Canale), much wilder in nature, with steeper, forest-covered slopes and very sandy-loamy soils that give wines of greater refinement.

Monteu Roero: Of Monteu Roero's roughly 150 hectares under vine, about 70.63 hectares and 17.26 hectares are planted to Arneis and Nebbiolo, respectively. Monteu Roero is a large, high-quality township for wines that are mostly saline and fresh, especially those made from soils at the easternmost tip of the denomination, right below the Rocche, where the loosely packed, sandy, fossil-rich soils really contribute to the making of such elegant wines. Moving in the direction of Vezza d'Alba and especially Canale, there is an increase in the soil content of marl, loam, and clay, making for richer, more-savory reds of greater alcohol power and size, and for more-tactile, savory whites.

Santo Stefano Roero: This commune's 50.09 hectares are planted mainly to Arneis (30.42 hectares), but there is a great deal of Nebbiolo also planted (19.67 hectares). Much as with Monteu Roero, the central part of the denomination is characterized by the marly-loamy soils of lacustrine and fluvial origin. Generalizing somewhat, the easternmost soils below the Rocche MGAs are best for very elegant Arneis wines and elegant, light-bodied Nebbiolo wines, while the more central parts of this subzone are noteworthy for rich, deep Nebbiolo wines.

Vezza d'Alba: A very large township, with 85.21 and 17.23 hectares planted to Arneis and Nebbiolo, respectively. The soils are mostly marly loam, with pockets extremely rich in clay (50 percent). The wines of this subzone are some of the most typical of what the Roero can offer—rich and spicy, though with the freshness and lightness of being that distinguish them from the wines of the Langhe.

The Best Roero Crus

Occhetti (Monteu Roero): There are five different sites that carry the Occhetti moniker: Occhetti, Occhetti Castelletto, Occhetti San Pietro, Occhetti San Vincenzo, and Occhetti Violi. The historic Occhetti site is attached to Occhetti San Pietro to the northeast and Occhetti San Vincenzo to the north and west. Occhetti Castelletto and Occhetti Violi are separate from Occhetti, to the south and east, respectively. Wines are powerful but suave and balanced. Renato Ratti made a famous Nebbiolo wine named Occhetti, but the name has been changed to Ochetti (one "c" only) because grapes don't necessarily come from that specific site anymore.

Renesio (Canale): Actually four different sites carry the Renesio name: Renesio, Renesio Incisa, Renesio Montorone, and Renesio Valbellina. Renesio is the historic center and is in fact surrounded in 180-degree fashion by, from west to east, Renesio Valbellina, Renesio Montorone, and Renesio Incisa.

S. S. Trinità (Canale): Adjacent to the Anime MGA (also in the Canale township) to the east of the large Mombeltramo MGA (divided between the townships of Santo Stefano Roero, Montà d'Alba, and Canale) and to the west of the Santa Margherita MGA of Canale, S. S. Trinità is a site planted to both Nebbiolo and Arneis. I personally believe that it reaches its qualitative zenith with the latter variety, though producers such as Malvirà have considerable success with its Roero reds.

Valmaggiore (Vezza d'Alba): The Valmaggiore hill is very steep: a 100 percent grade (45 degrees) in places. The soil is composed almost entirely of sand from shallow sea and beach deposits; fossils are common. There's almost no organic matter in the soil, and the vines have to grow deep down for nutrients. Because the sandy site is so well drained, in dry years the vines may suffer. The steepness of the site prohibits any mechanical work; everything must be done by hand. The single-lane road that winds up through the vineyard allows a tractor access to the top, but work on the rows of plants is entirely done by hand. At harvest, a specially designed "sled" that holds ten picking crates at a time is winched up in the aisles between sections of the vineyard to haul up the just-picked grapes.

BENCHMARK WINES

Bruno Giacosa /Azienda Agricola Falletto Valmaggiore***, Brovia Valmaggiore***, Francesco Rosso***, Giovanni Almondo Bric Valdiana***, Giovanni Almondo Riserva***, Luciano Sandrone Valmaggiore***, Malvirà Trinità***, Malvirà Renesio***, Negro Prachiosso***, Negro Ciabot San Giorgio***.

Valtellina

The Valtellina is the home of Chiavennasca, a local Nebbiolo biotype: the word *chiavennasca* derives from the dialect term of *ciù venasca*, meaning "a grape variety with great vigor" or "a grape variety that gives more wine." In fact, Nebbiolo has a long and distinguished history in the Valtellina; Benedictine monks were growing the variety as early as the tenth to twelfth centuries (Zoia 2004) The word *chiavennasca* first appears in the literature in 1595 (D'Agata 2014a). In relation to Nebbiolo's long-standing presence in the Valtellina, an extremely interesting 2006 study by Schneider et al. demonstrated the close genetic ties of Nebbiolo to local Valtellina varieties such as Brugnola, indicating that Nebbiolo is most likely original to this part of Lombardy rather than Piedmont. The wines can be either mono-variety wines (100 percent Nebbiolo) or blends containing up to 10 percent of other local cultivars such as Pignola, Rossola, and Brugnola. Nebbiolo Rosé is also common in the Valtellina, where it is called Chiavennaschino. The best wines are the DOC Valtellina Rosso; the DOCG Valtellina Superiore, with or without mention of subzones (these are Maroggia, Sassella, Inferno, Grumello, and Valgella); and the DOCG Sforzato di Valtellina (or Sfursat), which is made, Amarone-like, from air-dried Nebbiolo grapes. Some producers choose to make their Valtellina Superiore wines also with partly late-harvested or air-dried grapes; unfortunately, the back labels do not always give you that information—which, besides limiting your understanding and enjoyment of the wine, is also a grave marketing and communication error.

The Valtellina is located in Lombardy (about a two to three hours' drive north of Milan), just south of Switzerland, sandwiched between the Rhaetian Alps (Alpi Retiche, in Italian) to the north and the Bergamo Alps (Alpi Orobie, in Italian) to the south. These two parts of the Alps are not exactly low-lying hills but are true mountain ranges: at 3,905 meters, Mount Ortier is the highest peak in the Rhaetian Alps, while the Pizzo di Coca (at 3,052 meters) is the highest peak in the Bergamo Alps. In fact, the Valtellina is a famous summer and especially winter vacation destination, dotted as it is with beautiful mountain passes and famous ski resorts (such as Bormio) and spas, and it is blessed with great food (the local Bitto cheese is one of Italy's best) and wines. Clearly, what its geography and those altitudes also tell us is that the Valtellina is an area of mountain, even extreme, viticulture and winemaking. Its most famous wines are made with Nebbiolo, but they have very little in common with those of the Langhe, for example. If anything, they resemble those of the Alto Piemonte and the Valle d'Aosta a great deal more. The vineyard area of the Valtellina (occasionally spelled as two words in English, such as in Val Telline) snakes along in a rare horizontal or east–west direction along the lower course of the Adda River. (Most alpine valleys run in a north–south direction, and so do the vineyards.) The most important commune in the valley is Sondrio; other towns of note include Tirano, Livigno, and Morbegno. The Adda flows east to west from the Swiss Alps past Sondrio and toward Lake Como; the vineyards are planted along its north bank, so that the vines have southern exposures. The valley's east–west orientation and the presence of the river have important consequences for the area's weather; in fact, the rate-limiting step for successful viticulture in the Valtellina is not the climate, but the altitude. For the most part, planting any grapevines in the Valtellina above 750 meters above sea level even in these days of climate change is ambitious, or foolhardy. However, despite its mountain locality, the Valtellina is not as cold as one might expect it to be, and its flora of mostly deciduous trees including beech, elm, and chestnut (not the conifers you'd expect in truly cold climates) attests. In fact, during my walks up and down the Valtellina's vineyards over the years, I have come across numerous prickly-pear and cacti lookalikes—vegetation one would normally associate more with Sicily than upper Lombardy. This is because the area's topography and geographical location help mitigate inclement weather: the alpine ranges north and south of the Valtellina and the vicinity of the Adda River and Lake Como all contribute to making the climate less rigid. Therefore, summers and winters are devoid of temperature extremes and of excessive amounts of rain or snow; the mean average daily temperature range during the year is 11–13.5°C. The Winkler index ranges between 1400 and 1950 and the Huglin index between 1800 and 2300. As is often the case, the coldest month in the Valtellina is January, while the warmest months are July and August (Mazzoleni et al. 2006). The area is characterized by a generally bright, sunny, and dry climate. (Autumns are marked by strong diurnal temperature variations; in the Valtellina, day and night temperatures can differ by as much as 12°C.) Nevertheless, autumns and winters are not exactly balmy, and so farmers have taken steps to increase the chances of their crops surviving. The south-facing exposures combined with the steep slopes that bathe in sunlight greatly increase the grapes' exposure to the sun. The wealth of walled stone terraces, a characteristic feature of the Valtellina's vineyards (an unbelievable twenty-five hundred kilometers of walled terraces!), serve a dual purpose. Clearly, given the steep nature of the Valtellina's mountain slopes (in some places the gradient can be as much as 70 percent), terraces are necessary to allow the planting of vineyards (and for people to stand there, never

mind picking grapes); but they also serve an important thermoregulatory function (just as they do in the Valle d'Aosta and in Carema, in Alto Piemonte—other northern lands where conservation of heat is important). The large stones used to build the walls act as heat reservoirs, catching and storing daytime heat and releasing it slowly during the night to the hanging grapes. On average, the temperature within the walled vineyards is 4–5°C higher than it is in the Valtellina's flatland vineyards; for this reason, frost is a rare occurrence within the walled vineyards. Due to the steep slopes and the necessary presence of the stone walls, which are difficult to build and require constant maintenance, it follows that viticulture and winemaking in the Valtellina are costly endeavors, practically a labor of love. Farming mountain vineyards in this part of Italy means spending twelve hundred to fifteen hundred working hours per year per hectare—roughly four times the amount necessary for a normal hillside viticulture, and ten times more than what is required for flatland, machine-workable vineyards. Changing poles in a vineyard most often requires a helicopter, since it is nearly impossible to do this by hand or foot; even carrying the grapes downhill to the winery is difficult to do by hand in some areas, and even that may be done by helicopter. Small monorail trains, used in other parts of the world also characterized by extreme viticulture, might be a solution here, but their cost of upkeep far outweighs the financial benefits they might bring. In the end, viticulture in the Valtellina, for farmers and winery owners alike, is a social issue: the estates are responsible for the well-being of their stone walls and terraces, and are legally responsible should rocks or stones come tumbling down on passers-by below. The stone walls and the vineyards have hydrogeological importance, since they help prevent soil erosion and landslides. Rainfall is fairly regular between April and October, but is relatively scarce the rest of the year; autumns, when the harvest occurs, are mostly sunny and dry. Water stress is less likely in the Valtellina than in other mountainous areas of Italy (for example, the Valle d'Aosta).

The vineyard soils in the Valtellina are mostly the result of the degradation of the bedrock (in this case, mainly schist) and alluvial earth deposited over time by the flooding of the Adda River over the centuries. The topsoil is extremely thin in many places (in the Valtellina, it is never more than 40 to 120 centimeters deep), so much so that in order to plant vineyards, earth has had to be brought up by hand (or more precisely, by back), mule, small truck, and, believe it or not, even helicopter. Overall, Valtellina soils are sandy-loamy, characterized by good porosity ensuring good drainage, but clearly, roots do not dig particularly deep since their penetration is limited by the highly compacted glacial-rock substrate. The soils are often slightly deficient in boron and magnesium (Mazzoleni et al. 2006), and have an extremely acid pH (as low as 3.5 to 4.5), which is noteworthy (for example, the Langhe has alkaline soils with pH values of 8 or so) and very relevant to the Valtellina's Nebbiolo wines. Clearly, the thin, shallow, loosely packed, and nutrient-poor soils of the Valtellina greatly limit yields; the high age of Valtellina vines (fifty years on average) further helps reduce crop loads while delivering complex wines of noteworthy depth.

The Valtellina Subzones

Valtellina Superiore wines can be made from grapes grown in the area between Buglio in Monte and Tirano, which boasts about 215 hectares under vine. The wine labels can also carry the name of one of five subzones. Though the presence of five well-defined, historically recognized subzones ought to mean that it should be easy to distinguish between the wines of each, in practice it is not so. In my experience, it is very difficult, actually. This is because even within each subzone, wines are made from very small holdings, at varied altitudes and exposures, as described by Mariani and Failla (2006). Consequently, generalizing about a "Valgella-typical wine" or a "Sassella style" is difficult. Also, many of the wines taste all too similar (one might wonder why that is, actually), even though they are reportedly made in very different sections of a specific subzone or even between subzones. To what extent air-drying might contribute to this uniformity of taste is not clear to me, because there seems to be no such pattern present. Nevertheless, knowing the general characteristics of each subzone does help in discerning differences in wines being tasted. The five Valtellina subzones are as follows:

Maroggia: Located around the town of Berbenno, it is the smallest of the Valtellina subzones (roughly twenty-five hectares under vine) and was the last subzone to gain official recognition (in 2002). It is the first subzone one meets while driving up the valley toward Sondrio, but only a few producers make wine sporting this subzone's name on the label. For example, the Produttori Maroggia co-op makes lovely wines.

Sassella: At 114 hectares under vine, Sassella is the second-largest of the Valtellina subzones. Steep and sunny, it extends from the town of Castione Andevenna to the western reaches of Sondrio. Along with Grumello, it is the warmest of the five subzones, but differs from the Grumello subzone because of smaller diurnal temperature variations in September and a more direct angle of solar irradiation. Sassella takes its name from the sanctuary of the same name, and is probably the most famous and historic of all the Valtellina subzones. Its terroir is not homogenous, but such terroir differences do not always show in the wines made. The western portion of the Sassella subzone is known as Grigioni di Castione Andevenno (situated at about 370 to 430 meters above sea level); this part of Sassella is more protected from the winds, and in fact locals have always thought of it as a separate section of the subzone. Soils tend to be deeper and the wines rounder; by contrast, wines from the eastern section (where vineyards lie at 330 to 570 meters above sea level), toward the town of

San Lorenzo, are more mineral, and vertical in profile. The harvest can take place two weeks apart between the western and eastern portions of the subzone. I usually find notes of ripe raspberry, strawberry syrup, and rose petals in wines from the Sassella subzone.

Grumello: The Grumello viticultural subzone (seventy-eight hectares under vine) is located to the northwest of Sondrio, near the thirteenth-century castle of Grumello and the town of Montagna. Grumello's soils have more slate and limestone, and so, in theory, they tend to give wines with more finesse and minerality. In my experience, thanks to their graceful structure, these are the easiest of all Valtellina wines to recognize when one is tasting blind. However, Grumello does not perform especially well in hot years, when aromas and flavors of cooked fruit often emerge in its wines. Hazelnut, dried herbs (cilantro, marjoram), and strawberry are common descriptors I associate with wines from Grumello.

Inferno: Though small (only fifty-five hectares under vine), Inferno, located between Poggiridenti and Trevisio, is the Valtellina subzone most people recognize immediately— no doubt thanks to its evocative name, which means "hell" (most likely because of the steep, sunny, hard-to-work slopes that vineyard workers compare to a flaming inferno). Its wines have a strong note of violet, but it is notes of ripe plum, even prune, that dominate.

Valgella: Valgella is the largest of the subzones (137 hectares), divided between the communes of Teglio and Chiuro. It is characterized by being a rocky promontory that juts out into the open, breaking up the smooth procession of one Valtellina subzone after another. Valgella is also the easternmost of the Valtellina subzones, which contributes to its generally fresher microclimate. (It has more rainfall, too, and the angle of solar irradiation is more oblique, making for a less-warm mesoclimate.) And Valgella's soils, though similar to those of the other subzones (sandy-loam), have a slightly deeper layer of topsoil. The wines tend to be suaver, and less aromatically pungent and mineral, than those of other subzones but often show the best balance; I usually find a delicate spicy pepperiness and a note of sweet almonds in these wines.

Over the years, many Valtellina producers (such as the Fay family) have told me they do not believe that subzones play as important a role in defining the area's wines as we might like to think. Research studies have investigated the effect of climate and soil on possible zonations of the Valtellina (Failla et al. 2004; Mariani and Cola 2004). Interestingly enough, it appears that differences between grapes grown and wines made in different areas within the production zone are not mostly the result of a diversity in topography or soil composition, but rather of three different altitude ranges characterized by two different levels of photosynthetically active radiation (or PAR— that part of the spectrum of solar radiation ranging from four hundred to seven hundred nanometers that organisms are able to use for photosynthesis). Of course, this is not to say that the soil throughout the denomination is homogenous (it's not)—just that climate and altitude, as in many other mountain viticultural areas, appear to play a more important role in determining the qualities of the finished wines. In fact, this study showed that achieving technological maturity was positively correlated only with altitude (ranging from three hundred to seven hundred meters above sea level). By contrast, achieving good polyphenol maturity of Nebbiolo grapes in Valtellina is a more complex issue, influenced by the yield per vine and the interaction of altitude and PAR. According to the study, the Valtellina terroir can be divided, independently of the subzones, into three bands located at different altitudes: below four hundred meters above sea level, between four hundred and five hundred meters, and greater than five hundred meters. The area below four hundred meters is characterized as a harvest period that is usually neither too early nor too late, and by grapes that give deeper-colored wines than usual, provided that yields and PAR are relatively low. When the yields are allowed to creep upward, polyphenolic maturity is invariably diminished, though reportedly the sugar levels tend to remain high. Vines growing in the middle-altitude band seem to be less affected both by the PAR and the yield, and the polyphenolic and technological maturity levels of the grapes fall squarely in the middle of the three groups of grapes under examination. Instead, the grapes culled from the vineyards where the harvest takes place last (planted above the five-hundred-meter cutoff) achieved the highest degree of polyphenol maturity but barely adequate technological maturity (this with a relatively low PAR). Therefore, it appears that in the Valtellina, at least, the decisions made by the producer relative to his or her viticulture (such as training and pruning choices, canopy management, and choice of rootstock) become even more important than usual. Nebbiolo wines made at the lowest altitudes (below four hundred meters above sea level) offer classic Nebbiolo aromas of faded red rose petals and sweet spices, are medium- to full-bodied, and show good balance overall if not mind-blowing complexity; those made from medium-altitude vineyards (roughly those planted between four hundred and five hundred meters

above sea level) are characterized by riper fruit notes and less floral tones, and seem fleshier than the wines of the first group; last but not least, the wines made at the highest altitudes showcase noteworthy elegance, high acidity, and rigid tannins, with strong notes of sour red fruit. However, while the altitude undoubtedly plays a role in the style of Valtellina wines produced, in order to recognize Valtellina terroirs in the glass, other factors are also important. For example, I appreciate obvious differences in wines made in the eastern and western sections of the Sassella subzone, and those wines are made from grapes grown at the same altitudes. Most importantly, I know for a fact that, tasted blind, Grumello wines are easily distinguishable from those of all other Valtellina subzones; when comparing wines from different subzones (made with grapes picked at similar altitudes), Grumello's wines stand out thanks to a different mouthfeel and lighter structure.

BENCHMARK WINES

Fay Valgella Carteria***[PS].

AR.PE.PE. Sassella Riserva Vigna Regina***, AR.PE.PE. Sassella Riserva Rocce Rosse***, Fay Sforzato di Valtellina Ronco del Picchio***, Mamete Prevostini Sforzato di Valtellina Albareda***, Mamete Prevostini Sassella Sommarovina***, Nino Negri Sfursat Cinque Stelle***.

Nebbiolo Rosé

THE GRAPE VARIETY

Nebbiolo Rosé is one of my favorite Italian wine grapes. It has historically always been grown in Piedmont (Langhe, Roero, Carema, and Alto Piemonte), the Valle d'Aosta, and Lombardy's Valtellina, providing Nebbiolo wines with considerable perfume and greater alcohol presence. In the Valtellina, Nebbiolo Rosé is often called Chiavennaschino (once erroneously thought to be Grignolino) and was always appreciated for its resistance to drought (more so than Nebbiolo). Unfortunately, the variety's pale-red, pale-violet, almost translucent grapes do not (as its name implies) confer much color to the finished wines. (Interestingly, Nebbiolo Rosé actually has higher concentrations of malvidin, a dark-colored anthocyanidin, than Nebbiolo, but it releases its pigments with greater difficulty and tends to drop its color during fermentation.) The pale color of its wines, plus a certain juiciness of its round, medium-size berries (on average, bigger than those of Nebbiolo), had producers everywhere frowning back in the 1980s and 1990s when everyone was, very misguidedly, out to make the biggest, blackest wine possible. The end result being, of course, that Nebbiolo Rosé was uprooted everywhere—in my opinion, a real tragedy, because including 10 to 20 percent Nebbiolo Rosé in Barolo and Barbaresco adds a penetrating quality to those wines' perfume. However, the color remains a big problem at many estates: still today I hear producers routinely apologizing for their wine's light color, failing to realize that the 1980s have been over for a long while and nobody with even a modicum of wine knowledge nowadays believes that a red wine has to be deep and dark to be meaningful. Actually, and I'll be blunt: in my experience, inky, ruby-red wines make up the greatest percentage of completely meaningless wines made in Italy today. (Witness, for example, many ultradark red wines of Lombardy, Tuscany, Umbria, Emilia-Romagna, and Molise, all without any recognizable features of grape variety or place.)

Nebbiolo Rosé is a distinct variety from Nebbiolo (Botta et al. 2000), though the two are extremely closely related, according to Schneider et al. (2004). The studies on Nebbiolo genetics based on the analysis of microsatellite markers clearly indicated Nebbiolo Rosé as a separate cultivar, related to Nebbiolo by a first-degree parentage. There is only one clone currently available, CN III (where CN stands for Cuneo); it was actually one of the first Nebbiolo clones to have ever been developed. It is a very vigorous and fertile cultivar, less affected by shatter, and has fewer flowering problems during cold and rainy springs than Nebbiolo. Nebbiolo Rosé is usually picked quite late in the year independently of weather conditions, save for extreme years. In fact, this seems to be the best way to go about increasing the finished wine's plumpness and fruitiness. (Otherwise, Nebbiolo Rosé wines can seem a little shrill and tannic, without much obvious fruit, though their perfume is always glorious.) For example, in 2013 and 2014 (weather-wise, one normal and one very cold, wet year, respectively) grapes were picked at the Elvio Cogno winery at more or less the same time—on October 2 and October 3, respectively. Valter Fissore of Elvio Cogno likes to pick his Nebbiolo Rosé as late as possible and in fact has planted his Nebbiolo Rosé in the slowest-maturing site he owns in the Ravera cru of Novello. However, in a much warmer year such as 2015, according to Fissore, even the more drought-resistant Nebbiolo Rosé had to be picked on September 13 (but for comparison's sake, at Sordo, where their Galina vineyard in La Morra is planted to about 50 percent Nebbiolo Rosé, in 2015 they still picked their Nebbiolo Rosé in mid-October). By contrast, in 2016 the Nebbiolo Rosé harvest took place at Cogno on October 26, mainly because of a wet late season that stirred fears of rot problems. Nebbiolo Rosé has a less resistant skin than Nebbiolo, and so rain can pose problems; on the other hand, its loosely packed bunch allows air and wind currents to dry the wet grapes faster than would happen with Nebbiolo. Nebbiolo Rosé wines, or those that contain at least 20 percent of the variety, tend to have garnet rims early on in life, but the wine is very ageworthy. Aromas and flavors are similar to those of Nebbiolo wines, perhaps with a more intense

note of violet and rose and curious nuances of brown spices and of leather that emerge with time and most often in cold years. Some producers say that Nebbiolo Rosé wines have more alcohol and lower acid concentrations than do Nebbiolo wines, but others disagree. It may be a slightly more rustic variety than Nebbiolo, but when made by competent producers the wines are as great as any made wholly with Nebbiolo, and even more perfumed. Today the only two 100 percent Nebbiolo Rosé wines I know of are made by Elvio Cogno and Cascina Baricchi (see "Benchmark Wines" below). Another close to 100 percent Nebbiolo Rosé Barolo is the Sylla Sebaste Bussia bottling, everything you want a Bussia wine to be. Other producers make wines with hefty doses of Nebbiolo Rosé: look for the wines by Marchesi di Gresy (his regular Barbaresco Martinenga is made with at least 20 percent Rosé), the Vietti Barolo Lazzarito (also 20 percent Nebbiolo Rosé), and the Gianni Canonica Barolo Grinzane Cavour (40 percent Nebbiolo Rosé). (It is especially interesting to try this last wine and compare it with Canonica's Barolo Paiagallo, which does not have any Nebbiolo Rosé in it.) In past decades there were many wines made partly or wholly with Nebbiolo Rosé, and some of these wines belong in the pantheon of the greatest Barolos and Barbarescos ever made. Giovannino Moresco's Podere del Pajoré Barbaresco (he also used to pick his grapes as late as possible, just like they do at Cogno) is one of the greatest Barbarescos you are ever likely to try, and was reportedly made with 100 percent Nebbiolo Rosé : take a swig of the 1978 or 1979 to see exactly what I mean. (In fairness, I must point out that Gaja, the current owner, says there was only 50 percent Nebbiolo Rosé at most in the vineyard at the time he bought it.) Vietti's 1971, 1978, and 1979 Barolo Briacca, another 100 percent Nebbiolo Rosé wine, was just as memorable (especially the 1971 and 1978), as was the 1971 Giuseppe Mascarello Barolo Pugnane, which unfortunately was made just one year. Mauro Mascarello doesn't care much for the variety, and rather tellingly, when he replanted part of his estate to make his top-of-the-line and ultraexpensive Barolo Ca' di Morissio, it was two parcels of Nebbiolo Rosé he uprooted. A lovely Barbaresco made with Nebbiolo Rosé I still have fond memories of was the 1974 Scarpa Barbaresco Podere Barberis. All these wines prove what a crying shame it is that Nebbiolo Rosé was banished from most vineyards. Happily, it seems to be making a comeback as producers go looking for more elegance and fragrance in their wines rather than brute power.

BENCHMARK WINES

Cogno Barolo Riserva Vigna Elena***[PS].

Sylla Sebaste Barolo Bussia*** (only 50% Nebbiolo Rosé).

Cascina Baricchi Barbaresco Rosa delle Casasse**.

Nerello Mascalese and Nerello Cappuccio

THE GRAPE VARIETIES

Nerello Mascalese

The variety was selected by farmers centuries ago in the Piana di San Leonardello near the port of Mascali (hence its name), on the eastern side of Etna near the sea (Zappalà 2000). And in fact, Nerello Mascalese likes heat: Salvo Foti, consultant winemaker and owner of the I Vigneri estate (not to mention the single biggest living expert on Etna and its wines), jokes that the variety is a "beach bum." Above eight hundred meters above sea level near Randazzo and Castiglione di Sicilia on Etna's northern slope, it fares poorly. It can manage slightly better on the volcano's southern flank, even as high up as one thousand meters above sea level, but this is mostly dependent on the type of soil. (There it needs loam.) Salvo Foti very bluntly states that those who speak about their very "refined Nerello Mascalese" wine made from grapes grown above one thousand meters simply don't know what they are talking about because the wines are, in his estimation, most often made with old-vine Grenache. (Foti believes that 50 percent or more of the vines grown on Etna's western slopes, where the towns of Biancavilla, Santa Maria di Licodia, and Adrano are found, are mostly Grenache rather than Nerello Mascalese.) At least, Nerello Mascalese cannot be confused (not easily, at least) with Nerello Cappuccio, its partner in Italy's extremely popular Etna Rosso wine blends: Mascalese's berries are medium-small, oval, and light blue, and it has small and conical-cylindrical-shaped bunches; Nerello Cappuccio has medium-large, round, and dark blue berries and medium-large, pyramidal, compact bunches.

Nerello Mascalese is a natural crossing of Sangiovese and Mantonico Bianco (Cipriani et al. 2010), which would also make it a sibling of Gaglioppo (as also shown in another study, by Di Vecchi Staraz et al. [2007]). Physiologically and viticulturally, Nerello Mascalese is characterized by numerous important features that tell us a lot about what its wines are going to be like. Relative to polyphenols, Nerello Mascalese is low in anthocyanidins and high in tannins. (This is precisely why it is usually blended with

Nerello Cappuccio, which is instead characterized by dark pigments and low tannins.) However, anthocyanin concentrations can vary noticeably in Nerello Mascalese depending on growing conditions. With Nerello Mascalese, the grape variety genetics appear to dominate the influence of terroir in the expression of aroma molecules in its wines; the aromatic profile in Nerello Mascalese wines remains unchanged independently of where the grapes are grown (Foti 2012). In one study, three different Etna sites were compared, but concentrations of the aromatic molecules did not differ significantly; and the same was true of Nerello Cappuccio, another variety that appears to dominate the terroir it is grown in. However, the quantitative and qualitative expression of aroma molecules differed greatly between the two varieties in each terroir, showcasing how the two Nerellos are very distinct varieties, despite the similar name and similar area of cultivation. While both Nerello varieties express similar concentrations of hexanol, 1-phenylethanol, and eugenol, Nerello Mascalese wines express a slightly higher (though not statistically significant) concentration of terpenes such as geraniol and nerol, whereas Nerello Cappuccio delivers much higher concentrations of benzaldehyde (especially) and 4-vinyl guaiacol. It follows that Nerello Mascalese wines are marked more by musky and tobacco notes, whereas Nerello Cappuccio wines offer more vanilla and ripe-fruit notes, especially cherry (given the high benzaldehyde concentration) and clove-like herbal and spicy notes (4-vinyl guaiacol and eugenol). In this study, neither variety appeared to express significant amounts of molecules associated with floral aromas. One thing that helps us understand why this is so is the fact that Nerello Mascalese wines have low concentrations of terpenes, and those that are present are bound; what this tells us is that floral notes will develop as the wine ages, since the bound terpenes will be freed over time thanks to enzyme and acid hydrolysis (wine being an acid medium). Ansaldi et al. (2104) confirm that the terpenes most present

are 8-hydroxylinalool and 8-hydroxygeraniol (both of which smell of rose, with linalool evoking musk as well). The same study showed that ionone molecules (which recall violet) such as 3-oxo-α-ionol are also present. Clove and cinnamon are also typical of the variety, and this study also confirmed the presence of high doses of eugenol (responsible for such aromas) in Nerello Mascalese wine.

Nerello Mascalese being a late ripener (how much so depends on the altitude at which it is grown), the quality of its wines is strongly influenced by the year's weather, the site where it is planted, training method, and density of planting. Very vigorous, it's an abundant but irregular producer, and short pruning is essential in order to decrease yields and increase concentration. This also helps offset asynchronous maturation of the grape bunch (the bunches farthest along on the canes have pink berries that fail to ripen completely). What this means is that green streaks in Nerello Mascalese wines often result from improper terroir management due to deficient human intervention in the vineyards. The best training system for Nerello Mascalese is the bush vine or *alberello etneo*. Salvo Foti is adamant that experience is key in producing world-class Nerello Mascalese wines, since it is a difficult variety growing in a difficult terroir and experience is required to bring out the best of both the variety and terroir.

Nerello Cappuccio

Nerello Cappuccio lives mostly in the northeastern corner of Sicily; and though some also grows in Calabria, it is much rarer than its Etna Rosso wine partner Nerello Mascalese. (The latter is more common, accounting for 79 percent of all Etna red grapes.) It wasn't always so: as recently as the 1950s, Nerello Cappuccio was believed to account for over 30 percent of the area under vine in the areas of Messina and Catania. The two varieties are usually blended together, since Nerello Cappuccio provides color and tannins, and softens Nerello Mascalese's acidity. Its name derives from the cultivar's typically bushy canopy, resembling a cowl or cap (*cappuccio* in Italian), that hides the grapes behind a wall of leaves. This is also the reason why Nerello Cappuccio is thought to be a synonym of Nerello Mantellato, though there are those on Etna who believe these two to be distinct varieties (as does Marc De Grazia of Tenuta delle Terre Nere, for example). Nerello Cappuccio is an early-budding variety, and spring frosts and coulure (a condition that causes a failure of grapes to develop after flowering) can pose problems. It is easy to grow and not particularly demanding, and usually ripens a couple of weeks before Mascalese does. Studies have shown that Nerello Cappuccio wines offer more vanilla and ripe cherry fruit notes (because of high benzaldehyde concentrations) than do those made with Nerello Mascalese, as well as more clove-like herbal and spicy notes (because of the presence of significant 4-vinyl guaiacol concentrations). Normally, Nerello Cappuccio constitutes anywhere from 5 to 20 percent of an Etna Rosso blend; interestingly, it is in those areas where Nerello Mascalese tends to give even more fruit-challenged or paler wines than usual that Nerello Cappuccio really comes into play. For example, it's in the southern sector of Etna that most of the old vine Nerello Cappuccio vines are found nowadays, and this is where most of Etna's wines that feature 20 percent Nerello Cappuccio are made. All that being true, there is no doubt that Nerello Cappuccio's potential for giving bright, fruity, juicy, and less-structured wines is being reevaluated, and monovariety bottlings are starting to be made—something that was unheard-of twenty years ago (see "Benchmark Wines" below).

SPECIFIC TERROIRS

Etna

(For a detailed summary of Etna climate and terroir, see the Carricante entry.)

Etna wine fortunes have known nothing but skyrocketing success over the last fifteen years. A sign of the new interest in Etna wines is the increase in the number of hectares under vine during that time. For example, there were 1,308 hectares under vine in the Castiglione di Sicilia commune in 1970, being reduced to only 564 hectares by 2000; but in 2010 the number of hectares was back up to 608 (Militi 2016) and is reportedly increasing further. In addition, the number of outside investors (from Tuscany, Barolo, Belgium, and the United States, among other places) is also continuously on the rise. Investors who are smitten with Etna's almost magical terroir wines.

The simplest means by which to understand Etna's terroir relative to the wines made is to divide it into three viticultural subzones: the northern, southern, and eastern sections or slopes. In fact, the geographical positioning of Etna's wine terroirs is the result of the interactions among soil, site, and climate. (Exposure and altitude are all-important.) The average vine density per hectare ranges from forty-five hundred to sixty-five hundred, but can be closer to nine thousand to ten thousand thanks to the *alberello etneo* training system. Newer vineyards (such as those of Andrea Franchetti at the Vini Franchetti winery) can also be as tight planted as ten thousand vines per hectare.

The Contrade

Besides Barolo and Barbaresco, Etna is the best-known quality wine production area in Italy associated with specific crus. More importantly, and just like Barolo and Barbaresco, it is also one of the few where knowing the names of the *contrade* where the grapes grow actually tells you something about the wines made with them. Though *contrade* are essentially rural subdivision units that were never viewed as potential crus, there is no doubt that wines made with grapes grown in each are remarkably different. There are 133 officially recognized *contrade* on Etna, some of which are downright famous (Guardiola, Feudo di Mezzo, Rampante), others hardly known at all (Piano dell'Acqua, Fleri, Stella). This may soon change as producers and public alike begin to understand what each *contrada* can bring. Of course, human nature being what it is, this also means that we are already starting to hear about the supposed high quality of previously never before heard of *contrade*, so beware. On Etna, the individual *contrade* borders are defined on the basis of geologic and social constructs: geologic, because most *contrade* correspond to the paths of the various lava flows that have occurred over centuries; and social, since many *contrada* names refer to a fiefdom (such as "Feudo") or an activity (such as Porcaria, or "where hogs are raised"). *Contrada* labeling of Etna Rosso wines is becoming popular with most producers (and with the public, too) because it is both a great marketing tool (clearly, it associates Etna Rosso with some of the world's great wines, such as those of Burgundy, Barolo, and Barbaresco) and a means by which to stress the wine's bond with the local terroir. Given what we know about Etna's soil formation (characterized by multiple lava layers of different mineral composition) and myriad exposures, altitudes, and inclinations, this only seems logical. Clearly, the *contrada* labeling cannot be based only on differences in mineral constituents of the soil, for factors such as altitude and soil depth are just as important in creating a potential bond between site and wine flavor. Etna producers such as Marc De Grazia of Tenuta delle Terre Nere and Andrea Franchetti of Vini Franchetti (formerly Passopisciaro) strongly defend the *contrada* labeling concept. Clearly, at roughly 1.3 hectares of vineyards per estate (2005 data, AGEA), many of Etna's wine estates are very small family-run domaines; since their grapes come only from finite, well-delimited areas, *contrada* bottling for them is especially easy, and they have jumped on the bandwagon. Of course, this being Italy, not everyone agrees. Large-volume producers really don't want *contrada* labeling, for that ties their hands by binding them to a specific, finite place of origin as far as the grapes they use to name their wines: and so they object that not enough is yet known about the *contrade* and that Etna producers have jumped the gun on the issue. In fairness, that may partly be true: however, they, and we, also know that unless cru delimitations are set up very early in the course of a denomination's existence, they never get done, and waiting for them to happen "while we study the situation some more" is the clever way of ensuring they will never get done. (Witness Montalcino, a marketing disaster.) This is because once the existence of higher-quality areas within the denomination become apparent to everyone, nobody making wine in the production zone would ever accept or back the institution of a cru classification that might in some way expose the lesser quality of their vineyard sites.

THE NORTHERN SUBZONE

Nerello vineyards on the northern slope lie between five hundred to eight hundred meters above sea level. The townships are Bronte, Castiglione di Sicilia, Linguaglossa, Piedimonte Etneo, and Randazzo (Bronte being most famous for its pistachios, Italy's best). These townships have 50, 773, 250, 135, and 483 hectares under vine, respectively (2005 data, AGEA). The area is delimited by Etna on one side and the plain of Alcantara (and its river) on the other, separating the territory of Catania from that of Messina. This is where Etna's greatest red wines are made. (Bronte falls outside the Etna Rosso production zone.) It is also where most Etna wine is made: Castiglione di Sicilia and Randazzo alone account for close to 35 percent of Etna wine production. Of Etna's 133 *contrade*, the largest number are here: Castiglione di Sicilia boasts forty-six, Randazzo twenty-five, and Linguaglossa ten. Most of Etna's famous crus are in the administrative territory of Castiglione di Sicilia. Drawing a parallel between vineyard value (relative to the wines made) and real estate, you might say that Etna's Fifth Avenue, Bond Street, or Champs-Élysées corresponds to the slope just above and below the road (the *strada statale* 120) stretching from Linguaglossa to Randazzo. It is here that all of Etna's most famous crus are located; it is easy to pinpoint where these crus are by dividing the slope (west to east) into four sectors and then further subdividing these four sectors into two subsectors, one that falls above and one below the road in each sector.

The first sector of prime northern slope Etna vineyard real estate runs from the hamlets of Rovittello to Solicchiata: the subsector below this stretch of the road is the most interesting, where we find the *contrade* of Chiappemacine, Pietrarizzo, Pontale Palino, Zottorinoto, and Corvo. The most interesting of these are Chiappemacine and Zottorinoto. Chiappemacine is characterized by one of the richer and deeper soils of the northern slope, in which vine roots dig deep; wines from this *contrada* can be round but always bright thanks to an only thin surface layer of lava with limestone just underneath, and to the cool breezes that are typical of this site. By contrast, Zottorinoto gives more-flinty, compact, and sleek wines that offer hints of cedar and graphite, rather more reminiscent of Cabernet Sauvignon than Pinot Noir—a rare condition in Etna reds. A beautiful cru within a cru is Chiusa Spagnolo, located within the confines of Zottorinoto: you will see it on the right side of the road going from Solicchiata to Verzella. (The stuff on the left-hand side has nothing to do with Chiusa Spagnolo.) At 620 meters above sea level, it is situated slightly lower on the valley floor, a bit hidden in an amphitheater, surrounded by lava. Frank Cornelissen makes a lovely single-*contrada* wine from Chiusa Spagnolo that tends to be more Barolo-like than Burgundy-like; the vineyard was planted around 1925.

The second sector runs from Solicchiata to Passopisciaro: the *contrade* of Moganazzi and Marchesa are in the lower subsector, as is Arcuria, just on the outskirts of the town of Passopisciaro, while Pettinociarelle, Montedolce, Rampante, and Guardiola are found in the upper subsector. Arcuria, just outside of Passopisciaro, is a *contrada* that has recently come into the spotlight thanks to numerous outstanding mineral and high-acid red wines that are extremely refined and long. The Calcagno (called Calcaneus in the United States because of legal issues) and Graci estates both own vines here. Moganazzi is another up-and-coming *contrada*, the grapes of which were bought in the past by Benanti and Franchetti. Solicchiata can also give excellent wines, and given its slightly removed locality, it was long a favorite getaway destination for Castiglione's most well-to-do families. Rampante is a highly interesting and qualitative *contrada* characterized by its extremely steep gradient and a less sunny microclimate. It rises as high up as one thousand meters above sea level: the well-known estate Planeta farms vines at about nine hundred meters above sea level, and Franchetti at one thousand meters. Due to its large range in altitude, Rampante can be divided into a Rampante Soprana and Rampante Sottana, though I for one am not yet able to discern surefire differences in wines made from each. The Pietradolce estate makes a much-praised Etna Rosso named Vigna Barbagalli (centenary vines growing at about nine hundred meters above sea level) that is all Rampante grapes: Barbagalli was the family name of one of the previous owners of the site. The harvest here can take place very late in the year. (For example, in 2004, Franchetti harvested his Rampante grapes on November 17.) Thanks to its high-altitude location and very old lava that has been degraded over time to a sandy consistency Rampante gives extremely fragrant but chewy tannic wines that are very easy to recognize when tasted blind; in my experience, all Rampante wines, like Monforte Barolos, benefit from extended cellaring (much more so than do other Etna reds). But as good as Rampante is, for my money the single best cru of Etna (for red wines, at least) is Guardiola, located at eight hundred to one thousand meters above sea level and blessed with some of the geologically oldest soils of all the *contrade*. Guardiola wines are among the deepest and most complex of all Etna Rossos: though not as chewy and tactile at the outset as those from Rampante, they benefit from prolonged cellaring, too. Because Guardiola is situated very high up on Etna, in cold or weather-challenged years Nerello Mascalese will not ripen fully there (a big problem); but in good vintages Guardiola gives the most elegant, complex Etna Rosso wines of all. This is why I consider it to be the single best Etna *contrada* of all for the Nerello Mascalese variety.

The third sector stretches from Passopisciaro to Monte La Guardia: its lower sector is where the *contrade* of Calderara Sottana, Porcaria, and Feudo di Mezzo are located, while Santo Spirito and Sciara Nuova are *contrade* situated in the upper subsector. Tenuta delle Terre Nere makes its most penetrating, mineral wine from stony Calderara Sottana, the most Burgundian of all Etna Rosso. (I think the red Burgundy–Etna Rosso analogy is a little overstated, not finding that Etna Rosso wines resemble red Burgundy all that much, but I am more accepting of this comparison in the case of wines from Calderara Sottana.) Porcaria (roughly 680 meters above sea level) is another very high quality cru, the wines of which are much rounder and fleshier than those of Calderara Sottana but still exhibit a piercing quality that keeps them light on their feet. Nowadays, almost everyone includes Porcaria in the vast Feudo di Mezzo *contrada,* but this is a mistake; most likely, this happened because Porcaria is not considered an especially elegant name. (Porcaria translates to "hog's hollow," and this was an area where hogs were raised and sold; not unexpectedly, humidity can be a problem in this shallower area, and disease pressure is high.) It would be more accurate to say that Porcaria is the Sottana part of Feudo di Mezzo (which should be called Porcaria Soprana). Frank Cornelissen makes an outstanding Porcaria Etna Rosso, as do Franchetti and Tenuta delle Terre Nere. In general, Porcaria is prone to water stress in hot years and therefore gives slightly deeper-colored Nerello wines than other *contrade,* and I find their tannins usually tougher than those of Feudo di Mezzo wines. In fact, Etna Rossos from Feudo di Mezzo are some of the roundest, most luscious and ready to drink, but they also have noteworthy depth and complexity. If not quite at the same level as Guardiola, this is certainly one of Etna's top five or six crus of all. There is also a small piece of Feudo di Mezzo unofficially called *sottostrada,* where the vines sit in a small depression and where frost poses a major risk.

Two *contrade* worth knowing in the upper subsector are Santo Spirito (roughly 800 meters above sea level) and Sciara Nuova. Santo Spirito gives some of the readiest-to-drink, softest, and roundest Etna Rosso of all (and for this reason is often a big hit with wine writers and the wine-loving public alike), but with enough acidic backbone to extend the flavors on the usually long back ends. The estates of Pietro Caciorgna and Tenuta delle Terre Nere farm Santo Spirito grapes, but only the latter currently bottles a wine with this *contrada* name. Sciara Nuova differs noticeably from the other *contrade:* it is characterized by geologically very young soil (the lava flow dates back only to the 1700s, so the soil is more gravelly than sandy in texture compared with the soils that distinguish *contrade* situated on more-ancient lava flows), and so roots have a difficult time digging deep though the bedrock. In this situation, choosing the right rootstock is important: the Ruggeri 140 helps roots penetrate farther down. Etna Rossos from Sciara Nuova should never be fat or rich (in other words, they should be nothing like Feudo di Mezzo or Chiappemacine) but rather medium-bodied, fresh, and refined (to be expected on the basis of the high altitude of the vineyard; for example, Franchetti's Nerello Mascalese vines in this *contrada* grow at 850 meters above sea level).

The last sector stretches from Monte La Guardia to Randazzo: the Feudo, Calderara, and Allegracore *contrade* are in the lower subsector, and the Monte La Guardia and San Lorenzo *contrada* are located in the upper subsector. In Allegracore, only those vineyards farther removed from the nearby Alcantara River deserve premier cru status; otherwise, humidity levels are such that grapes are prone to rot. San Lorenzo gives suave, elegant wines with sneaky concentration and size. Monte La Guardia, which is located at a high altitude (seven hundred meters above sea level and upward), gives wines that are at once powerful and perfumed; it is a *contrada* characterized by very good drainage, and of all the Etna *contrade,* it is probably the one that gives the best results year in and year out. Donnafugata's new Fragore wine, just released in 2018, showcases the quality of this site. In the ultimate analysis, it is the northern slope of Etna that harbors this terroir's greatest crus, and their wines have met with skyrocketing success in just a very short time.

THE SOUTHERN SUBZONE

The communes of the southern sector include Belpasso, Biancavilla, Nicolosi, Pedara, and Santa Maria di Licodia. There are respectively 111, 284, 129, 82, and 73 hectares under vine in each of the communes (2005 data, AGEA). In general, the southern sector of the Etna is characterized by vineyards but few wineries; most here are growers who sell their grapes to other estates. For example, Nicolosi and Pedara now form one big urban sprawl, but back in the nineteenth century Nicolosi boasted 465 hectares under vine and produced fifteen thousand hectoliters of wine a year, with Pedara producing even more wine (thirty thousand hectoliters per year), its territory having 534 hectares under vine (Mirone 1875). However, it is noteworthy, according to Salvo Foti, that a great deal of Grenache grows among the vines of Nerello Mascalese on Etna's southern slope. Biancavilla has five *contrade* (for example, Maiorca and Stella), several of which might be promising in their winemaking potential, but about which currently very little is known; and clearly, nobody has produced any wines of note there in the last fifteen years. Santa Maria di Licodia has but one *contrada,* Cavaliere, but that has always enjoyed a good reputation for its wines. This part of the Etna is noteworthy for it harbors old vines of high-quality Nerello Cappuccio. Some of the wineries worth following in the area include Feudo Cavaliere, Masseria Setteporte, and Scammacca del Murgo. Recent news that has made headlines is that Piedmont's Angelo Gaja has entered a partnership with Alberto Graci of Etna's Graci winery to develop a winery project in this sector of Etna—specifically, in the Biancavilla township. It cannot hurt Etna as far as visibility goes to have an important, world-famous producer like Gaja investing in the area, and hopefully the wines will show well.

THE EASTERN SUBZONE

The eastern slope of Etna includes the communes of Giarre, Mascali, Milo, Sant'Alfio, Santa Venerina, Trecastagni, Viagrande, and Zafferana Etnea. The hectares under vine in each commune are 80, 120, 137, 103, 120, 213, 120, and 233, respectively (2005 data, AGEA). Wines from this area were much appreciated in older times, and there were country restaurants (or *osterie,* locally called *putìe*) that specialized in the sale of "vini di Mascalucia." The steep slopes (40 percent gradients are not uncommon) and the soil of the eastern slope greatly reduce Nerello Mascalese crop yields, but the wines are especially refined. Viagrande boasts nine *contrade,* and was historically famous for its wines, especially in the Monte Serra cru, where as early as 1474 there was a winery named "Serra della Contessa" (nowadays, also the name of an Etna Rosso wine made by Benanti). Monte Serra is another site prone to water stress and known for slightly deeper-colored Nerello Mascalese wines. (I stress that "deep color" is a very relative term with Nerello Mascalese wines, which by definition can never be inky or pitch-black.) Zafferana Etnea has twenty *contrade,* but most are not very well known yet, such as Piano dell'Acqua and Fleri. Last but not least, Milo is another important commune in this part of the Etna: there are eight *contrade* here, best known for their white-wine production, but there are also some standout crus for Nerello Mascalese. The names of the *contrade* of Milo are Caselle, Rinazzo, Pianogra32de, Praino Crisafulli, Fornazzo, Salice, Villagrande, and Volpare. Of these, Caselle is the best for Carricante, while Villagrande is probably best for Nerellos. Trecastagni has nine *contrade,* of which the best known are most likely Ronzini and Monte Ilice. (The word *ilice* derives from the Latin name of the holm oak, *Quercus ilex,* which grew abundant in this area; interestingly, the same tree has given Montalcino its name; see the Sangiovese entry.) Monte Ilice being an impervious, high-altitude, and hard-to-work area, most of its vineyards were abandoned in time; like Porcaria, Monte Ilice, and Monte Gorna, too, are prone to water stress in hot years, and therefore their Nerello wines are often slightly deeper in color than those of other *contrade*. Biondi makes wines from grapes grown in this sector. (Biondi's vineyards are near Trecastagni and so would be more accurately placed in an eventual southeastern Etna sector.) The red wines are especially successful. Actually, while the northern sector's red wines are more powerful and deep, the southern sector delivers refined juicy red wines of earlier appeal and charm. The Il Cantante estate, owned by Simply Red front man Mick Hucknall, also farmed grapes from the eastern subzone of Etna until it was sold.

The Best Nerello Mascalese and Nerello Cappuccio *Contrade*

This classification refers primarily to Nerello Mascalese; what little Nerello Cappuccio exists is confined mostly to the southern slope of Etna—for example, in the townships of Biancavilla and Santa Maria di Licodia. The classification is the result of a combination of my tasting results of Etna Rosso wines and monovariety Nerello wines since 2000 (at a time when nobody anywhere was drinking, talking about, or writing anything about these wines; for example, as recently as 1995 even Veronelli mentioned only Villagrande as a possible cru), with the information obtained over the years in interviews and winery visits. Clearly, literally nothing is known about the winemaking potential of *contrade* such as Corvo, Maiorca, or Stella, for example. Now it might be that one day there will be fine wines made with grapes grown in these and other similarly little-known *contrade,* but for the time being, beware jumping on the bandwagon of media-savvy estates and their soon-to-be-released hotshot, much-hyped wines from less-than-stellar sites. Clearly, such *contrade* have little or no history of terroir: Musigny, Doktor, or Cannubi they are not. Furthermore, be aware that, given the popularity and the rising importance of *contrade* labeling, wines are now being attributed to *"contrade"* that are not officially recognized as such: for example, Frank Cornelissen makes an outstanding Monte Colla red wine, but for accuracy's sake it's good to know that the *contrada* Monte Colla is in the township of Bronte, outside of the Etna DOC limits.

Eccezionale Sceltissima (Grand Cru *Hors Classe*)
Township of Castiglione di Sicilia: Guardiola.

Eccezionale Scelta (Grand Cru)
Township of Castiglione di Sicilia: Arcuria, Barbabecchi, Chiappemacine, Cottanera, Feudo di Mezzo (Porcaria Soprana), Marchesa, Montedolce, Piano dei Dani, Porcaria Sottana (today part of Feudo di Mezzo, but I believe these two give distinct wines and should be separate *contrade*), Rampante, Rovittello, Santo Spirito, Trimarchisa, Verzella, Zottorinotto. (Arcuria, Marchesa, and Santo Spirito are more precisely situated in the Passopisciaro hamlet of the Castiglione township, where in my experience wines tend to often showcase different aroma and flavor profiles than those of the rest of the Castiglione township.)

Township of Randazzo: Croce Monaci, Montelaguardia.
Township of Viagrande: Monte Serra.

Eccezionale (Premier Cru)
Township of Castiglione di Sicilia: Diciasettesalme, Pontale Palino (the latter more precisely in the hamlet of Solicchiata, township of Castiglione di Sicilia).
Township of Milo: Villagrande.
Township of Randazzo: Allegracore, Bocca d'Orzo, Calderara, Calderara Sottana, Feudo, Muganazzi, Pignatuni, San Lorenzo, Sciara Nuova.
Township of Santa Maria di Licodia: Cavaliere.
Township of Trecastagni: Carpene, Monte Gorna, Monte Ilice, Monte San Nicolò, Ronzini.

(I limit myself to a small selection of wines only, and one wine per estate, or this list would be too long.)

I Vigneri Vinupetra***PS, Franchetti Contrada G***PS, Tenuta delle Terre Nere Guardiola***PS.

Biondi Cisterna Fuori***, Calcagno (Calcaneus in the United States) Arcuria***, Calabretta La Contrada dei Centenari*** (not labeled as an Etna Rosso), Cottanera Feudo di Mezzo***, Cusumano–Alta Mora Feudo di Mezzo***, Donnafugata Montelaguardia Fragore***, Famiglia Statella Pettinociarelle***, Federico Graziani Profumo di Vulcano***, Frank Cornelissen CS***, Graci Arcuria***, Le Vigne di Eli Pignatuni***, Pietradolce Archineri***, Tenuta di Fessina Erse***.

Nerello Cappuccio: Benanti Nerello Cappuccio***, Calabretta Rosso Cappuccio***, Tenuta di Fessina Laeneo***.

Nero d'Avola (Calabrese)

THE GRAPE VARIETY

Calabrese is the official name in Italy for a grape variety that everyone, producers and experts alike, call instead Nero d'Avola. The name Calabrese derives from the words *calau avulisi*, meaning "down from Avola." (Avola is the little town near Ragusa considered by most everyone as Nero d'Avola's birthplace.) Over time the name morphed into "Calabrese" by way of *calaurisi, calavrisi, calabrisi*, and finally *calabrese*. (Interestingly, *cala, calea*, and *caleu* are Sicilian-dialect synonyms for *racina*, which means "grape.") Use of the Nero d'Avola name is a more modern event, stemming from the habit of calling dark grapes "Nero-Something"; it was in the nineteenth century that the dark grape from Avola became Nero d'Avola in popular parlance. Long a part of the Sicilian landscape and of the lives of Sicilians, Nero d'Avola was not always as plentiful everywhere on the island as it is today. According to 1961 data, Nero d'Avola was then mainly grown in the province of Siracusa (where it was planted on about 80 percent of the surface under vine, and

especially so in flatland vineyards and those up to two hundred meters above sea level). It also was reported to grow, but very sparsely, in the provinces of Caltanisetta (Gela), Enna, and Catania (only 4 percent of the surface under vine at that time, roughly 1,480 hectares), while there was apparently very little Nero d'Avola growing in the province of Palermo.

As early as the early seventeenth century, Cupani wrote of a round-berried *Calavrisi* (which is an important detail, since Nero d'Avola is characterized instead by a more elongated, oval grape shape), meaning that there were either distinct varieties called with the same name or different Nero d'Avola biotypes living in the vineyards. From a morphologic standpoint, Nero d'Avola has medium-to-large, compact bunches of conical shape with one or two wings and medium-to-large, oval berries. Despite a number of Nero d'Avola certified clones, a walk in any vineyard will easily demonstrate the myriad biotypes resulting from centuries of adaptation to Sicily's many different terroirs. Nero d'Avola is Sicily's second-most-planted cultivar, with over eighteen thousand hectares under vine (2010 data), or almost three times more than Ansonica (Inzolia), which is the third-most-planted Sicilian wine grape. (Nero d'Avola is Italy's seventh-most-planted cultivar.) This despite its not being free of problems: for example, it buds early and ripens late, meaning there is a potential frost risk at both ends of the growing season; but since it is mostly planted in warm, dry areas, there is not much of a risk for farmers. And so Nero d'Avola is grown all over the island, though it is less abundant in the northeastern corner of the island (in the countryside surrounding the cities of Messina and Milazzo), where it is the Nerello varieties that rule (because northeastern Sicily is too wet and humid for Nero d'Avola to perform beautifully and farmers prefer to plant other varieties, such as the outstanding Nocera). Nero d'Avola has an almost uncanny ability to tolerate highly saline soils—so much so that in areas of Sicily characterized by such soils (for example, the Agrigento province and southwestern Sicily in general), wines actually offer greater intensity of aromas and flavors in soils of medium high to high salt content compared with those of lower salt content (Scacco et al. 2010). Nero d'Avola is also a heat-resistant variety, and does not drop its acidity easily. (It is a variety that is very rich in malic acid and so tends to give high acid wines with at times shrill mouthfeels.) Numerous authors have studied the aroma and flavor molecules of Nero d'Avola and its wines, and have tried to link concentrations and profiles to specific parts of Sicily (Di Stefano, Foti, and Borsa 1993; Di Stefano et al. 1996). According to Genovese et al. (2005a), ethyl esters play a large role in generating the aromas of red fruits in Nero d'Avola wines. However, as any serious or expert wine taster knows, Nero d'Avola wines do not remind one especially of red fruits, save for when the vines grow in the island's southeast corner (but then it is more a matter of superripe, if not downright overripe, red fruits). Nero d'Avola wines are also rich in furaneol, which has an aroma of strawberry or caramel depending on its concentration (Pickenhagen et al. 1981), and it accounts for a candied note. The wines always have a floral smell, of course this is due to terpenes—in Nero d'Avola's case, due to linalool and citronellol (Verzera et al. 2014). Professor Rocco Di Stefano, one of Italy's premier wine grape researchers, told me in an interview years ago that Nero d'Avola has a strong tendency to produce terpinol molecules, such as cis-8-hydroxylinalool—something that distinguishes it neatly from Cabernet Sauvignon, Merlot, and Syrah.

SPECIFIC TERROIRS

There are numerous excellent terroirs in Sicily for Nero d'Avola, and undoubtedly these terroirs result in very different wines. For example, the Nero d'Avola wines of Vittoria are very different from those of Noto. The most striking of all Nero d'Avolas are made in Pachino, with an almost painful intensity of aromas and flavors, but any Sicilian DOC wine is likely to include Nero d'Avola. Analyzing Sicily's terroirs for Nero d'Avola, the wines associated with each specific terroir can be described in terms of geographical location as follows:

1. Nero d'Avola grapes grown at higher altitudes in north-central Sicily give wines that tend to have paler colors and more mineral and spicy personalities. These are the most refined Nero d'Avola wines of all (think of Tasca d'Almerita's Rosso del Conte and Feudo Montoni's Vrucara).

2. Lower-altitude vineyards in central Sicily are usually blessed with warmer mesoclimates, and so wines are richer and more tannic, with stronger notes of licorice, tobacco, and tar.

3. Farther south and toward the east, the Agrigento and Riesi areas are characterized by Nero d'Avola wines that are astringent yet fruity.

4. Nero d'Avola wines from areas farther southeast such as Noto and Eloro are very ripe, with herbal and saline notes (and can showcase almost anchovy-like notes at

times), while those made in nearby Vittoria are lighter and very floral. In fact, they resemble wines made with Frappato, another Sicilian native grape variety typical of Sicily's southeast. Pachino is where Nero d'Avola reaches its most concentrated zenith, characterized by superripe, pungently fragrant wines.

Southeastern Sicily

Southeastern Sicily is dominated by the Iblei mountain range (the Hyblaean Mountains, in English). Shaped like a half moon, this geographical feature delimits an important viticultural part of Sicily that boasts, north to south and east to west, the denominations of Siracusa, Noto, Eloro, and Vittoria. Vineyards are a common sight on the lower slopes of the mountains as well as on the coastal plains separating them from the sea. Each one of these four DOCs holds bragging rights to some of Italy's best wines: Siracusa and Moscato Bianco combine to give the wonderful but unfortunately now rare Moscato di Siracusa; Noto is another privileged site for Moscato Bianco (it is home to the famous and delicious Moscato di Noto and Noto Passito) and not, I point out, Nero d'Avola (see below); Eloro is a grand cru for Nero d'Avola (see below); and Vittoria is the home of Cerasuolo di Vittoria, a Frappato and Nero d'Avola blend, but also the best terroir in the world for Frappato. Last but not least, it is necessary to distinguish the district of Pachino within the Noto denomination, since it gives unique Nero d'Avola wines, unlike those of any other part of Sicily. There is no official recognition of districts in Italy, so you have to accept my deciding that it should be so (and hopefully the local politicos will one day wake up to the smell of the coffee . . . er, the wine). Nevertheless, much as Lamole and Panzano are to be considered districts of Greve but separate from the main denomination, given that their wines have little or nothing in common with those made elsewhere in the Greve denomination, so it should be with Pachino.

Eloro

The Eloro denomination was officially named in 1994. It is an overlap denomination that straddles two provinces, Ragusa and Siracusa, but its Nero d'Avola wines from its Siracusa portion, which falls within the jurisdiction of Noto, are excellent. Very intelligently, the minimum Nero d'Avola requirement for Nero d'Avola Eloro wines has to be 90 percent, and so it is for Eloro Rosso. Not so intelligently, the Eloro Pachino category stipulates a need for less Nero d'Avola in the blend (80 percent). That's Italy for you.

Pachino

Pachino is a grand cru for Nero d'Avola, pure and simple. Noto is not (although it is for Moscato Bianco; see the Moscato Bianco entry), but it is by far the most beautiful and famous town in this part of Sicily, and so clever officials thought it wise to use Noto's name for the wine denomination, too. (Therefore, Noto became a DOC in 2008—a territory that includes the municipalities of Avola, Pachino, and Rosolino, all of which are situated in the province of Syracuse). You cannot blame those legislators, actually: Noto really is a mesmerizingly beautiful town and a tourist-worthy destination, a treasure chest full of amazing Baroque architecture. Given that towns immediately close by such as Ragusa and Modica are also pretty and loaded with outstanding restaurants, ice-cream parlors, and chocolate shops (some of the best in Italy), it all adds up to a UNESCO World Heritage stamp for the area. (That we even have Noto to talk about today is wonderful: in 1693 a horrible earthquake destroyed Noto entirely, and so a new city was built in its place, roughly eight kilometers south of where the old one stood.) In the aftermath of the phylloxera scourge, farmers intelligently abandoned the promiscuous agriculture typical of the area and concentrated on just one grape, Nero d'Avola. Turns out they could not have picked a better one for their specific terroir. After all, it is in the nearby town of Avola (9.2 kilometers away from Noto, more or less a fifteen-minute drive) that the cultivar is believed to have been born. In fact, when people speak or write of "Noto Nero d'Avola" or of "Nero d'Avola of/from Noto," it is actually Nero d'Avola from Pachino they are really talking about, a town located twenty-three kilometers or fourteen miles (twenty-nine minutes by car) to the south of Noto. There are very few vineyards immediately around Noto, as any visit to the area will confirm. (In 2003, Tuscany's Mazzei family of Castellina's famous Fonterutoli winery did create the Zisola estate right outside Noto). But most everyone who moved quickly had already bought their vines down toward Pachino while there were sufficiently large tracts of land still available (Baglio di Pianetto, Duca di Salaparuta, Gulfi, Planeta). In fact, as early as the 1800s the countryside of Pachino was famous for its Nero Pachino or Rosso Pachino wines (made mostly with Nero d'Avola). According to Vito Catania (the founder of the stellar Gulfi winery and, sadly, no longer with us), the wine of Pachino was very much in demand, especially in France (Gironde and Burgundy), and vineyards were everywhere. At Pachino, the Baron Rudinì owned over two thousand hectares under vine and huge tanks capable of storing up to fifty thousand hectoliters of must. Wines labeled Noto Rosso need be made with only 65 percent minimum Nero d'Avola (and it is a still-too-low 85 percent for those labeled Nero d'Avola Noto). Unfortunately, Pachino is not officially recognized as a denomination or district, and so its name does not appear on labels. And so another great opportunity to create wines with not just a sense of place, but value and increased income for an Italian viticultural area is completely lost.

The topography and mesoclimate of the Pachino area contribute greatly to the style of Nero d'Avola wines made there. In the countryside of Augusta, Avola, Pachino, Noto, Rosolini, Floridia, Siracusa, and Sortino, the soils have a subalkaline pH and are prevalently brown in color (but not only) and are rather calcareous in nature. They can have up to 25 percent clay with high mineral concentrations, but one of the key characterizing features of Pachino soils especially is that the mineral content and soil types vary immensely over even short distances. For example, at Noto and Rosolini there are regosols (shallow, medium- to fine-textured soils of usually alluvial origin common in arid or semiarid soils) with clay-rich rocks but much less mineral content; there are sandy dunes between Marzamemi and Capo Passero; and at Porto Palo and Pachino there are also red Mediterranean-type soils, with plenty of iron, copper, and calcium, depending on the exact area. Flatland and hillside vineyards are bathed in a hot, arid environment with annual average temperatures around 17.6°C (among the highest of the island) and higher in July and August. The coldest month of the year is January (at a not exactly freezing 11.4°C, you can tell we're in Sicily), and the warmest month is August (average daily temperature 25.3°C, but long stretches of 30°C or more are common). This can lead to dehydration directly on the vine—as much as 30 to 35 percent of the total berries in the hotter vintages. The harvest in Pachino occurs two weeks earlier than around Noto in most vintages. Diurnal temperature variations are minimal (so these Nero d'Avola wines are more about texture and flesh than fragrance). The average annual precipitation is 450 millimeters, and though the winters are much rainier than the summers, the wettest month of the year is October (on average, there are 100 to 105 millimeters of rain in this month); the driest month of the year is July (only one millimeter of rain). The preferred training system in eastern Sicily is the nonirrigated *alberello* (bush vine) system, with vines in the Pachino area generally planted from 0.9 by 0.9 meters to 1.25 by 1.25, but more commonly vines stand at 1.20 by 1.20. Because bush vines require a lot of work and high costs, many estates are (unfortunately) trying newer plantings with irrigation and cordon spur training systems. In fact, at Gulfi they have created a mechanized *alberello* training system that allows faster harvesting and cuts costs. More than any other estate in

Sicily, Gulfi has forwarded the concept of Nero d'Avola crus to the extreme, making world-class Nero d'Avola wines from specific Pachino crus, the famous *contrade*.

Case Study: Gulfi and the Single-Contrada Nero d'Avola Wines of Pachino

Gulfi's four Nero d'Avola cru wines allow a lesson in terroir as few other Italian wines do. The wines are made by the same technical team, in exactly the same way, from grapes grown in four different vineyards that have basically the same grape variety, rootstocks, exposures, slopes, and altitudes (the difference in altitude between them being forty meters at most); and yet the four wines are completely different, bringing to the fore the spectrum of Nero d'Avola expressions in southeastern Sicily. The vineyards of Baroni, Bufaleffi, Maccari, and San Lorenzo are located at a short distance from each other roughly between the towns of Pachino to the south, Noto to the northeast, and Rosolini to the northwest. The whole area is more commonly referred to as Noto, but as I have written above, Pachino's wines are completely different from those of Noto. Gulfi's *contrade* wines (called by the name of the respective *contrade* and a "nero" prefix: Nerobaronj, Nerobufaleffj, Neromaccarj, and Nerosanlorè) are among Italy's very best wines. Undoubtedly, it helps to have passionate, dedicated owners (the Catania family) and Sicily's greatest living native grape expert (Salvo Foti) as the acting consulting enologist.

Baroni: One of southeastern Sicily's most famous *contrade* for Pachino wine, Baroni was producing much-sought-after wines as early as the 1800s. Gulfi's vineyard in Baroni is 2.8 hectares large, divided between four parcels, situated at fifty meters above sea level. Vine density is seven thousand vines per hectare; the bush vines are south-facing, average thirty years of age (many were planted before 1976), and are planted on Ruggeri 140 rootstock. Yields are low at forty quintals per hectare. The clay-calcareous soil is downright white or whitish-looking (high limestone content) and

is marked by high levels of potassium, magnesium, and calcium. Maceration and fermentation last about twenty days in stainless steel (at a maximum temperature of 28°C), and the wine is aged twenty-four months in used French oak barriques (225 liters) and *tonneaux* (500 liters). The Nero d'Avola wines of Baroni are powerful and pungently perfumed, with a rich, viscous (but not opulent) mouthfeel. In my experience, these are always the Gulfi Nero d'Avola wines that age best, though all four single-*contrada* wines age well.

Bufaleffi: Another *contrada* that has always been extremely renowned for its wines. The 2.5-hectare parcel is divided into ten plots and is characterized by an interesting mix of soils visible to the naked eye; more than that of any other Gulfi single-*contrada* vineyard, the soil here offers a kaleidoscope of colors ranging from blackish (clay) to reddish (sand) to whitish (limestone). The clay portions are obviously rich in organic matter (hence the soil's dark color), while the calcareous sections are characterized by a lighter-colored clay base and plenty of small calcareous pebbles, also making for an interesting granulometric mix. The south-facing vines are planted on Ruggeri 140 and Fercal rootstocks and lie at 50 meters above sea level. The plant density is seven thousand vines per hectare, and the bush vines are about forty years of age; yields are low, hardly reaching forty quintals per hectare. I always find Nerobufaleffj to be the most complex and powerful of Gulfi's four crus; it can be downright opulent in some vintages, almost Amarone-like (a good Amarone, that is) in its velvety and suave delivery of super-ripe red cherry, raspberry nectar, caper, and aromatic herb notes.

Maccari: This 1.55-hectare vineyard comprises five plots situated in the eponymous *contrada*—one of the historically most prestigious in terms of wine. (And just to confirm that there is no accounting for tastes, despite all its fame, it is almost always the Gulfi single-*contrada*

Nero d'Avola wine I like least, every vintage.) The soil is characterized by thin layers of reddish calcareous-clay base with little organic matter and small stones. The vineyard is situated at thirty meters above sea level. Plant density is seven thousand vines per hectare; the rootstock is Ruggeri 140; and the bush vines average thirty years of age (although the exact number is unknown, since a large portion of the vines were planted before 1976 and therefore nobody knows their exact age); the yields are just slightly higher than those of San Lorenzo, but still low (fifty quintals per hectare). The wines strike me as having a ferrous quality, and no, I am not being influenced by the soil's color; they are also strongly marked by notes of aromatic herbs, honey, and confit tomatoes. (The tomatoes of Pachino are world-famous, though few people get to taste the real ones, since most of the tomatoes labeled "Pachino" in Italy and elsewhere are conveniently "Pachino-like," rather than the real thing.)

San Lorenzo: I know minerals in the soil cannot be tasted as such in wines. I know that the concept of minerality in wine is a slippery slope. I know "minerality" has become the escape hatch of people who have to speak about wine in public and do not know what to say. That we all know. Then I open a bottle of Nerosanloré (the name of this wine was originally Nerosanlorenzo, but it was changed to avoid confusion with the many other Sanlorenzo or San Lorenzo wines made all over Italy), and I can swear I taste the sea and its minerals in every glass. Who knows where the truth lies? Anyway, San Lorenzo is the Gulfi vineyard most influenced by the sea; and it probably could not be otherwise, given that it lies right at the water's edge, less than seven hundred meters from the deep blue. The vineyard is about 2.5 hectares large and is divided into two plots of vines planted on Ruggeri 140 rootstock, situated at a whopping ten meters above sea level. The area's climate is cooler than you would expect when looking at a map and noting that this part of Sicily is situated farther south than the African city of Tunis, the capital of Tunisia. The south-facing bush vines are planted at about seven thousand vines per hectare and are over forty years old on average. The calcareous-sandy soil is very obviously reddish in color, rich in both iron and copper. Nerosanlorè is always the most refined of Gulfi's four crus, with noteworthy floral aromas and flavors complicated by notes of iodine. In the past, Nerosanlorè was made in a much riper, concentrated wine that seemed bent on outripening Nerobufaleffj; but over the years it has become the most elegant and austere of Gulfi's four splendid cru wines.

BENCHMARK WINES

Gulfi Nerobufaleffj***PS.

Gulfi Nerosanloré***.

Curto Nero d'Avola Eloro Riserva Fontanelle**, Gulfi Nerobaronj**, Gulfi Neromaccarj**, Marabino Nero d'Avola Riserva Eloro Pachino**, Planeta Noto Santa Cecilia**, Riofavara Eloro Sciavè**.

Baglio di Pianetto Sicilia Cembali*, Curto Eloro*, Gulfi Nerojbleo*, Gulfi Rossojbleo*, Riofavara San Basilio*.

Pecorino

THE GRAPE VARIETY

Pecorino has been Italy's hottest white cultivar and wine for the last five or six years. Its popularity does not seem to be decreasing any: the wine's unique combination of generous, rich mouthfeel and its bright, crisp aromas and flavors of fresh citrus fruits and sage seemingly make new converts at every tasting I go to. And to think that as recently as the late 1970s, there was no monovariety Pecorino wine being made. The two people who have done most for Pecorino have been Guido Cocci Grifoni, of the Cocci Grifoni estate in the Marche, and Luigi Cataldi Madonna, of the Cataldi Madonna estate in Abruzzo; curiously enough, in the beginning neither man seems to have been aware of the other. Cocci Grifoni essentially saved the variety while Cataldi Madonna broadcast knowledge about the variety and was the first to label his wine with the Pecorino name. (Cocci Grifoni preferred to call his wine "Colle Vecchio," without the Pecorino moniker.) There are different clones and at least three main biotypes of Pecorino; differences in the latter are mostly in

morphology of the leaf and the bunch. (Pecorino's leaf is actually easy to recognize: it's small and round, with very few indentations.) It is a rustic variety at home in the mountains, and so prefers cooler climates; rootstocks that push vigor such as Kober 5 BB and 1103 P seem most suited to it, since Pecorino, characterized by sterile basal buds, is a naturally low-yielding variety (provided you haven't planted new, very productive clones that give wines hardly reminiscent of the variety). Today, Pecorino is grown mainly in the Marche and Abruzzo, but in small amounts as well in Lazio, Tuscany, and Umbria (in the latter region, it is called Dolcipappola). Due to its success, plantings have been steadily increasing since 2000 (when there were only about eighty-seven hectares in Italy, whereas now there are well over three hundred hectares). Today, the best Pecorino wines are made by Cocci Grifoni in the Marche and by Abruzzo's Cataldi Madonna and Tiberio wineries. Nobody else comes even close to the level of quality achieved by these three estates. Studies on the Offida Pecorino grapes of Cocci Grifoni have shown that Pecorino has significantly high levels of β-phenethyl alcohol (a molecule that gives off a smell of roses), isoamyl acetate (banana), ethyl hexanoate (apple), and ethyl octanoate (citrus). High acidity is very typical of Pecorino wines (the variety is especially rich in malic acid). Cristiana Tiberio and Luigi Cataldi Madonna have always told me that the biggest difference between their Pecorino wines and that of others is that they actively seek acidity, while everybody else tries reducing it. According to them, that's a big mistake, since acidity defines Pecorino wines. The other big difference between Pecorino wines is that in the Marche producers will generally macerate the must on the skins, while in Abruzzo they don't. Pecorino is a sugar pump, packing in sugar easily (especially in hot climates), and so planting it in low-lying vineyards is a huge mistake and a travesty of terroir (Pecorino having no business being planted by the sea), because the wines will never showcase much complexity. Clearly because the variety does build sugar up quickly, wines can have noteworthy alcohol levels (14 percent is common, but levels may be as high as 14.5 percent). Hyperreductive winemaking has been used with Pecorino, heightening the lemony aromatics of the variety, because it is especially rich in thiol precursors, and as star consultant winemaker Lorenzo Landi says, "It makes no sense to oxidize this wine and lose what the terroir and cultivar combine to showcase." Though very perfumed, in my experience these Pecorino wines age less well.

SPECIFIC TERROIRS

Pecorino is a mountain grape variety that, because of its popularity, is now being forced to do things it does not have the genetic predisposition for. Now that it is planted practically everywhere short of in closets and on highways, good Pecorino terroirs are few.

Ofena (L'Aquila)

Ofena is a town located in the Abruzzo province of L'Aquila. It sits in a very mountainous area (right in the middle of the Gran Sasso massif), on soils that have a higher gravel content than those of other parts of Abruzzo (such as Vestina, for example). Parts of this area are just too cold to grow grapes, but the more temperate areas of Capestrano, Ofena, and Sulmona are fine. Viticulturally, the L'Aquila province (or l'Aquilano, in Italian) is made up of two important subzones: Ofena to the north, and the Val Peligna to the south (the latter being important for Montepulciano production; see the Montepulciano entry). The two are separated by the westernmost reaches of the Casauria Abruzzo subzone. Despite Ofena's mountainous landscape (vineyards lie at an average of 350 meters above sea level), it is nicknamed the "forno d'Abruzzo" (the Abruzzo oven) because it can get quite hot there in the summer. (The Cataldi Madonna estate is located here.) Soils in the area can vary noticeably: for example, Cataldi Madonna's Frontone vineyard (where the estate's oldest Pecorino vines grow) has roughly 36.4 percent sand, 32.1 percent clay, and 31.5 percent loam, with about 6 percent active lime, compared with the Macerone vineyard's 53 percent sand, 10 percent clay, and 37 percent loam, with about 9.5 percent active lime. These numbers are interesting, especially in light of those pertaining to the soil analysis of Tiberio's vineyard in Casauria in the province of Pescara, a slightly warmer (but still cool) mesoclimate; vineyards there also grow at 350 meters above sea level, but the soil percentages are 19 percent sand, 34 percent clay, and 47 percent loam, with 11.3 percent active lime. In other words, both these producers, who make Abruzzo's two best Pecorino wines, have a significant percentage of lime in the soil; the higher lime content in Tiberio's soils probably helps offset the effects of the slightly warmer microclimate. The Frontone's clay component's water-retaining capacity is very important, for it allows Pecorino to express itself to the utmost, with richer, spicier, more aromatically interesting wines. Also important is Ofena's relatively cold climate, because this is in fact what Pecorino wants: being a mountain grape, it thrives in colder habitats. Rootstocks of choice are the SO4, Kober 5BB, and the 420A. Another sign of Ofena's viticultural quality is that many other Abruzzo estates own or have recently bought vineyards in the Ofena area, including Marramiero, Masciarelli, Pasetti (in the Capodaqua *contrada*), and Valle Reale (at Capestrano). That never happens by chance, or because people like to throw money away.

BENCHMARK WINE

Cataldi Madonna Pecorino Frontone***PS.

Casauria

For an in-depth analysis of the Casauria subzone, see the Trebbiano Abruzzese entry.

BENCHMARK WINE

Tiberio Pecorino***PS.

Offida

Thanks to Guido Cocci Grifoni, the Offida area in the Marche is the birthplace of modern Pecorino wines. Offida's topography is that of a slowly rising plateau from the coastline toward the west, and the nearby Adriatic Sea has a cooling effect on the area's climate. July and August are the warmest months, January and February the coldest. The average annual temperature is 13.5°C, and diurnal temperature variations are highest in the summer and autumn; only the denomination's most coastal section is characterized by really warm weather. The Winkler index is 1750–2100, and the Huglin index is 2250–2500. Soils vary within the denomination, but are mostly either sand- or clay-based. The coastline and lower hillsides have mainly sandy-gravel soils, but vineyards there are few. Soils are for the most part clay with an alkaline pH (7.5–8.5) and quite deep, with roots easily digging one hundred centimeters below the surface. This rooting depth and the high clay content are ideal for Pecorino: on clay, Pecorino gives wines that are balanced and blessed with generous acidity levels and very intense notes of yellow flowers such as broom, while wines from sandy soils are simpler, if more intensely fruity and saline.

BENCHMARK WINES

Cocci Grifoni Pecorino Offida Colle
    Vecchio***PS.

San Savino Pecorino Offida Ciprea***.

Petit Rouge

THE GRAPE VARIETY

Petit Rouge is a variety that has called the Valle d'Aosta home for centuries. Not surprisingly, it is related to many other local grape varieties: it is a sibling of Fumin and is most likely the grandfather, uncle, or half-brother of most of the other Valle d'Aosta red grapes, such as Cornalin, Roussin, and Neyret de Saint-Vincent. Also, because it has hung around for quite some time (in order of historical citation among the Valle d'Aosta natives, it is fourth in line, after Prié [1691], Fumin [1785], and Mayolet [1787]), numerous biotypes exist. It is a member of the ancient Oriou family of grapes (named after a hamlet near Saint-Vincent that includes such Oriou biotypes as the Oriou Curaré, Gris, Lombard, Voirard, and others). Clearly, Petit Rouge has long been popular in the Valle d'Aosta, with an all-pervasive presence in the region similar to that of Sangiovese in Tuscany; although other Valle d'Aosta native red grapes (Cornalin, Mayolet, Vuillermin) risked extinction only twenty years ago, this was never true of Petit Rouge. Petit Rouge wines are easygoing, fruity midweight wines that offer savory red berry and herbal aromas and flavors lifted by juicy acidity. They are almost always deeply red in color (Petit Rouge is rich in malvidin and conjugated anthocyanidins) and are gently tannic since the variety is not especially rich in tannin molecules. If poorly made, they can have off-putting reductive smells that are hard to get rid of even with prolonged aeration in the glass.

SPECIFIC TERROIRS

Torrette

Torrette is the name of a DOC wine but also of a specific place in the Valle d'Aosta that was historically linked to the best and deepest Petit Rouge wines—specifically, the steep mountain area near the town of Saint-Pierre. So, just like Barolo and Barbaresco, it is the name of a specific area that gives a wine its name. There are about seventy hectares of Petit Rouge mainly planted in the Valle d'Aosta's middle valley, from Saint-Vincent to Arvier, especially around Aymaville, Saint-Pierre, and Villeneuve. Unfortunately, Torrette's fame means it now has the largest production area in the Valle d'Aosta; with the institution of the DOC in 1985, it can be made in the territories of the communes of Aymaville, Charvensod, Gressan, Introd, Jovençan, and Villeneuve, on the right bank of the Dora Baltea; and in the territories of Aosta, Quart, Saint-Christophe, Saint-Pierre, Sarre, and Villeneuve on the left bank. It was not always so. With the establishment of the DOC, the production zone was enlarged to the areas immediately around Torrette (or Torretta, as it was called by Gatta in 1838). And so whereas the best Torrette wines ought to be those made mostly with Petit Rouge grapes grown immediately around the Torrette toponym, there are now myriad Torrette wines made in the Valle d'Aosta, many of which are good despite the fact that the grapes come from elsewhere in the denomination. Apparently, the local government truly believed that the other communes had a terroir that was suitable to high-quality Torrette wine production and moved to have the production area increased; understandably, this did not sit well with the *vignaioli* of Saint-Pierre, who lobbied long and hard not to have this happen. Ultimately, they were convinced by the government who put up the cash to build a new social cooperative (the Cave des Onzes Communes, which makes outstanding wines), which gave locals another outlet for selling their grapes. Depending on where you sample within the denomination, the soils of the Torrette DOC are mostly sand (70 percent), loam (25 percent), and clay (5 percent) over fissured granite bedrock that allows for very good drainage (actually, far too good in droughty years). Petit Rouge grows at high altitudes (600 to 850 meters above sea level), and diurnal temperature shifts are noteworthy. Overall the meso- and microclimates of the area are warm; almond trees are able to survive here, which they would not be able to do in a cold environment. The grapes are usually harvested in mid-September, but in some vintages they can be picked at the end of October. Unfortunately, the official guidelines ask for only a minimum 70 percent Petit Rouge in the DOC Torrette wine, plus small percentages of Mayolet, Fumin, Vuillermin, and other local varieties. (Each cannot exceed 10 percent of the total.) Most of the better Torrette wines have at least 80 to 90 percent Petit Rouge. You might find yourself thinking that, given that Mayolet and Vuillermin are extremely high-quality varieties, adding 15 to 20 percent or more cannot be a bad thing: unfortunately, those two are moderately aromatic varieties, and including any more than 10 percent in the blend ends up hopelessly obfuscating Petit Rouge's expression. In general, Torrette wines are deeper, richer, and more tactile than those labeled Petit Rouge; comparing Petit Rouge wines with Torrettes is a little like comparing entry-level Chianti with *riserva* or *gran selezione*. I actually love well-made Torrette wines, often finding that with Torrette Supérieurs producers are trying too hard (either via the use of expensive oak air-drying excessively, or by adding large percentages of other cultivars). In this respect, a well-made entry-level Petit Rouge wine is often great fun to drink and a perfect accompaniment to just about any meal. In general, wines made from grapes grown on the left bank of the Dora Baltea (what is locally called the *adret* side) are richer and riper (the vines face full south), while those from the right bank (the *envers*, in local parlance) are usually characterized by greater freshness (as are those made from grapes grown at higher elevations—for example, 700 to 800 meters above sea level instead of 600 to 650 meters).

The Torrette's Bests Crus

Aymavilles: Champcognein.

Quart: Vigne Rovettaz.

Saint-Pierre: Chateau Feuillet, Conze, Torrette.

Sarre: Les Toules.

Villeneuve: Borne de Veyne.

BENCHMARK WINES (TORRETTE AND TORRETTE SUPÉRIEUR)

Di Barrò Torrette Clos de Chateau Feuillet***, Grosjean Torrette Supérieur Vigne Rovettaz***, Les Crêtes Torrette Supérieur***.

Anselmet Torrette Supérieur**, L'Atouéyo Torrette Supérieur**, Chateau Feuillet Torrette Supérieur** (100 percent Petit Rouge grapes that are lightly air-dried), Chateau Feuillet Torrette** (no air-dried grapes are used), Elio Ottin Torrette Supérieur**, Feudo di San Maurizio Torrette**, Les Crêtes Torrette**.

L'Atouéyo Torrette*, Di Barrò Torrette*, La Cave des Onzes Communes Torrette*.

Picolit

THE GRAPE VARIETY

Picolit is one of Italy's five greatest grape varieties, and its wine can be a true nectar. Unfortunately, a series of miscues and the Italian not-so-charming *vivi e lascia vivere* attitude ("live and let live," in English) have not helped Picolit hold on to its rightful place among the world's great wine grapes and wines. And so, over the centuries, Picolit slowly lost the international appeal it once had. And it had *immense* international appeal. The list of Picolit "number one" claims to fame is almost endless. To begin with, no other native Italian wine grape has a similarly illustrious a history: not Nebbiolo, and certainly not Sangiovese or Aglianico—all of which are wines with very recent pedigrees. (The Grecos and the Malvasias enjoyed very good press throughout history, but those were wines made with a variety of grapes, and not associated with one specific cultivar.) Picolit is one of Italy's oldest native varieties also in terms of official documentation; apparently its presence in Friuli–Venezia Giulia is documented back to the twelfth century, though

most usually cited is the 1682 wedding banquet of Alvise Contarini, doge of Venice, at which Picolit was served. Picolit is routinely mentioned in documents as early as 1699 and most often in association with gifts to the nobility or visiting dignitaries, and it met with enormous success in the royal courts of Europe. By the second half of the eighteenth century, it was exported to the king of France, the Russian tsar, the Austrian emperor, and, of course, the papal court—something that is not true of any other modern Italian wine you can think of. In the late eighteenth and early nineteenth centuries, Count Fabio Asquini from Fagagna was bottling the Picolit wine he produced in hand-blown Murano glass bottles and selling it all over Europe in personally owned wine shops. At that time, Picolit wine was viewed in the same light as the famous Hungarian Tokaj, quite an honor indeed. Also, Picolit was the only Friuli variety included in Giorgio Gallesio's famous *Pomona italiana* (1817–39), and many illustrious scientists, *buongustai,* and wine experts have lauded its virtues. Not the least of whom was Veronelli, who compared it with no less than Château d'Yquem (not in aroma or flavor profile, but in its significance relative to its country of origin).

The reasons why more people are not aware of Picolit as one of the world's great wine grapes are varied. One reason is that because of the wine's scarcity, there have always been attempts to "creatively increase" its production volumes—the simplest way being of course that of adding other varieties' juice or wine to the little Picolit that one had. (Historically, that role fell to Verduzzo, another Friuli–Venezia Giulia native that can give very sweet wines.) For people to do so could hardly be unexpected, given that most estates that produce Picolit wine can at most make one thousand half bottles a year; and even the biggest producer of all still makes only four thousand to six thousand half bottles a year (D'Agata 2007b). And given the high prices Picolit wine sells at, wanting to have more to sell (independently of exactly how that may come about) is only human nature. The *vivi e lascia vivere* attitude I mentioned previously was in reference to the fact that lawmakers have never really come down hard on this practice, preferring to let sleeping dogs lie. However, in so doing, or rather, *not* so doing, they have allowed Picolit's reputation to be tarnished by far too many bottles of poorly made wines, or wines that didn't smell or taste of Picolit, or wines that didn't justify their high prices. Another problem for Picolit's well-being is a much more recent happening, and that was the misguided creation of the DOCG for Picolit. Although the DOCG promotion might seem to those not well versed in Italian Byzantinisms like a great idea, even a deserved and logical one for as famous a wine as Picolit, the reality is different. In fact, the new legislation, passed in 2006 (and modified in 2010), determined that the DOCG Picolit wine could be made by using a minimum of 85 percent Picolit. Simply put, this is a travesty, enabling producers to make more Picolit wine. The problem is that now we have Picolit wines that taste of Chardonnay and Sauvignon Blanc, and not of Picolit. For all intents and purposes what the new production

guidelines have done is nothing more than legalize the habit of adding other juice to Picolit wine. Clearly, making people spend a lot of money on a half bottle of what is supposed to be a unique wine only to have them realize it tastes of Sauvignon Blanc is hardly the way to gain new customers (or hold on to your old ones, for that matter). Another huge problem with the creation of the DOCG was that it caused the elimination of subzones. And that's just insane, since Picolit is one of the few Italian wines to be historically associated with specific places in the FCO (see "Specific Terroirs," below).

Why is Picolit wine so scarce? Picolit's rarity is due to male sterility of its pollen (a condition charmingly referred to as floral abortion), because it lacks germination pores. Fertilization of the essentially female flowers therefore cannot happen as it does in most other hermaphrodite cultivars but requires the help of the wind and other grapevines, or the co-planting of pollinating species such as Verduzzo. Even then, the grape bunch is small (a typical Picolit grape bunch has about fifteen berries, whereas most other cultivars have grape bunches with as many as two hundred grapes), scrawny, and very loosely packed: only if complete fertilization occurs (a rare event) does it appear pyramidal in shape, with one wing, slightly more compact, and reaching as much as 130 grams in weight (again, this is not the norm); the grapes are small and oval, almost translucent (hold them up to the light and you can see the two large pips clearly) and have very thick skins with a good amount of bloom. After all, the name "Picolit" most likely derives from *piccolitto*, meaning "small." (For other possible derivations, see my book *Native Wine Grapes of Italy*.) In fact, because Picolit is an extremely ancient variety, it expresses more intravarietal variability than is commonly believed. (Most likely, few had noticed because there was not much Picolit around to begin with.) Of the various biotypes I have studied in vineyards on my own and then again with the likes of Paolo Rapuzzi and Andrea Felluga, there is a Picolit with a green stalk and bright yellow berries and a Picolit with a red stalk and smaller berries; there is apparently also one with a blood-red stalk described by Pietro di Maniago as early as 1823, but I am not sure I have ever seen it. According to Andrea Felluga of the Livio Felluga winery, the best of these is the red-stalked biotype, while the biotypes that have very large, compact bunches are modern nursery creations selected to give producers the chance to make more wine. There were once two different Picolits described in Slovenia—Pikolit Vienna and Pikolit Italia—but Štajner et al. showed them to be identical in 2008. Picolit is unrelated to the similarly named red grape Piculit Neri, also a Friuli–Venezia Giulia native. Picolit is a very vigorous variety, but unfortunately directs its vigor in the wrong direction (toward the shoots especially), and so grape production is extremely low. It is susceptible to peronospora and oidium (especially the latter) and grows better where there is plenty of sunlight, though excessively hot sites that lack ventilation are contraindicated. In my experience, Picolit grapes will have anywhere from 5 to 5.5 grams per liter total acidity (1.1 to 1.3 grams per liter malic acid) and accumulate sugars easily, such that, on average, concentrations of 240 to 300 grams per liter are not rare. The wine is redolent in terpenes (linalool and nerol especially) and norisprenoids (β-damascene and 3-OH-β-damascene). These molecules help explain the presence in Picolit wines of aromas and flavors reminiscent of rose petals, oranges, tangerines, grapefruit, candied apricot, honey, ginger, and dried peach.

The Picolit wine you will drink most often is the result of air-drying the grapes in suitable winery rooms. The other alternative is the late harvesting of grapes on the vine, something that many Friuli–Venezia Giulia producers resist because of the vagaries of fall weather (sudden autumn showers being not all that rare in the region). The air-dried Picolits are rich and jammy and very tropical, as are many other of the world's sweet wines; the variety's unique grace and nobility, though, comes through when the wine is the product of a late harvest. In this latter case, the wine is light-bodied, almost dainty, gently honeyed and floral—a far cry from the many marmelady behemoths that are all the rage in sweet winedom. Depending on how ripe and air-dried the grapes are when pressed, the color of the wine runs from pale yellow to bright golden yellow. Most Picolit wines are best drunk up within five years from the harvest.

SPECIFIC TERROIRS

Friuli Colli Orientali

Due to its low productivity and the world wars of the twentieth century, by the 1920s Picolit had virtually disappeared, and it was only thanks to the work of another count, Gaetano Perusini, that the grape and wine have come back with a vengeance. Beginning in the 1930s, Perusini scoured the hillside vineyards of his family's Rocca Bernarda castle and selected the vines that looked healthiest and strongest. He then propagated them, and if Picolit is here today to tell its story, it is Perusini we have to thank. Picolit is now grown in the provinces of Udine and Gorizia, which means in the Friuli Colli Orientali (FCO) and the Collio denominations, respectively. However, it is the former that is Picolit's home. For sure, Picolit loves the *ponca,* that soil typical of the FCO that is made up of alternating layers of marl and compacted sands (sandstone). However, as I have discussed elsewhere in this book (see the "Collio" section of the Ribolla Gialla entry), there is not just one *ponca,* contrary to what you will see written in articles and books. And neither is the term *ponca* synonymous with flysch, as you will also hear and read; furthermore, there are also many different types of flysch. These geologic-related soil differences are important, for the various terroirs of Friuli–Venezia Giulia are characterized by slightly different soils; this is true of Picolit's best terroirs, too, and all seem to add their own twist to the wines. The best Picolit wines have always been, and still are, clearly linked to four subzones, characterized by very specific terroirs: Cialla, Rosazzo, Rocca

Bernarda, and Savorgnano del Torre. The uniqueness of the Picolit wines made in these subzones has been known for a long time, and officially recognized in 1996 with the creation of two official Picolit subzones—an extremely rare occurrence in Italian wine circles. Once again, Picolit shows itself to be an Italian grape precursor in this realm, too.

Cialla

I have affectionately defined Cialla, one of my favorite places on earth, as a "shadow zone," an area that is not just beautiful but also much cooler and much less sunny than almost any-where else Picolit grows in Friuli–Venezia Giulia. As you stand on the hill where the ter-raced vines grow in small pockets literally sto-len from forests teeming with wildlife, a beauti-ful natural panorama unfolds before your eyes, with nary a house in sight. You will find your-self thinking how beautiful it all is—unless you forgot to bring a sweater along, because in that case you'll be thinking instead about how beau-tiful a warm cup of coffee or tea would also be. Cialla is not lacking for ventilation or breezes, that's for sure. Such ventilation has a physical basis. Cialla is located in the province of Udine, in the municipality of Prepotto, in what is the easternmost prolongation of the FCO; it is equi-distant from the Adriatic Sea and the Julian Alps, whose two main peaks are Mount Man-gart (2,677 meters above sea level) and Mount Montasio (2,754 meters above sea level). Essen-tially a valley that rises from 140 to 600 meters above sea level up against Mount Plagnava, Cialla is oriented east-northeast to west-south-west (essentially east to west), differing from the orientation of most other valleys in the FCO, which are directed north to south. What this orientation translates to, relative to wine terroir, is the ventilation I just mentioned: the east–west orientation is in the same direction in which the area's two main winds, the bora and the borino (you guessed it, it's a weak bora), also blow. The name Cialla derives from the Slovenian word *cela*, which means "stream";

certainly a lack of water is another problem that Cialla does not have. Cialla is not just more ven-tilated; it is also more rainy: the annual precipi-tation average is 1,550 millimeters, compared with the FCO average of 1,360 millimeters, and sometimes it seems like it rains all the time, though in fact the rainiest periods of the year are toward the end of the fall and in the spring. Not surprisingly, then, the average daily tem-perature is also lower than the average of the FCO (13.4°C versus 14°C, respectively). The same is true of the average temperature from April through October (17.8°C in Cialla, 18.4°C in the FCO). Of note is Cialla's diurnal tem-perature variation, which can easily reach 20°C in parts of the year. All this has the practical consequence that the yearly harvesting in Cialla takes place one or two weeks later than any-where else in the FCO. The soils are essentially made up of the flysch of Grivò, which differs from other types of flysch due to its greater con-glomeratic nature, with calcarenite and calcare-ous inclusions (see the Ribolla Gialla entry); soil concentrations of calcium are high, those of magnesium and potassium are average, and those of phosphorus are low.

Cialla's only Picolit wines are those of the Ronchi di Cialla estate, and they are the most delicate and dainty of all Picolit wines you will ever taste, a reflection of the microclimate more than the soil. Of course, these wines get blown away in blind tastings in which they get sand-wiched between too-jammy supersweet behe-moths, but that's not on Picolit, but rather on those who organize such blind tastings poorly.

BENCHMARK WINE

Ronchi di Cialla Picolit di Cialla FCO***PS.

Prepotto

See the Schioppettino and Tazzelenghe entries for a discussion of the Prepotto terroir.

BENCHMARK WINE

Vigna Petrussa Picolit FCO***PS.

Rocca Bernarda

A historic Picolit production area (and the home of count Gaetano Perusini), the Rocca Bernarda area is not a cold one, as demonstrated by its monthly temperature average of 18.9°C from April through October (as calculated over the period from 2003 through 2015). For the same time period, the Winkler index is 1910. On average it also rains less here than in other parts of the FCO; for example, the total rainfall average from April to October from 2003 through 2015 was 836 millimeters in Rocca Bernarda, 917 millimeters in Cividale, and 1,188 millimeters in Ramandolo; the average in the FCO during that same time frame is 920 millimeters. On average, only May and June in Rocca Bernarda have more than five days of rain a month; by contrast, in the FCO every month but one (April) has at least six or more days of rain. (These data refer to monthly averages calculated from 2003 through 2015.) Soil is also important in the Rocca Bernarda, because its chemical composition changes with altitude and with the slope. The Rocca Bernarda's soil has a lower pH than that of other FCO subzones (pH 6.5 in Rocca Bernarda, pH 8.0 in Rosazzo), yet one old vineyard owned by the Specogna family has a soil pH of 8.0. All this translates to Picolit wines that are more fleshy and luscious than most, but lifted by lively acidity. The Rocca Bernarda also boasts extremely old Picolit vines: besides many that were planted in the 1960s, Specogna owns a 0.6-hectare plot (named "Picolit Sud") that was planted in 1949.

BENCHMARK WINES

Valentino Butussi Picolit FCO***, Specogna Picolit FCO***.

Gigante Picolit FCO**, Nadalutti Picolit FCO**.

Rocca Bernarda*.

Rosazzo

Rosazzo is one of those truly blessed places on earth where just about anything grows well, beginning with the roses that made the Abbey of Rosazzo famous and that gave the abbey its name. Tocai Friulano, Pignolo, Ribolla Gialla, and Picolit all fare magnificently there; the wines made with those grapes are not just some of Friuli–Venezia Giulia's best, but all of Italy's. The Picolit is especially memorable: richer and thicker than any other Picolit you will taste from Cialla, the Rocca Bernarda, or Savorgnano (though unless the grapes are very heavily air-dried, "rich" and "thick" are not terms usually associated with Picolit), it still showcases the variety's unique refinement and elegance. The warm and well-ventilated microclimate of Rosazzo is just what the doctor ordered for the variety. Compared with the Rocca Bernarda, slope gradients are larger (20 to 35 percent versus 3 to 15 percent) but soil depth is shallower (30 to 90 centimeters versus greater than 110 centimeters). These two subzones differ greatly also because of the soil pH, much higher in Rosazzo than at the Rocca Bernarda (on average, roughly 8 for the former and 6.5 for the latter). The differences in pH certainly explain why at Rosazzo they can push ripeness levels without losing much in the way of acid thrust—not that Rocca Bernarda's Picolit wines lack for acidity, but when the ripeness envelope is pushed full tilt, the wines can become a little heavy.

Clearly, I am not the only one who believes Rosazzo to be a grand cru for Picolit. Lawmakers and politicians also felt as much when they declared Rosazzo a subzone for Picolit (only one of two; the other is Cialla); that sign of distinction was unfortunately lost with the creation of the DOCG Picolit, something that the local producers of Pignolo (another wine grape that benefits from the Rosazzo subzone), who are DOCG-less and are proud to make Pignolo di Rosazzo wines, don't have to worry about. Remember that DOCG status does not allow official subzones (see "The Italian Job" section in part 1), which is insane—and, not unreasonably, the Pignolo producers don't wish to lose their uniqueness. (For more information on the Rosazzo subzone terroir, see also the Ribolla Gialla and Pignolo entries.)

Livio Felluga Picolit FCO***PS.

Savorgnano del Torre

As I have had occasion to say and write before, I first fell in love with Savorgnano del Torre (or Savorgnano, for short) one day back in the early 1980s while visiting the town's local wine and food fair. Those were fun mother-and-son times; I used to visit the yearly fair with my mother, who was the happy chauffeur (she loves to drive); in fact, while I tasted the wines and met the producers, my mom used to do the same with the food products available. (She loves grilled sausage and prosciutto sandwiches even more than she does driving.) I distinctly remember that I came away from the fair thinking just how crazy good Picolit wines from the area could be. And after I had tasted all the other wines that were being poured, too (the usual Friuli–Venezia Giulia array of Ribolla Gialla, Friulano, Pinot Bianco, and other wines), it was obvious even to someone who wasn't at the time writing a book on wine terroirs that there was something about Savorgnano (a hamlet of the town of Povoletto) that turns everyone into a star Picolit producer. Today's outstanding wines made by the Aquila del Torre and Marco Sara estates are a case in point. I have often asked myself what it is that makes this area so special for Picolit. Old vines count for something: Marco Sara owns two half-hectare parcels in the Riu Falcon vineyard area; one of the two is at least fifty years old. Also, like Cialla and Prepotto, Savorgnano is cooler than Rosazzo, which enables Picolit to give the more elegant wines (though that is tricky, for Picolit is a variety that actually likes, even needs, heat to show its best). Savorgnano's alternating hot and cold mornings also help the development of noble rot, which has always flourished in the area and contributes greatly to the overall complexity of Savorgnano's wines. Should you visit the area, be warned: it's remarkably beautiful, wild, and alive with nature (the Aquila del Torre estate has studied its flora with the University of Udine's help and has found 237 species of flowers living on its property; normally there are 25 species living on most estates), with charming hamlets and folksy locals that will make you feel like you have stepped into an Italian Norman Rockwell painting. It will also strike you that the landscape there resembles Cialla's, to a degree. (Not by accident, it is in these two areas that you also find remarkably great, and rare, dry Picolit wines.) And so the lay of the land provides the first clue as to why Picolit is such a happy little camper in Savorgnano's countryside.

Aquila del Torre Picolit FCO***PS, Marco Sara Picolit FCO***PS.

Pignolo

THE GRAPE VARIETY

Pignolo takes its name from the word *pigna* (Italian for "pine cone") because of its very compact, small bunch that is in fact highly reminiscent of a pine cone. Pignolo is a red grape of good quality native to the Colli Orientali. For the longest time, it grew practically only there; and not much of it, either, since by the mid-twentieth century the variety was, for all intents and purposes, extinct. Historically Pignolo thrived in the countryside around the Abbey of Rosazzo, and it was thanks to the abbey that Pignolo has ultimately been able to make a comeback of sorts, thanks to a farmer named Casasola, who worked at the abbey, along with winemakers Silvano Zamò and Walter Filiputti. Based on different leaf morphology, three different Pignolo biotypes were selected and propagated elsewhere. (Of the three, the biotype characterized by the heavily indented or jagged leaf is the most miserly producer.) Everything worth knowing about Pignolo revolves around its appearance: one look at its very small, tightly packed bunch and berries with thick skins transmits information about the variety. Pignolo clearly needs well-ventilated sites to ward off disease pressure. Therefore, planting it at the summit of hills is always a good idea. (Pignolo is very sensitive to oidium, but in general, thanks to its polyphenolic clout, it has plenty of antioxidative protection and so does not succumb much to diseases anyway.) Such placement has the added benefit of guaranteeing maximum sunlight exposure— and this is important, for whereas Pignolo does not perform well if subjected to extreme temperatures, it does need plenty of heat to reach optimal ripeness; otherwise the tannins, which are tough at the best of times, are downright impossible to put up with. So deleafing judiciously at the right moment is also important. Some producers try to get around the ripeness problem by air-drying the grapes partially or wholly, but this is not a solution if the grapes were picked with unripe polyphenols to begin with (because in that case the air-drying only concentrates the green notes as well); also, to my taste, air-drying modifies the typical aroma and taste profile of Pignolo wine too much.

Pignolo is hard work not just in the vineyard (to add more fun to Pignolo's equation, it is also a highly irregular producer), but in the cellar as well. Because of its concentration of polyphenols, yeasts have a difficult time fermenting Pignolo must, and stuck fermentations are always a potential problem. Producers have also tried many different winemaking approaches to soften the at times brutal tannins, but no one generally agreed-upon method by which to reach this objective exists. Without doubt, Pignolo gives what are Italy's most tannic wines (or at worst, dukes it out with Sagrantino for top spot in that particular pecking order). In fact, I have never found that a Pignolo wine is anywhere near drinkable prior to eight years after the vintage; before that, its tannic cloak is so vehement that it just takes over your palate, locking it into its polyphenol grip without letting go no matter how much you drink or eat alongside it.

SPECIFIC TERROIRS

Friuli Colli Orientali

Nowadays, Pignolo is grown in many parts of Friuli–Venezia Giulia, because the variety enjoyed a popularity boom a decade or so ago. But its ancestral home, and where it is still mostly grown today, is the Friuli Colli Orientali (FCO). One of the reasons for this is that Pignolo is Friuli–Venezia Giulia's only red variety that can give truly full-bodied reds; all the others, such as Schioppettino, the various Refoscos, and Tazzelenghe, do not. If there is one real positive about Pignolo today, it is that producers do seem to be finally getting their heads around it; in other words, whereas as recently as ten years ago Pignolo wines were, almost invariably, simply not enjoyable to drink because of their monolithic chunkiness and astringency, that is no longer true, and many fine full-bodied but refined wines exist (at least, those of producers who do not choose to overextract). In the past, my suspicion was strong that a good deal of Merlot was finding its way into vats in order to soften things up, but I do not believe that to be the case anymore. Hats off, then, to the talented and passionate wine producers of the FCO, some of whom, at least, have really turned things around for Pignolo. All that Pignolo wines really need to be enjoyable is time—something well demonstrated by a producer who is not from the FCO: talented Josko Gravner in the Collio makes one of the best Pignolo wines of all, and as most people know, he releases his wines after about seven years from the harvest. Granted, Gravner is one of Italy's most talented winemakers, but his Pignolo wines have remarkably soft tannins nonetheless. Not as in "Merlot soft," mind you, but quite soft regardless.

Today Pignolo grows most abundantly in the countryside around the towns of Albana, Premariacco, Prepotto, and Rosazzo in the FCO, and DOC wines labeled FCO Pignolo are made there. (There is also the special category of Pignolo di Rosazzo.)

Rosazzo

Rosazzo is a small hamlet of the commune of Manzano, and its viticultural area is one of the most important subzones not just of the FCO and Friuli–Venezia Giulia, but of all of Italy. This is because Rosazzo has a unique historic link to specific high-quality cultivars that once grew practically nowhere else but there, and because, still today, it is where some of Italy's greatest wines are made. Clearly, Rosazzo's viticultural and winemaking history is intimately linked to the beautiful abbey; though the site was originally the home of a hermit who founded an oratory there, over time the abbey came under the watchful eye first of the Augustinians, then of the Benedictines, and last, of the Dominicans. It was always a very important winemaking center, and it contributed to saving and propagating many long-forgotten grape varieties. The Rosazzo subzone is especially suited to varieties that seek warmth and that do best in warmer microclimates; not by chance, other varieties that perform extremely well in Rosazzo are Picolit and Ribolla Gialla, wine grapes that if they could would go through life wearing nothing but sunglasses and a beach towel. But just as with those two, Rosazzo's terroir, and its penchant to give truly great Pignolo wines, have as much to do with the mesoclimate and soil as they do with the cultivar itself. Or more precisely, with the particular Pignolo biotype that is most typical of Rosazzo. The most common "true" Pignolo of Rosazzo has a cylindrical bunch, with small, round grapes that have thick skins and not much must at all. These characteristics allow for Pignolo to be late-harvested. (In Rosazzo, it is most usually picked in the first two weeks of October.) This prolonged hang time allows for the full maturation of the polyphenols to be reached in most vintages (hopefully). The best trellising system is the double-arched cane or *cappuccina*, which allows the vine to grow in a most-balanced fashion. Note that the Pignolo di Rosazzo is recognized officially as one of the wines that can be made in the Rosazzo subzone, and that it requires one more year of aging (it is released four years after the vintage) than do Pignolo wines made in other parts of the FCO and simply labeled as such. (For more information on the Rosazzo subzone terroir, see also the Ribolla Gialla and the Picolit entries.)

BENCHMARK WINES

Abbazia di Rosazzo***, Nadalutti Pignolo di Rosazzo***, Petrucco***.

Prié

THE GRAPE VARIETY

Prié is more commonly known nowadays as Prié Blanc, a name recently created to differentiate the variety from Prié Rouge or Primetta. Another synonym for Prié is Blanc de Valdigne (the Valdigne is the northernmost part of the Valle d'Aosta and Prié's natural home). The variety's name derives from the word *prier,* harking back to the wine's use in Sunday Mass by priests (from the French *prier,* or "pray"). Prié is the oldest documented variety of Valle d'Aosta and one of the oldest of Italy. A manuscript dated January 22, 1691, concerning the sale of specific goods excluded from the sale a plot of vines of Prié situated in the Clos Morant, near the town of Saint-Pierre, and is probably the first documentary evidence we have of Prié's existence in the region. Because it is an ancient variety, Prié is one of the parents of many other Valle d'Aosta grapes, including Roussin de Morgex, Prëmetta, Mayolet, and Blanc Comun. Prié tolerates cold habitats extremely well, and so is the only variety able to survive and ripen fully in the cold weather of Morgex and La Salle, in the upper third of the Valle d'Aosta (the Alta Valle). It is a very resistant wine grape, but its thin skins make it prone to botrytis. Historically, Prié was also consumed locally as a table grape.

SPECIFIC TERROIRS

Morgex et La Salle

In Valle d'Aosta there are over twenty-five hectares of Prié, and it grows practically everywhere in the upper third of the Valle, that northernmost third of the Valle d'Aosta region that hugs the French border. I have said and written before that I believe Italy's most beautiful vineyards to be those of Prié in the Valle d'Aosta. The Lilliputian plots of canopied vines hugging cliff-like mountaintops on little stone terraces (Prié grows at some of the highest altitudes in Europe, as high as twelve hundred meters above sea level) are beautiful to see. Actually, in order to see the Prié grapes hanging from the vines, you usually have to bend down to the ground and look up to the ceiling of leaves and pale straw-green grapes above. And since phylloxera does not survive cold mountain environments, most of these old Prié vines are ungrafted.

Prié is used to make one of Italy's best light-bodied white wines: the Blanc de Morgex et La Salle, the only wine of any commercial significance in the Alta Valle. The grapes can be grown only in the territories from Morgex and Pré-Saint-Didier to La Salle and Avise, but the highest-quality grapes come from the vineyards situated closest to the towns that give the wine its name: Morgex and La Salle. I believe the Morgex area to be a real grand cru area for Prié; the area around Morgex has very poor, nutrient-deficient mineral soils of morainic origin, and the resulting wines are very steely, floral, and brightly acidic. The wines of La Salle, due to a slightly higher alluvial-soil content, are less steely and are softer, and when blended with those of Morgex help round out the final wine. With a little practice, it's not hard to tell, when tasting Blanc de Morgex wines, where most of the grapes came from. A well-made Blanc de Morgex et La Salle is fresh and fragrant, with delightful aromas and flavors of green apple, nectarine, thyme, chlorophyll, mint, and white flowers. In warmer years, hints of apricot emerge. There are also sweet and sparkling versions made, which is not surprising, given the high natural acidity the variety is blessed with. But the best Prié wines are the dry still ones.

The Subzones and Crus

To my taste and in my experience, the best cru areas are Chaffery, Châtelard, Eicheru, Piagne, Tzanta Merla, and Vignal. Almost as good are Coureau, Labie, and Porettes. Other crus (Barrière, Moreau, and Ruie) have been mentioned in the past as being noteworthy (Veronelli 1995) but I have had no experience with them—and anyway, nobody is making wines from those specific vineyards today (which is a shame). La Piagne is an especially good 0.25-hectare southeast-facing single vineyard planted ungrafted at 1,050 to 1,100 meters above sea level in the zone of Piagne in 1997 in Morgex near the Cave du Mont Blanc.

BENCHMARK WINES

Piero Brunet*** (who owns some of the best vineyards of all for the variety), Cave du Mont Blanc Vini Estremi***, Cave du Mont Blanc Rayon***, Albert Vevey***.

Cave du Mont Blanc Metodo Classico Blanc de Blancs**, Cave du Mont Blac Metodo Classico Cuvée du Prince**, Ermès Pavese**, Marziano Vevey**.

Refosco del Peduncolo Rosso

THE GRAPE VARIETY

Refosco del Peduncolo Rosso is Friuli–Venezia Giulia's best-known and most-planted native red grape variety. It was always lumped in with other Refosco varieties, and so documentation on it prior to the nineteenth century is scarce and what there is not that accurate. Still, Poggi (1939) wrote that this Refosco was the one member of the group that was especially worthy of attention, because of superior wines. We know that it is a very old cultivar with a number of very important relationships. According to Grando, Frisinghelli, and Stefanini (2006), Refosco del Peduncolo Rosso is a grandson of Teroldego and a nephew of Lagrein. Refosco del Peduncolo Rosso has a medium-large pyramidal bunch with one small wing; the very dark blue berries are medium-small, with thin but resistant skins. An adaptable variety, it prefers nutrient-poor, calcareous-clay soils; and because it is also a vigorous cultivar, hillside locations are best. Achieving optimal physiologic ripeness is key, for otherwise vegetal aromas and flavors are common. Refosco del Peduncolo Rosso wines are the most complex of any made with Refosco varieties, hinting at fresh and dried red cherries, fresh herbs, and almonds, plus a complicating floral note. Being a reductive variety, it requires a lot of air in the immediate postfermentation phase, because off odors pose a real problem should they develop: they're very hard to get rid of. Aging the wine in barriques also helps round it out.

SPECIFIC TERROIRS

It is by far most common in Friuli–Venezia Giulia, though it is also grown in the Veneto (and outside of Italy, small plantings are found in Slovenia and in Greece.). The best wines to try are those of the DOC Colli Orientali del Friuli of Friuli–Venezia Giulia. Friuli Grave, Friuli Annia, and Friuli Latisana can also be good, but it is often too rainy, especially in central and western Grave, or yields are too high, to achieve truly great wines.

Torreano

Located in the FCO, Torreano represents a cool-climate expression of Refosco del Peduncolo Rosso wine, and this even though most of the vineyards devoted to the Refosco variety are located in the warmer Togliano fraction of Torreano. Unfortunately, in the 1980s the craze for international varieties led to almost all the Refosco del Peduncolo Rosso in the area being uprooted and replaced with Merlot, but that tendency has since been overturned and the local Refosco del Peduncolo Rosso variety replanted. It follows that most of the vines planted in the area are on the young side. Despite the increased number of sunlight hours that Togliano can boast relative to Torreano, most producers find it necessary to air-dry their grapes to achieve better levels of ripeness. The red wines are also aged in small oak barrels to provide further body and mellowness. (For a description of the Torreano terroir, see also the Tocai Friulano entry.)

BENCHMARK WINES

Valchiarò**, Volpe Pasini**.

Refosco Nostrano (Refosco di Faedis)

THE GRAPE VARIETY

Refosco Nostrano is also known as Refosco di Faedis (after the town that is the epicenter of this grape's production), but the official name is the former. This wine grape has a unique story to tell, because besides being used for making a pretty good red wine, it is marketed and sold in a truly novel way. A group of estates in and around Faedis formed an association called the Associazione Volontaria Viticoltori del Refosco di Faedis in which about ten member producers work together to promote and market the wine. They have also created an internal committee, consisting of a representative from each winery, that tastes the wines prior to bottling and determines whether the wines submitted are worthy of the association's labels. In fact, the Refosco di Faedis of the association is sold with two different labels: a white label that represents the entry-level wine, generally unoaked and offering early appeal; and a black label that represents each estate's top wine that has been aged a minimum of two years. Very interestingly, or

very curiously (I guess it depends on your point of view), the wines are then all bottled with exactly the same label: the only difference is that on each there is a small first and last name written in freehand diagonally across the label telling potential buyers whose wine that is. (The back label states in more conventional block letters the name of the estate that made the wine.) Producers also encourage each other to ask for more or less the same price per bottle. It is an interesting concept and one I hope will bring them fame and fortune, if nothing else, for their creativity and energy in promoting themselves the way they do.

All of that would be moot if the wine weren't good, and thankfully, it is. Much of the "goodness" of the wine is the merit not just of the producers but also of the little-known but high-quality Refosco Nostrano grape variety. (Refosco del Peduncolo Rosso is the more famous Refosco variety of Friuli–Venezia Giulia.) According to Poggi, who wrote about it in 1939, Refosco Nostrano was considered a potentially high-quality if little-known variety even at that time. Poggi wrote that it was then the most planted of all Refoscos since it was the one that, in light of its bigger berries, yielded the largest amount of must. And so Refosco Nostrano was able to hang around vineyards (literally, you might say) for centuries, though it has really surged to the attention of wine lovers only in the last twelve years or so. In fact, we now know it boasts a number of biotypes and relationships with other local varieties—always the sign of a variety of some age. (By definition, the genesis of new biotypes as well as of parent-offspring relationships requires time, and lots of it.) For example, Refosco Ronchis is a biotype of Refosco Nostrano: the two grapevines exhibit minor differences from both an ampelographic and a behavioral standpoint, but there is currently very little Refosco di Ronchis left. Refosco Nostrano also has a parent-offspring relationship with Tazzelenghe (also known as Refosco del Boton, but this name is no longer used) and the very rare Refosco Gentile (also called Refosco di Rauscedo), which is yet another Refosco biotype still occasionally found (when it's recognized, that is) in scattered rows of old vineyards throughout the FCO. Refosco Nostrano is characterized by very strong vigor and susceptibility to peronospora, but its large berries and generous yields have quite understandably endeared it to farmers. Refosco Nostrano is more productive than other Refoscos because of its obviously larger bunch than that of other Refoscos, and because its basal buds are more fertile. In general, Refosco Nostrano prefers clay-alluvial sites, since it suffers water stress easily. Wines made with Refosco Nostrano can be quite tannic in their youth, but if the winemaking allows for lowish fermentation temperatures and a short fermenting time, the variety's very red fruity personality is allowed to show. And though Refosco Nostrano's larger grapes ensure a higher pulp-to-skin ratio, the tannins are not exactly wimpy—a sensation that is reinforced by noteworthy acidity. (Refosco Nostrano wines tend to be slightly higher in acidity than those made with other Refoscos.)

SPECIFIC TERROIRS

Faedis

Faedis is a charming little town located in the province of Udine close to the Slovenian border, about thirteen kilometers (or eight miles) northeast of Udine itself (and seventy kilometers or forty-three miles northwest of Trieste). It lies at an altitude of 172 meters, but the vineyards lie slightly higher up at around 200 to 250 meters above sea level. The Refosco di Faedis production area can be subdivided into three areas or sections: a section of hills surrounding Faedis like a horseshoe (roughly 10 to 15 percent of the area under vine); a foothill section (another 10 to 15 percent of land under vine); and the plains or flatlands leading up to the foothills and hills. The hills have mostly marly soil, with a little sandstone; the foothills have mostly clay soil; and the flatlands are made up of alluvial soils derived from the Grivò stream, a mixture of loam-clay-gravel. About 70 percent of these flatland vineyards are located on the left bank of the stream at about 150 to 170 meters above sea level. In my experience, the Refosco di Faedis wines made from grapes grown on the hills are potentially higher in alcohol and quite structured; those made from foothill grapes are slightly more perfumed and have about equal structure with those from the hills; and those from flatland grapes are especially fruity and fragrant, if a little lighter-bodied. As I mentioned earlier, Refosco di Faedis is sold as an entry-level white label and a black-label top wine. The flatland vineyards are where most estates produce grapes for their white-label wines, bright and cheerful potables offering fresh red berry and aromatic herb aromas and flavors with gentle tannins. These crisp wines have an uncanny resemblance to a very good Beaujolais cru wine or a juicy, fruity Burgundy Villages red. Clearly, no matter where it is planted, it is of utmost importance that Refosco di Faedis achieve full polyphenolic ripeness before it is picked; because all Refosco grapes tend to give wines with a noteworthy green quality when the grapes are unripe, the hillside vineyards are planted with southern exposures in the hope of obtaining optimally ripe grapes. The climate is more or less similar to the FCO average—cooler than Buttrio, but not especially cold.

Besides Faedis, there are other towns worth knowing in the area since some of the wineries are located there. Vines at Rachiaccio and Campeglio are planted on hillsides and foothills very similar to those of Faedis (the wines are similar, too); however, the flatlands of these two towns are not associated with a body of water and soils are mostly very heavy clay not ideal for grapevines. (The tightly packed clays cause root asphyxia; the clay is used mainly to make bricks or for growing cereals.) Canebola, Clap, Costapiana, Cotalunga, and Valle are small hamlets located in mountain environ-ments where grape growing has always been looked at mostly as a hobby or as a way to make wine for family and friends. This may yet prove to be a very good terroir for white grapes, the caveat being that historically Faedis's upper reaches were always hit by at times serious hail episodes. One township that I think does grow very good grapes and whose wines are delicious (comparable for sure to those of Faedis) is Col-loredo. Colloredo's hillside terroir is similar to that of Faedis and Campeglio but is situated higher up, at 273 meters above sea level.

BENCHMARK WINES

Ronc dai Luchis (black label)***, Flavia De Gaspero (black label)***, Macor (white label)***, Claudio Zanni (black label)***.

Ribolla Gialla

THE GRAPE VARIETY

Ribolla Gialla is one of my favorite Italian native grapes and wines, and I am saddened to see that it has become, in the hands of far too many producers, a fad. The variety gives lovely, delicate white wines that are crisp and bright, with delicate citrus fruit and floral nuances, but needs old vines, hillside vineyards, and strict viticultural practices; otherwise the wines will unfailingly be insipid at best, or tart and thin at worst. Then, about ten years ago or so, one famous producer (Gravner) decided to try macerating it on the skins (because of the cultivar's underlying tannic nature), and the wine met with success; heaven help us, a plethora of wannabes with young vines in less than ideal plots began emulating the master (or trying to, and not successfully at that), producing myriad charmless, earthy, astringent, undrinkable wines. And yes, I do say all that as if it were a negative thing. Other producers have decided to take advantage of Ribolla Gialla's natural high acidity and are making sparkling wines with it, both with the Charmat-Martinotti method (in an obvious attempt to duplicate the success of Prosecco with another local grape) and by secondary fermentation in the bottle, in the manner of Champagne. All we need now is for someone really clever to start making ice-wines and air-dried wines with it, and poor Ribolla Gialla will have seen it all. And unfortunately, so will our palates.

Ribolla Gialla (yellow Ribolla) is a lovely grape to look at. It is not called *gialla* (yellow) by chance; even when fully ripe, the grapes rarely turn anything more than a deep yellow. Another variety, called Ribolla Verde, exists, and it has, as you would expect, green-tinged grapes. (The two have been known for a very long time, too: for example, Ribolla Verde and Ribolla Gialla were listed as numbers 213 and 214, respectively, in Acerbi's important 1825 treatise on Italy's wine grapes.) Historically Ribolla Verde was grown more in what is now ex-Yugoslavia, whereas in Italy it was much rarer (it gives poor wines) and its cultivation limited to flatland vineyards only. Some studies also referred to a Ribolla Nera, but we know this to be Schioppettino and not related to the other Ribollas (see the Schioppettino entry). Costacurta (1978) published a very detailed and informative study on Ribolla Gialla and pointed out that in what was then called the Yugoslavian Collio, there existed a third Ribolla variety, called Ribolla Castel Dobra, the characteristics of which fell somewhere in between the other two. Di Rovasenda (1877) also mentioned a Ribolla Bianca, but this was most likely another, unrelated variety. Also called Rebolla, Ribuèle, Ràbuele, Ribuèle Zale, Ribolla di Rosazzo, Raibola, Ràbola, and Rèbula, Ribolla Gialla is, more than any other Friuli–Venezia Giulia variety (along with Tocai Friulano), very close to the hearts of the locals, who view it as "one of them"—a piece of the region's fabric itself. (Ask for a *tajut* of wine in any local osteria, and it's Ribolla Gialla or Friulano they serve you; a *tajut* is the house wine served from a big bottle or dispenser into a small glass, and is akin to the Veneto's *ombra*.) The relationship between Ribolla Gialla and Slovenian Rebula (and its many subvarieties) was investigated by a number of authors, including Costacurta et al. (2006) and Rusjan, Jug, and Štainer (2010). We also know it is distinct from both the similarly named Rébola of the Romagna portion of Emilia-Romagna, which is identical to Pignoletto, and Ribolla Spizade, which is a synonym of Glera Lungo (Calò and Costacurta 1991). Recently, Crespan et al. (2011) have proven it is completely unrelated to Schioppettino, also called Ribolla Nera.

Ribolla Gialla was long considered one of Italy's greatest wines, and in the thirteenth century it was a regular presence on the dining tables of Venice's nobility. However, as I wrote in *Native Wine Grapes of Italy*, what these documents were referring to was a wine, not a variety: in centuries past, Ribolla was a name used for a wine made with various grapes (and specifically, a wine made on the hillsides, differentiating it neatly from poorer wines made with grapes grown on the plains). Enos Costantini has documented this in his book *Ribolla Story* (Costantini 2017). In fact, Ribolla Gialla itself has been mentioned with any real assiduity

only over the last two hundred years or so. One of Friuli–Venezia Giulia's most knowledgeable wine writers, Claudio Fabbro, has written numerous erudite articles on Ribolla's important history and cites that a "Rebula" wine was mentioned as early as 1170 (Fabbro 2008). A "Ribolla" is first mentioned in a 1299 deed of sale written by notary Ermanno di Gemona in *Notariorum Joppi* (Filiputti 1983). A legal document from 1376 concerning a land sale near Barbana in the Collio specified that the farmer had been producing "*sex urnas raboli.*"

Ribolla Gialla has pyramidal-cylindrical-shaped bunches that are very small. They can weigh as little as 80 grams, and rarely exceed 130 grams, with medium-large berries that can weigh up to 1.5 grams each. In flatland vineyards Ribolla Gialla tends to give a prodigious amount of grapes, and consequently the wines cannot help but be neutral and insipid. There are a number of outstanding clones available, such as VCR 72, VCR 100, VCR 394, and VCR 417, selected by Carlo Petrussi (2017). Good Ribolla Gialla wines offer fresh white flower, tangerine, and lemon aromas and flavors (with a hint of white pepper and saffron that is absolutely typical and adds noteworthy complexity in the really good wines); lip-smacking acidity is always a hallmark of this wine. Data that I have elaborated from vineyards in the Collio and Colli Orientali tended to by producers with similar work habits (and yields) show that the total acidity in Ribolla Gialla grapes varies from 6.2 to 7.7 grams per liter, of which as much as 2 grams per liter are of malic acid. For the most part, Ribolla Gialla wines have simple if fragrant aromas: most are due to fermentation esters (which means delicate grassy or herbal and white flower notes). Clearly, when the result of long macerations on the skins, the must is enriched by the presence of carotenoid-breakdown products. In Ribolla Gialla wines, the aroma of acacia flowers has been linked to p-methoxybenzaldehyde and the fresh citrus notes to 3-mercaptohexanol levels. Very typical of the variety is that it can express β-isophorone—a molecule that smells of saffron (Panighel et al. 2014). According to

D'Auria, Mauriello, and Rana (2004), in Ribolla Gialla grapes it is present at much lower concentrations than it is in saffron (0.70 milligrams per kilogram and 1.6 to 6.6 milligrams per kilogram, respectively), but its presence is very discernible and really adds something special to the best wines. Exceptionally interesting are those (unfortunately rare) Ribolla Gialla wines in which the grapes have been partially hit by noble rot; in this case the wine picks up a honeyed note and a far more complex aromatic profile that is truly enticing and thrilling. Enzo Pontoni of Miani makes a wine like this from time to time (the 2012 is to die for), but his 2006 Ribolla Gialla is just as good, and there was no noble rot that year to speak of (D'Agata 2017). Gravener also makes a noble-rot-affected Ribolla Gialla wine that is not just unique but amazing. Furthermore, back in the 1980s he also used to make an outstanding dry Ribolla Gialla wine without resorting to maceration (the 1983 was especially good), so that is all the proof you need that there was no need to start macerating the poor grape at all in order to make a great wine. In my opinion, Ribolla Gialla is at its best when grown in ideal hillside vineyards by limiting yields, and the wine made like any other white wine: with low fermentation temperatures that help the variety express its delicate aromas. Avoiding oak is also a very good idea, since the cultivar's delicate aromas and flavors of white flowers (acacia flowers), fresh citrus, yellow peach, banana, and white pepper are easily overwhelmed by oak.

SPECIFIC TERROIRS

Ribolla Gialla is typical of Friuli–Venezia Giulia and of the Friuli Colli Orientali (FCO) and Collio denominations, which are also the only two DOCs that contemplate monovarietal Ribolla. I believe there are two grand crus for the variety, historically recognized as such: Rosazzo in the FCO and Oslavia in the Collio (though the FCO's Buttrio area can also boast remarkably good Ribolla Gialla wines, most likely as a result of its having a hot microclimate). Since Ribolla Gialla loves heat, it's not surprising that it thrives in Rosazzo, too, another warm microclimate. Rosazzo's wines are generally deeper and richer than most (though rich is a very relative term with Ribolla Gialla, which makes a fresh, fragrant white wine of sneaky concentration and complexity), while the Ribolla Gialla wines from Oslavia (where it grows in a cooler microclimate at higher altitudes) are mineral, lemony, and higher in acid. Both are characterized by the variety's telltale nuance of white pepper, though this is never found when yields are high. Poorly fertile, mineral-salt-rich soils (such as those of Buttrio, Rocca Bernarda, and Spessa in the Colli Orientali and Dolegna del Collio and San Floriano, near Oslavia in the Collio) are all also outstanding sites for the variety, while clay, which retains water, is not ideal, because it tends to increase Ribolla Gialla's already naturally high vigor.

Collio

Ribolla Gialla has always been linked to the Collio, where it was the most-planted variety at the beginning of the twentieth century. The Collio (also known as Collio Goriziano, since the territory is historically and geographically linked to the city of Gorizia), much like the adjacent Colli Orientali denomination, is geologically and topographically very complex. As a result of this, there are a plethora of different grape varieties grown, each matched (in theory, at least) to specific areas throughout the Collio. When the right combination of grape variety, rootstock, site, and viticultural methods is achieved, it is here that some of Italy's potentially greatest white wines are made. There is no doubt that specific parts of the Collio are of grand cru quality—for Ribolla Gialla and Pinot Bianco especially, though very good Friulano and Malvasia wines can be made there as well. Of course, locals will also go on poetically about how well something like twelve other grape varieties perform on Collio soils, but I am afraid that's just the usually delusional Italian wine talk, completely devoid of any grounding in reality: for example, Italian Chardonnay wines, Collio's included, are for the most part uninteresting (and by world standards, possibly even worse than that). Most importantly, and yet another lesson in the intricacies of terroir, whereas the Collio is in many respects geologically identical to the neighboring Friuli Colli Orientali, the varieties that do best in each of the two denominations are not the same (such as, for example, Picolit, which has historically always been associated with the Colli Orientali).

At a total of 1,234 hectares under vine and roughly sixty thousand hectoliters per year of wine produced (ISTAT data 2014), the Collio is a relatively small wine-production area but is still the third-largest of all the Friuli–Venezia Giulia denominations, after Friuli Grave (far and away the biggest in terms both of hectares under vine and of hectoliters per year of wine produced). The Collio is an enclave delimited to the northwest by the Judrio River and by the Isonzo River to the southeast (the Judrio was once the border between the Austrian and Venetian empires); to its east is Slovenia (the Collio sits right at the Italian-Slovenian border: in fact, your cell phone, even as you find yourself still in Italy though only a kilometer or two from the border, will start sending you greetings in Slovenian and welcoming you to that country), while to the west of Collio lie the Colli Orientali and the rest of Friuli–Venezia Giulia. Unlike other well-known Friuli–Venezia Giulia denominations such as Friuli Isonzo and Friuli Grave, which are mostly made up of flatlands, the Collio is practically all hilly (save for the Preval depression or plain, and the area around Farra d'Isonzo, though in the view of the locals, the latter area is hilly as well; to me it looks so flat you could pour maple syrup over it, but so be it). In any case, the hillside topography of Collio is a very important aspect of the denomination—one that goes a long way in characterizing the wines made within it. It is in this series of hills and hillsides, arranged in a semicircle spreading from the town of Dolegna to the hamlet of Oslavia, that most of the Collio's greatest vineyards lie. Geologically, the area belongs to the Julian Prealps mountain system and is characterized by an undulating topography with numerous valleys, slopes, and summits. It follows that the Collio is characterized by many different subzones that can give very different wines, even when made from the same grape variety. Therefore, a "generic" Collio white wine is hardly an enlightened idea.

The main geological formation of the Collio (and the nearby Colli Orientali del Friuli) is the flysch—stratified sedimentary rocks characterized by a repeating succession of two or more lithologic types, such as marls and compacted sands (what in Friuli–Venezia Giulia is a little too generically called *ponca*) or calcareous rocks and clays. In fact, it would be more accurate to divide the Collio's soils into four main types: marly, arenaceous (sandstony), marly-arenaceous, and conglomerates; when grapes are grown on such different soil types, the resulting wines are invariably different, and so it is here. Marly-arenaceous soils are a mix of the two types, and this is what the locals refer to as *ponca*. Actually, there is also a very small portion of Collio's soils that is heavy clay in nature, located near the Preval depression or plain near Plessiva and Giasbana, but this acid soil type is not characteristic at all of the denomination. For accuracy's sake, please note that flysch and *ponca* are not interchangeable words. Flysches are stratified rocks that can be found all over the world; the *ponca* is a specific rock formation that is found only in an area straddling Friuli–Venezia Giulia, Slovenia, and Istria. The geologic difference between the *ponca* and other sedimentary formations is that the former originated in mostly shallow lacustrine basins, not deep in the sea. In general, the *ponca*, a rather friable rock, is made up of alternating layers of compacted sands cemented together by calcium and by marly layers (clay-loam weakly cemented together); but depending on the presence of turbidity currents, different *ponca* formations were born. In fact, the *ponca* is not even called *ponca* everywhere in

Friuli–Venezia Giulia; in the valley of the Vipacco River (one of my favorite trout-fishing haunts) it is known as *soudan* or *laporn;* in the Carso area, around Trieste, it is called *tasel* or *tassel.* (For an analysis of the Carso, see the Malvasia Istriana entry.) Therefore, it is far more appropriate to speak not of one *ponca* but of *ponche,* each differing by bedrock, soil, and the expression of the wines that can be made from grapes grown on them. For the most part, these soils have neutral or slightly alkaline pH; when red-tinged, they tend to have a weakly acid pH. The presence of *ponca* is so important because the sandstone component ensures very good drainage while the marl acts like a sponge, holding on to water and releasing it in times of drought. It is an excellent soil type on which to grow grapevines. Clearly, the *ponca* works best on slopes, hence hillside vineyards.

The name "flysch" derives from a Swiss German dialect word meaning "slippery slope" (I kid you not). It is a relatively frequently encountered geological formation within and outside of Italy: for example, many of the soils of Chianti Classico have derived from the marine Apennine class of flysch (which is different from Friuli's). To be precise, flysch deposits are those that are created when mountain ranges form; if the sedimentary deposit occurred after this event took place, we would speak of molasses (and so will wine producers when you listen to them, and it's always good to know what they're talking about). The flysch that typifies the Collio is mostly the flysch of Cormons formed during the middle Eocene period and is classically composed of alternating layers of marl and compacted sands (sandstone) rich in conglomerates (Venzo and Brambati 1969). There are at least three different flysch formations based on their clay, marl, and sandstone content and evolutionary origin. (According to a 2006 study by Carulli, these are the Superior Cretaceous flysch, the flysch of Cormons, and the flysch of Grivò.) The Superior Cretaceous flysch was formed roughly seventy-two to sixty-five million years ago and is located where the Collio sits at the border with

Slovenia. Clay-rich flysch formations derive from deep marine deposits, as opposed to those flysch formations (such as the flysch of Cormons) that derive from deposits in fluvial delta habitat (Tunis and Venturini 1989). While it is true that the flysch of Cormons (formed fifty-three to forty million years ago) is the predominant one in most of the Collio, in the northwestern reaches of the denomination, above Dolegna, it is the flysch of Grivò (formed sixty-five to fifty-three million years ago) that is most abundant (Martinis 1993). The latter flysch differs from that of Cormons for a greater conglomeratic nature, with calcarenite and calcareous inclusions not found to the same degree in the flysch of Cormons, which has a greater presence of sandstone. Knowing such differences is not a matter of being too granular in one's approach to Italian wine, but rather helps understand at least in part the contributing factors that make the wines of Dolegna recognizably different (wines marked by greater, zingier acidities and a citrusy quality that are related to the greater calcareous content of the soil) from those of other high-quality wine Collio subzones like Cormons and Capriva, which sit on different flysches. It is exactly the same level of knowledge that most people take for granted when dealing with French wines, such as whether the Chablis they are drinking stems from grapes grown on Kimmeridgean as opposed to Portlandian soil; so we need to start thinking and talking about Italian wines in the same way. In any case, all these slightly different *ponca* soils have the same important qualities. For one, a high pH, and this coupled with the surrounding cool temperatures helps produce grapes with a high amount of malic acid. Unfortunately, these soils are also prone to landslides (especially in the case of those *ponche* that are lower in sandstone content; this is just one of the many reasons why it is important to be aware of the differences between the soils, because, among other things, it can change the direction in which a producer chooses to plant his grapevine rows, and that's terroir, too). This is also the reason why many estates have planted fruit trees (apple trees are most common) in the hillside vineyards: doing so helps avoid having entire sections of the hill slide away. Marly soils are mostly gray-blue in color, plus or minus brown-yellow spots or streaks; arenaceous (sandstone) components are most often yellow-brown in color, but can be dotted with gray-blue and even slightly violet inclusions. (When you start seeing something violet in the soil, either you have been drinking way too much Collio wine or you are standing in a vineyard growing on plenty of sandstone.) Clearly, as the Collio denomination slopes down from the hillsides toward the Isonzo River alluvial plain and the Friuli Isonzo denomination below, the prevalent soil type changes, becoming, not surprisingly, much richer in loam and clay (colluvial soils typical of the area around Farra d'Isonzo and the plain of Preval). There are also frankly alluvial deposits derived from flows of the Isonzo (mainly gravel and sand) and the Judrio (mainly loam, gravel, and sand) Rivers. Ribolla Gialla can grow in all these flatland soils, but it gives poor results (high-acid grapes and wines of very little body that are turned into sparkling wines). It follows that in the Collio there are essentially two landscape types where vineyards grow: the hillsides and the alluvial plains. In general, the hillside vineyards grow between fifty and two hundred meters above sea level, though grapevines are mostly planted at heights between fifty and ninety meters. Gradients are generally soft, ranging from 15 to 30 percent (hence Condrieu-like walled terraces are rarely if ever seen in the Collio, because they are not needed there). On average, roots dig down eighty to one hundred centimeters. By contrast, the alluvial plain sits at an altitude of fifty to one hundred meters above sea level, roots dig down between fifty and one hundred centimeters, and the degree of water drainage varies greatly depending on the prevalent soil type; those sections richer in clay have outstanding water-retention capacity, and excessive water availability can pose a problem in terms of fine wine production. (Too much water, and vines tend to become very vig-

orous, pushing foliage first and foremost, and what grapes there are will be hopelessly bloated and dilute.) Clearly, there is usually no such concern on hillside sites. Trellising methods are mostly single and double Guyot, spur cordon, and double-arched cane (or *cappuccina*). Planting density is usually three thousand to four thousand vines per hectare. The most common rootstocks used in the Collio are the 420A, the 3309 De Couderc, Rupestris du Lot, and Kober 5BB; use of the Kober 5BB rootstock is not ideal in droughty terroirs. It would seem only natural to me to choose a rootstock, such as Rupestris du Lot, that would tend to curb the variety's naturally high vigor. According to Gianni Menotti, one of Italy's most famous consultant viticulturalists and winemakers (for years, responsible for the great wines of Villa Russiz), what characterizes the soils of the best vineyard areas of the Collio is their marly component. These marls have an alkaline pH, with normal concentrations of nitrogen, boron, and magnesium, high concentrations of potassium, and low phosphorus levels. Menotti believes it is the potassium that contributes mostly to the remarkable finesse of Collio wines (and, I would add, to their volume, too). Interestingly, when it comes to the Collio, Menotti believes that the single most important soil-related factor is soil texture, because the marly soils are not characterized by especially high available water capacities, meaning that drip irrigation can become necessary in droughty years and even at veraison. The annual mean daily temperature of the Collio is 13–14°C (slightly lower, 12°C, if only the north-facing sites of the Collio's northern section are considered). Between April and September, the average daily temperature is 17°C; the average minimum and maximum daily temperatures for the same time period are 13°C and 25°C, respectively (Winkler index, 1750–2100; Huglin index, 2250–2500). In fact, the ever-changing topography of the Collio creates myriad mesoclimates. January and February are the coldest months of the year and July and August the warmest. Importantly, rainfall is very evenly distributed in the Collio (however, the northern reaches of the denomination are some of the rainiest in all of Friuli), and except in occasional extreme vintages, there are essentially no periods of drought. Annual precipitation rates range from 1,450 to 1,600 millimeters per year (52 percent of the rain falls from April through September). Clearly, the higher part of the precipitation range (1,600 millimeters) refers to the Collio's northern sector, such as the area around Dolegna (Mennella 1977; Menezes and Tabeaud 2000).

The Collio Subzones

The Collio's extreme variability in exposures, gradients, and wind currents, coupled with the plethora of mesoclimates, creates many different subzones within the denomination. Wines made in each are rather easy to identify (granted, with a lot of practice). For example, the northernmost part of the Collio around the town of Dolegna is much cooler than the town of Cormons; it can be subdivided into Brazzano (better for red wines) and Plessiva (a much cooler mesoclimate, and so better for white varieties). Given the very recognizably different wines made in this very small part of the Collio alone (the distance between Dolegna and Cormons is only 10.6 kilometers—roughly fourteen minutes away, for those who know the area), you realize that writing about Collio wines generically is really of very little use, and is actually downright wrong. (It would be akin to speaking of Cote de Nuits wines generically, rather than differentiating between Vosne-Romanée and Gevrey-Chambertin.) Moving eastward, Capriva is very famous for its whites in the areas of Spessa di Capriva and of Russiz Superiore, but again, it is not so simple. First, it's important to specify that there are three different Spessas (two of which aren't even in the Collio), with very different topographical and climatic features, and so it is easy to get confused. Russiz Superiore is different from Russiz: both are exceptional grape-growing areas, but the former has a much cooler microclimate than the latter, and, you guessed it, wines made from the same variety in each of the two areas

are quite different. Other Collio municipalities that are important to know well are Farra, which is actually located in the Isonzo River plain; Oslavia (one of the two truly great grand crus for Ribolla Gialla); and San Floriano del Collio, a very cool subzone where some of Friuli–Venezia Giulia's most refined wines are made. Tocai Friulano grown on the hills and cooler microclimate of Dolegna invariably gives wines showing higher acidity levels and less ripe-fruit aromas and flavors: these wines offer notes of white flowers (acacia and peony), plus hints of fresh citrus and green apple. Tocai Friulano grown around Spessa di Capriva offers wines that are more yellow apple, almond, and a hint of ginger. By contrast, Collio Malvasia Istriana wines are far fruitier when grown on the hillsides, and are also characterized by noteworthy salinity and uncommon complexity. Flatland vineyards tend to give Malvasia Istriana wines that are more herbal and spicy (at times excessively so); the wines then have a rustic quality that is less than desirable.

To summarize, the complex Collio territory can and should be subdivided into five major subzones (and numerous smaller districts) that revolve around the following five townships, which I describe below: San Floriano, Oslavia, Capriva, Cormons, and Dolegna. In each of these subzones, there are crus that deserve to be well known—for example, Ruttars and Venco in Dolegna. Zegla is a separate district of unique wines located near Plessiva, but I have not included it in my subzoning of Collio because the area is now mostly associated with Collio Bianco wines, made from a blend of grapes that varies between producers and that renders terroir identification next to impossible (despite what they tell you). However, Tocai Friulano has always done very well in Zegla, and there are many delicious old bottlings from the likes of Edi Keber and Renato Keber that attest to this. In the five subzones I have listed, soils are mostly the same (it is the clay content that will change most, but my analysis is that variations are not so marked); by contrast, differences in topography and especially microclimate are most significant. Given the same grape variety, it is the combination of these different associations, plus human intervention, that leads to the wonderful and complex diversity of the Collio's wines from different subzones.

SAN FLORIANO DEL COLLIO

Along with Oslavia, the commune of San Floriano del Collio sits in the easternmost section of the Collio denomination. At roughly 250 meters above sea level, this subzone has historically been linked to outstanding Ribolla Gialla (especially), Friulano, and Sauvignon Blanc wines. As in the Oslavia subzone, dry winds from Slovenia and the Adriatic Sea blow regularly through the subzone, and the mesoclimate ensures that this is one of the latest subzones to be harvested in the Collio. San Floriano's wines are always characterized by higher average total acidity than similarly made wines in other Collio subzones. Mario Schiopetto used to tell me that even the most structured and biggest white wines of San Floriano, such as, for example, those made with grapes grown in vineyards with full southern exposures, were still fresher and livelier than any other wines made in the Collio. Both Lorenzo Landi and Gianni Menotti, two of Italy's most knowledgeable winemakers, confirm this impression.

OSLAVIA

The wonder and complexity that is terroir is in full evidence when you stop to consider the wines of San Floriano and those of Oslavia. Differently from those of San Floriano, the wines of Oslavia, which is located very close to San Floriano but at a lower altitude (about 150 to 180 meters above sea level), have a similar aroma and flavor profile but are more tactile and relatively fleshier. A good demonstration of the relevance of this observation is that this seemingly minor difference in mesoclimate and altitude means that Merlot (and Pignolo) fare relatively well in Oslavia, but not so famously in San Floriano. As in the San Floriano subzone, dry winds from Slovenia and the Adriatic Sea are strong, and so the sunny, dry

microclimate ensures that this is one of the latest subzones to be harvested in the Collio. As we have seen, Ribolla Gialla has long been associated with exceptional wines from Oslavia, and most likely the very strong diurnal temperature variations play an important role in helping fashion deeper Ribolla Gialla wines than those made anywhere else. While daytime temperatures can be quite hot in and around Oslavia (I know, I spent long parts of my adolescent summers here), the cold night winds help create this strong aromatic expression in Oslavia's Ribolla Gialla wines. This explains why the best Ribolla Gialla vineyards in Oslavia have full southern or southwestern exposures; otherwise the cultivar has trouble accumulating sugar there. When that happens, the finished wines lack body and have a hint of underlying bitterness—the telltale sign of a Ribolla Gialla wine that was either poorly made or from grapes planted in an unsuitable terroir. The best examples of Oslavia's Ribolla Gialla wines are deep, rich, complex, and piercingly fresh and perfumed. Once you taste a good Ribolla Gialla wine from Oslavia (not the macerated or orange stuff that we'll leave to those always in search of the latest flavor of the month), the greatness and uniqueness of a great terroir dawns on you immediately. The territory and history of Goriziai has been well described by Carl von Czoernig in *Il territorio di Gorizia e Gradisca* (1969).

CAPRIVA DEL FRIULI

Situated at only forty-nine meters above sea level, Capriva has a warm microclimate, at least by Collio's not-exactly-tropical standards. Vineyards are planted up to about one hundred meters above sea level and are especially characterized by more sunlight hours than those of other Collio subzones. Capriva's white wines are certainly the Collio's most powerful from an olfactory perspective; personally, I also find them to be very savory. Gianni Menotti believes this to be the single greatest subzone of the whole Collio, not because of one specific great wine made here (Tocai Friulano, Pinot Bianco,

Sauvignon Blanc, and Merlot all seem to grow well here and can potentially give outstanding wines), but because in his view the wines always seem to have outstanding balance. At times the extreme savoriness and outright size that characterize this subzone's wines are not especially to my taste, but they may be to yours.

CORMONS

Cormons is the biggest of the Collio's townships (over seven thousand people live in what is a small city), and its wines are some of the most famous of Friuli–Venezia Giulia. Like Capriva, it sits at a low altitude (56 meters above sea level), essentially where the hills meet the flatter portion of the denomination (the two being separated by another subzone, called Pradis). However, Cormons has a microclimate that is very slightly cooler and less sunlit than Capriva's; this is because Cormons lies at the base of Mount Quarin (276 meters above sea level). One can further subdivide this area into the southern side of the mountain and the vineyards of the north-facing slope, where clearly temperatures are cooler. The Cormons subzone includes the viticultural areas of Pradis to the southeast of Cormons, Brazzano to the north and northeast, and Plessiva farther northeast still of Cormons. (As one moves in the direction of Plessiva, the climate turns cooler.) Pinot Bianco, Tocai Friulano, and Malvasia Istriana all perform well in the Cormons subzone, but in my view no single variety excels and outperforms the others. The wines are similar to those of Capriva, rather large-scale and fleshy, though not nearly as savory, and I daresay not as complex, either, but offering softer fruit flavors and early appeal. Cormons is the prettiest of the Collio's communes, with a lovely *enoteca* in the center of town where it is wonderful to sit down and have a drink after a long day of tastings and winery visits. In some respects, that's terroir, too.

DOLEGNA DEL COLLIO

Dolegna is the northernmost of the Collio subzones, and though it does not lie at an especially high altitude (ninety meters above sea level), it is closer to the Alps, rainier, and cooler than all the other Collio subzones. And despite its weather, I absolutely love its wines. Dolegna boasts a world-class wine terroir relative to Pinot Bianco and Ribolla Gialla. (Only Terlano in Alto Adige can match Dolegna's Pinot Bianco.) Curiously, even though Dolegna is not a warm area, Ribolla Gialla does extremely well there, with wines showcasing uncanny refinement, a penetrating mineral mouthfeel, and memorable perfume. Last but not least, it is important to remember that Dolegna has a number of small hamlets (essentially small groups of houses), of which two have been most linked with high-quality vineyards: Ruttars and Vencò.

The Best Ribolla Gialla Crus

Over the last twenty to thirty years or so, I have been able to taste microvinifications from many different small plots of land in the Collio, and based on these and the anecdotes and statements of locals who either grew the grapes or made the wines, I think the following list includes the highest-quality vineyard areas for Ribolla Gialla. (Unfortunately, there are no single-vineyard-designated bottlings as such.)

Capriva: Russiz.

Cormons: Pecol di Lupi, Roncada, Subida, Monte Plessiva.

Dolegna: Cavezzo.

Oslavia: Hum, Runk.

San Floriano: Uclanci.

BENCHMARK WINES

Gravner***PS, Toros***PS.

Ca' Ronesca***, Doro Princic***, Primosic***.

Muzic**, Tercic**.

Friuli Colli Orientali (FCO)

A DOC since 1970, the Colli Orientali is a strip of land roughly sixty kilometers long and fifteen kilometers wide situated between the high

Friuli plains to the southwest and the southern section of the Julian Prealps to the northeast. This is the second-largest denomination of Friuli, both in terms of hectares under vine (1,807 hectares) and in terms of hectoliters of wine (77,000 hectoliters) produced (2014 ISTAT data). The denomination has seventeen different municipalities, all in the province of Udine: the biggest and most important is Cividale, a very pretty town founded by Julius Caesar as Forum Iulii in 50 B.C. The others are Attimis, Buttrio, Corso di Rosazzo, Faedis, Magnano in Roviera, Manzano, Nimis, Povoletto, Premariacco, Prepotto, Reana di Roiale, San Giovanni al Natisone, San Pietro al Natisone, Tarcento, Tricesimo, and Torreano. Wine lovers will have immediately recognized some of these names, since territories of some of these municipalities have long been associated with fine wine production. (Buttrio, Corso di Rosazzo, Faedis, Nimis, Premariacco, Prepotto, and Torreano spring to mind, but some small fractions are also very famous; see the Picolit entry.) In the area south of Cividale, east of Buttrio and Manzano, Corno di Rosazzo lies at an altitude of about 120 meters above sea level and has a temperate, relatively warm climate with gently rolling hills. By contrast, the area north of Cividale is characterized by a much cooler and rainier climate, with steeper, more jagged hills (where Savorgnano del Torre, Faedis, Nimis, and Attimis are located). Annual precipitation here ranges from twelve hundred millimeters in the southern portion of the FCO (with roughly ninety-six days of rain) to over two thousand millimeters (with one hundred fourteen days of rain) in the northern section. (The area of the Musi Mountains just outside the denomination's northern limits records more than three thousand millimeters of rain a year, one of the highest amounts in Europe.) About 40 percent of the rain falls between May and October; importantly, the longest periods without rain occur in the autumn (up to eighteen to twenty-one days), when harvest takes place. This means eventual water stress in Friuli–Venezia Giulia vineyards is not due to lack of rainfall

(there is almost too much of it, actually), but rather the poor water-retention capacity of some soils. The average daily temperature from January to December in the denomination is roughly 13°C, with minimum and maximum temperatures of 8°C and 18°C, respectively (actually, with surprising little difference between the northern and southern sections of the DOC that I wrote about above). The Winkler index is 1500–1650 in the southern portion of the DOC, and only 1400–1500 in its northern reaches. The Huglin index is 2050–2250 in the southern part of the denomination and only 1950–2050 in the northern part.

The cultivation of fifteen white and sixteen red wine-grape varieties is allowed in the FCO, but understandably, not all varieties reach the same outstanding results. The varieties that perform best in the FCO are Picolit, Ribolla Gialla, Tocai Friulano, and Verduzzo among the white grapes, and Pignolo, Refosco del Peduncolo Rosso, Refosco di Faedis, Schioppettino, and Tazzelenghe among the red grapes. Two official, and very important, FCO subzones were introduced in 1995: Cialla (for Bianco, Rosso, Picolit, Refosco del Peduncolo Rosso, Ribolla Gialla, Schioppettino, and Verduzzo only; roughly twelve hectares under vine between Prepotto and Manzano) and Rosazzo (for the production of Bianco, Rosso, Picolit, Pignolo, and Ribolla Gialla only; roughly forty-six hectares under vine that fall within portions of the townships of Manzano, Premariacco, Corno di Rosazzo, and San Giovanni al Natisone). In general, all the white wines of the FCO are less weighty and savory than those of the Collio. They usually also have fresher acidity.

Analyzing the terroir of the Colli Orientali is extremely hard because the area under vine is so vast, but a number of conclusions can be reached, and these help qualify the wines. The plains have soils of alluvial origin, while the hillsides of the southern reaches are the natural continuation of those of the Collio. By contrast, the northern part of the FCO has steep slopes and generally cooler, rainier weather. This is the section of the FCO that leads to Ramandolo, a downright cold, steep, and mountainous area. (Snow is common there in the winter.) It comes as no surprise, then, that the majority of the FCO's vineyards are found mainly in the southern portion next to the Collio, around the hamlets of Buttrio, Cividale, Corno di Rosazzo, and Prepotto. There are very few areas in the country that can boast so many different high-quality native grape varieties that give very terroir-specific wines such as can the FCO.

The Friuli Colli Orientali Subzones

There are a number of FCO subzones, but I think those linked to highest-quality, distinctive wine production are nine: Buttrio, Cialla, Faedis, Prepotto, Ramandolo, Rocca Bernarda (Corno di Rosazzo), Rosazzo, Savorgnano del Torre, and Torreano. There are many other townships that are excellent, such as Premariacco, but given the limited time and space I can devote to this particular chapter, I have been forced to make some hard choices. (For this reason I have had to also omit Ramandolo, situated in the FCO's far north and a grand cru for Verduzzo; I will broach it and other grapes and terroirs in another upcoming book.) Please note that I broach in this specific section devoted to Ribolla Gialla only those subzones that are especially linked to high-quality Ribolla Gialla wines. I discuss the subzones that are most suited and historically important for other varieties in their respective chapters: for example, I discuss Cialla, Rocca Bernarda (Corno di Rosazzo), Rosazzo, and Savorgnano del Torre in the Picolit entry, since these four subzones are also associated with grand-cru-quality Picolit wines. But because Rosazzo is also amazing for Ribolla Gialla, I will also discuss it here, where I list the FCO subzones and the grape varieties that give the best results in each:

Buttrio: Ribolla Gialla, Refosco del Peduncolo Rosso, Tazzelenghe, Tocai Friulano.

Cialla: Picolit, Refosco del Peduncolo Rosso, Schioppettino, Verduzzo.

Faedis: Tocai Friulano, Refosco di Faedis.

Prepotto: Picolit, Schioppettino, Tazzelenghe.

Ramandolo: Verduzzo.

Rocca Bernarda (Corno di Rosazzo): Picolit, Pignolo, Tocai Friulano.

Rosazzo: Picolit, Ribolla Gialla, Pignolo.

Savorgnano del Torre: Picolit.

Torreano: Friulano, Refosco del Peduncolo Rosso, Tazzelenghe.

The FCO Ribolla Gialla Subzones

BUTTRIO

Roughly ten kilometers southeast of Udine, the town of Buttrio is one of Friuli's oldest, certainly inhabited by A.D. 588 but most likely in much earlier times too; the name *Butrium* appears for the first time only around A.D. 1000. The town's name signifies a chasm or very deep ravine, and its immediate territory has long been associated with the FCO denomination's best red wines. The reason for this is an essentially warmer mesoclimate that allows red grapes to reach optimal polyphenol maturity; for the same reason, a variety like Ribolla Gialla also thrives there. The soil is usually assumed to be the classic *ponca*, but in fact Buttrio is especially characterized by red loamy soils rich in clay, which contribute an aromatic spiciness and tactile mouthfeel that the wines lack when the same grape varieties are grown elsewhere in Friuli–Venezia Giulia. Buttrio's soil has about average concentrations of phosphorus, nitrogen, and potassium; low magnesium and active lime; and scarce calcium levels. A very important fact about Buttrio is that the diurnal temperature range is wide, and so grapes rarely overripen, with both red and white wines fresh and crisp.

ROSAZZO

The Rosazzo subzone, Friuli–Venezia Giulia's most famous of all, falls within the municipalities of San Giovanni al Natisone and Manzano. It is an especially beautiful part of Friuli–Venezia Giulia, long associated with the Abbey of Rosazzo, the *Monasterium rosarum* ("monastery of the roses") built in the eleventh century. (But the hermit Alemanno, looking for spiritual peace and rest, had already settled there in the ninth century, establishing an oratory that turned into a full–fledged monastery over the course of the following centuries.) The area is very open and breezy, with lots of sunlight and gently sloping hillsides; the unique microclimate of the Rosazzo area is influenced by marine breezes blowing in from the Adriatic Sea, only twenty-five kilometers away. The presence of the warm marine breezes and of the Colle Santa Caterina d'Alessandria (239 meters high), situated next to the Abbey of Rosazzo, protects the Rosazzo subzone from the cool tramontana winds, and all add up to an especially warm microclimate. Also, the vineyards lie at 180 to 220 meters above sea level and are for the most part fully south-facing, which further contributes to the illumination and Rosazzo's warm climate (attested to by the olive trees that grow there). In any case, these conditions also mean that at Rosazzo, Ribolla Gialla can be harvested late, since its skins will be able to withstand any late-season inclement weather. The grape biotype is always important in the creation of an especially high-quality terroir: in fact, the authentic Ribolla Gialla "of Rosazzo" (it looks different from other biotypes growing elsewhere in the region) is characterized by a large but loosely packed bunch, with relatively big grapes armed with a fairly resistant skin. Thanks to the not-compact bunch and the tougher-than-usual skin, this Ribolla Gialla ecotype is a perfect fit for Rosazzo and allows not just better wines to be made, but site-specific ones, too. Unfortunately, producers have planted just about any nursery Ribolla Gialla in the area over the years, and this is a real shame; for Rosazzo was always associated with one specific Ribolla Gialla biotype, which should have been protected. Rosazzo's soil is mostly marl and compacted sands (the classic *ponca*, but I caution readers that there is more than one type of *ponca;* see the Collio section in this chapter) that are poor in organic matter but rich in mineral elements and fossils. The fact that this soil does not hold on to water is especially important with Ribolla Gialla, since it is a vigorous variety and too much water causes it to become overproductive and give dull wines. An old Friuli–Venezia Giulia admonition is to "always plant Ribolla Gialla where the grass doesn't grow"—in other words, in those soils so poor in nutrients that not even grass manages to grow (but Ribolla Gialla will). This is one of the secrets to Rosazzo's success with this specific cultivar. Well-made Ribolla Gialla wines of Rosazzo are magically balanced, deep, and long, but blessed with a crystalline acidity and a lovely saline nuance that is a far cry from the intense, almost chewy savoriness of the wines made in some of the better Collio subzones. Typically, the Ribolla Gialla wines of Rosazzo are also larger framed and more full-bodied than many Ribolla Gialla wines made outside of the Rosazzo district.

BENCHMARK WINES (RIBOLLA GIALLA FCO)

Miani Pettarin***[PS].

I Clivi***, Isidoro Polencic***, Meroi***, Nadalutti***, Ronchi di Cialla***, Sirch***, Volpe Pasini Zuc***.

Gigante**, Iole Grillo**, Paolo Rodaro**, Ronco delle Betulle**, Torre Rosazza**.

Ruchè

THE GRAPE VARIETY

An aromatic red grape variety, it is easy to either love or hate Ruchè, but most everybody loves it. Though floral and spicy, the wines have a discreet aromatic nature, and so never risk turning into too much of a good thing. In fact, in my experience, most people who try a Ruchè wine for the first time end up liking the experience (after a moment of understandable bewilderment). Even better for Ruchè producers, they end up wanting to repeat it.

Ruchè is a crossing of croatina and Malvasia Aromatica di Parma. The thinking today is that it was born in the hills to the northwest of Asti at Castagnolis Casalensis, a site that now falls within the municipality of Castagnole Monferrato, the modern-day home of Ruchè wines. The cultivar's French-sounding name itself might derive from Piedmont's long-standing association with France or from a viral disease (*roncet*, a.k.a. *court-noué*) to which Ruchè is more resistant than other local Piedmontese varieties such as Barbera. At first, Ruchè was most often a sweet wine reserved for special

occasions such as birthdays, christenings, graduations, and marriages. It was also used in small amounts to "kick up a notch" the perfume of more straightforward wines made with Barbera, Dolcetto, or Grignolino. And so, by the twentieth century Ruchè's future did not exactly compete in brightness with that of Alpha Centauri, its cultivation reduced to a few rows in vineyards scattered throughout the Monferrato. However, in a story line similar to that of many other quality native wine grapes resurrected from oblivion, one man's vision and passion ensured that Ruchè would one day rise from the ashes (D'Agata 2007b). That person was Don Giacomo Cauda, the father of modern Ruchè wines and the man who most likely saved the variety from extinction. Cauda was Castagnole Monferrato's town priest, and he loved viticulture: more than one local I have talked to over the years told me that the good man spent nearly all his time in the vineyards—so much so that there are whispers he was late for a couple of weddings and even a funeral once, much to the understandable chagrin of the locals. In fact, it was those very locals who rallied around Cauda's battle cry of "Save Ruchè," making the priest's belief in Ruchè's great qualities their own. Cauda realized that the area had something unique in Ruchè, a wine grape unlike any other growing in Piedmont. Along with the Medda family, he selected old Ruchè vines and had them propagated, establishing the first all-Ruchè vineyard of the 1960 and early 1970s. He also had his parishioners pay more attention to their extant Ruchè vines, and pushed to make the wine a dry one. His own wine, then called "Ruchè del Parroco" (which translates to "Ruchè of the priest"), was the best Ruchè wine made for a very long time and provided a shining example to all those making a Ruchè wine. In time, Cauda sold the vineyard to a local *vignaiolo,* Francesco Borgognone, who made the wine until very recently (the 2015 vintage); because the wine was no longer "of" the town priest, Borgognone had to change the wine's name, and he intelligently chose "Vigna del Parroco," or "vineyard of the priest." By then the seeds for Ruchè's revival had been sown. Between 1995 and 1998, university researchers scoured local vineyards and identified thirty-five different biotypes of Ruchè, eventually choosing four that appeared to have the best potential for making fine wine, and in so doing developed the modern Ruchè nursery clones now available to everyone. In 2015, getting long in the tooth, Borgognone sold the vineyard to Luca Ferraris, the energetic local golden boy of Ruchè wines and current president of the Ruchè consortium (likable, very talented, and with a keen business mind; the consortium could not be in better hands). He released his first (absolutely outstanding) Ruchè wine (2016 vintage) from the vineyard, renaming it "Vigna del Parroco—Don Giacomo Cauda." An early-ripening cultivar, Ruchè is fairly resistant to most diseases, though oidium is troublesome. It does very well in dry, well-exposed calcareous soils that help enhance the wine's perfume; clay-rich soils are good, too, and in this case Ruchè wines exhibit more power and size. No matter the type of soil on which Ruchè is planted, a great Ruchè wine smells of red cherry, raspberry, cinnamon, nutmeg, coriander, lavender, violet, and white pepper, but the aroma profile of an outstanding Ruchè wine can be far more complex. Lip-smacking freshness and mouth-cleansing acidity are hallmarks that make the floral mark of the variety's wines stick out even more. Locals have always told me that Ruchè needs cool sites, and for this reason it is often planted in vineyards with northern exposures; the goal is to avoid the risk of baking the grapes and thereby lose the wine's unique aromatics.

SPECIFIC TERROIRS

The Ruchè DOC and wine are known as Ruchè di Castagnole Monferrato; the wine is produced mainly in the countrysides of the small municipalities of Castagnole Monferrato and Scurzolengo, but also in nearby Grana, Montemagno, Portacomaro, Refrancore, and Viarigi, all in the province of Asti. The highest altitude in the denomination is reached at Grana, 270 meters above sea level; Castagnole Monferrato reaches 240 meters above sea level. The denomination's topography is dominated by a series of hillside ridges that run north–south, meaning that vineyards face mostly east-southeast or west-southwest. The denomination is characterized by mainly clay-calcareous soils formed during the Pliocene epoch (roughly 5.3 million to 2.5 million years ago), rich in fossils, with clay or limestone dominating specific subzones of the denomination. With Ruchè, the effect of terroir is alive and well, and depending on where the grapes are grown, wines can be very different. Better still, with a little practice, it is easy to tell where the grapes used to make a specific wine were grown. An initial breakdown of the Ruchè di Castagnole Monferrato wines is into those of Castagnole Monferrato and those of Scurzolengo. The wines of the former are often said to be fruiter, bigger, and fleshier; those of the latter are lighter-bodied, more fragrant, and higher in acidity, but this is not really so even though the soils of Castagnole Monferrato are richer in clay than those of Scurzolengo, which are more limestone based and are instantly recognizable by their intensely whitish color (*terre bianche,* in Italian). All these municipalities have areas where soils are either richer in clay or richer in limestone. In fact, a more accurate interpretation of the Ruchè production area's terroir is arrived at by knowing that the denomination's landscape is characterized by two main hillside ridges. The first ridge runs from the town of Castagnole Monferrato in the direction of Scurzolengo and Portacomaro, and is characterized mostly by the white-colored chalky limestone soils. Specific, very high-quality Ruchè crus in this area are Bricco della Rosa and Montiò. It is in this area that one finds well-known estates such as Cascina Terra Felice, Crivelli, and Luca Ferraris (the latter, at roughly 130,000 bottles a year, being the second-largest producer of Ruchè di Castagnole Monferrato). Montiò is essentially a Crivelli monopole; Bricco della Rosa is the name of Terra Felice's Ruchè wine. A second, more northerly ridge runs from Castagnole Monferrato in the direction of the municipalities of Grana, Montemagno, and Viarigi. Here soils are darker, fresher, poorer in organic matter, and richer in clay, with wines showcasing greater flesh and structure. Estates such as Livio Amelio and Evasio Garrone are located near Grana, where vineyards grow at the denomination's highest altitudes and the Ruchè wines are remarkably light-bodied and refined (think of wines from the Grana area as being the Margaux of the denomination); at lower altitudes, between Castagnole Monferrato and Montemagno, there is the Montalbera estate. (At something like 240,000 to 300,000 bottles a year of various Ruchè wines, Montalbera is by far the largest producer of Ruchè di Castagnole Monferrato.) At slightly lower altitudes still (but still around 220 meters above sea level) there are the famous vineyard areas of Santa Eufemia, where the Vigna del Parroco is located. Interestingly, some white soils in the area have reddish-hued veins; unlike in other cases, where the reddish color is due to high iron concentrations, here the color is the result of a strong presence of clay. These soils offer an interesting lesson in terroir-related cause and effect: should you look carefully at the ground you are walking on and at the rows of vines above, you will realize that the Ruchè vines planted on the reddish streaks are roughly three times more vigorous (showing fatter trunks and more copious, intensely green foliage, for instance) than the rows of vines growing parallel to their side on the whitish-only soil. (To the best of my knowledge, there is no one attempting microvinifications of these single rows of vines.) Last but not least, at the southern tip of the denomination, there are highly draining, mostly alluvial, sandy soils that can pose problems in droughty years; but when the weather cooperates, this is where some of the most structured of all Ruchè wines are made; a very famous cru of this area is Poggio Varolino. Though it is interesting and at times even illuminating to taste Ruchè wines from specific soil types, wines made from blends of Ruchè grapes can be thrilling, too: for example, the vineyard used to make the Ruchè di Castagnole Monferrato Bric d' Bianc by Luca Ferraris (despite the wine's name referring to white soils only) actually straddles both the white soils and the darker clay soils of the denomination; for this reason, he now calls the wine "Sant'Eufimia."

Ruchè di Castagnole Monferrato's Best Crus

I began tasting Ruchè wines assiduously in 2001, and over the years I have carefully catalogued where the grapes used to make each one had grown. What follows is a precise list of the best crus or sites for the Ruchè grape variety. Some of the names of the sites listed are not used currently on wine labels, but just knowing that the grapes were grown within their boundaries gives you a ton of information: first, you know that you are in for a potential treat, and second, you know a little something about the wines as well. (Each of these sites speaks of a specific soil type and terroir admirably well.)

Bricco della Rosa (white soils; near Castagnole Monferrato).

Castlet (dark clay soils; near Montemagno and Viarigi).

Montiò (white soils; on the way from Castagnole Monferrato toward Portacomaro; Montiò is a true grand cru for Ruchè).

Poggio Varolino (mostly sandy soils; completely removed from the Castagnole Monferrato center of the production zone, it is located in the southern reaches of the denomination, in the direction of Asti; very few vineyards are left in this part of the denomination, but in my experience, Poggio Varolino was a source of Ruchè grapes that gave great wines).

Ferraris Vigna del Parroco***PS.

Cantine Sant'Agata 'Na Vota***, Cantine Sant'Agata Pro Nobis***, Crivelli***, Dacapo***, Ferraris Opera***.

Amelio Livio**, Bersano San Pietro Realto**, Bosco Tommaso**, Caldera**, Garrone Evasio & Figlio**, Gatto Pierfrancesco**, La Miraja**, Marengo Massimo**, Montalbera La Tradizione**.

Bava*, Cantina Sociale Di Castagnole Monferrato*, Capuzzo Renato*, Tenuta Goggiano*, La Fiammenga*, Montemagno*, Poggio Ridente*, Tenuta Dei Re*, Tenuta Della Cascinetta*.

Sagrantino

THE GRAPE VARIETY

Whether or not the ancient *hirtiola* grape variety described by Martial and Pliny the Elder as typical of the territory of Mevania (once located in the area between Bevagna and Montefalco, the main towns in the Montefalco Sagrantino DOCG) was Sagrantino is unclear. Sagrantino has become famous anyway, and characterizes today an Italian region, Umbria, much as Chianti does Tuscany and Barolo does Piedmont. Sagrantino was once most famous as a sweet wine; the DOC Montefalco Sagrantino was created in 1977 for the *passito*. (The DOC guidelines for dry Sagrantino wines were created a few years later.) Both wines have been since elevated to DOCG status (in 1992). There are a number of different nursery clones available, some of which have been developed by individual estates, such as Arnaldo Caprai's "Cobra" clone (appropriately enough, given its name, I find the wines marked by almost toxic tannin levels). Sagrantino's polyphenol endowment can be limiting: wines can be very tough and astringent, and in my experience, no amount of cellar time will reduce the stubbornly tannic personality of less successful wines to any great extent. Hence, managing Sagrantino's tannins is everything. The variety does not like water stress, and actually needs good water availability because of its huge canopy (differently from, for example, Sangiovese, where leaves are fewer and more evenly distributed on the plant). Sagrantino shows above-average vigor but is not particularly productive; plenty of sunlight and heat are necessary for it to ripen properly, but it is important that these make their presence felt gradually rather than all at once or in short, intense bursts. This is because the main problem with Sagrantino is that it accumulates sugars quickly, which makes reaching optimal physiologic maturity a problem (though achieving technological maturity is not). According to Filippo Antonelli, of the Antonelli San Marco estate and back for a second round as president of the Montefalco consortium, the majority of Sagrantino's polyphenols are in the skins and not the pips, so enological choices depend largely on this reality. If one chooses to harvest early, long macerations are out because the pips are never going to be ripe (this is less of a problem with Sagrantino than it is with Montepulciano, for example, for most of Sagrantino's tannins derive from the skins), but the quality of what little pip tannins there might be does pose a problem when long macerations (more than two to three weeks) are contemplated. Recent work from San Michele all'Adige on the tannic structure of Sagrantino has led some producers (such as Antonelli–San Marco) to harvest ten to fifteen days earlier, and use shorter fermentation times, lower temperatures, and no oak. (Not by chance, Antonelli has named this wine "Contrario," which means "opposite," since the Sagrantino variety is not usually used to give light-bodied wines of early appeal and easy accessibility.) In general, Sagrantino does best on clay soils, but those with high loam content also give good results. The variety is sensitive to soil magnesium deficiency and can suffer from desiccation of the stem, especially with the SO4 rootstock. When well made, Sagrantino wines offer lovely, intense black-fruit and violet aromas and flavors that linger nicely, almost always complicated by a (more or less) delicate herbal note that can add freshness. Not surprisingly, scientific studies have looked at Sagrantino's polyphenol makeup. It appears that chain esters such as ethyl 2-methyl butanoate (the methyl ester of butyric acid, it is also known as methyl butyrate) are responsible for some of the fruit aromas of Sagrantino. This may come as a surprise given that methyl butanoate smells mostly of apple and banana, and Sagrantino is a red grape; however, the presence of ethyl cinnamate helps augment the note of small red fruits. Sagrantino's floral aromas are instead owing to the presence of terpenes (Di Stefano et al. 2009). However, anybody experienced in Sagrantino wines knows that the strong (at times very strong) herbal/green streak and notes of balsamic oils and pine needles are even more characteristic. The latter are due to the presence of α-terpineol, which is still active after many years of cellaring. Dehydration techniques lead to degradation of the polyphenols in the skin (especially) and the pulp (Ribeiro

Cunha de Rocha 2013), and this is why some producers choose to use a small portion of air-dried grapes even in their dry red wines.

SPECIFIC TERROIRS

Sagrantino di Montefalco

More than in other regions in Italy, in Umbria there is an uncanny (and for wine lovers, useful) correspondence between DOC and DOCG boundaries and the regional geology and pedology (soil science). Would that analyzing terroir in Italy were so easy all the time. Moving northeast to southwest, soils in Umbria vary from the calcareous-rich soils of the Apennine range, to the sandstone of the pre-Apennine chain of hills and the Trasimeno basin, the fluviolacustrine deposits of the valleys snaking through the mountain and hillside ranges, the deposits of marine origin hugging the course of the Paglia River, and the volcanic-ignimbrite deposits of Lake Bolsena. On this note, discussing Umbria's Sagrantino variety and understanding its terroir is made relatively easier, since the cultivar does not grow in significant numbers anywhere outside of the immediate Montefalco denomination. The Montefalco Sagrantino DOC covers the territory of the commune of Montefalco, and parts of the territories of the communes of Bevagna, Castel Ritaldi, Giano dell'Umbria, and Gualdo Cattaneo. As a general rule, the geology around Bevagna and Montefalco is more complex than that around Gualdo Cattaneo. According to Calandra and Leccese (2007), the soils of the Montefalco denomination are mostly alluvial clay, turbidites, sand, and conglomerates; these authors failed to find any correlation between the various types of soil and grape or wine quality—a finding confirmed by Palliotti et al. (2007). De Ribeiro Cuhna (2013) reported that soil organic matter is abundant in Montefalco (on average 1.8–2.2 percent) and the CEC is 14.3 to 31.5 milliequivalents per one hundred milligrams.

In fact, the entire Montefalco Sagrantino denomination coincides with the fluviolacustrine deposits of the rather unfortunately named Bastardo Basin (Bacino di Bastardo, in Italian) located between the Montefalco hill to the west and the Martini Mountains to the east. Tectonic movements occurring during the Plio-Pleistocene (a geological pseudo-period occurring from roughly five million to about twelve thousand years ago; see table 2 in the appendix) caused the lifting of the earth's crust at the eastern slope of the Martini mountain range, leading to the formation of the Montefalco hill and the Bastardo Basin roughly two million years ago. As correctly pointed out by Gregori (1988), the boundaries of the Montefalco denomination correspond to those of the lacustrine deposits of the Bastardo Basin. Furthermore, there is a clear association between the characteristics (and, dare I say it, the quality) of specific Montefalco subzones (terroirs) and the morphotectonic events that led to the formation of said terroirs. For instance, the fluvial deposits dragged downstream by rivers and brooks hurtling down the slopes of the Martini Mountains and the newly formed Montefalco hill mixed with the originally pure deposits of lacustrine origin in the basin below. This activity led to the formation along the basin's coasts of soils that were not clay-dominated but instead characterized by complex deposits made up of gravel, clay, and sands over a highly calcareous bedrock. (Montefalco soils have an alkaline pH ranging from 7.8 to 8.2.) Montefalco's best Sagrantino terroirs are those that are located upon the coastal areas of the ancient basin; according to Gregori (2006), this unique geologic feature contributes heavily to the unique aroma and flavor profiles of Sagrantino wines made in the Montefalco production area (and I would tend to agree). The climate of the Montefalco denomination is of the continental type; January is the coldest month (3.8°C average annual January temperature from 1960 to 1991) and July the hottest month (25.3°C average annual July temperature from 1960 to 1991). July is the driest month, November the wettest. Annual rainfall in the Montefalco DOCG is roughly 650 to 700 millimeters per year. Vines are now planted at roughly five thousand vines per hectare; it used to be just sixteen hundred vines per hectare only twenty years ago. (For this reason, and because of the onslaught of Esca disease, most of the vines in the Montefalco denomination have been replanted recently, so vine age is very low overall.) The most common training method nowadays is the cordon spur, but, as late as into the 1980s, it was the traditional *palmetta* system, with more than one fruiting cane superimposed on others—a system not ideal for heavy planting densities, because the higher, fruit-bearing branches created shade for those below (and in fact, planting densities in *palmetta* vineyards were roughly seventeen hundred vines per hectare). The Arnaldo Caprai estate investigated training methods most suitable for the Sagrantino variety at length beginning in 1989, and published subsequently (Valenti et al. 2004). While the Cordon de Royat, Guyot, and *palmetta* systems were compared initially at five different planting densities and each comparison was made on five different rootstocks in different experimental vineyards, further research was extended to seven different training systems. It is research such as this that led to the cordon spur and Guyot training and pruning systems being implemented, at least in part, all over Montefalco.

There has been quite a jump in Montefalco's wine production in the twenty-first century, with the number of hectares under vines climbing from 122 to 522 in the first five years of the new decade; there are 610 hectares under vine nowadays (2016 data). Over the same time span, the number of bottles also increased greatly (from roughly six hundred thousand to two million per year). The unique beauty of the Umbrian and Montefalco landscape, the fact that Sagrantino grows only there, the emergence of Trebbiano Spoletino as a high-quality white grape variety, and the ability to tame the Sagrantino variety's at times ferocious tannins led many outside investors to the area, including the likes of Cecchi, the Lunelli family of Trentino's famed sparkling-wine estate Ferrari, and Lungarotti, all of whom have set up estates here.

The Sagrantino Subzones

Sagrantino di Montefalco can be made in the territory of five Umbrian townships: in all of Montefalco, and in parts of the territories of Bevagna, Castel Ritaldi, Giano dell'Umbria, and Gualdo Cattaneo. Bevagna is the northernmost commune in the denomination. Montefalco is to the east, Gualdo Cattaneo to the west (a small section if its territory runs north up next to Bevagna), Castel Ritaldi to the southeast, and Giano dell'Umbria to the southwest. In my experience, there are clear-cut differences in wines made with grapes grown in at least some of the Montefalco townships. For example, the Sagrantino wines of Montefalco are more structured yet refined (when the tannins are kept in touch), those of Bevagna more floral and relatively gentler but with a very good core of acidity and minerality not found in all Sagrantinos, and those of Castel Ritaldi and Gualdo Cattaneo softer and readier to drink. Some of my empiric observations stem from comparing wines tasted blind in polyphenol zonation studies begun at the end of the 1990s, when the accumulation of polyphenols in Sagrantino grapes was studied relative to the terroir the grapes grew in (first by Andrea Gozzini in his 2000 university thesis and then in 2006 by Valenti et al.). Other studies investigated how best to manage Sagrantino's polyphenols not just by viticultural techniques but by enological ones as well (Valenti and Nicolini 2001). Results showed clearly that there were significant differences both in the total buildup of polyphenols and in their rate of rise, and this even in viticultural areas that were close to each other. These differences in Montefalco Sagrantino wines are easy to pick up because, for the most part, Montefalco estates all own vineyards immediately around the winery; furthermore, the denomination never had the grape buyers and brokers (*négociants,* if you will) of Barolo.

However, defining Sagrantino di Montefalco's subzones strictly by township is too limiting. To define the Montefalco production area more precisely, it is best to further divide it into ten districts, each of which can potentially give distinctive wines.

NORTHWESTERN SUBZONE (BETWEEN BEVAGNA AND GUALDO CATTANEO)

1. Bevagna North: The northernmost subzone, extending between Limigiano in the north, Castelbuono to the west, Cantalupo to the east, and Torre del Colle to the south. Estates worth knowing: Bellafonte, Dionigi, Fattoria Colsanto, Tenuta Castelbuono.

2. Rotolone: Immediately west of Bevagna, with mostly east-facing vineyards at about 450 meters above sea level. Estates worth knowing: no wineries are located here, but many estates own vines.

3. Colcimino: Located south of Bevagna. Soils here are poor, mainly marly arenaceous, and offer very good drainage; this subzone can suffer water stress in droughty years. The harvest occurs earlier than in other parts of the denomination; vineyards lie at three hundred to four hundred meters above sea level. In my opinion, this subzone is characterized by wines of greater elegance than those of other subzones, but poorly made wines can be lean and thin. Estates worth knowing: Villa Mongalli.

NORTHEASTERN SUBZONE (BETWEEN BEVAGNA AND MONTEFALCO)

4. Arquata: Very close to and southeast of Bevagna. For my money, this is the greatest of all wine crus of Montefalco. Wines are powerful yet exceptionally nuanced and balanced, long and complex. Estates worth knowing: Adanti, Antano Milziade.

5. Belvedere: Immediately to the southeast of Arquata, vineyards here lie at generally lower altitudes. Good clay content of the soils and plenty of sunlight. Estates worth knowing: Arnaldo Caprai, Ruggeri, Virili.

6. San Marco–Pietrauta: A roughly rectangular swath of land south of Bevagna and Colcimino, straddling the imaginary line that joins Gualdo Cattaneo in the west and Montefalco in the east. This is the only subzone that straddles two sectors—San Marco to the west and Pietrauta to the east. There is generally

more clay in this subzone, and so wines have generally more structure. The vineyards are exposed south-southwest and are located especially between three hundred and four hundred meters above sea level. Estates worth knowing: Antonelli–San Marco, Colle Ciocco.

7. Montefalco–San Clemente: Farther southeast still from Belvedere and immediately northeast of the town of Montefalco. Vineyards are mainly east-facing; the subzone makes fresher, less tactile wines mainly because of the exposure. (If poorly made, they can be the leanest and thinnest of all Montefalco Sagrantinos.) Estates worth knowing: Romanelli.

8. Montefalco South: That part of the Montefalco commune's territory facing toward Spoleto, which includes the towns of Cerreta, Casale, Gallo, and Turrita. Vineyards lie at around 300 to 380 meters above sea level (below the town of Montefalco) and in my experience give very decisive wines with plenty of personality; high acidities and tannins combine for a real palate presence. Estates worth knowing: Bea, Lungarotti, Pardi, Tabarrini; farther east, in the direction of Casale, Perticaia and Scacciadiavoli; farther west, at the hamlet of Fabbri, the estate of Tenuta Rocca di Fabbri.

9. Castel Ritaldi/Alzatura: Where the hamlets of Torre Grosso, Torvenano, and Colle del Marchese are located. Castel Ritaldi itself was born of the fusion of three smaller medieval hamlets: Colle del Marchese, Castel San Giovanni, and Castel Ritaldi itself. Alzatura is a subdistrict within the district, located farther north, between the territory of Castel Ritaldi and that of Montefalco. Estates worth knowing: Tenuta Alzatura (Cecchi), Colle Capoccia.

10. Giano dell'Umbria: This is the area facing in the direction of Todi; it is located between the towns of Marcellano to the northwest, Le Torri to the southwest, and Montecchio to the southeast. It comprises what is almost a west-southwestern sector, since it is quite far west of Giano dell'Umbria. Soils here are very rich in clay, and these wines are among the most powerful of the whole Montefalco denomination. Estates worth knowing: Colpetrone, Terre dei Capitani.

Most likely, there are other wine areas capable of giving distinct wines within the five Montefalco subzones, but neither have I built up enough experience with the wines of each to want to venture to identify them, nor have wines been made in each long enough for reliable assessments to be made. In fact, it is probably unfair on my part not to recognize as a separate winemaking district the hillside that slopes from the Attone River toward Giano dell'Umbria. (This is the slope of the valley that looks toward where Cerreta, Turrita, and Casale are located.) Wines from this potential district are lighter-bodied, mainly because of a very cool climate: though not far removed from Bevagna or Montefalco, the area commonly experiences snow and frost. (Should you be as interested in the physical factors determining terroir in wines as I am, perusing the climate charts and temperature tables of Montefalco's last thirty years will confirm the cool climate of this district.) I actually think this district may be better suited to white wine production, and for this reason I do not include it here since this chapter is dedicated to Sagrantino. Moretti Omero, a big believer in organic wines, would be the example of a solid producer who owns vines in this district.

Adanti***, Antano Milziade Colleallodole***, Antonelli Chiusa di Pannone***, Antonelli ***, Caprai Collepiano***, Caprai 25 Anni***, Fratelli Pardi Sacrantino***.

Bocale**, Perticaia**, Fratelli Pardi**, Ruggeri**, Sportoletti**, Tabarrini**, Villa Mongalli**.

Sangiovese

THE GRAPE VARIETY

Sangiovese is the most common wine grape of Italy (plantings are twice those of Trebbiano Toscano, which sits in second place on that list), and it is also one of the ten most-planted grape varieties in the world. Sangiovese's parentage is unclear as yet, with different research papers reporting contrasting results. While one study reported that Sangiovese is a Ciliegiolo × Calabrese Montenuovo crossing (Vouillamoz et al. 2007), another determined that Ciliegiolo is an offspring of Sangiovese and Muscat Rouge de Madère (Di Vecchi Staraz et al. 2007). Therefore, as I wrote in *Native Wine Grapes of Italy* (D'Agata 2014a), while we already knew that Ciliegiolo was a relative of Sangiovese (Crespan et al. 2002), we are left with the issue of whether Ciliegiolo is a parent or an offspring of Sangiovese. At the present state of knowledge, we simply do not know where the truth lies. Sangiovese offers plenty of opportunity to study terroir: since it is Italy's most planted cultivar, there exist hundreds of different Sangiovese wines in Italy, many of them remarkably different from each other. The diversity in aromatic and flavor profiles of such wines is, however, most often the result of Sangiovese being blended with other cultivars (whether the addition of other grapes is declared or not). Therefore, it is imperative to know what Sangiovese can and cannot deliver, or run the risk of being made to believe that such differences are due to some hypothetical "terroir" effect.

There are numerous synonyms of Sangiovese. (For a very long list, please refer to my book *Native Wine Grapes of Italy*.) Of these, Sangiovese Grosso and Sangiovese Piccolo were once in vogue to describe what were believed to be the two main biotypes of Sangiovese, but this is incorrect, because there are over one hundred morphologically different Sangiovese wine grapes and so the *piccolo* and *grosso* distinction should be abandoned. Furthermore, it was once believed that Sangiovese Grosso was typical and exclusive of Montalcino, but we now know that not to be true, either. According to Bertuccioli (2004), Sangiovese's skins are rich in linalool and α-terpineol, which contributes to the floral aromas typical of wines made with it, while the pulp is richer in norisoprenoids like vitispirane, TDN, ß-damascenone, and actinidols, which account for the notes of camphor, flint, and incense that develop as the wine ages; nerolidol and citronellol determine instead a dried-orange-peel nuance after a few years of bottle age, but the presence or absence of this descriptor may depend on the choice of yeasts used (Vernocchi et al. 2011). However, it is the color of Sangiovese wines that is the variety's single distinguishing feature, since it is at the core of a simple fact: monovariety Sangiovese wines are never extremely dark in color because the variety cannot deliver that sort of hue. So any supposedly 100 percent Sangiovese wine you may be served that is inky or black is a travesty. The anthocyanidin (grape pigment) profile of Sangiovese is rich in malvidin, cyanidin, and peonidin, and there are virtually no conjugated anthocyans (anthocyanidin molecules bound to a sugar molecule), which characterize instead varieties such as Merlot and Cabernet Sauvignon. Cyanidin and peonin are relatively pale-colored pigments that oxidize easily, so any variety that has them in spades simply cannot give wines that are purple-ruby or darker. More importantly, Sangiovese's lack of conjugated anthocyans (acylated or cumarated) means that finding them in higher-than-normal percentages (and in Sangiovese, they cannot be more than 1 percent of the total anthocyanidin concentration) is an impossibility in truly monovariety Sangiovese wines. Numerous studies have shown this to be the case—such as, for example, a recent highly interesting report by Costantini et al. (2010). Among other findings, it confirmed that soil type can modify the anthocyanidin patterns in Sangiovese wine, but never, as expected, does a soil type push this grape variety to express inky-black hues. Even more to the point, the study showed that absolute values in each of the five anthocyanidins can vary with soil type (but the ratios do not): for example, more cyanine and peonine (two of the five main pigments in wine grapes) were expressed in wines born from grapes grown on soils rich in organic matter and calcarenites. (Calcarenite, the carbonate equivalent of sandstone, is a clastic limestone characterized by sand-grade particles, one-sixteenth to two millimeters in diameter [Folk 1959]; A. W. Grabau, one of the world's greatest sedimentary geologists, had originally used the term "calcarenite" in his 1903 carbonate classification system based on the size of the limestone granules.) By contrast, wines made from Sangiovese grapes grown on *alberese* soils (a typical soil of Chianti Classico; see "The Geography and Climate of Chianti Classico" below) richer in stones and with limited water reserves expressed much lower concentrations of these two anthocyanidins; Sangiovese grapes grown in those *alberese* soils with high water-retention capacity (a lesser-quality type of soil that is associated with lower buildup of sugar in the berries) accumulated even less of these two anthocyanidins. Concentrations of the other three main anthocyanidins (delphinidine, petunidine, and malvidine) were never higher than those of cyanidin or peonidin, no matter what soil the grapes grew in. (And remember that cyanidin and peonidin are the easily oxidized, unstable pigments that account for Sangiovese wine's garnet-tinged light red color.)

This observation clearly underscores how the genetics of the Sangiovese grape variety, at least in this respect, supersedes any effect linked to the physical aspects of terroir (such as soil type): in other words, no matter where you plant Sangiovese, it will continue to produce wines of the same ilk (i.e., of a relatively pale red, even orange-tinged color) it is genetically programmed to give. In general, the best soils for Sangiovese are not very fertile, are well drained, and have minimal water retention especially from the time of color change of the berries until the ripening period. Clearly, Sangiovese does not help itself any by being both demanding and very irregular in its production outcomes: light, juicy wines and big, complex ones are common from the same site depending on many factors (degree of work in the vineyard, exposure, altitude, rootstock, and more). Given that the variety is an early budder and late ripener, both ends of the growing season can be a source of never-ending fun for growers (my tongue firmly in cheek as I write that), and it requires a warm (but not hot) climate. For example, in cool Chianti Classico (where snow is common in the winter), the best wines are often made by planting vines on south- and southwest-facing slopes between 250 and 500 meters above sea level. Relative to climate's role in inducing site specificity in Sangiovese wines, in Tuscany the variety ripens better in generally warmer, more southerly Montalcino than it does in Chianti Classico. It ripens even more in Tuscany's coastal Maremma region, where a drier, hotter climate and shorter growing season produce broader wines that are, however, also plagued by too much alcohol and overripe aromas, causing them to be lacking in the proverbial finesse of Sangiovese's best wines. Therefore, cool climates where large diurnal temperature differences and long growing seasons are common are essential to achieving success with Sangiovese; warm summers and autumns are just as necessary for Sangiovese to ripen properly.

Numerous studies have analyzed the biochemical parameters in Sangiovese grapes grown in different vineyards and the wines made from each. Gatti et al. (2011) specifically analyzed the relationship between Sangiovese, soil type, and the quality of resulting wines. The researchers characterized twenty-five sites on the basis of different geological origin, and analyzed the stilbene content of each wine made in the different sites to determine whether geological origin and soil composition had any effect on the concentrations measured. A positive relationship was found between site elevation and *trans*-resveratrol concentration in the Ravenna area, as well as between altitude and *trans*-piceid level in the Forlì and Ravenna areas. Furthermore, the richer the active lime content of the soils, the higher the stilbenes in the wines. The researchers concluded that site suitability for the cultivation of Sangiovese might be successfully evaluated by the grapevine's production, or lack, of significant concen-

trations of stilbenes. Egger et al. (1998) reported a statistically significant correlation between changes in soil (especially), the resulting grape makeup, and Sangiovese wine quality. The previously mentioned 2010 study by Costantini et al. also found vintage characteristics to be less important in determining Sangiovese wine quality, possibly because the three years in which the tests were conducted (1992, 1993, and 1994) were marked by uniformly poor weather patterns. (Of the three, only 1993 is remembered as a decent vintage.) In that study all the terroirs examined produced very good Chianti Classico wines of early appeal meant to be drunk young; by contrast, differences in terroirs became more relevant when ageworthy wines were the goal. Overly dense planting leads to shading of the vines and problems of under-ripeness, so 5,000 to 7,000 plants per hectare is now the suggested vineyard density of choice, but I point out that some of Italy's greatest Sangiovese wines are made from old vines planted at rather low, but traditional, densities of 2,700 to 3,300 plants per hectare. Of course, how much of that is due to the presence of old vines (a lot, would be my guess) and how much to other factors of terroir is up to debate. Various training systems all seem to work well with Sangiovese, including short ones (*alberello* or bush vines; spur cordon), mixed (Guyot, *capovolto*), and long pruning (*tendone* or canopy; *archetto*), depending on the prevailing climate and soil fertility of the site. Clearly, since Sangiovese is usually planted on stony soils, it is best to prune the vines short, but long pruning can be used in valleys and on cool soils. There are numerous suitable rootstock choices: in Italy at least, 420A is the one most commonly used, but Paulsen 775 is optimal when Sangiovese is planted on clay, since it helps reduce the tannic clout of the wines. Rootstocks like SO4 and Kober BB5 allow for too much vigor; by contrast, where there is little or no risk of extended drought, less vigorous rootstocks such as 161–49 and 101–14 are the pick of the litter, especially with a high-density plantation.

By contrast, 110R is used where droughty conditions are relatively common.

THE ART OF THE BLEND

Clearly, it is easiest to judge which terroirs are most suitable to Sangiovese by analyzing monovariety wines. However, there are Sangiovese blends in which it is still relatively easy to discern terroir-related differences: almost invariably, these are wines in which the blending cultivars are the historic, traditional partners of the Sangiovese grape. Canaiolo Nero or one of the two Malvasia Neras, and to a lesser extent one of the four true Colorino varieties (I refer you to *Native Wine Grapes of Italy* for an in-depth discussion of the Colorino group of grapes) and Mammolo, partner best with Sangiovese. This is because, unlike international varieties such as Cabernet Sauvignon and Merlot, these native grapes complement rather than overpower Sangiovese; and the wines still end up speaking clearly of Sangiovese and its specific terroir despite their presence. After over thirty years of extensive wine tastings and visits to Sangiovese production areas, I am absolutely convinced of the validity of this observation. Really, it is hardly surprising: after all, native grapes have historically been partnered with Sangiovese for centuries, and obviously there are reasons why this was, and is, just so. Though a monovariety Sangiovese from a quality terroir is a thing of beauty, I also find that, more often than not, a small percentage of these native grapes usually helps bring out the best Sangiovese has to offer. This is especially true of Canaiolo Nero, which is Sangiovese's perfect soul mate: after all, it was not by chance that the inventor of the Chianti formula, Bettino Ricasoli—a man of great culture (and Italy's first ever prime minister, by the way) who was very aware of the existence of the Cabernets and Merlot—believed that adding two-tenths of Canaiolo Nero to the Sangiovese blend was the right thing to do. (For accuracy's sake, I point out that Ricasoli's recipe for Chianti was seven-tenths Sangiovese, two-tenths Canaiolo Nero, and one-tenth Malvasia

Bianca Lunga, and that he did not wish for Trebbiano Toscano to be included—a position that further makes the man seem a genius.) Canaiolo Nero appears to accentuate Sangiovese's floral personality and to reduce the tannic clout of the finished wine while adding a juicy quality. I compare Canaiolo Nero's role in the wine blend with that of a cofactor (i.e., a molecule that helps biochemical reactions work more efficiently; vitamins are outstanding examples of cofactors that help our bodies run better and more smoothly). In its presence, a Sangiovese wine often tastes better than it would without the Canaiolo Nero. Clearly, it is not only a matter of which other grape is blended with Sangiovese, but also how much. Giuseppe Mazzocolin, director of the famous Felsina estate in Chianti Classico, states matter-of-factly that adding even 1 percent of Cabernet Sauvignon or Merlot to a Sangiovese wine will immediately modify it in a recognizable manner. (In his charming Tuscan-accented English, he says flatly that the "Sangiovese gets ruined" by even that small an addition.) Giovanni Manetti, another of Italy's most knowledgeable Sangiovese experts and the owner of Fontodi, a Chianti Classico estate just as famous and qualitative as Felsina, has repeatedly told me the same thing over the years. Paolo De Marchi, owner of the outstanding Isole e Olena estate in Barberino Val d'Elsa and responsible for what is generally acknowledged to be perhaps Italy's single best massal selection of Sangiovese (known as "selezione De Marchi"), does not mind adding up to 8 percent Cabernet Sauvignon in poor vintages to help Sangiovese out (by providing a little backbone, alcohol, and even fruit). However, he admits to being aware that in so doing he changes the organoleptic characteristics of his wine; this is why he chooses to do so only when weather conditions force his hand. Actually, I have routinely sat down over the years with graduated cylinders and bottles of monovariety Sangiovese and wines made with international grapes to study the effect these have on a 100 percent Sangiovese wine. (I normally use Merlot wines.) Through repeat trials, I have found the presence of Merlot to be practically always recognizable at 10 percent of the total—the point being not that such blends were not good; often they were lovely wines, but at more than 10 percent Merlot of the total blend, the wines stopped speaking of Sangiovese and told a different tale. At that point, inferring about the terroir I was tasting was next to impossible: for the wine spoke of chocolate, cocoa, and a very deep, almost opaque, purple-ruby hue, and not of any specific somewhereness. In an effort to verify whether these observations held any real merit, I took the experimentation one step further. Courtesy of the kindness and patience of Maurizio Castelli (one of Italy's foremost consultant winemakers and Sangiovese experts) and Castello di Radda, I repeated the same experiment in blinded fashion. The blind tasting included one glass of the blend that would be sold as that vintage's Chianti Classico; one glass of the estate's best Sangiovese wine, which would become the Chianti Classico Riserva; and a series of glasses in which increasing percentages of Merlot had been added (1 percent, 5 percent, 10 percent, 15 percent, 20 percent, and 30 percent, respectively). Arthur Conan Doyle–like, I went sleuthing about and found the 20 percent and 30 percent solutions immediately recognizable as not 100 percent Sangiovese; identifying the 5 percent, 10 percent, and 15 percent solutions requires a few more minutes of focus. (There was in fact no 7 percent solution.) In all honesty, I think that a 5 percent addition of Merlot wine or any other international grape will escape most tasters but that most everyone with a little experience should always pick up additions of 10 percent or more. Clearly, such an experiment leaves a lot to be desired from the scientific point of view. (For one, it was not a double blind, because although I did not know which glasses contained the wine to which Merlot had been added, I did know that it had been added to some.) But it reinforces impressions that I have built up over the years. Interestingly, Lamberto Frescobaldi of the famous Frescobaldi wine estate has told me that in regards to Italian Syrah, he finds that 30 percent needs to

be added to Sangiovese wines for the Syrah to become obvious—most likely as a result of the fact that most Italian Syrahs are not (yet?) concentrated and deep enough to add much to a blend (possibly because of still-young vines).

In the ultimate analysis, what matters most is that Sangiovese, when taken care of, doesn't need any help at all from international varieties to give great wines, just as great red Burgundies or Napa Cabs don't. Furthermore, my laboratory experiments clearly showed that the 10 percent, 20 percent, and 30 percent blends did not speak either of Sangiovese or of Radda (the latter having such a distinctive terroir that it should be identifiable in wines made from grapes grown there) because Merlot was all that was being tasted. The point is that those who have a truly great terroir to work with and know what they are doing (like Mazzocolin, Manetti, and De Marchi) have no need to add any other grape variety to their Sangiovese: all those who would like for international varieties to be added to Sangiovese wines that have to be monovariety by law (and therefore clamor to change the current production guidelines) do so because they have a less-than-great terroir. It really is that simple.

SPECIFIC TERROIRS

The boundaries of the Chianti Classico territory correspond (more or less) to that tract of land identified in the famous 1716 edict by Grand Duke Cosimo III de' Medici. This was one of the first official delimitations of a wine-producing zone anywhere in the world. At the beginning of the twentieth century, spurred on by high demand, "Chianti wine" began to be made outside of the official production zone, which of course did not sit well with those whose vineyards grew or whose estates were situated within the historic zone. And so in 1924 the producers of the originally delimited zone banded together to form the Consortium per la Difesa del Vino Tipico del Chianti e della Sua Marca d'Origine (which translates to something like the "Consortium for the Defense of the

Typical Wine of Chianti and Its Original Brand"). The logo chosen to represent the association was that of the well-known *gallo nero* (or black rooster), the symbol of the Lega Militare del Chianti (the "Military League of Chianti"), which as most wine lovers know was reproduced by the very famous painter Giorgio Vasari on the ceiling of the Salone dei Cinquecento in the beautiful Palazzo Vecchio in Florence. In 1932, a ministerial decree added the word *classico* to the name of Chianti to differentiate those bottles of wine made within the original boundaries of the Chianti production zone from all those made outside it and labeled either generically as Chianti *tout court* or Chianti from specific zones (other than the classic or historical one), such as Colli Aretini or Colli Fiorentini. Unfortunately, there are very big differences in the topography, climate, and soils of these many various Chianti denominations, most of which are far too large and diverse to hold really any meaning. I have been studying areas like the Chianti Colli Fiorentini for about ten years now and have come away convinced that it is pointless to look for unifying elements of terroir there: the area is simply too vast. Even worse, producers do not get along especially well or don't speak enough to each other, and so you have the dead-end situation of one estate making wine with Sangiovese and Colorino, the one next to it mostly with Syrah, and another just a little farther away with Sangiovese and a (very) healthy dollop of Cabernet Sauvignon. And so the wines made reflect individual producers' creativity rather than any sense of place. There are of course delightful wines to be had in non–Chianti Classico zones, such as those of the Colli Fiorentini's Fattoria di Lucignano or the Colli Senesi's Poggio Salvi. But the Chianti Colli Senesi was never taken seriously, and was long abandoned or used as a second-tier, fallback denomination. Only recently does it appear that the reality of what producers have and have not valued is slowly starting to sink in. Steps may at last be undertaken to better characterize the wines of the area. Of all the non–Chianti Classico denominations, only Chianti Rufina can boast a terroir of a quality comparable to that of Chianti Classico and an easy-to-grasp set of characterizing features that make for a very logical, altogether different subzone of Chianti. (See the Chianti Rufina section below.) In my view, it is these two areas of the "Chianti galaxy"—Chianti Classico and Chianti Rufina—that are worthy of a discussion in terms of Sangiovese, wine, and terroir.

Chianti Classico

Make no mistake about it: today, Chianti Classico is where you'll find some of Italy's greatest red wines. A big reason for this is that the wines are finally showcasing the great and unique results possible thanks to the interaction between Sangiovese and Chianti Classico's terroir. Line up ten Chianti Classico wines of some renown today and you'll see nothing but a range of bright red or dark red hues, with aromas and flavors that are mostly variety-accurate (violet, red currant, sour red cherry, tea leaf, and licorice—or, in other words, Sangiovese). Do that with the same wines from the 1990s and early 2000s and get ready to admire *tutti i colori del buio*.

The Geography and Climate of Chianti Classico

The Chianti Classico denomination is limited to the east by the Monti del Chianti range, which separates it from the Val d'Arno (or Arno River valley, in English). At 892 meters, Monte San Michele is the highest peak in what is, despite the lofty-sounding *monti* name above, little more than a chain of hills that are, however, rather impervious, and covered with trees. (What little vines there are grow at significant heights of 400 to 600 meters above sea level.) However, these hills do provide some defense against harsh continental weather—for example, cold easterly winds; and the Arezzo's Pratomagno mountain range, located east of the Monti del Chianti and rising higher than they do, further helps seal off Chianti Classico's eastern border. The southeastern corner of the production zone is more open, thanks to the upper Arno River valley basin, and this is in fact a much sunnier part of Chianti Classico. The rest of the Chianti Classico borders are: to the south, flatlands leading up to the city of Siena; to the north, flatlands leading up to the city of Florence; and to the west, the valleys of the Pesa and the Elsa Rivers.

There are very big differences in the topography, climate, and soils within the Chianti Classico denomination: obviously, at seventy-two hundred hectares under vine, it really could not be otherwise. And so Chianti Classico boasts numerous differences in exposures, inclines, soils, altitudes, and microclimates; and these factors combine, along broad lines, to give a very characteristic look and feel to the single townships of the production zone and their wines. However, it is not an easy task to go about recognizing somewhereness in a glass of Chianti Classico. One of the main problems is to obtain homogeneity of production, in that there are hills everywhere, with different exposures and inclines that often change within the confines of the same vineyard, and so there are different-quality grapes in each section of the rows of the vineyards. In general, the wines made in each of Chianti Classico's nine townships are potentially very different from each other, and each glass of wine does broadcast a general, if not always highly specific, sense of place. In short, much as the more knowledgeable wine public at large is becoming increasingly comfortable with distinguishing between Barolos, say, of Monforte and of Castiglione Falletto, so it should be with Chianti Classicos from Gaiole and Castelnuovo Berardenga. Most Chianti Classico vineyards are planted between 250 and 500 meters above sea level, though in theory vines could be planted as high up as 700 meters above sea level. With climate change, we may yet come to see this happen: even now Chianti Classico wine estates are planting new vineyards with eastern and northeastern exposures (when not even full north—something that would have been unthinkable only fifteen years ago) and at higher altitudes. Whereas in the 1970s vineyards at 350 meters above sea level were the most sought after and were thought to be at an ideal altitude to have Sangiovese ripen fully, today most estates are looking to plant vineyards at about 500 meters above sea level.

The climate of Chianti Classico varies greatly from northern to southern sectors, but even in these days of climate change, come winter, it is surprisingly cold in Chianti Classico. Not surprisingly, January and February are the coldest months of the year, and snow is not at all uncommon then. However, climate has changed, and now both budbreak and harvest have moved up in most vintages by at least a couple of weeks, if not more. Of course, an earlier budbreak leaves the vineyards exposed to the vagaries of unexpected late spring frosts, such as those of 1997 and 2001. Those two well-known episodes helped make better-than-average wines overall in Chianti Classico (by naturally reducing crop yields), but since the spring frost can also damage buds slightly, the ensuing uneven ripening in such years will lead to hardly stellar wines at less-than-attentive and less-hard-working wine estates. In contrast to the winter, summers can be hot and dry in Chianti Classico. July and August are the warmest months of the year, and days with temperatures soaring above 35°C are not rare (Amato and Valletta 2017). Diurnal temperature variations are high, however, and especially so, in most vintages, in the period immediately prior to harvest. In fact, diurnal temperature variations are highest in Chianti Classico's eastern section closest to the Monti del Chianti and farthest from the Tyrrhenian Sea to the west. Rainfall in Chianti Classico is highest in the autumn, especially in November and December (159 and 124 millimeters of rain, respectively). April is the third-wettest month of the year (93 millimeters) while, at 26 millimeters, the driest month of the year is July (Cantini et al. 2015). In general, strong winds and hail are rare in Chianti Classico (but not unheard of: the area immediately south of Castellina's Fonterutoli hamlet is a well-known hail hot spot, and in general, Radda and Gaiole are hit by hail slightly more often than other Chianti Classico subzones). Interestingly, and not dissimilarly from the Camigliano area in southeastern Montalcino, the Poggibonsi area is reached by the hot and humid winds blowing in from the Tyrrhenian Sea, and thus salt deposition can result in vine damage after budburst has occurred. Of all the factors that help define a specific wine terroir, besides grape variety, climate is probably the single most important in Chianti Classico—an area of almost interminable tight winding roads, hills, steep climbs, woods, clearings, and seemingly perennial shade. Unlike in Barolo or Barbaresco, where entire hillsides are covered with nothing but grapevines, in Chianti Classico vineyards often give the impression of having found a spot literally stolen from the forest, and small vineyards are often planted in similarly small clearings surrounded by trees. This is especially true of the northern part of Chianti Classico (starting immediately after Panzano) and the central portion (in the territories of Gaiole and Radda), the areas of which are reminiscent of a subalpine habitat. By contrast, the southern Chianti Classico opens up toward Castelnuovo Berardenga and then Montalcino, and is airier and sunnier, with little in the way of forests encroaching on the vines. In fact, Chianti Classico's communes exhibit much bigger differences in heat units than they do in soil. For example, the Winkler index average of Castellina from 2010 to 2016 is 1947 (this number is the average Winkler index that I calculated using the single Winkler indices of each of these seven vintages); Greve's average Winkler index for the same time period is 1732, and Gaiole's is smaller still, at 1604. I point out that the altitudes of the recording stations where the annual Winkler indices for each township were recorded (and then averaged out by me) are fairly similar: Greve, at 254 meters above sea level; Castellina, at 286 meters above sea level; and Gaiole, at 360 meters above sea level. Now factor in the average annual precipitation rates of each of these townships—Castellina, at 770 millimeters per year; Greve, at 920 millimeters

per year; and Gaiole, at 970 millimeters per year—and it should become immediately clear that Castellina is the warmest and the (relatively) driest of the three communes under exam; and that Greve falls somewhere between the extremes of Castellina and Gaiole. As useful as this analysis is, I stress that it is only a baseline evaluation of the climatic conditions of these three townships. For example, the vineyards located at the higher reaches of Castellina do not have the same warm and dry microclimate as the rest of the commune; but along general lines my breakdown remains valid, if for no other reason than that the average altitudes of the communes are loosely comparable: Castellina, at 403 meters above sea level; Greve, at 415 meters above sea level; and Gaiole, slightly higher at 478 meters above sea level. Without bogging this chapter down with too many facts and figures, I will just add that Radda's climate and altitude data are very similar to Gaiole's, while Castelnuovo Berardenga's data are similar to Castellina's (the average temperatures in a large part of Castelnuovo Berardenga's production zone being actually higher than those of Castellina). In any case, such data are extremely useful and correlates clearly with the style of each commune's wines: there is no doubt that the wines of Gaiole and Radda resemble each other more than they do those of Castelnuovo Berardenga. Clearly, in order to further characterize the wines of each commune, the soil type of each has to be analyzed as well. Unfortunately, it is not possible to assign a specific soil type to each commune because of considerable overlap, and so subdividing Chianti Classico's soil diversity into broad bands of different geologic origin and placing the different townships within each of them, as can be done instead with Barolo and Barbaresco, is not possible. Broadly (very broadly) speaking, there are three main soil types in Chianti Classico: *alberese, galestro,* and *macigno,* as defined by a 1924 statute of the Gallo consortium (Giannetto 2008). *Alberese* is a mix of whitish calcareous marls and yellowish calcareous deposits—a very hard, marly stone not unlike limestone; its name derives from the Latin word *albus* (meaning white) and refers to the stone's whitish color because of its very high calcium carbonate content. It is not unlike the *albariza* of Jerez, but Chianti's *alberese* is darker, more compact, and richer in stones. *Galestro*, highly friable (unlike *alberese*), is a metamorphic medium-grained clay schist made of flaky layers (what geologists describe as "foliated"). Though often said to be "shaley" (schist and shale are related), true *galestro* is more schistous than shaley; *galestrino* is the term that ought to be used to describe Chianti's finer-grained, shale-like soils. *Macigno* is a mix of sands and compacted sands but is more accurately defined as one of the layers in a flysch of turbiditic origin (the geologic deposit of a turbidity current) formed during the Oligocene and Inferior Miocene (Migliorini 1943; Kuenen and Migliorini 1950). It has a lower calcium carbonate content than both *alberese* and *galestro*, and its soils are characterized by excellent drainage (even too good drainage in droughty hot years). These three have always been viewed as being the heart of the soils that characterize true Chianti Classico, while areas at the periphery of the denomination (for example, areas to the northwest of Mercatale Val di Pesa, southwest of Castellina, and south of Castelnuovo Berardenga) are of a different (sedimentary) origin, and some experts do not think they should be included within the Chianti Classico boundaries (Rezoagli 1965).

The Issue of Subzones

Though history has dictated otherwise (and I have a very healthy respect for history and tradition), the irony is that Chianti Classico, more than most other wine denominations in Italy, really is, or ought to be, a cru smorgasbord. The combination of a grape variety that translates sense of site well and a plethora of extremely different soils, exposures, slope gradients, and more make Chianti Classico a highly interesting place for wine-terroir lovers. Chianti Classico extends over roughly seventy thousand hectares (to be precise, 71,800 hectares), of

which about ten thousand are under vine; of these, seventy-two hundred hectares are officially registered to produce Chianti Classico. Nine townships can produce Chianti Classico: Castellina in Chianti, Gaiole in Chianti, Greve in Chianti, and Radda in Chianti, the territories of which fall completely within the boundaries of the Chianti Classico production zone; and parts of the townships of Barberino Val d'Elsa, Castelnuovo Berardenga, Poggibonsi, San Casciano in Val di Pesa, and Tavarnelle Val di Pesa. (In the latter case, using the Val di Pesa suffix rather than just Tavarnelle is a good idea, in order to avoid confusion with the almost identically spelled and sounding Tavernelle, which is a hamlet of the Montalcino denomination.) Hopefully, the name of the township where the grapes were grown to make a Chianti Classico will soon be found on the labels, much as Pauillac and Margaux appear on the labels of Bordeaux wines. A step such as this would undoubtedly help Chianti Classico, since non-Italians can hardly be expected to know where towns such as Roddi or San Gusmè are located (in the Barolo and Chianti Classico production zones, respectively). Not indicating subzones where they can be easily seen (i.e., on the front label) seems like a lost opportunity for producers to better broadcast where they are, where their wines are from, and what they are about.

In fact, the concept of crus was never a strong one in Chianti Classico; historically the goal was always to promote an estate's wine thanks to the family's name or the estate brand—in other words, more in the manner of Bordeaux than Burgundy. In any case, to generate a system of subzones in Chianti Classico will not be easy, for a variety of reasons. An absence of historical reference points and official delimitations will make it hard in today's politically charged and commercially driven world to define the boundaries of each subzone in the most accurate manner possible. Furthermore, only four townships allowed to make Chianti Classico fall completely within the Chianti Classico production zone, leaving the discussion open as to what to do with the likes of

Barberino Val d'Elsa or Poggibonsi, parts of whose territories fall outside the Chianti Classico production zone. Nesto and Di Savino (2016) propose to incorporate those townships whose territories do not fall entirely within the denomination under the banner of San Donato in Poggio (a town that is close to all the communes that do not fall entirely within the denomination's borders), which seems like a perfectly reasonable option to me. Last but not least, identifying the subzones will be made that much more difficult by the existence of high-quality hamlets (or township "fractions": *frazioni,* plural of *frazione,* in Italian) that would like their "independence": these include Greve's Lamole and Panzano, and Gaiole's Monti. These hamlets give very different wines from those of the main subzone. (For example, the wines of Lamole have virtually nothing in common with those of Greve or Panzano.) The problem with hamlets is that for the most part, they have not yet been officially delimited, and so they lack precise geographic boundaries on which to hang one's subzoning hat.

Chianti Classico Subzones, Sectors, Subsectors, Districts, and Crus

The territory of Chianti Classico falls within two provinces: Florence (30,400 of Chianti Classico's total 71,800 hectares) and Siena (the remaining 41,400 hectares). The division between a Chianti Classico of the province of Florence and one of Siena is important. A hillside ridge running west from Gaiole (essentially where the Badia a Coltibuono estate is located) toward Radda and then Castellina conveniently hugs the geographic boundary separating the province of Florence to the north and the province of Siena to the south. This ridge is responsible for creating a boundary that is more than just an administrative one, because the wines from the northern sector are very different from those of the southern part. Because most cold winds blow in from the northwest, it is the northern sector that is colder and rainier, while the southern sector, especially its lower subsector, is characterized by much greater luminosity and heat units. Both sectors can be further subdivided into subsectors; for example, the southern sector can be divided into an upper southern subsector (essentially the territories of Radda and Castellina) and a lower southern subsector (of which Castelnuovo Berardenga is the most important territory). The northern or Florentine sector is characterized topographically by two river valleys, that of the Pesa and the Greve Rivers, which run roughly parallel to each other (plus the Monti del Chianti in the easternmost part of this sector). The northern sector can be divided into various subsectors: one subsector is that of the town of San Donato in Poggio, which is west of the Pesa, and another is that of Panzano, which is to its east (or to the west of the Greve). East of the Greve we have the northern sector's last subsector, characterized by the sparsely planted viticultural territories of the towns of San Polo (more north) and Lucolena (more to the east). I think the area of San Polo, today little known but not so in the past, is a site potentially capable of delivering high-quality Sangiovese wines. In fact, the territory of Panzano is so small and precisely delimited, and its wines so specific to the area, that Panzano should be more accurately referred to as a district (see below).

Relative to the southern sector, its upper subsector stretches just above and just below an imaginary line that joins Radda to Castellina; the area immediately below this line is that of Lecchi, which, given the specificity of its wines, ought to be considered a district of its own. The lower southern subsector is divided in two by the Arbia River: the territories of Castelnuovo Berardenga and San Gusmé are to the east, while the less well-known Vagliagli territory is to the west. Last but not least, in each subsector and district there appear to be specific cru or single vineyard areas of note, but these have never existed as such in Chianti Classico. And so today most "crus" you hear about are nothing more than estate single vineyards; however, these are not crus in the real sense of the word; rather, they are mostly just single vineyards that the individual estates believe to be special but that have no real history or tradition to back up such claims (a problem generalized to all of Italy, as we have seen).

The Chianti Classico Subzones

Focusing on single townships, Castellina has three predominant types of soil: *alberese* along with the *formazione di Sillano* (according to Merla and Bortolotti's in-depth 1967 study, the latter appeared in the Superior Cretaceous and Inferior Eocene, and is a mix of gray to olive-green calcareous marls, brown and gray marls, calcarenites, and other rock formations); *macigno toscano,* the least common of Castellina's three main soil types; and blue clays (which are quite frequent). By contrast, Castelnuovo Berardenga has two predominant soil types of sedimentary and alluvial origin (dating back to a more recent geologic origin): the Chianti Classico typical mix of *alberese* and *galestro,* and the loamy sands and yellow-reddish clays with a high content of tufa (this commune's most typical soil type). This soil strongly characterizes Castelnuovo Berardenga's wines, which tend to be fuller-bodied than most other Chianti Classicos (especially when the vines grow on sedimentary soils—as opposed to alluvial soils, which give lighter-bodied wines) and in fact are the closest in style to the wines of Montalcino (and for this reason, I find it a shame that the Chianti Colli Senesi was completely forgotten and a practically abandoned denomination by producers until recently; instead, it has potentially one of the more easily recognizable terroir signatures of all the non–Classico Chianti denominations). Greve is mostly characterized by *alberese* soils; Panzano's bedrock is mainly a bioclastic shelf limestone that is hard and compact, with a high calcium carbonate content called *pietraforte* that was formed in the Cretaceous period (Carmignani and Lazzarotto 2004) and is not to be confused with the younger geologic formation (born in the late Oligocene to early Miocene) called *pietra serena.* (Throughout history, the former was used as a building and load-bearing material, the latter for mainly decorative purposes.)

Radda has a very complex geology, with *galestro* (here characterized by a particularly strong calcareous content) more present at the midrange altitudes while *macigno toscano* (with a stronger presence of sand) is more common in Radda's higher reaches. The basic soil formation is known as *formazione di Monte Morello* (mostly *alberese* and *galestro*), with elements of the *formazione di Pietraforte* and *di Sillano*. In the ultimate analysis, it is only by combining information about the soil types, microclimates, and altitudes of each vineyard site that quality inferences can be made relative to Sangiovese wine production in each site.

It is worth knowing that not all the Chianti Classico communes carry the same weight as far as volumes of Chianti Classico produced. The percentage of land under vine in each commune giving rise to Chianti Classico wines is as follows (Enoproject 2017 data):

Castellina in Chianti: 20.62 percent

Greve in Chianti: 18.61 percent

Castelnuovo Berardenga: 17.27 percent

San Casciano in Val di Pesa: 15.34 percent

Gaiole in Chianti: 12.76 percent

Radda in Chianti: 8.54 percent

Tavarnelle Val di Pesa: 3.28 percent

Barberino Val d'Elsa: 3.08 percent

Poggibonsi: 0.5 percent

Of the nine official townships, a broad generalization might be that those linked to the best Chianti Classicos are Barberino Val d'Elsa (where estates such as Castello di Monsanto and Isole e Olena are located); Castellina (where Tenuta di Lilliano, Rocca delle Macie, and Fonterutoli are found); Castelnuovo Berardenga (where you find the fantastic wines of Felsina and Castell'in Villa); Gaiole (Badia a Coltibuono, Castello di Ama, Castello di Volpaia, Capannelle, Rocca di Montegrossi, and San Giusto a Rentennano are all there); Greve (with a world-class list of estates including Fontodi, I Fabbri, Le Cinciole, and Vecchie Terre di

Montefili, among others); and Radda (where Monte Vertine has made, and still makes, some of not only Italy's greatest red wines, but the world's). Of course, there are fine wines made in the other townships, too.

So what are the wines of each commune like? According to superstar wine consultant Lorenzo Landi, who works with numerous Chianti Classico estates in different communes and so is well equipped to make statements of broad scope on the matter, Chianti Classico offers a spectrum of wines. At one extreme are those of Castellina and Castelnuovo Berardenga (the most powerful wines, with the latter having a touch more opulence); at the other extreme are those of Gaiole and Radda (the most refined wines). Greve's wines fall somewhere in between those two opposites. Another interesting and learned point of view is that of Maurizio Castelli, another Italian star winemaking consultant, who understands Sangiovese like few others do: he has been at Badia a Coltibuono practically all his life and was the historic winemaker at Castello di Volpaia during the time the estate made its greatest wines. He believes that Radda makes the most elegant wines of all, wines of such refinement they can taste almost lean. In his view, Radda's wines are usually the most penalized in blind tastings, with those of Gaiole following closely behind in what could be defined as the "classification of the unlucky." Simply put, the two communes make nonflashy wines that can be easily overlooked by inexperienced tasters in favor of fleshier, jammier wines. Another Sangiovese superexpert is Franco Bernabei, whose office is in Panzano's pretty if small city center: he has been the winemaker at Felsina and Fontodi in Chianti Classico (and of Selvapiana in Chianti Rufina) ever since I can remember. His views are that Panzano can offer wines combining power, velvet, and refinement, while the wines of Castelnuovo Berardenga showcase an opulence that is not found in the wines of any other Chianti Classico commune. And now, it's my turn: in my opinion, the characteristics of the wines of each Chianti subzone and their most important crus are as follows.

BARBERINO VAL D'ELSA AND POGGIBONSI

The town of Barberino Val d'Elsa, which gives the subzone its name, was founded in the thirteenth century. The subzone itself is located in the west-central part of Chianti Classico, and extends over the hills of the Elsa and Pesa river valleys. Though soils are rich in conglomerates and stones, it is nearly impossible to generalize about the wines; the range in wine styles from this subzone is too vast, and it's difficult to identify features that would help anyone (myself included) recognize wines from this subzone in any blind tasting. For sure, the southeastern reaches (where famous estates Castello di Monsanto, Castello della Paneretta, and Isole e Olena are found) closest to the border with Castellina give full-bodied, savory wines that are some of Chianti Classico's largest and richest (second only to those of Castelnuovo Berardenga). The irony is that this small slice of Chianti Classico is probably as close to a grand cru terroir as any in Chianti Classico, but the rest of the subzone does not give wines of the same depth and complexity. Some estates worth seeking out: Casa Emma, Castello della Paneretta, Castello di Monsanto, Cinciano, and Isole e Olena.

CASTELLINA IN CHIANTI

Located in the western south-central part of the Chianti Classico zone, Castellina (for short) is mostly a large amphitheater that looks in the direction of Monteriggioni, Colle Val d'Elsa, Siena (partly), and the valleys of the Arbia, the Elsa, and the Pesa Rivers. A large subzone, it contains at least two famous wine districts within its boundaries: Fonterutoli and Castagnoli. Castellina can potentially deliver some of the most balanced of all Chianti Classicos, but its wines are some of the hardest to organize into a stylistic whole because altitudes, soils, and exposures vary greatly in the subzone. In general, Castellina, because of its warm and dry microclimate and the mostly *alberese* and calcareous soils, tends to give Chianti Classicos of sneaky power and relatively deep color, but also high in acidity and refinement. (The calcareous presence in the soil is very important in allowing Castellina's wines to have that acidity and that elegance.) I believe the best vineyards of Castellina lie mostly between 250 and 500 meters above sea level and look toward the Val d'Elsa. The key about the wines of Castellina is that the acidity levels are such that the intrinsic power of the wines is held in check and that the wines are more perfumed than one might expect. Some estates worth seeking out: Bibbiano, Casale dello Sparviero, Castellare di Castellina, Castello di Fonterutoli, Lilliano, and Rocca delle Macie.

CASTELNUOVO BERARDENGA

Castelnuovo Berardenga owes its name both to a Frankish nobleman called Berardo di Ranieri (who settled in the area in the second half of the tenth century) and to the decision of the general council of Siena to build a castle there (in the area of Poggio in Frati) in 1366. While wines from Castellina seem to hint at underlying power but rarely come across as especially big wines, this is not the case with the wines of Castelnuovo Berardenga, which everyone recognizes as powerful and fleshy. However, this assumption is only partly true. In fact, the Castelnuovo Berardenga subzone has the shape of a butterfly, with the eastern and western "wings" separated by Gaiole's southern sector (where Monti is located) snaking downward between the two. In my opinion, the wines of the western wing, which looks toward Radda, are generally lighter-bodied, but succulent and juicy (such as those of Borgo Scopeto, Fattoria di Petroio, and Villa di Geggiano); those of the eastern wing (where world-famous estates such as Felsina and Castell'in Villa are located) are deeper, richer, and ultimately more complex. The typical Castelnuovo Berardenga combination of warm microclimate and tuff-rich soils leads to a slightly earlier harvest in most vintages and fuller-bodied, more opulent wines that have a tactile, fleshy mouthfeel unlike that of any other Chianti Classico. Specific wine crus of Castelnuovo Berardenga include San Gusmè and Vagliagli. Some estates worth seeking out: Borgo Scopeto, Castell'in Villa, Fattoria di Petroio, Felsina, Le Bonce, San Felice, and Villa di Geggiano.

GAIOLE IN CHIANTI

Gaiole in Chianti is first mentioned in 1086, and by 1215 it was an important marketplace; more than other Chianti Classico subzones, it is dotted with castles and medieval fortifications (Meleto, Monteluco, San Polo in Rosso, and Vertine, among others). The subzone is located in the southeastern part of Chianti Classico and overlooks the upper Val d'Arbia. The wines of Gaiole (for short) are probably the hardest to assign to a specific wine style, since the topography, altitudes, and soils of this large subzone vary greatly. Gaiole is also the subzone that contains a specific district where outstanding Chianti Classico wines are made: Monti, the home of rich, dense, tannic Chianti Classicos that have more refinement and less power than those of Castelnuovo Berardenga. I can actually make a very good case that this subzone probably boasts a few other distinct districts as well: Fietri (very light wines) and Lecchi (richer but still graceful and nervous wines) are examples. In general, Gaiole produces wines that are more vertical and shut down in the first few years of life, but age gracefully and long. Not all Gaiole wines are just so, and the subzone has its share of richer and thicker wines, especially when produced from grapes grown near the border with Castelnuovo Berardenga. Some estates worth seeking out: Badia a Coltibuono, Capannelle, Castello di Ama, Rocca di Montegrossi, and San Giusto a Rentennano.

GREVE

Greve is located in the northernmost part of the Chianti Classico just a short car's drive from Florence. (Should you decide to rent a car in Florence and drive to Greve, be aware of numerous speed traps along the way and resident-only streets through which you should not drive unless you enjoy receiving fines in the mail.) It is another subzone that harbors many different crus and slopes within its boundaries, but generally speaking, Greve wines fall in between those of Gaiole and Castellina in style. Two Greve districts stand out especially, because their wines are so different from all others made in the subzone, and in all of Chianti Classico: Lamole and Panzano. Some estates worth seeking out: Filette di Panzano, I Fabbri (Lamole), Villa Calcinaia (Greve), Fontodi, Le Cinciole, and Vecchie Terre di Montefili (Panzano).

RADDA IN CHIANTI

The Radda (for short) subzone is situated in the east-central part of the Chianti Classico, in the upper Pesa Valley. Here the river (but it's more like a big stream) does a ninety-degree turn such that its right bank (the best for vineyards) looks due south—a compensating factor for the relatively high altitudes of most of Radda's vineyards. Its wines (especially those of its upper hillsides) are the sleekest and most refined of all Chianti Classicos (Lamole's are, too, but lack the underlying power of most of Radda's wines.) However, this depends on where in the Radda subzone the grapes grow. For example, in specific parts of Radda (for example, the northernmost quarter of the subzone) the presence of *macigno toscano* (and therefore of sand) in the soil means the harvest occurs earlier than you might expect in vineyards planted at such high altitudes (such as five hundred meters above sea level). A look at the landscape and the maps tells you that from a geographical perspective Radda's subzone could be subdivided into four roughly parallel sections running east–west (the high or arenaceous section, the Pesa bank, the central section, and the Arbia bank at the southernmost point of the Radda subzone), but I am not entirely convinced that wines from the four areas clearly reflect where the grapes grew. In any case, Radda's wines are Chianti Classico's easiest to misjudge when young, when they are often mistakenly thought to lack concentration. This impression is heightened in wines made with grapes from specific parts of the Radda territory (such as where some of the vineyards of Zonin's Castello d'Albola and of Castello di Volpaia's vineyards are located), where the combi-

nation of a very specific limestone-type soil and high elevation makes for especially high-acid, very steely red wines of real purity but not much flesh. However, this really is a mistaken impression, for the wines fill out in time and prove very ageworthy—wines that are of mind over matter, if you will. An estate worth seeking out: Monte Vertine.

SAN CASCIANO VAL DI PESA

The farthest north of all of Chianti Classico's communes, San Casciano Val di Pesa is located in the northwestern part of Chianti Classico. The Val di Pesa runs north–south, parallel to the Valle della Greve, but is sunnier and broader in its topography, and in general I find the wines from this area to be easily accessible in an endearing lighter, easy-drinking style. Some estates worth seeking out: Fattoria Ispoli and Podere La Villa.

TAVARNELLE VAL DI PESA

This subzone is located in the west-central part of Chianti Classico, on the hills dividing the Elsa from the Pesa valleys. Though soils vary from richer (Badia a Passignano) to stonier (Poggio al Sole), the wines are characterized by generally early appeal and plenty of juicy fruit but with a sleekness that confers subtle refinement. These can be lovely wines whose sum is more than their individual parts. Some estates worth seeking out: Badia a Passignano and Poggio al Sole.

BENCHMARK WINES

(I will limit myself to a selection of three-star wines or this list would risk being much too long.)

Badia a Coltibuono***, Castellare di Castellina***, Castello di Ama Vigneto Bellavista***, Castello di Monsanto Riserva Il Poggio***, Felsina Riserva Rancia***, Fontodi Vigna il Sorbo***, I Fabbri***, Isole e Olena***, Le Cinciole***, Monteraponi***, San Giusto a Rentennnano***, Vecchie Terre di Montefili***, Villa Calcinaia***.

Chianti Rufina

Chianti Rufina has always been famous for the high quality of its wines. In 1716, this fact was officially recognized in the by-now-famous edict of Cosimo III de' Medici, grand duke of Tuscany. Rufina (with Pomino) was one of the four areas he identified officially as the best wine production areas of Tuscany, and its wines are still outstanding today. Chianti Rufina is located northeast of Florence and north of Chianti Classico. Chianti Rufina (or Rufina, for short) is by far the best and most interesting non–Classico Chianti denomination. It boasts a small but cohesive group of producers (about thirty) and a terroir that is very well defined, easy to grasp in its general outline, and characterized by unique Sangiovese wines. Despite its limited number of producers, the Chianti Rufina is not small (12,483 hectares total, of which 1,500 hectares are registered for DOCG production). It is the "highest of all Chiantis," as the consortium's slogan dictates, but the average altitude at which vineyards grow in the Chianti Rufina (roughly two hundred to five hundred meters above sea level) is actually not that high; however, the slogan is reasonable enough given that some vines do grow at the highest altitudes—in almost mountainous environments—of any Chianti denomination. (Near the town of Dicomano, in the northern Rufina, vineyards are planted up to seven hundred meters above sea level.) The denomination stretches along the summit of Mount Senario from the town of Dicomano in the northeast to Pontassieve in the southwest. The most important towns of the Rufina linked to specific subzones are Dicomano in the north, Pontassieve in the south-central part, Rufina in between Dicomano and Pontassieve, and Pelago to the southeast. It is the Rufina's location that creates much of its uniqueness as a territory and explains its wines. Differently from other Chianti denominations and Chianti Classico itself, Chianti Rufina is closer to the Apennines—the mountain range that runs down Italy's spine and divides Tuscany from Emilia-Romagna.

The Sieve River, which runs through Chianti Rufina, is also important. The combination of the proximity to the Apennines and the river's presence leads to especially cold nights and dramatically large diurnal temperature shifts. This means that Chianti Rufina is characterized by very slow and long-ripening growing seasons, with wines potentially of very good balance. Furthermore, the area's wealth of variable altitudes, soils, and topographies leads to the establishment of numerous different mesoclimates and terroirs that give radically different wines within the Rufina. The numerous pockets of vineyards created are so distinctive that one district, Pomino, is considered a separate area altogether and is not included within the denomination. (It is so cold there that Sangiovese does not ripen well: the area is best known for Pinot Nero, Pinot Bianco, Riesling, Chardonnay, and Sauvignon Blanc wines.) Most of Rufina is nowhere near as cold as Pomino, and some areas, such as those around Pelago, can be downright warm. Broadly speaking, Rufina's coldest months of the year are January and February, while the warmest is August. Rainfall peaks occur in November and in April; by contrast, the liquid refreshment is at its lowest in mid-January and July; drought in Chianti Rufina is rare. The essentially temperate climate boasts mean average temperatures of 14°C over the course of the year (Winkler index, 1700–2100; Huglin index, 2100–2500).

Chianti Rufina's soils are varied and include limestone, sand, *galestro-alberese*, marly clays, and others. Summarizing broadly, there are four major soil types: marly silt, marl and clay, marly clay, and chaotic and differentiated soils (Scienza et al. 2015). The first soil type is typical of the Dicomano area but extends as far south as Pomino; the yellow-gray or brown colored mix features very good water drainage. The marly clays are more typical of Rufina's southern reaches, characterized by yellow-brown alkaline soils that can hang on to water. (A fertile area, this part of Rufina absolutely requires low cropping.) Chaotic soils are found west of Pontassieve and Tigliano, and take their name from their highly varied composition (but mostly clay). Last but not least, the differentiated soils are those of Molino del Piano and Santa Brigida. Soil nature aside, though, the area's steep gradients and cool average temperature give Sangiovese a hard time, so wines can be especially edgy in their youth (but age and develop very nicely).

The Rufina Subzones

Chianti Rufina is characterized by three valleys. The first extends along the Sieve River; the second is in the southeastern part of the denomination, along the Pelago; the third is to the west of Pontassieve. As a result of these three valleys, there are six wine-related sectors in Chianti Rufina, defined by these three valleys, the Sieve River, and other natural landmarks.

1. The area that runs from the towns of Dicomano to Colognole, which should be divided into a northern and southern subsector: to the north, the Sieve Valley is narrower and cooler, very late-ripening, and with a long growing season. The high elevations (up to seven hundred meters above sea level) and extreme weather (there are easily nine hundred millimeters of rain a year) make for extreme viticulture and beautiful wines of uncanny refinement, offering bright red fruit perfume and penetratingly juicy licorice, floral, and tobacco flavors. These can be the most lithe and refined Sangiovese wines of Tuscany. Frascole is this area's best estate, ideally situated off in a side valley so its vines see less rain and more sun. (I find this estate's Chianti Rufinas to be remarkably Pinot Noir–like in some vintages.) The area is so extreme that another estate, Il Lago, resorted to air-drying part of its grapes to ensure it could make suitably ripe reds. The area around Colognole comprises the southern subsector and is located between Dicomano and Rufina. It is where I always seem to flush out more pheasants in the vineyards than anywhere else in Italy, and

is characterized by less-extreme weather, much greater luminosity, and open topography (there's little in the way of Dicomano's nooks and crannies), with slightly more sandy soils. Noteworthy acid bite but surprising flesh characterize graceful and ageworthy wines.

2. Londa: a narrow valley edging out in a northeastern direction, but lacking in wineries and any recent wine production of note.

3. The central part of Sieve Valley (right bank): wines of greater structure, less perfume, deeper hue, and tannins. Podere Il Pozzo, a true jewel created by Gianfranco Caselli (of the large Cantina Bellini; this is his pet project), Fattoria Lavacchio (owned by the Lottero family), and the Fattoria di Grignano (owned since 1972 by the Inghirami family of textile fame) are three outstanding estates.

4. The central part of the Sieve Valley (left bank): less morning sun in this part of the Rufina means a generally cooler climate and wines that speak of licorice, sweet spices, and savory plum—the latter an element not typical of wines from elsewhere in Rufina. The most famous estates here are world-renowned: Fattoria Selvapiana and Frescobaldi's Castello di Nipozzano.

5. The area that extends from Pontassieve to Pelago: the Pelago Valley has plenty of sunlight hours and so is fairly warm, with an average annual rainfall that is much lower than in other parts of Chianti Rufina. (It is therefore an early-ripening area.) Some of the denomination's richest, ripest wines are made here. (Clearly, they never reach Castelnuovo Berardenga levels of power; they are perhaps more similar to Panzano's.) Notes of cinnamon, dried violet, and dry spices in the wines are copious. I Veroni makes outstanding wines here (though I wish they would drop the use of Cabernet Sauvignon). This is the

part of Chianti Rufina that is most associated with historic, standout crus: I Sodi, San Martino, Bucerchiale, Camperiti, Altomena, Cafaggio, Nipozzano, and Virgilio.

6. Pian del Molino and Santa Brigida: due east from the Sieve River, this area produces wines that have more of a blue fruit note than is common in Chianti Rufina wines. Herbs and licorice are also typical findings. Castello del Trebbio is the best-known estate of the area; Frescobaldi owns vines at Poggio Remole, at slightly lower altitudes than Castello del Trebbio's vineyards.

BENCHMARK WINES

Fattoria Selvapiana Bucerchiale***PS.

Colognole***, Frascole***, Il Pozzo***, Lavacchio***, Nipozzano Vecchie Viti***.

Castello del Trebbio**, Grignano**, Nipozzano Riserva**, Travignoli**, Vetrice**.

Montalcino

Mons ilcinus, or "the mountain of the holm oak," has long been the wet dream of Italian wine *terroiristes* everywhere. Unlike Barolo and Barbaresco, it does not appear that an official listing of Montalcino's historic and less historic production areas (such as *menzioni geografiche,* or "geographic indications") is likely to appear anytime soon, so that gets everyone taking a shot at it (and at the denomination, but that's another story). Clearly zonation isn't of any interest in an area where a number of the larger producers (the majority of whose vineyards are planted on soils less than ideal for growing grapes with which to make high-quality mono-ovariety Sangiovese wines) are still trying to have the official production guidelines changed to allow Merlot and other international grape varieties into at least the Rosso di Montalcino blend (the *real* goal being, of course, to achieve this for the more important Brunello di Montalcino category). If many in Montalcino seem

hell-bent on dropping out of the great-wines-of-the-world sweepstakes, that's really of no concern to us; and anyway, the great, good, and poor viticultural areas of Montalcino are very obvious for all to see (and taste), as has been noted elsewhere (D'Agata 2009b; Galloni 2014).

My view is that creating meaningful, well-defined subzones is never a bad thing, for this increases curiosity about a denomination, encourages more listings in wineshops and on wine lists, and creates a sense of somewhere-ness for the wines that is always a plus, both culturally and commercially. Of course, you would expect me to say that, given I have written a book on wine terroirs; but I have always been in favor of establishing, and fostering, wine-township self-identity, though I realize it is a complex issue. And when it comes to Montalcino, it is even more complex than usual.

A Little History of Montalcino and Its Wines

The difficulties in launching an official zonation study of Montalcino are a direct result of the denomination's only very recent rise to wine fame, as I have had occasion to write before (D'Agata 2009; D'Agata 2012). Although Brunello di Montalcino is a relative newcomer to the ranks of world-famous wines, with barely 150 years of history, the area of Montalcino itself has a long and distinguished history as far as vineyards are concerned. For example, documents show that Niccolò di Nuccio bought a vineyard (as well as a chicken and pigeon coop) in Montalcino as early as 1364; and the Montosoli hill and its vines were being mentioned in medieval times. Initially the area's fame was mainly due to a sweet white wine made from a local biotype of Moscato Bianco (the wine known as Moscadello di Montalcino), but it's the reds that most excite people nowadays. Brunello made its entrance in society only in the mid-nineteenth century, thanks to Clemente Santi (his family name was not yet Biondi-Santi), who isolated what he believed to be a special clone of Sangiovese. Given the large berries and their brownish coloration, it became known as Sangiovese Grosso or Sangiovese Brunello. Around 1870, his grandson Ferruccio Biondi-Santi (the son of Clemente's daughter Caterina, who had married Jacopo Biondi) perfected the wine, and Montalcino has become synonymous with Sangiovese ever since. Well-made examples of Brunello di Montalcino rank with the world's best wines, mainly because parts of Montalcino's terroir are uniquely suited to Sangiovese, just as the Côte d'Or is magical for Pinot Noir and the Mosel for Riesling. This match made in heaven has resulted in Montalcino's rocket-like success. But this success is only a very recent one, and therein lie the roots of the problem that has caused modern Montalcino's unwillingness to legislate on matters related to terroir. Sometimes, too much success can be a bad thing. It was because of the wine's success that Brunello di Montalcino's production zone was thoughtlessly expanded over the last fifty years. Whereas at the 1933 Siena wine exposition there were only four Brunello wines (one of which was not even being bottled regularly at that time), there were twenty-five producers and eight hundred thousand bottles produced in 1975, and the numbers have continued to climb inexorably. There are now a whopping 250 producers of Brunello wine, and a just as whopping 6.7 million bottles of Brunello made (2004 vintage). The numbers are similar when you examine the hectares under vine: whereas in the mid-twentieth century there were roughly only 46.6 hectares of land specifically devoted to viticulture in Montalcino (Wasserman and Wasserman 1991), there are now a ridiculous 2,100 hectares from which Brunello can be made, plus another 250 hectares for the production of Rosso di Montalcino, Brunello's little brother. Clearly, it is impossible to make truly great wine from as large an area under vine as Montalcino's. In a telling example I have used before, consider that the whole of Burgundy's grand cru Musigny amounts to only 10.7 hectares, and all the twenty-four Chambolle premier cru vineyards add up to only sixty-plus hectares. Unfortunately, the

great success of Brunello attracted many large estates to the area (exactly what is happening in the Etna denomination nowadays) that were faced with two problems: the heart of the production zone (which is the most qualitative) was in the hands of small family-run estates whose owners had no intention of selling, and even if they had been open to the idea, disposable hectares were few and far between. Clearly, it is doubtful that those who make millions of bottles a year are really that interested in owning just a few scattered vineyards here and there, since the goal is always to reduce costs by owning very large contiguous swaths of land from which many thousands of bottles can be made at the lowest cost possible from machine-harvestable lower-lying flatland vineyards. So what happens in these cases is that the big boys move in, buy as much land as possible on the outskirts of a denomination, and then push political buttons and pull legislative strings to have the denomination enlarged so as to have their land included within the denomination. (Rumors are rampant that this is exactly what is happening currently on Etna, where the pressure to have the denomination enlarged is apparently enormous.) This course of action is unfortunately common (not just in Italy) but is fraught with peril. In the case of Montalcino, it has clearly blown up in many people's faces. This is because Sangiovese is a uniquely site-sensitive variety, and requires very specific climate and soil conditions to give a truly world-class wine (not to mention the right biotype, specific exposures, altitudes, and a whole lot more). Sangiovese simply does not give memorable results when planted just anywhere (as they have found out the hard way in California and elsewhere). Unfortunately, by expanding the Montalcino denomination's boundaries in all directions, too many new sites have been included that are loaded with heavy, clay-rich soils that are unsuitable for the production of great Sangiovese (but are just fine for Merlot; hence the push to change the 100 percent Sangiovese-only guidelines of Rosso and Brunello to include other wine grapes). Many locals and producers I have talked to over the years believe that only one-quarter to one-third of the current Montalcino production zone is ideally suited to making top-flight 100 percent Sangiovese wines. Clearly, if and when grown in suitable sites, Sangiovese does not need help from any other variety, as most enologists and producers point out. There is plenty of evidence that 100 percent Sangiovese wines (for example, the Chianti Classicos from Badia a Coltibuono, Le Cinciole, Felsina, Fontodi, Isole e Olena, Montevertine, San Giusto a Rentennano, and Selvapiana in Chianti Classico and Chianti Rufina; or the Brunellos from Baricci, Canalicchio di Sopra, Case Basse, Costanti, Franco Pacenti, Fuligni, Le Potazzine, Pian dell'Orino, Poggio di Sotto, San Filippo, and Salicutti in Montalcino) can effectively rival the world's best—something that far too many people conveniently seem to forget. It follows that, like it or not, outside of enological alchemy there are many estates in Montalcino that simply cannot make great Brunello wines. Good ones? Sure. Truly great? Forget it. I am not the only one who thinks that in Montalcino, terroir matters (Galloni 2016). And so in Montalcino the (huge) problem is that there really are areas in the denomination that are poor (for Sangiovese), and the wines made there nothing to write home about.

Montalcino's Terroir

The Montalcino production zone extends over roughly 24,000 total hectares, 15 percent of which (about 3,500 hectares) are currently under vine. These are subdivided into roughly 2,000 hectares from which Brunello is made, 250 hectares for Rosso di Montalcino production, and 900 hectares for Sant'Antimo and other different wines. The hill is located mainly (but not exactly) in the central part of the production zone, and the town is situated at 564 meters above sea level. (The highest point in the denomination is the Passo del Lume Spento, at 661 meters above sea level.) The hill gently slopes down to the valleys below, and in fact the entire production area is a nearly circular territory surrounding the hill and delimited by the valleys of the Asso, the Orcia, and the Ombrone Rivers; these rivers are the boundaries of the Montalcino denomination to the east, the southeast and south, and the west, respectively. Rosso and Brunello di Montalcino are both 100 percent Sangiovese wines; often, but not always, the former are just declassified Brunellos. Terroir speaks loudly in this case, for *rosso* wine made from non-Brunello vineyards is fairly easy to recognize in the glass: bright, juicy, and lovely, but without the supple texture and power that characterize the *rosso* wines made from Brunello vineyards. Precipitation in Montalcino is roughly seven hundred millimeters per year, and the rainiest times of the year occur in spring and the fall. I have obtained ten-year averages for the Winkler and Huglin indices relative to Montalcino: in the ten years from 2008 to 2017, the average Winkler index of Montalcino is 1973, and the average Huglin index is 2294. Interestingly, according to a 2005 study by Orlandini et al. correlating the meteorological data of Montalcino from 1961 to 1990, vintage quality is influenced most by increased heat accumulation and less so by excessive precipitation. A very interesting conclusion emerges from analyzing the climatic data and correlating them to my tasting notes and scores accumulated during the same time period that I spent writing for *International Wine Cellar* first, and *Decanter* and *Vinous* later. I find that the best vintages for Brunello di Montalcino are those with especially low Winkler indices: for example, the very underrated 2008 (Winkler index 1898), the outstanding 2010 (Winkler index 1787), and the classic 2013 (Winkler index 1960). The only outlier in the ten-year period under review is the generally poorly regarded 2014 vintage, the Winkler index of which is 1859 (and therefore not that different from the other three vintages). By contrast, the Winkler index of a disappointing (hot) year such as 2009 is 2044 (and it was 2197 in the extremely hot and dry 2003 vintage). This analysis suggests that there may be a higher likelihood of making better wines in

Montalcino when the Winkler index is less than 2000, but I would need to study more decades' worth of data in order to reach a more definitive conclusion. Generally speaking, Montalcino's soils vary from the limestone-rich *galestro* soils of the northern sector of the Montalcino production zone to the loamier, siltier sandy clays of the southern sector (though there is a huge sector- and district-related diversity, as we shall see below). The soils are not especially deep save for some areas at higher altitudes like Romitorio; soils need to be worked in order to allow roots to dig deep. Training systems throughout Montalcino are for the most part similar (there are always exceptions, of course); rootstocks are mostly 110 R (universally good in Montalcino) and 101–14, whereas SO4 is popular only with nurseries because of its higher rate of planting/grafting success.

The Montalcino Subzones

The first step in understanding Montalcino's terroir is to divide the production area into a northern and a southern sector, and then into four quadrants: the northeast, the northwest, the southeast, and the southwest, with the town of Montalcino at the center. Each quadrant represents a Montalcino production area identified with a township of origin (such as is the case with, for example, Bordeaux's Pauillac and Margaux, or Burgundy's Chambolle-Musigny and Vosne-Romanée). Torrenieri is the main commune in the northeast quadrant. I use Buonconvento as the identifying commune of the northwest quadrant, which has the lowest density of vines of the denomination, though this is not especially accurate. In fact, this quadrant lacks a major town with which it can be identified, and Buonconvento itself is located outside of the Montalcino production zone; however, this quadrant's eastern border is made up of the road leading to Buonconvento (the same road is therefore the western border of Montalcino's northeastern quadrant) and Buonconvento has long been associated with Montalcino wines (if perhaps not Brunello). Castelnuovo dell'Abate is the commune of the southeast quadrant, and Sant'Angelo (Sant'Angelo in Colle and Sant'Angelo Scalo) the commune of the southwest. Clearly this subdivision is indicative only, but it is helpful for novices since it is clearly linked to the individual style of Montalcino's wines.

Broadly speaking, Montalcino wines of the two northern quadrants reflect the cooler microclimate (lower average temperatures and cooling winds); they are sleeker, more floral and mineral, with generally higher total acidity levels. The wines of the southeastern sector are some of the broadest, most powerful Montalcino wines of all, while those of the southwestern quadrant vary from the rich but graceful wines of Sant'Angelo in Colle to the larger, often superripe wines of Sant'Angelo Scalo. The southern half of Montalcino has a Mediterranean climate, and the sea's influence is especially strong in Montalcino's southwestern sector. (These vineyards are only about an hour's drive from the Tyrrhenian Sea and, given the lack of natural barriers, are exposed to winds from the east.) No one quadrant routinely gives wines superior to those of the others: many sections of the Montalcino production zone make great Brunellos, though some do so more regularly than others.

Although the subdivision of Montalcino's territory into four quadrants is very helpful in providing baseline information about the wines, it is not the best way in which to go about characterizing Montalcino's terroir or its wines. Clearly, while the subdivision into the cooler northern sector and the warmer, sunnier southern sector is entirely acceptable (Montalcino is a hill, after all), the breakdown into four quadrants is a little too simplistic, because there are a number of specific wine-production areas within the denomination that are not taken into account with a four-quadrant subdivision. The specific subzones of Montalcino are therefore best identified by the towns and their territories for which we have enough climatic, geologic, and tasting data to allow us to characterize the wines well. These would be Torrenieri in the northeast, Montalcino in the center, and Camigliano, Castelnuovo dell'Abate, Sant'Angelo in Colle, Sant'Angelo Scalo, and Tavernelle in the south (with no identifying commune in the northwest). Given some highly specific and unique wines, a number of distinct wine districts within each township can also be identified (similarly to Chianti Classico's Lamole or Panzano). Some of the distinct districts of Montalcino have long and distinguished histories: the Canalicchios (Canalicchio di Sopra, Canalicchio, and Canalicchio di Sotto), Cerbaia-Rasa, Montosoli, and Pellagrilli in the northeast; Castiglion del Bosco and La Pisana–Collelceto in the northwest; and Sesta in the south. All these present enough geologic and altitude diversity to warrant being classified separately from the larger subzones. In summary, there are Montalcino subzones (Camigliano, Castelnuovo dell'Abate, Nordovest ["northwest"], Sant'Angelo in Colle, Sant'Angelo Scalo, Tavernelle, Torrenieri) and Montalcino districts (Argiano, I Canalicchio, Castiglion del Bosco, Cerbaia-Rasa, La Pisana–Collelceto, Montosoli, Pellagrilli, Sesta) within the subzones.

Every Montalcino commune boasts at least one great wine estate and interesting wines. Some of Montalcino's greatest Brunellos are made in the north (Baricci, Fuligni), but also in the southeast (Biondi-Santi, Pian dell'Orino, Poggio di Sotto, Salicutti, Stella di Campalto) and the southwest (Col d'Orcia, Cupano, Il Poggione). I hope to shed some light on the little-known communes (and their wines) on which there is a paucity of information available. For example, most of the various terroirs of the southwestern sector of Montalcino—Sant'Angelo in Colle, Sant'Angelo Scalo, Tavernelle, Argiano, and Camigliano—are lumped together, mainly because their supposedly warmer microclimate and proximity to the Tyrrhenian Sea give their wines a slightly homogenous bent, but this is an oversimplification that ignores local factors.

CAMIGLIANO

Camigliano, located at 234 meters above sea level in the extreme western reaches of the southwestern section of Montalcino (and not to be confused with the town of same name in Campania's Caserta province), has a highly different terroir from all other areas of the production zone. It is associated with idiosyncratic wines whose idiosyncrasies are not always understood, especially when young. The first document to mention Camigliano dates back most likely to A.D. 948, when a document from the Abbey of Sant'Eugenio mentions a sale by the Abbott Devoto to a *camugliano* (most likely the term used to indicate an inhabitant of Camigliano). Camigliano's vineyards lie at roughly 250 to 280 meters above sea level, but there are some flatland vineyards; according to a few expert specialists on organic and biodynamic farming who live in the area, this means that air-flow currents are at a premium in this subzone. The area has a Mediterranean climate, with warm, dry, salty winds blowing in from the sea to the east (about seventy kilometers or forty-four miles away), but vineyard exposures are varied. In this light, a Winkler index of 2000 is not even that high; I calculated the Winkler indices for Camigliano over seven years, from 2010 through 2016. The annual precipitation over the same seven years was 650 millimeters. Lorenzo Landi, who worked for many years at the Camigliano wine estate (it has the same name as the subzone), remembers how the numbers (Winkler index and annual rainfall) showed that Camigliano's climate was not that different from that of other Montalcino areas reputed to be slightly cooler, like Sesta. Rootstocks that help delay picking times seem to be the best-suited to this area. Camigliano's soils are highly variable, but are among the richest in clay and lowest in limestone of the whole denomination. Water stress is therefore a concern in this subzone, because this specific clay releases water with difficulty. Wines are never short on power (in fact they're downright chunky, in some vintages), and they can have relatively low acidity and lack freshness in years characterized by especially hot, dry weather. In fact, Camigliano's soils are especially rich in mineral elements (magnesium, potassium, calcium), and this factor, coupled with the marine influences, helps give the commune's wines a saline or briny (*salmastro,* in Italian) tang that is a hallmark of the Brunellos of Camigliano.

CASTELNUOVO DELL'ABATE

Castelnuovo dell'Abate is a small hamlet located at about 385 meters above sea level that takes its name from a palace built within its city walls by the Abbot of Sant'Antimo. In fact, the town is most famous for the magnificent abbey (Abbazia di Sant'Antimo) nearby, said to have been built by Charlemagne in A.D. 781. (Some historians believe this to be a legend.) Castelnuovo dell'Abate's huge potential for fine-wine production was not immediately seized upon by either locals or tourists. Only in the last twenty years has Castelnuovo dell'Abate taken its place among the best terroirs of Montalcino, and this thanks to one memorable wine after another made in different vintages from many different producers (especially Poggio di Sotto). Castelnuovo dell'Abate is a very warm part of Montalcino (at times almost too hot), and Sangiovese has no trouble ripening here, unlike Montalcino's northern sector (before climate change arrived). However, Monte Amiata looms large over this subzone: it is 1,740 meters high and protects the hamlet and its vineyards from warm, salt-loaded air currents. For these two reasons, the Brunellos of Castelnuovo dell'Abate are not just big, ripe, and fleshy, but also marked by ripe red fruit and sweet spices, without any saline tang. Monte Amiata also ensures a noteworthy diurnal temperature range, and so these are wines of remarkable freshness—an important trait given just how fleshy and ripe the wines can be. One Achilles' heel is a greater-than-usual concentration of sodium in the essentially clay-rich soils; sodium-rich clay soils are not ideal for Sangiovese, or for grapevines in general (high levels of soil sodium will displace calcium and lead to poor soil structure and possible sodium toxicity to the vines), plus the sodium does not allow flocculation of the clay. And so when it's hot and dry, the clay tends to crack. High sodium concentrations in the soil usually also mean the wines will likely show high pH and low acidity values. Therefore, this subzone's wines are readier to drink and full of early appeal even at a young age, but also age well. I find that all the Castelnuovo dell'Abate Brunellos I have aged in my various cellars have kept remarkably well fifteen years or more. Some estates worth seeking out: Mastrojanni, Poggio di Sotto, and Stella di Campalto/San Giuseppe.

MONTALCINO

This is the sweet spot of the Montalcino production zone, the area at the top of the hill and surrounding the town. It is characterized by the denomination's oldest *galestro*-rich soils, which give the most-balanced Brunellos of all, the best of which magically combine the sleekness and elegance of the northern sector with the fleshy richness of the southern sector. Well-known estates are Il Marroneto at 400 meters above sea level and Costanti at about 350 to 400 meters above sea level; the two make remarkably similar wines. To the northeast of Montalcino, the Fuligni estate makes one of the ten best Brunellos of all Montalcino; it is located in the Cottimelli district, situated between Montalcino and Torrenieri. The La Fortuna estate is also in the area of Cottimelli. This specific area's wines tend to be more structured and less sleek than those of wineries immediately around Montalcino (like Costanti) but they are not anywhere near as structured and large as those of the Canalicchios or of Pellagrilli that are farther to the northeast. To the southeast, in the direction of Castelnuovo dell'Abate, a stretch of exceptional Brunello terroir is home to world-famous estates such as Biondi-Santi, Barbi, Pian dell'Orino, and Salicutti. Their often spectacular wines have a touch less refinement and a touch more body than those of the Cottimelli district, as one might expect given the more southern position. Some estates worth knowing: Biondi-Santi, Costanti, Fuligni, Il Marroneto, Pian dell'Orino, Salicutti.

NORDOVEST

Some producers refer to Buonconvento as the main town in the Nordovest ("northwest") sector, but it is not included within the official Montalcino production zone. The most famous estates to be situated in this sector are Silvio Nardi, at its beautiful Tenuta Casale del Bosco, and the equally beautiful Castiglion del Bosco. Unfortunately, there is only a very small critical mass of data relative to wines made in the north-western sector, for the simple reason that very few if any single vineyards or even single-area wines were made there. (At most estates, the grapes were usually blended with grapes from other subzones to make an entry-level Brunello.) So we have only specific wine examples to go by.

Silvio Nardi's Sangiovese vines are located at about 250 meters above sea level, and the soil composition varies greatly all over the property: for example, Nardi's Brunello di Montalcino Poggio Doria is made from grapes grown in the Oria vineyard, which has a very different soil from other Casale del Bosco vineyards. (Oria is rich in jasper, a sedimentary rock that is essentially an aggregate of microgranular quartz with different mineral inclusions, plus some clay and calcarenites.) Drainage is very good in this vineyard, and the wine is characterized by a refined mouthfeel and a medium-bodied weight on the palate. It is an absolutely lovely wine that helps put to shame all the guffaws one is liable to hear about the northwestern sector's ability to deliver on high-quality-Brunellos. At Castiglione del Bosco, talented winemaker Cecilia Leoneschi has really turned things around, and the estate's Brunellos have gone from rather soft (when not jammy), coffee- and cocoa-laced wines to sleeker, more austere wines more in tune with their terroir. The estate has two very large Sangiovese vineyards, the forty-two hectare Capanna and the twenty-hectare Gauggiole. The Capanna is a huge hill that has been subdivided into many plots; the most important is situated at the summit and is known as Campo del Drago, from where the estate's excellent single-vineyard Brunello of same name is made. The vines grow at 350 to 400 meters above sea level, and the roots have to dig very deep to find water and nutrients, given the very rocky soil (one of the most gravel rich in all of Montalcino). Capanna

gives wines of very good structure and complexity due to plenty of sunlight hours and good water retention. The vines have a southwestern exposure, and this helps add a little flesh. The Gauggiole vineyard is located in the northern section of the large estate grounds (which amount to two thousand hectares, of which forty-two are under vine). The vines grow at 200 to 250 meters above sea level, the soil is very rich in clay, and it has a relatively high sodium content that, as described previously in the Castelnuovo dell'Abate subzone, contributes to making wines that are lively and ready to drink early. Paradoxically, of Castiglione del Bosco's two vineyards, it is the less-prestigious Gauggiole that I find gives wines that have an easier-to-recognize Montalcino northwestern-subzone somewhereness. Gauggiole grapes are used mainly to make the estate's excellent Rosso di Montalcino: its wines are sleeker and higher in acidity, and always make me salivate more than those made with grapes of Capanna. It is a *rosso* not dissimilar from Nardi's Brunello Poggio Doria (the clear-cut differences in palate weight and drag inevitably present between a Brunello and a Rosso notwithstanding). I should also note that Luciano Ciolfi's very pretty San Lorenzo estate is also physically located within the north-western sector, far down in its southern reaches right at the border with the southwestern sector. But the estate's 4.7 hectares of vines are actually situated in the southwestern sector planted at high altitudes (up to 500 meters above sea level), but all have southwestern exposures and look out toward the sea, so the specific site where they grow in has nothing in common with that of Castiglion del Bosco or that of Casale del Bosco (and San Lorenzo's Brunellos are fleshier and riper than Silvio Nardi's Poggio Doria or Castiglion del Bosco's Brunello). Some estates worth seeking out: Castiglion del Bosco, Silvio Nardi.

SANT'ANGELO (SANT'ANGELO IN COLLE AND SANT'ANGELO SCALO)

The Sant'Angelo area is home to some of Montalcino's largest estates, but should really be divided into two districts, Sant'Angelo in Colle and Sant'Angelo Scalo, the wines of which differ greatly. Sant'Angelo in Colle is a small town with two very good trattorias, in addition to top-notch Brunello vines. The town itself is only an agglomeration of a few houses located at 444 meters above sea level, on the slope immediately southwest of Montalcino. Sant'Angelo Scalo is located lower down the mountain and was well known as a train stop of the Asciano–Monte Antico railroad line, which was closed in 1994 when the more modern (more or less, actually) Siena–Buonconvento–Monte Antico railroad line was opened. (A tourist train runs on the old line now for visitors to the area.) The two Sant'Angelo towns are often simply united into one Sant'Angelo (because some estates do not wish to be linked to the word *scalo* [meaning "port" or "dock"], thinking that the association makes the area sound less like a high-quality, bucolic vineyard area and instead rather urban and industrial, which it is not). Sant'Angelo in Colle vines have very good exposure to the sun and, coupled with the area's clay-rich soils, give rich, relatively deeply colored and very classic Sangiovese wines boasting noteworthy balance. These grapes are also blessed by uncanny acidity levels, so the wines rarely seem overripe—a fact that makes grapes from Sant'Angelo in Colle very different from those of Sant'Angelo Scalo and much sought after for estate blends. The vines of Sant'Angelo Scalo are planted in much wider, open habitats that are sunlit and easy to work (to mechanize, especially) and give very ripe wines heavy on the alcohol but possibly flat and overripe, since water stress is a problem in warmer years. Good examples of Sant'Angelo Scalo Brunellos are broad and luscious; over the years, I have found wines from this specific part of the Sant'Angelo subzone to often have Syrah-like spicy qualities. Some estates worth seeking out: Banfi (their Brunello Poggio all'Oro is the wine to buy), Campogiovanni, Col d'Orcia, Ferrero, and Il Poggione.

TAVERNELLE

Located in the central southwestern sector of Montalcino, Tavernelle (which also includes the hamlet of Santa Restituta) is characterized by mainly *galestro* soils and clays. At higher altitudes, the main geologic formation of the area is the Formazione di Santa Fiora (which—according to Abbate and Sagri [1970], who confirm previous work by Boccaletti and Sagri [1965]—is a variation of the Formazione di Sillano; however, according to more-recent geologic opinions, these two formations can be taken to be synonymous). Essentially, the soil consists of a series of layers of argillites with marly clays and calcareous marls (*galestro*). At lower altitudes, the soil becomes clay rich, and the main geologic formation is the Formazione di Pietraforte. According to Giacomo Bartolommei of the Caprili estate, there is a strong marine breeze (the sea is only forty kilometers away), and so especially in the summer, despite day–night temperature shifts, the Tavernelle subzone is characterized by a hot microclimate with daily temperatures as high as 35–38°C. There is plenty of ventilation since there is very little in the way of natural barriers. Selecting drought-tolerant rootstocks (like the 110 Richter) and sward management (which shades the soil without competing with vines for water) can help ward off the risk of drought-related effects in the hotter, drier years. In fact, because of the windy nature of the area, Bartolommei points out, especially in the summer, on days it rains in Montalcino it does not do so in Tavernelle. Wines have luscious fruit flavors and good acid spines (for example, as much as six grams per liter of total acidity), though different winemaking styles make recognizing such similarities more difficult. Bartolommei plans to release a single vineyard wine (with the commercial release of the 2015 vintage) made from his Cepponero cru planted in 1997. Some estates worth knowing: Caprili, Case Basse, Pieve di Santa Restituta.

TORRENIERI

The Torrenieri subzone of the northeastern quadrant of Montalcino is characterized by soils rich in minerals (iron and magnesium), with alluvial and volcanic rocks mixed with clay. The wines of Torrenieri range from light and full of early appeal to richer and dense. It is a cool climate, and in fact the harvest can take place three to four weeks later than at Castelnuovo dell'Abate. Vineyards lie at altitudes of 350 to 480 meters above sea level, which helps accentuate the wine perfume. There is an almost archetypal note of flint in wines from this district in almost every vintage and independently of the estate making them. However, the wines can border on the thin in poor years, and then notes of graphite, green coffee beans, and bell pepper can be downright excessive. Some estates worth knowing: Casanova di Neri (which, according to owner Giacomo Neri, is more correctly placed in an area he refers to as Fiesole, rather than in Torrenieri, but other producers I talked to do not agree), and La Rasina.

Montalcino Districts

ARGIANO

Argiano is a hamlet in the southwest section of Montalcino that appears to have been first mentioned in A.D. 830 when Ludovico il Pio wrote that all the holdings of the church of Argiano had been gifted to the abbot of Sant'Antimo. The hamlet is located at about 242 meters above sea level, on what are mainly alluvial clay soils with sand and marine fossils. The vineyard area is open to the sun, broad, and totally exposed. This creates all-important airflow, and drainage is further helped by some gravel in the soil. The area has long been associated with quality wines that are, in my opinion, characterized by a supple texture and a perfumed menthol note. It's a fascinating terroir, with the potential for making truly great wines, rather than the very solid, well-rounded wines that have been made there thus far. There are locals who believe that Argiano is one of the best terroirs of the whole southern sector of Montalcino, and that sits perfectly well with me. Some estates worth seeking out: Argiano, Sesti–Castello di Argiano.

I CANALICCHIO (THE CANALICCHIOS)

Located in the northern half of Montalcino on the road that leads to Buonconvento (not Torre-

nieri), there are, Léoville-like, more than one Canalicchio, but it is a pretty confusing state of affairs (which is very un-Léoville). According to Francesco Ripaccioli of the Canalicchio di Sopra estate and Franco Pacenti of the Franco Pacenti/Canalicchio estate, the name Canalicchio (meaning "small canal") derives from the large number of manmade canals in the area. There is a Canalicchio di Sopra (Upper Canalicchio, or, in Burgundian terms, Canalicchio-dessus), a Canalicchio proper, and a Canalicchio di Sotto (Lower Canalicchio, or Canalicchio-dessous), resulting mainly from family divisions and inheritances. Since 1988, Franco Pacenti has been at the helm of his family's winery, originally known as Fratelli Pacenti and founded in 1966, and now called Franco Pacenti/Canalicchio. Despite its name, the estate is located in Canalicchio di Sopra (only in Italy, I guess). Franco's vineyards are mostly located right around the winery at about 280 meters above sea level and have a mainly northeastern exposure, which helps account for the freshness and deceivingly lightweight frame of his outstanding wines. Just across the small street (loftily named Strada Provinciale del Brunello) that runs in front of the Franco Pacenti winery is the Canalicchio di Sopra estate, which has vineyards in Canalicchio, in the extended Montosoli vineyard (known as Le Gode di Montosoli), and in Casaccia, an area removed (it's lower down) from Canalicchio. (However, Francesco Ripaccioli, who now runs the estate with siblings Marco and Simonetta, considers Casaccia to be part of the Canalicchio cru.) All of Canalicchio di Sopra's vineyards range from about 270 to 325 meters above sea level, with mainly northeastern but also southeastern exposures. The wines from each site are very different: those of *vigna* Cerrino are always fresher and slightly more balsamic in nature than those of the *vigna* Cantina (the former looks east-northeast, while the latter looks east-southeast). Soils here are mostly rich in clay, with less loam and sand but with many minerals (manganese, magnesium, and phosphorus) that make for surprisingly rich and fleshy wines. Those areas slightly richer in sand often have higher soil calcium concentrations, which seem to me to give wines with a more saline and aromatic character. La Gerla is another winery that owns a sizable chunk of the Canalicchio real estate: six hectares, planted in 1976 and 1982. Owner Sergio Rossi (who passed away in 2011) bought the estate (which had been previously owned by the Biondi-Santi family) in 1976 and launched it with its brand-new name, La Gerla, in 1978. The estate is located in Canalicchio just past Franco Pacenti's winery, at about 320 meters above sea level; exposures and soil types are mostly similar to the other Canalicchio estates. The wines have the sleek, refined personality and balsamic touch that is typical of all Canalicchio wines. Last but not least, there is a Canalicchio di Sotto estate, too, located—you guessed it—at Canalicchio di Sotto; the estate, located just below Franco Pacenti's Canalicchio estate, is actually better known as Lambardi and is run by Maurizio Lambardi. Maurizio's father, Silvano, bought the farm in 1965 and made his first Brunello in 1973. Like all the Brunellos made in the Canalicchio district, I find his wines to have a strong menthol and savory quality. To give readers a breakdown of what the Canalicchio Brunellos taste like, Lambardi's wines are less perfumed and more savory than those of Franco Pacenti/Canalicchio (the sleekest wines of the district and those most dominated by fresh red berry notes) but are balsamic, similarly to those of Canalicchio di Sopra, though with a fleshier, richer mouthfeel.

CERBAIA–LA RASA

Located in Montalcino's northeastern sector, the Cerbaia-Rasa area is a very visible, rather wind-swept promontory exposed due east so that vines planted on its slopes catch mostly the morning sun. Originally, the area belonged to the large Cerbaia estate, which was later divided up into various pieces that are now well-known wine estates: La Cerbaiola (Salvioni), Cerbaiona, Palazzo, La Rasina, San Filippo, and La Serena. I have arbitrarily added the "Rasa" name to Cer-

baia, since there is a Cerbaia estate (founded in 1979 and having made its first wine in 1985) in another part of Montalcino. La Rasa is the name of the farm owned by the Mantengoli family of the Palazzo estate. Salvioni's best parcel of vines is here (Giulio Salvioni owns twenty hectares, of which four are under vine and divided into three parcels, the vines ranging between five and thirty years of age) lies at about 420 to 440 meters above sea level, just above the Cerbaiona estate on a small *poggio,* and undoubtedly there are similarities between the wines, as pointed out by Matthew Fioretti, the new technical director at Cerbaiona. Fioretti brings up an interesting point about terroir when he says, "Terroir is not cut-and-dried: for example, Diego Molinari of Cerbaiona used to make wines by cropping at seventy to eighty quintals per hectare, which is high by anyone's standards, and yet his were some of the greatest Brunellos to have come out of Montalcino in the last thirty years. Some sites are able to weave magic; not all can." I agree wholeheartedly. (Fioretti's first full vintage since the ownership change at Cerbaiona will be the 2016 since the 2015 grapes had already been harvested by the time he arrived.) At Cerbaiona, the relatively cool microclimate and the *galestro*-rich soils express an outstanding version of Montalcino Sangiovese, characterized by an underlying refinement and salinity and a full-bodied texture. In this district, there is none of the ripe jammy fruit typical of Montalcino's southern reaches, but plenty of acid-related sleekness and refinement. Some wines worth seeking: Cerbaiona, La Cerbaiola–Salvioni, La Serena, Palazzo.

LA PISANA–COLLELCETO

La Pisana–Collelceto is a district located in the very farthest-west confines of the Montalcino denomination. Its vineyards lie at roughly two hundred meters above sea level, and the exposure is mostly southwestern. The annual precipitation over the seven-year period from 2010 through 2016 was 650 millimeters. The Winkler index is 2000 (so, not exactly cool), calculated as an average over the same seven years.

Collelceto has soils that are fairly similar to those of Sesta, but with a bit more clay and less limestone, and with schistose rocks and clay pockets. Clearly, this means that the wines have more power and less freshness than those of Sesta. Estate worth knowing: Collelceto.

MONTOSOLI

Montosoli is one of Montalcino's most famous vineyard sites, and it provides a benchmark lesson in the difference between "site" and "cru." Famous since medieval times for its vineyards, it has maintained its reputation into the twenty-first century, and so it will not surprise anyone to know that many producers interpret Montosoli's boundaries with considerable largesse. The true Montosoli is easily visible as you drive on the road from Montalcino to Buonconvento and is characterized by vineyards that, though located on the northern side of the hill, have a mainly southeastern or southwestern exposure and are awash in sunlight most of the time. Its soils are rich in *galestro* (with a good presence of gravel that ensures Montosoli has outstanding drainage, with some calcarenites and limestone); for comparison's sake, many of the much-less-prized soils around Buonconvento (the nearest town) are richer in clay. At roughly 340 hundred meters above sea level, the Montosoli hill is not especially high, yet high enough to ward off spring frosts and autumn fog. Most of the vineyards lie slightly lower down, between 250 and 300 meters above sea level. Grape ripening on the Montosoli hill occurs very evenly—one of the main reasons this cooler, northern microclimate has been so coveted in Montalcino throughout its brief history.

Montosoli is thirty hectares large, but only fifteen are under vine. The villa of Montosoli (now a little run-down), built in 1555 by the well-known architect Baldassare Peruzzi, was once owned by the Angelini family and is now owned by the Daviddi and Carratelli families. As was common in the Angelinis' times, the property was also engaged in agricultural activities under the name of Fattoria Montosoli. There were numerous smaller houses and farming buildings on the villa's property that had names: Colombaio, La Casa, Le Gode, and Casa Lovina (the latter not associated with vineyards). These farms have since been sold off, leading to the creation of wine estates, some of which are very well known today. The most famous of all these estates are Baricci, Altesino, and Caparzo. (The Altesino and Caparzo estates are run separately but have the same ownership.) In the 1950s, Nello Baricci was looking to buy land and set up his home and estate somewhere. He had always been aware of Montosoli and wanted to buy land there if possible because the site had always had a great reputation for outstanding wines. Furthermore, at the annual wine competition run by the Enoteca Italiana di Siena, it was almost always the wine from the Fattoria Montosoli that took first place. And so when the opportunity to buy arose, he did so without flinching (in 1955). Baricci bought the farm called Il Colombaio di Montosoli (*colombaio* translates as "dovecote" in English: a dovecote is a structure, either freestanding or built into the wall at the end of a mansion, that was meant to house pigeons or doves), and it is still the full name of the winery. His was the first Montosoli farm to come to life, but he was also the first to register its Brunello vineyards (in 1966) at the Chamber of Commerce of Siena. (In 1967 he was among the founding members of the Consortium of Brunello di Montalcino, along with Siro Pacenti, Silvio Nardi, Emilio Costanti, Silvano Lambardi, and a few others.) Montosoli is a name that refers to a hill, and so it is a site with different crus of varying quality levels that are the result of the presence and interaction of a specific mesoclimate and soil in a specific, well-defined and finite area. The grand cru area of Montosoli is the south-southeastern side of the hill; for comparison's sake, the western side of the same hill is quite different, since it does not have the same soil type (much more clay rich and less gravelly than the grand cru). It might be unfair on my part to refer to Le Gode of Montosoli as only a premier cru: if it is, then it's an extremely high-quality premier cru, practically of grand cru level, in the manner of Gevrey-Chambertin's Clos Saint-Jacques and Chambolle-Musigny's Les Amoureuses. Nevertheless, Le Gode is situated on the Montosoli hill; interestingly, other estates such as the outstanding Capanna and Ridolfi make wines I love and state that they are situated in the "Montosoli area" (I point out that so am I, when I happen to drive through there), and Paradiso di Frassina reports that it is "at the foot of the Montosoli hill." But the estates that truly farm the best part of Montosoli are few: Altesino, Baricci, Caparzo (La Casa), Casanuova delle Cerbaie, and Pietroso. Baricci owns five hectares of vines subdivided into six different plots of vines (*vigne*) planted immediately around the estate: among these are the Vigna Sottostrada, Vigna Imposto (the old name of this vineyard was actually Vigna dell'Incrocio, or "*vigna* of the intersection"; Baricci replanted it in 1988), Vigna di Casa (planted in 2001, this vineyard is the estate's youngest and was so named because it was planted right in front of the Baricci winery and home), and Vigna Sopramuro (meaning "over the wall," in English, since there is a stone wall there). Altesino, the smallest of owner Elisabetta Gnudi Angelini's four wine estates but the one she herself describes as a "jewel," first made a Brunello Riserva from Montosoli grapes in 1975, then with the 1978 vintage turned it into Montalcino's first-ever single-vineyard wine. Caparzo is another important property owned by Gnudi Angelini: the Brunello di Montalcino La Casa (in my opinion a slightly underrated wine given the wonderful quality that ends up in every bottle) has long been one of the denomination's best and most dependable Brunellos. Besides soil, altitude, and exposure, the La Casa Brunello may also reflect a genetic background of the grapes used. In fact, up until 1982 Caparzo used Sangiovese clones from the large Rauscedo nursery, and after studying six different clones for a number of years, they have selected to use clones F9, Cl19, and R24 because sensory analysis of the wines made with those three clones always placed the wines in the top three spots three years in a row.

Casanuova delle Cerbaie also owns 1.5 hectares in Montosoli's sweet spot, and its vines were planted in 1999. It does not make a single-vineyard wine from these vines. The relationship between Montosoli and the Pietroso estate is an interesting one and worth knowing about. Pietroso is run by Gianni Pignattai, who made wine from a small vineyard at the top of the Montosoli hill he had rented in 2015 from its owners, the Caratelli family. From 2010 to 2015, he made an *indicazione geografica tipica* (IGT) wine called Villa Montosoli from a blend of 95 percent Sangiovese and other local native grapes (Colorino del Valdarno, Canaiolo Nero, and Ciliegiolo). In 2016 he bought the vineyard and then replanted it, and he plans to make a Brunello di Montalcino wine from this cru also. Estates worth knowing: Altesino, Baricci, Canalicchio di Sopra, Caparzo, Le Gode.

PELLAGRILLI

Located in the northeastern sector of Montalcino not far removed from the crus of the Canalicchios, Pellagrilli has been producing wines made famous by the Siro Pacenti estate and especially the über-talented current owner, Giancarlo Pacenti. In fact, the wines of Pellagrilli share similarities with those of both areas. There is a certain fleshy ripeness and balsamic note that recalls the Canalicchio wines, while the subtle flinty, inky nuance that is present in most vintages (especially the cool ones) brings Torrenieri to mind. The main differences from the Canalicchios are due to the exposures: north-northeastern for most of the vines that grow there, south-southwestern for those of Pellagrilli. The wines of Pellagrilli are also a great deal more austere when young than those of the Canalicchios, and are at their best (depending on the vintage) about ten years after the harvest, whereas those of the Canalicchios are readier to drink about five years earlier. Pellagrilli has soils that are more or less like those of the Canalicchios, so mostly a mix of clay-loamy soil and gravel. One section of the Pellagrilli subzone seems to have different soil from the rest of the district: it is where

Giancarlo Pacenti farms grapes that he uses to make his Brunello PS bottling, made only with Pelagrilli grapes (while the almost-as-good Brunello Vecchie Vigne is made in part with old vines growing in Castelnuovo dell'Abate). The 1.5-hectare plot of vines used to make the Brunello *prima scelta* are the oldest on the estate and grow on a gravelly soil unlike any other in the district—one giving wines that have a strong note of graphite (something rare in Montalcino wines), fresh earth, and flowers. In fact, some of the peculiarities of Pacenti's wines (such as the graphite note) may well be due to the genetic factor of terroir: he has been studying his Sangiovese vines closely over the years, and it appears he has been able to select three biotypes that will soon be released as clones 3, 13, and 19. All three have very small but loosely packed bunches but exhibit noteworthy aromatic differences. (The aromatic analysis has been conducted with the help of researchers from the University of Pisa and the University of Florence.) An estate worth knowing: Siro Pacenti.

SESTA

Sesta makes outstanding Brunello and Rosso di Montalcino wines. The historian Emanuele Repetti writes that Sesta was already known and spoken about in the seventh and eight centuries, when Longobards ruled. It is a specific high-quality area for Brunello production because of its climate and position. It is located between Castelnuovo dell'Abate and Sant'Angelo in Colle, in one of the few areas in Montalcino particularly rich in gravel and rocks; this distinctive mineral component of Sesta's wines is a trait not usually found in Brunellos made elsewhere. Sesta's vineyards lie at three hundred meters above sea level, and the exposure is mostly full south. The Winkler index average from 2010 to 2016 is 1950, and the annual precipitation over the same time period is 640 millimeters per year. There is never any fog because of continuous ventilation that comes from the sea. Sesta has high daytime temperatures typical of the southeastern area of Montalcino but has much

lower temperatures at night. Soils are a mix of mainly alluvium and clay (the clay's presence really increases about one to two meters below the surface), plus limestone with high iron concentrations, especially at lower elevations (characterized by the presence of red clay soil that is visible to the naked eye). This latter area is known as Sesta di Sotto, characterized by a very warm microclimate and plenty of gravel and rocks strewn in the highly reddish clay soils. The presence of clay and limestone helps bring a note of freshness to the wines, which might otherwise taste heavy because of the mostly southern, sunny exposure. (The limestone helps reduce absorption of potassium, keeping acidity levels interesting, and the clay retains water.) Parts of Sesta are also still remarkably wild, with large forested areas right next to the vineyards, such as at Sestidisopra estate. Other Sesta estates or estates with vineyards there include Piancornello, Agostina Pieri, Il Ventolaio, Lisini, Tenuta di Sesta, and Collosorbo, and the wines of each present unique terroir-related features. Il Ventolaio has a vineyard in Sesta that is more than 400 meters above sea level; Sestidisopra's vineyards are more than 330 to 380 meters above sea level, like those of Lisini, which helps make the latter's top Ugolaia wine (Lisini only barely fits into the Sesta district). Piancornello and Agostina Pieri are located much lower down, where the soils become pink in color due to their higher ferrous oxide concentrations. However, the secret to the success of Sesta Brunellos resides in a combination of Sesta's many unique factors: "Everybody wants to own vines here," says Maurizio Castelli. Estates worth knowing: Agostina Pieri, Collosorbo, Piancornello, Sestidisopra, Tenuta di Sesta.

Torgiano (Umbria)

Torgiano is a small, pretty town that came to wine lovers' attention thanks to the hard work and passion of the Lungarotti family. Their most famous wines, the Rubesco and Rubesco Riserva Monticchio, are essentially 70 percent

Sangiovese and 30 percent Colorino blends, and thanks to those flag bearers, Torgiano is now considered an excellent site for Sangiovese. Today most of Lungarotti's Sangiovese vineyards are located in the hills of Brufa, between Torgiano and Perugia, at an altitude ranging between 220 and 300 meters above sea level. The soils are of lacustrine origin, deriving from the progressive drying up of Lake Umbro. Clearly, the best site for Sangiovese in Torgiano is the Monticchio hill, which has a long history of excellent wines. Monticchio is an amphitheater in which the vines face mostly west: the highest part of the hill reaches 300 meters above sea level, while the lowest sits at 250 meters above sea level. The Monticchio site has been divided by Lungarotti into seven different parcels: Vigna del Prete, Vigna sotto Martello, Vigna sopra Martello, Vigna del Toppo della Breccia, Vigna Gigliarelli, Vigna della Scesa Grande, and Vigna del Cimitero, the only one of the seven planted to Canaiolo Nero. The seven parcels have been subdivided into two zones based on soil types: zone A is characterized by frankly clay soils of average depth, without much gravel or limestone; zone B is characterized instead by loosely packed soils that are sandy-loamy, friable, and well draining. When the vineyard plots needed replanting, the Lungarottis chose to use high-quality clones such as R24, T-19, Janus10, and Janus 20, plus low-vigor rootstocks such as 3309 De Couderc and 161–49, which push the vine to ripen as early as possible. In general, I find the Sangiovese wine from Torgiano to have a definite spicy and savory quality that complements the ripe red-cherry fruit. The very fresh acidity keeps the wines from becoming too heavy or chunky.

BENCHMARK WINE

Lungarotti Rubesco Riserva Monticchio***.

Addendum: Another high-quality terroir for Sangiovese in Italy (in fact the only other grand cru for the variety in my books) is Emilia-Romagna's Predappio, which I will address in an upcoming book.

Schioppettino

THE GRAPE VARIETY

Schioppettino is one of Italy's most noble red grapes, and its wines can be truly unforgettable. My judgment might be tainted by the fact that I grew up with Picolit and Schioppettino as my university-days liquid soul mates, but I have had ample evidence presented to me over the years that I am not the only out there who sees Schioppettino's greatness. I have been guiding tastings for the past thirty years; over the last four I have led many tastings devoted to the red native grapes of Friuli–Venezia Giulia—not just in Italy, but all over the world. Well, it cannot be an accident or sheer luck that Schioppettino is always the wine that people like best. Schioppettino's rather cute name derives from its explosive large, round grapes that literally blow up (from the Italian verb *scoppiettare*, "to crackle") in your mouth when you bite into them; another hypothesis is that the name is due to the explosion of closed bottles because of unexpected secondary refermentation thanks to residual sugar left over in unfiltered wines.

Schioppettino risked extinction only thirty years ago: scattered vines were still present in most grower's vineyards, but nobody was making a monovariety wine from Schioppettino. The first monovariety Schioppettino wine was launched by Paolo and Dina Rapuzzi of the Ronchi di Cialla estate in 1977 (their first vintage), prodded on to do so by friends Luigi Veronelli (Italy's first serious wine journalist) and the Nonino family (distillers of Italy's most famous grappas). Rapuzzi knew that Friuli had always been the home of many grape varieties that by the 1970s had all but disappeared from the Friuli–Venezia Giulia countryside. He spoke with the mayor of Prepotto, Bernardo Bruno, who, in Rapuzzi's estimation, owned about thirty of the only seventy or so Schioppettino vines he believed were still alive in the area. The problem was that Schioppettino had not been inserted into the list of "officially recognized varieties" and could not be planted, much less used to make wine. Grappa superstars Benito and Giannola Nonino came to the rescue while looking for pomace of the Schioppettino and Ribolla Gialla varieties. (The husband-and-wife team wished to begin making monovariety Schioppettino and Ribolla Gialla grappas, just as they had done with Picolit the year before.) They realized that although many producers in Albana, Prepotto, and a few other areas within the Colli Orientali such as Dolegnano were still growing a little Schioppettino out of habit and tradition, the variety was essentially unknown. In 1975, the Noninos created what has since become a major award, called the "Premio Nonino Risit d'Âur," with the objective of promoting Friuli–Venezia Giulia's culture. Part of that culture is clearly its grape varieties, and so "stimulating, rewarding, and recognizing officially the ancient Friuli varieties, including Schioppettino" was a good reason to acknowledge all those involved for their foresight and dedication. Giannola Nonino has forwarded me private documents in which it is clear that she was at that time moving to have Schioppettino officially recognized as a wine grape, and had initiated the necessary bureaucratic proceedings. Therefore, the first edition of the Risit d'Âur placed the spotlight on the Rapuzzi family, who were selected for their courage in planting a grapevine they might never have been able to make a wine from. Other awardees that year included Luigi Bolzicco of the Count Trento di Dolegnano estate, where Schioppettino had been grown and nurtured since the 1800s, and Professor Guido Poggi, the author of a then state-of-the-art historical, ampelographic, and technical treatise on Schioppettino. The rest, as they say, is history: Paolo Rapuzzi began selecting old Schioppettino vines in Bernardo Bruno's vineyards and elsewhere, too, going as far as Slovenia to look for suitable Schioppettino grapevines (called Pocalza in Slovenia). By 1975, Rapuzzi had planted about thirty-five hundred Schioppettino vines at Cialla, a completely illegal vineyard at the time, but one that benefited from Schioppettino's rehabilitation, which had been set in motion thanks to the Risit d'Âur. Schioppettino's fall into oblivion is hard to fathom. In 1907, the Consorzio Antifilosserico (the antiphylloxera consortium) recommended Schioppettino as one of the varieties

worth planting in lieu of all the dead vines in vineyards ravaged by phylloxera. In 1912, Marinelli wrote that Pocalza was one of the most commonly cultivated varieties around Cividale in the aftermath of phylloxera. Perhaps Schioppettino's demise was due to the fact that making great wines with it is not easy. Terroir is important, since Schioppettino is a variety that does not travel well. In the early twentieth century, winemakers such as Luigi Rieppi and historians like Poggi had already noticed that only a few kilometers removed from the Prepotto terroir the wine was no longer interesting. Schioppettino has a fragile stem, a plethoric grape bunch with one or two large wings, and similarly well-fed-looking round grapes. It is not a very resistant variety (very susceptible to peronospora). In rainy, cold springs *millerandage* and floral anomalies are a big problem, leading to heavily curtailed yields. It's also a late ripener, which means that poor autumn weather, always a possibility in Friuli–Venezia Giulia, poses another problem. Because its basal buds are practically sterile, its yields are low, and long pruning systems are best. Schioppettino is now grown all over Friuli–Venezia Giulia but nowhere else in Italy, and it is most common in the Colli Orientali del Friuli (FCO), where over 90 percent of the vines are located, mainly near Cividale. Schioppettino gives Friuli–Venezia Giulia's most elegant red wines, bursting with black currant, black cherry, and green peppercorn aromas and flavors. (Schioppettino, like Vespolina and Grüner Veltliner, is a variety rich in rotundone, a type of sesquiterpene ketone that smells of pepper.) Schioppettino's wines, unless the grapes are air-dried, never provide an especially fleshy, large-bodied drink, but rather offer a refined medium-bodied palate presence and freshness.

SPECIFIC TERROIRS

Colli Orientali del Friuli

The best terroirs for Schioppettino are those of Prepotto and Cialla. In fact, Cialla is a hamlet of Prepotto, but the microclimate is so different between the two that the wines from each are radically different. Furthermore, Prepotto's terroir is different from that of nearby Albana, and so in a very small portion of the FCO we actually have a number of different Schioppettino expressions. Albana and Prepotto Schioppettino wines differ greatly: such differences are partly due to soil differences between the two (more marly soils in Albana, slightly more alluvial soils in Prepotto). Nearby is Centa, another excellent terroir for Schioppettino: it is characterized by red clay soil rich in iron and so its wines are also recognizably different. Clearly, Schioppettino is uniquely sensitive to site: in less qualitative areas it can fail to ripen properly, in which case the wine can have a not-too-thrilling green streak à la unripe Cabernet Sauvignon.

Schioppettino Subzones

CIALLA

Compared with the Schioppettino wines of Prepotto, those of Cialla are even more refined and vibrant, but lack the flesh of some of the best Prepotto wines. (For an analysis of the Cialla terroir, see the Picolit entry.)

PREPOTTO

The Prepotto Valley is narrow, surrounded by wooded hills in what is an almost mountainous setting. Ventilation is strong, and diurnal temperature variations are noteworthy. The valley is characterized by three types of soils on which Schioppettino grows:

1. To the north at about 250 meters above sea level there are the red marls that are typical of Centa and give wines that are intensely colored, spicy, and full-bodied.

2. The plateau of Albana and Prepotto, at about 110 meters above sea level, has mostly clay-loamy soils on a marly-sandstone bedrock. These are the soils that give the wines with the most striking note of rotundone and noteworthy refinement.

3. The hills of Novacuzzo to the south are characterized by marly soils on the hillsides and loamy-clay soils in the flatlands. The microclimate is generally cooler here; the ventilation is good throughout the Prepotto subzone, and rain is mostly present in the fall and the spring. The wines usually show very good balance and early drinking appeal but can have a green streak in years of poor weather. According to Carlo Petrussi, there are specific Prepotto wine crus of real note, but I cannot say that I have much firsthand experience with wines made there. According to Petrussi, and from what microvinifications I have been able to taste over the years, the main crus are Brischis (characterized by red marls; structured, perfumed wines); Fregelis (with Cretaceous calcareous stones; there is noteworthy perfume to the wines); Cladregis (offering a mix of red soils and reddish arenaceous soils; the wines are perfumed yet structured); and Craoretto (which has calcareous soils on the hillsides and loamy-clay soils with reddish pockets in the flatlands).

BENCHMARK WINES

Cialla: Ronchi di Cialla***PS.

Albana/Prepotto: Iole Grillo***PS, La Viarte***PS, Vigna Petrussa***PS.

Colli di Poianis**, La Buse del Lôf **, Pizzulin**.

Marinig*, Petrussa*, Stanig*, Vie d'Alt*.

Tazzelenghe

THE GRAPE VARIETY

Let me be crystal-clear about one thing relative to Italy's native red grapes: Tazzelenghe is simply one of the three or four most underrated and also one of the best Italian cultivars of all. I have been guiding tastings, running certification courses, and training students to become experts on Italian wine for universities and Italian wine academies, and tasting hundreds of Friuli–Venezia Giulia wines from the new vintage each year and writing about them for longer than I care to remember (my liver, too, I'm quite sure), and one thing has become apparent to me. People *really* like Tazzelenghe wines— that is, if and when they get a chance to taste them. Unfortunately there are only seven or eight estates bottling Tazzelenghe wines anymore, and only four or five do so as a monovariety wine. Let me be blunt: the only reason Tazzelenghe runs the risk of disappearing is because it cannot give big, fat jammy wines, blessed as it is with sky-high acidity and tannins that are no shrinking violets. And so, in what were the dark ages of wine (the 1990s and early twenty-first century), when what most everybody wanted was big, jammy, fat, black, high-Ph caramel-vanilla-cocoa-coffee infusions that were being passed off as wine, poor Tazzelenghe got uprooted left and right in order to plant Merlot and other more "in" varieties. The result is that ten hectares of Tazzelenghe remain scattered around in the countryside, and that is a crying shame. I still remember just how magnificent the 2001 Dorigo Tazzelenghe Ronc di Juri was (the Tazzelenghe, not the Pignolo, also made from the Ronc di Juri vineyard) when I tasted it after about twelve years. Simply put, a wine that good does not happen by chance nor does it happen with a non-noble-grape variety.

The name Tazzelenghe derives from the Friulian word *tàce-lenghe* (my Friuli friends and relatives always point out that Friulian is not a dialect but a real language), which means "cuts the tongue," in reference to the variety's laser-like acidity and tannin clout. The grape was first documented around Udine in 1863, and has always been grown mostly in the countrysides of Buttrio, Manzano, and Prepotto in

Friuli–Venezia Giulia's Colli Orientali del Friuli. In the past, Tazzelenghe was believed to be one of the many Refoscos, and was also called Refosco del Boton. In fact, thanks to genetic testing we know that Tazzelenghe is closely related to Refosco Nostrano but is its own distinct variety. Tazzelenghe's grape bunch has a very recognizable shape similar to that of a medium-size truncated cone; the medium to medium-large, almost oval grapes are loosely packed. The grapes have thin but very resistant skins, which allows for a long hang time since the grapes are less prone to common diseases. In fact, Tazzelenghe is not an especially late-ripening variety, but because of its skins, it can be left out in the vineyards for a few days more so as to get a very slight air-drying effect directly on the vine. This is a useful step because Tazzelenghe grapes have, on average, more total acidity than any other red grape of the FCO (most commonly, six to seven grams per liter of total tartaric acid). One clone is available today: ERSA-Friuli–Venezia Giulia 435. The only DOC wine made is Colli Orientali del Friuli Tazzelenghe. A good Tazzelenghe wine offers a precise and crisp aroma and flavor profile that is just ideal with most foods. The tannins especially, often reputed to be harsh and massive, are nothing of the sort. Some producers purposely harvest Tazzelenghe as late as possible in order to naturally decrease acidity levels as much as possible. But with or without the air-drying, Tazzelenghe always gives a very elegant red wine that ages extremely well. Talented Gionata Ottogalli, the winemaker at the high-quality La Viarte estate, is one who believes that a little air-drying with Tazzelenghe goes a long way, in that the extra time out on the vine allows for a touch less acidity in the grapes and stable color and tannins. Ottogalli's point of view is mine, too: Tazzelenghe is not genetically capable of giving huge wines, but rather can produce wines of real grace and refinement. Delicately air-drying its grapes just a little helps make the wine that much more drinkable and enjoyable. Deep purple in hue, with intense aromas and flavors of violets and

fresh blackberries complicated by delicate hints of roses, underbrush, and tar, this is a complex, very interesting, and unique red. As it ages it smoothens out and picks up a complexity that I have yet to find in Pignolo wines, generally (and in my view, erroneously) considered by locals the much better variety of the two.

SPECIFIC TERROIRS

Friuli Colli Orientali

For an in-depth analysis of the Friuli Colli Orientali terroir, see the Ribolla Gialla entry.

Tazzelenghe Subzones

BUTTRIO

There is not much written documentation about Tazzelenghe wines even from those years when they were made in larger volumes than they are today. Therefore, precise data relative to the most suitable altitudes, exposures, slopes, and rootstocks for Tazzelenghe in Buttrio (or anywhere else, for that matter) are hard to come by. That said, it is impossible to forget just how great some of those Tazzelenghe wines were. It follows that Buttrio must be an especially blessed terroir for this variety, since not one, but a few producers made truly great wines with Tazzelenghe from Buttrio. Dorigo made truly memorable wines with Tazzelenghe, while Conti d'Attimis Maniago's and Gianpaolo Colutta's Tazzelenghe wines (all made with Tazzelenghe grapes grown around Buttrio) are modern classics that deserve to be much better known. Undoubtedly, Buttrio's warmer microclimate contributes to the achievement of full polyphenolic ripeness of the Tazzelenghe grapes, making for more-luscious wines devoid of any green streaks. However, it cannot be only a matter of heat units: there must be more to Buttrio's terroir (relative to Tazzelenghe) than meets the eye, because the variety actually does well in cooler climates, too (such as that of Prepotto). In the ultimate analysis, the exact reasons for Tazzelenghe's success in Buttrio may not yet be in our grasp, but it is undeniable that the terroir there is a great one for this variety. (For more information on Buttrio, see the Ribolla Gialla entry.)

PREPOTTO

Prepotto is a magical wine-production area of the FCO, most famously associated with Schioppettino (see the Schioppettino entry); but Tazzelenghe also seems to do remarkably well within its boundaries. In many ways, Prepotto offers the perfect link between the wines of the Collio and those of the FCO. In fact, Prepotto (in the FCO) sits on the border with Dolegna (in the Collio), and Dolegna is a cool climate area, too. The area is characterized by a great diversity of soils, including the classic *ponca* with high sandstone content, but also a *ponca* that is much richer in marl. (These two are flysches of different geologic origins: see the Ribolla Gialla and Picolit entries for a more in-depth discussion of flysch formations and of the different *ponche*.) And it is the latter that characterizes Prepotto. (It also differentiates Dolegna's soils from those of other subzones of the Collio.) Prepotto's soils are generally very poor in organic matter (humus) and have a gravel component that in the presence of rainfall can contribute to stress for the vines. It is important to keep yields low (which usually involves throwing down some grapes, or green-harvesting) and not add any unnecessary work to that which the poor grapevines already have to do. The Prepotto mesoclimate is also very area-specific, with hot summer days and cold nights, adding up to strong diurnal temperature variations. Annual precipitation rates are lower than the average of the FCO, whereas ventilation is stronger; the latter is an important fact that helps explain why Prepotto suffers fewer hail episodes than other parts of the FCO. What this also means is that Prepotto's white wines are aromatically complex, like those of the Collio, while the reds are fresh,

medium-bodied, and less deep in color than those of Buttrio or Albana.

TORREANO

The Torreano territory can produce very site-specific Friulanos and Refosco del Peduncolo Rosso wines, but it's exceptionally suited to Tazzelenghe as well. And just as there is a specific district of Torreano—Togliano—ideal for quality Refosco del Peduncolo Rosso production, so there is one for Tazzelenghe, too: Montina. The Montina terroir lies at about 130 to 150 meters above sea level, and it is characterized by a very particular topography. (It is an amphitheater that opens toward the south, allowing for a warm mesoclimate.) The soils are characterized by the presence of the *pietra piasentina*, a sedimentary, extremely hard calcareous gray rock characterized by white and brown streaks. Its name derives from the saying *"una pietra che la piase,"* or "a stone one likes," in reference to its many uses such as in making pavements. It is a calcarenite/biosparite and so is characterized by a finer granulometry; in Friuli–Venezia Giulia it is essentially found only around Torreano, and makes up the specific flysch formation of the area, known as flysch of Grivò, formed during the Paleocene (from 66 million to 56 million years ago) to the Lower Eocene (56 million to 47.8 million years ago) through tectonic movements of the earth's crust that led to compaction and cementification of previously deposited calcareous stones. It is this strong calcareous presence that leads to Tazzelenghe wines of almost lemony acidity and extreme perfume, lifting Torreano to grand cru level for Tazzelenghe. (For more information on Torreano's terroir, see the Tocai Friulano entry.)

BENCHMARK WINES

Buttrio: Conti D'Attimis Maniago***, Gianpaolo Colutta***.

Prepotto: La Viarte***.

Torreano: Jacuss***.

Tocai Friulano

THE GRAPE VARIETY

Tocai Friulano is the name of a Friuli–Venezia Giulia grape variety, whereas Friulano is the name of the wine made from those grapes. That name alone tells you how dear to people in Friuli–Venezia Giulia this cultivar is. In fact, Friulano is the house wine of most *osterie* or *gostilne* (pubs) you might visit in the region, where the *tajut* of wine (a *tajut* is a small glass of wine, comparable to the *ombra* of the Veneto) poured is almost always of Friulano (or Ribolla Gialla). However, due to one of the many Byzantinisms of Italian law, although the wine can no longer be called "Tocai" in observance of European Union laws (they allow only Hungary and Slovakia to use the name "Tokai," "Tokaj," or "Tokay"), in Italy the grape's name continues to be Tocai Friulano. (Hilariously, non-European wine estates can still label their wine Tocai Friulano if they wish to do so.) Apparently, Tocai Friulano has long graced Friuli–Venezia Giulia soil with its presence, as documents dating back to the twelfth century indicate, and it's even more popular today, grown in practically every denomination of the region. The other very important thing to know about this cultivar is that it has been identified with Sauvignonasse, which used to be very common in France but is now more common in Chile. With Tocai Friulano, matters such as nursery clones and biotypes are very important, for wines can be very different depending not just on where the grapevine is planted, but also on *which* Tocai Friulano is being planted. There are at least three different biotypes of Tocai Friulano: the most common has yellow berries, while the green-berried and the red-stalked biotypes are much rarer, especially the latter, which was only recently discovered (Petrussi 2013). Of the three, it appears that it is the green-berried biotype that gives wines with more intense aromatic power, while the exact winemaking potential of the red-stalked biotype has yet to be determined because of the paucity of such vines. The exact worth of the yellow-berried type is not yet clear to me: while some producers and experts, such as Carlo Petrussi or Cristian Specogna, swear by it, others like Lorenzo Landi believe that it gives heavier, broader wines that are slightly oxidative. For the most part, Tocai Friulano is a fairly resistant cultivar, though its thin skin is always a cause for concern because of the frequent autumn rains during harvest time. A good Friulano is a pale straw green, with delicate aromas of white flowers, sage, thyme, white peach, sweet almonds, and citrus fruits. These aromas have been correlated to significant levels in both grapes and wines of 8–mercaptomenthone (nuances of white peach) and 3-mercaptohexanol acetate (citrus fruits). These molecules seem to be especially present in Tocai Friulano wines from the Collio. They can stand up to a judicious oaking, but can also be very easily overwhelmed by overly enthusiastic use of the same. The first to have bottled Friulano as such was Mario Schiopetto in 1965 (when, of course, the wine was labeled as Tocai Friulano); his wine was the gold standard for this variety for the better part of three decades. (The estate still owns some of Friuli–Venezia-Giulia's oldest Tocai Friulano vineyards.) Nicola Manferrari of Borgo del Tiglio and Enzo Pontoni of Miani make Italy's best oaked Friulanos.

SPECIFIC TERROIRS

Collio

Many renowned winemakers swear by Tocai Friulano in the Collio (then again, it's hard to find *anyone* in Friuli–Venezia-Giulia who doesn't have a kind word for this variety), but most also mention that it is imperative to identify a good site for it. Tocai Friulano, in order to produce the best results, needs the right soil and maturity of grapes. If the variety is picked unripe, the levels of catechins are just too high and the wine tastes unfailingly bitter. Clones or biotypes are also fundamental with Tocai Friulano because of the potentially aromatic component of the grapes and the variety's well-known, fairly tightly packed bunch. The more compact the bunch ooecia Friulano, the less aromatic the wine will be. (Loosely packed members of the Tocai Friulano population are more aromatic also, because they carry fewer grapes, allowing the vine to concentrate aromatic precursor molecules in fewer grapes.) For example, the R14 Friulano clone is loosely packed and is much planted, since it offers more of an aromatic component similar to that of Sauvignon Blanc. Friulanos made with that specific clone have strong thiol-derived notes, and terpen-derived nuances as well; norisoprenoids are instead never especially high with Tocai Friulano. Being a versatile variety, Tocai Friulano adapts easily to many different terroirs, which is a big help to producers; but the wines have different aroma and flavor profiles as a result. If Tocai Friulano is well positioned— say, midslope and facing south-southeast— results are almost always good in the higher hillside Collio vineyards. However, including about 10 to 20 percent grapes picked from vineyards with a south-southwestern exposure really helps provide the wine with a little extra (and often much-needed) fat, but it can then drop its acidity very quickly. Last but not least, noble rot, when present, also really helps bring out aromas, but it has to be left on the grapes for a very short time only (two days at most) for maximum results. (With Tocai Friulano, noble rot can make the wine taste heavy and earthy if it is left on the grapes too long.) In some areas, such as Ronco Blanchis (in the area around Mossa in the Collio) and San Floriano, noble rot forms more easily, and this is why Friulanos from these terroirs can boast a greater degree of complexity, at least in some vintages.

Collio Tocai Friulano Subzones and Districts

I have always believed San Floriano to be an important Tocai Friulano subzone in the Collio, if for no other reason than that the area was long known for a specific high-quality Tocai Friulano biotype and very old vines (some up to eighty years of age). However, its cool microclimate makes for pungent wines (a different pungency than the minerally one of Zegla; wines from San Floriano can be downright pyrazinic in cold, rainy years; when the hint of greenness is not there, San Floriano deserves grand cru status for Tocai Friulano, especially in the areas of Scedina and Uclanci). Capriva vines face mostly south, as opposed to Russiz, which is north-facing, and so is known for voluptuous, full-bodied Friulanos. Pradis gives very elegant wines, while Zegla gives very warm wines rich in alcohol clout. About the only negative I can think of is that Zegla is a little prone to hail, but otherwise it is undoubtedly a grand cru for this variety. Brazzano gives at once powerful and balanced wines, and was traditionally nicknamed *"la zona del Tocai"* (the area of Tocai). Based on work by Veronelli (1995) and my own experiences tasting Tocai Friulano wines over the last thirty years, I would say that the following list includes most of the high-quality sites for this variety in the Collio:

Capriva: Russiz, Russiz Superiore.

Cormons: Plessiva, Roncada, Subida, Zegla (Zegla's is an especially interesting and in my view high-quality territory that, like Oslavia's, is situated close to the Italian-Slovenian border; a much colder microclimate that looks mainly north, it gives Friulano wines of truly pungent proportions and a minerality that will make you think you are licking stones anytime a Friulano made here should grace your lips).

Brazzano: Ronco della Chiesa.

Dolegna: Ronc di Zora, Ruttars.

Gorizia: Trebes Zardin.

Lucinico: Belvedere.

San Floriano : Kebrisce, Scedina, Uclanci.

BENCHMARK WINES

Brazzano: Borgo del Tiglio Ronco della Chiesa***PS, I Clivi Brazan***PS.

Borgo del Tiglio**, Livio Felluga**.

Capriva: Schiopetto***PS; Attems**.

Cormons: Dario Raccaro**, Doro Princic**, Drius**, Polencic**, Ronco dei Tassi**.

Dolegna: Toros***, Venica Ronco delle Cime***; Alessandro Pascolo**, Ca' Ronesca**.

Faedis: Ronc dai Luchis***PS.

San Floriano: Gradis'ciutta**, Tercic**.

Friuli Colli Orientali (FCO)

Not surprisingly, Tocai Friulano grows very well in the FCO as well, and there are numerous areas where it does especially well. I personally believe that the areas of Buttrio, the Rocca Bernarda near Premariacco, and Torreano give especially noteworthy Friulano wines in this denomination, but there are other very good ones, such as Manzano.

Specific FCO Subzones

BUTTRIO

Buttrio is blessed with slightly warmer microclimates than other viticultural zones of Friuli–Venezia-Giulia, and this makes for slightly richer, fleshier Friulanos. Provided the acidity levels stay refreshingly high (much easier with old vines and their long rooting systems), these are some of the most concentrated, luscious, almost opulent Friulano wines you will get to taste. (For more information on Buttrio's terroir, see the Ribolla Gialla entry.)

ROCCA BERNARDA

Rocca Bernarda is characterized by a climate in between a continental and Mediterranean one, since the area sits between the Julian Alps to the north and the Adriatic Sea to the south. The mountain massif helps protect the area from cold northerly winds; the warmer breezes from the Adriatic help buffer temperature further; and the cold bora winds from the northeast that blow through strongly help in creating significant diurnal temperature excursions, to the advantage of the aromatics in wine. Another aspect of the Rocca Bernarda terroir is that the soil (and its mineral composition) changes greatly with altitude and with the side of the hill on which one does the analysis. Overall, the Friulanos of Rocca Bernarda have a balance unlike that of any other FCO Friulano; they might lack the "impression of opulence" given by the Friulanos of Buttrio or the nervous, chiseled freshness of the Friulanos from Torreano, but they have a harmony that in the best wines from this subzone is both unique and magical. (For more information on the Rocca Bernarda terroir, see the Picolit entry.)

TORREANO

Torreano is located close to Cividale, the main town of the FCO. Its fundamental characteristic is that it has a generally cooler microclimate, and therefore, provided one has a little tasting experience with Friuli–Venezia-Giulia wines, the Tocai Friulano wines of Torreano are easily distinguished from those of Buttrio, for example. The Chiarò stream slows through Torreano, and many of the vineyards lie close to the water's edge, about 100 to 150 meters away. This narrow windswept valley, called Pradis, extends from the stream's edge to the first major hillsides in the distance, and lies at about 150 meters above sea level, with the majority of the small vineyard plots facing south-southwest. The soil is mostly alluvial but with a strong gravel component; strong ventilation is always present in both summer and winter, so disease pressure is not a big issue, and the grapes retain freshness easily. Good diurnal temperature variation helps heighten the aromatics of the Friulano wines. The largest number of planted vines in Torreano grow in its hamlet known as Togliano; as described earlier, the Togliano is a viticultural district of Torreano. (For more information on Torreano's terroir, see also the Refosco del Peduncolo Rosso and Tazzelenghe entries.) Togliano's vineyards are mostly south-facing and lie at about 125 meters above sea level. Differently from Torreano, Togliano's subsoil is richer in clay and the ventilation not as noteworthy; but there are more sunlight hours, and so this is actually the part of the Torreano viticultural area that is most suited to red grapes. Therefore, Torreano was always most planted to Tocai Friulano (and a little Picolit, too, that has always struck me as being of high quality; see the Picolit entry), while Togliano has always been planted mostly to Refosco del Peduncolo Rosso.

BENCHMARK WINES

Buttrio: Meroi Le Zittelle***[PS], Miani Friuli Colli Orientali Friulano Buri***[PS], Miani Friuli Colli Orientali Friulano Filip***[PS].

Manzano: Torre Rosazza***. Premariacco: Ermacora**, La Tunella**, Scubla**.

Rocca Bernarda (Corno di Rosazzo): Gigante 50 Anni***, I Clivi Galea***, Specogna***; Nadalutti**, Sirch**.

Spessa di Cividale: La Sclusa**.

Torreano: Valchiarò***, Volpe Pasini***.

Trebbiano Abruzzese

THE GRAPE VARIETY

Trebbiano Abruzzese is the grape; Trebbiano d'Abruzzo is the wine. One of Italy's many Trebbiano varieties, Trebbiano Abruzzese is, along with Trebbiano Spoletino, the most interesting. (Not surprisingly, according to the landmark 2001 study by Labra et al., the two are the only Trebbiano group members that are somewhat related.) For the longest time, it was thought to be a poor-quality cultivar because it was confused with the likes of Mostosa, Bombino Bianco, and even Trebbiano Toscano. This means that farmers were growing different cultivars in their vineyards yet were treating them as one and the same—clearly not a good situation, since different grapes have different needs: exposures, gradients, soil types, and rootstocks, for example, are all variety dependent. In fact, it should have been obvious to all that Trebbiano Abruzzese was a noble cultivar: Valentini makes his Trebbiano d'Abruzzo with it, and for many people, that is Italy's greatest white wine. There are at least two biotypes of Trebbiano Abruzzese: Sbaganina (typical of the area of Vasto and characterized by a medium-large bunch, very thin-skinned berries, and as many as three wings) and Svagarina (more typical of the Marruccina area, with a larger bunch, thicker skins, and usually two wings). Trebbiano Abruzzese is vigorous but susceptible to oidium and fares poorly in excessively windy sites. (The real problem is that its acidity, though usually sky-high, drops very quickly if the grapes overripen.) Greco-like, it has high polyphenol concentrations (but curiously, the wine tastes nothing like a Greco), and so the must oxidizes easily. Trebbiano d'Abruzzo is characterized by delicate aromas and flavors of pomaceous orchard fruits, white flowers, and mint. Poor examples are remarkably thin and neutral, and that's why the grape and the wine had previously earned a reputation for being nothing special. When good, though, it has crystalline acidity, a honeyed mouthfeel, and a pure mineral edge, with an at times uncanny resemblance to France's outstanding Chablis. It is also very ageworthy. Two of Italy's fifteen white wines, Valentini's Trebbiano d'Abruzzo and Tiberio's Trebbiano d'Abruzzo Fonte Canale, are made with this variety.

SPECIFIC TERROIRS

Casauria (Terra di Casauria) and Loreto Aprutino

Unlike Montepulciano, which performs best in relatively cooler mesoclimates that guarantee long hang times, Trebbiano Abruzzese likes gently rolling hills closer to the sea, with more sunlight and less humidity. The best terroirs for this variety in Italy are Casauria and Loreto Aprutino. (See the Montepulciano entry).

BENCHMARK WINES

Casauria: Tiberio Trebbiano d'Abruzzo Fonte Canale***[PS].

Valle Reale Popoli***.

Tiberio**, Valle Reale Capestrano**.

Loreto Aprutino: Valentini***[PS].

Verdicchio

THE GRAPE VARIETY

Ampelio Bucci, the dean of Verdicchio wine producers, has a background in the world of fashion, and this has helped him put things into perspective. According to him, the classic marketing mantra of "think global and act local," which works well for mass products, is not ideal for artisanal ones such as wine. He prefers instead to "think local and act global"— an axiom that he finds is especially well suited to the Verdicchio grape variety. This is because Verdicchio is a noble wine grape that can make wines of international appeal. However, its reputation had been ruined by decades of cheap wines and folkloristic amphora-shaped glass bottles that have done little to help its image. And yet there are fewer white grapes in Italy that give more ageworthy, site-specific wines. I believe that along with Carricante, Garganega, Fiano, and Trebbiano Abruzzese, Verdicchio gives Italy's best white wines. No other grape variety can claim four wines in Italy's top twenty-five whites, but Verdicchio can: the wines by Bucci (Villa Bucci Riserva), Garofoli (Podium), Sartarelli (Balciana), and the Verdicchio di Matelica by Collestefano (which, unlike the first three wines, does not carry a fantasy name) are simply world-class wines. They are also ageworthy, and drinking a good ten-year-old Verdicchio wine can be an eye-opening experience. Happily, Verdicchio's great potential is now becoming increasingly clear to everyone, with producers realizing they had a Ferrari in their hands but were driving around at only forty miles an hour. In other words, a waste.

Verdicchio is one of the many green-something grapes of Italy. The country boasts myriad wine grapes that have green (*verde*) somewhere in their name: Steppa Verde, Verdealbara, Verdello, Verdesse, Verduschia, and Verduzzo are just some of those that spring immediately to mind. The reference to the color green is usually because either the grapes or the wine (and often both) are characterized by a strong green hue. In fact, Verdicchio's less common synonyms all revolve around the same: for example, Verdone, Verzana, Verdetto, and Verzello all bring Verdicchio's color to mind. There are two cultivars that are closely related to Verdicchio that wine lovers need to be aware of: Trebbiano di Lugana (now called Turbiana) and Trebbiano di Soave. In 1991, Calò et al. demonstrated that Trebbiano di Soave is identical to Verdicchio (but because DNA testing was not available at that time, this research group was able to study the grapevines only by means of ampelographic and isozyme analysis). Ten years later, in 2001, Labra et al. were able to add DNA testing to the grape-identification tools at their disposal (by then that particular molecular biotechnology had become available) and confirmed the findings by Calò and associates. These results helped everyone understand that Verdicchio and Trebbiano di Soave are, at the current level of genetic knowledge, the same grape variety (in theory) and that the variety adapted over time to very different habitats (the Marche for Verdicchio, the Veneto for Trebbiano di Soave; therefore, the two are best thought of as biotypes, and give different wines). Shortly thereafter, Vantini et al. (2003) also performed DNA profiling, not just on Verdicchio and Trebbiano di Soave, but on Trebbiano di Lugana, too. This later study, while confirming the identity between Verdicchio and Trebbiano di Soave, revealed that Verdicchio and Trebbiano di Lugana are not genetically identical. (There is an abnormal allele of five hundred nucleotide bases in the VVMD36 locus that allows genetic differentiation between Trebbiano di Soave and Trebbiano di Lugana.) This was all the Lugana producers needed to declare their grape variety as distinct from all others, prompting the name change from Trebbiano di Lugana to Turbiana (just to ensure nobody would miss the message). On the basis of these results, it is correct to view Verdicchio and Trebbiano di Soave as biotypes, and both as varieties distinct from Turbiana.

There exist different clones of Verdicchio, characterized by different viticultural behaviors and fairly different wines—all things worth knowing when hunting for terroir in wines. The R2 clone is very productive but allows for good everyday table wines; the CSV clones have thicker skins and are ideal for late harvest and for sparkling-wine production (though in my experience wines made with these clones are not particularly ageworthy). Since the ERPT 155 and CVP 01–162 clones are derived from Turbiana, it would be not only more precise, but also respectful of the wine and its terroir, if these were no longer allowed to be planted in the Verdicchio production zones; but of course such precision is not the coin by which Italy works. As with other Italian native grapes, a surefire sign of the quality of any grape is given by the number of clones and crossings that have derived from it: therefore, it is not surprising that Verdicchio has been the source not just of many different clones but also of new crossings: Incrocio Bruni 54 (or IB54), developed in the 1930s (it is a Verdicchio × Sauvignon Blanc crossing), is an especially successful crossing, the wines of which manage to deliver the delicate aromatic note typical of Sauvignon Blanc and Verdicchio's more minerally characteristics. The Verdicchio variety is characterized by high natural acidity: therefore, it is an ideal cultivar with which to make not just dry wines, but sparkling and sweet wines also. The sparkling wines have charm, but maybe not quite the complexity of the world's best sparklers. Likewise, sweet wines can be delicious (Verdicchio takes to noble rot fairly well, and its naturally high acidity ensures that the wines rarely induce palate fatigue), but because it is not an aromatic variety, they are ultimately less interesting and complex than those made with the likes of Riesling or Zibibbo, for example.

Verdicchio wines are floral and delicately fruity when young and develop a note of diesel fuel with age. Also, both young and older Verdicchio wines are typically characterized by a delightful and recognizable sweet almond note, which becomes much stronger (veering to marzipan) in Verdicchios with some age on them. (This almond note usually becomes especially noticeable at eight years from the vintage.) And while all Verdicchio wines have vibrant freshness thanks to the variety's intrinsically high tartaric acid levels, wines can be very different depending on the habitat the grapes grow in. In fact, there are fewer wines in Italy made with the same grape variety in neighboring denominations that are as radically different as the Verdicchio dei Castelli di Jesi and the Verdicchio di Matelica. Knowing how and why Verdicchio's typical aromas and flavors form and how these deviate from the baseline is very helpful in putting into context terroir-related differences of Verdicchio wines from the two different denominations. In fact, modern-day Verdicchio wines are being increasingly characterized by notes of fresh citrus fruit (lime, most noticeably, but grapefruit, too); this is especially true of the Verdicchio dei Castelli di Jesi, many of which are being made via gentle prefermentation macerations and hyperreductive techniques (in other words, vinification in absence of oxygen by use of inert gases). This has led to the attenuation (and even the disappearance, in some cases) of the typical almond note of Verdicchio wines of the past, which was partly due to problems related to incipient oxidation. That said, Verdicchio is not Sauvignon Blanc, and it does not have the thiol (or sulfahydril) wealth to allow its turning into a passion-fruit–gooseberry cocktail, though the lime and tropical-fruit notes (the former quite strong, the latter most often delicate) certainly echo those of some Sauvignon Blanc wines. These notes of lime and tropical fruit are the result of the increase in antioxidant molecules (Di Lecce et al. 2013) and the synergy that exists between molecules such as 3-mercaptan-hexenol and 3-mercaptan-1-hexenol acetate (Fedrizzi et al. 2007). In the 2013 study, Di Lecce and associates showed that skin contact in low-oxygen conditions leads to an increase in phenolics and glutathione in both must and white wine (but both glutathione and tyrosol, another antioxidant typical of white wines, were found to decrease in older wines). Therefore, the strong citrus notes that tend to dominate the nose of some of today's Verdicchio wines are the result of enological techniques used, and so I would not tend to associate them with physical factors of a specific Verdicchio terroir, but rather

human intervention. Without the use of such techniques, Verdicchio's typical, gently floral and herbal aromas and flavors steal the show; they are due to fermentation esters, though their nuances can be made more complex or modified by the presence of isoamyl acetate (which gives a note of banana), hexanoate (notes of pineapple, pear, and apple), and butanoate (more apples and pineapple) in different concentrations. The notes of riper tropical fruit such as pineapple are due to the development of aromatic molecule precursors formed in carotene catabolism; their concentration is correlated to the amount of sunlight radiating onto the berries in the early phases of the growth cycle. (As a general rule, the warmer and brighter the climate, the faster wines made with a few specific varieties will develop hydrocarbon-like aromas and flavors.) Last but not least, there is apparently more to these molecules than just creating variety-specific and terroir-related aromas and flavors. Believe it or not, there are experimental data showing that Verdicchio may help in treating liver disease. In an interesting 2009 study by Boselli et al., it was found that ethyl caffeate (or caffeic acid ethyl ester) present in Verdicchio wines has a strong antifibrotic activity that helps reduce liver injury. Ethyl caffeate is one of the main natural phenol antioxidants present in Verdicchio wine. Intraperitoneal administration of a purified extract of ethyl caffeate from Verdicchio wine in rats previously treated with ten milligrams per kilogram body weight dimethylnitrosamine (a liver toxin) prevented the dimethylnitrosamine-induced loss in body and liver weight that would otherwise occur, and reduced the degree of liver injury (as determined by alanine aminotransferase values, necroinflammatory score, diminished hepatic stellate-cell activation, and an increase in proliferation of stellate cells in hepatic inflammatory states, as well as collagen synthesis—all markers of inflammation). What can I say? Should there be more articles like this one confirming Verdicchio's medicinal properties, and if it can be determined which terroirs give grapes with the highest concentrations of ethyl caffeate, some producers out there might be able to start charging Montrachet-like prices for their wines. Honestly now, this will likely never happen; but on more than one level, it would be nice, wouldn't it?

SPECIFIC TERROIRS

In the Marche, Verdicchio is best represented by two different DOCG wines: Verdicchio dei Castelli di Jesi and Verdicchio di Matelica. Unlike many of Italy's DOCs and DOCGs that are devoid of any real meaning (at least in terms of any potential somewhereness of the wines), the two Verdicchio denominations are especially well characterized, and the wines of each speak clearly of the specific areas in which the grapes that are used to make them grow. In fact, it is only fair to give local and national politicians credit on a job well done, at least in this one case. As a general rule, the Verdicchio di Matelica mountain mesoclimante gives wines of a higher acidity level, but also more body and alcohol (thanks to copious solar radiation and the reflection of heat from the mountain cliffs onto the grapes) than the wines of Jesi (which are usually lighter and more floral than those of Matelica). Both Verdicchio wines share the telltale varietal note of almond, sometimes with a pleasantly bitter twist.

Verdicchio dei Castelli di Jesi

The Castelli di Jesi are very pretty medieval towns all characterized by having been under the influence and leadership of Jesi, the birthplace of Emperor Frederick II (1194–1250), Holy Roman emperor from 1220 to 1250. (Freddy must have liked being busy, since he was also king of Sicily from 1197 to 1250, Duke of Swabia—as Frederick VI—from 1228 to 1235, and German king from 1212 to 1250. Obviously feeling like he had some free time to spare, he joined in the Sixth Crusade from 1228 to 1229, becoming king of Jerusalem and reigning from 1229 to 1243.) So the name Castelli (or castles,

in the sense of "affiliated with," or "dependences of") is the least this bucolic part of Italy's Marche region might want to lay claim to. In fact, Jesi is also the birthplace of Giovanni Battista Pergolesi (1710–36), the famous organist, violinist, and composer (of comic opera, serious opera, and sacred work; his *Stabat Mater* composition is especially famous). Nowadays, Jesi and its Castelli can be just as proud of their Verdicchio wines, which rank with Italy's best. What is most noteworthy about the wines is their extremely high and regular level of quality: though insipid and neutral wines are still being made, it is rare to drink a downright bad Verdicchio dei Castelli di Jesi today.

At three thousand hectares, the modern-day Verdicchio dei Castelli di Jesi production zone is not small and falls within two provinces of the Bassa Vallesina Valley: Ancona (which at twenty-two communes covers by far the largest part of the Castelli di Jesi denomination) and Macerata (involving the territories of only two municipalities). The production zone is located in the hills of the Esino River basin (only 10 percent of the denomination involves plains or flatlands), which are not especially high—lowest at Jesi (96 meters above sea level) and highest at Cingoli (630 meters above sea level). Most vineyards are planted between 80 and 270 meters above sea level (though a few are planted as high as 700 meters above sea level), with slope gradients mostly between 2 and 25 percent (though some mountain vineyards have gradients of 70 percent); the steeper gradients help with drainage. Average rainfall is eight hundred millimeters per year; spring frosts are not rare (but Verdicchio is usually unscathed, since it does not bud especially early; the coldest month of the year is January (4–6°C), while the warmest month of the year is July (average daily temperatures of 21–24°C). The warm microclimate is well shown by the fact that September and October rarely have days in which the temperature falls below 10°C. The Winkler index generally cited by scientists I have talked to over the years is always above 1600 (most often, between 1800 and 2200).

The gentle, softly fruity personality of Verdicchio dei Castelli di Jesi wines is partly the result of this warm climate; the denomination lies very close to the sea (most of the vineyards lie within twenty to at most forty kilometers from the sea). It is this marine influence and the protection offered by the Apennine mountain range that creates a relatively warm microclimate. For the most part, soils are rich in clay and calcium carbonate (especially higher hillside locations), while flatland vineyards grow in mainly alluvial soils richer in organic matter and are poorly permeable, but they vary greatly within the denomination. The wines from the various Castelli territories can be very different. For example, the Verdicchio dei Castelli di Jesi produced from grapes grown around the charming town of Montecarotto are more structured, like those of Matelica, while those of Cupramontana are more vibrant and characterized by higher total acidity levels. (In fact, the latter grapes have long been sought after for the production of sparkling wines.)

The Verdicchio dei Castelli di Jesi
Townships and Specific Contrade

On the basis of roughly two hundred Verdicchio wines per year tasted for the past twelve to fifteen years, I have a pretty good idea of what the Castelli di Jesi townships and their *contrade* can offer. In my view, the following are the most significant *contrade* of Verdicchio wines in the Castelli di Jesi production zone (though I am sure there are others that would be worthy of this list and that I have not included because of minimal experience with the wines made in them).

Cupramontana: Barchio, Brecciole, Carpaneto, Manciano, Morella, San Bartolomeo San Marco, Palazzo, San Michele.

Maiolati Spontini: Colle del Sole, Monteschiavo, San Sisto.

Morro d'Alba: Laureto, Sant'Amico Marziano, Santa Maria del Fiore.

Montecarotto: Busche, Passetto, Sabbionare, San Lorenzo, Villa.

Poggio San Marcello: Balciana, Coste del Molino, Fossato, Giuncare, Tralivio.

San Paolo di Jesi: Cesola, Colle San Giuseppe, Coroncino, San Nicolò, Santa Maria d'Arco, Scappia, Versiano.

Serra de Conti: Farneto, Montefiore, San Paterniano, San Sebastiano.

Staffolo: Coroncino, Salmagina, Crocefisso, Castellareta, San Francesco, San Lorenzo San Martino, Santa Caterina.

BENCHMARK WINES

Bucci Villa Bucci Riserva***[PS], Garofoli Podium***[PS], Sartarelli Balciana***[PS].

Casalefarneto***, Colonnara (Cuprese)***, La Staffa***, Marotti Campi Salmariano***, Montecappone Utopia***, Tenuta di Tavignano Misco***.

Andrea Felici Vigna Cantico della Figura**, Montecappone Federico II**, Musone**, Pievalta**, Sartarelli Tralivio**.

Verdicchio di Matelica

Verdicchio di Matelica is one of my favorite Italian wines, one that winemaker Roberto Potentini, perhaps the single greatest expert of this wine, has aptly defined as "hidden" (Potentini 2010), due to its inland production area located far from international wine lovers' eyes. It's a shame: Verdicchio di Matelica wines are blessed with intense minerality, high extract and acidity, and a generally refined mouthfeel, despite being usually very powerful wines. I am not the only fan of this wine. In 2017, the Verdicchio di Matelica DOC celebrated its fifty-year anniversary. (It was launched in 1967, a year before the fiftieth anniversary of the Castelli di Jesi denomination, designated in 1968). In Italy, it is the most important wines that were awarded the DOC first. In 2009, the Verdicchio di Matelica Riserva became a DOCG wine. At roughly three hundred hectares (there were only sixty-six in 1969), the Verdicchio di Matelica denomination is much smaller than that of Verdicchio dei Castelli di Jesi and produces much less wine (ten time less). Verdicchio di Matelica is made in a landlocked valley, the Alta Vallesina, which is only one of two in the Marche that runs in a north–south direction (all the others run east–west, perpendicular to the Adriatic Sea to the east). The denomination is located between the towns of Castelraimondo to the south and Cerreto d'Esi to the north and includes the townships of Matelica, Esanatoglia, Gagliole, Castelraimondo, and Camerino in the province of Macerata, and Cerreto d'Esi and Fabriano in the province of Ancona. The denomination is characterized by a mountain viticulture, with very steep gradients and a cool microclimate; in this sort of habitat, Verdicchio tends to produce very little, and so Verdicchio di Matelica benefits from a natural yield reduction, making for potentially very concentrated, deep wines. However, though winters are very cold, the summers are quite warm, with the sun's rays captured by the mountain rocks and then reflected onto the grapes; the few grapes hanging on the vines accumulate a great deal of sugar, leading to powerful, high-alcohol wines, but the growing season is a long one. Vineyards grow at an average of 350 meters above sea level; roughly 80 percent of the vineyards lie between 280 and 480 meters above sea level. (The highest vineyard in the denomination was planted at 720 meters above sea level.) Lower-lying vineyards grow on alluvial soils, while the higher hillsides have complex soils of calcarenites, marl, limestone, gravel, and conglomerates. The Winkler index is 1800–2000. Silvestroni (2010) shed a very interesting light on the Verdicchio di Matelica wines of centuries past and those made today. In the five-year period of 1874 to 1878, forty-four tests were conducted on the grapes from ten different sites, and showed that the average sugar concentration of the grapes was 20 percent, while the total acidity was 8.86 grams per liter; both values showed very wide ranges, however: 15.9 to 26.7 percent and 3.98 to 14.0 grams per liter, respectively. The harvest in the ten sites took place between the last ten days of September and the first twenty of October. Much later, in 1962, Bruni reports a range of total sugar and total acidity in Verdicchio grapes of 17 to 23 percent and 7.5 to 9.0 grams per liter, respectively. Clearly, these figures tell us that, over the course of roughly one century, producers most likely reduced yields and picked harvest times with more care. More recent data still (relative to the years 1987–90) have shown average values of 19.7 percent and 9.6 grams per liter—numbers that are not all that different from those obtained years before. Interestingly, data obtained from 1993 and 1994 have shown that the average sugar concentration of Verdicchio di Matelica grapes is increasing (21.1 percent) and total acidity values slightly decreasing (7.82 grams per liter)— findings that, not surprisingly, researchers believe to be linked to climate change.

In my experience, though Matelica is rather small and fairly uniform in its soil and microclimate, there are differences between wines made in similar manners within the Matelica denomination. For example, the towns of Camerino and Castelraimondo have generally cooler microclimates, since they are located more inland. Snow, for example, is much more common here than it is in other parts of the Matelica denomination. Diurnal temperature variations are also much larger than they are in other sections of the denomination, and I believe this to be the single most important factor (certainly more than possible soil diversity) in determining major differences in Verdicchio di Matelica. In this respect, there are slight differences between wines made with grapes from the Monte San Vicino area (northeastern exposure) and from the Monte Gemmo area (southwest exposure). The Esino River's source is in the latter area (it is born in the territory of the town of Esanotoglia, which is located in the valley between Monte Gemmo and Monte Corsegno), which is characterized by a generally cooler microclimate; thus wines made from grapes grown here offer even more salinity and freshness than other Verdicchio di Matelicas, all of which are, however, no slouches in the freshness and salinity department.

The Verdicchio di Matelica Townships and
Specific Contrade

Castelraimondo: Collestefano.

Macerata: Podere Cavaliere, Podere
  Fornaciano.

Matelica: Fogliano, Monacesca.

Collestefano***PS.

Belisario Cambrugiano***, Bisci Fogliano***,
  Borgo Paglianetto***, La Monacesca
  Mirum***, La Monacesca***.

Belisario Vigneti B**, Bisci**.

Vermentino

THE GRAPE VARIETY

Vermentino is currently one of Italy's hottest grape varieties, with its wines selling like hotcakes and producers scrambling to plant the grapevine everywhere they can. Its success is such that even the French have paid their Italian cousins the ultimate compliment: rather than continue calling the grape variety and its wines by the French name of Rolle (not to be confused with Rollo, which is a distinct, rare Italian wine grape), they, too, are now calling grape and wine "Vermentino" (of course, the French charmingly pronounce it as "Vermentinò," with the accent on the o, but that's another story). Vermentino's qualities are so obvious that in Italy, too, producers have changed the way they go about things: for example, the Tuscan coast's estates, all typified by a rather pro–international-grape-variety mind-set, have essentially stopped blending Viognier and/or Sauvignon Blanc in their Vermentino wines. Producers have become aware that Vermentino is a noble grape variety, and have begun at last lavishing it (and its wines)

with the viticultural and winemaking care previously reserved for other, more highly thought of wine grapes. Lower yields, more-attentive grape selection, and picking at optimal ripeness levels have all led to wines that are not just everyday quaffers of early appeal and little else, but delicious wines of real depth and complexity (and it is only fair to recognize that the great wines of Capichera have been showing Vermentino's true colors all along). Second, Vermentino is an extremely plastic variety that can give wines differing immensely in style and sweetness scale but that are always lively and crisp, with easy-to-like herbal and fruity nuances. In short, its wines are perfect for today's busy lifestyles and desire for wines that aren't caricatural fruit or grass bombs (as far too many Chardonnay and Sauvignon Blanc wines tend to be). Even better, Vermentino ticks all the boxes when it comes to making wines redolent of flintiness and minerality, the current passwords to wine success. In fact, Vermentino is truly a unique grape variety that has a great deal to offer: but knowing the grape variety's characteristics is of paramount importance in understanding all the possibilities Vermentino offers.

The first thing to know about Vermentino is that it is a rare grape variety that likes, even wants, heat. Actually, Vermentino doesn't just want heat, it craves it. According to star consultant winemaker Maurizio Castelli (who follows Badia a Coltibuono, Grattamacco, Le Ragnaie, and many other top Italian wine estates, many of which make Vermentino wines), what Vermentino really wants is not just heat (and lots of it) but rather a sudden temperature surge—what he humorously refers to as a "hot flash" (or the rather more carnal-sounding *vampa*, in Italian). Research bears this out: environmental factors (exposure to sun, wind, and drought conditions during ripening) greatly influence the concentration of secondary metabolites (such as amino acids and organic acids) in Vermentino grapes. These changes are prevalent in different parts of the grape bunch, meaning that Vermentino expresses noteworthy intra-bunch variability depending on the terroir it is exposed to (Mulas et al. 2011).

In this, it is of great help that the variety does not drop its acidity all that quickly, and can withstand hot and droughty conditions. In fact its distribution range coincides with that of the Mediterranean basin (this cultivar is most typical of southern France, southern Spain, and Italy's Liguria, Sardinia; and the coastal part of Tuscany). The fact is, Vermentino has a bipolar personality. Really. Harvest the grapes early, and the variety expresses very strong thiol-related notes of passion fruit, grapefruit, boxwood, and sage; harvest the grapes late, and the wines exude a strong smell of terpen-related molecules that produce notes of musk, underbrush, camphor, candied citrus fruits, and pungent flowers. Depending on the vintage (often only a two-week difference in picking date is necessary), two completely different wines can be made, and I do mean *completely* different. Be aware that this dichotomy is not at all typical of most cultivars: for example, you can harvest Pinot Bianco as early or as late as you want, but you will never achieve the thiol- or terpen-

related notes that Vermentino can offer in spades. This behavior has a biochemical background, and so Vermentino's aromas and flavors can be easily explained. Harvesting Vermentino grapes late also allows for the production of a delicious, potentially complex late-harvest wine (*vendemmia tardiva* in Italian, and you'll find these words on the label) that, due to the variety's being lightly aromatic, holds much more interest than late-harvest wines made with nonaromatic cultivars such as Chardonnay and Verdicchio.

Aldave de las Heras, Le Fur, and Feuillat (1992) studied both lightly macerated and air-dried grapes and showed that the at times pungent floral aromas of Vermentino wines are due mainly to the presence of linalool. By contrast, what the mineral and flinty notes are caused by is still the subject of some debate in academic circles; at the current state of scientific knowledge, Vermentino's well-known marine and/or saline notes are most likely due to new hyper-reductive winemaking techniques that reduce the must's contact with oxygen. In this manner, dimethyl sulfate and other sulfur compounds produced by yeast metabolism, and smelling of matches, flint, and stones, are freed rather than bound or destroyed (Rauhut 1993). The most suitable rootstocks for Vermentino are the Rupestris du Lot (especially good for droughty areas of Sardinia and Liguria), the 110R (best for Corsica and the Tuscan coast), and even the 1103P and SO4 in specific parts of Liguria where it appears to preserve total acidity better. Different training systems are used, too, depending on the area of cultivation, with *alberello* not surprisingly preferred in Sardinia and in Corsica's droughtiest areas (while the canopy and *tendone* systems are the choices when more water is available), *pergola bassa* in the Cinque Terre, and Guyot and cordon spur most everywhere else. Vermentino can be a very vigorous variety, and if it is allowed to yield too high, the quality of the grapes regresses considerably. In general, Vermentino prefers poorly fertile soils anyway.

There is one more extremely important fact about Vermentino, and that is the role of biotypes and or distinct varieties. In Italy, there exist two other cultivars that current scientific knowledge tells us are genetically identical to Vermentino. These are Liguria's Pigato and Piedmont's Favorita, two varieties that don't look or behave very much like Vermentino at all. In my view, and in accordance with what has already been very clearly enunciated by the likes of Pelsy et al. in 2010 and Emanuelli et al. in 2013, these three grapes are at the very least site-specific biotypes (ecotypes), if not downright distinct grape varieties. The reasoning behind such a statement is simple: the three wine grapes present noteworthy morphological and viticultural differences, and their wines have very little in common. When differences between wines made with varieties that are said to be genetically identical are sufficiently strong, the correct way in which to proceed is to consider said grape varieties as distinct. Numerous wine producers in Italy (a number that is increasing all the time) feel exactly the same way that I do. In fact, these three Italian natives provide an outstanding example of how terroir works: in Liguria, Vermentino grows mostly in the eastern half of the region, while Pigato grows mainly in the western half: not by chance, the wines of these two areas have separate DOCs: Riviera Ligure di Levante and Riviera Ligure di Ponente, respectively. For example, as Pigato, it is especially grown in the Valle Arroscia up to Pieve di Tenco, where the provinces of Savona and Imperia meet. (The best Riviera Ligure di Ponente Pigato wines are 95 to 100 percent Pigato.) And though Vermentino and Pigato wines might not offer quite the same diversity in the glass that Pinot Gris and Pinot Noir do, with a little tasting experience anyone can pick them out when tasting blind, for Pigato gives much bigger, more luscious, and less aromatic wines than does Vermentino. As these things happen, it is quite likely that the two grapes have adapted over the centuries to rather different terroirs, leading to different morphologic, viticultural, and enological expressions that most likely have an as-yet-unidentified genetic basis. In fact, Vermentino,

Favorita, and Pigato are all listed in Italy's national registry of grape varieties as separate entities. (This correct classification, though, was due to a stroke of luck: their inclusion preceded the availability of genetic testing, which would have led to erroneous conclusions.)

SPECIFIC TERROIRS

Sardinia and the Gallura

Vermentino grows all over Sardinia, but there are two very different wines made with it on the island: Vermentino di Sardegna and Vermentino di Gallura. The former wines are fruitier and offer earlier, uncomplicated appeal; the latter are deeper, more complex, and austere, and can showcase surprising ageworthiness. Over the years, I have tasted enough Vermentino wines released for sale and numerous experimental microvinifications to feel very comfortable in identifying the specific aromas and flavors associated with the different Sardinian subzones, as well as the Gallura denomination. I identify five different subzones for Vermentino di Sardegna wines based on the main communes within each subzone. (These subzones are not valid for Sardinian wines in general: for example, the subzones of Cannonau di Sardegna are very different from those of Vermentino di Sardegna.)

The Vermentino di Sardegna Subzones
Alghero: In Sardinia's central northwest, Vermentino grapes grow in different soils such as mainly gravel and mainly sand (these are the most abundant), but also reddish-colored soils rich in iron, calcareous-marly soils that are whiter in color, and even gray soils that are clay-rich and poor in organic matter but have relatively high potassium and phosphorus levels. The clay soils give weightier wines; the calcareous soils give wines that are more perfumed and refined.

Cabras: Located in the central-west part of Sardinia (south of Alghero), these Vermentino wines are a bit more opulent and creamy than the other Vermentino di Sardegna, with generally lower total acidity levels. These wines offer plenty of easy-to-grasp, early appeal, but I don't find them to be especially complex or nuanced.

Cagliari: Sardinia's southeast is characterized by mainly calcareous soils, and Vermentino wines made here exude especially strong notes of capers.

Serdiana: In Vermentino wines made just north of Cagliari (in the south-central part of the island), note of capers, thyme, and rosemary are especially prominent. Vermentino wines from Serdiana are easily recognizable because they are less saline than those of Alghero and those of the Cagliari area.

Usini: From Sardinia's northwest, near the city of Sassari, come wines with strongly herbal, almost vegetal nuances, that are a touch less refined than the helichrysum notes of the Vermentino di Gallura.

Gallura

The Gallura is a completely different part of Sardinia, characterized by granite soils, a rarity in Italy. However, it is wrong to view the Gallura as an area of granite only. For the most part, the soil is a very particular pink granite with high acidity and minerality, but some sections also have a presence of sand and clay. Generally speaking, Vermentino di Gallura wines are characterized by notes of green apple, white flowers (acacia and hawthorn, especially), and helichrysum (the latter being the archetypal finding in all Vermentino di Gallura wines). Vermentino di Gallura is also much more flinty and saline than Vermentino di Sardegna. However, this short synopsis of the Vermentino di Gallura aroma and flavor profiles is too simplistic and limited, given that the Gallura has wildly different terroirs and the wines reflect this.

There is an internal and a coastal Gallura, and wines from each can be very different. The internal area around the towns of Aggius, Tempio Pausania, Calangianus, and Luras is practically mountainous, and the wines are marked by a strong stoniness, as well as notes of capers, apricot, and peach.

Monti and Berchidda are towns usually associated with the internal part of the Gallura denomination but are on the border between the Gallura and Luguodoro to the west. Here the hills are gentler, with soft slopes, less steep (especially at Berchidda) than in the internal part of the Gallura. The wines are some of the most balanced of all Vermentino di Gallura, but always showcase the denomination's telltale savoriness and herbal notes. The coastal Gallura is where the towns of Badesi, Palau, Arzachena, Olbia, and Lori Porto San Paolo are located; soils are granite and warm. The climate is characterized by strong diurnal temperature variations, but the Vermentino usually ripens earlier in the year than in the mountainous Gallura. However, I believe the area around Badesi to be different from the rest of the coastal Gallura, and the wines made there are different, too: a preponderance of old bush vines planted right by the sea and a finer, sandy-like disgregated granite account for Vermentino di Gallura wines that are extremely balsamic and mineral.

BENCHMARK WINES (ONLY THREE-STAR WINES ARE MENTIONED)

Capichera***^{PS}, Capichera Vendemmia Tardiva***^{PS}.

Cantina del Vermentino Funtanaliras***, Cantina di Gallura Canayli***, Cantina di Gallura Vendemmia Tardiva***, Capichera Vigna 'Ngena***, Pala Stellato***, Paolo Depperu Ruinas***, Mura Sienda***, Masone Mannu Petrizza***, Surrau***.

Vuillermin

THE GRAPE VARIETY

As much as I love Mayolet, I really do think that Vuillermin is its equal. In fact, I think these two are among Italy's most exciting native grapes. There is not that much planted currently, but the few monovariety wines that exist are simply outstanding. Documentation on Vuillermin is relatively thin: the first to document Vuillermin's existence was Louis Napoléon Bich in 1890, who wrote of its resistance to sunburn—a real plus in mountain habitats. Vuillermin as such was probably not written about much because it was confused with Eperon or Spron, a variety that some confused with Cornalin, too. If it was a separate variety, it is now extinct (Moriondo et al. 1998). Vuillermin is related to Fumin, Rouge du Pays, Rèze (a Valais variety), and also, strangely enough, to Trentino's Nosiola, a white variety.

SPECIFIC TERROIRS

The wine is labeled DOC Valle d'Aosta Vuillermin. It is simply outstanding, combining the aromatic perfume of Mayolet with the body and tannins of Cornalin, though it is gentler in perfume and body than both those varieties. Good Vuillermin wines are never structured behemoths but rather medium-bodied, and offer a magical mix of floral and spicy perfume and fresh flavors of crisp red and blue fruit with aromatic herb nuances and a long floral finish. (For a full description of the Valle d'Aosta terroir, see the Mayolet entry.)

BENCHMARK WINES

Feudo di San Maurizio***[PS].

IAR Vuillermin**.

Zibibbo

THE GRAPE VARIETY

Zibibbo is one of the world's great wine grapes, a unique variety that can withstand heat and droughty conditions better than most other wine grapes. Better known as Moscato di Alessandria but officially called Zibibbo in Italy, the name derives from the Arab word *zibibb*, meaning "dried grape" or "raisin." Zibibbo is in fact the oldest name for this variety, since the name "zibibo" (with only one *b*) was first documented in Sicily in 1563 by Pietro Andrea Mattioli (whereas "Moscato di Alessandria" first appears only in 1713 in the catalogue of the Certosini brothers in Paris). Zibibbo is the second-oldest Muscat variety known (after Moscato Bianco), born from the crossing of Moscato Bianco and a table grape called Axina de Tres Bias (Cipriani et al. 2010). Not surprisingly, then, since Zibibbo is an extremely old variety, it is also the progenitor of at least fourteen different wine grapes, at least a couple of which are extremely important and of high quality: Sicily's Grillo (a Moscato of Alexandria × Cataratto Bianco crossing) and Lazio's Malvasia del Lazio (Moscato of Alessandria × Schiava Grossa). That so many Italian native grapes have originated in Italy from Zibibbo and another parent tells us that Zibibbo is undoubtedly a native Italian grape. A variety with many positives, Zibibbo has been planted all over the world, especially in hot and dry places. For example, we know it is identical to the Spanish Moscatos called Moscatel de Jerez, Moscatel de Malaga, and Moscato Gordo Blanco, but it is also identical to the Portuguese cultivar Moscatel de Setúbalin (Lopes et al. 1999) and the Greek Moschato Alexandreias (Lefort et al. 2000). There are also numerous red-berried mutations of Moscato di Alessandria, including the United Kingdom's Black Muscat of Alexandria, California's Flame Muscat, and Australia's Brown Muscat. Moscato di Alessandria has a plethoric look compared with the other two main Moscato varieties (Bianco and Giallo). Large, compact bunches, conical-pyramidal and slightly elongated in shape, with medium-large oval/round berries (they are much larger than those of Moscato Bianco, for example) with yellow-green, thick skins represent the habitual look for this member of the very large Moscato family. Cordonnier and Bayonove (1974) demonstrated it to be very rich in aromatic precursor molecules. In fact, when they eliminated all aromas from a Zibibbo wine (by distillation *sous vide*), they found that the aromas immediately returned when the wine was blandly reheated or if an enzyme was added. What this tells us is that heat and enzymes can liberate aroma molecules lying dormant within the wine since they are most likely bound to other molecules that impede their aromatic expression. But through acid hydrolysis and enzymatic digestion, the free aromatic molecule are liberated and can weave their odorous magic. Cabaroglu and Canbas (2002) reached similar conclusions. They identified forty-one free-volatile and twenty-eight bound aromatic compounds in Zibibbo wines (the study used the Muscat of Alexandria name); the researchers showed that prolonging must contact with the skins increased the aromatic intensity of the wines. In contrast to other Italian sweet wines such as Caluso Passito (see the Erbaluce entry) and Sciacchetrà (a Ligurian sweet wine made with air-dried local grapes), Giordano et al. (2009) found that Passito di Pantelleria wines are rich in potassium (greater than two grams per liter) and sodium (one hundred milligrams per liter); similar findings have been reported for other wines made in marine habitats, such as those of the Canary Islands (Frías et al. 2003). And yet Sciacchetrà is also made with grapes grown near the sea, but lacks Passito di Pantelleria's salt concentrations. That's terroir talking: the high potassium content is most likely owing to the volcanic nature of Pantelleria's soil (it's a volcanic island, remember) and to the high sodium levels due to the seawater-salt-saturated winds also typical of Pantelleria (to which the grapes are exposed continuously). The habitat where Sciacchetrà is made is completely different. The high potassium content in Passito di Pantelleria also helps explain the wine's fleshier, richer mouthfeel compared with that of other Italian sweet wines.

SPECIFIC TERROIRS

Pantelleria

Pantelleria is an Italian volcanic island in the Mediterranean Sea that is actually closer to Africa than it is to Italy: in fact, it lies roughly 70 kilometers from Tunisia (in Africa) and 110 kilometers from Mazzara del Vallo in Sicily. Eighty-three square kilometers large, it has a population of seventy-seven hundred. Though grown all over the world (in France, Greece, Spain, Portugal, Chile, Peru, South Africa, Australia, and California), Zibibbo or Moscato di Alessandria is absolutely at home in this beautiful island habitat. In fact, Pantelleria makes arguably the world's best Zibibbo wines, of which there are two versions: the dry DOC Moscato di Pantelleria, exuding fresh and aromatic aromas and flavors of dried herbs, fig, ginger, and dried apricot; and the Passito di Pantelleria (made from air-dried grapes), a very sweet and luscious wine redolent of honey and orange marmalade, with nuances of raisin and macerated fig. These wines are born of the interplay between marine environment, volcanic soil, a hot and windy climate, and the ingenuity and passion of men and women. Pantelleria's unique island terroir is remarkably interesting and much more varied than one might think at first glance. Dismayingly, grape production on the island has greatly decreased over the last twenty years (down from the 450,000 quintals of grapes picked in 1973 to 28,000 in 2009). Today there are 1,562 hectares under vine on the island. (There were 5,890 hectares under vine in the 1930s, for example: clearly, working windswept and sunstroked volcanic rocks is no walk in the park, so this decrease in production is not hard to understand.) Geologically, the denomination is easily divided into two parts: a northwestern portion that is made up of basaltic lava soils, and the southeast, which is characterized by mainly siliceous soils. In both portions, green ignimbrite abounds.

Pantelleria is an example of a terroir where climate plays a role of paramount importance.

Clearly, Pantelleria's soil of volcanic ash is not exactly a nutrient feast for any of the plants growing there, and its inability to hold on to water only makes matters more difficult. Looking at a vineyard landscape on Pantelleria will bring to mind more a forest of bushes rather than an open area of neat rows of vines. In fact, the vines on Pantelleria are planted in bushes lying very low to the ground, which as we have seen is a means by which to reduce water evaporation. The vines also tend to be planted in small circular pits, which serve the double function of acting as water collectors the few times it rains on the island and of helping to limit water evaporation. The climate is dry and hot, typically Mediterranean, with only 485 millimeters of rain per year; there is very little summer rainfall to speak of, and 320 millimeters per year being concentrated over the autumn and winter seasons. The average monthly temperature in February is 11.5°C, whereas it is 25°C in August. The Winkler and Huglin indices are respectively 2340 and 2800, and the general humidity is 78.8 percent, ranging over the year from 75 to 85 percent. In fact, Pantelleria's name in the Arab language is Bent el Rhia ("daughter of the wind"), which is understandable, given the almost constant presence of the winds (mainly mistral or scirocco) that blow on average 337 days a year at speeds of more than twenty kilometers per hour. As a consequence of the rather windy habitat, the trellising system in Pantelleria is the *alberello pantesco* or island bush vine; in order to have the vines escape the wind, these bush vines are buried within concave pits so that the grapes grow very close to the soil, which consists of mainly disgregated volcanic rocks. Soil phosphorus and potassium concentrations are high. For this reason, the soils are very sandy, brown in color, and have neutral or lightly acid pH; they are not especially deep but are decently fertile. Thanks to the hot, very dry and windy climate, plus the porous nature of the soils, there is very little disease pressure on the island. Northerly winds help the ripening process, while the scirocco winds bring about dehydration without much of a gain in polyphenol ripening.

Pantelleria is characterized by a very diverse topography, with a central mountainous high point reaching 836 meters above sea level, two large lateral valleys, and hence various slopes that have cone-like shapes with different exposures and gradients. These *cuddie*, as they are called locally, originated during the course of different volcanic eruptions, and therefore the soils of each (depending on the geologic period in which the eruption took place) can be relatively different. Pantelleria's soils are volcanic in origin (not by chance, legend and popular beliefs have it that it is a vestigium of the mythical Atlantis, though I know they say the same thing about the Greek island of Santorini and a few other spots as well) and of the effusive acid type called pantellerites and trachites, though there are also areas rich in green tuff (rich in green imbrignite and basalt). They are rich in organic matter and aluminum, which tend to combine, forming stable complexes together. It is the older soils that are better able to hold on to water, and this is of crucial importance to Pantelleria site quality. Pantelleria can therefore be divided into four different zones based on when Zibibbo optimal ripeness is reached. Of these four areas, three are distinct, while the fourth is located within one of the others. The earliest-ripening area of the island is its northwestern section. The medium-ripening area corresponds to the eastern half of the island. A large circular area in the island's center is where grapes ripen latest.

The Pantelleria Subzones and Contrade

Moscato and Passito di Pantelleria made with grapes grown in different sectors of the island differ appreciably in aroma and flavor profiles. Pantelleria can be divided into subzones that correspond to finite viticultural areas (known as *contrade*, similarly to the custom at Etna). Areas in the southern half of the island, such as Dietro Isola, Bukkuram, Martingana, and Coste di Barone, lend themselves to earlier ripening and are especially suited to air-drying:

but even in this part of the island, there are noteworthy differences between subzones. For example, wines made with grapes from Barone, located higher up, at four hundred meters above sea level, tend to be lighter and more fragrant than those of Martingana, characterized by a warmer microclimate. Vineyards on Pantelleria lie between twenty meters and four hundred meters above sea level and are generally planted with densities of twenty-five hundred to thirty-five hundred plants per hectare. Rather paradoxically, on Pantelleria it is the grapes harvested in the early-maturing sites that are richest in terpenes and achieve the best balance. (Normally, these are the warmest and usually give grapes that are aromatically compressed.) The presence of stones helps avoid excessive water evaporation, as do the mostly southeastern exposures and steep gradients. Vineyards planted at higher altitudes and not directly in the valleys also have better ripening of the grapes thanks to the warming anabatic currents, compared with the cooler nighttime katabatic currents that cool the site and even the rare presence of fog. The best known *contrade* of Pantelleria are Bukkuram, Martingana, and Khamma, but in fact some of the less famous sites give much more perfumed wines, such as Baroni (or Piana di Baroni, one of my favorites). Other noteworthy quality *contrade*: Dietro Isola, Favarotta, Ghirlanda Monastero, Mueggen, Mulini, Gibbiuna, Punta Karace, and Serraglia.

Martingana: At roughly thirty meters above sea level, characterized by pumice and pantellerite, Martingana has soil that is not especially porous but is rich in organic substance. Soil texture is sandy, and roots can dig down to one meter or more below the surface. Medium-good water-holding capacity.

Bukkuram: Roughly 150 meters high, Bukkuram has mainly lava soils with trachite, with a good quantity of organic substance on the surface, then fairly impermeable below. Mainly sandy, with medium-good water-holding capacity, but roots dig down thirty-five centimeters at most.

Khamma: Situated at roughly 130 meters above sea level, Khamma has rather deep (roots dig down to eighty centimeters below the surface) and porous volcanic soil that is characterized by ignimbrites, plenty of organic substance, and medium-good available water capacity.

Monastero: A lesser known *contrada* of Pantelleria, Monastero, situated at about 230 meters above sea level and characterized by fluviolacustrine deposits, gives very interesting wines; the soil is deep and porous, but tends not to accumulate much organic matter. Characterized by a very sandy texture, roots can dig down one meter below the surface. Medium water-holding capacity.

Piana di Baroni: At 350 meters above sea level, Piana di Baroni is one of the highest of all *contrade* and the one that in my opinion and experience gives the most elegant Pantelleria Zibibbo wines of all. Soils are not too evolved, are porous and deep, and have good amounts of organic matter. Roots can dig down over one meter below ground, and there is very good water-retention capacity.

Readers might wonder why, differently from other parts of this book, I insist so much on the ripening time at each site. This is because early-maturing sites do best by Zibibbo: early-maturing sites are those at which the vine's growth cycle occurs in a part of the year during which better weather is more likely (Barbeau, Morlat, and Asselin 1998), but it is important to know that "better weather" in a hot Mediterranean area such as Pantelleria means not just sunlight but also plenty of water availability in the early part of the cycle. This, along with the soil temperature of the superficial layers, helps determine an acceleration of the various phenological steps in the growth cycle, thereby increasing the rate of terpenic synthesis in the skins and the pulp at a time when it is still warm (in the months of June and July), which favors the buildup of a particularly good mix of terpenes. In other words, one is helped in identifying the best possible terroirs for Zibibbo on Pantelleria by verifying which sites allow for ripening of the grapes in such a way as to obtain the most interesting and intense mix of aromatic molecules (terpenes) possible. By contrast, harvesting too late has a negative effect on both the quality and the quantity of terpenes in the wine (Dirninger, Schneider, and Schaeffer 1997). It is these sorts of studies that provide some scientific basis for the empiric notion of the "best terroir" or "grand cru" of a wine grape—in this case, Zibibbo on Pantelleria. Clearly, terpen concentration and blend is not going to be the only important factor in determining which site may potentially give the best Zibibbo wine, but I trust you'll agree that if we are to identify which are the best possible sites on the island for the variety, it is probably better to have this information than not. In an extraordinarily interesting 1998 study by Brancadoro and associates, in which twenty-six different sites were evaluated on the island of Pantelleria, with each site described and classified according to USDA soil-taxonomy and FAO soil-classification methods, Zibibbo grapes were collected at technological ripening and Moscato di Pantelleria wines made following the same protocol. Five months later the resulting wines were evaluated by gas chromatography according to methods described by Di Stefano (1991) and by sensory analysis. The study showed what was already obvious to those working on the island: that different island sites characterized by different altitudes, soils (in terms of their depth), and types of horizons and exposures gave significantly different wines. Of the three factors under investigation, exposure was the single most important in determining the final wine outcome. Interestingly, grapes reached optimal ripeness as much as forty to fifty days later when planted in the later-ripening sites, a truly jaw-dropping difference given that Pantelleria is generally thought of as having a uniformly hot climate (obviously, not so). Wines made from the early-maturing sites differed from those made from late-ripening sites, with the former expressing notes of flowers and fresh citrus fruit, and the latter having aromas and flavors of fruit jam and raisins (Brancadoro et al. 1998). The study found that linalool and α-terpineol were present at a higher concentration than geraniol and that early sites had berries with the highest sugar levels.

BENCHMARK WINES

Donnafugata Passito di Pantelleria Ben Ryè***[PS], Ferrandes Passito di Pantelleria***[PS].

Coste Ghirlanda Jardinu***, Coste Ghirlanda Silenzio***, Donnafugata Moscato di Pantelleria Kebir***, Donnafugata Lighea***.

Dietrolisola**.

APPENDIX

TABLE 1

Possible associations of soil type with wine in the Barbera d'Asti denomination

Subzone	Winery	Denomination	Vintage	Name of wine
S1	Cascina Gilli–Vergnano Giovanni	Barbera d'Asti DOCG	2016	Le More
S1	Cascina Galarin	Barbera d'Asti DOCG	2016	Le Querce
S1	Bersano	Barbera d'Asti DOCG	2015	Costalunga
S1	Garrone Evasio & Figlio	Barbera d'Asti	2015	[none]
S2	Michele Chiarlo Srl	Barbera d'Asti DOCG	2015	Le Orme
S2	Castello di Gabiano–Marchesi Cattaneo Adorno Giustiniani	Barbera d'Asti DOCG	2015	La Braja
S2	Rovero F.lli	Barbera d'Asti Superiore	2014	Rouvè
S2	Coppo	Barbera d'Asti DOCG	2014	Pomorosso
S1-S2	Tenuta Il Falchetto	Barbera d'Asti DOCG	2016	Pian Scorrone
S1-S2	Franco Roero	Barbera d'Asti DOCG	2016	Carbunè
S1-S2	Cantina Sociale di Vinchio e Vaglio	Barbera d'Asti Superiore DOCG	2011	Vigne Vecchie
S3	Az. Agr. Marchesi Incisa della Rocchetta	Barbera d'Asti Superiore	2015	Sant'Emiliano

Subzones: S1 includes silty-clay, silty-marly, and silty-arenaceous soils; S2 includes sandy-marly and sandy-arenaceous soils; S3 includes Villafranchian soils; S4 includes sandy soils and ancient terracing soils (but no wine example I can think of).

TABLE 2

Geologic time line, including major historical events and when specific Italian wine terroirs were formed
(adapted from Zangheri 2003)

Era	Period	Epoch	Time	Wine terroir
		Holocene *Human domination begins.*	10,000 years ago to present	Gattinara
	Quaternary *Humans first appear.*	**Pleistocene** *First primitive humans appear.*	1.7 million– 10,000 years ago	Franciacorta Montefalco / Sagrantino Taurasi Torgiano Rosso Riserva Valtellina Superiore Vino Nobile di Montepulciano
		Pliocene *Apelike humans appear. An ice age nears.*	5 million– 1.7 million years ago	Brunello di Montalcino Chianti Chianti Classico Gavi / Cortese di Gavi Montefalco / Sagrantino Vernaccia di San Gimignano Vino Nobile di Montepulciano
CENOZOIC *The formation and beginning of today's world as we know it, with recognizable plants, animals, and geographic formations.*	**Tertiary** *Mammals replace reptiles.*	**Miocene** *Extremely important epoch for the formation of numerous famous Italian wine terroirs; raccoons and horses are plentiful.*	23 million– 5 million years ago	Asti / Asti Spumante / Moscato d'Asti Barbaresco Barolo Brunello di Montalcino Chianti Chianti Classico Montefalco / Sagrantino Taurasi Torgiano Rosso Riserva Vermentino di Gallura

TABLE 2 *(continued)*

Era	Period	Epoch	Time	Wine terroir
CENOZOIC (continued) *The formation and beginning of today's world as we know it, with recognizable plants, animals, and geographic formations.*	**Tertiary** (continued) *Mammals, replace reptiles.*	**Oligocene** *The first true primates make their first appearance. Horses appear for the first time on American soil.*	35 million– 23 million years ago	Chianti Chianti Classico
		Eocene *Another very important epoch for wine terroir formation in Italy; mammals adapt to marine life.*	57 million– 35 million years ago	Brunello di Montalcino Chianti Chianti Classico Recioto di Soave
		Paleocene *The modern continents as we know them begin to form.*	65 million– 57 million years ago	Brunello di Montalcino Chianti Chianti Classico
MESOZOIC *When the big dinosaurs ruled (age of reptiles).*	**Cretaceous** *Flowering plants and modern trees appear. Tyrannosaurus rex lives.*		145 million– 65 million years ago	Brunello di Montalcino Franciacorta
	Jurassic *Reptiles dominate land; Archaeopteryx, the first birdlike dinosaur, appears;* Allosaurus *is the dominant carnivore reptile. South America breaks away from Africa.*		210 million– 145 million years ago	Franciacorta
	Triassic *Dinosaurs and primitive mammals first appear. Breakup of Pangea.*		245 million– 210 million years ago	
	Permian *Conifers appear in the north. Pangea, the first major continent, forms by the fusion of different land masses.*		290 million– 245 million years ago	

(continued)

TABLE 2 *(continued)*

Era	Period	Epoch	Time	Wine terroir
	Carboniferous *Amphibians move out of the sea and onto land.*		360 million– 290 million years	
	Devonian *Bony fish appear. Land is covered with giant ferns.*		410 million– 360 million years ago	
PALEOZOIC *Life moves from the oceans onto land.*	**Silurian** *Vertebrate, jawed fish, and corals appear in the seas. Vascular plants appear on the land.*		440 million– 410 million years ago	
	Ordovician *Fish and corals appear.*		510 million– 440 million years ago	
	Cambrian *Invertebrates are present in the seas along with seaweed, while lichens are present on land.*		570 million– 510 million years ago	
			2.5 billion– 570 million years ago	
PROTEROZOIC *Marine invertebrates and algae appear in oceans.*			3.8 billion– 2.5 billion years ago	
ARCHEAN *Prokaryotic cells only; bacteria and blue-green algae appear in the oceans, where algae begin producing oxygen that reaches the atmosphere (an absolutely necessary step for the subsequent evolution of higher animals).*			4.6 billion years ago	
Formation of the universe and the Earth			20 billion– 7 billion years ago	

TABLE 3
Important Italian wine terroirs discussed in this book, their prevalent geologic substrate, geologic age, and topography (adapted from Zangheri 2003)

Wine terroir	Prevalent geologic substrate	Geologic age	Topography
Moscato d'Asti (also applies to Asti)	• Mostly blue-gray marls with a strong sandy-clay content • Sulfur-gypsum marls with clays • Serravallian compacted sands	Miocene epoch—three different stages: Tortonian (St. Agathe's fossil marls); Messinian (sulfur-gypsum marls with clays); Serravallian (compacted sands)	Hillsides (mostly 250–600 meters above sea level)
Barbaresco	Mostly blue-gray marls with a strong sandy-clay content	Medium (mainly) and Superior Miocene period (Serravallian and Tortonian stages)	Hillsides (mostly 200–400 meters above sea level, with areas in Treiso reaching 500 meters above sea level)
Barolo	• Blue-gray sandy-marly clay and compacted sands • Sulfur-gypsum marls with loamy clay	Miocene epoch—three different stages: Tortonian (St. Agathe's fossil marls); Messinian (sulfur-gypsum marls with clays); Serravallian (compacted sands)	Hillsides (mostly 250–500 meters above sea level)
Brunello di Montalcino	Clay-calcareous and tufa-rich soils	Superior Cretaceous period: Eocene epoch (calcareous rocks typical of the Ligurian facies); Superior Miocene and Superior Pliocene epochs (the neoautochthonous complex)	Hillsides (less than 677 meters above sea level)
Chianti	Large area characterized by multiple substrates (calcareous-sandy-marly . . .)	Mostly Tertiary period	Hillsides
Chianti Classico	Large area characterized by multiple substrates (calcareous-sandy-marly . . .), but more homogenous than Chianti	Mostly Tertiary period	Hillsides (250–800 meters above sea level)
Franciacorta	Partly calcareous rocks and flysches and partly moraine deposits (Lake Iseo Amphitheater)	Jurassic-Cretaceous and Quaternary periods (moraine deposits)	Hillsides
Montefalco Sagrantino	Sandy clays and lacustrine conglomerates (Lacustrine Formation) plus alternating clay and compacted sandy clays	Pliocene, Pleistocene, and Miocene epochs (Tortonian and Langhian stages)	Hillsides
Soave	Prevalently nummulitic calcareous rocks plus other sedimentary calcareous formations (Biancone and Scaglia Rossa) and tertiary vulcanites	Eocene epoch (nummulitic calcareous rocks); Cretaceous period (Biancone and Scaglia Rossa Formations); Tertiary period (Vulcanites)	Hillsides with sedimentary rocks and magmatic inclusions (basalt)

(continued)

TABLE 3 *(continued)*

Wine terroir	Prevalent geologic substrate	Geologic age	Topography
Taurasi	Clay-calcareous, with tufa and volcanic elements	Miocene epoch and Quaternary period	Hillsides
Torgiano Rosso Riserva	Loam and clay-rich compacted sands	Miocene epoch (compacted sands) and Quaternary period	Hillsides
Valtellina Superiore	Crystalline schists and glacial deposits	Prevalently pre-Permian period (mostly schists); Quaternary period (moraine deposits)	Mountains
Vermentino di Gallura	Mostly granites with the presence of volcanic and carbonate rocks	Primary period and Miocene epoch	Hillsides

TABLE 4

Breakdown of the Quaternary, Neogene, and Paleogene periods

Period (system)	Epoch (series)	Stage (age)
Quaternary	Pleistocene	Gelasian
Neogene	Pliocene	Piacenzian
		Zanclean
	Miocene	Messinian
		Tortonian
		Serravallian
		Langhian
		Burdigalian
		Aquitanian
Paleogene	Oligocene	Chattian

Adapted from International Commission on Stratigraphy 2017.

GLOSSARY

BASALT: potassium-rich, it is typical of volcanic rocks.

CALCAREOUS (SOIL): any soil with high calcium and magnesium carbonate concentrations. These soils are usually alkaline, with very good drainage (unless the clay content is too high, as in some calcareous clays), and may be low in phosphorus.

CLAY: the smallest soil particle size, usually defined as less than two micrometers. Clay-rich soils are cold, acid, compact, and hard to work. (I caution readers that clay soils are thought of as being acid because they can theoretically hold more hydrogen atoms than other soils, but they do not actually always do so. Therefore, they are not necessarily always acid soils.) If clay soils are too packed, they can suffocate roots. Clays usually have outstanding water-retention capacity, and vines are less likely to go into water stress on clay-rich soils (but this is not always so). Of the three granulometric fractions that can make up soils (loam, sand, and clay), it is clay that interacts most with the plants' roots in helping to regulate exchanges in water and minerals. Clays have plate-like crystalline structures and are essentially made up like a sandwich, with numerous layers one on top of another. The flat layers (for the most part, hydrated silicates of aluminum, and also of iron and magnesium) have permanent negative charge and therefore attract cations (which are positively charged ions and are different from anions, which are negatively charged); the negative charge and the large surface area of clays

ensure that these are the site of many physical and chemical reactions. It is the different composition of these tetrahedrally or octahedrally shaped layers that account for differences in clay types: vermiculites, illites, smectites, and chlorites are just a few of the many different clays out there. Different clays soil properties range from the low cationic exchange capacity of chlorites to the great plasticity of smectites.

CLAY-LOAM: fertile loam characterized (depending on the clay content) by good water retention.

FERRUGINOUS CLAY: iron-rich clay.

GRANITE (SOIL): a high-pH soil that contains roughly 40 to 60 percent quartz and 30 to 40 percent potassium feldspar. (Feldspar is a silicate of potassium-aluminum or sodium-calcium-aluminum.)

GRAVEL (SOILS): characterized by pebbles and stones of all shapes and sizes. These soils are most often acid and infertile, and offer outstanding drainage depending on the nature of the subsoils (not a good thing in droughty years).

LOAM: a mix of silt, sand, and clay in varying proportions (usually in a 40–40–20 percent mix). When none of the three predominate, we use the term "loam"; otherwise it is "loamy clay" or "sandy loam," depending on which component prevails.

MARL: a cold, calcareous clay (a mixture of clay and lime) that delays ripening. Whereas lime is roughly 95 percent lime and 5 percent clay, calcareous clay is more like a 75–25 percent mix of the two, with marl being a roughly 65–35 percent mix.

SAND (SOIL): usually acid soil that is not especially fertile, made up of very small particles of small rock that is loosely packed; characterized by excellent drainage. Based on the size of the particles, sand can be divided into fine sand (with particles ranging in size between fifty and two hundred micrometers) and coarse sand (any sand made up of larger particles).

SCHIST: a laminated, crystalline rock usually rich in potassium and magnesium. It derives from shale.

SILT: a very fine deposit (at between two and fifty micrometers, silt particles are just next up in size from clay) characterized by poor drainage.

TUFA: a limestone resulting from deposited groundwater. Unlike tuff, it is not volcanic in origin.

TUFF: volcanic soil.

VOLCANIC (SOILS): volcanic soils are referred to as lava-based, and are mainly composed of basalt, with small percentages of andesite, rhyolite, and trachyte. Volcano lavas are differentiated by their chemical characteristics, the most noteworthy being the content of silica in the magma they expel. Silica strongly influences the characteristics of the volcano's magma and how this will behave in an eruption. When magma is rich in silica, it is a great deal more viscous and tends to hold noxious gases within that can cause horrific explosions, with numerous rocky fragments (at times very large ones) being jettisoned at a considerable distance from the volcano, with a thick layer of smoke extending for kilometers. These type of eruptions are called "explosive" and are extremely dangerous, in that not just the far-reaching explosion but also the highly toxic gases liberated in the eruption are noxious to any surrounding life. Such volcanic soils produce plenty of either pumice (molten particles that cool down in the atmosphere and drop to the earth) or ash (highly fragmented particles pulverized by the explosive forces at work). Examples of such volcanos in Italy are Vesuvius and Stromboli (the latter is the name of one of the Lipari or Aeolian Islands and is essentially a volcano emerging from the water). When lava is poor in silica content, it is less viscous and tends to flow freely; eruptions such as these are called effusive and are characteristic of slowly sloping volcanos with large bases, such as those of the Hawaiian Islands. However, most volcanos are of an intermediate type, such as, for example, Etna.

BIBLIOGRAPHY

Abbate, E., and M. Sagri. 1970. "The eugeosyncli-
nal sequences." In "Development of the Northern
Apennines Geosyncline," ed. G. Sensini.
Special issue, *Sedimentary Geology* 4 (3–4):
251–340.

Accigliaro, W., G. Boffa, and D. Destefanis. 1993.
*Castiglione Falletto: Dai Saluzzo ai Savoia
attraverso tre diocesi.* Turin: Gribaudo.

Acerbi, G. 1825. *Delle viti italiane ossia materiali per
servire alla classificazione, monografia e sinonimia,
preceduti dal tentativo di una classificazione delle
viti.* Milan: G. Silvestri.

Aldave de las Heras, L., Y. Le Fur, and M. Feuillat.
1992. "Skin contact effects on Vermentino and
Semillon grapes varieties." *Sciences des Aliments*
12 (3): 483–92.

Anderson, K. 2014. "Changing varietal distinctive-
ness of the world's wine regions: Evidence from a
new global database." *Journal of Wine Economics*
9 (3): 249–72.

Anesi, A., S. Dal Santo, M. Commisso, S. Zenoni,
S. Ceoldo, G. B. Tornielli, T. E. Siebert, M.
Herderich, M. Pezzotti, and F. Guzzo. 2015.
"Towards a scientific interpretation of the *terroir*
concept: Plasticity of the grape berry metabo-
lome." *BMC Plant Biology* 15:191.

Ansaldi, G., D. Cartabellotta, V. Falco, F. Gagliano,
and A. Scienza. 2014. *Identità e ricchezza del
vigneto Sicilia.* Palermo: Regione Sicilia,
Assessorato dell'Agricoltura, dello Sviluppo
Rurale, e della Pesca Mediterranea.

Arbabzadeh-Jolfaee, A. F. 1982. "Response of grapes
to saline irrigation water." PhD diss., University

of Arizona, 1981. *Abstracts International* B 42 (7):
2624B–2625B.

Archetti, G. 1997. "La vite e il vino a Brescia nel
medioevo." *Civiltà Bresciana* 6 (3): 3–24.

Bandinelli, R., G. Dicollalto, A. Fabbri, G. B.
Mannini, F. P. Nicese, and E. Rinaldelli. 1986.
"Osservazioni sul danno da freddo alla vite in
Toscana." *Notiziario di Ortoflorofrutticoltura*
12 (6): 249–55.

Barbeau, G., R. Morlat, and C. Asselin. 1998.
"Relations entre la précocité de la vigne et la
composition des baies des différents cépages du
Val de Loire: Suite et fin." *Le Progrès Agricole et
Viticole* 6 (115): 127–30.

Baroncini, D. 2016. "Presentazione." In G. La
Greca, *Passolina, uva passa e Malvasia: L'economia
vitivinicola delle Eolie.* Lipari: Edizioni Centro
Studi Eolano.

Bazin, J. F. 2012. "L'émergence de la notion de
climat en Bourgogne." *Pays de Bourgogne: Les
Climats* 231:4–6.

Belancic, A., E. Agosin, A. Ibacache, E. Bordeu,
R. Baumes, A. Razungles, and C. Bayonove.
1997. "Influence of sun exposure on the aromatic
composition of Chilean Muscat grape cultivars
Moscatel de Alejandría and Moscatel Rosada."
American Journal of Enology and Viticulture
48 (2): 181–86.

Belfrage, N. 2001. *Brunello to Zibibbo: The Wines of
Tuscany, Central and Southern Italy.* London:
Faber and Faber.

Berget, A. 1904. "Maïolet." In *Ampelographie*, edited
by P. Viala and V. Vermorel. Paris: Masson et Cie.

Bertuccioli, M. 2004. "Idoneità e peculiarità del Sangiovese e gusto internazionale." In Atti del Simposio Internazionale, "Il Sangiovese vitigno tipico: Identità e peculiarità," 253–63. Florence: Arsia–Regione Toscana.

Bich, L. N. 1896. *Monographie des cépages de la Vallée d'Aoste et leurs systèmes de culture*. Aosta: L. Mensio.

Boccaletti, M., and M. Sagri. 1965. "Strutture caotiche nell'Appennino 1) Età, assetto giacitura del complesso argilloso-calcareo affiorante nella parte occidentale del Foglio 129 'S. Fiora.'" *Bollettino della Società Geologica Italiana* 83 (4): 461–524.

Bogoni, M., O. Failla, R. Minelli, C. A. Panont, and P. L. Villa. 1997. *La zonazione della Franciacorta*. Brescia: Amministrazione Provinciale.

Boni, I. 2006. "La zonazione vitivinicola in Piemonte: Gli esempi del Barolo e della Barbera d'Asti." *Il Suolo*, nos. 1–3.

Bordiga, M., G. Piana, J. D. Coïsson, F. Travaglia, and M. Arlorio. 2014. "Headspace solid-phase micro extraction coupled to comprehensive two-dimensional with time-of-flight mass spectrometry applied to the evaluation of Nebbiolo-based wine volatile aroma during ageing." *International Journal of Food Science and Technology* 49 (3): 787–96.

Borgo, M., A. Cartechini, L. Lovat, and G. Moretti. 2004. "Nuove selezioni clonali dei vitigni umbri." *Vignevini* 5:73–80.

Borsa, D., D. Carniel, A. Asproudi, L. Ponticelli, M. Crespan, and A. Costacurta. 2005. "Caratterizzazione di uve Malvasia attraverso lo studio dei metaboliti secondari." *Rivista di Viticoltura e Enologia*, nos. 2–4: 167–82.

Boselli, E., E. Bendia, G. Di Lecce, A. Benedetti, and N. G. Frega. 2009. "Ethyl caffeate from Verdicchio wine: Chromatographic purification and *in vivo* evaluation of its antifibrotic activity." *Journal of Separation Science* 32 (21): 3585–90.

Boselli, M., B. Volpe, and C. Di Vaio. 1996. "Effect of seed number per berry on mineral composition of grapevine (*Vitis vinifera* L.) berries." *Journal of Horticulture Science* 70 (3): 509–15.

Bosellini, A., F. Carraro, M. Corsi, G. P. De Vecchi, G. O. Gatto, R., Malaroda, C. Sturani, S. Ungaro, and B. Zanettin. 1967. *Note illustrative della carta geologica d'Italia alla scala 1:100,000. Foglio 49, Verona*. Rome: Nuova Tecnica Grafica.

Botos, E. P., and A. Bacsó. 2003. "Tokaj zonation, traditions and future prospects." In *Terroir, zonazione, viticoltura: Trattato internazionale*, ed. M. Fregoni, D. Schuster, and A. Paoletti, 345–55. Rivoli Veronese, Italy: Phytoline.

Bott, L., and E. Chambers. 2006. "Sensory characteristics of combinations of chemicals potentially associated with beany aromas in foods." *Journal of Sensory Studies* 21 (3): 308–21.

Botta, R., A. Schneider, A. Akkak, N. S. Scott, and M. R. Thomas. 2000. "Within cultivar grapevine variability studied by morphometrical and molecular marker based techniques." *Acta Horticulturae* 528:91–96.

Brajkovich, M. 2017. "Revealing vineyard terroir: A New Zealand perspective." Paper presented at the 2nd Terroir Renaissance International Wine Symposium, Shanghai, December 8–10.

Brancadoro, L., C. Pilenga, A. Scienza, D. Lanati, F. Guaitoli, M. Perciabosco, and A. Pumo. 1998. "Influenza del sito di coltivazione nella espressione aromatica del Moscato liquoroso di Pantelleria." In *Territorio e Vino, Atti del Simposio Internazionale, Siena, 19–24 maggio, 71–83*. Siena: Città del Vino.

Broadbent, M. 2003. "Terroir: Place, time and people." In *Terroir, zonazione, viticoltura: Trattato internazionale*, ed. M. Fregoni, D. Schuster, and A. Paoletti, 18–19. Rivoli Veronese, Italy: Phytoline.

Brousset, J., D. Picque, L. Guerin, E. Goulet, and N. Perrot. 2010. "Potentiel des sols viticoles et qualité des vins." Paper presented at the 8th International Terroir Congress, Soave, Italy, June 14–18.

Bruwer, J., and R. Johnson. 2010. "Place-based marketing and regional branding strategy perspectives in the California wine industry." *Journal of Consumer Marketing* 27 (1): 5–16.

Cabaroglu, T., and A. Canbas. 2010. "The effect of skin contact on the aromatic composition of the white wine of *Vitis vinifera* L. cv. Muscat of Alexandria grown in Southern Anatolia." *Acta Alimentaria* 31 (1): 45–55.

Cai, J., B. Q. Zhu, Y. H. Wang, L. Lu, Y. B. Lan, M. J. Reeves, and C. Q. Duan. 2014. "Influence of pre-fermentation cold maceration treatment on aroma compounds of Cabernet Sauvignon wines fermented in different industrial scale fermenters." *Food Chemistry* 154:217–29.

Calandra, R., and A. Leccese. 2007. "Indagini ambientali." In *Caratterizzazione vitivinicola dell'area a denominazione di origine controllata Montefalco*, ed. Agenzia Regionale Umbra per lo Sviluppo e l'Innovazione in Agricoltura, 15–38. Todi, Italy: Edizioni 3 A–Parco Tecnologico Agroalimentare dell'Umbria.

Calò, A., and A. Costacurta. 1991. *Delle viti in Friuli*. Udine: Arti Grafiche Friulane.

Calò, A., A. Costacurta, S. Cancellier, M. Crespan, N. Milani, R. Carraro, E. Giusti, et al. 2000. *Delle* viti Prosecche: Ovvero della distinzione fra Prosecco tondo e Prosecco lungo. Pordenone, Italy: Libra.

Calò, A., A. Costacurta, S. Cancellier, and R. Forti. 1991. "Verdicchio bianco, Trebbiano di Soave: Un unico vitigno." *Vignevini* 11:49–52.

Campis, P. 1980. *Disegno historico della nobile e fedelissima città di Lipari.* Lipari: Bartolino Famularo.

Cancellier, S., and U. Angelini. 1993. "Corvina Veronese e Corvinone: Due varietà diverse." *Vignevini* 20 (5): 44–46.

Cantini, C., T. Ceccarelli, G. Sani, and F. Nizzi Grifi. 2015. *La zonazione olivicola e miglioramento della filiera oleicola del Chianti Classico.* Florence: Consorzio dell'Olio DOP del Chianti Classico.

Carboni, D., and S. Ginesu. 2010. "The Malvasia wine of Bosa as an example of Sardinian *terroir* through its history, economy, traditions and exploitation." *Revista de Ciencias Humanas* 24:59–98.

Carmignani, L., and A. Lazzarotto. 2004. *Geologic Map of Tuscany (Italy): Regione Toscana.* Special edition for the 32nd International Geologic Congress. Florence: Litografia Artistica Cartografica.

Carulli, G. B. 2006. *Carta geologica del Friuli Venezia Giulia, scala 1:150.000.* Regione Friuli Venezia Giulia, Direzione Regionale Ambiente e Lavori Pubblici, Servizio Geologico. Florence: S.E.L.C.A.

Cavazza, D. 1907. *Barbaresco e i suoi vini: Estratto dall'almanacco dell' "Italia agricola."* Piacenza: V. Porta. Reprint, 2009. Barbaresco, Italy: Tipografia Artigianale di Alba con la collaborazione della Produttori di Barbaresco.

Cellino, A., and M. Soster. 1998. "Studio per la caratterizzazione delle produzioni vitivinicole dell'area del Barbera d'Asti DOC." In *Atti del Simposio Territorio & Vino,* 341–54. Siena: Associazione Nazionale Città del Vino.

Cerreti, M., M. Esti, I. Benucci, K. Liburdi, C. De Simone, and P. Ferranti. 2015. "Evolution of S-cysteinylated and S-glutathionylated thiol precursors during grape ripening of *Vitis vinifera* L. cvs Grechetto, Malvasia del Lazio and Sauvignon Blanc." *Australian Journal of Grape and Wine Research* 21 (3): 411–16.

Cerreti, M., P. Ferranti, I. Benucci, K. Liburdi, C. De Simone, and M. Esti. 2017. "Thiol precursors in Grechetto grape juice and aromatic expression in wines." *European Food Research and Technology* 243 (5): 753–60.

Chambers, E., IV, and K. Koppel. 2013. "Association of volatile compounds with sensory aroma and flavor: The complex nature of flavor." *Molecules* 18:4887–905.

Cipriani, G., A. Spadotto, I. Jurman, G. Di Gaspero, M. Crespan, S. Meneghetti, E. Frare, et al. 2010. "The SSR-based molecular profile of 1005 grapevine (*Vitis vinifera* L.) accessions uncovers new synonymy and parentages, and reveals a large admixture amongst varieties of different geographic origin." *Theoretical and Applied Genetics* 121 (8): 1569–85.

Cita, M. B., S. Chiesa, and P. Massiotta. 2001. *Geologia dei vini italiani: Italia settentrionale.* Milan: BE-MA.

Coelho, E., M. A. Coimbra, J. M. Nogueira, and S. M. Rocha. 2009. "Quantification approach for assessment of sparkling wine volatiles from different soils, ripening stages, and varieties by stir bar sorptive extraction with liquid desorption." *Analytica Chimica Acta* 635 (2): 214–421.

Cordonnier, R., and C. Bayonove. 1974. "Mise en évidence dans la baie de raisin variété Muscat d'Alexandrie, de monoterpènes liés révélables par une ou plusieurs enzymes du fruit." *Comptes Rendus de l'Académie des Sciences Paris,* ser. D, vol. 278: 3387–90.

Corino, L., P. Ruario, G. Renosio, M. Rabino, and G. Malerba. 1991. "Esperienze di diradamento grappoli sul vitigno Barbera in alcuni ambienti del Monferrato." *Vignevini* 18 (7–8): 51–58.

Costacurta, A. 1978. "Ribolla." *Agricoltura delle Venezie* 8:364–65.

Costacurta, A., S. Gianneto, S. Meneghetti, and M. Crespan. 2006. "Does it exist a Greek ampelographic heredity in southern Italy? SSR profiles comparison of cultivars growing in both countries." Paper presented at Ampelos 2006, the 2nd International Symposium on the Evaluation and Exploitation of Grapes of Corresponding Terroir through Winemaking and Commercialization of Wines, Santorini, June 1–3.

Costantini A., M. Lazzarotto, M. Maccantelli, R. Mazzanti, F. Sandrelli, and E. Tavarnelli. 1990. *Carta geografica della provincia di Livorno a sud del fiume Cecina.* Florence: S.E.L.C.A.

Costantini, E., ed. 2017. *Ribolla story: Vini e vitigni che hanno sfidato i secoli.* Udine: Forum.

Costantini, E., S. Pellegrini, P. Bucelli, R. Barbetti, S. Campagnolo, P. Storchi, S. Magini, and R. Perria. 2010. "Mapping suitability for Sangiovese wine by means of $\delta^{13}C$ and geophysical sensors in soils with moderate salinity." *European Journal of Agronomy* 33 (3): 208–17.

Costantini, L., A. Monaco, J. F. Vouillamoz, M. Forlani, and M. S. Grando. 2005. "Genetic relationships among local *Vitis vinifera* cultivars from Campania (Italy)." *Vitis* 44 (1): 25–34.

Cravero, M.C., and R. Di Stefano. 1992. "Composizione fenolica di alcune varietà di vite coltivate in Piemonte." *Vignevini* 19 (5): 47–54.

Crespan, M., F. Cabello, S. Giannetto, J. Ibanez, J. Karoglan Kontic, E. Maletic, I. Pejic, I. Rodriguez-Torres, and D. Antonacci. 2006. "Malvasia delle Lipari, Malvasia di Sardegna, Greco di Gerace, Malvasia de Sitges, and Malvasia dubrovačka: Synonyms of an old and famous grape cultivar." *Vitis* 45 (2): 69–73.

Crespan, M., A. Calò, A. Costacurta, N. Milani, M. Giust, M. Carraro, and R. Di Stefano. 2002. "Ciliegiolo ed Aglianicone: Unico vitigno direttamente imparentato col Sangiovese." *Rivista di Viticoltura ed Enologia* 55 (2/3): 3–14.

Crespan, M., A. Calò, S. Giannetto, A. Sparacio, P. Storchi, and A. Costacurta. 2008. "Sangiovese and Garganega are two key varieties of the Italian grapevine assortment evolution." *Vitis* 47 (2): 97–104.

Crespan, M., G. Crespan, S. Giannetto, S. Meneghetti, and A. Costacurta. 2007. "'Vitouska' is the progeny of 'Prosecco tondo' and 'Malvasia bianca lunga.'" *Vitis* 46 (4): 192–94.

Crespan, M., S. Giannetto, S. Meneghetti, C. Petrussi, F. Del Zan, and P. Sivilotti. 2011. "Recognition and genotyping of minor germplasm of Friuli Venezia Giulia revealed high diversity." *Vitis* 50 (1): 21–28.

Crespan, M., and N. Milani. 2001. "The muscats: A molecular analysis of synonyms, homonyms, and genetic relationships within a large family of related grapevine cultivars." *Vitis* 40 (1): 23–30.

Crupi, A., A. Coletta, and D. Antonacci. 2010. "Analysis of carotenoids in grapes to predict norisoprenoid varietal aroma of wines from Apulia." *Journal of Agriculture and Food Chemistry* 58 (17): 9647–56.

Cuadros-Inostroza, A., P. Giavalisco, J. Hummel, A. Eckardt, L. Willmitzer, and H. Peña Cortés. 2010. "Discrimination of wine attributes by metabolome analysis." *Analytical Chemistry* 82:3573–80.

Cupani, F. 1696. *Hortus Catholicus*. Naples: Benzi.

D'Agata, I. 2001. "Educazione: Viva l'Italia; Il vitigno autoctono." *Porthos* 6 (June): 90–94.

———. 2004. "Speriamo sia autoctono, parte seconda." *Cucina e Vini* 60 (November): 128–34.

———. 2007. "Picolit, un amore antico per un ricordo d'infanzia." In *Colli orientali del Friuli: Dedicato al Picolit DOCG*, ed. B. Puciarelli, 159–61. Cividale del Friuli, Italy: Consorzio Tutela Vini Colli Orientali del Friuli.

———. 2008. *The Ecco Guide to the Best Wines of Italy*. New York: HarperCollins.

———. 2009. "A modest proposal for updating and protecting Brunello di Montalcino." *International Wine Cellar*, July.

———. 2012a. "Wine's true colours." *Decanter* 37 (6): 52–55.

———. 2012b. "Don't lose Brunello's unique magic." *Decanter* 37 (7): 38.

———. 2014a. *Native Wine Grapes of Italy*. Berkeley: University of California Press.

———. 2014b. "Italy's most famous vineyard." *Decanter* 39 (8): 24–30.

———. 2016. "Italy's 10 best terroirs." *Decanter* 41 (8): 24–33.

———. 2017. "The 2000–2015 Miani Ribolla Gialla vertical." *Vinous*, December.

———. 2018. "Giovanni Battista Columbu Malvasia di Bosa vertical." *Vinous*, February.

D'Agata, I., L. He, and M. Longo. 2019. *Barolo and Barbaresco: Listening to Nebbiolo in the Langhe*. independently published by Amazon.

D'Alatri, M., and C. Carosi. 1976. *Gli statuti medioevali della Città di Alatri*. Alatri, Italy: Tofani.

Dall'Asta, C., M. Cirlini, E. Morini, and G. Galaverna. 2011. "Brand-dependent volatile fingerprinting of Italian wines from Valpolicella." *Journal of Chromatography* 1218 (42): 7557–65.

Dalmasso, G., I. Cosmo, and G. Dell'Olio. 1939. "I vini pregiati della provincia di Verona." In *Annali della sperimentazione agraria*, vol. 35. Rome: Failli.

D'Ambra, S. 1962. "La vite e il vino nell'isola d'Ischia." *Atti dell'Accademia Italiana della Vite e del Vino* 14: 37–54.

D'Ascia, G. 1867. *Storia dell'isola d'Ischia*. Naples: Gabriele Argenio.

D'Auria, M., G. Mauriello, and G.L. Rana. 2004. "Volatile organic compounds from saffron." *Flavour and Fragrance Journal* 19:17–23.

de Villaine, A. 2010. "La vraie modernité." In *Le réveil des terroirs: Défense et illustration des climats de Bourgogne*, ed. J. Rigaux. Messigny-et-Vantoux, France: Éditions de Bourgogne.

Di Giovannatonio, C., and G. Pica. 2016. "Il comparto vitivinicolo regionale: Qualità e garanzia." Paper presented in Cori, Lazio, June 8.

Di Lecce, G., E. Boselli, G. D'Ignazi, and N.G. Frega. 2013. "Evolution of phenolics and glutathione in Verdicchio wine obtained with maceration in reductive conditions." *International Journal of Food Science and Technology* 53:54–60.

Di Rovasenda, G. 1877. *Saggio di una ampelografia universale*. Turin: Loescher.

Di Stefano, R. 1991. "Proposal for a method of sample preparation for the determination of free and glycoside terpenes of grapes and wines." *Bulletin de l'O.I.V* 721: 219–23.

———. 2001. *Dell'uva e dei vini di Casorzo.* Asti: Istituto Sperimentale per l'Enologia in collaboration with the Consorzio per la Tutela del Vino Malvasia di Casorzo.

Di Stefano, R., S. Foti, and D. Borsa. 1993. "Indagine sulla natura e sul contenuto di alcuni classi di polifenoli di alcune uve prodotte nella Sicilia orientale." *L'Enotecnico* 29:67–73.

Di Stefano, R., F. Mattivi, M. Caburazzi, and L. Bonifazi. 2009. "Profilo aromatico dell'uva e del vino Sagrantino." *Rivista di Viticoltura ed Enologia* 62 (2): 57–68.

Di Stefano, R., R. Pigella, D. Borsa, N. Gentilini, and S. Foti. 1996. "Precursori d'aroma presenti in alcune uve della Sicilia Orientale." *Annali Istituto Sperimentale per l'Enologia* 27:83–89.

Di Stefano, R., E. Vaudano, D. Borsa, L. Panero, N. Gentilini, R. Follis, S. Gaetani, V. Gerbi, G. Zeppa, and L. Rolle. 2001. "Barbera: Studio per la caratterizzazione del territorio, delle uve, e dei vini dell'area di produzione del Barbera d'Asti–Aspetti enologici." *Quaderni della Regione Piemonte Agricoltura* 26:107–22.

Di Vecchi Staraz, M., R. Bandinelli, M. Boselli, P. This, J. M. Boursiquot, V. Laucou, T. Lacombe, and D. Varès. 2007. "Genetic structuring and parentage analysis for evolutionary studies in grapevine: Kin group and origin of the cultivar Sangiovese revealed." *Journal of the American Society for Horticultural Science* 132 (4): 514–24.

Dirninger, N., C. Schneider, and A. Schaeffer. 1997. "Quelques aspects de l'influence du terroir sur l'expression aromatique des vins Gewurztraminer alsaciens." *Les Vins d'Alsace*, February, 20–23.

D'Onofrio, C., and G. Scalabrelli. 2015. "Grechetto." In *Italian Vitis Database*, www.vitisdb.it, ISSN 2282-006X.

Dosi, A., and F. Schnell. 1992. *Le abitudini alimentari dei Romani.* Rome: Quasar.

Du, X. F., A. Kurnianta, M. McDaniel, C. E. Finn, and M. C. Qian. 2010. "Flavor profiling of 'Marion' and thornless blackberries by instrumental and sensory analysis." *Food Chemistry* 121:1080–88.

Duchêne, E., J. L. Legras, F. Karst, D. Merdinoglu, P. Claudel, N. Jaegli, and F. Pelsy. 2009. "Variation of linalool and geraniol content within two pairs of aromatic and non-aromatic grapevine clones." *Australian Journal of Grape and Wine Research* 15 (2): 120–30.

Ducruet, V. 1984. "Comparison of the headspace volatiles of carbonic maceration and traditional wine." *Lebensmittel-Wissenschaft & Technologie* 17:217–21.

Egger, E., M. G. Greco, M. Pierucci, and P. Storchi. 1998. "Zonazione aziendale nel territorio del Chianti Classico e valorizzazione dei vini." In *Atti del Simposio Territorio & Vino*, 341–54. Siena: Associazione Nazionale Città del Vino.

Eggers, N. J., K. Bohna, and B. Dooley. 2006. "Determination of vitispirane in wines by stable isotope dilution assay." *American Journal of Enology and Viticulture* 57 (2): 226–32.

Emanuelli, F., S. Lorenzi, L. Grzeskowiak, V. Catalano, M. Stefanini, M. Troggio, S. Myles, et al. 2013. "Genetic diversity and population structure assessed by SSR and SNP markers in a large germplasm collection of grape." *BMC Plant Biology* 13 (1): 39.

Esti, M., R. L. Gonzáles-Airola, E. Moneta, M. Paperaio, and F. Sinesio. 2010. "Qualitative data analysis for a sensory study of grechetto wine." *Analytica Chimica Acta* 660:63–67.

Etiévant, P. X., S. N. Issanchou, and C. L. Bayonove. 1983. "The flavour of Mucat wine: The sensory contribution of some volatile compounds." *Journal of the Science of Food and Agriculture* 34 (5): 497–504.

Eynard, I., A. Morando, G. Gay, and M. Olivero. 1975. "Ricerche su differenti potature effettuate sula vite dopo una forte potatura." *Il Coltivatore e G.I.V.* 121 (4–5): 70–90.

Fabbro, C. 2008. *Il vino in Friuli Venezia Giulia.* Vol. 1, *Storia, Terra e Vitigni.* Udine: Editoriale FVG.

Fabiani, L. 1968. *La Terra di S. Benedetto: Abbazia di Montecassino.* Vol. 2. Cassino, Italy: Franco Di Meo & Figli.

Fabiani, R. 1913. *I bacini dell'Alpone, del Tramigna e del Progno d'Illasi nei Lessini medi.* Vols. 44 and 45. Venice: Uff. Idrogr. Mag. Acque.

Failla, O., L. Mariani, L. Brancadoro, A. Scienza, G. Murada, and S. Mancini. 2004. "Spatial distribution of solar radiation and effects on vine phenology and grape ripening in an alpine environment." *American Journal of Enology* 55 (2): 128–38.

Failla, O., A. Scienza, P. Fiorini, and R. Minelli. 1998. "La zonazione della Valle d'Illasi (Verona)." In *Atti del Simposio Territorio & Vino*, 401–16. Siena: Associazione Nazionale Città del Vino.

Fang, Y., and M. C. Qian. 2006. "Quantification of selected aroma-active compounds in Pinot Noir wines from different grape maturities." *Journal of Agricultural Food Chemistry* 54 (22): 8567–73.

Fedrizzi, B., E. Tosi, B. Simonato, F. Finato, M. Cipriani, G. Caramia, and G. Zapparoli. 2011.

"Changes in wine aroma composition according to botrytized berry percentage: A preliminary study on Amarone wine." *Food Technology and Biotechnology* 49 (4): 529–35.

Fedrizzi, B., G. Versini, I. Lavagnini, G. Nicolini, and F. Magno. 2007. "Gas chromatography–mass spectrometry determination of 3-mercaptohexyl acetate in wine: A comparison of headspace solid phase microextraction and solid phase extraction methods." *Analytica Chimica Acta* 596 (2): 291–97.

Ferrara, F. 1810. *I Campi Flegrei della Sicilia e delle isole che le sono intorno*. Messina: Stamperia dell'Armata Britannica.

Ferrarini, R. 2014. "L'effetto appassimento su Corvina, Corvinone and Rondinella." *L'Enologo, no. 4: 26–34.

Ferrarini, R., V. Guantieri, F. Mattivi, S. Carlin, U. Vrhovsek, and F. Lonardi. 2015. "Determinazione del rotundone, l'aroma pepato, nelle varietà principi della Valpolicella: Corvina e Corvinone." *L'Enologo*, nos. 1–2: 79–83.

Ferreira, V., N. Ortin, A. Escudero, R. Lopez, and J. Cacho. 2002. "Chemical characterization of the aroma of Grenache Rose wines: Aroma extraction dilution analysis, quantitative determinations and sensory reconstitution studies." *Journal of Agricultural Food Chemistry* 50:4048–54.

Fila, G., F. Meggio, L. M. Veilleux, and A. Pitacco. 2010. "Analysis of spatial-temporal variability in the Conegliano-Valdobbiadene DOCG district." Paper presented at the 8th International Terroir Congress, Soave, Italy, June 14–18.

Filippetti, I., O. Silvestroni, and C. Intrieri. 1999. "Individuazione di omonimie e di sinonimie in alcune varietà di *Vitis vinifera* attraverso metodi ampelografici e analisi del DNA a mezzo di microsatelliti." *Frutticoltura* 7/8: 79–84.

Filiputti, W. 1983. *Terre, vigne e vini del Friuli–Venezia Giulia*. Udine: Angelico Benvenuto.

Fitzgerald, F. S. 2011. *On Booze*. New York: New Directions.

Flamini, R. 2013. "Aromatic potential of some Malvasia wine grapes through the study of monoterpene glycosides." Paper presented at the 4th Symposium Malvasia of the Mediterranean, Monemvasia, Greece, June 23–27.

Folk, R. L. 1959. "Practical petrographic classification of limestones." *American Association of Petroleum Geologists Bulletin* 43 (1): 1–38.

Forlani, M., D. Gioffré, and V. Coppola. 1991. "Osservazioni sulla fertilità delle gemme in otto vitigni (*Vitis vinifera* L.)." *Rivista di Viticoltura ed Enologia* 34:334–41.

Foti, S. 2012. *I vini del vulcano*. Catania: Giuseppe Maimone.

Fregoni, M. 1998. "La zonazione strumento della valorizzazione del territorio." In *Atti del Simposio Internazionale Territorio & Vino, Siena, 19–24 Maggio*, 17–18.

Frezier, V., and D. Dubordieu. 1992. "Ecology of yeast strain *Saccharomyces cerevisiae* during spontaneous fermentation in a Bordeaux winery." *American Journal of Enology and Viticulture* 43 (4): 375–80.

Frías, S., J. E. Conde, J. J. Rodriguez-Bencomo, F. Garcia-Montelongo, and J. P. Pérez-Trujillo. 2003. "Classification of commercial wines from the Canary Islands (Spain) by chemometric techniques using metallic contents." *Talanta* 59 (2): 335–44.

Frojo, X. 1878. *Elenco dei vitigni della provincia di Napoli*. Bollettino ampelografico 9, no. 878. Naples: Ministero Agricoltura, Industria e Commercio.

Gallesio, G. 1817–39. *Pomona Italiana ossia Trattato degli alberi fruttiferi*. Rare Book Division, New York Public Library Digital Collections. Accessed November 30, 2017. http://digitalcollections.nypl .org/items/510d47dd-d8c0-a3d9-e040- e00a18064a99.

Galloni, A. 2014. "The 2009 Brunello di Montalcino: The day of reckoning." *Vinous*, May.

———. 2016. "The 2011 Brunello di Montalcino: Terroir matters." *Vinous*, February.

Gambelli, L., and G. P. Santaroni. 2004. "Polyphenols content in some Italian red wines of different geographical origins." *Journal of Food Composition and Analysis* 17:613–18.

Gambuti, A., S. Lamorte, R. Capuano, A. Genovese, M. T. Lisanti, P. Piombino, and L. Moio. 2005. "Study of the influence of grape ripeness degree on aroma characteristics of Aglianico wines by instrumental and sensory analysis." *International Workshop on Advances in Grapevine and Wine Research* 754:533–40.

Garner, M. 2018. *Amarone and the Fine Wines of Verona*. Oxford: Infinite Ideas.

Garner, M., and P. Merrit. 1990. *Barolo: Tar and Roses: A Study of the Wines of Alba*. London: Century.

Garofolo, A. 1998. "Diversificazione e valorizzazione di produzioni tipiche sul territorio: I Cesanesi." In *Atti del Simposio Territorio & Vino*, 753–63. Siena: Associazione Nazionale Città del Vino.

Gatta, L. F. 1838. *Saggio intorno alle viti ed ai vini della provincia d'Ivrea e della Valle d'Aosta*. Turin: Chirio e Mina.

Gatti, M., M. Zamboni, S. Civardi, N. Bobeica, M. Zanetti, D. Elothmani, and L. Bavaresco. 2011. "Relationship between soil origin and wine stilbene concentration in the 'Sangiovese di Romagna' appellation area." In *Comptes Rendus du 17th International Symposium of the Group of International Experts for Cooperation on Vitivinicultural Systems (GiESCO)*, 147–50. Asti: Le Progrès Agricole et Viticole.

Gay, G., F. Mannini, L. Giunchedi, R. Credi, and V. Gerbi. 1981. "Relazione fra attitudini agronomiche ed enologiche e condizioni sanitarie rilevate nelle prime fasi della selezione clonale della vite." In *Proceedings of the 3rd International Symposium on Clonal Selection in Vines, Venice*, 392–96. Conegliano, Italy: Istituto Sperimentale Per La Viticultura.

Genovese, A., A. Gambuti, P. Piombino, and L. Moio. 2007. "Sensory properties and aroma compounds of sweet Fiano wine." *Food Chemistry* 103 (4): 1228–36.

Genovese, A., M. T. Lisanti, A. Gambuti, P. Piombino, and L. Moio. 2005a. "Relationship between sensory perception and aroma compounds of monovarietal red wines." *International Workshop on Advances in Grapevine and Wine Research* 754:549–56.

Genovese, A., P. Piombino, M. T. Lisanti, and L. Moio. 2005b. "Occurrence of furaneol (4-hydroxy-2,5-dimethyl-3 (2h)-furanone) in some wines from Italian Native Grapes." *Annali di Chimica* 95 (6): 415–19.

Gerbi, V., L. Rolle, S. Giacosa, and E. Cagnasso. 2016. "Il Nebbiolo e la ricerca enologica." *L'Enologo*, no. 9: 26–32.

Gerbi, V., G. Zeppa, L. Rolle, I. Boni, F. Petrella, M. Piazzi, F. Spanna, A. Schubert, and C. Lovisolo. 2000. "Barolo: Studio per la caratterizzazione del territorio, delle uve e dei vini dell'area di produzione." In *Analisi statistica e valutazione delle interazioni tra i diversi aspetti considerati*, 87–100. Turin: Regione Piemonte, Assessorato all'Agricoltura.

Giannetto, R. F. 2008. *Medici Gardens: From Making to Design*. Philadelphia: University of Pennsylvania Press.

Giordano, M., L. Rolle, G. Zeppa, and V. Gerbi. 2009. "Chemical and volatile composition of three Italian sweet white Passito wines." *Journal International des Sciences de la Vigne et du Vin* 43 (3): 159–70.

Girardi, M. 2008–9. "Determinazione dell'attività pectin metilesterasica e polifenolossidasica in vitigni a bacca bianca." Thesis, Department of Food Technology, University of Padua.

Gómez-Míguez, M. J., M. Gómez-Míguez, I. M. Vicario, and F. J. Heredia. 2007. "Assessment of colour and aroma in white wines vinifications: Effects of grape maturity and soil type." *Journal of Food Engineering* 79:758–64.

Gougeon, R. D., M. Lucio, M. Frommberger, D. Peyron, D. Chassagne, A. Hervé, et al. 2009. "The chemodiversity of wines can reveal a metabologeography expression of cooperage oak wood." *Proceedings of the National Academy of Sciences of the United States of America* 106: 9174–79.

Gozzini, A. 2000. "Caratterizzazione di alcuni ambienti vitati del territorio a DOCG del Sagrantino di Montefalco." Thesis, Department of Agriculture, University of Milan.

Grando, M. S., C. Frisinghelli, and M. Stefanini. 2006. "Identità e relazioni genetiche dei vitigni autoctoni trentini." *Terra Trentina* 52 (8): 24–27.

Graziotin, M. 2016. "Cartizze, il pentagono d'oro tra terra e cielo." In *Herbarium, 116 erbe in Cartizze*, ed. I. Bisol. Valdobbiadene/Treviso: Ruggeri.

Gregori, L. 1988. "Il bacino di Bastardo: Genesi ed evoluzione nel quadro della tettonica recente." *Bollettino della Società Geologica Italiana* 107:141–51.

———. 2006. "La geologia del vino (in Umbria)." *Il Suolo*, nos. 1–3: 58–74.

Habsburg Lothringen, L. S. 1893–96. *Die Liparischen Inseln*. Vol. 8. Prague: H. Mercy. Reprinted in Italy as L. S. D'Austria, *Die Liparischen Inseln*, ed. P. Paino. Lipari: Edinixe, 1979.

Hashizume, K., and T. Samuta. 1999. "Grape maturity and light exposure affect berry methoxypyrazine concentration." *American Journal of Enology and Viticulture* 50 (2): 194–98.

International Commission on Stratigraphy. 2017. "Chart/Time Scale." www.stratigraphy.org.

Jarnut, J. 1980. *Bergamo 568–1098: Verfassungs-, Sozial- und Wirtschaftsgeschichte einer lombardischen Stadt im Mittelalter*. Vierteljahrschrift für Sozial- und Wirtschaftsgeschichte 67. Wiesbaden: Steiner.

Jenny, H. 1941. *Factors of Soil Formation*. New York: McGraw-Hill.

Khalil, W. 1961. "Studi sulla morfologia, differenziazione, fertilità delle gemme in due cultivar di *Vitis vinifera* L." *Atti Accademia Italiana della Vite e del Vino* 13:431–84.

Kotseridis, Y., and R. Baumes. 2000. "Identification of impact odorants in Bordeaux red grape juice in the commercial yeast used for its fermentation and in the produced wine." *Journal of Agricultural and Food Chemistry* 48 (2): 400–406.

Koundouras, S., V. Marinos, A. Gkoulioti, Y. Kotseridis, and C. van Leeuwen. 2006. "Influence of vineyard location and vine water status on fruit maturation of nonirrigated Cv. Agiorgitiko (*Vitis vinifera* L.): Effects on wine phenolic and aroma components." *Journal of Agricultural and Food Chemistry* 54:5077–86.

Kramer, M. 1990. *Making Sense of Burgundy.* New York: William Morrow.

———. 2010. *Matt Kramer on Wine: A Matchless Collection of Columns, Essays, and Observations by America's Most Original and Lucid Wine Writer.* New York: Sterling Epicure.

Kuenen, P. H., and C. I. Migliorini. 1950. "Turbidity currents as a cause of graded bedding." *Journal of Geology* 58 (2): 91–127.

Kumsta, M., P. Pavlousek, and J. Kupsa. 2012. "Influence of terroir on the concentration of selected stilbenes in wines of the cv. Riesling in the Czech Republic." *Horticultural Science* 39 (1): 38–46.

Kurin, E., P. Mučaji, and M. Nagy. 2012. "In vitro antioxidant activity of three red wine polyphenols and their mixtures: An interaction study." *Molecules* 17:14336–48.

La Greca, G. 2009. *Nel regno di Efesto.* Lipari: Edizioni Centro Studi Eolano.

———. 2016. *Passolina, uva passa e Malvasia: L'economia vitivinicola delle Eolie.* Lipari: Edizioni Centro Studi Eolano.

Labra, M., M. Winfield, A. Ghiani, F. Grassi, A. Sala, A. Scienza, and O. Failla. 2001. "Genetic studies on Trebbiano and morphologically related varieties by SSR and AFLP testing." *Vitis* 40 (4): 187–90.

Lacombe, T., J. M. Boursiquot, V. Laucou, F. Dechesne, D. Varès, and P. This. 2007. "Relationships and genetic diversity within the accessions related to Malvasia held in the Domaine de Vassal grape germplasm repository." *American Journal of Enology and Viticulture* 58 (1): 124–31.

Lamorte, S. A., A. Gambuti, A. Genovese, and L. Moio. 2007. "Volatile components of *Vitis vinifera* L. cvs. Uva di Troia, Aglianico and Fiano at different stages of ripening." Paper presented at the 30th World Congress of Vine and Wine, Budapest, June 10–16.

———. 2014. "Volatile secondary metabolites of Greco (*Vitis vinifera* L.) must." *International Journal of Food Science and Technology* 49 (3): 711–17.

Lamorte, S. A., A. Gambuti, A. Genovese, S. Selicato, and L. Moio. 2015. "Free and glycoconjugated volatiles of V. vinifera grape 'Falanghina.'" *Vitis* 47 (4): 241.

Lavalle, J. 1885. *Histoire et statistique de la vigne et des grands vins de la Côte d'Or.* Ivry-sur-Seine, France: Phénix Éditions. English translation in C. Curtis, *The Original Grand Crus of Burgundy* (New York: Wine Alpha, 2014).

Lawley, F. 1865. *Manuale del vignajuolo o modo di coltivare la vite e fare il vino.* Florence: A. Bettini.

Lazzaroni, S., and L. Mariani. 1997. "Inquadramento climatico." In *La zonazione della Franciacorta*, ed. C. S. Panont and G. Comolli, 41–54. Brescia: Assessorato Agricoltura Provincia di Brescia.

Le Roy de Boiseaumarié, P. 1967. "Les organismes nationaux." In *L'élite des vins de France, spiritueux, eaux-de-vie et liqueurs*, ed. C. Quittanson and F. Des Aulnoyes. Paris: Centre National de Coordination.

Lee, J., L. Vazquez-Araujo, K. Adhikari, M. Warmund, and J. Elmore. 2001. "Volatile compounds in light, medium, and dark black walnut and their influence on the sensory aromatic profile." *Journal of Food Science* 76 (2): C199–204.

Lefort, F., M. Anzidei, K. A. Roubelakis-Angelakis, and G. G. Vendramin. 2000. "Microsatellite profiling of the Greek Muscat cultivars with nuclear and chloroplast SSR markers." *Quaderni della Scuola di Specializzazione in Scienze Viticole ed Enologiche* 23:56–80.

Leicht, P. S. 1949. "Un contratto agrario dei paesi latini mediterranei." In *Studi in onore di Gino Luttazzo*, 1:18–29. Milan: Giuffrè.

Levadoux, L. 1951. "La sélection et l'hybridation chez la vigne." *Annales de L'École Nationale d'Agriculture de Montpellier* 28 (3–4): 165–358.

Lojacono Pojero, M. 1878. *Le Isole Eolie e la loro vegetazione.* Reprint, Bologna: Arnoldo Forni, 1987.

Longo, M. 2017. "Barbera d'Asti and its terroirs: An overview of the different soils and their influence on the wines." Paper presented at Collisioni Vino & Food Project Festival, Costigliole d'Asti, Italy, July 11.

Lopes, M. S., K. M. Sefc, E. Eiras Dias, H. Steinkellner, M. Laimer da Câmara Machado, and A. de Câmara Machado. 1999. "The use of microsatellites for germplasm management in a Portuguese grapevine collection." *Theoretical and Applied Genetics* 99:733–39.

Lotteri, C. 1852. *Memorie storiche di Villa di Serio e il suo Santuario di S. Maria sotto il titolo del Buon Consiglio.* Bergamo: Natali.

Lund, S. T., and J. Bohlmann. 2006. "The molecular basis for wine grape quality: A volatile subject." *Science* 311:804–5.

Magnoli, M. 2004. "Una storia di Barolo." In *100Barolo*, ed. G. Brozzoni. Alba, Italy: Go Wine Editore.

Mancini, C. 1888. *Il Lazio viticolo e vinicolo*. Reprint, Rome: Grafica MGF, 1989.

Mannini, F., R. Credi, and N. Argamante. 1994. "Changes in field performances of clones of the grapevine cv. Nebbiolo after virus elimination by heat-therapy." In *Proceedings of the 6th International Symposium on Grape Breeding*, 117–19. Paris: Office International de la Vigne et du Vin.

Mannini, F., D. Santini, A. Mollo, G. Mazza, P. Cascio, and D. Marchi. 2015. "Influenza della componente ambientale sui composti aromatici dell'uva e del vino della cv. Nebbiolo." *L'Enologo*, no. 5: 73–85.

Manzo, A., and C. Trucchi. 1927. "Barbaresco, per la difesa del suo nome e dei vini tipici: Memoriali inviati all'onorevole prefetto di Cuneo, alle autorità e gerarchie; Pareri tecnici e cenni storici ed enologici." Reprint, Barbaresco, Italy: Enoteca Regionale del Barbaresco in collaboration with Produttori di Barbaresco, 2010.

Margalit, Y. 2005 *Elementi di chimica del vino*. Reggio nell'Emilia, Italy: Eno-One.

Mariani, L., and G. Cola. 2004. "Il clima e la zonazione viticola in Valtellina." *Informatore Agrario* 1:46.

Mariani, L., and O. Failla. 2006. "Agroclimatic characterization of European mountain viticultural areas." In *Proceedings of the "Premier congrès international sur la viticulture de montagne et en forte pente."* Saint-Vincent, France: CERVIM.

Martinis, B. 1993. *Storia geologica del Friuli*. Udine: La Nuova Base.

Mas, A., and V. Pulliat. 1874–79. *Le vignoble; ou, Histoire, culture et description, avec planches coloriées, des vignes à raisins de table et à raisins de cuve les plus généralement connues*. 3 vols. Paris: G. Masson.

Masnaghetti, A. 2015. "Barolo MGA." *L'Enciclopedia delle Grandi Vigne del Barolo*. Monza: Alessandro Masnaghetti.

———. 2016. "Barbaresco MGA." *L'Enciclopedia delle Grandi Vigne del Barbaresco*. Monza: Alessandro Masnaghetti.

Mateo, J.J., and M. Jimenez. 2000. "Monoterpenes in grape juice and wines." *Journal of Chromatography A* 881 (1): 557–67.

Matthews, M.A. 2015. *Terroir and Other Myths of Winegrowing*. Oakland: University of California Press.

Maule, C. 2013. *Valtellina: La vite, il vino, il paesaggio*. Sondrio, Italy: Amici della Vecchia Accademia.

Mazzei, P., N. Francesca, G. Moschetti, and A. Piccolo. 2010. "NMR spectroscopy evaluation of direct relationship between soils and molecular composition of red wines from Aglianico grapes." *Analitica Chimica Acta* 673 (2): 167–72.

Mazzoleni, G., A. Aldighieri, A. Conforto, L. Mariani, and G. Murada. 2006. "Valtellina: Un tipico terroir per il vitigno Nebbiolo." Special issue, *Bollettino della Società Geologica Italiana* 6:97–106.

McSpadden, K. 2015. "You now have a shorter attention span than a goldfish." *Time*, May 14. http://time.com/3858309/attention-spans-goldfish/.

Mendes-Pinto, M.M. 2009. "Carotenoid breakdown products the norisoprenoids in wine aroma." *Archives of Biochemistry and Biophysics* 483 (2): 236–45.

Meneghel, M. 1979. "I terrazzi fluviali della Valle d'Illasi (Monti Lessini)." *Studi Trentini di Scienze Naturali: Acta Geologica* 56:153–68.

Meneghetti, S., A. Costacurta, L. Bavaresco, and A. Calò. 2014. "Genetic variability and geographic typicality of Italian former Prosecco grape variety using PCR-derived molecular markers." *Molecular Biotechnology* 506 (5): 408–20.

Meneghetti, S., A. Costacurta, G. Morreale, and A. Calò. 2012. "Study of intra-varietal genetic variability in grapevine cultivars by PCR-derived molecular markers and correlations with the geographic origins." *Molecular Biotechnology* 50 (1): 72–85.

Menezes, A., and M. Tabeaud. 2000. "Variations in bora weather type in the North Adriatic Sea, 1866–1998." *Weather* 55:452–58.

Mengarini, F., 1888. *La viticoltura e l'enologia del Lazio*. Monografia Roma. Roma: Tipografia della Accademia dei Lincei.

Mennella, C. 1977. *I climi d'Italia*. Naples: Fratelli Conte.

Mercado, L., A. Dalcedo, R. Masuelli, and M. Combina. 2007. "Diversity of Saccharomyces strains on grapes and winery surfaces: Analysis of their contribution to fermentative flora of Malbec wine from Mendoza (Argentina) during two consecutive years." *Food Microbiology* 24 (4): 403–12.

Mercury. 2009. *Rapporto sul turismo italiano, 2008–2009*. Edited by E. Becheri. Milan: Franco Angeli.

Merla, G., and V. Bortolotti. 1967. *Note illustrative della carta geologica d'Italia alla scala 1:100,000. Foglio 113, Castelfiorentino*. Rome: Nuova Tecnica Grafica.

Mielke, E.A., and G.R. Dutt. 1977. "Evaluation of wine grapes in Arizona: Production on a salt-treated catchment." *HortScience* 12 (4): 402.

Migliorini, C. I. 1943. "Sul modo di formazione dei complessi tipo macigno." *Bollettino Società Geologica Italiana* 62:48–49.

Militi, L. 2016. "La viticoltura a Castiglione di Sicilia, volàno dell'economia e rilancio del territorio." *Humanities* 5 (9): 53–88.

Mirone, S. 1875. *Monografia storica dei comuni di Nicolosi, Trecastagni, Pedara e Viagrande*. Catania: E. Coco.

Miyazaki, T., A. Plotto, E. A. Baldwin, J. Reyes-De Cuercuera, and F. G. Gmitter. 2012. "Aroma characterization of tangerine hybrids by gas-chromatography-olfactometry and sensorial evaluation." *Journal of the Science of Food and Agriculture* 92:727–35.

Moio, L. 2005. *Colori, odori ed enologia della Falanghina*. Naples: Assessorato Agricoltura Regione Campania.

———. 2012. *Colori, odori ed enologia del Fiano*. Naples: Assessorato Agricoltura Regione Campania.

———. 2016. *Il respiro del vino*. Milan: Mondadori.

Monaco, A., and L. Branca. 2016. "Aglianico storia e ricerca." *L'Enologo*, no. 11: 26–30.

Montanari, V., and G. Ceccarelli. 1950. *La viticoltura e l'enologia nelle Tre Venezie*. Treviso: Longo e Zoppelli.

Morassut, M., and F. Cecchini. 1999. "Caratterizzazione dei profili fenolici di vitigni coltivati nella regione Lazio." *L'Enotecnico* 35 (5): 73–80.

Moriondo, G., G. Praz, and L. Rigazio. 1998. "Primi risultati della selezione massale dei vitigni autoctoni valdostani a minor diffusione: Fumin, Mayolet, Premetta, Prié e Vuillermin." *Vignevini* 5:76–80.

Morlat, R., A. Jaqueta, and C. Asselin. 1997. "Variabilité de la précocité de la vigne en Val de Loire." *Revue Française d'Œnologie* 165:11–22.

Mulas, G., M. G. Galaffu, L. Pretti, G. Nieddu, L. Mercenaro, R. Tonelli, and R. Anedda. 2011. "NMR analysis of seven selections of Vermentino grape berry: Metabolites composition and development." *Journal of Agriculture and Food Chemistry* 59:793–802.

Nasi, A., P. Ferranti, S. Amato, and L. Chianese. 2008. "Identification of free and bound volatile compounds as typicalness and authenticity markers of non-aromatic grapes and wines through a combined use of mass spectrometric techniques. *Food Chemistry* 110 (3): 762–68.

Nesto, B., and F. Di Savino. 2013. *The World of Sicilian Wine*. Berkeley: University of California Press.

———. 2016. *Chianti Classico: The Search for Tuscany's Noblest Wines*. Berkeley: University of California Press.

Nicolini, G., G. Versini, M. Falcetti, A. Dalla Serra, P. Barchetti, and S. Inama. 1995. "Müller-Thurgau: Aspetti compositivi, di tecnica enologica, e sensoriali dei vini." *L'Enotecnico* 31 (11): 67–74.

Novello, V. 2005. "Lo stato delle conoscenze viticole sul 'Barbera.'" Paper presented at the 1st International Congress on Barbera, Alessandria, Italy, December 2–3.

Orlandini, S., D. Grifoni, M. Mancini, G. Barcaioli, and A. Crisci. 2005. "Analisi della variabilità meteo-climatica sulla qualità del Brunello di Montalcino." *Rivista Italiana di Agrometeorologia* 2:37–44.

Palliotti, A., A. Cartechini, S. Vignaroli, D. Petoumenou, A. Taticchi, G. F. Montedoro, M. Servili, R. Selvaggini, P. Guelfi, and R. Luneia. 2007. "La viticoltura della DOC Montefalco." In *Caratterizzazione vitivinicola ed enologica dell'Area a Denominazione di Origine Controllata Montefalco*, ed. Agenzia Regionale Umbra per lo Sviluppo e l'Innovazione in Agricoltura, 61–110. Todi, Italy: Edizioni 3 A–Parco Tecnologico Agroalimentare dell'Umbria.

Paloc, J., A. Seguin, and P. Torres. 1996. "Effet terroir et aromes des Muscats." In *1er Colloque Int. Les terroirs viticoles*, 444–52. Montpellier, France: INRA.

Palumbo, L. 2012. "Risposte quali-quantitative del vitigno Aglianico coltivato in diversi terrori di Taurasi." N.p.: Università degli studi di Torino, Milano, Palermo, Sassari, Foggia; Facoltà di Agraria, Corso di Laurea Magistrale interateneo in Scienze Viticole ed Enologiche.

Panighel, A., I. Maoz, M. De Rosso, F. De Marchi, A. Dalla Vedova, M. Gardiman, L. Bavaresco, and R. Flamini. 2014. "Identification of saffron aroma compound β-isophorone (3,5,5-trimethyl-3-cyclohexen-1-one) in some *V. vinifera* grape varieties." *Food Chemistry* 145:186–90.

Panont, C. S., and G. Comolli. 1998. "La zonazione della Franciacorta: Il modello viticolo della DOCG." In *Atti del Simposio Territorio & Vino*, 321–39. Siena: Associazione Nazionale Città del Vino.

Parr, W. 2016. "Unravelling the nature of perceived complexity in wine." *Practical Winery & Vineyard*, January.

Pasa, A. 1954. "Carsismo e idrografia carsica nel gruppo del Monte Baldo e dei Lessini veronesi." In *Ricerche sulla morfologia idrografia carsica*, ed. CNR, Centro Studi per la Geografica Fisica, 5. Bologna: Mareggiani.

Pasquali, G. 1990. "Vite e vino in Piemonte (secoli VIII–XII)." In *Vigne e vini nel Piemonte medievale*, ed. R. Comba, 17–33. Cuneo, Italy: L'Arciere.

Paulsen, T. 1929. "Salviamo la Malvasia!" *L'Avvenire Eoliano* 3 (23): 1.

Pejić, I., and E. Maletić. 2005. "'Malvazija istarska' and 'Malvasia dubrovacka': Croatian or Greek cultivars?" Paper presented at the 17th Symposium of History and Art, Monemvasia, Greece, May 30–June 1.

Pelsy, F., S. Hocquigny, X. Moncada, G. Barbeau, D. Forget, P. Hinrichsen, and D. Merdinoglu. 2010. "An extensive study of the genetic diversity within seven French wine grape variety collections." *Theoretical Applied Genetics* 120 (6): 1219–31.

Perusini, G. 1935. "Note di viticoltura collinare." *L'Agricoltura friulana* 25.

———. 1972. "È provata l'esistenza di tre vitigni di Picolit." *Il Vino* 2 (4): 71.

Pesavento Mattioli, S. 1996. "Gli apporti dell'archeologia alla ricostruzione della viticoltura cisalpina in età Romana." In *2500 anni di coltura della vite in ambito Alpino e Cisalpino*, ed. G. Forni and A. Scienza, 391–408. Trento: Istituto Trentino del Vino.

Petrozziello, M., M. Guaita, S. Motta, L. Panero, and A. Bosso. 2011. "Analytical and sensory characterization of the aroma of Langhe DOC Nebbiolo wines: Influence of the prefermentative cold maceration with dry ice." *Journal of Food Science* 76 (4): C525–34.

Petrussi, C. 2013. "Tocai Giallo e Tocai Verde: Due facce della stessa medaglia." In *Tocai e Friulano: Un racconto di civiltà del vino*, ed. E. Costantini, 241–47. Udine: Forum.

———. 2017. "La selezione clonale del vitigno Ribolla Gialla." In *Ribolla story: Vini e vitigni che hanno sfidato i secoli*, ed. E. Costantini, 141–60. Udine: Forum.

Pezzotti, M., G. B. Tornielli, and S. Zenoni. 2015. "Il terroir del Soave: Una interpretazione molecolare." In *Il Soave: Origini, stili, e valori*, 193–203. Soave: Consorzio Tutela Vini Soave.

Piano, F., M. Petrozziello, E. Vaudano, F. Bonello, V. Ferreira, J. Zapata, and P. Hernandez-Orte. 2014. "Aroma compounds and sensory characteristics of Arenis Terre Alfieri DOC wines: The concentration of polyfunctional thiols and their evolution in relation to different ageing conditions." *European Food Research and Technology* 239 (2): 267–77.

Pickenhagen, W., A. Vellus, J. P. Passerat, and G. Ohloff. 1981. "Estimation of 2,5-dimethyl-4-hydroxy-3 (2H)-furanone in cultivated and wild strawberries, pineapples and mangoes." *Journal of the Science of Food and Agriculture* 31 (11): 1132–34.

Pineau, B., J. C. Barbe, C. Van Leeuwen, and D. Dubourdieu. 2007. "Which impact for β-damascenone on red wines aroma?" *Journal of Agricultural and Food Chemistry* 55 (10): 4103–8.

Pioletti, A. 2012. "Il paesaggio vitivinicolo: Espressione del terroir e promozione di un territorio." In *Annali del Turismo*, vol. 1. Novara: Geopress.

Piombino, P., R. Pessina, A. Genovese, J. L. Le Queré, and L. Moio. 2004. "Gli odori dei frutti di bosco dell'aroma del vino: Parte II, Analisi strumentale." *L'Enologo* 40 (4): 97–102.

Poggi, G. 1939. *Refosco d'Istria: Atlante ampelografico.* Udine: Consorzio della Viticoltura.

Poisson, L. 2008. "Characterization of the most odor-active compounds in an American Bourbon whisky by application of the aroma extract dilution analysis." *Journal of Agricultural Food Chemistry* 56 (14): 5813–19.

Pollini, C. 1824. "Osservazioni agrarie per l'anno 1818." *Memorie dell'Accademia di Agricoltura, Scienze e Lettere Verona* 10.

Ponchia, G., D. Tomasi, F. Gaiotti, L. Lovat, P. Marcuzzo, F. Battista, E. Tosi, and A. Lorenzoni. 2010. "Il Soave: Esempio di cultura e scienza." Paper presented at the 8th International Terroir Congress, Soave, Italy, June 14–18.

Potentini, R. 2010. "Che cos'è il Verdicchio di Matelica." In *Il Verdicchio di Matelica DOC e il Verdicchio di Matelica Riserva DOCG: Quando un vino è un racconto*, ed. Roberto Potentini. Rome: Retecamere.

Racheli, G. 1983. *Eolie di vento e di fuoco.* Milan: Mursia.

Ratti, R. 1991. *Carta del barolo.* Alba, Italy: Museo Ratti dei Vini.

Rauhut, D. 1993. "Yeasts-production of sulfur compounds." In *Wine Microbiology and Biotechnology*, ed. G. H. Fleet, 6:183–223. Chur, Switzerland: Harwood Academic Publishers.

Razungles, A., Z. Gunata, S. Pinatel, R. Baumes, and C. Bayonove. 1993. "Étude quantitative des composés terpéniques, norisoprénoïds et de leurs précurseurs dans diverses variétés de raisins." *Science des aliments* 13 (1): 59–72.

Regione Campania. 2009. *Carta dell'utilizzazione agricola del suolo.* Naples: CUAS.

Repetti, E. 1833. "Camigliano." *Dizionario geografico fisico storico della Toscana*, 1:4045. Florence: Mazzoni.

Rezoagli, G. 1965. *Il Chianti.* Rome: Società Geografica Italiana.

Ribeiro Cunha de Rocha, L. A. G. 2013. "Effects of dehydration conditions in grapes of Sagrantino variety dried in climatic chambers for the production of Sagrantino Passito wine." Master's thesis, Department of Agronomy, University of Trás os Montes and Alto Douro, Villa Real, Portugal.

Ribéreau-Gayon, P., Y. Glories, A. Maujean, and D. Dubourdieu, eds. 2006. *Handbook of Enology*. Vol. 2, *The Chemistry of Wine Stabilization and Treatments*. 2nd ed. New York: John Wiley & Sons.

Rigaux, J. 2018. "How to understand Burgundy terroir philosophy." Paper presented at the 3rd Terroir Renaissance International Wine Symposium, Shanghai, November 30–December 2.

Rigazio, L., G. Praz, G. Lale Demoz, O. Zecca, L. Mariani, R. Minelli, O. Failla, and A. Scienza. 2006. "Zonage du terroir viticole de la Vallée d'Aoste: Primo Congresso Internazionale sulla Viticoltura di Montagna e in Forte Pendenza." Quart, Italy: Musumeci.

Riou, C., R. Morlat, and C. Asselin. 1995. "Une approche intégrée des terroirs viticoles: Discussions sur les critères de caractérisation accessible." *Bulletin de l'O.I.V.* 68:93–106.

Ristuccia, M. 1957. *L'album dei ricordi: Le Eolie da "Illustrazione Italiana" Garzanti*. Reprint, *Il Giornale di Lipari*, May 25, 2015. http://www .giornaledilipari.it/lalbum-dei-ricordi-le-eolie-da-illustrazione-italiana-garzanti-1957/.

Robinson, J. 2005. *Wines, Grapes and Vines: The Wine Drinker's Guide to Wine Grape Varieties*. London: Mitchell Beazley.

Robinson, J., J. Harding, and J. Vouillamoz. 2012. *Wine Grapes: A Complete Guide to 1,368 Vine Varieties, including Their Origins and Flavours*. New York: Ecco Press.

Rodriguez, C. 1841. "Breve cenno storico sull'isola di Lipari." *Giornale Letterario* (Palermo), no. 277.

Roland, A., J. Vialaret, A. Razungles, P. Rigou, and R. Schneider. 2010. "Evolution of S-cysteinylated and S-clutathionylated thiol precursors during oxidation of Melon B. and Sauvignon blanc musts." *Journal of Agriculture and Food Chemistry* 58 (7): 4406–13.

Roullier-Gall, C., L. Boutegrabet, R. D. Gougeon, and P. Schmitt-Kopplin. 2014. "A grape and wine chemodiversity comparison of different appellations in Burgundy: Vintage vs terroir effects." *Food Chemistry* 152:100–107.

Rusjan, D., T. Jug, and N. Štainer. 2010. "Evaluation of genetic diversity: Which of the varieties can be named Rebula (*Vitis vinifera* L.)?" *Vitis* 49 (4): 189–92.

Saenz-Navajas, M., E. Campo, J. M. Avizcuri, D. Valentin, P. Fernandez-Zurbano, and V. Ferreira. 2012. "Contribution of non-volatile and aroma fractions to in-mouth sensory properties of red wines: Wine reconstitution strategies and sensory sorting task." *Analytica Chimica Acta* 732:64–72.

Sagrantini, G., F. Maggi, G. Caprioli, G. Cristalli, M. Ricciutelli, E. Torreggiani, and S. Vittori. 2012. "Comparative study of aroma profile and phenolic content of Montepulciano monovarietal red wines for the Marches and Abruzzo regions of Italy using HS-SPME-GC-MS and HPLC-MS." *Food Chemistry* 132 (3): 1592–99.

Sakellariades, H. C., and B. H. Luh. 1974. "Anthocyanins in Barbera grapes." *Journal of Food Science* 39 (2): 329–33.

Sannino, F. A. 1913. "Note ampelografiche sulle tribù del Prosecco e del Verdiso." *Rivista di Viticoltura e di Enologia di Conegliano* 19:5.

Sansovino, F. 1575. *Ritratto delle più nobili et famose città d'Italia*. Venice.

Sauro, U. 1978. "Forme strutturali e neotettoniche nei Monti Lessini." *Gruppo Quaternario Padano* 4:31–60.

Sauro, U., and M. Meneghel. 1980. "Dati preliminari sulla neotettonica dei fogli 21 (Trento), 35 (Riva), 36 (Schio) e 49 (Verona)." In *Contributi alla realizzazione della carta neotettonica d'Italia* 33–57. Rome: Centro Nazionale Ricerche.

Scacco, A., A. Verzera, C. M. Lanza, A. Sparacio, G. Genna, S. Raimondi, G. Tripodi, and G. Dima. 2010. "Influence of soil salinity on sensory characteristics and volatile aroma compounds of Nero d'Avola wine." *American Journal of Enology and Viticulture* 61:498–505.

Scaglione, G., C. Pasquarella, and M. Boselli. 1998a. "Evoluzione delle temperature ed andamento climatico della maturazione nel vitigno Aglianico: Risultati di un quadriennio di osservazioni in Campania." In *Atti del Simposio Territorio & Vino*, 503–5. Siena: Associazione Nazionale Città del Vino.

———. 1998b. "Indagini sul fabbisogno del vitigno Fiano nell'ambiente campano." In *Atti IV Giornate Scientifiche S.O.I.*, 447–48.

Schneider, A., P. Boccacci, and R. Botta. 2003. "Genetic relationships among grape cultivars from north-western Italy." *Acta Horticulturae* 603:229–35.

Schneider, A., P. Boccacci, D. Torello Marinoni, R. Botta, A. Akkak, and J. Vouillamoz 2004. "Variabilità genetica e parentele inaspettate del Nebbiolo." Paper presented at the Convegno Internazionale sul Vitigno Nebbiolo, Sondrio, Italy, June 23–25.

Schneider, A., D. Torello Marinoni, P. Boccacci, and R. Botta. 2006. "Relazioni genetiche del vitigno

Nebbiolo." *Quaderni di Scienze Viticoli ed Enologiche dell'Università di Torino* 28:93–100.

Scienza, A., and M. Boselli. 2003. *Vini e vitigni della Campania: Tremila anni di storia.* Naples: Prismi.

Scienza, A., A. Giorgianni, D. Tomasi, F. Gaiotti, F. Graziani, L. Mariani, and P. Carnevali. 2015. *Atlante geologico dei vini d'Italia: Vitigno, suolo e fattori climatici.* Florence: Giunti.

Scienza, A., R. Miravalle, M. Boselli, and G. Dorotea, 1981. "Effetto della boro: Carenza sullo sviluppo e la composizione chimica sulle bacche di 'Barbera.'" *Vignevini* 8 (11): 37–42.

Scienza, A., D. Tomasi, A. Garlato, and Gruppo Tecnico Masi. 2011. *Le Venezie: Le diversità di terroir riflesse nel bicchiere.* Gargagnago, Italy: Fondazione Masi.

Scienza, A., L. Toninato, D. Bacchiega, R. Pastore, R. Minnelli, and N. Bottura. 2008. *La zonazione viticola della Valpolicella.* San Pietro in Cariano, Italy: Consorzio per la Tutela Vini dei Valpolicella.

Scienza, A., G. Versini, and F. A. Romano. 1989. "Considérations sur l'influence du génotype et du milieu sur la synthèse des arômes dans le raisin: Cas particulier du Chardonnay." In *Atti del 1° Simposio Internazionale, "Le sostanze aromatiche dell'uva e del vino,"* 9–53. San Michele all'Adige, Italy: Istituto San Michele all'Adige.

Seguin, G. 1986. "'Terroirs' and pedology of wine growing." *Experientia* 42 (8): 861–73.

Selli, R. 1960. "Il Messiniano Mayer-Eymar 1867: Proposta di un neostratotipo." *Giornale di Geologia* 27:1–33.

Sergent, E., and H. Rougebief. 1925. "Mutualism between Drosophila and wine yeast." *International Entomology Kongress Zurich* 2:94–99.

Servizio Geologico d'Italia. 1969. *Carta geologica d'Italia alla scala 1:100.000. Foglio 119, Massa marittima.* Rome: Istituto Superiore per la Protezione e la Ricerca Ambientale.

Shepherd, W. R. 1964. *Shepherd's Historical Atlas.* 9th ed. New York: Barnes and Noble.

Silvestroni, O. 2010. "Il mondo Verdicchio: I vitigni e i vigneti." In *Il Verdicchio di Matelica DOC e il Verdicchio di Matelica Riserva DOCG: Quando un vino è un racconto,* ed. R. Potentini. Rome: Retecamere.

Simpson, R. F., and G. C. Miller. 1984. "Aroma composition of Chardonnay wine." *Vitis* 23 (2): 143–58.

Smith, W., W. Wayte, and G. E. Marindin. 1890. *A Dictionary of Greek and Roman Antiquities.* London: John Murray.

Smyth, W. H. 1824. *Memoir Descriptive of the Resources, Inhabitants, and Hydrography, of Sicily and Its Islands: Interspersed with Antiquarian and Other Notices.* London: John Murray.

Sommers, B. J. 2008. *The Geography of Wine.* London: Plume/Penguin.

Soster, M., and A. Cellino. 1998. "Caratterizzazione delle produzioni vitivinicole dell'area del Barolo: Un'esperienza pluriennale." *Quaderni della Regione Piemonte Agricoltura,* no. 13.

Spallanzani, L. 1793. *Viaggi alle Due Sicilie e in alcune parti dell'Appenino.* Pavia: Baldassare Comini.

Speranza, F. 1953. *L'isola di Salina studio geografico economico.* Catania: Università degli Studi di Catania; Zuccarello & Izzo.

Spiers, J. C., H. J. C. Chen, and N. A. Lavidis. 2015. "Stress alleviating plant-derived 'green odors': Behavioral, neurochemical and neuroendocrine perspectives in laboratory animals." *Phytochemistry Reviews* 14 (5): 713–25.

Staglieno, P. F. 1835. *Istruzione intorno al miglior metodo di fare e conservare i vini in Piemonte.* Reprint, Alessandria, Italy: Edizioni dell'Orso, 2003.

Štajner, N., Z. Korošec-Koruza, D. Rusjan, and B. Javornik. 2008. "Microsatellite genotyping of old Slovenian grapevine varieties (*Vitis vinifera* L.) of the Primorje (coastal) winegrowing region." *Vitis* 47 (4): 201–4.

Stevenson, T. 1993. *The Wines of Alsace.* London: Faber and Faber.

Stocking, M. 1994. "Soil erosion and conservation: A place for soil science?" In *Soil Science and Sustainable Land Management,* ed. J. K. Syers and D. L. Rimmer, 40–58. Wallingford, UK: CAB International.

Stow, D. A. V., S. C. R. Rainey, G. Angell, F. C. Wezel, and D. Savelli. 1984. "Depositional model for calcilutites: Scaglia Rossa limestones, Umbro-Marchean Apennines." *Geological Society London Special Publications* 15 (1): 223–41.

Strucchi, A. 1908. *I migliori vini d'Italia.* Milan: Ulrico Hoepli.

Strucchi, A., and M. Zecchini. 1895. *Il Moscato di Canelli.* Turin: UTET. Reprint, Canelli, Italy: Dalmasso, 1986.

Taglienti, A. 1985. *Il Monastero di Trisulti e il Castello di Collepardo.* Rome: Terra Nostra.

Tandon, K. S. 2008. "Linking sensory descriptors to volatile and nonvolatile components of fresh tomato flavor." *Journal of Food Science* 68 (7): 2366–71.

Tarr, P. T., M. L. Dreyer, M. Athanas, M. Shahgholi, K. Saarloos, and T. P. Second. 2013. "A metabolomics based approach for understanding the influence of terroir in *Vitis vinifera* L." *Metabolomics* 9, supp. 1: 170–77.

Tempesta, G., and M. Fiorillo. 2011. "Patrimonio varietale della vite." De Vulpe et Uva. www .devulpeetuva.com/DeVulpeetUva%20NEW/C2 /Patrimonio%20Varietale.html.

Terribile, F. 2016. "I suoli e i territori del vino: Le DOCG Taurasi e Aglianico del Taburno." L'Enologo, no. 11: 32–39.

Thomas, A. 2011. Garrisoning the Borderlands of Medieval Siena: Sant'Angelo in Colle, Frontier Castle under the Government of the Nine, 1287–1355. Farnham, UK: Ashgate.

Tomasi, D., A. Calo, G. Pascarella, A. Pitacco, D. Borsa, and F. Gaiotti. 2015. "Effetto dell'incremento termico sulla quantità aromatica dell'uva: Il caso della Garganega e delle sue forme di allevamento." In Quaderni CRA Istituto Sperimentale per la Viticoltura. Conegliano, Italy: Amministrazione Comunale.

Tomasi, D., and F. Gaiotti. 2011. I terroirs della denominazione Conegliano-Valdobbiadene. Conegliano, Italy: CRA–VIT.

Tomasi, D., F. Gaiotti, and G. V. Jones. 2013. The Power of the Terroir: The Case Study of Prosecco Wine. Basel: Springer.

Tominaga, T., G. Guimbertau, and D. Dubourdieu. 2003. "Contribution of benzenemethanethiol to smoky aromas of certain Vitis vinifera L. wines." Journal of Agricultural and Food Chemistry 51 (5): 1373–76.

Tominaga, T., C. Peyrot des Gachons, and D. Dubourdieu. 1998. "A new type of flavor precursors in Vitis vinifera L. cv. Sauvignon Blanc wines: S-cysteine conjugates." Journal of Agricultural and Food Chemistry 46 (12): 5215–19.

Tonietto, J., and A. Carbonneau. 1998. "Facteurs mésoclimatiques de la typicité du raisin de table del'A.O.C. Muscat de Ventoux dans le département de Vaucluse." Le Progrès Agricole et Viticole 115 (12): 271–79.

Tornielli, G. B., E. Rovetta, E. Sartor, and M. Boselli. 2010. "A zoning study of the viticultural territory of a cooperative winery in Valpolicella." Paper presented at the 8th International Terroir Congress, Soave, Italy, June 14–18.

Tosi, E., B. Fedrizzi, M. Azzolini, F. Finato, B. Simonato, and G. Zapparoli. 2012. "Effects of noble rot on must composition and aroma profile of Amarone wine produced by the traditional grape withering protocol." Food Chemistry 130 (2): 370–75.

Tunis, G., and S. Venturini. 1989. "Geologia dei colli di Scriò, Dolegna e Ruttars (Friuli orientale): Precisazioni sulla stratigrafia e sul significato paleoambientale del flysch di Cormons." Gortania Atti del Museo Friulano di Storia Naturale 11:5–24.

Tura, D., O. Failla, D. Bassi, S. Pedò, and A. Serraiaocco. 2008. "Cultivar influence on virgin olive (Olea europea) oil flavor based on aromatic compounds and sensorial profile." Scientia Horticulturae 118 (2): 139–48.

Ubigli, M., M. Rissone, V. Gerbi, and P. Anfosso. 1991. "Analisi strumentali e sensoriali del Barbaresco D.O.C.G." Rivista di Viticoltura e di Enologia 44 (2): 47–65.

Ummarino, I., and R. Di Stefano. 1996. "Influenza del numero di semi per acino sulla composizione dell'uva." Rivista di Viticoltura e di Enologia 49 (4): 29–37.

Usseglio-Tomasset, L. 1969. "I costituenti aromatici delle uve." Rivista di Viticoltura e di Enologia 22:223–42.

Vagni, M. 1999. "Aspetti della viticoltura monastica medievale." In La vite e il vino: Politiche e tecniche a confronto per un progetto di sviluppo. Rome: ARSIAL.

Valenti, L., F. Cisani, F. Mattivi, and F. Carletti. 2004. "Utilizzo di tecniche agronomiche innovative per il vitigno Sagrantino: Sette differenti forme d'allevamento ad alta densità di impianto." L'Informatore Agrario 48:49–55.

Valenti, L., F. Mattivi, M. Compagnoni, L. Mariani, and A. Gozzini. 2006. "Caratterizzazione di alcuni ambienti vitati del territorio D.O.C.G. del Sagrantino di Montefalco attraverso le componenti polifenoliche." Paper presented at the 1st Convegno Nazionale di Viticoltura (CONAVI), Ancona, June 21–23.

Valenti, L., and G. Nicolini. 2001. "Indagini sul corredo polifenolico di vini Sagrantino con metodiche applicabili ai controlli di processo." Rivista di Viticoltura ed Enologia 54 (1): 47–63.

Van Leeuwen, C., P. Friant, X. Choné, O. Tregoat, S. Koundouras, and D. Dubourdieu. 2004. "Influence of climate, soil, and cultivar on terroir." American Journal of Enology and Viticulture 55:207–17.

Van Leeuwen, C., and G. Seguin. 2006. "The concept of terroir in viticulture." Journal of Wine Research 17 (1): 1–10.

Vantini, F., G. Tacconi, M. Gastaldelli, C. Govoni, E. Tosi, P. Malacrinò, R. Bassi, and L. Cattivelli. 2003. "Biodiversity of grapevines (Vitis vinifera L.) grown in the province of Verona." Vitis 42 (1): 35–38.

Vaudour, E. 2003. Les terroirs viticoles. Paris: La Vigne/Dunod.

Venditelli, M. 1988. Statuta Civitatis Ferentini. Rome: Miscellanea della Società Romana di Storia Patria.

Venzo, G., and A. Brambati. 1969. "Prime osservazioni sedimentologiche sul flysch Friulano." *Studi Trentini di Scienze Naturali*, sec. A, vol. 46 (1): 3–10.

Vernocchi, P., M. Ndajimana, D. I. Serra Zanetti, C. C. López, A. Fabiani, F. Gardini, M. E. Guerzoni, and R. Lanciotti. 2011. "Use of *Saccharomyces cerevisiae* strains endowed with β-glucosidase activity for the production of Sangiovese wine." *World Journal of Microbiology and Biotechnology* 27 (6): 1423–33.

Veronelli, L. 1964. *I vini d'Italia*. Rome: Canesi.

———. 1981. *Bere giusto*. Milan: Rizzoli.

———. 1995. *Repertorio Veronelli dei vini italiani*. Bergamo: Veronelli.

Versini, G., G. Nicolini, and A. Dalla Serra. 1996. "Caratterizzazione dell'aroma dei vini Müller-Thurgau." *Vignevini* 23 (7–8): 37–43.

Versini, G., A. Rapp, F. Reniero, and H. Mandery. 1991. "Structural identification and presence of some p-menth-1-enediols in grape products." *Vitis* 30 (3): 143–49.

Versini, G., and T. Tomasi. 1983. "Comparison of the volatile components of red wine obtained by traditional maceration and carbonic maceration (differentiating the effects of ethyl cinnamate)." *L'Enotecnico* 19:595.

Verzera, A., G. Tripodi, G. Dima, C. Condurso, A. Scacco, F. Cincotta, and A. Sparacio. 2016. "Leaf removal and wine composition of *Vitis vinifera* L. cv. Nero d'Avola: The volatile aroma constituents." *Journal of the Science of Food and Agriculture* 96 (1): 150–59.

Viala, P., and V. Vermorel. 1909. *Ampélographie*. Paris: Masson.

Villa, P. L., O. Milesi, and A. Scienza. 1997. *Vecchi vitigni Bresciani*. Brescia: Queriniana.

von Czoernig, C. 1969. *Il territorio di Gorizia e Gradisca, 1891*. Gorizia, Italy: Cassa di Risparmio.

Vouillamoz, J. F., A. Monaco, L. Costantini, M. Stefanini, A. Scienza, and M. S. Grando. 2007. "The parentage of 'Sangiovese,' the most important Italian wine grape." *Vitis* 46 (1): 19–22.

Webb, A. D., R. E. Kepner, and L. Maggiora. 1966. "Gas chromatographic comparison of volatile aroma materials extracted from eight different Muscat-flavored varieties of *Vitis vinifera*." *American Journal of Enology and Viticulture* 17:247–54.

Williams, P. J., M. A. Sefton, and B. Wilson. 1989. *Nonvolatile Conjugates of Secondary Metabolites as Precursors of Varietal Grape Flavor Components*. ACS Symposium Series 388. Washington: American Chemical Society.

Wilson, B., C. R. Strauss, and P. J. Williams. 1986. "The distribution of free and glycosidically-bound monoterpenes among skin, juice, and pulp fractions of some white grape varieties." *American Journal of Enology and Viticulture* 37 (2): 107–11.

Yilmaz, E. 2001. "The chemistry of fresh tomato flavour." *Turkish Journal of Agriculture* 25: 149–55.

Yoder, W. M., S. W. Currlin, A. Larue, K. M. Fernandez, D. King, and D. W. Smith. 2012. "Interactions of guaiacol and methyl salicylate in binary mixture significantly lowers perceptual threshold in human observers." *Journal of Sensory Studies* 27 (3): 161–67.

Zamboni, M., A. Iaconi, and L. Bozzalla. 1997. "Influenze ambientali sulle caratteristiche produttive e qualitative dei vitigni Biancolella e Forastera nell'isola d'Ischia." Supp., *Vignevini* 24 (4): 9–15.

Zamorani, A., G. Borin, C. Giulivo, and A. Maggioni. 1987. "Il Moscato dei Colli Euganei." *Vignevini* 5:23–33.

Zangheri, P. 2003. "I terroir delle DOCG italiane." In *Terroir, zonazione, viticoltura: Trattato internazionale*, ed. M. Fregoni, D. Schuster, and A. Paoletti, 281–89. Rivoli Veronese, Italy: Phytoline.

Zappalà, A. 2000. *La vite e il vino sull'Etna nel tempo*. Siena: Associazione Nazionale Città del Vino.

Zenoni, S., F. Guzzo, and G. Tornielli. 2012. "Genes and the metabolome reveal the dynamics of grape appassimento." Paper presented at the 23rd Technical Seminar, "Appassimento: Which Grapes? The Answer in Genetics and the Glass," Verona, March 26.

Zoia, D. 2004. *Vite e vino in Valtellina e Valchiavenna: La risorsa di una valle alpina*. Sondrio, Italy: Officina del Libro.

GENERAL INDEX

Barberani, 124
Bard, 200, 201
Baricci, 286, 290, 296, 297
Barile, 4, 40, 41–42, 44
Barolo, 171, 172–190
Barolo Classico, 173
Barolo Vecchio, 172
Bartolo Mascarello, 126
Basilisco, 38, 46
Basilium, 38
Bava, 53, 55, 158, 264
Beaujolais cru, 248
Belisario, 318
Benanti, 67, 216, 220
Benito Favaro, 90
Benito Ferrara, 38
Benzaldehyde, 213
Benzenoids, 113
Bera, 158
Bergamo, 160
Bernabei, Franco, 281
Berrouet, Jean-Claude, 1
Bersano, 264
Berzano San Pietro, 171
Berroeut, Jean-Claude, 1
Bersano, 53, 55
Berta Paolo, 55
Beta-damascenone, 30, 71, 168, 271
Beta-cymene, 168
Beta-isophorone, 250
Beta-myrcene, 168
Beta-phenethyl alcohol, 228
Bianco di Custoza, 107
Biava, 162
Bibbiano, 282
Big 'd Big, 185
Biondi, 219, 220
Biondi-Santi, 286, 287, 290
Biondi-Santi, Ferruccio, 287
Biotypes, 15
Bisci, 318
Bisol, 83, 118
Blazic, 145
Bocale, 269
Boccella, 38
Bolla, Emanuela, 182
Bolla (Nebbiolo), 168, 169
Bolnego-Strambino landform system, 89
Bolognano, 153, 154
Bolzicco, Luigi, 301
Borgo del Tiglio, 145
Borgognone, Francesco, 262
Borgo Maragliano, 158
Borgomasino, 89
Borgo Paglianetto, 318

Borgo Scopeto, 282
Borin, 165
Boroli, 190
Bortolomiol, 118
Boscaini, Raffaele, 76
Boscaini, Sandro, 76
Bosco del Merlo, 118
Botrytis cinerea. See noble rot.
Braida, 53, 128, 158
Brandolini, 148
Bricco Rocca, 186
Broom, 65, 108
Brovia, 51, 204
Bruno Giacometto, 90
Bruno Giacosa, 186, 188, 190, 194, 197, 204
Bruno Rocca, 194, 197
Bucerchiale, 286
Bucci, 312, 316
Bucci, Ampelio, 312
Burgundy: history of terroir, 7–8
Bussia, 178
Bussia stream, 177
Bussola, 80

Ca' d'Gal, 158
Ca' del Baio, 197
Ca' di Morissio, 211
Ca' Mariuccia, 172
Ca' Ronesca, 257
Ca' Rugate, 86
Ca' Ronesca, 255, 257
Cafaggio, 286
Cagliari, 322
Calabretta, 220
Calcagno (Calcaneus), 67, 216, 220
Calcarenite, 271
Caldera, 264
Calore river, 35
Caluso Passito, 89, 325
Camp Gros, 193
Caminella, 162, 166
Camperiti, 286
Canalicchio di Sopra, 287, 294, 295
Canavese, 88
Candida, 102
Canelli, 157
Cantatore, Luigi, 132
Cantiani, Riccardo, 191
Cantina Altarocca, 124
Cantina Cooperativa Erbaluce di Caluso, 90
Cantina del Barone, 101
Cantina del Glicine, 194
Cantina del Taburno, 32
Cantina del Vermentino, 312
Cantina di Gallura, 322

INDEX OF GRAPE VARIETIES

INDEX OF TERROIRS